EUROPE SINCE 1945

FROM CONFLICT
TO COMMUNITY

EUROPE SINCE 1945

FROM CONFLICT TO COMMUNITY

WM. LAIRD KLEINE-AHLBRANDT
Purdue University

WEST PUBLISHING COMPANY

Minneapolis/Saint Paul   New York   Los Angeles   San Francisco

Copyediting by Patricia Lewis

Text design by John Rokusek/Rokusek Design

Cover design by Pollock Design Group

Composition by Parkwood Composition

Art by Alice Thiede/Carto-Graphics

Index by Sandi Schroeder/Schroeder Indexing Services

Cover image by D. Aubert/Sygma

Production, prepress, printing, and binding by West Publishing Company

West's commitment to the environment

In 1906, West Publishing Company began recycling materials left over from the production of books. This began a tradition of efficient and responsible use of resources. Today, up to 95 percent of our legal books and 70 percent of our college texts are printed on recycled, acid-free stock. West also recycles nearly 22 million pounds of scrap paper annually—the equivalent of 181,717 trees. Since the 1960s, West has devised ways to capture and recycle waste inks, solvents, oils, and vapors created in the printing process. We also recycle plastics of all kinds, wood, glass, corrugated cardboard, and batteries, and have eliminated the use of styrofoam book packaging. We at West are proud of the longevity and the scope of our commitment to our environment.

Photo credits follow the index.

Library of Congress Cataloging-in-Publication Data

Kleine-Ahlbrandt, W. Laird (William Laird)
    Europe since 1945 : from conflict to community / W. Laird Kleine-Ahlbrandt.
        p.   cm.
    Includes index.
    ISBN 0-314-00735-0
    1. Europe—History—1945-   I. Title.
    D1051.K57   1992
    940.55—dc20   92-4518
                                                        ∞ CIP

To Sheila and Stéphanie

in recognition of their loyalty and love

CONTENTS

PREFACE

Most people who lived in Europe during the Cold War have some story that reminds them how close the world came to blowing itself up. I remember the third Berlin crisis of 1961. I was in Geneva studying at the Graduate Institute of International Studies. Like many others, I feared that the direct confrontation between American and Soviet tanks at the Brandenburg gate would precipitate a nuclear holocaust. Only later did we learn that none of the soldiers carried live ammunition. I lost one night's sleep, the Soviets built the Berlin Wall, and the Cold War became comfortably predictable.

The possibility of the Soviets sweeping through the Fulda gap into Western Europe became as remote as the possibility that American forces would cross the Elbe blasting a trail to Moscow. Nonetheless, as long as East and West remained in the posture of war readiness that characterized the Cold War, no one could truly relax. The collapse of the Soviet Union has made moot any fear of a confrontation between Communist and democratic Europe. However, if the Cold War experience taught us anything, it is that true European security is indivisible; the security of one state depends on the security of the rest. The current turmoil in Eastern Europe has replaced anxiety about the Cold War with concern that the instability of nascent democratic nations, inexperienced in the mechanics of self-governance, will pose a threat to the peace of Europe. The story of post–Cold War Europe, however, will be the subject of future histories. Here I have tried to tell the story up to that point as fairly and honestly as I could, albeit with the fortuitous assistance of others who have shared with me their specialized knowledge and advice.

I am particularly grateful to those who have read various parts of the manuscript and provided me with constructive criticism: L. Margaret Barnett of the University of Southern Mississippi, Robert Cole of Utah State University, Lawrence E. Daxton of the University of Southern Colorado, Charles F. Delzell of Vanderbilt University, Kees Gispen of the University of Mississippi, Dan L. LeMahieu of Lake Forest College, Howard M. Sachar of George Washington University, Jose M. Sanchez of Saint Louis University, Marshall S. Shatz of the University of Massachusetts at Boston, Hans A. Schmitt of the University of Virginia, Joanne Schneider of Rhode Island College, James F. Tent of the University of Alabama at Birmingham, and John B. Wilson of DePauw University.

I am also grateful to others who have expertise in particular subject areas and have given me the benefit of their counsel: William Buffington, the post-Stalinist Soviet Union; Randy Roberts, the impact of sports in society; Lois Magner, the development of medicine; Donald Paarlberg, the agricultural practices of the Common Market; Stéphanie Kleine-Ahlbrandt, the social policy of the Treaty of Rome; and Sheila Hégy Swanson on women's and cultural affairs. My opinions were also formed and tested by conversations with friends: Gordon Young of West Lafayette; Harold Dierickx of Luxembourg City; Roland Bernay of Geneva; Joseph Haberer of West Lafayette; Stephen Pallay of Geneva; Engin Baraz of Izmir; Roger Pethybridge of Swansea; Ramsay Radi of Geneva; Marc Cornu of Ferney-Voltaire;

Dorothy and Andon Jurukov of Glendale, California; Mara Safurtlu of Geneva; and Rolf Bergs of Melle, Germany. I would like to pay tribute to Jacques Freymond, former director of the *Institut de Hautes Études Internationales* in Geneva. I also acknowledge those who have provided me with secretarial assistance: Judy McHenry, Julie Mántica, and Eleanor Gurns.

Finally, my thanks go to the staff at West Educational Publishing for their dedicated professionalism, especially Laura Evans, production editor, and Diane Colwyn, development editor. In addition my gratitude goes to cartographer Alice Thiede. Most of all thanks to Robert Jucha, an extraordinary project editor. Bob gave freely of his friendly counsel and his patient assistance in helping to make less formidable the task of bringing this project to completion.

Wm. Laird Kleine-Ahlbrandt

AN AGE OF TOTAL WAR

PREFACE   World War I sounded a death knell for Europe's great continental empires. The Russian empire collapsed first in 1917; it was followed a year later by the Ottoman, next the Austro-Hungarian, and then the German empire. Nevertheless, the imperial age in Europe was far from over. The Bolsheviks, who seized power in Petrograd in November 1917, wanted to recover and refashion as much of the tsarist territory as they could. Furthermore, they sponsored a new sort of imperialism with their call for world revolution. They regarded all "capitalist" states as illegitimate and created the Third International to be the instrument through which those states would be destroyed. The Germans also refused to accept their losses in the war as final. They dreamed of recovering all the national territory once ruled by the kaiser. The National Socialists, who came to power in 1933, wanted even more. Their leader, Adolf Hitler, made *Lebensraum* (living space) his goal. By this he meant the expansion of the German "racial community" eastward into the vast plains of Russia. The expansionist ambitions of these two powers determined the course of European politics for much of the twentieth century. Although the Nazi and Soviet empires differed in important respects, each was a messianic system controlled by a brutal totalitarian dictatorship. Both threatened the independence of the other European states.

After 1945, the Soviets created a ring of satellites in Eastern Europe and arrogated to themselves the right to intervene whenever they thought the integrity of the regimes they had established was threatened. Although the division of the continent into Eastern and Western zones of influence initiated an era of intense rivalry and danger, it also brought Europe an unusual period of peace. Ironically, during the Cold War, Europe enjoyed one of the longest periods without war in its history.

The threat of nuclear destruction did not prevent the states of Western Europe from raising their economies to new heights of prosperity while, at the same time, ending their brutal national rivalries. Many of these states went farther and created common institutions that brought them closer to political unity. In the East, however, the Soviet-imposed order brought no similar lasting integration. The Communist regimes promised a material paradise and harmony of peoples, but the standard of living in Eastern Europe did not keep pace with the life-style enjoyed in the West. Below the surface, national tensions and hatreds continued to simmer and were kept in check only by dictatorship. When the Soviet Union withdrew its support, all these regimes collapsed. By then the Soviet Union itself was declining, pulled apart by its own contradictions and divisions. Few would have thought that this nation, which had emerged from the chaos of World War I to become the strongest power in Europe, would come apart at the seams a mere generation later. Less than half a century after its great victory over Nazi Germany, the Soviet Union disappeared with astonishing rapidity.

THE TWENTY YEARS' TRUCE

The Legacy of World War I

Rusting barbed wire, caved-in parapets, wide craters, villages reduced to rubble— the visual reminders of the great bloodletting were everywhere. World War I had become a clash of popular wills in which the participants were inspired by a sense of national mission. Many had been imbued with a spiritual fanaticism absent from Europe since the days of the wars of religion. As the conflict dragged on, many people despaired that it would never end. Only the entry of the United States in April 1917 had tipped the balance toward victory for the coalition led by Britain and France. Woodrow Wilson, the American president, knew that his country had to join the war if he wanted a seat at the peace conference where the great decisions affecting the destiny of the world would be made. The Americans, protected by a vast ocean from the power struggles of Europe, had once been willing to let the warring nations fight it out among themselves. The Americans had no territorial ambitions and did not believe their security would be endangered no matter which side won. Their country enjoyed absolute political domination in its own hemisphere and had heretofore avoided participating in the creation or maintenance of a European equilibrium. Wilson, however, had a revolutionary vision. He wanted to establish a world organization that would collectively guarantee the security of its members. But Wilson's lofty ideas for a new world order simply did not conform to present realities. The ensuing settlement was not based on the kind of objectivity that might have made the world safe for his version of democracy.

The mobilized fury of nations could not easily be staunched once the conflict no longer raged. All the European participants came out of the war demonstrably poorer. The strong commercial relationship between Germany and Britain had been damaged. The economic unity of the Danube valley lay in ruins. Trade between Russia and the West had been suspended. The Austro-Hungarian Empire was gone for good, killed by defeat and ethnic militancy. The new beneficiary states, with no experience in self-government, struggled with economic problems and national divisions that proved impossible to resolve. Eastern Europe became a vast power vacuum of squabbling peoples. Many of these countries became beggars, unable to survive without handouts from abroad. Even the more economically viable states were mired in inflation and recession. The collapse of empires and the rekindled ethnic hatreds diverted energy from reconstruction and efforts to build harmony among states.

Everywhere government power had increased enormously during the war and became a permanent feature of all societies even after demobilization. Many aspects of wartime control stayed in place. In many countries, the older generation of leaders remained in power and tried unsuccessfully to apply the lessons they had learned before the war to the new, often insurmountable problems of the present.

World War I destroyed the traditional European balance of power, but not the power of the sovereign state. Germany, though humiliated, was still potentially the strongest nation in Europe. The power of Russia was also temporarily in eclipse, but it too would eventually rearm and develop its economic and political strength. Its new Communist masters wanted to re-create the old Russian empire by recovering Finland, Bessarabia, the Polish territories, and the Baltic states of Latvia, Lithuania, and Estonia. The Communist call for world revolution sowed the seeds of an East-West confrontation that would persist for most of the twentieth century. Denunciation, propaganda, and subversion, learned and practiced in the war, became front-line weapons—a national policy reduced to slogans.

By the middle of the 1920s, most European countries had halted the depreciation of their currencies and returned to prewar levels of productivity. Many hoped that free and healthy commerce would gradually develop through the application of the most-favored-nation principle, even though they were reluctant to reduce their own protectionist measures. Tariffs, restrictive quotas, exchange controls, and marketing agreements continued to flourish. Income from exports declined. As foreign exchange reserves were depleted, the national currencies weakened. Governments struggling to pay for the war found their hands tied by high fixed costs, particularly for welfare, reconstruction, and war pensions. They tried quick fixes, borrowing to cover deficits or inflating their currencies. For a time, production continued to expand and prices remained stable, but with the Great Depression of the 1930s, nations again looked inward. They became defensive and increasingly listened to demagogic leaders who promised national regeneration by appealing to xenophobia.

The Nazi Imperium

The hardships brought on by the depression in Germany converted large sections of the middle and lower-middle classes and the peasantry to the doctrines of Adolf Hitler. Hitler believed that the main conflict of history was racial and that his personal intuition surpassed the sovereign will of the state. Accordingly, he preached obedience to his will. In foreign affairs, he wanted to recover the territory Germany had lost after World War I, incorporate German peoples outside the Reich into a Greater Germany, and expand the German racial community into the eastern border states, the Ukraine, and western Russia.[1]

He began by destroying the Treaty of Versailles. He withdrew Germany from the League of Nations, repudiated the arms limitation clauses of the Versailles treaty, proclaimed his intention to build a peacetime army of thirty-six divisions (about 550,000 troops), and, on 7 March 1936, sent German troops into the demilitarized Rhineland. In March 1938, claiming that he was fulfilling the Wilsonian principle of self-determination of peoples, he invaded Austria; six months later, he annexed the German-speaking districts of Czechoslovakia. Many western statesmen, including British prime minister Neville Chamberlain, thought that the Führer was essentially reasonable, that his goals were definable, and that he could be appeased without destroying the balance of power. They accepted the disappearance of Austria with only mild protest and, at the Munich Conference in September 1938, gave him the slices of Czechoslovakia he demanded. But Hitler had no intention of quitting. Driven by unlimited ambitions, he was immune to any restraint or reason. His strong belief in his personal destiny encouraged him to conduct foreign affairs on the basis of his self-delusive intuition.

After his triumph over Czechoslovakia, Hitler concentrated on the destruction of Poland. To do so, he needed an agreement with the Soviet Union and, on 23 August 1939, signed a nonaggression pact with Joseph Stalin. The two dictators carved Eastern Europe into German and Soviet spheres of influence. They partitioned Poland by dividing the country down the middle along the Narew, Vistula, and San rivers. The Germans accorded the Soviets a free hand in determining the fate of the Romanian territory of Bessarabia along with Finland, Estonia, and Latvia. (The Germans later ceded Lithuania to the Soviets in exchange for more Polish territory.) Stalin had gone a long way toward recovering the territory lost after World War I.[2] He also erroneously believed that, in the process, he had avoided war by turning Hitler's attention westward.

WORLD WAR II

The Days of Nazi Triumph

Wehrmacht Panzer units rolled across the Polish frontier at 4:45 in the morning on Friday, 1 September 1939. Britain and France declared war on Germany two days later. In contrast to 1914, no cheering crowds greeted the outbreak of this war. Even in Germany, where the leaders' desire for combat was strongest, the people did not respond with a sense of exhilaration. On 17 September, the Soviets invaded Poland from the east to take possession of the territory promised them in the Nazi-Soviet pact. Shortly afterwards, Stalin concluded treaties of mutual assistance with Estonia, Latvia, and Lithuania. All three treaties gave the Soviets the right to garrison armed forces in the Baltic countries—a preliminary for the Soviet annexation of the entire region ten months later. Stalin also demanded and received the province of Bessarabia from Romania plus, for good measure, northern Bukovina, which had once been part of the Austrian Empire.

On 10 May 1940, the war shifted to the west, as Germany invaded Belgium and Holland. The Low Countries fell after four days. The Germans then invaded France, which surrendered after a five-week struggle. At Hitler's insistence, the Germans occupied the most valuable and strategic areas—about 60 percent of the country. These included the entire Channel and Atlantic coastline and the prosperous industrial north and east, which included the Loire and Paris basins, the Flemish and Champagne lowlands, and Alsace. France was allowed to have its own government in the unoccupied part of the country, but this "Vichy" regime clearly functioned at the sufferance of the conquerors. Moreover, France was to pay the occupation costs, its armed forces would be demobilized, and its war fleet neutralized. Hitler insisted that the French capitulation on 22 June be signed in the railway carriage used for the German surrender in November 1918. The same table and chairs were used, with Hitler seating himself in the chair once occupied by Generalissimo Ferdinand Foch.

The Germans next attempted the conquest of Great Britain, but were never able to gain the necessary control of the skies. Hitler, however, considered an invasion of the British Isles secondary to his goal of establishing a great German empire in Eastern Europe. Even while the Battle of Britain was raging, the Germans were shifting their strength into Poland for an invasion of the Soviet Union. The attack began on 22 June 1941 along a broad front from the Black Sea to northern Finland. By the end of the year, the Wehrmacht had advanced to the outskirts of Moscow and Leningrad and pushed deep into the Ukraine to position itself for a thrust into the Caucasus, planned for the following year.

In his first two years of war, Hitler had thrust his Panzer army beyond Paris, into North Africa, and to within twenty miles of Moscow. Germany had achieved almost complete hegemony of continental Europe. The lands not occupied by its armies were either docile neutrals, like Sweden and Switzerland; allies, like Romania, Bulgaria, and Italy; collaborators, like Vichy France; or distinctly pro-Axis, like Spain. Hitler triumphantly designated 1941 as the "year of a great European new order," the supreme hour for the Greater German racial community.

The Grand Alliance

The European war became a world war on 7 December 1941, when 350 Japanese dive-bombers attacked the American naval base at Pearl Harbor with devastating results. The United States answered with a declaration of war on Japan. Germany and Italy responded by declaring war on the United States. But neither Hitler nor Italian dictator Benito Mussolini had managed to prevail against their current opponents in Europe, much less draft plans for a war against a new adversary. Hitler did not consider such plans necessary because he believed the Americans were already demoralized and economically weak and on the verge of a social upheaval. He incorrectly calculated that the European war would be over before American participation could have an effect. Winston Churchill, the British prime minister, knew better. He realized that with the entry of the United States into the war Hitler's fate was sealed: "All the rest was merely the proper application of overwhelming force."[3] Churchill convinced the American president Franklin D. Roosevelt that the Americans should make Europe, not the Far East, the primary theater of war.

Until the Americans assembled enough force to make a difference, the Soviet Union carried the brunt of the fighting. The Germans had concentrated about three-fourths of their total strength on the Eastern Front and, in June 1942, began an offensive aimed at the Caucasus. By August, they had achieved most of their objectives. German forces had captured the oil fields at Maikop in the foothills of the western Caucasus Mountains and had reached the Volga above Stalingrad. After two months of bitter fighting, the Wehrmacht gained control of the city. However, a Soviet counterattack cut off the German garrison and forced it to surrender. The capitulation of 31 January 1943 was the first great defeat of the vaunted Wehrmacht, which for three and a half years had never lost the initiative. The Soviets now began a counteroffensive that pushed the Germans back to the battle lines of the previous summer. Within six weeks, they had liberated the Don basin and reached the Dnieper River at Dnepropetrovsk. In the north, the Soviets lifted the siege of Leningrad. In July 1943, they managed to crush a German counterattack at the Kursk salient in the greatest tank battle in history. From then until the end of the war, the Soviets were constantly on the attack. At Moscow, they had halted the Germans at the end of their offensive. At Stalingrad, they had smashed them during the height of an offensive. At Kursk, they stopped the offensive as soon as it began.

Meanwhile, in June 1944, the British and Americans had opened a second front by successfully landing forces on the beaches of Normandy. They liberated France and struck eastward into the Rhineland. At the same time, the Red Army swept all the way to the Oder River, crossed Silesia, and Brandenburg, and proceeded until its advance units were just forty miles from Berlin. While the Soviets began their all-out attack on the German capital, the Allies crossed the Rhine and started to move into central Germany. On 30 April 1945, Hitler committed suicide in his bunker below the Reichschancellery by biting into an ampoule of cyanide. His wife Eva Braun also took poison.[4] The two bodies were then burnt in the chancellery garden.[5] Hitler's designated successor, Admiral Karl Dönitz, carried out the instrument of capitulation, which was signed on 7 May in General Dwight D. Eisenhower's headquarters at Reims, France.

The war against Japan now became the major preoccupation of the coalition. By the end of April 1945, the Japanese position had become hopeless. American marines had reconquered most of the Philippines, secured Iwo Jima, and held Okinawa. The imperial fleet had practically ceased to exist. The Japanese concentrated most of their offensive power in massed attacks by Kamikaze suicide planes, flown directly from the home islands. Nevertheless, it took the explosion of two atomic bombs—the first at Hiroshima on 6 August, the other at Nagasaki on 9 August—to end the war. The same day the bomb was dropped on Nagasaki, the Soviet Union declared war on Japan and invaded Manchuria. On the morning of 10 August, the Japanese government announced it was willing to surrender. The formal ceremony took place on 2 September, on board the U.S. battleship *Missouri* anchored in Tokyo Bay. One of the flags the Americans flew that day was the ensign with thirty-one stars that Commodore Matthew Perry had displayed when he first landed in Japan ninety-two years before.

The Goals of Victory

For Churchill bringing the United States into the war was a high priority. However, he feared that his reputation for having a "reactionary Old-World outlook" might make the task more difficult. He therefore worked out a set of war aims that he hoped would appeal to the ideological sensitivities of President Roosevelt. Churchill knew that the Americans would never fight under banners that promised a restoration of the European balance of power. Churchill's moral agenda called for the self-determination of peoples, the reduction of armaments, the guaranteeing of security through an international organization, and the establishment of government with the consent of the governed. Although these ideals were somewhat platitudinous, they became fixtures in postwar international relations.

Churchill discussed this program with Roosevelt at their meeting on board the U.S. warship *Augusta* in Placentia Bay off the Newfoundland coast on 11 August 1941. At that time, Churchill also proposed that the United States and Britain "strive to bring about a fair and equitable distribution of essential produce, not only within their territorial boundaries, but between the nations of the world."[6] Roosevelt liked what he heard and added a few principles of his own, namely "a peace to establish for all safety on the high seas and oceans" and "that all the nations of the world must be guided in spirit to the abandonment of the use of force." Both leaders advocated "improved labor standards, economic advancement, and social security" throughout the world, goals long espoused by the British Labour party, which lobbied for their inclusion. Roosevelt suspected that Churchill might try to use the war to shore up the British Empire. Therefore, to avoid giving the impression that he was making any specific commitments to Great Britain, the president insisted on a strong endorsement of the principles of international justice and civilization. He hoped this Atlantic Charter, which reflected his own idealism, would have a positive impact on American public opinion. Not the least striking feature of the charter was the admission that after the war the United States would join with Britain in establishing a better order.[7] Clearly, Roosevelt, like Wilson before him, was determined to reorganize international relations.

The American president believed that the old balance of power system was no longer workable and should be replaced by a new international peacekeeping organization. Specifically, he wanted a new United Nations to replace the defunct League of Nations. In the United Nations, the major powers would police the world.[8] They would disarm all other states and require them to submit to inspection. "If any nation menaced the peace, it would be blockaded and then if still recalcitrant, bombed."[9]

Roosevelt also wanted Stalin's cooperation and insisted that the Soviet dictator add his signature to the Atlantic Charter. Stalin agreed, but not in the spirit Roosevelt had envisioned. Stalin suspected the charter was "directed against the U.S.S.R."[10] He had specific territorial objectives and wanted a clear definition of the political geography of Europe after the defeat of Germany. Specifically, he wanted the frontiers delineated in the nonaggression pact with Germany to be recognized along with Soviet control of Latvia, Lithuania, and Estonia. The Balkans were to be regarded as a Soviet security zone. The Soviet Union would get Bessarabia, military bases in Romania, the eastern half of Poland, and its 1941 boundary with Finland. Stalin also desired an independent Austria and the separation of the Rhineland and possibly Bavaria from Germany. He wanted East Prussia to be ceded to Poland and the Sudetenland returned to Czechoslovakia. He thought Yugoslavia should receive territory from Italy and that Turkey should be given the Dodecanese Islands, certain pieces of Bulgaria, and possibly northern Syria. Stalin suspected that the British and Americans had purposely delayed the invasion of France and the opening of a second front so that the Soviet army would continue to bear the brunt of the German onslaught. He therefore refused to participate in top-level discussions with Roosevelt and Churchill until he felt he was in an unassailable position militarily. For this reason, he had refused to come to the Casablanca conference in January 1943 during the Battle of Stalingrad.

Churchill was caught in the middle between Roosevelt and Stalin, between Wilsonianism and realpolitik. The British prime minister viewed the Anglo-American partnership as the cornerstone of the wartime alliance, but he feared that failure to satisfy Stalin's fundamental aims might prompt him to make another arrangement with Hitler. Churchill was willing to recognize the Soviet incorporation of the Baltic republics, but he hesitated to do so without Roosevelt's consent. He therefore agreed that such questions "could only be settled upon the termination of the war."[11]

The Strength of Armies

Few Soviet soldiers who had lived through the hell of the Nazi invasion of their homeland had much sympathy for the sacrifices of the Americans and British whose countries had escaped occupation. Understandably, they tended to dismiss the contribution their allies had made to the defeat of Hitler. They resented the fact that the Western Allies built their postwar strength on the sacrifices of the Red Army. In return, the British and Americans frequently slighted the Soviets. Such mutual underestimation had serious consequences after the fighting ceased. The political geography of postwar Europe was determined by where the troops were when the fighting stopped. Stalin declined to invite his allies to help determine the fate of the countries the Red Army had liberated, nor did the United States and Britain invite Stalin to share in the governance of the areas they controlled—Italy, France, the Low Countries, and Japan. Both sides believed that what they controlled was theirs to dispose of as they wished. Thus, the shape of postwar Europe owed more to the disposition and number of divisions than to the discussions of diplomats (see Table 1).

POSTSCRIPT   World War II was both a war between nations and a war between peoples—a civil war between collaborators and resisters, between ethnic and racial groups, between political enemies and class enemies. Europe's multinational states were extremely fragile. Nor were they all-encompassing communities. The Nazis and Soviets spent a great deal of time in battle with domestic adversaries. Hitler had enemies in very high places. In the Soviet Union, separatist ambitions persisted despite Stalin's efforts to stamp them out.

Even before the rubble had been cleared away, people began to ask how the outcome would have been changed if different tactics had been used. In particular, the decision to use the atomic bomb was questioned. Sir Basil Liddell Hart wrote that Hiroshima had been destroyed merely to demonstrate the overwhelming power of a new weapon. It "had done no more than hasten the moment of surrender."[12] This the Americans freely admitted. They believed the Japanese might not have surrendered so quickly without the bomb. Restraint, whatever its merits, was not seriously considered because its risks were unacceptable. No state engaged in war has ever failed to use a new weapon if the advantages of deploying it have outweighed the disadvantages. Some suggested that President Harry S Truman wanted to give the Soviets a practical demonstration of the awesome power of the atomic bomb to encourage them to be more cooperative in resolving the problems of Europe.[13] Others wondered if he would have used it as willingly against the Germans. The question is moot because the surrender in Europe took place before the bomb was operational. Certainly, the Americans were not concerned about saving German lives. More Germans died in the daylight precision bombing raids on German cities than in the blast at Hiroshima.

The world has been haunted by Truman's decision ever since. It is fortunate that the use of such a powerful weapon did prompt such strong emotions. One of the most persistent safeguards against a future nuclear explosion has been in the demonstration of its practical horror. People sometimes adopt civilized behavior because they are frightened into restraint. The blasts at Hiroshima and Nagasaki certainly forestalled any ro-

TABLE 1
FRONT-LINE STRENGTH IN EUROPE, 1941–1945

	German Divisions*		Soviet Divisions	Allied Divisions		
	Eastern Front	Western Allied Fronts		Total	American	Chronology of Events
June 1941	162	6	158	5		German armies invade Soviet Union, June 22. Atlantic Charter, Aug. 14.
December 1941	180	11	236	9		Soviet counterattack at Moscow, Dec. 6. Japanese attack on Pearl Harbor, Dec. 7. Second British drive into Libya, Dec. 11.
August 1942	216	13	345	15	0	Churchill begins four-day visit to Moscow, Aug. 12. German offensive against Stalingrad begins, Aug. 22. Third British offensive in Africa, Oct. 23. American invasion of North Africa, Nov. 8.
January 1943	220	9	375	15	4	Casablanca Conference, Jan. 14–24. Tripoli occupied by British Eighth Army, Jan. 24. Germans capitulate at Stalingrad, Feb. 2.
December 1943	250	18	450	20	9	Soviets recapture Kiev, Nov. 6. Teheran Conference, Dec. 2–7. Allied forces land at Anzio, Jan. 22.
August 1944	228	79	460	70	28	Allies capture Florence, Aug. 12. Allies land in southern France, Aug. 15. Romania surrenders, Aug. 24. Paris liberated, Aug. 24. Russians reach East Prussia and Poland, end of Aug.
February 1945	150	95	480	93	49	Yalta Conference, Feb. 7–12. Russians within 30 miles of Berlin, Feb. 20. American Third Army crosses Saar River, Feb. 22.
May 1945	—	—	500	111	68	End of war in Europe, May 8. Allied Control Committee assumes control of Germany, June 5.

*Includes German satellite divisions.

Note: An average Soviet rifle division contained 8,000 men, while a comparable American division contained 15,000. A British division contained 14,000 men, and a German division had 16,000. However, while the level of manpower in the Allied divisions remained fairly constant during the war, the number of men in the German units steadily declined with a comparable falling off in training and equipment. When the Germans invaded the Soviet Union, one German division was equal in size to three Soviet divisions. After Stalingrad, the size of the German divisions had begun to decline, while the number of Soviet divisions increased. Thus, by mid-1943, the Germans had 3 million men on the Eastern Front while the Soviets had 5 million. At war's end, the Soviets outnumbered the Germans 6 million to 1 million in total front-line strength (just over three to one in total divisions, though). After the Battle of the Bulge (December 1944), German division size declined dramatically, with many German divisions having only 10 percent of their strength on paper. Another important generalization should be kept in mind: although the Soviet divisions were numerically inferior, their combat effectiveness was always much greater than that of the Americans, which had much more extensive support services.

mantic illusions about what a future world war would be like. Obviously, no such conflict would be winnable.

World War II was a total war and total victory was its logical outcome. The essence of war is violence; the atomic bomb showed just how violent war could be. Even in an age when mutually assured destruction became accepted policy, its presence had a sobering effect. Seldom has justice been better served than with the defeats of Nazi Germany, Fascist Italy, and imperial Japan. Although a heavy price was paid in the destruction of property and the loss of life, those costs do not seem too high given what the world would have experienced had the Axis won.

ENDNOTES

1. Hitler had expressed his goals in his book *Mein Kampf (My Struggle)*, a complete English translation of which appeared only in 1939. Adolf Hitler, *Mein Kampf* (New York: Reynal and Hitchcock, 1939).

2. A future Soviet premier, Nikita Khrushchev, wrote that from a territorial point of view the reacquisition of the western Ukraine from Poland gave the Soviet Union "practically nothing except what we were legally entitled to." Nikita Khrushchev, *Khrushchev Remembers* (Boston: Little, Brown, 1970), 139.

3. Winston S. Churchill, *The Grand Alliance* (Boston: Houghton Mifflin, 1950), 607.

4. Robert Waite, "Hitler's Anti-Semitism," in Bruce Mazlish, *Psychoanalysis and History* (New York: Universal Library, 1971).

5. Shortly afterwards, a detachment from *Smersh*, the Soviet counterintelligence organization, discovered the charred remains and took them with other corpses to a surgical field hospital in the Berlin suburb of Buch for autopsy. For some unknown reason, Stalin never told his allies of the discovery of Hitler's body, nor of its postmortem examination. The record was only made public a decade and a half after the Soviet dictator's death. Lev Bezymenski, *The Death of Adolf Hitler* (New York: Harcourt, Brace & World, 1968), 44–50.

6. Churchill, *The Grand Alliance*, 434.

7. Churchill, *The Grand Alliance*, 444.

8. *Foreign Relations of the United States*, 1942, 3:568.

9. Ibid., 568–69.

10. Ibid., 502. Stalin revealed these goals to British Foreign Secretary Anthony Eden, when he visited Moscow in December 1941. Stalin assumed that on certain of these points, namely, the permanent incorporation of the Baltic states into the Soviet Union, no agreement with the West was necessary. He became terribly annoyed when Eden insisted that formal agreement on *all* matters was essential.

11. Ibid., 521.

12. Basil H. Liddell Hart, *History of the Second World War* (New York: G. P. Putnam's Sons, 1970), 698.

13. Martin J. Sherwin, *A World Destroyed: The Atomic Bomb and the Grand Alliance* (New York: Alfred A. Knopf, 1975), 199.

PART ONE

EUROPE IN THE AGE
OF THE SUPERPOWERS,
1945–1960

CHAPTER 1

WAR AIMS AND POSTWAR RECONSTRUCTION, 1943–1948

PREFACE   The British and Americans and the Soviets came from different worlds with vastly different attitudes toward international politics. Just as Woodrow Wilson had minimized the security needs of the French in 1919, so Franklin D. Roosevelt a quarter of a century later also ignored crucial historical differences between his country and the Soviet Union. The United States was protected by two oceans and had traditionally viewed its security as absolute. Russia, as part of a great landmass, was surrounded by hostile neighbors with which it constantly competed for territory and power. The Communists did not need Marxist-Leninist doctrine to tell them that they occupied a precarious position in a hostile world. Stalin took his fears to the point of paranoia with his belief that the Western democracies were ganging up on him; yet, from the Soviet perspective, this seemed to be a safe assumption. In Russia, friendship was always a fragile straw upon which to base a policy. Thus, Stalin suspected that every decision the British and Americans made concerning the conduct of the war had a malevolent purpose. He refused to consider a combined command for fighting the war and put off meeting with Roosevelt until he believed he was in an advantageous position militarily; even then he selected a site for the conference that was close to the Soviet Union in territory occupied by the Red Army.

A dictator as brutal as Stalin was an affront to the very ideals Roosevelt espoused. Nevertheless, the American president was determined to win Stalin's confidence, even at the risk of chilled relations with Churchill. The task was impossible, however, and not just because of differences in background and attitude. As long as Roosevelt insisted on the right of self-determination of peoples, it was impossible to satisfy the Soviet demands for security. Moreover, Roosevelt could not even convince Stalin that the United States was wholeheartedly committed to the defeat of Nazi Germany. (Stalin believed only a cross-channel invasion of France could prove their determination.) Roosevelt, though, had high hopes that the global war would be followed by a global peace. Only the United States and the Soviet Union could guarantee this. Roosevelt's opportunity to discuss his great plans with Stalin came at Teheran in November 1943. This first summit conference of the three Allied powers set the stage for others to follow, but also showed the extent of the disagreement among the victors—differences that would determine the future shape and character of Europe.

THE END OF THE GRAND ALLIANCE

Negotiations at Teheran

Anglo-American Dissension. Britain wanted to fight the war as economically as possible, not out of stinginess but of necessity. Its efforts were truly heroic. Churchill knew that if his country suffered losses on the scale it had experienced in France during the last war, its position might be further weakened in the postwar world. For this reason, he refused to consider a cross-channel invasion until the Allied advantage was overwhelming. The British preferred to continue their efforts in the Mediterranean until the American buildup was so massive that there was no possibility of defeat. Only in August 1943 at Quebec did Roosevelt and Churchill finally agree to give priority to the invasion of France, setting a target date of 1 May 1944, a delay they knew carried risks. The Soviet victory at the Battle of Kursk in July 1943 had been so impressive that Churchill and Roosevelt thought the German defeat might come sooner than expected. The overthrow of Mussolini at the end of July showed how rapidly political circumstances could change. Therefore, the Americans presented a contingency plan, code-named "Rankin," calling for the immediate deployment of Anglo-American forces to the continent should suddenly German resistance end. In that event, Roosevelt was confident that the Allied armies could reach Berlin at the same time as the Soviets.

When the Teheran conference opened on 28 November 1943, the military situation was decidedly to the Soviet's advantage. The Red Army had an almost two-to-one superiority against the Germans. It had crossed the Dnieper the previous month and had liberated Kiev on 6 November. Meantime, the British and American advance in Italy was stalled along the Gustav line south of Rome, less than halfway up the peninsula. Nevertheless, the situation might change, and Stalin wanted an agreement on spheres of influence before Allied troops advanced farther north and closer to Central Europe. Stalin had chosen the capital city of Iran for the meeting because it was currently under joint Soviet-British protection, and because the Soviets controlled direct land communications to Moscow.[1] Roosevelt, however, protested that the remoteness of Teheran might prevent him from fulfilling his constitutional duty to sign or veto legislation within the required ten-day congressional limit.[2] Stalin replied that unless Teheran was chosen he could not attend, as he was obliged "to direct military operations day in and day out."[3] Roosevelt therefore gave way and worked out an arrangement whereby he would quit Teheran temporarily and fly to Tunis if a bill required his attention.

The foul mood of Churchill offset the high spirits and optimism of Roosevelt. When the prime minister arrived at the airport on 27 November 1943, his throat was so sore that he could speak only with difficulty. However, his cold was of small concern compared to the cold shoulder he felt Roosevelt was giving him. The two had not worked out a common conference strategy although they had flown to Teheran directly from Cairo, where they had just met with the Nationalist Chinese leader, Chiang Kai-shek.[4] Roosevelt had spent the whole time discussing the Far East situation and, at one point, had even suggested that Britain give up Hong Kong as a *"beau geste."* He avoided all private discussions with Churchill on the forthcoming conference and wasted enormous amounts of time posing for pictures. In fact, he was doing everything he could to avoid giving Stalin the impression that the Soviet Union would be faced by an Anglo-American front at Teheran. Churchill thought Roosevelt was "a charming country gentleman," but was appalled at his lack of professionalism.[5] Roosevelt was preoccupied with his grand plans for rearranging the affairs of the world. His great affection and personal friendship for Churchill did not erase his suspicion that the prime minister's foreign policy was geared toward the preservation and strengthening of Britain's imperial interests.

Once in Teheran, Roosevelt accepted Stalin's invitation to take up residence in a villa on the Soviet embassy grounds. Ostensibly, this housing solved the problems of security and discomfort due to Roosevelt's physical handicap, but it also gave Stalin an opportunity to disturb the current diplomatic equilibrium. When Roosevelt arrived, Stalin paid him a personal visit, setting a precedent for similar private meetings that were to continue throughout the conference.

Discussions on Strategy. The Americans and Soviets were in general agreement on how to fight the war. Churchill, though, keenly aware that the politics of postwar Europe would be determined by where the troops were when the fighting ceased, wanted to continue operations in the Mediterranean as part of a drive into Central Europe. He wanted to advance to Rome, push the Germans out of central Italy, and then launch an expedition across the Adriatic to help the Yugoslav partisans. He further believed that Turkey should be pressured into the war in order to "open up the Aegean Sea and assure an uninterrupted supply route to Russia into the Black Sea."[6] Turkish belligerency, Churchill said, would "undoubtedly have an effect on Rumania from whom peace feelers had already been received, and also from Hungary and might well start a landslide among the satellite states."[7] He wanted to exploit these opportunities even if it meant delaying the invasion of France. Churchill hoped this eastern strategy would limit Soviet influence in Eastern Europe at the end of the war.

Stalin opposed Churchill's scheme for that very reason, but, politics notwithstanding, the Soviet leader's arguments against the plan made sense militarily. He doubted the Turks would enter the war and questioned the wisdom of scattering Allied forces in various Mediterranean operations. Italy, he felt, was a poor place from which to launch an attack on Germany because the Alps constituted an almost insuperable barrier. He insisted that, after the capture of Rome, the Allied troops should be readied for an invasion of southern France to support the cross-channel attack in the north. "Russian experience," he remarked, "had shown that an attack from one direction was not effective and that the Soviet armies now launched an offensive from two sides at once which forced the enemy to move his reserve back and forth."[8] Roosevelt agreed, and the invasion of France, planned for spring 1944, was given top priority. The Soviets had wanted a second front in

1942, when the danger of Nazi victory was strong. Now they were to have it, two years later. Stalin believed the delay was deliberate to allow the West to profit from the further destruction of his country.

The British and Americans contemplated invading France with a combined force of thirty-five divisions, which in size were about the equivalent of fifty German divisions—an unimpressive army by Soviet standards. The Soviets currently had five million men fighting to Germany's three million. It was therefore romantic nonsense to believe that Churchill's southern strategy could have prevented a Soviet movement into Eastern Europe. As Churchill himself told Stalin, only two or three divisions were available for capturing the islands of the Aegean Sea and a scant "20 squadrons of fighters and several anti-aircraft regiments"[9] to send to aid Turkey, hardly a force capable of making any great impact. Had the British and Americans been capable of invading the Romanian and Hungarian plains in sufficient numbers to launch an attack up the Danube, had they been able to overcome the enormous problems posed by extended supply lines, they would still not have been able to prevent the eventual division of Europe between the Soviet Union and the democracies. An army as vast and powerful as the Soviet force would not have stood idly by while the British and Americans were butting their heads against mountainous defenses in unfamiliar terrain, possibly waiting for the military effort of their adversaries to collapse quickly as had occurred in the Balkan theater at the end of World War I. The Soviets most likely would have concentrated their efforts in eastern Prussia and Poland, striking across Germany to the Low Countries and dividing Europe north and south rather than east and west. Certainly, Stalin was protecting his country's right to a clear field in the Balkans, a traditional area of Russian interest, by insisting that the second front be opened in France, but his strategy also promoted the best interests of the Western powers. How lasting would have been any British and American guarantees in the Balkans, a part of Europe to which they had never before felt any particular obligation?

The British had always shied away from commitments in Eastern Europe; the Americans had difficulty accepting political responsibility for *any* part of Europe. George C. Marshall, the American chief of staff, dismissed Churchill's contention that Europe had a "soft underbelly." In the fall of 1943, he wrote: "Even though we were now firmly entrenched in North Africa to have attempted to force Germany from the South across the Alpine barrier was on the face of it impracticable. In Europe's innumerable wars no vigorously opposed crossing of the Alps had ever been successfully executed."[10] Any major Allied offensive in the Balkans would have given the Germans the welcome advantage of fighting all their major enemies on the same front.

The German Question. The problem of how to treat Germany proved even more ticklish. Faced with the persistent brutality of the Nazi regime, the three leaders assumed that the best way to guarantee a future free of German aggression was to break up the country into smaller units. Roosevelt proposed cutting up the country into seven parts: five would be self-governing areas; the other two would be placed under international control. Stalin wanted Germany dismembered to avoid a rebirth of militarism.[11] The Soviet dictator believed that the Germans would always follow men such as Hitler, an opinion that contained no little amount of irony considering his own brutal style of leadership.[12] Stalin insisted that the subjugation and control of Germany must last indefinitely. At a dinner at the Soviet embassy on 29 November, he said that effective control of Germany required the physical liquidation of between 50,000 and 100,000 German military leaders—a conservative number by Stalin's murderous standards. An angry Churchill declared that he would rather "be taken out into the garden here and now and be shot myself than sully my own and my country's honour by such infamy."[13] Whereupon he left the table and walked into the next room. Stalin followed him and, smiling broadly, tried to pass off the remark as a joke. Churchill believed that Stalin was serious.[14]

Churchill believed that wars were fought to restore balances of power. Germany, therefore, should not be defeated so badly as to allow the Soviet Union to rise in its place. Such an outcome to the war could only threaten the security of the rest of Europe, including Great Britain. The prime minister wanted a united, economically prosperous, democratic Germany, but agreed to settle for a three-way split. Churchill believed that a European equilibrium had to be ensured with the reconstruction of France as a strong nation, friendly to the West. Stalin wanted France kept weak as punishment for French collaboration with Germany. He believed that the whole French nation, particularly its leaders and upper classes, was rotten and that it did not deserve to play an important part in the immediate postwar world. Roosevelt seemed to agree. "Many years of honest labour would be necessary before France would be re-established. He said the first necessity for the French, not only for the Government but the people as well, was to become honest citizens."[15]

Stalin was full of other friendly advice. He suggested "that Great Britain and the United States install more suitable government in Spain and Portugal, since he was convinced that Franco was no friend."[16] He also encouraged the British to annex more land around Gibraltar.

On the Future of Poland. Britain and the United States were both committed to the reestablishment of a strong and independent Poland. However, the Soviet Union intended to determine that nation's future. Churchill recognized the irony of going to war to defend a state that lay outside the traditional British sphere of interest. Roosevelt had shed his previous reluctance to consider Soviet revisionism in Eastern Europe, but he did not want to appear as if he were participating in an arrangement that would jeopardize Poland's national independence. He explained that six or seven million Americans of Polish extraction dictated his attitude. As a practical man, he did not wish to lose their vote.

The West was not in a very strong position to establish Poland's future frontiers. Churchill had reconciled himself to this loss of influence and told Stalin that "he personally had no attachment to any specific frontier between Poland and the Soviet Union; [but] that he felt that the consideration of Soviet security on their western frontiers was a governing factor."[17] Stalin insisted that Poland's eastern frontiers would be those established by the 1939 German-Soviet Nonaggression Pact; he felt these were "just right."[18] He intended to compensate Poland with German territory, pushing the country's western boundary to the Oder River and into eastern Prussia. Furthermore, since it seemed unlikely that Stalin could be coaxed into recognizing the Polish government in exile in London, any future Polish government would exist only at Soviet sufferance. The same was true of the Baltic peoples. Stalin did not consider the future status of Latvia, Lithuania, and Estonia subject to negotiation: these states would be reincorporated automatically into the Soviet Union. When Churchill expressed a desire to see Finland remain independent, Stalin agreed, but insisted "they must pay half of the damage they had caused."[19]

The Four Policemen. Stalin's authority at Teheran flowed naturally from the power of his army, which was more than adequate to ensure Soviet domination of Eastern Europe. The negotiations helped him gauge Western intentions. He saw that the British and Americans had serious disagreements over the character of their future political commitments to Europe. Churchill wanted to prevent Great Power—that is, Soviet—domination of the continent. Roosevelt was preoccupied with creating a new world organization, which, as he explained on the first day of the conference, meant establishing sovereignty in a collective body such as the United Nations, "a concept which had never been developed in past history."[20] Roosevelt envisioned the basic power of this postwar organization in the hands of the "Four Policemen"; that is, the Soviet Union, the United States, Great Britain, and China—states with the strength to deal with any emergency and threat to peace. As policemen, they would have the right to threaten aggressive nations with "immediate bombardment and possible invasion."[21] When Roosevelt explained his personal commitment to worldwide organization, he gave the Soviets the impression that they need not fear the United States as a powerful rival in postwar European affairs. The Americans, in keeping with their past record in foreign wars, would initiate a disengagement as soon as victory was achieved. Roosevelt told Stalin that only in the most extreme case, such as the current crisis, would the Americans ever again contemplate sending troops to Europe. In a lesser crisis, he envisaged the "sending of American planes and ships," but "England and the Soviet Union would have to handle the land armies in the event of any future threat to peace."[22]

Stalin wanted to recover the territory lost by Russia at the end of World War I, and he wanted to establish a sphere of influence in Eastern Europe. Beyond this, his aims seemed dependent upon "what form of security organization would be developed after the war and how far the United States and British governments were prepared to go in implementing the police power of such an organization."[23] Although no final decisions were made at Teheran, the discussions revealed the fears and hopes of the participants, and the conference established the agenda for future meetings of the Big Three. Stalin was always more an opportunist than a rigid doctrinaire. In his determination to wield absolute power, he had made the Communist dialectic his servant. Thus, the future confrontation with his Western allies developed more from the practical concerns of projecting power than from an inevitable clash of contradictory ideologies. Stalin made it clear at Teheran that Soviet security would not be satisfied with anything less than the domination of Poland. Furthermore, he would set that country's new boundaries.

Roosevelt would have preferred a sovereign Poland, but he was not prepared to risk antagonizing Stalin and thereby losing Soviet cooperation after the war by insisting on freedom for the Poles. Roosevelt also set the strategy that would bring final victory in Europe by definitively agreeing on the two-pronged invasion of France from the west and the south—an operation Churchill had tried to delay as long as possible.[24]

The Conference at Yalta

Soviet Hegemony in Eastern Europe. By the late summer of 1944, the western Allies had liberated Paris and were across the Seine; meanwhile the Soviet army had reached the borders of prewar Poland and was driving into Romania. The German invaders had been successfully cleared from almost the entire country. Romania capitulated on 23 August; Bulgaria surrendered the following month.

At a reception in the Livadia Palace during the Yalta Conference, host President Franklin Roosevelt seems to be the only one paying attention to the toast being offered by Secretary of State Edward Stettinius. Josef Stalin and Winston Churchill on Roosevelt's right and left have their attention focused elsewhere, while Soviet Foreign Minister Vyacheslav, at the end of the table, peruses the menu. Many more toasts will be offered before this banquet is over.

Stalin knew that the Red Army would assure the Soviets control of Eastern Europe, but not until the war against Germany was as good as over did he consent to another summit meeting, this time at Yalta, the favorite summer residence of the last tsar. The Germans had evacuated the town the previous year and had left it in shambles. The Soviets worked hard to refurbish the place, completing the job just weeks before the conference opened on 4 February 1945. Every effort was made to ensure the comfort of the guests. A member of the British delegation casually remarked that the cocktails contained no lemon peels, and "the next day a lemon tree loaded with fruit was growing in the hall."[25] This courtesy made up in part for the bedbugs and toilets that did not flush. Stalin was friendly, charming, and confident. He had good reason to be.

While the British and the Americans were still recovering the ground they had lost during the Battle of the Bulge, the Red Army was forty miles from Berlin, a bit more than a day's march if unopposed. German resistance in Hungary had been crushed, and the road to Vienna lay open, with the Soviets in control of most of the territory of Eastern and Southeastern Europe. Stalin had largely decided what he wanted and was now determined to keep it. In December 1944, much to the dismay of the West, he had recognized his own creation, the Communist Lublin government, as the basis upon which he would construct the future political administration of Poland. He was also entrenching Communist leaders in positions of power in Bulgaria, Romania, and Hungary.

Churchill and Roosevelt wanted to prevent the communization of Poland, but with the Soviets already occupying most of the country, Churchill could only complain that Poland should be mistress of her house and captain of her soul. Roosevelt, by this time a very sick man with only a few months to live, again tried to coax Stalin into making a gesture by reminding him of the six or seven million Polish-Americans who formed part of the Democratic party's electorate. Stalin was not inclined to be generous. He insisted that the security of the Soviet Union depended upon a subservient Poland. He did agree to "add to the Provisional Polish (Lublin) Government some democratic leaders from Polish émigré

circles . . . . and from inside Poland," a vague concession more than offset by maximum demands over Poland's future boundaries. Stalin had decided that Poland's
western frontiers should be traced from the town of Stettin southward to and along
the Oder River and then south along the Neisse River.[26] Since the hundreds of
thousands of Germans who lived in this area would be cleared out, its separation
from the Reich might cause permanent Polish-German hostility and allow the
Soviet Union to assume the role of Poland's protector. The British and Americans
realized this would be the likely outcome, but they could do little to prevent it.
They saved face by deferring the question to an eventual postwar peace conference.

Although the Polish question was discussed at seven of the eight plenary sessions, the Western leaders had more important things on their minds. Churchill,
still trying to get the Soviet Union's help in restoring a general European balance
of power, lobbied for an occupation zone for France in Germany. Roosevelt pushed
for amplification of the authority of the United Nations through which he hoped
to re-create international order and extend American influence.[27] He also wanted
China to be elevated to Great Power status, and he wanted the cooperation of
the Soviet Union in the war against Japan.

As a result of the desperate, suicidal resistance by the Japanese on Okinawa
and Iwo Jima, the Americans assumed that an invasion of the Japanese home
islands would be necessary to end the war. General Leslie Groves, the head of the
Manhattan Project to develop an atomic bomb, had judged that a bomb equivalent
to ten thousand tons of TNT, enough power to wreck a large city, would be
operational only by August 1945. Less than two weeks before the beginning of the
Yalta Conference, the Joint Chiefs of Staff informed Roosevelt that "Russia's entry
at as early a date as possible consistent with her ability to engage in offensive
operations is necessary to provide maximum assistance to our Pacific operations."[28]
Roosevelt was therefore prepared to offer the Soviets powerful inducements to fight
the Japanese. Specifically, he promised the restoration of Russia's former rights
"violated by the treacherous attack of Japan in 1904," including the southern half
of Sakhalin Island, the lease of Port Arthur as a Soviet naval base, and the joint
operation of the Chinese-Eastern and South-Manchurian Railroads. The Soviets
would also get the Kurile Islands.[29] In exchange, Stalin agreed to attack Japan
within ninety days after the end of the war in Europe, enough time for the Soviets
to transfer their armies to Asia. He also pledged to conclude a pact of friendship
and alliance with the National Government of China "in order to render assistance
to China with its armed forces for the purposes of liberating China from the
Japanese yoke."[30] The Americans assumed that China would emerge as a major
East Asian power and wanted to promote the stability of the Nationalist government. They also believed that since the Soviet Union was a Far Eastern as well
as a European power, it was better to offer the Soviets something and win their
support for the status quo rather than risk making them perpetual antagonists.

How to Treat Germany. The major problem facing the Big Three continued to
be the question of Germany. Roosevelt and Stalin were still disposed to treat the
defeated with great severity. The American president had once advocated a plan,
advanced by his secretary of the treasury Henry Morgenthau, that proposed to
destroy Germany's industrial potential and return the country to a pastoral economy. Churchill had gone along, especially when (at the second Quebec Conference in September 1944) his acquiescense had produced an American commitment to lend Britain $6.5 billion after the war.

No sooner had he agreed than he began to have second thoughts. Roosevelt was also becoming somewhat less extreme. Both Secretary of State Cordell Hull and Secretary of War Henry Stimson thought the impoverishment of Germany would be disastrous for rebuilding a prosperous Europe. Although the stern approach had gradually lost favor, the attitudes that had inspired it nevertheless remained and helped prolong the discussions on dismembering Germany. At the session on 5 February, Stalin said he assumed that everybody was still in favor of partition and asked what this would involve. Would the Allies establish one German government, or would they set up separate governments for each of the various parts? Since Churchill was unwilling to go further than recognizing the principle of dismemberment, no agreement was possible. Therefore, the Allies recognized the likelihood of dismemberment only if that became necessary for future peace and security.

The Big Three confirmed the zones of occupation, which had been agreed upon in principle at the Moscow Conference of Foreign Ministers in October 1943. In February 1944, the foreign ministers set the future zone of Soviet occupation and agreed on the joint occupation of Berlin. These decisions were confirmed and further defined at Yalta. Under the plan, each of the three powers would occupy its own zone but would coordinate administration and control through a central commission consisting of the Supreme Commanders of the Three Powers. This would mean that roughly 40 percent of pre-1938 German territory (with 36 percent of the population) would be under Soviet control with the rest divided between Britain and the United States. Berlin was to be administered under the combined control of all three. Mainly through pressure from Churchill, Stalin agreed that France could have a zone of occupation and participate in the administration of postwar Germany, providing the French share came from the area allotted to the British and Americans. The inclusion of France marked a major change in attitude from the Teheran Conference where Stalin and Roosevelt had maintained that France would not be allowed to play a major role in European politics after the war. Only Churchill had put in a good word for the French, saying that he could not conceive of a civilized world without a flourishing and lively France. The inclusion of France in the occupation plan had positive and negative aspects. On the one hand, France, not being a party to the Yalta accords, did not feel bound by them; on the other hand, the Western powers had enlarged their stake in German affairs, especially their position in Berlin, a city completely surrounded by Soviet territory. French inclusion enhanced the legal independence of the city and increased the determination of the Western powers to hold on to their share during the Soviet blockade of 1948.[31]

Stalin demanded that Germany pay heavy reparations. He wanted certain industries, like machine tools, to be transferred to the Soviet Union; he wanted the rolling stock, plus yearly payments in kind for a decade. He also demanded a general reduction of German heavy industry by 80 percent and insisted that "in the interests of the orderly execution of the reparations plan and for the security of Europe there should be an Anglo-Soviet-American control over the German economy which would last beyond the period of the reparations payment."[32] Roosevelt favored giving the German people only enough to keep them from starvation, while Churchill warned that the exaggerated demands made on Germany after World War I eventually proved self-defeating. The question was not settled. The Allies declared Germany responsible for the losses it caused during the war and left it to the Reparations Commission to work out the details.

Lesser Issues. The British and Americans tried to obtain an agreement for the development of independent governments in Eastern Europe; they settled for a confirmation of the Atlantic Charter in the "Declaration of Liberated Europe," which promised that "the restoration of sovereign rights and self-government [would go] to those people who have been forcibly deprived of them by the aggressive nations."[33] Stalin showed a willingness to reach an agreement on the establishment of the United Nations, an area that he believed Roosevelt considered important largely to satisfy American popular opinion. Stalin emphasized that "he was prepared in concert with the United States and Great Britain to protect the rights of the small powers but that he would never agree to having any action of any of the Great Powers submitted to the judgment of the small powers."[34] The five permanent members of the United Nations Security Council (the Soviet Union, the United States, Britain, France, and China) had to agree unanimously on how to enforce the peace. None of them believed that a system of world security could really prevent aggression.

Stalin did not consider the Yalta agreements an inhibition on his freedom of action in Eastern Europe. His promise to allow free elections in Eastern Europe was not sincere. He once remarked to Marshal Georgi Zhukov: "Churchill wants the Soviet Union to border with a bourgeois Poland, alien to us, while we can not allow this to happen. We want to have, once and for all, a friendly Poland as our neighbor, and that is what the Polish people want too."[35] Stalin apparently believed Roosevelt's assurances that American troops would be gone from Europe within two years.[36] Therefore, once he had consolidated his hold in Eastern Europe, there would be nothing to prevent him from extending Soviet influence westward if he so desired.

SPHERES OF INFLUENCE

The Potsdam Conference

A Campaign of Stalinization. Shortly after the end of the Yalta Conference, Stalin dispatched Andrei Vyshinsky to Romania. Vyshinsky's job was to pressure King Michael into dismissing his present government, which the Soviets deemed terroristic and incompatible with the principles of a people's democracy, and replacing it with one totally controlled by Communists. The king gave way. In the new ministry, representatives of "bourgeois" parties held only two portfolios. Roosevelt charged that the Soviet action was incompatible with Stalin's promises at Yalta, which were embodied in the Declaration of Liberated Europe. But the protests changed nothing.

Stalin's heavy hand in Romanian politics was the prelude for a general purge of all non-Communists from the left-of-center coalition governments that had emerged elsewhere in Eastern Europe. When in March 1945 the West protested the arrest of certain non-Communist Polish underground leaders, Stalin defiantly replied:

> You evidently do not agree that the Soviet Union is entitled to seek in Poland a Government that would be friendly to it, that the Soviet Government can not agree to the existence in Poland of a Government hostile to it. I do not know whether a genuinely representative government has been

established in Greece, or whether the Belgian Government is a genuinely democratic one. The Soviet Union was not consulted when those governments were being formed, nor did it claim the right to interfere in these matters, because it realized how important Belgium and Greece are to the security of Great Britain.[37]

Stalin insisted that the arrests were necessary for military security.[38] The Czechs tried to head off similar Soviet pressure by voluntarily reorganizing their government to include Communists. This action did not dissuade Stalin from demanding Ruthenia. Historically, this territory had never been part of Russia, but Stalin wanted it because it would move the Soviet frontier across the Carpathian Mountains and create a common border with Hungary. Stalin also retained a piece of prewar Romanian territory that gave the Soviet Union part of the mouth of the Danube River; and he lopped off the northern part of East Prussia, which bordered on the Baltic and included the famous ice-free port of Königsberg. The Soviets claimed to be merely administering the area pending a German peace treaty, but the acquisition became permanent.

The British and Americans had been willing to recognize the Soviet Union as a paramount power in Eastern Europe, but they were horrified at Stalin's systematic extinction of the area's political independence. They hoped the example of Finland might provide a suitable alternative to tight control. Finland had recognized Soviet hegemony, yet retained its independence. The campaign of stalinization in Eastern Europe seemed to be motivated by more than a desire for security, and it only confirmed their suspicions that Stalin was developing bases from which he would project Soviet power westward. The Soviets also continued to pressure Turkey to cede the Transcaucasian areas that the Treaty of Brest-Litovsk had detached from Russia in 1918. They also demanded revision of the Montreux Convention to allow their warships free passage through the Istanbul Straits, and they wanted to establish a Soviet military and naval base on the Sea of Marmara, in effect blocking the passage of others from the Aegean to the Black Sea. Moreover, the international Communist movement, though not the Comintern, which had been dissolved in 1943 to appease the British and the Americans, was being reactivated and reorganized to prepare for a new era of revolutionary militancy.

The Soviets wanted to avoid any direct confrontation with the West, at least until they had established firm control over Eastern Europe. They therefore cooperated in the establishment of the United Nations and freely signed proclamations in favor of democratic liberties and national independence. Stalin had learned to count on what he regarded as Roosevelt's generous idealism. He was therefore greatly disturbed by news of the American war leader's death on 12 April 1945. Harry Truman, Roosevelt's successor, was an unknown quantity. He had little experience in foreign affairs, but intended to show that he could be firm and would make no concessions from basic principles or traditions in order to win Soviet favor.[39] Stalin, anxious to discover whether Truman contemplated any policy changes, had Foreign Minister Vyacheslav Molotov stop off in Washington on his way to the United Nations meeting at San Francisco. Molotov found that the new chief executive regarded the Polish question as the acid test of Soviet willingness to cooperate. Truman accused the Soviets of violating the Yalta accord, and when Molotov became evasive, the president became more forceful. "I have never been talked to like that in my life," protested Molotov. "Carry out your agreements and you won't get talked to like that," the president replied.[40]

The Strains of Diplomacy. The final defeat of Nazi Germany made another summit conference necessary. On 6 May, the day before the German surrender at Reims, Churchill proposed that one be held "in some unshattered town in Germany, if such can be found."[41] The prime minister was particularly delighted that President Truman, whom he had never met, intended to stand firmly on "our rightful interpretation of the Yalta Agreements," but the Americans' intention to pull their troops out of Europe deeply worried him. Churchill feared that if the outstanding differences between the West and the Soviet Union were not settled before this withdrawal occurred, there would be no satisfactory solution and very little chance of preventing a third world war.[42]

The conference finally got under way in Potsdam, near Berlin, on 17 July. Its meetings were held at the Cecilienhof Palace, the country estate of Crown Prince Wilhelm, the last Hohenzollern heir to the throne. The purpose of the meeting was to prepare for an eventual peace conference that would draft a treaty of peace with Germany. The task of drafting treaties of peace with Italy, Romania, Bulgaria, Hungary, and Finland was assigned to a special council of foreign ministers from the five major victorious governments: the United States, Britain, the Soviet Union, France, and China.[43] Truman hoped the Foreign Ministers Council would expedite the final peace, but with the heads of government so divided, the group's ability to propose solutions to problems was limited.

Stalin came to Potsdam to get the West to accept his new order in Eastern Europe. The British and Americans had officially rejected, but privately accepted, the Soviet presence there, but they disagreed over important details. Churchill protested the Soviet scheme to turn the parts of Germany that were to form Poland's western frontier over to Polish administration. He said this would admit the Poles as a fifth occupying power and "would undoubtedly mark a breakdown of the Conference."[44] Stalin claimed that these territories were practically all Polish because the local German population had fled before the Red Army had arrived.[45] Truman supported Churchill and asked if Germany were going to be given away piecemeal. But nothing was going to stop Stalin from carrying out the changes he thought necessary. All Germans in the lands east of the Oder-Neisse line were systematically being rounded up and expelled. The Poles did not want any repetition of the irredentist agitation that had followed World War I.

There were acrimonious exchanges over German reparations. The Soviets insisted they immediately be paid half of the $20 billion they claimed at Yalta. Churchill and Truman feared that such an amount would critically damage the German economy, contribute to revolution, civil disorder, and starvation, and force the West to subsidize the German standard of living. In short, Britain and the United States would bankroll Soviet reparations. Churchill knew that his country was in no condition to undertake such support, even had it desired to do so. He told Truman that Britain itself needed aid. In order to fight the war, he said, Britain "had spent more than half her foreign investments for the common cause when we were alone, and now emerged from the war with a great external debt of three thousand million pounds . . . . we should [therefore] have to ask for help to become a going concern again, and until we got our wheels turning properly we could be of little use to world security."[46] The Soviets also continued to demand official recognition of their Eastern European puppet regimes. The Americans countered by asking that the Soviets honor the Declaration of Liberated Europe. Stalin pushed for greater Soviet influence in Iran and Turkey; a share in

**At Potsdam, two
newcomers to
international diplomacy,**
Prime Minister Clement
Attlee and President
Harry Truman, stand
next to veteran
negotiator Josef Stalin,
who as usual is backed by
his faithful henchman
Molotov. Attlee defeated
Churchill in the British
general election and
replaced him halfway
through the conference.

the administration of Libya, the old Italian colony of Tripoli; and the annexation
of the port of Königsberg. At a banquet in Churchill's honor on 23 July, he asked
in the middle of the toasts, "If you find it impossible to give us a fortified position
in the Marmara, could we not have a base at Dedeagatch [Alexandroúpolis]?"[47]

A Proposed Compromise. Midway through the conference, the British electorate
replaced Churchill with Clement Attlee. The new prime minister, who arrived in
Potsdam on 28 July, brought no change to British policy—he had been Churchill's
deputy and needed no special briefing—but, lacking the prestige of his predecessor,
he was not as forceful in pressing the Soviets. This opened the way for Truman,
who was becoming impatient and wanted to conclude the negotiations as quickly
as possible. The Americans proposed a compromise: they would agree to the Polish
western boundary if the Soviets would give in on German reparations. Truman
allowed the Poles to administer all the German territory east of the Oder-Neisse
line, pending a final settlement at the peace conference, in exchange for Stalin's
agreement to take most of his reparations from the Soviet zone.[48] The compromise
was not an entirely happy one for either party. Reparation was the issue on which
the Soviets had the greatest moral claim, but the one on which they received the
least satisfaction; and by informally recognizing the Soviet frontiers for Poland,
the Americans seemed to be sacrificing liberty for expediency.[49]

The exchange of promises was not significant in political terms; both reparations
and Poland were lost causes. However, the compromise did allow agreement to be
reached on a series of minor issues. There was to be no immediate reestablishment
of a German central government, although the division of the country into zones
was not intended to be permanent. (Had Stalin then considered politically separating the Soviet zone from the rest of Germany, it does not seem likely that he
would have given so much valuable German territory to Poland.) Finance, transport, communications, foreign trade, and industry would be administered collectively, and the country would be treated as a single economic unit with common
policies on industrial production, wages and prices, currency and banking, central
taxation, and customs. But, despite these accords, the wartime alliance was fin-

ished. The Potsdam decisions were intended to be provisional pending final negotiations at a peace conference. It was doubtful such a meeting would ever be
held. Furthermore, the agreement was achieved without the participation of France. The Big Three had assumed that Charles de Gaulle would automatically give
his assent. This was a mistake. De Gaulle did not feel bound by the decisions of
any conference to which he had not been invited.

Great Power Rivalry

Efforts at Peacemaking. The two meetings of the Council of Foreign Ministers
immediately after Potsdam, held in London in September 1945 and in Moscow
in December 1945, produced little progress toward peacemaking and only reaffirmed existing disagreements. When the Americans continued to push for free
elections in Eastern Europe, the Soviets took their insistence as evidence of an
unfriendly attitude, a charge the Americans staunchly denied. Yet establishing
Western-style democracies was difficult in a region with such a strong authoritarian
tradition. Only the Czechs had really succeeded. Moreover, the Soviets feared that
allowing free elections would have resulted in the victory of anti-Soviet, anti-
Communist leaders. The Soviets, therefore, assumed the Americans were only
interested in weakening Soviet control so they could extend Western influence.
The Soviets, with a certain amount of truth, pointed out that the United States
wanted entry to the Soviet sphere of interest while excluding the Soviet Union
from the Western sphere. The Soviets also feared the United States might threaten
them with nuclear weapons. At the September meeting in London, when Molotov
asked Secretary of State James Byrnes if he had an atomic bomb in his side pocket,
Byrnes replied, "We carry our artillery in our hip pocket. If you don't cut out this
stalling and let us get down to work, I am going to pull an atomic bomb out of
my hip pocket and let you have it."[50] The remark did not actually reflect American
nuclear diplomacy, but the sour-faced Molotov could hardly be expected to appreciate the American brand of humor.

The atmosphere was not nearly so tense at the December conference. Nevertheless, the failure to reach any agreement over levels of German production and
economic unity convinced Secretary of State Byrnes that the Soviets were eager
to profit politically from the country's weakness. The Soviets did consent to
broaden the Communist-dominated regimes in Bulgaria and Romania to include
other anti-fascist parties. And they agreed to attend a general peace conference to
be held in Paris the following year and to help prepare for the peaceful use of
nuclear energy through a United Nations Atomic Energy Commission.

Truman thought such gestures meaningless. Yet, while he talked about con-
fronting the Soviets with an iron fist, his administration was presiding over one
of the most complete and rapid military demobilizations of modern times. In less
than two years after Hitler's defeat, only two American, four British, and three
French divisions were stationed in Western Europe, all uncoordinated by any effective military alliance. The Soviets had also demobilized, though not as significantly. They had reduced the 500 divisions in existence at the time of Germany's
surrender down to 175, concentrating 60 percent of these forces in the occupied
countries of Europe and the proximate western border regions of the Soviet Union.
In East Germany alone, the Soviets had 22 divisions, 18 of them armored. The
cutback had actually resulted in a more efficient and better equipped force. Moreover, as soon as hostilities ended, the Soviets launched a major arms modernization

program, with emphasis on the development of a long-range air force and a first-class oceangoing navy. The Americans believed such military strength vastly exceeded what the Soviets needed for legitimate self-defense.

George Kennan, the American chargé d'affaires in Moscow, sounded the alarm about Soviet intentions when he called the Soviet Union:

> a political force committed fanatically to the belief that with the U.S. there can be no permanent *modus vivendi* that it is desirable and necessary that the internal harmony of our society be disrupted, our traditional way of life be destroyed, the international authority of our state be broken, if Soviet power is to be secure. This political force . . . . is borne along by deep and powerful currents of Russian nationalism. . . . For it, the vast fund of objective fact about human society is not, as with us, the measure against which outlook is constantly being tested and re-formed, but a grab bag from which individual items are selected arbitrarily and tendentiously to bolster an outlook already preconceived. . . . [But] Soviet power, unlike that of Hitlerite Germany, is neither schematic nor adventuristic. It does not work by fixed plans. It does not take unnecessary risks. [It is] impervious to [the] logic of reasons, [but] it is highly sensitive to [the] logic of force. For this reason it can easily withdraw—and usually does—when strong resistance is encountered at any point. Thus, if the adversary has sufficient force and makes clear his readiness to use it, he rarely has to do so.[51]

Kennan got support from a welcome quarter. Winston Churchill, in his famous speech at Fulton, Missouri (5 March 1946), said:

> Nobody knows what Soviet Russia and its Communist international organization intends to do in the immediate future, or what are the limits, if any, to their expansive and proselytizing tendencies. . . . From Stettin in the Baltic to Trieste in the Adriatic an iron curtain has descended across the continent. . . . The communist parties, which were very small in these eastern states of Europe, have been raised to pre-eminence and power beyond their numbers and are seeking everywhere to obtain totalitarian control.[52]

Stalin's attitude clearly was "I control what I conquer," but to belabor the point, the West was also unwilling to allow Soviet influence in its zones of occupation. Churchill, who was no longer prime minister, was unlikely to have made this speech without the approval of President Truman, who was in the audience.

Stalin took the words as conclusive evidence of an Anglo-American cabal. He described the speech as "an unfriendly act and an unwarranted attack on himself and the U.S.S.R. which, if it had been directed against the United States, would never have been permitted in Russia."[53] Stalin thought that Churchill was trying to instigate war against the Soviet Union with the participation of the United States, as had been done in 1919. In response, Soviet propaganda became more violently anti-American. American leaders were denounced for having abandoned Roosevelt's heritage and succumbed to "militarist, imperialist, and expansionist tendencies incompatible with international peace and security."[54] The United States was Fascism in another guise, "a manifestation of capitalist society in its imperialistic phase." The Soviets believed that both the United States and Great Britain were supporting Fascism to fight democracy and the Soviet Union. However, the United States was "much the greater menace since it emerged from the war as the strongest of capitalist countries."[55] In this tense atmosphere, the victors met to try to produce a peace settlement.

The Results of the Plenary Conference. Representatives of twenty-two states gathered in Paris in the Luxembourg Palace, on 29 July 1946, to draft peace treaties between the Allies and Italy, Bulgaria, Hungary, Romania, and Finland. The contrasts between this peace conference and the one that followed World War I were striking. The 1919 conference had moments of high drama and genuine accomplishment; the participants in 1946 were men of lesser stature—although South Africa's Jan Christian Smuts was present at both—and their deliberations seemed lackluster. Most of the preparatory work had been done the previous spring by experts who labored over the texts of the treaties, trying to produce drafts that would win final approval. Their efforts were far from conclusive. The Plenary Conference continued the work, deliberating for almost three months over a host of amendments. Even when the "final" texts were submitted to the Council of Foreign Ministers the second week of October, the deadlock continued. The representatives of the Great Powers decided to continue the discussions at a later date among themselves. Thus, the Plenary Conference ended without achieving its purpose. Georges Bidault, the French foreign minister and later premier, wrote, "When everyone got together, there were no results at all." Nor was anything accomplished when the four countries discussed things by themselves. Only "the tone changed slightly."[56] Bidault's judgment may have been too harsh. Although the council failed to reach an overall agreement on Central Europe, peace treaties were eventually worked out with the lesser enemy powers. Moreover, the Soviets were willing to permit the existence of a reasonably independent Finland.

The Council of Foreign Ministers finalized the treaties at sessions held at the Waldorf Astoria in New York (4 November–6 December). The signing ceremony took place in Paris on 10 February 1947 at the French Foreign Ministry in the Salle de l'Horloge, the same room where the plenary sessions of the Paris Conference negotiating the Treaty of Versailles in 1919 were held. Each of the five treaties contained an affirmation of the inviolability of human rights and fundamental freedoms as well as reparations clauses and disarmament provisions. Their territorial provisions were heavily influenced by former treaties, especially those negotiated at Paris in 1919–1920. The previous summer each of the enemy countries had an opportunity to make comments and observations on the draft treaties. They all sought to mitigate the terms, claiming that they were not the same nations they had been previously. Little of this special pleading had been effective.

Italy was shorn of all the territory it had annexed during the Fascist period and was deprived of its colonial possessions. Its losses included Rhodes and the Dodecanese, which went to Greece; most of the territory on the Dalmatian coast (the greater part of Venezia Giulia with Istria, Fiume, and the Adriatic islands), which went to Yugoslavia; and some small northwestern frontier areas, which went to France. The Italians also surrendered sovereignty over Ethiopia, Libya, Eritrea, and Italian Somaliland. Italy was allowed to keep the South Tyrol, and it managed—in 1954—to recover the city of Trieste, which the treaty originally created a free city under the protection of the Security Council of the United Nations.[57] The Italian armed forces were limited to 300,000 troops; and the country was required to pay a total of $360 million in reparations to the Soviet Union, Greece, Yugoslavia, Ethiopia, and Albania.

The other Axis states were also stripped of their ill-gotten gains. Romania was forced to give Bessarabia and northern Bukovina to the Soviet Union, surrender the Black Sea province of Dobruja to Bulgaria, and cede Transylvania to Hungary. In addition, Romania was required to pay the Soviets $300 million in reparations and limit the size of its armed forces to 138,000 troops. Hungary returned to the

GERMAN ZONES
OF OCCUPATION

SOVIET TERRITORIAL GAINS
1946

From Poland

From Finland

From Germany

From Czechoslovakia

From Romania

From Estonia, Lithuania,
and Latvia

POLISH TERRITORIAL GAINS
1946

From Germany

Soviet Republic Boundary

Iron Curtain

Map 1

frontiers of the Treaty of Trianon. Its armed forces were reduced to 70,000 men, and it was forced to pay an indemnity of $200 million to the Soviet Union and $100 million apiece to Czechoslovakia and Yugoslavia. Bulgaria lost the lands it had added as a result of its association with Nazi Germany but gained Dobruja from Romania. Finland did not get off so easily. In addition to the territories the Soviets had taken in March 1940 as a result of the Winter War (the Karelian isthmus, the strategic port of Vyborg, and the lands surrounding Lake Ladoga), the Finns lost the strategic northern area of Petsamo thereby cutting off direct Finnish access to the Arctic Ocean. (The Soviet Union now had a common frontier with Norway.) The Finnish armed forces were limited to 41,500 men, and Finland was forced to pay $300 million in reparations. Despite the severity of these terms, the Finns could consider themselves lucky that the Soviets had not chosen to control the whole country as they had done with Hungary, Romania, and Bulgaria.

Peacemaking after World War II was remarkable for the degree to which most of the former enemy states had become satellites or clients of the chief negotiators. Since the Soviet Union had by then established complete authority over Romania, Bulgaria, and Hungary, no formal peace settlement was really imperative. Regularizing the situation did offer certain advantages, however. The Soviets especially wanted to abolish the Allied Control Commissions that gave the Western powers an official presence in their satellites. Moreover, after the peace settlement, the American and British troops would leave Italy, allowing greater freedom of action for the Communist party. No similar provisions required the Soviets to withdraw their armies from Eastern Europe.

The Truman Doctrine

The Mediterranean Crises. The British had been the dominant power in the Mediterranean Sea since the eclipse of Turkish power a century earlier. Nevertheless, historically, the Soviets also had strong interests in the area. On 7 August 1946, the Soviets demanded that Turkey give them certain naval bases in the Dardanelles. Previously, the Soviets had tried to bully Turkey into returning the provinces of Kars and Ardahan lost by the Treaty of Brest-Litovsk. Washington viewed these moves as the beginning of a Soviet campaign to gain control of this vital waterway. On 15 August, Dean Acheson, under secretary of state, told Truman that if Stalin's claims against Turkey were not opposed, they "would be followed next by infiltration and domination of Greece . . . with the obvious consequences in the Middle East and the obvious threat to the line of communications of the British to India." Acheson thought this Soviet "trial balloon" should be strongly resisted even though it might lead to armed conflict. Truman was of a like mind.

The British no longer had the strength to protect Europe's southern flank, but were reluctant to disengage. In Whitehall, fear of a horrendous scenario took shape: Greece would go Communist, Turkey would follow suit, and the Soviet Union would gain control of the entire eastern Mediterranean. The policy that the British had laboriously shaped during the nineteenth century to contain Russian imperialism would be in ruins. The British hoped the Americans could be shocked into making long-range commitments, but until this new Soviet threat, the Americans had given little thought to making a major commitment in the Mediterranean.

Truman now ordered Acheson to canvass the secretaries of war and navy and the chiefs of staff for their views on whether "to take a firm attitude on the Russian *démarche* or whether we should do as we have in the past—protest, but ultimately give in."[58] The situation was tricky because the Americans had not yet developed a military capacity to back up a strong response. They had some warships in the Mediterranean, including the aircraft carrier *Franklin D. Roosevelt*, but a very large number of ships in the "active" fleet could not go to sea "because of lack of competent personnel." The air strength available in Europe was then 460 fighters, only 175 of which were first-line, and about 90 bombers.[59] Even if these bombers had all been operational, and if the United States had been able to arm each with an atomic bomb, there was little assurance they would reach their targets, given the strength of the Soviet air defenses. Yet, to prevent the Red Army from over-running Western Europe and depriving the Americans of their strike bases, the bombers would have had to knock out the Soviets in the first assault. Furthermore, if the Red Army had moved into Western Europe, would the United States have used its atomic weapons to try to stop the Soviets—that is, would the United States have bombed targets in Western Europe? It is impossible to say. Truman, for all his determination, was probably not prepared to go to such lengths to keep the Soviets from acquiring Turkish bases. Fortunately, the crisis never came to that. Stalin was more cautious than the Americans gave him credit for being. His main concern was, as usual, the strengthening of Stalinism at home. He had learned it was easier to make war on his own people than to risk one with foreigners. He had no desire to push the Turkish crisis to the point of confrontation.

The Allies were not so sure of the Soviet dictator's restraint. Ever since the withdrawal of German troops from Greece, beginning in September 1944, the British had been actively involved in preventing the Greek Communists, who had built up a powerful military force during the resistance, from taking power. Churchill apparently believed that Moscow was not interested in helping out its Greek Communist comrades. In December 1944, Stalin did nothing to prevent the British from putting down a local Communist insurrection in Athens. Soviet neutrality changed with the breakdown of the wartime alliance, however. In the fall of 1946, the Greek Communists made another bid for power, this time with help from Albania, Bulgaria, and Yugoslavia; undoubtedly, this assistance had Stalin's approval. The Communist guerrilla armies were particularly successful in the northern border areas close to these foreign sources of supply. Intervention in the Greek civil war put a tremendous strain on the resources of the British who were then in the midst of a major economic crisis. The London government realized that it must withdraw. On Friday, 21 February 1947, the British embassy in Washington informed the U.S. Department of State that as of the following 30 March, Britain would discontinue all aid and support to the governments of Greece and Turkey. The Americans had been expecting such a move, but did not anticipate it so soon. Coming in the wake of the Turkish affair, however, it had not caught them completely off guard.

To Support Free Peoples. President Truman quickly summoned leaders of both houses of Congress to the White House on 27 February 1947. Under Secretary of State Dean Acheson painted a grim picture. He said that the Soviet "corruption of Greece would infect Iran, and all to the East" and "would also carry infection to Africa through Asia Minor and Egypt, and to Europe through Italy and France." To hear him tell it, the United States had reached a great turning point in history: "The Soviet Union was playing one of the greatest gambles in history at minimal cost. It did not need to win all possibilities, even one or two offered immense gains. We and we alone were in a position to break up the play."[60] Acheson's appraisal of Soviet intentions and the aggressive nature of Communism became a basic American belief; this article of faith persisted for over a generation, giving U.S. foreign policy a monumental rigidity and simplicity. At the time, however, Truman feared that others did not share the same sense of danger. He particularly feared that Republican majorities in the House and Senate might refuse to appropriate the additional funds the United States needed to move into the power vacuum the British withdrawal from the Mediterranean had created.

On 11 March, he told a joint session of Congress that he intended "to support free peoples who are resisting attempted subjugation by armed minorities or by outside pressure." He said he believed the United States must help free peoples work out their own destinies by giving them massive economic and financial aid, beginning with $400 million for Turkey and Greece. He also wanted authority to send those countries civilian and military personnel to help them maintain internal stability and independence. Truman said he was determined to defend a system "based on the will of the majority . . . distinguished by free institutions, representative government, guarantees of individual liberty, freedom of speech and election and freedom from political oppression" against one "based upon the will of a minority forcibly imposed on the majority, . . . [relying] upon terror and oppression, a controlled press and radio, fixed elections and the suppression of personal freedoms."[61] In a more tangible way, his doctrine committed the United States to the protection and reconstruction of Western Europe. Many French and British critics of the "Truman Doctrine" were not convinced that the Soviet Union was a real threat to their security. They argued that the policy would ensure the permanent division of Europe. Some wanted to create a third force between the United States and the Soviet Union, even though such a federation could hardly become effective without the economic recovery that could only be achieved with assistance from the United States.

In Greece the new doctrine had its first dramatic success. American military aid started to arrive in August 1947, and shortly thereafter a joint Greek-American military command was formed. Although it would be another two years before all resistance ended, the Americans had already shown that they would not allow the Greek Communists to take power. The arrival of General James A. Van Fleet as effective commander of operations inaugurated a period of more aggressive field tactics that gradually cleared the Communist forces from one sector of the country after another. Finally, the closing of the Greek-Yugoslav border by Tito in July 1949 led the Communists to abandon their struggle altogether.[62] Their defeat marked the first time in the Cold War when a Communist army trying to seize power had been crushed by force of arms. The victory was a perfect tonic to convince the Americans that they were on the right road; it also provided an example to future Cold War planners who came to believe that American intervention would produce similar results in other situations.

INTERNATIONAL ECONOMIC AND POLITICAL ORDER

Creating International Monetary Stability

The Background. The same Cold War that had helped dash the hopes of the Atlantic Charter and had once again made Europe a dangerous place to live also contributed to a unification process that in time would determine the future course of European politics. While the Americans and the British contemplated Europe's political future, they were also engaged in discussions about postwar economic reconstruction. This emphasis on economic matters was in stark contrast to the almost total absence of such considerations during and at the end of World War I.

In the summer of 1941, British Treasury representative John Maynard Keynes came to Washington to arrange a Lend-Lease agreement with Secretary of the Treasury Henry Morgenthau. That subject was not the only one on Keyne's mind, however. He managed to broaden the negotiations into a discussion of the whole question of postwar economic recovery. He said that his country hoped to restore its foreign trade through a series of bilateral agreements that would induce other countries to buy British goods and thus would enable the British to avoid deficits in their balance of payments. The Americans were interested in the concept, but not the particulars. Keynes's trading scheme was too narrow; it also contained the seeds of discrimination against American products.[63] The Americans wanted to consider a system that established an equilibrium.

When Keynes returned home, he drafted his "Proposals for an International Currency Union" in which he advocated establishing a monetary system with fixed rates of exchange. He hoped this was closer to what the United States had in mind. The British had no economic resource that could balance the $30 billion they received in Lend-Lease aid. They were wary of being drawn into the American economic orbit, but hoped that an arrangement with the world's principal creditor nation would result in real benefits. Specifically, they wanted to ensure full employment at home and enhance the prestige of the pound as a world currency. They also desired to strengthen their economic and financial ties with the Commonwealth. The Americans needed little prompting. Roosevelt believed that his country had to exert a leading role in shaping the world's economic environment. This commitment to a new world order was the fundamental premise of the Atlantic Charter. It did not originate there, however.

Even before World War I, American leaders believed that the promotion of trade among nations was the best way to prevent war. In their view, the failure of the peace settlement in 1919 to create a proper economic foundation had led to the instability that prepared the ground for future conflict. Herbert C. Hoover, secretary of commerce from 1921 to 1928, hoped to stifle nationalistic rivalries and rebuild the shattered European economy through the extension of private investment. The administration tried to encourage American bankers to assume responsibility for stabilizing European currencies, while it brought order to foreign exchange by reconstructing the gold standard and resolving the issues of war debts and reparations. The Dawes and Young Plans were examples of this effort. Convertibility of national currencies would lead to the reestablishment of multilateral trade and check economic nationalism and discrimination against American goods. Cordell Hull, secretary of state from 1933 to 1944, believed that national rivalry was caused by economic discrimination and trade warfare, a view that implied that World War II had its roots in the economic chaos of the 1930s. This view was shared by Henry Morgenthau, secretary of the treasury, who thought that the currency disorders of the depression had contributed to unemployment and poverty and made people easy prey for demagogues and dictators. "Bewilderment and bitterness [became] the breeders of fascism and, finally, of war," he said.[64]

Americans not only wanted to make the world safe from exchange control and quotas, they also wanted to open markets to their products. Therefore, the planners of the Roosevelt administration were determined to construct an economic counterpart to the United Nations that would provide the foundation for recovery, reconstruction, prosperity, world peace, and the free flow of goods.

The Bretton Woods Arrangements. American leaders did not hesitate to use their country's economic power to achieve their ends. In that spirit they organized the Monetary and Financial Conference that opened, on 1 July 1944, at the Mount Washington Hotel in Bretton Woods, New Hampshire.[65] Forty-four states sent delegates, but the conclave was largely an Anglo-American show. Italy, Germany, and Japan had, of course, not been invited. France, currently under enemy occupation, participated only marginally. The Soviet Union, attending at the last minute, made no positive contribution. In these circumstances, it is difficult to see how the United States, the world's principal creditor nation, could have been prevented from achieving its goals.

Under Secretary of the Treasury Harry Dexter White proposed avoiding the competitive currency devaluations of the 1930s by establishing fixed rates of exchange that could not be substantially altered without the consent of the other parties. The Americans wanted to encourage multilateral trade by preventing restrictive controls on foreign exchange transactions; and they wanted an international stabilization fund, backed by gold and national currencies, that would extend credit to member states to alleviate foreign exchange difficulties caused by temporary fluctuations and speculation.[66] They also wanted to establish an international institution to facilitate the creation of credit for postwar reconstruction and development. This scheme of applied capitalism gave rise to the International Monetary Fund (IMF) and the International Bank for Reconstruction and Development (World Bank).

The member states created the IMF from their own currencies or stocks of gold, giving themselves drawing rights on the collective resources to cure temporary deficits in their balance of payments. The amount each subscribed was determined by taking into account national income, trade, gold reserves, and value of currency convertible into gold. The IMF was a gigantic insurance scheme in which countries paid premiums to protect themselves against disasters that could threaten the stability of their currencies. With this security, nations would no longer need to resort to protectionist measures like currency controls and could thereby maintain freedom of exchange. Economists and politicians did not forget that the rise of economic nationalism and the breakdown of international liquidity helped cause and deepen the Great Depression of the early 1930s.

The World Bank was established in like manner, its principal stockholders being the nations that subscribed a certain amount of capital and put up the credit for its basic operations. Backed by these funds, the bank could mobilize further capital by issuing bonds. The bank would also guarantee loans from other sources and would create a special reserve fund to encourage private investors to put their money into worthy ventures. Furthermore, it would investigate potential borrowers to make sure they could pay back their loans and would never guarantee an amount greater than its own capital and resources. The member states would proportionally share the risks of default. The bank, which would be run along conservative lines, expected profit from the ventures it financed. Morgenthau, in his closing address to the conference, tried to minimize American influence in the agreement by insisting that all countries had joined hands and worked in unity. The United States, he said, wanted to protect its own national interests, but he added that "the only enlightened form of national self-interest [lies] in international accord."[67] Considering the previous tendency of the United States to go it alone, commitment to a multilateral scheme to maintain financial security was a remarkable about-face.

Despite their denials, the Americans with their vast economic power dominated the two organizations established at Bretton Woods. The amount of money each country put into the system determined its share of operational control. The Americans contributed one-third of the total.[68] Washington became the headquarters of these organizations, and Americans monopolized the directorships, especially the presidency of the World Bank. The Soviets realized that they could hardly hold their own against such an American presence and refrained from membership.[69] They were not missed. The market-economy countries could not do business with a state that exercised such control over its economy, and the Soviets were unwilling to change the dictatorial, central-planning premises upon which their system was based. On balance, the Bretton Woods agreement was a success; it provided the basis for world trade and investment that helped sustain the postwar recovery for the next quarter of a century.

The European Economic Community

The Marshall Plan. Even before 1900, American leaders knew that their country's well-being depended on European economic prosperity. The failure of the Republican policies of the 1920s to ensure economic stability at home and abroad indicated that a different approach was required if the disappointing results of the past were to be avoided. With the increased threat of Stalinist expansion, the task was all the more urgent. Truman administration officials had hoped European currencies could be stabilized through the International Monetary Fund and that bilateral loans and relief provided through such agencies as the United Nations Relief and Rehabilitation Administration (UNRRA) would push Europe on the road to recovery.

The anticipated recovery did not take place, however. At the beginning of 1947, Europe was entering one of its bleakest peacetime periods with political turmoil mounting in France and Italy and the crisis brewing in the Mediterranean. Surveying the scene, American planners concluded that only a comprehensive plan for economic integration could assure European recovery and save Western Europe from the danger of Communism. An integrated approach had the added advantage of ensuring that Germany's recovery would be contained within a larger context and would therefore be less likely to threaten the security of its neighbors. Some officials in the administration also saw European integration as a way to reconcile the differences between East and West, preventing the permanent division of the continent into rival blocs; others, taking their cue from Kennan, despaired of ever doing business with the Soviets and believed the consolidation of Western Europe was the only solution compatible with the nation's strategic interests.[70] The stream of invective coming from Moscow gave credence to the arguments of the hard-liners. For example, the 1 May 1947 edition of *Pravda* contained a half-page article, signed by Ilya Ehrenburg, who likened Truman's March speech and Churchill's Iron Curtain speech to the speeches of Mussolini and Hitler. And "before Fulton and Washington," Ehrenburg said, "there were the Piazza Venezia balcony and Berlin Stadium."[71]

Following high-level discussions in Washington, the promotion of European economic integration became official American policy. Secretary of State George Marshall outlined this proposal in his commencement address at Harvard University on 5 June 1947. The speech, drafted by Marshall's special assistant, Charles E. Bohlen, proposed reviving Europe's economy "so as to permit the emergence of political and social conditions in which free institutions can exist." This, Marshall said, would be done through a continuing, coordinated program of massive American aid. He invited participation from "any government that is willing to assist in the task," provided it did not seek to perpetuate human misery for political profit. This meant that the scheme was open to Soviet participation, although few believed Stalin would actually agree to do so.

The Americans expected, in fact insisted, that the Europeans would advance concrete proposals for the plan's mechanics and cooperate substantially in its execution:

> It would be neither fitting nor efficacious for [the American] Government to undertake to draw up unilaterally a program designed to place Europe on its feet economically. This is the business of the Europeans. The initiative ... must come from Europe. The role of [the United States] should consist of friendly aid in the drafting of a European program and of later support of such a program so far as it may be practical for us to do so. The program should be a joint one, agreed to by a number, if not all, European nations.[72]

What the Americans wanted beyond the cooperation of the Europeans in their own recovery was specific proposals about how the strengths and assets of one country could be made to complement those of another. In a sense, they wanted to apply David Riccardo's laws of comparative advantage to the whole continent. By insisting that the Europeans work together, the Americans contributed to the systematic destruction of trade and exchange barriers among Western European states and initiated a movement toward integration that proved well-nigh irreversible. The Marshall Plan was further hard evidence that the Americans were not going to shy away from involvement in European affairs as they had done after World War I and that they were seriously committed to promoting economic recovery, a task already begun in a different form at the conference at Bretton Woods. The Americans were not just being Santa Claus—they needed a revived Europe to counter the Stalinist menace. In the process, however, they contributed to the greatest period of European prosperity and cooperation in history.

Ernest Bevin, the British foreign secretary, saw in this proposal the opportunity to establish the close Anglo-American cooperation he thought necessary for economic recovery and protection against the rise of Soviet power (the latter would be accomplished through a British-led European security system). He immediately arranged a meeting with his French counterpart, Georges Bidault. On 17 June in Paris, the two agreed to create a European economic commission. They invited the Soviet foreign minister, Vyacheslav Molotov, to join their discussions, but the invitation was only a tactic. Bevin knew that despite Marshall's lofty gesture,[73] Washington never really intended the Soviet Union to be a recipient of American aid and that it would be only too delighted if he and Bidault were to act as hatchet men, thereby ensuring their countries a greater share of American largesse. Bidault played the invitation for its propaganda benefits. He maintained that the offer to the Soviets showed how serious the French and British were about achieving a genuine detente in Europe, and said that it would give the Soviets a chance to display their similar good intentions.[74] Privately, he worked with Bevin to maneuver the Soviets out of participation.

Molotov joined the other two in Paris on 27 June for tripartite discussions, but suspected he was walking into a trap. He apparently believed that the recovery scheme was a ruse to build up Western, especially German, power at Soviet expense and weaken Soviet control over Eastern Europe. Molotov participated in the discussions for only four days, during which he denounced the British and French for causing the division of Europe and dismissed Bevin and Bidault as lackeys of the United States. Being disagreeable was one of the few talents this subservient and generally incompetent foreign minister possessed. He was also adept at following Stalin's orders. Stalin refused to participate further in the talks and forbade all the Eastern European countries within his sphere of influence to do so as well. The Soviets wanted American aid, guaranteed in advance, with no strings attached. Any participation, they believed, would liberalize their economy and reduce the dependency of their satellites. Their country would be at the mercy of the American Congress, which would dole out further loans only to enhance capitalism. Such risks were unacceptable.

Molotov's departure simplified the task of Bevin and Bidault. They now invited the other European states to help create the machinery through which the American aid would be channeled.[75] There was a great deal of disagreement over the scope and objectives of the program with the conferees deciding that each member country would retain control of its domestic economy but would coordinate its other activities through the Committee on European Economic Cooperation (CEEC). They subsequently committed themselves to the mutual reduction of tariffs, a multilateral system of payments, and the free convertibility of currencies. The British and French steered the conference toward endorsement of their desire to establish a long-term program of industrial modernization. The British, however, were reluctant to see any scheme for European economic integration interfere with their Commonwealth trade, which at the time was twice as large as Britain's trade with the continent. The French wanted to make their country the focal point of an economically integrated Europe. To that end, they sought limits on German steel production. Other countries, though, believed a revived Germany would aid their own recovery and were suspicious of French efforts to restrict Germany's production.

Such national priorities made the Americans dubious that the Europeans could transcend their national sovereignties and make the kind of adjustments necessary to promote recovery and economic integration.[76] Nevertheless, the U.S. Congress adopted the Marshall Plan as official national policy and, on 3 April 1948, appropriated an initial $13 billion. Bidault, who saw in the plan the means to contain a revitalized Germany, loftily claimed that there had "never been a finer, more far-sighted gesture in history than the Marshall Plan."[77] Far-sighted perhaps, but hardly unselfish. The dollars would return to the United States as the devastated Europeans bought American products. The Americans wanted to remake the European economy in their own image; their goal was an economy integrated like their own without trade barriers and with the forces of the free market determining rational development.[78] European institutions would have to become more supranational and develop the ability to transcend sovereignties, quell nationalist rivalries, and promote cooperation among private corporations. The balancing act between government and private business would be delicate but necessary if the European countries were to achieve mutual economic growth. Through such growth, the old political and class rivalries of Europe would diminish, and out of this shrinking area of conflict, the new European order would emerge.

The planners of the Democratic party envisaged a new reformed capitalist system for Europe that they had only incompletely achieved at home. In such a system, the working classes would share the fruits of their labor more equitably, the public sector would be significantly expanded, and professionals from business, labor, and government would rationally discuss the best means to solve society's problems. Interdependence would resolve the old problems of how to contain an expanding Germany and how to guarantee French security; increased wealth would enable the Europeans to repel the Communist threat at home and rearm against it abroad. While American planners were not trying to bring about a united states of Europe in the political sense, they did hope that increased integration would make the Europeans strong enough to play a major role in the containment of world Communism, thereby supporting America's global strategic objectives.

The Soviet Response. As relations between the two superpowers became more rigid, Stalin prepared for new encounters with his capitalist enemies by carrying out a major reorganization of the Communist International. In September 1947, the Poles hosted a meeting in Silesia of the representatives of the Communist parties of Bulgaria, Czechoslovakia, France, Hungary, Italy, Poland, Romania, and Yugoslavia. The Soviet delegation was headed by Stalin's main spearbearer, Andrei Zhdanov, who in his keynote address dismissed the Marshall Plan as a scheme for the political subjugation of Western Europe. "American imperialism," he said, "is endeavoring, like a usurer, to take advantage of the postwar difficulties of the European countries . . . to dictate to them extortionate terms for any assistance rendered. With an eye to the impending economic crisis, the United States is in a hurry to find new monopoly spheres of capital investment and markets for its goods. American economic 'assistance' pursues the broad aid of bringing Europe into bondage to American capital."[79]

Zhdanov believed the world was divided between the imperialists headquartered in Washington and the peacelovers based in Moscow. The "peacelovers" needed an organization through which they could maintain close ties with the European Communist parties outside the immediate satellite area. The answer was a refurbished international Communist movement, known as the Cominform (the Communist Information Bureau), an agency that would enlist "all anti-fascist and freedom loving elements in the struggle against the new American expansionist plans for the enslavement of Europe." In the struggle, the French and Italian Communist parties were accorded a special responsibility: "They must take up the standard in defense of the national independence and sovereignty of their countries."[80]

The Communists now took to the streets. Shortly after the formation of the Cominform, a series of strikes swept Western Europe. Their organizers hoped to kill the Marshall Plan and weaken Europe's ties with the United States, especially in France and Italy. Stalin apparently believed that the United States was itself on the brink of economic collapse. But, although Western Europe was still in a sorry state economically, political recovery was well under way, and by the end of the year, the Communist threat was successfully contained. The Communist parties were obviously not going to disappear, but parliamentary regimes, with their welfare states in place, were more securely entrenched than before. Failure to participate in the global economy developing in Western Europe helped condemn the Soviet Union and its satellites to economic backwardness and decline and led ultimately to the failure of the Communist system. Almost two generations would pass before that became evident, however; for the time being, Soviet power was real and serious enough.

The United Nations

The Charter. The Soviet-American confrontation stemmed from the same historic forces that had created, shaped, and conditioned earlier balance-of-power systems. For those who believed in the basic harmony of national interests and still had faith in collective security, the reality was harsh. On 26 June 1945, the fifty states that attended the San Francisco Conference resolved "to unite [their] strength to maintain international peace and security, and to ensure, by the acceptance of principles and the institution of methods, that armed force shall not be used, save in the common interest."[81] Poland was absent but was considered a charter member. The participants at the conference hoped the United Nations (UN) would succeed where the League of Nations had failed, but structurally the new organization for peace was remarkably like its predecessor.

It had a General Assembly, consisting of all member states, with the authority to discuss any questions related to "the maintenance of international peace and security"; in reality, its powers were largely consultative. There was an executive council, the Security Council, composed of five permanent members (France, Great Britain, the Soviet Union, the United States, and China) and six nonpermanent members elected for a term of two years. The League's Permanent Court of International Justice continued exactly as before, with only a slight change of name—the International Court of Justice. Both the League and the UN had secretariats, headed by a secretary-general, and various economic and social agencies.

The myth of sovereign equality was strong in both organizations, but the reality was less in the UN. All members of the UN agreed "to accept and carry out the decisions of the Security Council in accordance with the . . . Charter," but any of the Security Council's permanent members could block action by voting against any nonprocedural decision. The veto power, a recognition that the UN was incapable of effective operation without Great Power unanimity, was particularly opposed by the smaller powers who resented giving the Security Council's permanent members even more authority than they had enjoyed in the League.[82] Furthermore, Article 2, Section 7, forbade interference in matters that were essentially within a state's jurisdiction. The purpose of this clause was to provide special protection for nations with colonial possessions. Protection of a different sort was provided in Article 52, Section 1, which allowed "the existence of regional arrangements or agencies for dealing with such matters relating to the maintenance of international peace and security." Thus, all sorts of military alliances were perfectly legal, provided that "their activities are consistent with the Purposes and Principles of the United Nations." Nominally, of course, they all were.

Multilateral Problem Solving. The United Nations purported to be more than just a system of collective security. The League had left the final decision to apply sanctions against an aggressor to the individual states. Once sanctions were voted, however, the UN required each member to make a commitment in advance to "undertake to make available to the Security Council, on its call and in accordance with a special agreement or agreements, armed forces, assistance, and facilities, including rights of passage, necessary for the purpose of maintaining international peace and security." But the "agreement or agreements" needed to give this article (43) its teeth were never adopted; thus, in the long run, the UN was in no better position to enforce its decisions militarily than was the League.[83] Once again, the fault was not so much in the institutions of the organization but in the willingness to use them. When the major powers, especially the Soviet Union and the United States, agreed to cooperate, the original purposes of the organization could be achieved.

The failure of the UN to deal with international problems stemmed from the nature of the modern state system, especially as it confronted the political realities of the postwar world. The UN, like the League, had no independent sovereignty; it was simply one among many diplomatic devices, and exercised only the authority that the member states chose to confer upon it. Its agencies could be used for the peaceful settlement of disputes, but could also heighten the very tension they were supposed to dissipate. The speeches made in the Security Council or the General Assembly almost never influenced the actions of nations. In fact, UN speeches were usually carefully crafted monologues, intended primarily for propaganda. All permanent members of the Security Council favored the veto power as an ultimate safeguard, but only the Soviet Union used it as a normal diplomatic device to prevent consideration of any issue related to national security, no matter how distantly. Consequently, certain states, the United States among them, favored giving more power to the General Assembly, which reached decisions with a two-thirds majority of those present and voting. The Soviet Union, however, fought to keep supreme decision-making power in the Security Council.

The UN could be used as an agency for solving disputes when the United States and the Soviet Union were in agreement. This occurred over the question of Palestine and produced a resolution, calling for the establishment of two independent states, one Jewish, one Arab, to replace the British mandate. But the UN had no power to prevent the Arabs and Israelis from later fighting among themselves. The UN was sometimes used on problems related to the Cold War, but then usually as a forum for announcing decisions already made elsewhere. Thus, for example, a special UN commission was established to help bring an end to the civil war in Greece because the Soviet Union saw no further profit in supporting the cause of the Greek Communist guerrillas. The UN was also used during the Berlin crisis, when both sides accepted the invitation of the organization's secretary-general to begin informal discussions leading to the end of the blockade. By then, the success of the airlift had been established, and it was evident that the Western powers could not be forced out of the city, short of war. Thus, in these instances, the UN was only an instrumentality for putting the finishing touches on a settlement that would have come anyway.

Although many other issues, including the reunification of Korea, the Italian-Yugoslav dispute over Trieste, and the Soviet subversion of Czechoslovakia, were all brought to the UN's attention, the organization had no success in bringing about an accord. And only the temporary withdrawal of the Soviet representative from the Security Council made possible the UN's involvement in the Korean War in 1950.[84] Even here the real force behind the resolution to resist aggression was the United States, which would have committed its army in any case. The absence of the Soviet Union from the UN led to the passage, in November 1950, of the U.S.-sponsored "Uniting for Peace Resolution," which allowed the General Assembly to discuss, in emergency session, any important measure that had been vetoed in the Security Council. But this virtual revision of the Charter did not change the fact that the Great Powers still made the major political decisions outside the UN.

POSTSCRIPT   Allied diplomacy marched to the sound of battle and to the dreams of Wilsonian idealism. This blend of the real and the imaginary complicated the practical task of agreeing on the conduct of the war and building a firm structure for postwar Europe. Among the major questions to be decided were the boundaries of Eastern Europe, the nature of political and economic reconstruction, including the treatment of Germany, and the most difficult task of all, how to establish future security and harmony. The Americans were determined to avoid the cardinal mistake they had made after World War I when they refused to join the League. Roosevelt intended to work closely with a United Nations organization in conjunction with the Soviet Union to achieve the idealistic goals he first enumerated in the Atlantic Charter.

Until the Soviets open their archives, it is impossible to know whether Stalin's goals were clearer and better defined than those of Churchill and Roosevelt. His actions showed that he believed that Soviet security must be enhanced by creating "friendly" governments in those states bordering his country's western frontier. When he spoke of free and democratic development, his words had a special meaning. George Kennan, counselor of the American embassy in Moscow, affirmed:

> No one can stop Russia from doing the taking, if she is determined to go through with it. No one can force Russia to do the giving, if she is determined not to go through with it. In these circumstances, others may worry. The Kremlin chimes, never silent since those turbulent days when Lenin had them repaired and set in motion, now peal out the hours of night with a ring of self-assurance and of confidence in the future. And the sleep of those who lie within the Kremlin walls is sound and undisturbed.[85]

Stalin expected his allies to recognize that Eastern Europe was within the Soviet orbit and appeared willing to recognize that Britain and the United States were similarly free to arrange the affairs of Western Europe. Roosevelt was unwise to believe that he could gain Stalin's trust and work with him for a better world. Nor was Roosevelt on firm moral ground in his concept of collective security: his view of the Four Policemen obviously implied establishing the very spheres of influence he was to deride the Soviets for creating. The participation of the United States in both world wars was essential to prevent the destruction of the European balance of power. Whereas in 1914, and again in 1939, the United States had the capacity to be the holder of the balance, it preferred to leave the task to others, and even when forced into war, it hardly viewed its participation in terms of maintaining an equilibrium. A conscientious effort to counter Great Power domination of the European continent in times of peace was therefore something new.

In 1947, no country but the United States was capable of standing up to the Soviet Union. American leaders feared that their country's continued disengagement from Europe would result in an eventual Soviet takeover, but their interest went beyond the present crisis. The Americans had a concept of a peaceful Europe based on harmonization of national rivalries through economic integration. They believed that political problems were essentially technical problems and were consequently solvable. The greatness of the Marshall Plan lay in the way it managed to transcend the immediate political pressures and concerns to become a positive force for the stabilization and integration of Europe. However, the clash between the superpowers seemed to determine all action. Byrnes based his policy on the not preposterous assumption that the Soviets were prepared to bide their time until they developed local leaders who could make the communization of Western Europe a success. "By the threat of strikes and by encouraging discontent, they can in many states exert power without having responsibility."[86] Military occupation of the whole of Europe would have put an intolerable strain on Soviet resources, perhaps endangering Stalin's control at home. Then, too, for Stalin successful communization of such countries as Germany, France, and Britain was not without its dangers. Unless perfect Stalinist regimes could be installed and maintained, these states would compete with the Soviet Union for world Communist leadership. Nevertheless, the leaders in the Kremlin showed themselves willing to exploit any weakness they perceived in the Western camp. Even if the Soviets had no intent of using their massive position in Eastern Europe as a springboard for aggression against the West, the fact that they were there was a significant alteration of the European balance of power and was *ipso facto* threatening. Over time, however, the confrontation in Europe between the superpowers took on the comfortable predictability of a stalemate. Danger still lurked at the periphery where the two great spheres of influence had not become consolidated, but the superpowers had decided that whatever their differences and rivalries, these were not worth an all-out war. The longer the standoff continued, the more feeble became the conviction that any of their policies would lead to the creation of a brave new world, notwithstanding all the utopianism and chest puffing in which both indulged.

ENDNOTES

1. Iran had been invaded by British and Soviet forces in August 1941 to crush German influence and ensure a supply line to the Soviet Union. The occupation, following an arrangement worked out in 1907, gave the Soviets control of the north, the British control of the south, and put the capital under joint protection.
2. The president had suggested Cairo, Asmara in Eritrea, Ankara in Turkey, or some port in the eastern Mediterranean.
3. *Stalin's Correspondence with Churchill, Attlee, Roosevelt and Truman, 1941–45* (London: Lawrence & Wishart, 1958), 104.
4. Roosevelt, without informing Churchill, had also invited Vyacheslav Molotov to join the discussions. Molotov refused to attend because this might imply a commitment to the Nationalist Chinese.
5. Anthony Eden, *The Reckoning* (London: Cassell, 1965), 491.

6. United States, Department of State, *Conferences at Cairo and Teheran, 1943* (Washington, D.C.: U.S. Government Printing Office, 1961), 492.

7. Ibid., 493.

8. Ibid., 495.

9. Ibid., 494.

10. General Marshall's Report, *The Winning of the War in Europe and the Pacific* (War Department: Simon and Schuster, 1945), II.

11. *Conferences at Cairo and Teheran*, 602.

12. Stalin recalled that when he was in Leipzig in 1907, "200 German workers failed to appear at an important mass meeting because there was no controller at the station platform to punch their tickets which would permit them to leave the station." Ibid., 513. This was one of his favorite stories. See Milovan Djilas, *Conversations with Stalin* (New York: Harcourt, Brace and World, 1962).

13. Winston Churchill, *Closing the Ring* (Boston: Houghton Mifflin, 1951), 374.

14. Stalin had earlier suggested that Churchill nursed "a secret affection for Germany and desired to see a soft peace." *Conferences at Cairo and Teheran*, 533.

15. Ibid., 485.

16. Ibid., 554.

17. Ibid., 512.

18. Ibid., 595.

19. Ibid., 592.

20. Ibid., 511.

21. Ibid., 532.

22. Ibid., 531.

23. Ibid., 514.

24. On the importance of the neglected conference of Teheran, see Keith Eubank, *Summit at Teheran* (New York: William Morrow, 1985).

25. Winston S. Churchill, *Triumph and Tragedy* (Boston: Houghton, Mifflin, 1953), 347.

26. United States, Department of State, *The Conferences at Malta and Yalta, 1945* (Washington, D.C.: U.S. Government Printing Office, 1955), 716. Hereafter referred to as *Yalta Conference*.

27. The essential features of the United Nations had been adopted at the Dumbarton Oaks Conference, held from 21 August to 9 October 1944. It was not surprising that in scope and responsibilities the organization was a political agency of the superpowers.

28. *Yalta Conference*, 396.

29. This chain of thirty-six islands between Kamchatka and Hokkaido had been Russian during the eighteenth and most of the nineteenth centuries. The Japanese got them in 1875.

30. *Yalta Conference*, 984.

31. J. P. Nettl, *The Eastern Zone and Soviet Policy in Germany, 1945–1950* (New York: Farrar, Straus, and Giroux, 1977), 37–38.

32. *Yalta Conference*, 620.

33. Ibid., 972.

34. Ibid., 589.

35. Georgi Zhukov, *The Memoirs of Marshall Zhukov* (New York: Delacourte Press, 1971), 583.

36. The American president had repeated the assurance he had made at Teheran that Congress and the American people would support "any reasonable measures designed to safeguard the future peace, but he did not believe that this would extend to the maintenance of an appreciable American force in Europe." *Yalta Conference*, 617.

37. *Stalin's Correspondence*, 331.

38. Ibid., 348.

39. Harry S Truman, *Memoirs*, vol. 2, 71–72.

40. Ibid., 82.

41. United States, Department of State, *The Conference of Berlin (Potsdam) 1945*, vol. 1 (Washington, D.C.: U.S. Government Printing Office), 6. Hereafter cited as *Potsdam Conference*.

42. Ibid., 7.

43. These nations would only participate in the formulation of settlements if they had signed the respective terms of surrender. Thus, China could not participate in the decisions concerning the fate of Europe.

44. *Potsdam Conference*, 385.

45. At this point, Admiral William Leahy whispered to Truman. "Of course there are no Germans left. The Bolshies have killed them all." Truman, 369.

46. Churchill, *Triumph and Tragedy*, 631–32.

47. Ibid., 669.

48. Stalin renounced his rights to assets in defeated countries outside Bulgaria, Finland, Hungary, Romania, and eastern Austria and agreed to make no demands on the German gold that the other Allies had captured. He also abandoned his support of a scheme to internationalize the Ruhr.

49. Stalin helped to cushion the blow by promising that the Polish Provisional Government would hold "free and unfettered elections as soon as possible on the basis of universal suffrage and secret ballot in which all democratic and anti-Nazi parties shall have the right to take part and put forward candidates." *Potsdam Conference*, 2:1491.

50. In Lisle Rose, *After Yalta* (New York: Charles Scribner's Sons, 1973), 123–24.

51. Foreign Relations of the United States, 1946, VI, 706–7.

52. *New York Times*, 6 March 1946.

53. *Foreign Relations of the United States*, 1946, VI, 73–74.

54. Ibid., 768.

55. According to a 7 June 1946 attack delivered by Fedor Nesterovich Oleshchuk, the assistant-chief of the Agitation and Propaganda Administration of the Communist Party Central Committee. Ibid., 770.

56. Georges Bidault, *Resistance* (London: Weidenfeld and Nicolson, 1967), 127.

57. The "Free Territory of Trieste" had been divided into two zones, A and B. After much squabbling, the Trieste problem was solved in the agreement of 5 October 1954, which awarded zone A (the city proper) to the Italians and zone B (the hinterland) to the Yugoslavs.

58. Dean Acheson, *Present at the Creation; My Years in the State Department* (New York: Norton, 1969), 191.

59. Ibid., 196.

60. Ibid., 219.

61. *Department of State Bulletin*, 23 March 1947, 534–37.

62. Tito needed all his energy for his confrontation with Moscow. In addition, having a friendly non-Communist country on his southern frontier was infinitely preferable to a potentially hostile Communist one.

63. This caveat was subsequently incorporated into the Mutual Aid Agreement (of 23 February 1942) whose goal was "to promote mutually advantageous economic relations between [the United States and Britain] and the betterment of world-wide economic relations." (Article 7)

64. *Proceedings and Documents of United Nations Monetary and Financial Conference, Bretton Woods NH* (Washington, D.C.: Department of State, 1948), I, 71.

65. See: A. L. K. Acheson, J. F. Chant, and M. F. J. Prachowny, eds., *Bretton Woods Revisited* (Toronto: University of Toronto Press, 1972); Richard N. Gardner, *Sterling-Dollar Diplomacy: The Origins and the Prospects of Our International Economic Order* (New York: McGraw Hill, 1969); R. G. Hawtrey, *Bretton Woods, For Better or Worse* (London: Longmans, Green, 1946); Edward S. Mason and Robert E. Asher,

The World Bank since Bretton Woods (Washington, D.C.: Brookings Institution, 1973); Sidney Rolfe, *Gold and World Power: The Dollar, the Pound, and the Plans for Reform* (New York: Harper and Row, 1966); Armand Van Dormael, *Bretton Woods: Birth of a Monetary System* (New York: Holmes and Meier, 1978).

66. In 1942, Keynes had made a similar proposal when he advocated the establishment of a clearing union that would reinforce a state's currency through drawing rights on an international fund established by participating countries.

67. Van Dormael, *Bretton Woods*, 221–22.

68. The United States put up half of the original start-up capital, however.

69. They were joined by Liberia and New Zealand.

70. Michael J. Hogan, *The Marshall Plan: America, Britain, and the Reconstruction of Western Europe, 1947–1952* (Cambridge: Cambridge University Press, 1987), 29–45.

71. *Foreign Relations of the United States*, 1947, IV, 557.

72. *Department of State Bulletin*, 16 (1947), 1159–60.

73. The secretary of the navy, James Forrestal, described Marshall's objective as a tactic "to show to both the world and our country that every effort had been made on our part to secure [Soviet] cooperation so that we should have the support of public opinion in whatever policy we found it necessary to adopt thereafter." *The Forrestal Diaries*, ed. Walter Mills (New York: Viking, 1951), 192.

74. Bidault, *Resistance*, 150.

75. Sixteen nations attended: Austria, Belgium, Britain, Denmark, France, Greece, Iceland, Ireland, Italy, Luxembourg, the Netherlands, Norway, Portugal, Sweden, Switzerland, and Turkey. The Soviet Union vetoed participation by Bulgaria, Czechoslovakia, Hungary, Finland, Poland, and Romania.

76. Hogan, *The Marshall Plan*, 64–70.

77. Bidault, *Resistance*, 151.

78. Hogan, *The Marshall Plan*, 427–30.

79. *Documents on International Affairs, 1947–1948*, 127.

80. Ibid., 137.

81. The Charter of the UN can be found in *The United Nations in the Making: Basic Documents* (Boston: World Peace Foundation, 1947), 41–72.

82. The League Covenant had required any League Council decision to be unanimous, but any member who was a party to the dispute would *not* be allowed to vote.

83. Peace forces were created though from time to time to handle particular crises, but they never became permanent.

84. In 1990 and 1991, the United Nations was used to help forge the coalition that ended the aggression of Iraq against Kuwait. In that crisis, the Security Council could act because of the unanimity of the Great Powers.

85. *Foreign Relations of the United States*, 1944, IV, 909.

86. James F. Byrnes, *All in One Lifetime* (New York: Harper and Brothers, 1958), 294.

CHAPTER 2

GERMANY BETWEEN EAST AND WEST

PREFACE   Stalin considered Germany the most important country in Europe. Its control would ensure Soviet security, its loss would make all other gains meaningless. In Germany were fought the first great battles of the Cold War. During the closing weeks of World War II, the British and American armies entered parts of Germany that had been marked for Soviet occupation: Thuringia, Saxony, and Mecklenburg. Churchill favored keeping them as bargaining chips for the forthcoming negotiations at Potsdam, but Stalin refused to allow any Allied control machinery to be established until all these territories had been handed over to his armies. Only then did he allow the French, British, and American military commissions to come to Berlin to establish a government in accordance with the Yalta agreement.

When the Allied commanders arrived in the German capital on 5 June 1945, the Soviets kept them waiting. Dwight D. Eisenhower and Bernard Montgomery were so annoyed that they threatened to leave. Hasty apologies ensued and within half an hour the ceremony took place. The agreement confirmed the Allied Control Commission, the division of Germany into four zones of occupation, and the establishment of a special Inter-Allied Governing Authority (the *Kommandatura*) to administer Greater Berlin jointly. The post of chief executive would rotate every three months among the four Allied commanders.

Marshal Georgi Zhukov hosted a reception after the official business. It featured speeches and toasts and a huge groaning board of Russian delicacies. The Red Army Chorus presented a short concert. The affair "developed into a sort of mutual congratulation society, Field-Marshal Montgomery recalled."[1] All of this warmth and bonhomie could not cover up the fundamental divisions and hostilities, however. Stalin had already refused to recognize the right of the Allies to use certain routes into Berlin. Had he specifically done so, the Allies probably would not have accepted them anyway. The Allies feared that accepting such routes might mean forfeiting rights over all others. Instead, they concluded a temporary agreement with Stalin. The Soviets allocated a main highway, a rail line, and two air corridors and agreed that these would be freed "from border search or control by customs or military authorities."[2] Only the agreement on air corridors was put in writing.[3]

Stalin believed that his wartime allies were planning to use the resources of Germany for future aggression against the Soviet Union. These suspicions also permeated the upper echelons of the Communist hierarchy. When Marshal Zhukov visited Eisenhower in the ruined city of Frankfurt five days after the ceremony in Berlin, he noticed that the I. G. Farben chemical factory, in which the American general had established his headquarters, was undamaged. He concluded "that Washington and London had given the Allied High Command special instructions" to save it from destruction, along with I. G. Farben's property in other parts of Germany.[4]

Germany's recent attempt to destroy the balance of power had cost it heavily. Approximately 4.2 million Germans, soldiers and civilians, had been killed; 6 million more had been wounded; and some 2 million were prisoners of war. Countless more were refugees who had either fled before the advance of the Soviets or had been expelled as undesirable aliens from the Eastern European countries. About 10 million of these sought refuge in western Germany, where they currently were living in special camps.[5] The desperate plight of the Germans elicited little sympathy. In the eyes of the Allies, the Germans had brought such misery to others that they deserved to suffer. Now was their time of reckoning. Germany should atone for its sins and must never be allowed to threaten the peace of Europe again. Furthermore, the Germans should make financial reparation for the damage they had caused.

But how could the Germans pay if they were not allowed to recover? Yet if they were allowed to recover, would they not once again become a threat? These questions, which had also arisen after World War I, would now be answered in the context of a military occupation. A properly supervised recovery would keep Germany from threatening European security and prevent the rebirth of German militarism. To make the occupation work, however, the occupiers had to cooperate with each other—all the more so, since much of Germany's food and raw materials lay in the Soviet zone, while the bulk of the country's industry was in the Western zones. From the Soviet point of view, the solution was simple. They would tighten their hold over East Germany while preparing the ground for the eventual socialization of the rest of the country. They were prepared to take advantage of every opportunity presented to them.

FOUR-POWER GOVERNANCE

The Occupation

Diverse Styles. The Joint Chiefs of Staff directive 1067 of April 1945 instructed the American occupation commander that "Germany's ruthless warfare and the fanatical Nazi resistance have destroyed the German economy and made chaos and suffering inevitable and that the Germans cannot escape responsibility for what they have brought upon themselves."[6] Consequently, no action would be taken "that would tend to support basic living standards in Germany on a higher level than that existing in any one of the neighboring united nations."[7] Many Americans had Old Testament notions of collective guilt and took special pains to make the Germans aware of the suffering they had caused. They bused many citizens of Munich out to Dachau to view, and in some cases to clean up, the rotting corpses. They also showed films of Nazi atrocities to German elementary and secondary schoolchildren and to entire populations of some towns.

The Soviets, officially at least, tried to distinguish between the Nazis and other Germans. Toward the end of the war, Stalin was careful to emphasize that the Soviet Union was fighting to liberate the German people from the Hitlerites. When the Soviets entered Berlin, they pasted up posters, proclaiming, "The Hitlers come and go but the German people, the German state remain." Even before all the rubble was cleared from the streets, the Soviets erected a gigantic statue honoring the Soviet soldiers who had saved the German people from oppression.

Soviet occupation was very harsh. The Soviets immediately widened the gauge of the German railways to correspond with their own and confiscated and shipped anything of value to the Soviet Union. Montgomery received reports that in the Soviet zone the Germans "were living like beasts on whatever they could get, and that starvation was already evident."[8] The Red Army continued to terrorize the population. Film actress Hildegard Knef remembered "hiding in a shed in a Berlin suburb listening to the screams of the women being raped by Russian soldiers in the house across the street."[9] Every female was fair game, regardless of age. German Communist leaders, returning from exile, wanted "to see that no excesses took place in relations between the German population and the Soviet troops,"[10] but they had no control over the Red Army, and the terror ran its course.

Meanwhile the French viewed their zone as a source of industrial booty, which they deemed reparations. Since a large section of the area was rural, they took what they could, even cutting down trees in the Black Forest. Because the Germans had invaded their country three times in as many generations, the French felt completely justified in exploiting their zone to the fullest. The French also had a political agenda. As after World War I, France wanted to separate the Rhineland and the Saar from Germany and even encouraged separatist movements in the regions it occupied.

Despite their animosity for Germans and their tendency to treat Germany almost as a colonial possession, British leaders, possibly more than the other Allies, were concerned with not repeating old mistakes. Montgomery felt it necessary to "give the German people hope for the future; they must be made to realize that they could reach a worthwhile future only by their own work. That meant fixing the level of industry so that there would be a decent standard of living with the minimum of unemployment. If this were not done the Germans would merely look to the past and be ready to follow any evil leader who might arise."[11] Montgomery might have added that many of his own subordinates were helping to make that possible by engaging in all kinds of unsavory activities from black marketeering to theft and sexual concubinage. "German women," recalled one British second lieutenant, "were really no more than a commodity on the black market"; if a woman ran out of things to trade, "she could always trade herself."[12] The American record was not much better.

The occupation powers abolished the main Nazi administrative unit of the *Gau* and reorganized Germany into a series of states (*Länder*), ranging in size from 156 square miles (Bremen) to 18,000 square miles (Lower Saxony), and from 500,000 people in Bremen to 12 million in North Rhine–Westphalia (Table 1). By restoring Germany's federal character, the Allies hoped to curb and dissipate the country's aggressive nationalism. The new Länder emerged out of the combination or division of former states. The British, for example, combined Hanover, Oldenburg, Brunswick, and Schaumburg-Lippe into Lower Saxony. The French put together parts of Baden and Württemberg to form the Rhine-Palatinate. Prussia disappeared completely. This shifting of boundaries broke down the old federalist pattern and formed new units that the occupiers hoped would in time develop their own loyalties and identities. Only Bavaria, whose former boundaries remained virtually unchanged, preserved its regional integrity.

TABLE 1   GERMANY IN 1946

	Size (Square Miles)	Population
British Zone		
(North Rhine–Westphalia, Lower Saxony, Schleswig-Holstein, Hamburg)	37,721	22,304,509
American Zone		
(Barvaria, Greater Hesse, Württemberg-Baden, Bremen)	41,490	17,254,945
French Zone		
(Württemberg-Hohenzollern, Rhine-Palatinate, Baden)	15,527	5,077,806
Soviet Zone		
(Brandenburg, Saxony, Mecklenburg-Vorpommern, Thuringia, Saxony-Anhalt)	41,380	17,313,734
Berlin	344	3,199,938
Total	136,462	65,150,932

Note: Square kilometers have been converted to square miles.

Source: Survey of International Affairs: Four-Power Control in Germany and Austria, 1945–1946 (London: Oxford University Press), 191.

The terms of the Potsdam agreement specified that Germany would be governed as an administrative whole, but Charles de Gaulle, who had not been party to the accord, did not feel bound by its provisions. According to Georges Bidault, the French foreign minister, de Gaulle wanted "to go back to the treaty of Westphalia."[13] He still advocated the dismemberment of Germany and a special status for the Rhineland and the Ruhr, policies that the other powers had by now abandoned. De Gaulle wanted to annex the Saar and opposed the establishment of any machinery of central government. At the end of October 1945, he effectively vetoed a proposal to formulate common directives for the whole of Germany. As a result, henceforth, each power assumed responsibility for setting policy in its own zone. De Gaulle's policies were guided by his fear that a revived Germany under Soviet domination would eventually invade France. He suspected that the Americans were not going to stay long in Europe. On 3 November 1945, he told the U.S. envoy in Paris, Jefferson Caffery, that France viewed Europe as "a matter of life and death," while for the United States, it was "one interesting question among many others." Nor did de Gaulle expect help from the British; they "lack courage and are worn out," he said.[14]

De Gaulle's intransigence caught the Soviet Union off guard. Stalin had decided that the continuation of four-power control was less dangerous than a divided Germany in which the capitalists enjoyed unrestricted domination over the largest, most industrialized part of the country. Under four-power control, the Soviets could veto any measure they did not like, since decisions had to be made unanimously. The only serious obstacle to the rise of Communist power in Europe was the United States, but the Soviet dictator had every reason to expect that the Americans would not continually involve themselves in European affairs. German central government would, therefore, inevitably fall under Soviet domination. Meanwhile he consolidated Soviet power in his own sphere.

The Nuremberg War Crimes Trial. A rare example of successful Allied cooperation was exhibited in the first of the great war crimes trials that began on 20 November 1945 in Nuremberg, the sacred city of National Socialism. If Stalin had had his way, there would have been no trials. He no doubt was serious when he told Roosevelt and Churchill at Yalta that he favored summarily shooting 50,000 of Germany's leaders. The Nuremberg trial, however, served a double purpose: first, it fulfilled the desire for retribution, and secondly, it established rules of international law for future generations, outlawing aggressive war and holding those persons who caused it personally responsible. On trial were twenty-four Nazi leaders and six Nazi organizations. The 25,000-word indictment listed three categories of crimes: crimes against peace, war crimes, and crimes against humanity. The defendants were specifically charged with preparing and waging a war of aggression; being responsible for the murder of civilians and prisoners of war; wantonly destroying and plundering property; and preparing the extermination, enslavement, and deportation of people for political, racial, and religious reasons. The defendants were also charged with conspiracy to commit those crimes, a concept consistent with Anglo-American jurisprudence, but alien to French, German, and Soviet law. Until now, military aggression and the violation of treaties had never been considered illegal. Crimes against humanity were only justiciable if one side was capable of enforcing its concept of guilt on the other. At Nuremberg, the entire indictment was held to be valid "whether or not [any of the crimes were] in violation of domestic law of the country where perpetrated."[15]

The great room of Nuremberg's neo-Gothic courthouse looked like an avant-garde theater; the defendants sat side by side in two long rows, as if they were waiting for the house lights to dim. A line of white-helmeted American soldiers stood guard at their backs. The prisoners were seated more or less in order of political importance. In the best location—first row, first seat—sat Hermann Göring, the most imposing of the defendants, and in the last seat of the second row was Hans Fritzsche, the radio broadcasting chief in the propaganda ministry. Fritzsche, a comparative unknown, was really there at Soviet insistence as a stand-in for his old boss, Josef Goebbels.[16] Not all the indicted were present: Ernst Kaltenbrunner, chief of the SS Security Service, was suffering from a cerebral hemorrhage and could not make the opening session; Robert Ley, boss of the Nazi Labor Front, hanged himself from a pipe in his cell a month before the trial began; Gustav Krupp von Bohlen, the armaments manufacturer, was excused because he was too senile; and Martin Bormann, once deputy führer, could not be found.[17]

The legal problems were daunting. The Americans and the British used English common law; the French, Roman law; and the Soviets, their own brand of positive class-struggle law. This divergence led to enormous problems about presumed innocence or guilt, obscured the rights of the defense, and clouded the rules of evidence. The gathering of evidence was no problem, however, as the American prosecutor, Justice Robert Jackson, declared in his opening statement: "We do not ask you to convict these men on the testimony of their foes. There is no count of the indictment that cannot be proved by books and records. The Germans were always meticulous record keepers, and these defendants had their share of the Teutonic passion of thoroughness in putting things on paper."[18] Altogether, the proceedings produced over 4 million words of evidence and testimony. Three hundred sworn statements were admitted, 240 witnesses were heard, and 5,330 documents were produced. More than 40,000 pounds of paper were used. Every spoken word was simultaneously translated into French, English, Russian, and German and was recorded.

The trial became a gigantic history lesson. It examined Hitler's rise to power, the Reichstag fire (which Göring denied he had anything to do with), the origins and development of the concentration camps, the destruction of the trade unions, the Night of the Long Knives, and the persecution of the Jews. It detailed the assassination of Austrian chancellor Englebert Dollfuss, the remilitarization of the Rhineland, the Anschluss, the Axis intervention in the Spanish Civil War, the extinction of Czechoslovakia, and the invasion of Poland. The prosecution introduced the Hossbach Memorandum of the chancellery meeting of 5 November 1937 as prima facie evidence of the Nazi premeditation of World War II. The document, according to U.S. associate trial counsel, Sidney Alderman, destroyed "any possible doubt about the well-laid plans of the Nazis in their crimes against peace." He read it into the record in its entirety. Most of the testimony on World War II concentrated on Nazi behavior behind the lines—the treatment of civilians in the occupied countries, especially the organized extermination of the Jews. The prosecution augmented the written evidence by showing atrocity films, which disturbed some defendants. "When I see such things I'm ashamed of being a German," General Wilhelm Keitel remarked. Göring had a different reaction: "They were reading my telephone conversations on the Austrian affair," he complained, "and everybody was laughing with me—and then they showed that awful film, and it just spoiled everything."[19]

Hans Frank, former Nazi overlord in Poland, now a recent convert to Roman Catholicism, enthusiastically confessed his sins and willingly gave the prosecution his incriminating thirty-eight-volume diary. "A thousand years will pass and the guilt of Germany will not pass away," he said with religious fervor. Another approach was taken by SS Obergruppenführer Ernst Kaltenbrunner who denied all personal complicity. He put the blame entirely on Hitler and Himmler. When evidence was introduced showing that he had killings staged in his honor, he insisted he had been responsible only for problems of civilian morale. "You Americans . . . seem to think that our whole R.S.H.A. [SS Security Service] was nothing but an organized gang of criminals," he told the prison psychologist, G. M. Gilbert. "I must say that impression does exist," Gilbert replied. "Then how can I defend myself against such prejudice?" Kaltenbrunner snapped.[20]

Had the Germans won the war, they might have charged the Americans with the bombing of Dresden, tried the Soviets for their invasion of Finland, and indicted the British for their commando raids. Such evidence about Allied and Soviet conduct was ruled inadmissible at Nuremberg, however. When Göring's lawyer tried to justify Germany's treatment of Russian prisoners by describing how the Soviets had treated Germans, he was cut short. The president of the court, Sir Geoffrey Lawrence, explained: "The question is how can you justify in a trial of the major war criminals of Germany evidence against Great Britain, or against the United States of America, or against the U.S.S.R. or against France? If you are going to try the actions of all these signatory powers, apart from other considerations, there would be no end to the trial at all."[21] Contradictions were thus inevitable.

For example, the Germans were charged with the invasion of Poland, but the secret clauses of the Nazi-Soviet Non-Aggression Treaty that made the invasion possible were not admissible. Yet the Germans were accused of violating that treaty when they attacked the Soviet Union. The defendants were also disadvantaged by being denied access to the documents from which the prosecution prepared its case. If the defendants requested a particular order or letter, the Allies would conduct a search, but in asking for the document, the defense would have disclosed its strategy. The defendants' lawyers could not travel without permission from the prosecution, and their witnesses were often treated as enemies and harassed. The Soviets, who were used to a different type of trial procedure, expected the accused to be docile and their lawyers to cooperate in establishing a predetermined verdict.

Despite fundamental disagreement between the prosecution and the defense over the validity of the trial, the defense was accorded a certain latitude to present its case, and sometimes did so with telling effect. For example, the Soviets had insisted, against the advice of the Americans and British, that the massacre in the Katyn Forest be blamed on the Germans. Dr. Otto Stahmer, the attorney of Hermann Göring, so skillfully discredited the Soviet evidence that the charge was removed from the indictment and all mention of Katyn was dropped from the trial. In the end, nobody was held responsible. The American prosecutor Robert Jackson, who had little experience in cross-examination, proved to be a poor choice. He was much better at setting a moral tone. In his closing address on 26 July 1946, he said: "The future will never have to ask, with misgiving, 'What could the Nazis have said in their favor?' History will know that whatever could be said, they were allowed to say. They have been given the kind of a trial which they, in the days of their pomp and power, never gave to any man."[22] Of the twenty-one defendants, the court sentenced only eleven—Göring, Streicher, Frick, Ribbentrop, Kaltenbrunner, Sauckel, Keitel, Jodl, Frank, Rosenberg, and Seyss-Inquart—to death. It acquitted three of the accused: Papen, Fritzsche, and Schacht. The others were sentenced to prison terms ranging from ten years to life.

The Nuremberg tribunal delivers its judgment. For the twenty-one accused, seated in the two rows on the right, there were eleven death sentences, seven prison sentences, and three acquittals. Chief defendant Göring, wearing his dove-colored Reichsmarshal's uniform devoid of insignia and decorations, knew that he could cheat the hangman with the poison that had been smuggled to him in his cell.

Only Göring cheated the executioner by taking a cyanide capsule. The reichsmarshal had bragged, "In fifty years there will be statues of Hermann Göring in Germany." Göring apparently thought the Germans possessed a faith in their leaders that would transcend the bitterness of defeat.

The trials left an ambiguous legacy. Some people questioned whether it was right to try defendants for crimes that were defined after the fact. Yet, the trials also ensured that World War II would not give rise to a "stab in the back" myth or a mystique about the greatness of the National Socialist period.

The Nuremberg tribunal continued in session—by the end of 1946, 447 more cases, involving 1,341 suspects, were ready for prosecution. Over the next four years, however, only 199 persons were actually put on trial. Thirty-six received death sentences, half of which were carried out. Nuremberg was not the only city to hold war crimes trials. The Americans also convened courts at Dachau, and trials were held in the other three occupation zones and indeed throughout Europe. The Soviets led the way in death and prison sentences—over 10,000 in the decade and a half following the war. The British, French, and American courts, and the German courts that followed them, sentenced about 10,555 persons; 200 of the judgments resulted in executions. All these trials were part of a general program of denazification, the essential purpose of which was reeducation.[23]

The Eastern Zone

The Rebirth of the Communist Party. The Soviets pretended to govern with restraint. On 10 June 1945, Marshal Zhukov proclaimed that the Germans were free to engage in social and political activity through the formation of "anti-fascist parties" dedicated to "the consolidation of the foundations of democracy and civil liberties"; such parties should also recognize the right of the workers "to unite in free trade unions and organizations to protect the interests and rights of all working people."[24] This directive was in keeping with the party line established earlier in which political activity in Germany could only be developed "initially in the context of a large scale comprehensive anti-Fascist movement under the title of the 'Bloc for Militant Democracy.' "[25]

On 12 June 1945, the German Communist party (*Kommunistische Partei Deutschlands* or *KPD*) was officially reestablished before a small audience of two hundred people in the Berlin city hall. The proclamation stated that "the method of imposing the Soviet system on Germany would be wrong, since this method does not correspond to present-day conditions of development in Germany." The German Communists took the view "that the overriding interests of the German people in their present-day situation prescribe a different method for Germany, namely the method of establishing democratic rights and liberties for the people."[26] The decree also recognized the "complete and unrestricted development of free commerce and private enterprise on the basis of private property." Nowhere was there any mention of Marx or Engels or socialism. This public endorsement of independent political activity (as long as it was anti-Fascist) was at odds with what Communist party officials had been taught and would have come as a surprise had it been taken seriously.

The basic strategy for the ultimate triumph of Communism had been worked out in Moscow before the end of the war. Even before the Red Army had ended all Nazi resistance, German Communist leaders had moved into key areas to take over the local administration under the supervision of the Soviet military authorities. Walter Ulbricht took charge in Berlin. He wanted everything to appear democratic on the surface and therefore advocated a broad coalition of all anti-Fascist parties. These, in addition to the KPD, included the Social Democratic party (SPD), the Christian Democratic Union (CDU), and the Liberal Democratic party of Germany (LDPD). The Soviet Military Administration was to handle affairs in East Germany, but the Communists did not want to appear too greedy for political power. They usually installed a well-known non-Communist as mayor, while retaining for themselves the key position of deputy mayor and other important posts in the municipal government. In Berlin, for example, they took charge of personnel, education, social welfare, finance, the post office and communications, and labor deployment.[27] From this powerful base, the Stalinists began quietly to tighten their control over East Germany and in the process gave up their earlier prohibition against seeking an alliance with the Social Democrats.

One-Party Government. Many Social Democrats had favored joining with the Communists to form a single party in which they would be the senior partners. They remembered how the Communist and Social Democratic split had contributed to the triumph of Hitler. However, their growing strength at the polls and the opposition of the West German Social Democrats to a union with the Communists had given them second thoughts. In the meantime, the Communists, alarmed at this new mood of independence, also had a change of heart.

In November 1945, Ulbricht called for an immediate union of the parties. He had witnessed the drift away from Communism in nearby Hungary and Austria and the gains made by the Social Democrats, at the expense of the Communists, in the local elections in West Germany and Berlin. Promising a German road to socialism, the KPD launched a massive recruitment campaign. It formed local KPD-SPD action committees and held meetings and conferences. The Soviet Military Administration did its part by banning Social Democratic meetings and arresting those who spoke out against unification. Finally, the Communists decided the time for persuasion was over and announced that fusion with the Social Democrats was an accomplished fact.

At the unification congress on 26 April, Wilhelm Pieck, the head of the Communists, and Otto Grotewohl, chief of the Social Democrats, officially proclaimed the establishment of the Socialist Unity party (*Sozialistische Einheitspartei Deutschlands* or *SED*) with a strict Marxist-Leninist program: "the transformation of the capitalist ownership of the means of production into social ownership and the transformation of capitalist production of goods into socialist production."[28] The SED claimed to represent the people and made a genuine attempt to appeal to the voters. It refused to accept the eastern boundary with Poland as final, and it promised to give former Nazis fair treatment. Such public relations ploys were part of Stalin's strategy of trying to influence political developments in the rest of Germany. However, the Americans, British, and French prohibited the SED from operating in their zones.

Even with considerable help from the Soviet authorities, who constantly harassed opposition party members and refused to place their candidates on the ballots, the SED failed to win a majority of the votes in the Kreis and Landtag elections of October 1946.[29] The party assumed control anyway. Within a year it had risen to two million members, more than all the other parties combined. Between 1946 and 1948, it expelled, degraded, falsely accused, or purged most of the leading Social Democrats.[30] Other political groups were turned into Communist auxiliaries or similarly eliminated. The establishment of one-party Stalinist rule in East Germany confirmed the country's division into two halves. Stalin severed all East Germany's ties with Western political parties and ended any hope that the country might take an independent road to socialism.

The Sectors of the West

The Development of Grass-Roots Democracy. In accordance with the Potsdam provisions on "the decentralization of the political structure and the development of local responsibility,[31] the British, Americans, and French each developed their own brand of German government. The British treated their zone as a sort of colony, one that was in transition from complete military control "to an eventual civilian organization in which there would be a German administration with British control at the top."[32] Thus, the British would use the army only in emergencies and would gradually allow the Germans to assume greater responsibilities. At the end of 1946, the British accorded the Länder the power to regulate their own industrial development, enact housing and town planning ordinances, and adopt measures concerning freedom of the press and association. Nevertheless, no measure the Länder legislatures passed could become law until the regional British commander countersigned it. The British also changed the traditional function of the town mayor. Previously, a *Bürgermeister* (mayor) had been both a city's chief executive and its chief legislator—as such, the mayors were frequently more responsible to the central government than to their own constituents. The British made the mayor head only of the town council and gave the executive functions to a professional city manager, the *Stadtdirector* (town clerk). By separating these functions, the British hoped to make the elected city council responsible for policy and show that the administrators were its servants, "dependent on its good will."[33]

The Americans also tried to inculcate democracy by extending popular participation to all levels of village, city, county, and state government. They allowed the people to ratify the constitutions drafted for Bavaria, Württemberg-Baden, and Hesse.[34] At the same time, however, the Americans never let the Germans forget who ultimately pulled the strings. General Lucius Clay ran things from his "capital" at Stuttgart, personally presiding over the monthly meeting of the minister-presidents of the various states. He used the occasion to charge them with specific responsibilities and to issue warnings. At the first meeting, he announced: "Since you will in fact develop the measures necessary for full cooperation between your units, it must be assumed that each of you individually will carry out what you have agreed to collectively. I wish to emphasize that, within United States policy, yours is the responsibility. We will not dictate to you except as you violate expressed policy."[35]

As for the French, General Pierre Koenig ruled from Baden-Baden like a king's viceroy. He thought it unfair that East Germany, but not the West, should be under a harsh rule. Consequently, he stubbornly refused to coordinate his policies with those of the British and Americans. His country's own economic problems virtually precluded it from supplying the Germans with any aid or providing much logistical support for its forces of occupation. The French tried to live off the land as much as possible, even to the extent of bringing over hordes of relatives to dwell with the soldiers in requisitioned quarters. To conserve rations, the French refused to accept refugees from other parts of Germany. They were interested in getting reparations, and they also wanted to annex the Saar, persisting in their demand long after it was plain that their cause was hopeless. The question of the Saar poisoned Franco-German relations for over a decade until the issue was finally resolved in 1957. Then, just as they had done in 1935, the Saarlanders voted overwhelmingly to become a permanent part of Germany. In one way, though, the French were less harsh than the other occupying powers. They seldom turned Germans out of their homes. They simply moved in on them, occupying the best rooms, sitting in the best chairs, and sometimes relegating the former occupants to the basement. Still, this was better than in the other zones where if a house or an apartment was needed, the inhabitants were simply ordered to leave.

Denazification. The Americans were optimistic that they could change the German national character and therefore pushed denazification harder than any of the other occupying powers. The Joint Chiefs of Staff directive 1067 determined to purge from public office and positions of importance all members of the Nazi party who were "more than normal participants in its activities, all active supporters of Nazism or militarism and all other persons hostile to Allied purposes."[36] These included officeholders, party activists, organizers, participants in Nazi unions, and those who had voluntarily given substantial support or assistance to the National Socialist cause. The Americans believed that everyone who joined the party before 1937 had done so out of commitment, not necessity. To identify the suspects, they prepared a personal questionnaire (*Fragebogen*) with 131 questions. Every German over the age of eighteen had to complete one. The process was carried out through local registration boards somewhat reminiscent of the U.S. Selective Service System. The Americans examined the answers and assigned the respondents to the appropriate classifications: major offender, offender, lesser offender, follower, or exonerated. The table of punishments for each category (except major war criminals who were placed in a special category) ranged from imprisonment to loss of property, and from exclusion from public office to prohibition from voting.

The Americans ordered the Germans to create a Special Ministry of Political Education and establish their own denazification courts under the supervision of the Public Safety Branch of the Military Government. In its heyday, the operation was massive, comprising 545 separate tribunals with a combined personnel of over 22,000 people. Thirteen million Germans were registered, 3 million of whom were charged, but only 930 received sentences. Denazification concentrated a tremendous amount of energy on an essentially negative task, which was never completely successful. Nazism had, after all, been an indigenous movement, and people had many reasons for joining—some out of ideological enthusiasm, others because it was a good way to advance their careers. Some were required to become members because they held positions of responsibility and trust and the party officials ordered all such people to belong. If all Nazi party members had been excluded from participation in the political and economic life of postwar Germany, the society would have ceased to function. General George Patton, briefly military governor of Bavaria, had no difficulty using Nazi civil servants to run his province, and he was not alone. The Americans also suspected that the Germans were not particularly keen to pursue their compatriots.

The Soviets were more tolerant of a person's past—if that person were willing to join the Socialist Unity party. After all, the psychology of totalitarianism was the same whether it was from the Left or the Right—a person could serve one just as well as the other. The British endorsed denazification, but compiled dossiers on only two million persons. The French believed all Germans were guilty anyway so they saw little to be gained in pursuing former Nazis unless they had committed specific crimes against the French.

The way the denazification policy was implemented aroused considerable dissatisfaction. Nevertheless, a great many former Nazis *were* removed from active public life, thereby creating opportunities for those who were less politically compromised. The purge was necessary to encourage the democratic elements, who had been terrorized during the Nazi period, to once again play an active role in the political life of their country. The Germans may have been critical of the policy, but the society in which they lived was better for being at least partially cleansed of its unwholesome elements. Had the Weimar Republic carried out a similar purge of the old imperial bureaucracy, its democracy might have had a better chance of survival.

Removing the unsavory elements was only part of the process of denazification. The Allies believed that if Nazism were to be eradicated, the demons of the past would have to be exorcised through reeducation.[37] To this end, the Americans, British, French, and Soviets all wanted to make profound changes in the schools, including purging them of National Socialist books and curricula, screening teachers for the proper moral and political qualities, and imposing a new educational policy on Germany. Their philosophies varied as did their techniques and their degree of success.

The Soviets, who did not have to worry about imbuing the Germans with a love of democracy, accomplished the most significant structural changes. But then they had more and longer opportunities than the Western powers. The Soviet Military Administration (after 1949 the Soviet High Commissioner) and the SED, the official political party, did not have to face competition. East German teachers had already been schooled in obedience. The centralized Nazi educational administration continued under another guise with those who believed in Marxist Leninism replacing those who followed the Führerprinzip. Politics aside, the Soviets did effect a significant and lasting social alteration. Whereas the German system had previously trained different social classes for different tasks, the Soviets abolished the special advantages of the middle and upper classes and created comprehensive, more egalitarian schools.

The three Western powers were primarily interested in inculcating the Germans with democracy. The French rivaled the Soviets in reformist zeal, although they had less practical effect. They arrived with missionary enthusiasm, bringing elaborate plans and first-rate educators. Not since the old colonial days had they had such an opportunity to practice their *mission civilisatrice*. They left with their ambitions unfulfilled, but with the Germans less nationalistic and less parochial.

The British brought a similar array of experts, but theirs seemed content with giving advice rather than being coercive. The British and German systems operated on similar social wavelengths—both institutionalized the system of tracking. Within two years, the British began returning the school system to the Germans.

In contrast, the Americans were just getting their second wind in 1947. The Americans had first concentrated on denazification, carefully removing Nazi party members from the schools and starting to reform the curriculum. They replaced Nazi books with those of the Weimar Republic, forgetting that the Weimar schools were bastions of ultranationalism. The universities were immediately reopened with University Planning Committees to supervise who taught what and to whom. Following the precedent established at Marburg University, applicants were required to fill out a *Fragebogen*; after admission, they had to take a special orientation course that concentrated on Germany's relations with the world since 1935. The Americans gave feminism a big boost by abolishing the Nazi 10 percent ceiling on enrollments for women. The first postwar class admitted at Marburg was almost 40 percent female. The Joint Chiefs of Staff directive of July 1947 strongly linked educational reform with economic and political recovery, but the low status the American army accorded its educational specialists belied that contention.

Ultimately, Western plans to change the structure of German education by making the schools workshops for democracy and social unification fell short of their goals. The occupation only lasted four years, too short a time for rewards to keep pace with expectations. The United States had more influence through its cultural exchange programs than through its curriculum revisions. In addition, the educational programs of the Western democratic powers all contained a basic contradiction. The philosophe Jean-Jacques Rousseau had advocated liberating people from the chains of the past by forcing them to be free. In practice, though, military government proved to be a poor tutor for democracy.

The Demise of Central Administration

The Policy of Pauperization Ends. The Potsdam agreement mandated that the German standard of living be maintained at the European average—in effect, cut back to the levels that existed in the depression year of 1932. Despite the enormous destruction of the war, only 15 to 20 percent of German industry was irreparably damaged. In 1944, Germany actually produced 40 percent more goods than in 1938. In March 1946, however, a joint economics council directive set Germany's annual steel production at 7.5 million tons (a significant reduction from its prewar figure of 19 million tons). It reduced the production of chemicals to 40 percent of 1936 output, set machine tools at 11.4 percent of the 1938 level, and dropped heavy electrical equipment to 30 percent of the 1938 capacity. Under this directive German manufacturing would, on average, be stabilized at half the productive levels achieved in 1938. Most importantly, the Germans were prohibited from manufacturing all armaments and war materials, including ball bearings, synthetic rubber, heavy tractors, and radio transmitting equipment. The Germans were also to discontinue all experimentation with nuclear energy. The directive left only a few industries without limitations—building materials, bicycles, china dishes, and glass bottles. Even this was practically meaningless because the Germans did not have sufficient hard currency to purchase raw materials, which, for the most part, had to be imported.

Having set the policy, the occupying powers were sharply divided over how it should be carried out. The Russians and French pushed for even further reductions, while the British and Americans had come to the conclusion that maintaining artificially low levels of production was against their own national interests. For one thing, they reasoned that their exports were already keeping the Germans alive; with millions of refugees fleeing to the West from the Russian zone, this economic dependency would only get worse. Overriding these economic concerns was the British and American fear that unless the Germans were allowed to return to prosperity they would once again seek a solution to their problems in extremist politics, which now could only mean Communism. Therefore, German economic prosperity was a fundamental necessity.

Furthermore, the Soviets were insisting that the $10 billion due them in reparations be directly satisfied with goods from current production, including production from the Western zones. If the Soviet demand were met, the West would, in fact, be subsidizing the Soviet Union. The British and Americans tried to ease the economic tensions by advocating the establishment of a central import and export agency that would treat Germany as a single economic unit, but the Soviets (and also the French) were strongly opposed. Stalin withstood all attempts to conclude a formal treaty of peace until his demands were satisfied.

James Byrnes, the U.S. secretary of state, believed that Soviet intransigence was prompted by fear of another invasion. He, therefore, proposed a treaty to guarantee German demilitarization for twenty-five years. Byrnes hoped that such an agreement would pave the way for the early evacuation of all Allied military forces. The Soviets toyed with the idea and even induced Byrnes to extend the guarantee to forty years. Nevertheless, Stalin knew that any agreement that might lead to a Soviet evacuation from Germany would jeopardize the collection of reparations. Furthermore, the experiences after World War I suggested that German disarmament could not be ensured without occupation.

The Suspension of Reparations Payments. The British and Americans became convinced that Stalin was deliberately promoting German economic chaos to further the advance of Communism. On 3 May 1946, the United States suspended all payments of reparations from its zone to the Soviets. Byrnes concluded that the failure of the Soviet leaders to support his guarantee treaty meant that they did not want the United States involved in any system to maintain European security and that only the "pressure of American power would restrict the freedom of action which the Soviet Union, as the predominant military power in Europe, might otherwise enjoy."[38] The suspension of reparations payments to the Soviet Union was Byrnes's way of showing that a common German policy was impossible.[39] Britain and the United States refused to consider the resumption of reparations payments until there was a general willingness to share resources.

Byrnes then went further. On 11 July, he said that the United States was willing to join "with any other occupying government or governments in Germany for the creation of our respective zones as an economic unit."[40] On 6 September, Byrnes made the new policy more explicit when he told the minister-presidents of Württemberg, Bavaria, and Hesse at Stuttgart that the United States no longer considered the agreement to limit German production to be binding. "Germany must be enabled to use her skills and her energies to increase her industrial production and to organize the most effective use of her raw materials," he said. "Germany is a part of Europe, and recovery in Europe . . . will be slow indeed if Germany with her great resources of iron and coal is turned into a poorhouse."[41] Byrnes also stated that Germany must be permitted to develop democratically responsible government in which the central administrative agencies would function under an appropriate federal constitution. This, he emphasized, would take place under the full protection of the United States. "Security forces," he added significantly, "will probably have to remain in Germany for a long period. I want no misunderstanding. We will not shirk our duty. We are not withdrawing. We are staying and will furnish our proportionate share of security forces."[42]

Great Britain responded immediately to the American initiative, and the merger of their two zones was finalized in December 1946. The French at first tried to maintain a position of "nonalignment," hoping that they could, with Soviet support, annex the Saar and achieve internationalization of the Ruhr. The pursuit of such a policy, however, left them in the uncomfortable position of standing on the sidelines while a strong Germany once again emerged. No longer was there any possibility that Germany would be broken up into some sort of loose federal state. Therefore, Paris began negotiations toward joining the French zone with the British and American sector. At the same time, French leaders found the prospect so objectionable that they tried to delay the inevitable as long as possible by holding out for large concessions.

In creating Bizonia, the British and Americans nevertheless tried to avoid the complete breakdown of the policy of joint administration. They therefore allowed the continuation of the present currency system. This was a double-headed arrangement in which regular German reichsmarks were allowed to circulate alongside the special occupation currency that the Allies had issued to transact their own affairs. Both monies were highly inflated. During the war, the number of banknotes in circulation had quadrupled without a corresponding increase in goods and services. The occupation money was similarly inflated, largely because the Soviets, on their own, kept printing as much as they wanted to satisfy their needs. It thus became a way of collecting reparations. Since the real worth of both currencies was unrelated to their fixed rate, an active black market flourished. Under the circumstances, it was impossible to program any rational economic development. The Allies had tried to maintain economic stability by continuing the rationing and wage and price controls established under the Nazis. Still the amount of goods was small in relation to the superabundance of currency, and official prices were too low to stimulate production. Without any reliable currency, the Germans resorted to barter. In many areas, American cigarettes became a form of legal tender. The Soviets were clearly more interested in maintaining the financial chaos of Germany than they were in promoting its recovery. They refused to agree to any new banking scheme because that might weaken their hand.

Therefore, the British and Americans decided to act alone. In February 1948, they announced their intention to establish a new bank of issue, the *Bank Deutscher Länder*, under the supervision of the Allied Banking Commission. Before putting the scheme into effect, they asked the Soviets to help conclude a new four-power agreement. The Soviets came to the negotiations with the intention of sabotaging them. Stalin regarded the proposed reform as part of a plot to divide Germany. At the conference, the Soviets insisted that they had the right to continue printing money without restriction, but it was clear that the Americans and British were prepared to enact the reform without them—an obvious prelude to establishing a separate West German government. On 20 March, the Soviets withdrew their representatives from the Allied Control Commission. General Clay had seen the stiffening Soviet attitude and warned Washington to prepare for some major Soviet move. The Anglo-American determination to carry out the currency reform in Bizonia prodded France to merge its zone with theirs. Without waiting for parliamentary approval for the full merger plan, the French negotiators agreed to accept the new currency reform in their zone. At the same time, they continued to demand last-minute tax benefits. The French were of two minds: realizing they could not go it alone, they wanted to join the merger, but be independent at the same time.

The *Währungsreform* (currency reform) was announced on 18 June to take effect two days later when the new banknotes would be released simultaneously in the British, French, and American zones. Stalin was ready. He denounced the Western powers for violating the Yalta and Potsdam accords and suspended their rights to have access to Berlin by land. For Stalin the blockade was more than just a ploy to force a return to the status quo ante. The currency reform provided him with an opportunity to win a stunning Cold War victory by removing the West from Berlin. He had long viewed this outpost as a threat to the security of the whole Soviet position in Germany.

The Berlin Blockade. Stalin was in a much better position than he had been the previous year to seek a showdown with his former allies. In February 1948, he had considerably strengthened his hold over Eastern Europe with the formation of a Communist-controlled government in Czechoslovakia. The country had rapidly been integrated into the Soviet bloc. Stalinist governments were also in firm control of all the important Eastern European states, excluding Greece and Yugoslavia. Stalin chose Berlin for the showdown because it was completely surrounded by Soviet-controlled territory. The Soviets had been interfering with Western access to the city since January 1948. On 1 April, the Soviets demanded that Allied railroad traffic obtain special prior authorization before passing through the Soviet zone. Next came a claim that the Western allies had forfeited all their rights in the city because they had disrupted the four-power government of Germany. Now, Stalin argued that in organizing a West German government, the West had violated the Yalta and the Potsdam accords, and therefore he was not bound to follow these agreements on the status of Berlin.

On 24 June, four days after the Western currency reform went into effect, the Soviets stopped all surface freight and passenger traffic into the city from the West; a week later, they officially withdrew from the Berlin Kommandatura, bringing four-power rule to an end. Stalin had good reason to expect that his Berlin coup would succeed. The Western powers had only token forces in the city and were hardly mobilized for the kind of military action needed to challenge the might of the Red Army. Furthermore, there was no written agreement confirming ground access to the city. Such a formal reinforcement of rights had not seemed necessary in 1945, when few assumed that the military arrangements for the occupation of Germany would form the basis for two separate states. The Western powers could argue that Soviet acceptance of their presence in Berlin implied that they had an easement into the city to exercise their rights there. For this reason, they considered Stalin's behavior unacceptable and a violation of the agreements of 1944 and 1945.

Washington vetoed a plan advanced by General Lucius Clay to send an armored column up the autobahn to reassert Western rights. On paper, the only right of access the West had was a provision for the use of specific air corridors, which

A Skymaster flies low over the Berlin rooftops on its final approach to Templehof airport. The C-54 was the workhorse of the U.S. Air Force during World War II; the U.S. built more C-54s than any other cargo transport. Some three hundred of them participated in the Berlin airlift, and the last flight of the blockade was made by a C-54.

had been committed to writing more for the purpose of air safety than for politics. Yet upon this legality, the United States decided to base its countermeasure to the blockade. Until now the feasibility of supplying Berlin by air had hardly been considered. Commander R. N. Waite of the Royal Air Force (RAF) quickly concocted a plan showing it could be done, and the Americans and British scraped together practically every transport plane at their disposal to put it into effect.

The airlift began on 25 June with a flight of C-47s and was improvised as it went along. At first, people viewed it as a holding operation to give the politicians time to negotiate a settlement, but the longer the airlift continued, the more supplies it could fly into the beleaguered city. With the arrival of C-54s in late July, ten tons of goods could be carried per plane. At its height, the airlift supplied Berlin with 8,000 tons of food, raw materials, and fuel daily. On average, a plane landed at Berlin's Templehof Airport every three to five minutes, twenty-four hours a day. In all, some 2.3 million tons of provisions arrived; the United States Air Force carried two-thirds, the RAF was responsible for most of the rest. When the blockade began, the Americans moved their B-29 strategic bombers to Britain. The planes, armed with atomic bombs, were within striking distance of Moscow. President Harry S Truman saw the Berlin crisis as Stalin's attempt to test his resolve. He believed that if he gave in, there would be no end of bullying. The Berlin Blockade also prompted an Allied counterblockade. The West kept a broad range of products from being exported to the Soviet zone: machinery, chemicals, rubber, textiles, steel, tools, spare parts, and electrical goods.[43] The ban kept the East German government from fulfilling its Two-Year Plan.

Throughout the ordeal, the morale of the Berliners remained extremely high. Political cabarets were especially popular, as indeed were all sorts of cultural events and activities that brought the people of West Berlin closer together. The crisis ended all-city government, however. In December 1948, separate elections were held in West Berlin, resulting in the triumph of Ernst Reuter. Heretofore the Soviets had prevented this Social Democrat from becoming mayor. East Berlin then held its own separate elections. In addition to having two mayors, the city also separated economically, with each part having its own public services.

Berlin became divided educationally as well. The school system had already been marked by ideological and political confrontation as Social Democrats and Communists fought to control the administration and curriculum. The Communists had an advantage because the Soviets had entrenched themselves in power as soon as they arrived in the city, months before the others. Although the Allied Kommandatura had final authority, the constant East-West squabbles resulted in frustration and delays. The Soviets challenged every Western proposal. Meanwhile, they had taken over Berlin University (since 1949 Humboldt University), which was located in their zone, and shut everybody else out. Their secret police routinely harassed students, arresting and expelling those they found objectionable.

The Berlin Blockade presented the perfect opportunity to bring this impossible situation to an end by creating a separate elementary and secondary school system for West Berlin. At the same time, General Clay pushed for the creation of a new university. The proposal reached his desk in April 1948, and he immediately gave it his most enthusiastic endorsement, insisting that the new institution be opened in time for the autumn term. The Free University of Berlin was to be a German university run by Germans. It held its first classes in November. In addition to liberating Berlin's higher education from the grip of Marxist-Leninism, the university's founders wanted to promote free inquiry in all fields and avoid the traditional authoritarianism of German universities. On the occasion of the university's inauguration on 4 December 1948, Ernst Reuter, mayor-elect of Berlin and chairman of the Preparatory Committee, said, "Universities should be centers of free activity, free creativity, and free thinking, not centers where politics in the narrow sense of the word are perpetrated."[44] Thus, he linked the freedom of the university with the aspirations of Berliners for the freedom of their city.

The Berlin airlift dramatically confirmed the Western presence in Berlin. Truman did not think the Soviets really wanted to push the crisis to the point of war, but he feared that "a trigger-happy Russian pilot or hothead Communist tank commander might create an incident that could ignite the powder keg."[45] The crisis ended in a stalemate. The Soviets lifted the blockade on 12 May 1949. Berlin was divided, but so was all Germany. On 23 May, the British, American, and French zones officially became the German Federal Republic.

The Soviets denounced the *Bundesrepublik* as a Germany of warmongers, armaments tycoons, and large estate owners and established their own "sovereign" state. They claimed that their German Democratic Republic (*Deutsche Democratische Republik* or GDR) was the only regime to honor the Potsdam agreement's call for an independent and democratic Germany. The West saw the GDR as an illegitimate puppet regime, established by fiat, not by free elections. Thus, each side claimed its creation was legitimate and the only true basis for a united Germany. Rhetoric aside, none of the victors genuinely desired reunification, at least not then. They did not want a sovereign, independent Germany; nor did they want a united Germany under the control of the other party. Division was the most feasible solution. The Berlin crisis changed the character of the Cold War by ending the active competition for a unified Germany. The airlift also showed that neither side was willing to wage war to obtain more than it already had. Truman summed up the significance of the airlift succinctly: "When we refused to be forced out of the city of Berlin, we demonstrated to the people of Europe that with their co-operation we would act, and act resolutely, when their freedom was threatened. Politically it brought the peoples of western Europe more closely to us."[46]

THE BONN REPUBLIC

Constitutional and Political Reconstruction

The Basic Law. The Weimar Republic had foundered because most Germans thought that their problems could be solved by those who wanted to destroy democracy. In 1948, the framers of the new *Grundgesetz* (Basic Law) could hardly create an instant respect for representative institutions, but they did try to correct past structural weaknesses. They were not alone in their desire. On 1 July 1948, the Western allies issued a directive requiring the Germans to draft a "democratic constitution," establishing a "federal type" government to "protect the rights of the participating states, provide adequate authority, and contain guarantees of individual rights and freedoms."[47] During the drafting of the constitution, the military governors constantly offered advice and assistance, and, not surprisingly, the final document reflected their concepts of democratic practice as well as the Germans' notions of self-government.

The constituent assembly resurrected the parliamentary republic, but deprived the president of the power to issue emergency decrees and to act as commander-in-chief of the armed forces. To minimize the possibility of a cult of personality, a special Federal Convention would elect the president "without debate." The convention would be divided equally between representatives from the lower house of the legislature and from the local state diets. The president would have the authority to "propose" the head of the government, but could not participate in the process of selecting a cabinet; and an appropriate minister had to endorse all official acts (appointments and dismissals, proclamations of treaties, and official pardons). The president was clearly expected to be a figurehead, while the real executive power was concentrated in a cabinet, which was responsible to, and had to enjoy the majority support of, the lower house of parliament. The head of the government was the chancellor (*Bundeskanzler*), who could only be overthrown by a positive vote of no confidence: that is, the chancellor could not be ousted by a simple vote of no confidence; a viable successor had to be elected instead. This provision was inserted to avoid interregnums and to prevent the sort of situation that had occurred in the early 1930s when the Nazis and Communists overturned the government with the sole purpose of creating as much confusion as possible.

The legislative power, in keeping with the desires of the Western allies to promote federalism, was vested in two chambers. The lower house, the *Bundestag*, was the more powerful. Its deputies directly represented the whole people and were "not bound by orders and instructions and are subject only to their conscience."[48] In financial matters, the lower chamber had paramount authority. The upper house, the *Bundesrat*, directly represented the Länder and had to approve any laws that affected the states' administrative, territorial, and financial interests. On other legislation, it possessed only a suspensive veto.

In its "Letter of Advice," the Allied Military Government of the Western powers demanded that the Germans establish "an independent judiciary to review legislation, to review the exercise of executive power, to resolve conflict between the federal government and the states or between the states, and to protect civil rights and individual freedoms."[49] The principle of judicial review, which the United States strongly endorsed, was alien to the German tradition.[50] It was also foreign to the legal practices of the British and French, but they agreed that such a check on executive and legislative authority could prevent the central government from riding roughshod over the rights of the states and individual liberties. Accordingly, the Germans established a federal constitutional court to rule on the substantive and procedural rights of individuals and groups. The court had the authority to arbitrate jurisdictional disputes between the federal and the state governments; the responsibility of interpreting, supervising, and enforcing constitutional norms; and the duty to protect the basic rights of free speech, press, assembly, and equality before the law, even against private individuals and groups that sought to deprive citizens of these rights.[51] The court met in Karlsruhe to avoid making a single city the seat of the German government.

Allied Approval. The West Germans accepted judicial review, but they had difficulty achieving the amount of functional decentralization that the Allies demanded. The French, British, and American military governors, meeting in Frankfurt on 16 February 1949 to review a draft of the proposed constitution, feared that excessive authority had been given to the central government, especially in the fields of public health, public welfare, labor, revenue raising, and tax collection. They also mistrusted its power over the press. The Allies believed that giving broad concurrent legislative powers to both the federal government and the Länder would unnecessarily weaken the authority of the individual states. In addition, they were concerned that the new civil service would perpetuate undemocratic traditions.[52] The Allies were not unanimous in their demands. While the British were willing to accept the Basic Law, provided the provisions about the civil service were changed, the Americans and French wanted specific reductions in the financial and legislative powers of the central government.

Social Democratic party leader Kurt Schumacher announced publicly that he would try to force the constitution's ratification without change. His party felt that centralization was essential to carry out the socialization of the German economy. General Clay thought Schumacher was merely trying to score political points with the electorate: "If he and his party could defy the occupying powers and get away with it, they could go to the polls triumphantly proclaiming their success as defenders of the German people against the Allies."[53] Neither the Germans, nor the Allies, really wanted to delay the establishment of constitutional government. A major difference over financial authority was resolved by giving the federal government the receipts from customs, most excise taxes, and the sales tax and giving the Länder the income from property, inheritance, and motor-vehicle taxes. The states could also keep the tax revenues from the sale of alcoholic beverages—a concession that the 1871 constitution had accorded some states. Both the federal government and the Länder were to share the revenues from income and corporation taxes. These financial provisions, comprising ten articles of the Basic Law, were almost a constitution in themselves. The Basic Law is probably the only constitution in the world that specifically recognizes the right to collect a tax on beer.

Reestablishment of Party Government

A Multiparty System. The Basic Law came into force on 23 May 1949, after being ratified by two-thirds of the Länder. The first elections were held the following 14 August. The voting system combined proportional representation with single-member districts; each German cast two ballots—one for a specific candidate and the other for a particular party list. This device was supposed to promote the development of large, nationally organized political parties and discourage the growth of splinter groups. The election law also stated that any party receiving less than five percent of the vote would not be represented in the Bundestag. For the first time in German history, the constitution described the role of parties: "The political parties participate in the forming of the political will of the people. They may be freely formed. Their internal organization must conform to democratic principles. They must publicly account for the sources of their funds."[54]

The 1949 balloting gave seats in the Bundestag to ten political parties. Three of these won four-fifths of the seats. The Christian Democratic Union (with its Bavarian affiliate the Christian Social Union) had 139 delegates; the Social Democratic party, 131 delegates; and the Free Democratic party, 52 delegates. In subsequent elections, as the strength of the smaller parties dwindled, Germany came closer to having a two-party system than any other continental European nation. The new parliament met in Bonn in September 1949 and elected Theodor Heuss, leader of the Free Democrats, as first bundespräsident. The new chief of state had distinguished himself in the days of the Weimar Republic as a journalist and lecturer at the Berlin Institute of Politics. He had served in the Reichstag and was a convinced democrat. His conception of the presidency as a largely ceremonial office outside the main political arena helped to confirm the intent of the constitution. As part of the agreement to elect Heuss to the presidency, the Free Democrats supported the formation of a cabinet by Konrad Adenauer, the leader of the Christian Democrats. With additional support from several minor parties, he squeezed into office by 201 to 200 votes.

Adenauer's Christian Democratic Union (CDU) was a heterogeneous collection of old Center party veterans, Rhineland industrialists, landowners, economic free traders, Weimar liberals, and conservatives. Although the Christian Democrats were predominantly Roman Catholic, Adenauer wisely fought the creation of a confessionalist party and chose a Protestant, Ludwig Erhard, to hold the second position in the party. Adenauer's political acumen was demonstrated by his ability to hold these disparate elements together and, in less than a decade, mold them into a solid majority party. (For example, in the 1957 elections, the CDU received 50.2 percent of the votes and 270 of the 497 deputies in the Bundestag.) The CDU stood for the "maintenance of a socially-responsible free enterprise economy."[55] Accordingly, it adhered to the long-standing welfare goals of socialism, but balanced these with an endorsement of private initiative. The Christian Democrats called for the elimination of the monopolistic practices of the past that had acted as a hindrance to the free play of market forces. They wanted to strengthen small and medium-size private businesses and agricultural enterprises. They believed in a sound fiscal system and in the protection of savings and private property. In some regions, like Bavaria, the party posed as the champion of Roman Catholicism. However, it gained more support in the large urban areas of the north with its appeal to middle-class fears of socialism.

Despite the great loyalty to democracy that the Social Democratic party (*Sozialdemokratische Partei Deutschlands* or *SPD*) had shown during the Weimar Republic, many Germans were leery of turning power over to a group of Marxists. The SPD therefore remained the main opposition party, relying chiefly on working-class support. At their reorganization convention in October 1945, the Social Democrats advocated state economic planning and public ownership of the basic means of production. However, the party gradually became more moderate as it began to compete with the CDU for middle-class votes. Gallant though its leader Kurt Schumacher was, he proved a hindrance to creating a broad-based party. In order to win more than its usual 30 percent of the vote, the SPD needed to purge itself of all its revolutionary ideology. Schumacher's death paved the way for the Godesberg Program of 1959. This program advocated "freedom of choice in consumption and in employment, free competition and free economic initiative," and it pledged to protect and assist privately owned means of production "except where this may interfere with the development of a just social order."[56] The Social Democrats recognized that most Germans were no longer content with doctrinaire solutions to problems, and that the successful recovery of Germany meant a strong endorsement of the market economy.

Profile: Konrad Adenauer (1876–1967)

Until 1945, when Konrad Adenauer presided over the formation of the Christian Democratic Union—one of the four interregional parties that the Allied military government permitted to exist—he was practically unknown outside his native Cologne where he had served as mayor from 1917 to 1933. During this long tenure, he had exercised almost unchallenged control over the city's administration, dominating its council and requiring complete obedience from his subordinates. He was forced from office in 1933 when the Nazis accused him of embezzling money from the city treasury and of having betrayed Germany to the French by intriguing for the establishment of a separate Rhenish Republic. The charge of separatism was not without merit.

A key to understanding Adenauer's personality and subsequent career as chancellor of Germany can be found in the special characteristics of Cologne in the late nineteenth century where he was born on 5 January 1876. His father was a clerk of the city's Superior Tribunal, and his family was devoutly Roman Catholic. This was the time when Bismarck was conducting his famous *Kulturkampf* (Conflict of Beliefs) to subordinate the Roman Catholic religion to state regimentation. Adenauer grew up determined to combat the influence of Prussia. He became a lawyer in order to establish a power base within the local Cologne hierarchy. In 1897, he obtained his first position as an assistant in the public prosecutor's office. He joined the regionally powerful Catholic Center party, an alliance that led to his appointment as an administrative assistant in the city's taxation department. In six years, he rose to become vice-mayor, and in October 1917 he was elected mayor for his first twelve-year term.

After the fall of the kaiser, Adenauer tried to discern where his interest lay. On the one hand, he was sympathetic to Rhineland separatism, but at the same time he wanted to wait until he could obtain a clearer idea of the viability of the Weimar government. At one time, he advocated a West German Republic within the bounds of the Reich. This unit would have its own police force and diplomatic representation abroad. German nationalists suspected him of being pro-French, since his goals seemed to coincide with those of Paris, but Adenauer simply did not want to have his authority diluted by service to any foreign authority even that of the government in Berlin. When the independence movement fizzled, Adenauer redirected his energies to his duties as mayor of Cologne. The lord-mayors of German cities traditionally exercised power like the old prince-bishops of the Holy Roman Empire. Adenauer, in addition to holding the highest executive position, was also the permanent chief of every municipal department and used his authority to interfere routinely whenever he saw fit. Later, as chancellor, when the editor of *Die Zeit* criticized him for approaching politics like the director of a volunteer fire department, he shot back, "Herr Fuengel is probably quite right, but I'm sure he has no idea what a difficult time you can have with a volunteer fire department."[57]

Although he had little appreciation of democratic niceties, Adenauer wanted nothing to do with the Nazis, whom he regarded as upstarts and louts. Their raucous brutality conflicted with his high sense of moral purpose. It therefore came as no surprise when they gave him the boot. He quit active politics altogether, but not before making a pro forma declaration of obedience to the new regime in order to save his pension. Years of retirement kept him out of trouble. The Gestapo arrested him in April 1944, held him for a time, released him, and then arrested him once more. His status as a victim gave him a cachet with the Allies, who in March 1945 installed him once again in the city hall at Cologne. His appointment lasted only until the following August, when the British, dissatisfied with his performance, imperiously fired him. Three months after this dismissal, however, he became head of the largest branch of the Christian Democratic Union and thus began his march to the chancellorship, the post to which he was elected in August 1949.

As chancellor, Adenauer retained his authoritarian style. He took complete advantage of the powers given the chancellor under the Basic Law to appoint and dismiss ministers and to determine policy, especially in foreign affairs and defense. In 1951, he issued new rules of governmental procedure that recognized the chancellor's paramount responsibility to establish and supervise overall principles that were "binding on federal ministers and are to be put into practice by them in their departments independently and on their own responsibility. In cases of doubt the federal chancellor's decision must be sought."[58] Because of his age (he was seventy-three in 1949), Adenauer was expected to remain active in politics only a short time. However, from the outset, *Der Alte* (the old man) acted with the energy and determination of an immortal. He became the longest serving chancellor in twentieth-century German history, remaining in office a bit over fourteen years, until October 1963. He managed this impressive tenure not only because of his domestic political skills, but also in large part because he wisely retained the active support of the United States. Once again, he was denounced for subservience to foreign interests. The Social Democratic leader Kurt Schumacher called him the "chancellor of the Allies." Adenauer reacted with fury. He had Schumacher condemned for violating the parliamentary rules of order and suspended from participation in the Bundestag for twenty sitting days. Fortunately, Adenauer's successors were men of a different sort. Although Adenauer had helped to establish the viability of postwar German parliamentary government, German democracy was as yet too fragile to survive many chancellors with his readiness to manipulate the law when it served his purpose.

Growth and Readjustment

The Economic Miracle. Germany's phenomenal recovery (the *Wirtschaftswunder*) began with the currency reforms of 1948. Under the new currency law, old reichsmarks were converted into new deutsche marks at a graduated rate of exchange: 1 for 1 up to a total of 60; for amounts above that, the rate was 100 of the old for 6.5 of the new. Thus, those who had their money in savings suffered the most, while those who had their assets in commodities survived much better. The general effect on economic activity, however, was astounding. Hoarding ended almost overnight as goods and specialty foods returned to the stores. The Germans went on a buying spree. Production, spurred by demand, increased rapidly. It doubled during the last half of the year and continued to rise steadily over the next decade. In 1950, the West German gross national product was 97.2 billion marks (about $24 billion); ten years later, it had almost tripled, to 277.7 billion marks. In 1950, the millions of refugees from East Germany were considered a drain on the economy and helped push the overall unemployment rate to 10.3 percent. In 1960, despite the addition of 2 to 3 million more escapees from the Soviet zone, unemployment had fallen to 1.2 percent and, the following year, to a minuscule 0.7 percent. Between 1954 and 1961, real earnings increased by 42 percent, and personal consumption by 48 percent. The number of privately owned automobiles soared.[59] Although prestige models built by Mercedes-Benz and Porsche became the ultimate status symbol, the lowly *Käfer* (beetle), produced by Volkswagen, was the choice of most German car owners; the Volkswagen bug became the country's single most important export, helping to give Germany a consistent 3 to 4 percent surplus in its balance of payments.[60] Although the German recovery owed a great deal to American economic aid—from 1945 to 1961 over $3.5 billion worth—the Germans themselves were primarily responsible for their economic miracle.

The Germans worked hard for modest wages. Their small business owners and industrialists reinvested a great deal of the profits. Trade union leaders, realizing that sacrifice was essential to build a strong economy, refrained from strikes. (Besides, it was difficult to radicalize the proletariat in a period of full employment.) Codetermination, or labor-management decision making, helped keep labor peace. In the 1950s, Germans usually worked a 48-hour week. This was not reduced to 40 hours until 1961. At the beginning of the 1950s, the average worker earned one mark (25 cents) an hour; ten years later, he or she received three times as much. The increase represented a similar advance in real income. Inflation, as revealed by the retail price index, hardly ever exceeded two percent in any given year.

A Social Market Economy. The Christian Democrats and the Social Democrats both agreed on the necessity for social security and welfare. The Germans had a long tradition of social legislation, which at the level of the central government began with Bismarck's welfare program in the 1880s. The Christian Democratic Union proclaimed its desire to create a *Sozial Marktwirtschaft*, which, according to Economics Minister Ludwig Erhard, was "a simple Christian act" necessary "to free our fellow Germans from need and misery and give them back a sense of security and dignity."[61] Erhard had no intention of creating a total welfare state, which he believed would increase the collectivization of everyday life and produce a " 'social serf' whose material security is guaranteed by the almighty state, while economic progress in freedom becomes a thing of the past."[62]

Erhard's philosophical *éminence grise* was Wilhelm Röpke, then professor at the Graduate Institute of International Studies in Geneva, who believed that the study of economics was more than a matter of developing a methodology from the natural sciences. Economics was essentially "a moral science and as such has to do with man as a spiritual and moral being."[63] A neoliberal, Röpke was constantly aware that his discipline might move too far in the direction of mechanics, statistics, and mathematics to the neglect of human values:

Prosperous Berliners stroll through Tauentzienstrasse, one of the central city's principal shopping districts. The ruined tower of the Kaiser Wilhelm Memorial Church (center) stands as a witness to the destruction of the war and provides a stark contrast to the modern architecture that surrounds it.

It is a serious misunderstanding to wish to defend the mathematical method with the argument that economics has to do with quantities. That is true, but it is also true of strategy, and yet battles are not mathematical problems to be entrusted to an electrical computer. The crucial things in economics are about as mathematically intractable as a love letter or a Christmas celebration. They reside in moral and spiritual forces, psychological reactions, opinions which are beyond the reach of curves and equations. What matters ultimately in economics is incalculable and unpredictable.[64]

Röpke's contribution to the reconstruction of the West German economy earned him the Bundesrepublik's highest decoration, the Grand Cross of Merit.

The Adenauer government was committed to the market economy, which meant eliminating the monopolistic practices of the past. The Western allies, particularly the United States, had insisted on the destruction of the entire cartel system that had been so closely associated with the Nazi war machine. Erhard, a convinced free trader, agreed. Over the opposition of the Federation of German Industries, he convinced parliament to pass a bill (enacted in 1957) outlawing restrictions on competition (*Gesetz gegen Wettbewerbsbeschränkungen*). "If you reject state controls in industry," he told the Bundestag, "you cannot at the same time accept the collective control of industry by cartels or even regard it as useful and necessary. If you see political, social, and economic dangers in collectivism, you cannot at the same time defend cartels, which are a special form of collectivism."[65] The new law, which was mandated by membership in the supernational European Coal and Steel Community, replaced the anticartel legislation of the Allies. Nevertheless, a relatively small group of managers and directors still controlled German industry. The Christian Democrats were reluctant to enforce the law because a substantial amount of their political and financial support came from these same industrialists and bankers. Besides, cartels could exist legally if they were held to be beneficial to the overall economy. By 1964, some 136 cartels had been accorded this privilege, with many others operating clandestinely. The deconcentration policy was thus slowly undermined. The Krupp Steel Works survived virtually intact, as did most of the other great coal and steel combines. The three great commercial banks—the Deutsche Bank, the Dresdner Bank, and the Commerzbank—eluded a proposed breakup into thirty-odd successor institutions and, in 1957, were reintegrated under their former names. Erhard continued to warn that cartels were an extravagance Germany could not afford: "Where all groups want to have special protection and more security, people will enjoy less and less freedom and will lose more and more of genuine security. There can be no doubt that the advantages some people are out to acquire can only be acquired at the expense of others."[66]

Germany was prosperous, however, and with one-fourth of total state expenditures going to social services, few felt threatened. The German concept of proper economic management assigned the government a primary role in establishing a secure economic base for society. Government was expected to establish long-term conditions for growth by creating the proper infrastructure and stimulating areas lacking in development; thus, for example, government should boost the output of energy and promote the development of microtechnology. Government was also expected to work for a proper social partnership between capital and labor and encourage responsible collective bargaining. Above all, government was responsible for monetary stabilization. It relied on the banking industry to help identify weakness and assist with rescue operations.[67] The Germans did not forget the crippling experiences of the Weimar Republic with its two nightmarish bouts of inflation that led to the collapse of German democracy. The German term for economic order (*Wirtschaftsordunug*) suggested a harmony between economics and law in which the achievement of a secure political system is a logical counterpart of a properly run economy.

"Hitler? Never Heard of Him!" Even achieving the highest standard of living in their history did not automatically make the Germans enthusiastic about democratic values. They did become politically less extreme, however. Above all, they preferred to get on with the business of life and not be reminded of their past transgressions. By 1953, the apparent end to the prosecution of war criminals was generally greeted with approval. Adenauer rationalized that if those who had supported Hitler were too roughly handled, a backlash would set in and would actually contribute to the growth of neo-Nazism. Already the "refugee party" was trying to broaden its political base by appealing to all manner of dispossessed. As the pressure declined, former Nazis found little difficulty returning to important positions in industry and government—some even turned up in Adenauer's own cabinet.[68] One of the chancellor's most controversial appointments was that of Dr. Hans Globke as his chief administrative assistant in the chancellery. Globke had officially participated in drafting the racial laws against the Jews and Gypsies. Adenauer took the attacks on Globke personally, however, and continued to stand by him.

The sons and daughters of those who had supported Hitler seemed the most sensitive about war guilt. Yet many Germans seemed embarrassingly ignorant about how much suffering their country had caused others. Instead, they tended to concentrate on the barbarities of others: the bombing of Dresden, the massacre in the Katyn Forest, the rape of Freudenstadt. War was war. Heinrich Grüber, dean of the Evangelical church in Berlin and himself a victim of the Nazis, insisted that the extermination of the Jews, although immoral, was for some reason "part of

God's plan." Grüber continued: "God demands our death daily. He is the Lord, He is the Master, all is in His keeping and ordering."[69] Rabbi Richard Rubenstein joined the theological debate, charging that Grüber had failed to recognize the incongruity of regarding Hitler as an instrument of God's will. "Stated with the-ological finesse," Rubenstein remarked bitterly, "it comes to pretty much the same thing as the vulgar thought that the Christ-killers got what was coming to them."[70]

The degree to which such attitudes really reflected the sentiments of the mass of the German people or affected the functioning of their institutions was a matter of debate. Dr. Paule Sethe claimed that the Bonn judicial system was "still dom-inated by the spirit of the twenties which had caused the downfall of the Weimar Republic and had paved the way for Hitler." He added that justice would be better served "if the judges had some of the stench of the Auschwitz crematoria in their nostrils."[71] On the other hand, Sybille Bedford, an English author, sensed a new German compassion and respect for justice. "It would be hard for a Bismarck today to re-introduce the death penalty," she wrote. "There is the respect of man for man, the tending of liberty and the decencies and the due process of law, and with it goes a love, an almost avid love, of normality and all its trimmings."[72] Chronology frequently dictated which attitude would prevail. When Adenauer retired in 1963, most people in West Germany had either been born after Hitler had come to power or were too young to have been directly involved in Nazi atrocities. Most of the leaders of the Third Reich had been born at least ten years before the beginning of World War I and would have been 60 or more years old if they had lived until 1963. Had he lived, Hitler would have been 74, Göring 70, and Goebbels 66. The aging, lower-level Nazis increasingly made fit subjects for gerontologists. The Federal Republic was getting what the Weimar Republic did not have: peace, prosperity, and time with which to heal social wounds and adapt to democracy.

Nevertheless, the Germans were still reluctant to confront their Nazi past. Most of the current crop of teachers had been nurtured by a system that considered it unprofessional to teach democratic values. Since it was embarrassing for those who had served National Socialism to deal with events after 1933, most history lessons ended with World War I. Had Adenauer felt the matter deserved high priority, little would have stopped him from instituting a reform of German education. Instead, the federal government argued it could not be held responsible for the sorry conditions since education had been entrusted to the Länder. Educational reform was associated with the American efforts at reeducation and was discredited. All the direct efforts to restructure the universities, build comprehensive schools, and alter the authoritarian nature of German pedagogy met with strong resistance. The Western allies discovered that the time was too short and their methods too imperfect to teach democracy to a class that had no desire to learn.[73]

The educational system continued to foster social inequality. Primary and vo-cational schools were free, but most Länder charged tuition for secondary educa-tion. An official publication noted, with an obvious sense of embarrassment, that "exemption from the payment of school fees of any kind, and whenever possible from payment for instructional material, is something that has already been achieved in a varying degree in some of the Länder."[74] Only about 20 percent of the children from elementary schools continued their education in the secondary schools, and most of these came from the middle and upper-middle classes. In the universities, students from working-class families were practically nonexistent.[75] The universities remained institutions of specialization, run by faculty senates, which intentionally kept the number of professors small. In 1970, Heidelberg, a typical case, had only 190 full professors for 11,500 students. The lack of adequate facilities was equally scandalous: "Anatomy exercises become a macabre farce when 20 to 40 scalpel armed medical students crowd around one cadaver."[76] The Germans spent only 2.79 percent of their gross national product on their school system, about the same amount they expended for cigarettes and cigars.

The new generations rejoiced in their growing affluence. "It is our misfortune," wrote a German journalist, "that those outside Germany often form a picture of it today from this type of uninhibited, narrow-minded *nouveaux riches* who cannot see beyond the fenders of their Mercedes 400."[77] The citizens of this *Wirtschaftswunderland* sometimes showed an incredible lack of sensitivity. In the early 1960s, a manufacturer of women's fashions blithely called a new line of nylon hosiery the "Ouradour" line, apparently forgetting that Ouradour was the name of a French village in Haute Vienne where, on 10 June 1944, soldiers from the SS "das Reich" division massacred the entire population of 650 men, women, and children. When German tourists traveled to other European countries, they were often just as gauche. "I like your country," the visitor might say. "I was here during the war."

THE GERMAN DEMOCRATIC REPUBLIC

The Tightening of Soviet Control

A Posture of Independence. Stalin hailed the creation of the *Deutsche Demokratische Republik* as "a turning point in the history of Europe." A "peace-loving democratic Germany side by side with the existence of the peace-loving Soviet Union excludes the possibility of new wars in Europe, puts an end to bloodshed in Europe and makes impossible the enslaving of the European countries by the world imperialists."[78] In 1949, the Communist-controlled part of Germany officially became an independent state, but the Soviet Control Commission, backed by the Red Army, kept tight political control on the new government. Formal sovereignty was not accorded until after Stalin's death (1953), and even then the East Germans did not become masters in their own house.

At first, Soviet control was disguised under a posture of respect for the independent development of socialism. In December 1945, Anton Ackermann, one of the Moscow-trained leaders of the German Communist party, published an article entitled, "Is there a separate German road to Socialism?" Ackermann stated: "It was no less an authority than Lenin who emphasized that it would be a great mistake to exaggerate the general applicability of the Russian experience, or to extend it beyond more than a few features of our (i.e., the Russian) Revolution. In this sense we must unquestionably give our assent to the concept of a separate German road to Socialism." Ackermann noted some of the differences between his present-day Germany and Russia three decades earlier: Germany was more developed industrially, had a greater number of highly trained professionals, and a working class that represented a majority of the total population—a fact of great importance because "it will mitigate the domestic political struggle, reduce the burden of sacrifices, and hasten the evolution of Socialist democracy."[79]

The publication of Ackermann's theses encouraged many German Communists (and Social Democrats) to believe that Soviet political control was temporary and that Red Army occupation would soon end, leaving the natives free "from foreign tutelage to find their own road to socialism, in accordance with their own traditions and conditions."[80] But this theory was only a means of making the

German Communist party more acceptable to the Social Democrats whose support was deemed useful in stimulating a new national consciousness of unity. The Socialist Unity party accepted a separate road to socialism as part of its official program in order to mask Stalinization and blame the "Western imperialists" for promoting the division of Germany.

Before the establishment of the German Democratic Republic (GDR), the Soviets had already established a whole series of organizations befitting a people's republic. These included a single trade union for industrial workers, the Free German Trade Union Federation; a union for farmers, the Peasants Mutual Aid Union; an organization for women, the Democratic Women's Federation; an official youth group, the Free German Youth Movement; and a similar organization for intellectuals, the German Cultural Federation. These groups all were represented in the national legislature, which, like its Soviet counterpart, was a rubber stamp. After the founding of the GDR, the Soviet Military Administration gave way to a Soviet High Commissioner who like his predecessor still had the final authority.

The *Volkskammer*, the legislature, was purportedly the highest authority of the state; its members were elected by secret ballot according to proportional representation. However, like all Soviet-style governments, only one party exercised real authority. In East Germany, this meant the Socialist Unity party. Walter Ulbricht was its secretary-general; Wilhelm Pieck and Otto Grotewohl were its co-chairmen. Pieck was also state president and Grotewohl was prime minister. The GDR's most important political agency was the Ministry of State Security (the Stasi). This was responsible to the Politburo of the Socialist Unity party, not to the government. The Stasi had wide arbitrary powers to protect the state against its enemies both at home and abroad. The German Economic Commission (*Deutsche Wirtschafts Kommission*) directed the economy and ensured state control over industry and agriculture, banking and finance, foreign and domestic trade, transportation, labor, and energy. The commission, which issued directives to all governmental and administrative departments, planned the transformation of the East German economy into a Soviet-style system, integrated within the Eastern bloc. In 1949, a Two-Year Plan was inaugurated to boost heavy industry and increase productivity to 81 percent of the levels achieved in 1936. Building industrial socialism also meant the collectivization of agriculture and the regulation of the cultural life of the nation. As in the Soviet Union, socialist realism was the only standard of creativity. Ulbricht talked of the evolution of the new man and woman. The party expected writers, composers, and artists to extoll the heroes of socialist labor who raised productivity.

Resentment Turns to Protest. Until 1953, the Soviets continued to dismantle German factories, while the East Germans were obliged to pay about one-fourth of their total production to the Soviet Union as reparations. Special corporations were established to produce almost entirely for the Soviet account. Sovietization caused considerable malaise throughout the party cadres and provoked resentment among the general population. By 1951, between 11,000 and 17,000 people a month were leaving the GDR to live in West Germany. The following year, over 23,000 people left during September alone; in the first half of 1953, the monthly average climbed above 37,000. The East Germans, it was said, were voting with their feet. Such an enormous loss of labor power seriously threatened the viability of the German Communist regime, but Socialist Unity party leaders could offer no effective countermeasures. Their regime was not yet sufficiently strong to risk closing the frontier, and Ulbricht refused to admit that his hard line was wrong and inaugurate a program of reform. Still some concessions had to be made.

In June 1953, two months after Stalin's death, the regime called off the persecution of the Catholic and Evangelical churches. Some businesses and farms were restored to their former owners. At the same time, the regime promised to increase social insurance benefits and review the sentences of political offenders. Workers were told that, in the meantime, they were expected to produce more goods with no increase in wages. The reaction was immediate. On 16 June 1953, the workers in Berlin went out on strike. The authorities, eager to show that the East German proletariat could express itself freely, let the demonstration take place. The situation soon got out of hand. On 17 June, the strikers, with their ranks swelled by members of the "People's Police," attacked public buildings, set some on fire, and tore the Red Flag from the Brandenburg Gate. The local authorities, unable to handle the disturbance, called on the Soviet Union for help. But when Red Army tanks moved into East Berlin, the rioters began to attack the tanks with bricks and anything else they could find.

On the afternoon of 17 June, the Soviet commander in Berlin proclaimed a state of emergency and proceeded to crush the revolt by shooting and hanging the demonstrators. More than five hundred were killed. By nightfall order returned to the streets of Berlin, but the revolt had already spread to other cities—Magdeburg, Halle, Jena, Brandenburg, in all about three hundred towns and villages. The authorities blamed the rising on capitalist agents provocateurs.

The riots clearly demonstrated the weakness of the Communist regime, but lack of effective leadership prevented the masses from taking advantage of the weakness. Consequently, the Communist bosses, with full support of the Soviet authorities, were easily able to regain control. They emerged from the crisis more entrenched in power than before. Ironically, Stalinization in the GDR did not really reach its height until after Stalin's death. The ruthless suppression of any oppositionist tendencies was sweetened with a promise to increase the general standard of living and improve working conditions, but no real progress appeared for the next several years.

Communist party boss Ulbricht, who after 1954 had become the most important political leader in the GDR, proved to be the most durable of the Eastern satellite rulers. A prototypical ruthless, unimaginative bureaucrat, he systematically eliminated all rivals within the party. In 1960, when President Wilhelm Pieck died, Ulbricht, in a move reminiscent of Hitler's strategy in 1934, abolished the presidency and had himself appointed chairman of a newly created Council of State. The prime minister, Otto Grotewohl, who had already been neutralized with the creation of the SED in 1946, now became little more than an office boy. Resentment smoldered just under the surface awaiting another opportunity to plunge East Germany into chaos.

A Highly Controlled Economy

The Tempo of Socialism. East Germany had difficulty adjusting to the dismantling of its industry and the deportation of many of its most skilled workers. Under Operation Ossavakim, the Soviets deported the human and material resources of entire firms, including Karl Zeiss Optics at Jena, the Junkers Aircraft works at Dessau, and the Leuna Synthetic Petrol and Plastics company near Merseburg. The economy also was victimized by poor planning and the difficulty of adjusting to the economies of its Communist-bloc trading partners, although the Soviets

East German youths attack a pair of T-34/85s. Tanks like these participated in the Battle of Berlin in 1945; the T-34 was probably the best such weapon of World War II. It mounts an 85 mm gun, which is more than a match for these rock-throwers.

bore part of the costs of transition. In 1958, Ulbricht attempted to speed up socialism by pushing the collectivization of agriculture. Within five years, the total amount of arable land under direct state control was increased from 37 percent to 86 percent, or from 2,386,020 hectares to 5,456,143 hectares.[81] The same process was carried out in industry and business; by 1963, 90 percent was under government control.

Under Ulbricht's command, East Germany led the Soviet satellites in industrial capacity. During the 1950s, the production of brown coal rose from 137,050,000 to 214,783,000 metric tons; pig iron rose from 337,000 to 1,898,000 metric tons; crude steel from 1,257,000 to 3,615,000 metric tons; and the output of electrical energy from 19.47 to 37.25 million kilowatt hours. Most of the gains were registered in the last half of the decade.[82] The results were not so encouraging in agriculture, however. Wheat and oats production remained almost unchanged, sugar beets and corn increased only slightly, and production of rye and potatoes actually declined.[83] In 1961, food shortages prompted a reintroduction of rationing in certain commodities. Ulbricht tried to solve all problems with more controls; but no matter how dictatorial these became, it was impossible to achieve economic stability as long as great numbers of East Germans, often the most productive and best trained, continued to flee westward. Flight was simple: first, get to East Berlin, next take the subway or the elevated train from the Soviet sector into the Allied sector, and then fly from Berlin to the West. Finally, Ulbricht, secure of his hold over East Germany, obtained permission from the Soviets to close the border.

The Berlin Wall. Early Sunday morning, 13 August 1961, East German police and soldiers sealed off sixty-eight of the eighty crossing points into West Berlin.[84] There was no retaliation. The Western powers made only a written protest. In time, a wall of concrete replaced the hastily sprawled coils of barbed wire, lookout towers were erected, and guards were given orders to shoot anyone who tried to flee. The East German regime viewed such extreme measures as an absolute necessity, and from their perspective, the wall was a great success. The exodus of so

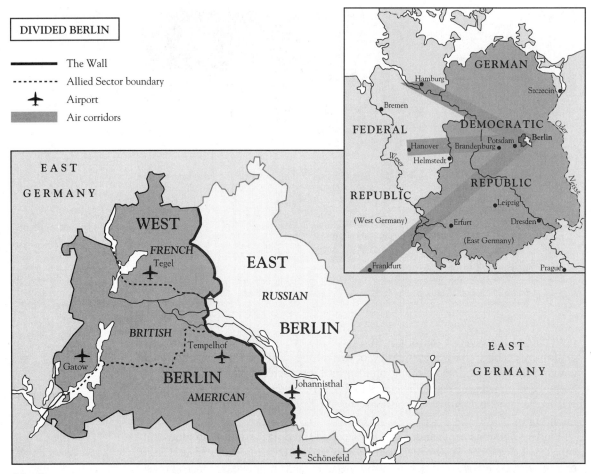

Map 2

much valuable laborpower virtually stopped, although every once in a while there would be news of a daring escape. In the West, the wall became a symbol of shame, but the East German regime appeared to become more viable. But the resignation of the East Germans was deceptive and proved temporary. The Communist regime had only bought time.

POSTSCRIPT   The problem of Germany remained the key to the security of Europe. The Soviets believed a weak but unified Germany was more in their interests than a divided Germany, but they were not prepared to ease their own rigorous standards of Stalinization. The Americans tried to calm Stalin's fears of a resurgent Germany with a security pact that guaranteed German disarmament for the next forty years. When this offer failed to reduce the tensions, the Americans assumed that Stalin had far-reaching and sinister intentions to extend his power westward. State Department adviser Robert Murphy thought the Soviets were seeking "not only to disarm Germany, but to render that country economically impotent."[85] His superior, Secretary of State James Byrnes, feared "that unless forced by world opinion to do so, the Soviet Union would not agree to a treaty of peace with Germany for years to come."[86] World opinion certainly seemed a curious weapon to consider using against a state that had the largest military force in Europe, but in time it did pay dividends. Nevertheless, any hopes that it would work in 1948 were quickly dispelled by the Berlin Blockade.

Both sides accused the other of causing the division of Germany, but neither appeared to have been disappointed when the division occurred. Ever since the end of World War I, many people had dreamed of dismantling the German colossus. Once it happened, only the West Germans seemed to take reunification seriously. The preamble of their constitution called upon the entire German people "to achieve in free self-determination the unity and freedom of Germany." In 1956, the Constitutional Court declared that this provision had "mainly political, but also legal significance, binding all national political organizations to strive with every means at their disposal for its fulfillment."[87] After his electoral victory in September 1953, Adenauer seemed to be setting a new foreign policy goal when he called for the liberation of "our 18 million brothers" who lived in East Germany,[88] but it is doubtful he really believed reunification was possible in the lifetime of most Germans. The accomplishment of such an objective seemed impossible without war; and furthermore the creation of the Bundesrepublik achieved Adenauer's goal of creating a Rhineland-dominated West German state purged of Prussian leadership.

The Bundesrepublik had to contend with the hegemony of the United States; the Democratic Republic had to accept the domination of the Soviets. Although West Germany, in particular, gradually became more independent, there was no question who had called the shots. World War II allowed the destiny of Germans to be decided by outsiders. Neither the United States nor the Soviet Union had wanted this conflict, which had extended their power, but neither showed any desire to give way. Their rivalries drowned out the wishes of the Germans themselves. But as friction between East and West diminished, and relations between East and West Germany improved, German unification, a dream that had never disappeared, moved closer to fulfillment.

ENDNOTES

1. Bernard Montgomery, *The Memoirs of Field-Marshal Montgomery* (New York: World Publishing Co., 1958), 339.
2. Lucius Clay, *Decision in Germany* (New York: Doubleday, 1950), 26.
3. In November 1945.
4. Georgi Zhukov, *The Memoirs of Marshal Zhukov* (New York: Delacorte Press, 1971), 662.
5. Furthermore, there were almost 5 million displaced persons; for the most part, these were people who had been forcibly brought to Germany to work for the Nazis.

6. *Documents on Germany under Occupation, 1945–1954* (London: Oxford University Press, 1955), 15.

7. Ibid., 22.

8. Montgomery, *Memoirs*, 356.

9. Hildegard Knef, *The Gift Horse* (New York: McGraw-Hill, 1970), 75.

10. Zhukov, *Memoirs*, 636.

11. Montgomery, *Memoirs*, 367.

12. Douglas Botting, *From the Ruins of the Reich: Germany, 1945–1949* (New York: New American Library, 1985), 252.

13. Georges Bidault, *Resistance* (London: Weidenfeld and Nelson, 1967), 83.

14. *International Herald Tribune*, 22 April 1968.

15. Ibid., 53.

16. Seated between Göring and Fritzsche were Rudolf Hess, former deputy führer who had flown to England in 1941; Joachim von Ribbentrop, the foreign minister; General Wilhelm Keitel, the army chief of staff; Alfred Rosenberg, the Nazi party ideologist; Hans Frank, the governor-general of Poland; Wilhelm Frick, the minister of interior; Julius Streicher, editor of *Der Stürmer* and gauleiter of Franconia; Walther Funk, economics minister; and Hjalmar Schacht, Funk's predecessor who had just been released from a Nazi jail and had no idea why he was there. In the second row, directly behind Göring, sat Admirals Karl Dönitz and Erich Raeder; then came Baldur von Schirach, Vienna gauleiter and one-time Hitler Youth leader; Fritz Sauckel, plenipotentiary for (Forced) Labor Allocation; Alfred Jodl, chief of operations for the Wehrmacht; Franz von Papen, Hitler's first vice-chancellor and the last Nazi ambassador to Turkey; Arthur Seyss-Inquart, reichscommissar for the occupied Netherlands and former chancellor of Austria; Albert Speer, minister of armaments and munitions; and Konstantin von Neurath, protector of Bohemia-Moravia and former foreign minister.

17. Bormann was tried and sentenced to death in absentia. In fact, he was already dead. Several hours after the Führer had committed suicide, Bormann had been killed while trying to leave Berlin. Supposedly, however, he had made it to South America on a Vatican passport. In December 1972, construction workers found some skeletal remains in Berlin's Tiergarten district. These were identified as Bormann's. On 11 April 1973, he was declared officially dead. *New York Times*, 12 April 1973, 2:4.

18. Robert Jackson, *The Nuremberg Case* (New York: Knopf, 1947), 35.

19. Gustav Mahler Gilbert, *Nuremberg Diary* (New York: New American Library, 1947), 46–50.

20. Ibid., 239.

21. Eugene Davidson, *The Trial of the Germans* (New York: Macmillan, 1966), 83.

22. Jackson, *Nuremberg Case*, 122.

23. Botting, *From the Ruins of the Reich*, 258–89.

24. *Documents on Germany*, 38.

25. Wolfgang Leonhard, *Child of the Revolution* (Chicago: Henry Regnery, 1958), 413.

26. Ibid., 414.

27. Martin McCauley, *The German Democratic Republic since 1945* (New York: St. Martin's Press, 1983), 10–17.

28. *Documents on Germany*, 124.

29. The SED received 4,658,483 to a combined total of 5,123,169 for its opponents. McCauley, *German Democratic Republic*, 31.

30. Leonhard, *Child of the Revolution*, 451.

31. *United States, Department of State, Potsdam Conference*, vol. 2 (Washington, D.C.: U.S. Government Printing Office), 1482.

32. Montgomery, *Memoirs*, 358.

33. *Survey of International Affairs: Four-Power Control in Germany and Austria, 1945–1946* (London: Oxford University Press), 188.

34. The Americans insisted especially on the establishment of an independent judiciary with powers of judicial review.

35. Clay, *Decision in Germany*, 98.

36. *Documents on Germany*, 17.

37. See James F. Tent, *Mission on the Rhine* (Chicago: University of Chicago Press, 1982).

38. James F. Byrnes, *Speaking Frankly* (New York: Harper, 1947), 176.

39. The action was aimed as much at the French as at the Soviets. De Gaulle had repeatedly vetoed plans for economic centralization. He objected to the creation of a unified transport administration, continued to insist on the annexation of the Saar, and advocated putting the Rhineland under French administration. He also demanded the internationalization of the Ruhr. Robert Murphy, the chief American political adviser, found it ironic "that Stalin, who always deplored French participation in the occupation of Germany, became the chief beneficiary of early French policy there." Robert Murphy, *Diplomat among Warriors* (Garden City, N.Y.: Doubleday, 1964), 287.

40. *Foreign Relations of the United States*, 1946, II, 897.

41. *Documents on Germany*, 156.

42. Ibid., 157.

43. Anthony Mann, *Comeback: Germany, 1945–1952* (London: MacMillan, 1980), 128–45.

44. James F. Tent, *The Free University of Berlin: A Political History* (Bloomington: Indiana University Press, 1988), 166–67.

45. Mann, *Comeback*, 131.

46. Harry S. Truman, *Memoirs*, vol. 2 (Garden City, N.Y.: Doubleday, 1956), 131.

47. *Documents on Germany*, 316.

48. *Grundgesetz*, Article 38.

49. Clay, *Decision in Germany*, 405–6.

50. The Italian constitution of 1948 contained a similar provision. See Chapter 19.

51. The court exercised this power in 1952 when it outlawed the neo-Nazi Socialist Reich party, and again, four years later, when it declared the Communist party disbanded and confiscated its assets. The court argued then that the minimum duty of any political party in a free society was to accept the paramount values of the constitution as binding and refrain from bringing that system into contempt. "Any party which consciously, continually, and systematically, undertakes a campaign of slander and mockery of these values and the order embodying them, is envisaging their impairment and even their destruction. It is unthinkable that such a party could constitutionally be called upon to cooperate in the formation of the will of the state in a free democracy." John J. Wuest and Manfred C. Vernon, eds., *Source Book in Major European Governments* (New York: World Publishing Co., 1966), 384.

52. They also disapproved of the inclusion of Berlin as one of the federal states because that was inconsistent with the legal position that Berlin was under quadripartite control by international agreement. Clay, *Decision in Germany*, 421–22.

53. Ibid., 431.

54. *Grundgesetz*, Article 21, para. 1.

55. Wuest and Vernon, *Source Book in Major European Governments*, 354.

56. Ibid., 356–57.

57. Rudolf Leonhardt, *This Germany: The Story since the Third Reich* (Baltimore: Penguin, 1968), 197.

58. Quoted in Richard Hiscocks, *The Adenauer Era* (New York: Lippincott, 1966), 91–92.

59. The number of automobiles per 1,000 people was 18.4 in 1938; 10.9 in 1950; 33.3 in 1955; 48.7 in 1957; 67.4 in 1959; 95.3 in 1961; and 112 in 1962. See the yearbooks of the *Statistisches Bundesamt* (Wiesbaden: Federal Statistical Office).

60. In 1969, Germany produced 145,000 passenger cars, second only to the United States. It also had one of the world's largest annual outputs of steel. In 1936, greater unified Germany produced 1,235,500 metric tons of crude steel: in 1956, West Germany (with only 53 percent of the former territory and 75 percent of the population) turned out 1,932,400 metric tons; in 1960, it produced 2,841,700 metric tons, an amount exceeded by only the United States and the Soviet Union. In 1960, West Germany's major customers were (in order) the Netherlands, France, the United States, Switzerland, Belgium-Luxembourg, Italy, Sweden, Austria, Great Britain, and Denmark. Trade with Eastern Europe, traditionally so important, had almost completely disappeared.

61. Ludwig Erhard, *The Economics of Success* (London: Thames and Hudson, 1963), 191.

62. Ibid., 184.

63. Wilhelm Röpke, *A Humane Economy* (London: Wolff, 1960), 247.

64. Ibid., 248.

65. Erhard, *Economics of Success*, 171.

66. Ibid., 177.

67. William E. Paterson and Gordon Smith, eds., *The West German Model: Perspectives on a Stable State* (London: Frank Cass, 1981), 41–43.

68. The East German regime was particularly adept at publishing lists and pictures of Nazi party members who were doing quite well in the Bundesrepublik. See, for example, *Grey Book: Expansionist Policy and Neo-Nazism in West Germany* (Dresden: 1967).

69. Richard L. Rubenstein, *After Auschwitz* (Indianapolis: Bobbs-Merrill, 1966), 54.

70. Ibid., 56.

71. T. H. Teters, *The New Germany and the Old Nazis* (New York: Random House, 1961), 167.

72. Sybille Bedford, *The Faces of Justice* (London: Collins, 1961), 152.

73. Tent, *Mission on the Rhine*, 312–18.

74. Helmut Arntz, *Facts about Germany* (Wiesbaden: Press and Information Office, 1966), 321.

75. By contrast, in East Germany at least two-thirds of the university student population came from the working class or peasantry.

76. *International Herald Tribune*, 2 April 1970.

77. Leonhardt, *This Germany*, 97.

78. *Documents of International Affairs, 1949–50*, 538.

79. Leonhard, *Child of the Revolution*, 440–41.

80. Ibid., 441.

81. *Handbuch der Deutsche Demokratischen Republik* (East Berlin: Staatsverlag, N.D.), 403. In 1952, only 3.3 percent of the East German land had been collectivized.

82. B. R. Mitchell, *European Historical Statistics* (New York: Columbia University Press, 1975), 366, 395, 402, 281.

83. Ibid., 270.

84. The Berlin crises are discussed in Chapter 21.

85. Murphy, *Diplomat among Warriors*, 302.

86. Byrnes, *Speaking Frankly*, 181.

87. Wuest and Vernon, *Source Book in Major European Governments*, 382.

88. Rudolf Augstein, *Konrad Adenauer* (London: Secker and Warburg, 1964), 28.

CHAPTER 3

PROSPERITY AND REFORM IN WESTERN EUROPE

PREFACE   Clement Attlee, the leader of Britain's Labour party, wanted to build a truly equitable, socially just society on the ruins of the selfish capitalistic society of the past. This could only be done if the prevailing economic system were brought under greater public control. Nationalization was not an end in itself, however. "Controls were desirable not for their own sake, but because they were necessary to gain freedom from the economic power of the owners of capital." Attlee had no desire to take revenge on the rich; he wanted wealth distributed more equitably "because a society with gross inequalities of wealth and opportunity is fundamentally unhealthy."[1]

Attlee's theme could be heard in all the countries of Europe. People expected that recovery from the war would include social change as well as political reconstruction. They thought the years of struggle and destruction would have been in vain if they did not result in a better world. Now was the time to fulfill the lofty goals of the Atlantic Charter—freedom from want and freedom from fear. It was also the time to discard the old ways.

Nowhere was this longing for a better tomorrow more pronounced than in Great Britain. Discontent with the prewar record of the Tories—their bankrupt policy of appeasement, their failure to cure unemployment, their obsession with class and tradition—was widespread. Even the Conservatives recognized the popular mood and, like the Labour party, promised the people a public welfare system. The aspirations for a better life were reflected in the Beveridge Report, which inspired so much optimism that Prime Minister Churchill recognized that "bringing the magic of averages nearer to the rescue of the millions, constitutes an essential point of any post-war scheme of national betterment."[2] A government policy statement, issued in 1944, accepted full employment, based on increased productivity, as a fundamental responsibility of government.

The French National Council of the Resistance set essentially the same goals. In March 1944, it advocated the nationalization of key industries, a comprehensive system of sickness and accident insurance, a guaranteed standard of living, a program of family allowances, price supports for agricultural commodities, and recognition of the right of workers to participate in factory management. The French had grown up under governments that had not made changing society a high priority. The Resistance, though, had spawned a new generation of leaders who were dissatisfied with the record of the past. They believed that if society were to change, the state had to play a greater role in directing the economy and helping to make the labor force more productive.[3] Social security was a right, not a gift. Great economic progress could be achieved if traditional private entrepreneurship were bolstered by planning for the modernization and expansion of the nation's industrial structure.

Italian aspirations for a new society were expressed in their new constitution, which recognized the obligation of the state "to remove the obstacles of an economic order which . . . prevent the full development of the human personality." It recognized the right of the worker "to a compensation proportionate to the quantity and quality of his [sic] labor and in any case sufficient to assure him and his family a free and dignified existence."[4] It endorsed the right to work and to be socially secure, guaranteed the equality of women, and endorsed the right of workers to share in the management of business. At the same time the Italians endeavored to form a new social order, they also had to create a democratic system. Under Mussolini, respect for individual rights had been of no concern. Furthermore, the economy's problem was not too little central direction, but too much. Fascist controls had petrified the economy, wasted precious resources, and replaced cooperation with subservience to authority. These were poor foundations upon which to build a new society.

SOCIALIST BRITAIN

Labour Takes Charge

The Campaign. Perhaps Churchill's irritation came from physical exhaustion—throughout the war he rarely slept more than four hours a night—or from the increasing dislike he had for a "socialist" Eastern Europe, but in his first radio broadcast of the 1945 electoral campaign, he said cuttingly:

> I declare to you, from the bottom of my heart, that no Socialist system can be established without a political police . . . no Socialist Government conducting the entire life and industry of the country could afford to allow free, sharp, or violently-worded expressions of public discontent. They would have

Labour election posters promise a better and healthier tomorrow with full employment. Although Winston Churchill was the most popular man in Great Britain in 1945, it was not enough to ensure his party's victory. Many British voters had not forgotten the failings of the Tories during the 1930s.

to fall back on some form of Gestapo. . . . And this would nip opinion in the bud, it would stop criticism as it reared its head, and it would gather all the power to the supreme party and the party leaders, rising like stately pinnacles above their vast bureaucracies of civil servants, no longer servants and no longer civil.[5]

Churchill's "Gestapo" speech caused many to doubt that the man who had led his country to victory in war should preside over its fortunes in time of peace. Moreover, the Labour party appeared as the staunchest champion of the proposed Beveridge reforms, and this dedication to social welfare swept it triumphantly into office in the 5 July 1945 election. Labour increased its seats in the House of Commons by 154 to 393 seats, while the Conservatives dropped from 373 to 213. The already weakened Liberals were practically wiped out, winning only a scant 11 seats. The total vote was more evenly distributed,[6] but the Labour triumph was nevertheless genuine, a true national victory, won at the expense of all other parties and in all districts of the country. Now, for the first time in its history, the party had the power to implement its welfare policy and carry out its program of nationalization.

On 26 July 1945, shortly after the results of the election were certain, Winston Churchill drove to Buckingham Palace to offer his resignation to the king. Half an hour later, Clement R. Attlee arrived and was confirmed as the new prime minister. The leaders of the Labour party had little doubt that Attlee's competent, moderate style of leadership was best suited to maintain the unity of the party while carrying out the sweeping social and economic program that would further reform British capitalism by expanding the welfare and public sectors. Attlee's cabinet reflected his conservative nature; it was composed largely of bourgeois middle-aged professionals. Attlee chose the trade unionist leader Ernest Bevin to be his foreign secretary. The appointment of a true son of the working class to represent Britain abroad was wildly popular with the rank and file. Furthermore, Bevin, despite his lack of experience in foreign relations, turned out to be one of the best foreign secretaries of his age.

Labour took charge at one of the worst times in modern British history. The war had cost the lives of 388,000 persons, and German air raids had destroyed 6.5 percent of British real estate. The public debt had risen from $3 billion in 1938 to $13.5 billion by war's end. During the same period, exports had fallen by $312 million each year. Shipping revenues were down 75 percent; and income from overseas investments had slid by one-half. With the end of Lend-Lease, the British went scrambling to Washington for a $6 billion loan with which to begin reconstruction. They got $3.75 billion, but this was quickly spent,[7] and Britain seemed to face a bleak future.

The Program of Nationalization. The Labour government did not believe that the extension of social security alone was sufficient; it felt that the state also had to establish control over the country's most important resources and services. However, the program of nationalization was never total and was limited to essential public services and basic industries. The issue of nationalization had risen during the war, but Churchill had discouraged spending much time on postwar planning. He was not particularly keen on nationalization to begin with, and in any case, he believed that winning the war should be the first priority. In choosing industries for public control, the Labour party seemed to have been motivated more by the desire to improve efficiency and increase production than by ideology. Experience showed that many owners either did not want to or could not afford to modernize to make their companies more competitive. A good example was the coal industry, which had been plagued by poor organization and even worse labor relations. The average output per miner was one of the lowest in Europe, and the owners had made little effort to improve productivity by reinvesting their profits. Furthermore, the British people felt a moral duty toward those who earned their livelihood by such backbreaking, dangerous work. This sense of duty was reinforced by the fact that this resource upon which Britain's industrial revolution was based had not provided the miners a reward commensurate with their contribution. The Conservatives shared the sense of obligation toward the miners, but many would have preferred a policy of government subsidy rather than ownership.

Labour presented the Coal Industry Nationalization Bill to Parliament in December 1945. The Tories and Labour differed more over the details than on the principle of state ownership. The bill became law the following July. The act—a "bill" becomes an "act" when it passes Parliament—combined more than eight hundred private companies into the National Coal Board (NCB), which was under the Ministry of Fuel and Power. The NCB inherited an industry plagued by mismanagement, high unemployment, an aging work force, poor labor relations, and insufficient mechanization. Even with proper capitalization, the rundown mines of Yorkshire and Wales could not be made efficient, and many were closed down, while production at the modern collieries of Derbyshire and Nottinghamshire was increased to compensate for the weakness of the others.

The Ministry of Fuel and Power was also responsible for the nation's electricity under the Electricity Act, which passed in August 1947 with little controversy. The municipalities already owned most of the various power stations (362 systems out of 563), and the old system was hopelessly disordered: voltages differed from place to place, and rates fluctuated inequitably. London alone had seventy-five different standards. Former owners were compensated by averaging representative share quotations on the stock exchange over a previous two-year period. The Labour government completed its program to control the basic sources of industrial power by nationalizing the gas industry; but as in the case of the coal and electrical industries, the government's motivation was less socialist than the industry's need for reorganization and modernization.

Government control and supervision were already so strong in central banking that nationalization hardly constituted a radical departure. The Bank of England was private in name only. However, the Labour party leaders never felt safe until the institution was completely state owned. They feared, for example, that the bank's directors might pursue a deflationary policy that could obstruct an official commitment to full employment. Even Churchill did not see what the fuss was about, since the Exchequer already decided all major policy.

The public transportation industry was also heavily regulated: civil aviation had been a public monopoly for some time, and the railroads were practically so. The most controversial aspect of the government's Transport Bill concerned nationalization of long-distance trucking, which Labour believed was necessary to provide proper coordination with rail services. The act was roundly denounced by Conservative spokesman David Maxwell-Fife as "the greatest disservice which the Government had so far done to the trade and industry of the nation."[8] The measure made public functionaries of one million more people, almost six percent of the total work force. It transferred to state control sixty railways, with 52,000 miles of single track and 600,000 railway cars, and 2,100 miles of navigable canals. Also affected by the act were 200,000 licensed truckers who operated nearly 450,000 vehicles.

Clearly, Labour's bill to nationalize iron and steel was the government's most "socialistic" measure because it could hardly be argued that the industry was inefficient and needed government support. Neither could it be said that the industry was a basic public service, nor that it needed drastic reorganization. The workers had not demanded nationalization, nor had the industry been subject to much public control in the past. Churchill denounced the bill as a Labour government plot to establish a base for the ultimate penetration and paralysis of all forms of free enterprise. Ivor Thomas called it "dogma run mad." The steel industry fought it. The press was hostile. Labour insisted, however, that this industry, which was important for national security, should be in public hands. The bill became law on 15 February 1951.

The benefits of nationalization were not always readily apparent. The nationalized industries operated as separate corporations with a certain amount of local autonomy, but they remained under the final authority of an appropriate cabinet minister who was answerable to Parliament for their operation. A special agency had acquired the leading steel firms through stock purchase. That agency also supervised the firms' operation under their old names and with the same managers. Thus, the firms were not government departments, and their employees were not civil servants. This arrangement, intended to minimize disruption, was itself the source of much added confusion. Since it was often impossible to distinguish between overall state policy and day-to-day operations, differences frequently arose over prices and wages. Furthermore, the government had great difficulty raising enough capital for the fundamental reorganization of industry. Financing was handled in different ways. The Treasury subsidized the coal mines directly, while allowing the transport, electricity, and gas industries to raise their own capital by issuing public bonds.[9] Private investors, though, were not eager to put their money in the state enterprises (even though the government guaranteed the investment), and the bond issues were usually undersubscribed. This necessitated large-scale borrowing, which led to a steady increase in the public debt and distorted the British money market as the government provided over 40 percent of all capital to industry. Trying to improve the situation by funding the industries through direct taxation could have led to a depression.[10] Nationalization also failed to produce some of the social benefits it had promised. The transition from private ownership to public ownership did not make mining a more desirable job than before. The miners now had to deal with government bureaucrats who often were just as indifferent as the previous company owners. The Labour government's social welfare programs changed their lives more, especially the program of socialized medicine.

Regulating the Nation's Resources

The Welfare State. The establishment of universal socialized medicine came on the heels of a long effort to improve Britain's health, reaching back at least as far as the National Insurance Act of 1911, which provided medical care to a portion of the lower classes from obligatory contributions of employees, employers, and the government. That act, however, covered only the workers themselves and did not extend to their families. In 1926, a Royal Commission advocated a national health service bill supported entirely by public funds. Though the Labour party could not claim credit for that scheme, it nevertheless gave its enactment the highest priority. Attlee wanted all classes to be included, even the well-to-do, for he felt that there was something patronizing and undemocratic about recognized exemptions for the "top people."

Several months after the 1945 election, the minister of health, Aneurin Bevan, presented the first draft of a national health service, which embodied the intent "to make medical and dental attention free to all who cared to avail themselves of its provisions, without qualification or limitation."[11] The legislation proposed the establishment of nationwide medical executive councils that would solicit and organize the services of the country's doctors and dentists. Membership in the system was strictly voluntary, but practitioners who joined would receive a regular annual salary, plus a stipulated fee per patient, and they could still maintain a private practice for patients who had not registered for socialized medicine. The country's entire hospital system would be nationalized and administered by various regional boards under the overall authority of the Ministry of Health. Bevan estimated that the National Health Service would initially cost 152 million pounds ($612,560,000) a year, but he had no illusion that this amount could be raised by some insurance scheme. It would have to come directly from the public treasury.

The passage of the National Health Service Bill in September 1946 launched a two-year struggle for its acceptance. A British Medical Association (BMA) poll revealed that 54 percent of the doctors were against affiliation, with opposition particularly strong among general practitioners (10,024 against, 5,479 for). In January 1948, the BMA denounced the act as "grossly at variance with the essential principles of the profession," to which Bevan replied: "Parliament has spoken and the country now awaits the cooperation of the medical world." The doctors feared that they would become badly paid civil servants and, in a second more comprehensive plebiscite, voted against participation by an even greater margin: 40,814 to 4,735. Bevan now became more conciliatory. He quieted fears that the state would deny individuals the right to choose their own doctors or would interfere with the delicate relationship between physician and patient, and he repeatedly emphasized that adherence to the scheme would be voluntary. Gradually, the BMA, realizing that socialized medicine was inevitable anyway, came around and advised its members to cooperate. The comprehensive medical scheme began operation as scheduled, on 5 July 1948. Shortly afterwards, Bevan announced that over 90 percent of the British people had enrolled in the scheme. In time most of the doctors also decided to participate. The success of the National Health Service was vital for the reputation of the Attlee government. It was possibly the most popular feature of the British welfare state.[12]

Benefits were not restricted to the practice of curative medicine. Community care included prenatal and postnatal assistance, a meals-on-wheels program for the aged and infirm, and rehabilitation and training for the physically and mentally handicapped. The National Health Service also practiced preventive medicine, supervising the relationship between health and the environment and raising the physical fitness of the British people. The program gave Attlee a tremendous sense of personal achievement: "I feel cheered when I look at the children and babies and compare them with those of past times."[13] Although the minister of health was given the right, in 1949, to charge aliens for medical services, the authority was not exercised, and foreigners received the same free services as British citizens, a benefit that was later discontinued.

The Labour government also extended social services to provide cradle to grave protection. When the Tories complained about the cost, Attlee answered his critics by declaring that if Britain could not afford the expense, it would be an admission that "the sum total of the goods produced and the services rendered by the people of this country is not sufficient to provide for all our people at all times, in sickness, in health, in youth and in age, the very modest standard of life that is represented by the sums of money set out."[14] The prime minister was aware, though, that only by utilizing fully the human and natural resources of the United Kingdom could the benefits of the welfare state be guaranteed. He expected people to work for social security. Labour party leaders knew that until Britain's economic recovery was assured, the welfare system could not be fully implemented. Unfortunately, current economic conditions did not encourage optimism.

A Crippled Economy. The prospects for a substantial increase in British production at first seemed good. The markets of Western Europe were starved for consumer goods. Investment capital was cheap. Inflation was harnessed by wartime controls, and there was full employment. The expansion did not live up to expectations, however. Exports increased, but only by 20 percent instead of the anticipated 75 percent. A world shortage of raw materials drove up commodity prices, causing foreign loans to be depleted twice as fast. The reduction of incentives and a serious housing shortage cooled the ardor of the workers. By 1947, the country was in the throes of a major economic crisis.

As the year began, the severest winter in over half a century pummeled the United Kingdom. Blizzards and freezing temperatures blocked roads, isolated villages, and brought chaos to the transportation system. Neither railroads nor barges could supply British industry with enough coal. Electricity stations, given the highest priority, were reduced to two-week reserves, and the government drastically rationed power. Emmanuel Shinwell, the minister of fuel and power, suspended service to industrial consumers in London, the southeast, the Midlands, and the northwest. Residents were prohibited from heating their homes with electricity between 9:00 A.M. and noon and from 2:00 to 4:00 P.M. The service of the London public transit system was curtailed, the BBC's Third Program went off the air, and the greyhound tracks stopped racing. When Shinwell blamed the weather, a critic countered, "the crisis is not due to an act of God, but the inactivity of Emmanuel."

By March the worst was over. Nevertheless, in late April, industries were still guaranteed only half their usual quotas of solid fuel. The workers who had expected the Labour victory to bring immediate prosperity expressed their disillusionment through official and wildcat strikes, which lost 2.4 million working days. From January to June, walkouts in the still depressed coal industry reduced coal production by 559,000 tons. The effect was disastrous for Britain's balance of payments and accelerated the drain on its foreign credits. On 20 August, the government enacted exchange controls. Britain henceforth obtained hard currency through the direct sale of gold. More than at any other time, British leaders were embarrassed by their country's complete dependence on help from abroad. "I do not like being tied to money lenders at all," grumbled Foreign Secretary Ernest Bevin, but he admitted that without American aid "the British people must face a descending spiral of depression, for they could not by themselves solve the sterling-dollar problem of the world."[15] The pressure became so great that, in September 1949, the British pound was devalued from its prewar level of $4.08 to the pound to $2.80.

The government feared inflation could jeopardize Britain's position in foreign trade and finance and endanger its social welfare obligations. To stimulate exports and stabilize the economy, it proposed to retard demand. Taxes and restrictions on credit curtailed consumer spending. Price controls, ceilings on purchases of essential goods, and prolongation of stringent wartime rationing of basic foodstuffs helped quiet the demands for higher wages. The middle- and higher-income groups paid comparatively more taxes than the lower-income wage earners. The standard rate of income tax was 45 percent of the earnings left after deductions, to which was added a progressive surtax for incomes over 2,000 pounds. Those in the highest brackets could pay 95 percent of their earnings before exemptions and adjustments to the public treasury. Nevertheless, the bulk of the overall revenue continued to come from the lower-income taxpayers, who formed the largest group in society. The British were no strangers to such taxes. Before the war, the scale ranged from 27.5 to 75 percent of income. Most of the revenue from the postwar hikes went to industrial reconstruction and defense spending, not to an extension of social welfare. Escalating costs in the latter sector forced Labour to cut back on some of the intended services.

Britain recovered its prewar level of industrial production within three years after the German surrender. By 1950, production had risen another 25 percent.[16] Nevertheless, the increase was inferior to the gains made by Germany, France, and Italy during the same period. Furthermore, the Labour government's austerity program dampened its popularity and set the tone for the 1950 general election.

The Conservatives attacked the devaluation of the pound and the high level of public expenditures. They scored points by criticizing Labour's nationalization of the iron and steel industry and pledged to denationalize it if they won. Their campaign manifesto pledged, "This is the Road. We shall bring nationalization to a full stop here and now," and they promised to repeal the Steel Act and return the trucking industry to private ownership. By and large, however, the Tories accepted Labour's reforms, although they placed more emphasis on private enterprise as a basis for economic expansion. They too were committed to full employment, and they talked about increasing pensions and extending social services. Churchill was now seventy-five and fighting the thirteenth general election of his career. The results were close. The Labour party, with 46 percent of the vote, barely squeaked out a victory; it now had only a 7-vote majority, down from a once-proud 136. Such a slender margin meant another election would soon be held. Wrote Attlee, "It was not pleasant to have members coming from hospital at the risk of their lives to prevent a defeat in the House."[17]

The new campaign came in October 1951. Attlee fought strenuously—he was practically the only remaining minister from the old guard of 1945—but it was a tight race. Labour edged the Conservatives by almost one percent in the popular vote, but received fewer seats in the Commons.[18] On 26 October, Attlee resigned. Every important piece of legislation that he had submitted had been enacted, yet his party was still uncertain of its future. Its moderates wanted to consolidate their gains, while its radicals wanted to use these gains as a base for continuing the revolution. Both sides showed more skill in attacking each other than in providing leadership capable of reconciliation. When Attlee finally retired from active politics in 1955, he left behind a party unsure of its direction.

The End of Empire. The Labour government intended to couple its policy of austerity at home with one of retrenchment abroad. In 1945, the British had over five million men under arms, the largest army in their history. They had helped to develop the atomic bomb, and their world influence was formidable, with troops stationed in Germany, Italy, Greece, Turkey, Egypt, and their numerous colonial possessions in Africa and Asia. Britain had been the holder of the European balance of power for as long as anyone could remember and seemed likely to maintain this position as long as anyone could imagine. Indeed, shortly after coming to power, the Labour government decided to continue conscription, the first peacetime draft in British history. The costs were staggering. The government was outspending its income by over two billion pounds a year.

In August 1945, the United States discontinued Lend-Lease, the principal source of British military aid. The British tried to negotiate further credits, but the Truman administration was unsympathetic. John Maynard Keynes cabled home disgustedly that what was good enough for the ultraconservative directors of the Bank of England was apparently not good enough for the Americans: "We are negotiating in Washington, repeat Washington, fig leaves that pass muster with old ladies in Threadneedle Street wither in a harsher climate."[19] The Americans finally agreed to lend $4.4 billion, to which the Canadians added another $1.5 billion, but this was insufficient to enable Britain to build up its strength at home while also maintaining its traditional position in world affairs. Indeed, without serious economies, Britain appeared headed toward bankruptcy.

Some old-time imperialists might complain. Churchill had remarked only three years before that he had not become the king's first minister in order to preside over the liquidation of the British Empire, but the British people, in addition to their growing doubts about the righteousness of ruling over alien peoples, thought empire was too costly to preserve. Attlee felt that the sooner decolonization could proceed, the better. Accordingly, at the end of July 1945, he announced his intent to seek "an early realization of self-government for India." In the spring of 1946, an interim native government was established, and the drafting of a constitution began. The British had hoped that the transfer of power to the local leaders could be accomplished without destroying the unity of the country, but tensions between the Hindu majority and Muslim minority were already making this prospect extremely doubtful. Since the British had very few means of maintaining order, the only practical solution seemed to be partition.

Attlee said, in February 1947, that the British would definitely give up all power in India not later than June 1948, "either as a whole to some form of central government, or in some areas to provincial governments or in such other ways as might seem reasonable." He appointed Lord Louis Mountbatten, former supreme allied commander in South East Asia, to handle the responsibility. The new viceroy, fearing an all-out civil war was imminent, advanced the day of the British transfer of power to August 1947. There would be two states: Hindu India and Muslim Pakistan. Parliament approved the Independence Act in July. No sooner had the Union Jack been lowered over India than the subcontinent exploded into a ferocious religious and ethnic war that left at least a half million dead and another 12 million homeless. Many felt that the sudden departure of Mountbatten helped make the situation more inflammable. Indeed, the disaster might have been attenuated through a prolonged presence and additional deployment of British troops, but these were unavailable. Even if they had been, their use would no doubt have been regarded by Hindus and Muslims alike as evidence of British perfidy, producing an even greater catastrophe in the long run.

Indian independence marked the beginning of the end of British colonial domination throughout the world. Ceylon went free that same year; Burma followed in 1948. Britain also relinquished its mandate over Palestine. The British had the good sense to realize that the days of empire were over, and they wisely took steps to adjust to the new situation before it blew up in their faces. The rapidity of divestment was amazing. The duke of Windsor recalled a state visit he made to India in 1922 as prince of Wales: "British dominance in India was the product of two hundred years of war, work, and wisdom. Had anybody tried to persuade me as I left Karachi, with a regimental band on the quay crashing out 'God Save the King,' that all this would be lost in my lifetime, I would have put the man down as a lunatic."[20]

The Duration of Reconstruction

The Return of the Tories. The Conservatives remained in office until 1964, during which time they won two more national elections (1955 and 1959) and were led by four different prime ministers.[21] Such continuous tenure in office had not been achieved by one party since the great Whig ministries of the nineteenth century. The Tories returned to power as a rise in prices, brought on by Labour's policies and commodity shortages, threatened to produce serious inflation. In addition, the acceleration of the rearmament program, boosted by the Cold War, was necessitating a reordering of domestic priorities,[22] and the outflow of gold and dollar reserves had reached crisis proportions.

The Conservatives responded by doing the very thing for which they had taken Labour to task: they restricted credit, notably through an increase in the bank rate, and reduced foreign expenditures by imposing exchange controls and curtailing imports. Luck was on their side. The terms of trade—the prices manufacturers paid for foreign commodities—swung in Britain's favor, relieving pressure on the balance of payments. World food production expanded, finally enabling the government to abandon wartime rationing. The general level of production, which had dropped four percent during 1951 and 1952, rose six percent in 1953 and seven percent the year after. Except for denationalizing the iron, steel, and trucking industries, the Tories tampered very little with the Labour legislation. They even expanded social services, taking tremendous pride in their ability to fulfill a campaign promise to build 300,000 units of public housing a year. In 1953, the coronation of Queen Elizabeth II gave the Conservatives a psychological boost by holding out the prospect of a new Elizabethan age.

Churchill retired in the spring of 1955, when the economic condition of the country was better than it had been at any time since the war. His successor, Anthony Eden, immediately called for new elections and succeeded in increasing the Conservative majority in the Commons to 60 seats. However, the new prime minister soon ran into trouble when he ordered British intervention in the 1956 Israeli-Egyptian war. Even then, he might have survived this crisis had his health not been so precarious. His doctors advised him to retire from politics. Thus, after being Churchill's heir-apparent for a decade and a half, Eden held office just twenty months. Harold Macmillan, his successor, recalled the day Eden told him the news: "I can see him now on that sad winter afternoon, still looking so youthful, so gay, so debonair—the representative of all that was best of the youth that had served in the 1914–18 war. That band of men had faced the horrors of this fearful struggle with something of an Elizabethan gallantry. The survivors of that terrible holocaust had often felt under a special obligation, like men under a vow of duty."[23] Eden had symbolized the Conservative party at a time when Britannia neither ruled the waves, nor dominated world trade and finance; a time when surviving balance of payments crises and inflation was more important than maintaining imperial splendor; a time when foreign competition threatened domestic prosperity and any return to a policy of austerity was political suicide.

Continuity Amid Change. Nationalization did not prove to be the salvation of Britain's sick industries. During the economic boom of the 1950s, the real productive advances came almost entirely from the nonpublic sector. The low output of the mines continued to be a particular disappointment. Before World War I, British coal mines were capable of producing 287 million tons a year, a third of which was exported. Between 1919 and 1939, they averaged 200 million tons annually. They declined further during the war, but by 1947, the first year of nationalization, they had just about recovered their prewar level. Over the next several years, they showed a steady, but not spectacular, improvement. In 1950, the National Coal Board called for a capital investment of $1,778 million to ensure an annual production of 230–250 million tons. That same year, the British produced only 216 million tons, not enough to cover domestic needs and foreign obligations. They made up the shortages by buying coal from the United States. Five years later, production again had to be supplemented with foreign purchases.

While past mistakes and abuses were in part to blame, the greatest potential asset—the enthusiasm of the coal miners for nationalization—failed to materialize. Despite the improved productivity brought about by mechanization, British workers were poor competition for their German or American counterparts. Militancy rose in direct proportion to the miners' expectations of higher wages and better working conditions. Absenteeism rose to 11.5 percent of the workers in 1948. The unions rejected the recommendation of the joint committee on coal production to impose fines on the truants. Ultimately, the problems of the coal industry were not so much solved as transcended. Oil and natural gas offered other, more convenient sources of fuel. The Clean Air Act of 1956 also affected the situation. The legislation outlawed heavy smoke pollution and required new furnaces to be outfitted with special filters, thereby eliminating the burning of bituminous coal in many urban areas. During the 1960s, the famous London pea soupers (part water vapor, mostly chimney grit) gradually disappeared, and with them the demand for some 19 million tons of coal. In 1959, the Coal Board revised the goals it had set a decade earlier and lowered its intended productivity to 200 million tons a year. Later, a government report estimated that only 170 to 180 million tons would be required in the 1960s.

Of all the government programs, socialized medicine was the most popular, albeit one of the most expensive. By 1952–1953, its yearly cost had jumped to 518 million pounds (roughly $1.5 billion); forcing the government to charge patients for various medical services: half the cost of a set of dentures, a shilling for each prescription, five to ten shillings for elastic hosiery, two and a half pounds toward the price of a wig, and three pounds for orthopedic footwear. The 20 million pounds received from these new charges could not begin to cover the 76 million pounds increase in doctors' salaries that was granted in 1951 to prevent a threatened mass resignation of general practitioners from the National Health Service. By 1958, the National Health Service cost 710 million pounds (almost $2 billion), of which the Treasury paid 80 percent. Still, if one believed that medical care was a matter of right, not privilege, the British received their money's worth. Protected by the National Health Service, the average citizen did not face the enormous expense of catastrophic illness.

The Labour party had been particularly keen to abolish the great inequities of wealth. In particular, it went after inherited wealth, but without much success. In 1938–1939, about one-third of 1 percent of the people owned at least 21.6 percent of the country's personal wealth.[24] Two decades later, despite an increase in death duties in the upper brackets to as much as 75 percent, slightly over 1 percent still commanded 17 percent of the total personal wealth. Obviously, more than one generation was needed to promote social egalitarianism. Popular ingenuity in avoiding estate duties was limitless. A favorite ploy was to make the intended beneficiaries stockholders in a special company that would be subject only to corporate taxation. In sum, keeping great fortunes seemed easier than amassing them.

In general, though, the real wages of the average worker rose during the period by about 40 to 50 percent. Between 1952 and 1960, the number of private car registrations climbed from 187,616 to 805,017. In 1960, consumers were buying 63 percent more goods and services than they had ten years before, and a certain amount of complacency set in for which the British would ultimately suffer.

Profile: Clement Richard Attlee (1883–1967) and Charles-André-Marie-Joseph de Gaulle (1890–1970)

Attlee

Their styles of leadership and their personalities were completely different. Attlee always seemed so understated, de Gaulle so overblown. Attlee made every speech sound boring; de Gaulle made his sound exciting. Attlee was called "Clem the Clam"; de Gaulle was "le grand Charles." Did the British and French people get the leaders they deserved? Well yes—but with such men they probably did much better. Attlee and de Gaulle, each in his own way, epitomized the desires of the people. Both served them extremely well.

They were born in the last years of the nineteenth century to solid bourgeois parents who had relatively large families. Attlee had four brothers and three sisters; de Gaulle had two brothers and two sisters. In both households, patriotism and religion were inseparable, and respect for authority was considered a virtue. Yet both abandoned the safe and sane in their desire to serve their countries.

Attlee was born in the London suburb of Putney on 3 January 1883. As the son of a solicitor of "high standing" in the City of London, he was educated at public (private prep) schools, which gave him entry into the old boy network with its shared sentiments, accents, and jargon. After graduating from University College at Oxford, he studied law. He passed the bar examination in 1905 and went to work in his father's office. The Attlees were a politically conservative family who had long been defenders of established authority, a tradition Clement would break.[25]

Charles de Gaulle was born in Lille on 22 November 1890. His father was the headmaster of the Collège Stanislas, a Catholic school in town. Charles was educated in schools run by the Jesuits and, before his teens, had already decided that he would become a soldier. He had a great passion for the heroes of the past and a deep interest in military strategy, stimulated by his father's participation in the ill-fated defense of Sedan in 1870. He dreamed of the day when France would recover the lost territories of Alsace and Lorraine. In France, revenge and romance were often mortar for robust nationalism.

de Gaulle

In the conservative milieu of the Attlee family, the Christian duty to improve the lot of those less fortunate often took the form of acts of genteel charity. While trying to establish a career in the legal profession, Clement became involved with a boys' club on London's East Side. The experience of working in the city's worst slums forced him to reexamine the whole social and economic system that could produce such poverty. "I soon began to realize the curse of casual labour. I got to know what slum landlordism and sweating meant. . . . I learned also why there were rebels."[26] In 1907 he became the live-in manager of the Haileybury Boys' Club in the borough of Stepney. He joined a Fabian Society discussion group and in 1908 became a member of the Independent Labour party, a socialist group that advocated radical change, including the collective ownership of the means of production, distribution, and exchange. Impressed by their arguments, Attlee completely abandoned the practice of law and committed himself to finding a way to change society.

De Gaulle had fewer doubts about where he was headed. In 1909, he passed a special examination for admission to the national military school of Saint-Cyr. He finished the course three years later, in the top ten of a class of two hundred, emerging as a second lieutenant. His first posting as an officer was to the 33rd Infantry regiment at Arras, then commanded by a certain Colonel Philippe Pétain, who became a valuable mentor. The General Staff rated Pétain's unit as one of the most efficient in the army. When World War I began, it immediately saw action near Dinant. De Gaulle was then a full lieutenant and leader of a platoon. His service in the war was distinguished, if not brilliant. He was wounded three times and cited in dispatches three times before taken prisoner in 1916 during the early days of the Battle of Verdun. Despite five escape attempts, he returned home only after the Armistice.[27]

The German violation of Belgian neutrality shocked Attlee into joining the army two days after his country's declaration of war. He was thirty-one years old, one year over the official age limit. Nevertheless, he became an instructor in the Officer Training Corps and, from there, managed to transfer to a South Lancashire battalion. Commissioned a second lieutenant, he got his first chance to see combat in 1915 at Gallipoli, serving at Suvla Bay. His unit was evacuated with the big British retreat in December 1915 and sent to Mesopotamia where Attlee was wounded. He rose to the rank of major and later saw action in France. Discharged in January 1919, he returned to the East End.

De Gaulle returned from the war looking forward to a promising army career. In 1919, he was sent to Warsaw to advise the Fourth Polish Light Infantry division during the Russo-Polish War. After the conclusion of peace, he stayed on to teach tactics at the Polish war college, an experience that led to his subsequent appointment as a professor of military history at Saint-Cyr. Next came appointment to the General Staff of the army of the Rhine at Mainz (1924); then to the staff of Marshal Pétain, vice-president of the Superior War Council (1925–1927). This was followed by assignment to the General Staff of the French army in Beirut (1929–1931); and to the general-secretariat of the Superior National Defense Council (1932–1936).

Meanwhile, Attlee had gone into politics. The Labour party saw his well-to-do background, his army record, and his commitment to the poor as decided assets. It obtained his appointment as mayor of the district of Stepney and invited him to serve on the executive committee of the London Labour party. He was offered a five-year term as a city alderman and became a candidate for Parliament from Limehouse. In 1922, he entered the Commons. Attlee epitomized Labour's tendency to be a party run by middle-class politicians with a proletarian following. Less than one-fifth of Labour's parliamentary delegation were from the working class. In 1923, Attlee won reelection and, in 1924, became under secretary of state for war in the ill-fated Labour government of Ramsay MacDonald. During the period of Tory ascendency from 1924 to 1929, his standing within his own party increased. When MacDonald became prime minister again in 1929, Attlee became chancellor of the duchy of Lancaster and postmaster general. In 1931, however, he refused to join the National Government and broke with MacDonald. The Labour party was in shambles, and Attlee's chances for national leadership had apparently collapsed.

In contrast, de Gaulle's future seemed assured. He had found a powerful mentor in Marshal Pétain, who had been shepherding his career. De Gaulle had dedicated his book *The Edge of the Sword* (1932) to him. *The Edge of the Sword* was an intellectual discourse on the philosophy of leadership, containing a wealth of aphorisms about the qualities necessary for effective command: "Great warriors have always been conscious of the role and value of instinct." "Nothing heightens authority more than silence." "The man of action can do nothing without a strong dose of egotism, pride, endurance, and guile." In downplaying the use of the airplane and the tank, the study hardly challenged conventional military thinking. De Gaulle's next book was more controversial. In *The Army of the Future* (1934), he advocated creating a professionally trained army composed of independent, highly mechanized, armored units capable of engaging in rapid offensive action. Although this concept had already been developed by certain pioneer military thinkers during the 1920s, de Gaulle's lucid prose infused it with new meaning.[28] The High Command rejected these proposals, however, believing its current doctrine of defense to be less costly in money and lives. The ambitious de Gaulle never really seemed comfortable in the role of courtier, and by the time the book was published, he had broken with Pétain. His career apparently was now in limbo. When his term at the General Staff Strategic Center was over, de Gaulle was sent to cool his heels in Metz as commander of the 507th tank regiment. Meanwhile the army brass continued to rely on the Maginot Line to protect France against invasion.

Attlee had managed to survive the National Government debacle and hold on to his seat in Commons. He became deputy party leader in 1931; and four years later, when George Lansbury was forced out of office because of his pacifist views, Attlee was elected leader. During the late 1930s, Attlee supported collective security against Hitler and urged aid for Republican Spain, but was reluctant to agree to a massive program of rearmament.

At the same time, de Gaulle had found a new mentor in Paul Reynaud. Reynaud, a former minister of finance, was a leading advocate of the creation of an offensive army to support France's diplomatic commitments to the countries of Eastern Europe. Reynaud lacked sufficient influence, however, and a Chamber of Deputies' army committee rejected his ideas. The Battle of France in 1940 gave both men an opportunity to be vindicated. De Gaulle put his ideas into practice on the battlefield and earned promotion to the rank of brigadier general; Reynaud became the head of the government. Reynaud then recalled de Gaulle from the front to become his under secretary for war, a transfer that added to de Gaulle's prestige. In the aftermath of the defeat, de Gaulle fled to London, the only minister to do so. He refused to obey the orders of the new Pétain government to accept the Armistice, thereby becoming an outcast at odds with his fellow officers, most of whom chose obedience over exile.[29] De Gaulle's isolation increased his determination to establish his legitimacy, although his famous appeal for continued resistance, issued over the British Broadcasting System on 18 June 1940, had no authority behind it other than his own pretensions.

The war brought Attlee back into the government. In 1940, Prime Minister Winston Churchill chose Attlee to be one of his top aides. In 1942, Attlee became deputy prime minister with responsibility over domestic affairs. He was therefore involved in much of the planning for a new postwar society. Attlee was always more of a pragmatist than an ideologue. Churchill had once warned his ministers that they should "be careful not to raise false hopes, as was done [after World War I] by speeches about 'homes for heroes.' "[30] But Attlee wanted to transform British society and was not prepared to take these warnings seriously.

De Gaulle also set his own standards. He believed that truly great leaders could not be judged by the rules applied to others. In *The Edge of the Sword*, he had written approvingly of a comment that Admiral John Fisher once made about Sir John Jellicoe who had failed to destroy the German fleet after the Battle of Jutland. Fisher said that Jellicoe had "all the qualities of Nelson save one; he does not know how to disobey." De Gaulle certainly had such qualities; but when he became head of the provisional government in 1944, he was not willing to admit that others shared them as well.

Both Attlee and de Gaulle were solitary men with no close personal friends. Both possessed a sense of purpose and a strong commitment to ideals. In their careers, they had both taken risks, and were extremely lucky in having them pay off. Now, in power neither doubted that he was the man best qualified to preside over the regeneration of his country.

THE RISE AND FALL OF THE FOURTH FRENCH REPUBLIC

The Provisional Government of Charles de Gaulle

The Liberation. General Charles de Gaulle entered Paris at four o'clock on the afternoon of 25 August 1944. Earlier that day, General Philippe Leclerc, the commander of the Second Armored Division, had received the official surrender of Paris from the German commander, General Dietrich von Choltitz. De Gaulle had insisted that the capitulation be accepted in the name of the French, not the Allied, Supreme Command. De Gaulle's ultimate destination was the Hôtel de Ville, the city hall and the traditional birthplace of French republicanism, where a vast cheering crowd had assembled to greet him. Here also were the leaders of the Paris Liberation Committee. When de Gaulle finally arrived, the committee's leader Georges Bidault asked him to officially proclaim the reestablishment of the Republic before the mass of French citizens who were chanting the general's name in the square below. De Gaulle cut him short. "The Republic has never ceased to exist," he snapped. "Since I myself am the President of the Government of the Republic, why should I go and proclaim it?" But it would take more than pretensions to restore the greatness of France.

World War II had cost the lives of approximately 600,000 soldiers and civilians. Although the human losses were less than those of World War I, the material damage was more widespread and the demoralization much greater. Only ten out of ninety départements had been left undamaged. The infrastructure was particularly hard hit: telephone and telegraph systems had been demolished; railroads were paralyzed; and roads were blocked with rubble and marked with gaping holes. All the major bridges over the Seine, Loire, and Rhone had been blown up. No trains ran between Paris and Lyons or from Paris to Marseilles, Toulouse, Bordeaux, Nantes, Lille, and Nancy. The war had caused a tremendous decline in both industrial and agricultural productivity.[31] The cost of living had tripled between 1937 and 1944 and would increase even more the following year.[32]

Large areas of the country, although liberated, had yet to be pacified. The national gendarmerie was disorganized, making it difficult to ensure personal safety. Before order was restored, thousands of people were killed in a massive settling of accounts. Many of the victims had indeed collaborated with the Germans—the militiamen who handed over French Jews to the Gestapo or the active agents of Nazi propaganda—but many others perished because of old political rivalries and personal hatreds. The Communists went after members who had earlier defied party discipline by denouncing the Nazi-Soviet Non-Aggression Pact. Villagers found violent solutions to long-standing private feuds, social bitterness, and interfamily squabbles. In some towns, resistance groups made the rounds of apartment buildings, asking concierges to finger the collaborators in their buildings. Women who had, or were suspected of having, slept with German soldiers had their heads shaved and were sometimes—in a blend of outraged patriotism and sanctimonious prurience—marched naked through the streets.

De Gaulle realized that mere physical recovery was not alone sufficient. In a speech at the Palais de Chaillot on 12 September 1944, he stated that his goal was "to subordinate private interest to public advantage; to exploit the national resources of the nation and administer them to the general advantage; to abolish coalitions of interest once and for all; and finally, to permit each of France's sons and daughters to live, to work and to raise their children in security and dignity."[33] Thus, de Gaulle publicly committed himself to the economic and social goals of the Resistance Charter. He wrote that there must either "be an official and rapid move to institute a marked change in the conditions of the working people, and profound limitations upon financial privilege, or the embittered and suffering mass of workers would founder upon those disturbances which risked depriving France of what remained of her substance."[34]

The Trial of Marshal Pétain. The establishment of de Gaulle's position depended on the destruction of the legitimacy of the previous regime and of its leader, Marshal Philippe Pétain. The old marshal's trial began on Monday, 23 July 1945. The High Court, which exercised special authority over persons who had participated in the Vichy government, was comprised of magistrates who earlier had sworn allegiance to the man on whom they now presumed to sit in judgment. Pétain imperiously refused to recognize the court's competence and in his opening statement emphasized the legality of the Vichy government. "Power was entrusted to me lawfully and recognized by every country in the world from the Holy See to the U.S.S.R. I used this power as a shield to protect the French people, for whose sake I went so far as to sacrifice my personal prestige."[35] The irony of a man who had faithfully served his country all his life betraying his country when he was eighty-four years old was not lost on the French. Novelist Jules Roy, a reporter at Pétain's trial, offered this explanation:

> On the point of leaving this world, with every day that passed taking him one step nearer the shadows, he was suddenly offered a crown of light. . . . What octogenarian can resist a display of interest in himself, and why are Academy meetings so well attended if not because old men are afraid of solitude and boredom? All of a sudden the Marshal found himself a magus, kneeling before the star of a grandiose redemption.[36]

On 15 August, the court convicted Pétain of treason and sentenced him to death. De Gaulle allowed no appeal of Pétain's sentence, but he did commute it to life imprisonment. No such clemency was shown toward Pierre Laval, Pétain's unsavory subordinate. Laval knew too much about everybody's dirty linen. He had much to answer for, but his trial was a procedural monstrosity. The judges shouted at him, preventing him from presenting his defense. He was sentenced to death, but on the eve of his execution, he tried to poison himself. His stomach was pumped out, and he was hastily shot before he could cheat the firing squad. Few doubted that Laval got what he deserved—here was a man who said he welcomed a German victory—but the outrageous handling of his case brought no credit to his judges.

Other trials were held, but the justice coming from these special courts remained far from evenhanded. Economic collaboration was often treated more leniently than intellectual collaboration. It was said that a person who had helped the Germans build the Atlantic Wall need not fear arrest, but that an individual who had called the wall a good thing would go to jail. Often the big fish got away while their subordinates were left to suffer. For example, Admiral Jean-Pierre Esteva was sentenced to life imprisonment for permitting the German landings in Tunisia in 1942, although he was only following the orders of his superior, Marshal Alphonse Juin, who at the moment of Esteva's trial was the chief of staff of the Fourth Republic.[37]

Constitution Making. De Gaulle had returned, after four years of exile without official British or American recognition of his government.[38] Indeed, for almost a year and a half, he had no constitutionally recognized status in his own country. This limbo ended with the general election of 21 October 1945—the first such since 1936 and the first in which women voted. De Gaulle was unanimously elected president-premier of the Provisional Republic and, for the time being, set the legislative agenda. He divided his ministries among the three major parties, but took special care to keep the important posts of Interior, Foreign Affairs, and Defense out of the hands of the Communists who, with 160 delegates, could claim at last to be the first political party of France. The other two parties in this so-called Resistance Coalition were the newly created Popular Republican Movement (*Mouvement Populaire Républicain*, or MRP), a Catholic social action party, which won 152 seats; and the Socialists with 142 seats.[39]

The electorate clearly desired significant social and political change and had called for the establishment of a new republic. The three leading parties had all committed themselves to accepting the Resistance Charter as the basis of future legislation. What this meant in practice, however, was more difficult to ascertain. From the start, the coalition was beset by old rivalries and antipathies. The Communists had not changed their basic Leninist-Stalinist goals. They hoped tripartism would ensure them a permanent role in governing France and wanted to merge with the Socialists, the better to dominate them. The Socialists strongly opposed any such alliance as they had in the past. The MRP, although committed to social reform, was too distrustful of the anticlerical Socialists to develop any real association with them. The parties did agree on the need to restore the prerogatives of the legislative branch of government, but they ran into opposition from de Gaulle.

Although de Gaulle rejected government by executive decree, he opposed a system based on parliamentary supremacy. In his view, the old political parties had failed to provide adequate leadership: "Some among them could obtain the votes of an important fraction of the citizens, [but] not a single one was thought of as representing the public interest as a whole."[40] De Gaulle preferred a strong presidency that would directly represent the nation and stand above party politics. However, sensing his influence beginning to wear thin and perhaps hesitant to lead a France so weak that it would be overly subservient to the United States, he announced his retirement in a special meeting of the Council of Ministers on 20 January: "The exclusive regime of parties has reappeared. I disapprove of it. But aside from establishing by force a dictatorship which I do not desire and which could certainly end in disaster, I have not the means of preventing this experiment. I must therefore withdraw."[41] De Gaulle calculated that he would soon be recalled on his own terms.

Drafting an acceptable constitution was no easy task. The first attempt, submitted to the voters on 5 May 1946, was defeated by 10.6 to 9.5 million votes. The constitution, which had the support of the Communists and the Socialists, provided for a single-chamber legislature with a figurehead president. The MRP had opposed the constitution, fearing that a unicameral legislature would lead to a Communist dictatorship. Elections were held on 2 June to choose a second Constituent Assembly. The MRP, which received the largest number of seats with 169 (followed by the Communists with 153 and the Socialists with 127), was able to obtain a two-chamber legislature, but in actuality the differences were not significant. The lower house, or National Assembly, held the real power of governance with control over the premier and the cabinet. The upper house, or the Council of the Republic, could only examine and express its opinion on legislation before the Assembly. The president was essentially a figurehead. This second constitution was presented to the voters for ratification on 13 October.

De Gaulle, who had kept his silence during the first referendum, lambasted the second constitution with an appeal to legitimacy over legality: "The public powers have no validity, in fact or in law, unless they are in accord with the superior interests of the country and repose on the confident approval of the citizens." He advocated a strong executive, thereby foreshadowing changes that would be enacted in 1958. In 1946, however, his intervention failed. The voters accepted the second constitution by 9.2 to 8.2 million votes. Significantly, 31 percent of the eligible voters (8,468,000) did not bother to go to the polls. The French were clearly bored with constitution making and voted for a system that did not seem much of an improvement over the one they had lived under during the Third Republic. Institutionally, this was true, but the attitude of the French people had changed. In contrast to the previous period, they expected their government to contribute to the economic prosperity of the country and provide them with expanded social and welfare services.

The New Republic

Politics and Reorganization. France continued to be governed by an uneasy coalition of Socialists, Communists, and Popular Republicans, The "big three" did not agree on constitutional issues, however, and they had differing views on economics, religion, and foreign policy. Soon the strain became too great. The Communists controlled the economic ministries of Labor and Social Security, Industrial Production, and Reconstruction, but these posts failed to give them an effective power base from which to dominate the government. Therefore the Communists resorted to obstructionism. They opposed any political or economic association with the Western powers, and they voted against the policy to stabilize wages. In May 1947, Socialist Premier Paul Ramadier threw them out of the cabinet and replaced their ministers with Socialists and Popular Republicans. The Communists became a party of opposition.

Great labor unrest, increasing inflation, and growing political dissatisfaction from the Right added to the turmoil. The first clear proof of the Right's growing strength came with de Gaulle's reentry into politics. At Strasbourg, on 7 April, the second anniversary of the liberation of Alsace, the general delivered a spirited denunciation of the institutions and political parties of the Fourth Republic and announced the formation of the Rally of the French Republic (*Rassemblement du peuple français* or *RPF*). Its goals were to bring about a fundamental transformation of the political and social life of France and to act as a stout bulwark against Communism. In the municipal elections of October 1947, the RPF candidates and their allies won about 40 percent of the total vote, more than the MRP and Socialists combined. In 1951, the party won over 100 seats in the National Assembly. This proved to be the peak of its popularity, however. Although the Gaullists were united in protesting the current inertia of the Fourth Republic, some were clearly antiparliamentary, while others wanted to retain democracy and make it more progressive and modern. De Gaulle seemed committed to constitutionalism, but as he had made clear many times before, it must be a constitution that would strengthen the powers of the president.

The Gaullist successes had diminished the Communists' local support, and in November, they seized the initiative by launching a wave of strikes to paralyze the country. Organized through the Communist-led General Confederation of Labor, the demonstrations involved three million workers from all sectors of industry, particularly metallurgy, iron and steel, and coal. The strikes were also intended as a protest against the receipt of Marshall Plan aid and were thus a battle of the Cold War. In fact, Moscow had instructed the French Communists to incite the workers against their government and, if necessary, to sabotage trains carrying troops.

The government reacted as if it were facing an insurrection. The new premier, MRP leader Robert Schuman (November 1947–July 1948), enlarged his cabinet to include the Radicals and appointed the tough Jules Moch as minister of interior. Moch, a Socialist, quickly organized special detachments of the gendarmerie for rapid deployment to the major strike areas: the Paris region, Lyons, and Marseilles area, and the northern départements. He activated 80,000 reservists and recalled units from Germany. The government accompanied these hard-line measures with efforts to appease the strikers. Economic benefits were significantly increased. The carrot and stick policy worked, but the crisis had a lasting effect on French trade unionism. The Communist test of strength had failed to destroy the Fourth Republic and had weakened the unity of the General Confederation of Labor. Many non-Communist unions had opposed the strike; even many of the Communist-controlled unions boycotted the official demonstrations. Old-time syndicalists, who had never fully accepted affiliation with any political party, now thought it was time to become independent. Some organized a separate organization, the General Confederation of Labor of the Working Force; others, like the Federation of Teachers, declared their autonomy; and still more, tens of thousands, abandoned their union affiliation altogether. The divisions among the trade unions weakened their ability to effect social change.

The events of 1947 frightened those loyal to the institutions of the Fourth Republic. The MRP with its 166 seats, the Socialists with their 102, and the Radicals and their affiliates with 69 seats—altogether more than half of the seats in the National Assembly[42]—formed a political alliance to halt further disorder. This "Third Force" remained inherently unstable because its member parties were rarely able to agree on anything more basic than the defense of democracy. Moreover, the parties themselves were divided internally on major economic, social, and religious issues: the Socialist party was based upon "a more or less imaginary class concept," the Popular Republican Movement on "a religious ideal," and the Radical party "on historical memories."[43] Nevertheless, the Third Force managed to survive until 1951, when the Socialists, frustrated by the continual opposition of their coalition partners to economic reform, refused to accept any more cabinet portfolios. They went into opposition thereby leaving control of the government to the MRP, the Radicals, and various other rightist groups. For the remaining years of its life, the Fourth Republic was unable to produce a solid consensus on any significant issue.

The growing strength of powerful lobbies that spoke for the interests of business, farmers, labor, veterans, and others compounded the problem. For the most part, these groups chose to influence legislation by working behind the scenes within the prevailing political parties. However, the Defense of Shopkeepers and Artisans movement had a taste for more direct action. This group, founded by shopkeeper Pierre Poujade, served as a rallying point for discontented independent merchants who wanted to protest high taxes and denounce the stagnation of the parliamentary system. The movement drew most of its strength from the small towns and rural areas. In the elections of January 1956, the group, now transformed into the French Brotherhood Union (*Union et fraternité française*), entered candidates in almost every electoral district and managed to win over 2.5 million popular votes and 52 seats in the National Assembly. However, Poujadism was essentially negative. It appealed to the fears of the independent small business owners who were against the forces of change. Without effective leadership, the group soon degenerated into anti-Semitism and ultranationalism as its deputies scrambled for alliances with other right-wing parties. However, the contempt for the Fourth Republic upon which the forces of the French Right fed remained.

Economic Planning. In France, nationalization began with those companies that had actively collaborated with the Germans: the Renault Motor Car factories were seized on 4 October 1944, followed by the Berliet Engine Works and the Gnôme and Rhone airplane factory. The newspaper *Le Temps* was also nationalized.[44] In December, the Provisional Government took an important step to implement the promises of the Resistance Charter when it reorganized most of the coal industry as "the National Coal Industry of the Nord and Pas-de-Calais" and put it under the supervision of the Ministry of Mines. The government felt that an energy resource so important to French national security had to be under public control. In April 1946, the gas and electrical industries were handled the same way. That same year, the government nationalized the four major depository banks.[45] State domination of credit, it was argued, would lead to a more rational allocation of national resources and result in an inevitable rise in productivity. Many of the current problems were long-standing, however, and could not be solved by such expedients. In this respect, the Resistance Charter called for an intensification of production "in accordance with a Plan to be decided upon by the state, after consultation with all those concerned with this production."[46] The Provisional Government therefore created the Plan for Modernization and Equipment, with Jean Monnet as high commissioner. A Council of the Plan, formed on 3 January 1946, began a survey of French resources to be used in formulating a series of goals for the next four years.

Fears arose that France was headed toward a controlled economy, but planning was to be accomplished with the assistance, not the destruction, of private enterprise. The planners hoped to provide businesses with the means to chart a rational course on their own. These technocrats tried to take a middle ground between rigid control and complete laissez-faire, but they recognized that priorities could not be established without a certain amount of coercion. Not being true ideologues, however, they often found that the best way to get people to do what they desired was to bribe them. Doing so was fairly easy since the government controlled most of the total investment capital,[47] which was made available, at preferential interest rates, to those who agreed to follow the plan's established priorities. The government offered additional incentives through special depreciation allowances, tax reductions, and outright subsidies.[48] The state was also responsible for approximately one-third of total French investment spending, which went mostly to the nationalized industries and to basic industries in dire need of modernization: iron and steel, cement, electricity, coal, agricultural machinery, and transportation.

The government also tried to repeat Poincaré's "economic miracle" by fighting inflation psychologically. To gain people's confidence, solvency had first to be restored to government finances through a policy of austerity, an unpopular measure that politicians were reluctant to endorse. Direct taxation accounted for less than one-third of national revenues, scarcely enough to meet the mounting deficits, which were covered by advances from the Bank of France and by issuing interest-bearing Treasury bonds. The state also borrowed money from the deposits in state savings banks, paid for goods and services with credit, and relied upon money from abroad. Between 1947 and 1954, foreign loans, principally from the United States, offset between 20 and 50 percent of the French budget deficits. Aid made available to France under the Marshall Plan accounted for about 30 percent of total French investment.[49]

Inflation and the huge military expenditures, which cut a large slice out of the budget, undermined the success of the First Plan for Modernization and Equipment (1947–1953).[50] Furthermore, resources were very limited, and frequently the planners were unable to gather reliable data on the extent of war damage and the availability of materials.[51] Then too, the goals of the plan were frequently confused and unrealistic. For example, one goal was to exceed 1929 levels of production by 25 percent, but it was unclear whether the planners were referring to industrial production or to gross national product. The plan also failed to address the inequities that existed between different regions of France, such as between the underdeveloped southwest and the more advanced regions of Paris, Lyon, and the north. In addition, the sectors emphasized by the plan drained funds from other programs. For example, of the half a million new dwelling units promised by 1950, only 174,000 were actually built. However, in the targeted sectors, growth was significant.[52] The Second Plan (1954–1957) was more sophisticated than its predecessor and was more concerned with lowering production costs. At the same time, it hoped to expand overall production by 25 percent. The planners concentrated on increasing efficiency by promoting the restructuring of certain industries by regrouping and mergers. They fostered the reorganization of agricultural marketing and distribution and emphasized scientific and technological research. Their success was impressive. Goals in certain categories were even filled to excess: electrical equipment by 233 percent, textiles by 213 percent, and chemicals by 280 percent. For the first time, the planners had to face the problem of economic disequilibrium because of too much growth.

Such an embarrassment of riches seemed a good augury for stabilizing the political system of the Fourth Republic. The derisive clamor of the Communists and the Gaullists continued, but the defenders of the present constitutional system still managed to hold on to the reins of power. Nevertheless, their disagreements were becoming increasingly acute. The issue of German rearmament was particularly divisive, both among and within parties.[53] But colonial policy ultimately proved the most destructive. Throughout its entire life, the Fourth Republic was involved in an exhausting struggle with independence movements in Indochina and Algeria. France was no longer powerful enough to make reality conform to its confused ambitions. And in trying to hold on to everything, the French were ultimately left with nothing.

The French population had remained stable for many decades. In 1901, the nation had 38.9 million people (about 40.5 million including the separated départements of Alsace and Lorraine); in 1946, it contained 40.3 million people. Even allowing for the wartime losses, the fact remained that, for one reason or another, the French preferred small families. Since 1830, the French population had grown more slowly than that of any other major European country. From 1935 until World War II, the death rate consistently exceeded the birthrate. If this trend had continued, the French population by 1985 would have been only 30 million.

Why the French started having more babies at the end of World War II is difficult to answer. Perhaps the fighting, or an increase in the level of fecundity, or the 1939 program of family allowances produced the change. Certainly, the higher standard of living the French achieved after the war had little to do with it, for the birthrate rose before the recovery began. In 1945, births exceeded deaths by 13,000, a year later the difference jumped to 298,000, and by 1950 to 328,000. The celebration of marriages postponed because of the war, the return of prisoners of war and deportees, and the coming of age of the pre-Depression generation (least affected by the losses of World War I) would sustain the increase, but they did not start it.

In any case, a growing population required more housing, schools, and hospitals. The consumer-oriented parents of this new generation demanded these services as a matter of right and had less patience than their elders with a system that failed to provide them. People wanted to live for the present. The traditional belief in the value of saving disappeared and was replaced by an increased demand for durable goods. This change in the economic reflexes of the French, though difficult to quantify or depict in charts and graphs, was one of the most significant aspects of growth and development during the Fourth Republic.

The rising birthrate seemed to indicate that the dynamic France was winning out over the static France, a distinction usually based on regional differences. The northern area of the country, stretching from Paris to the Belgian frontier, drained population and resources from the rest of France. The steady growth of industrialization in this region contributed to the general decline of small farms, small-scale industry, and local handicrafts in such an alarming way that the planners would later turn their attention to the development of backward regions affected by this exodus of workers and talent. The French economy was both progressive and backward. For all its expansion, it remained an economy of small family businesses. Even in 1952 when production had returned to its prewar high, only 332 industrial companies employed more than 1,000 workers, and only 653 had between 500 and 1,000 workers; the number of large firms had actually declined since the Great Depression. As long as the marginally efficient French industries functioned within the confines of a protected domestic market and were so strongly rooted in class values, they were incapable of competing with foreign industries. Many small business owners and industrialists appeared more concerned with the preservation of social stability than with higher production.

Meanwhile, inflation continued to threaten those on fixed incomes. In 1958, the government decided to abolish any pensions that, due to the successive monetary depreciations, were worth less than the cost to the Treasury of printing and making out the checks. The decision provoked a protest by some World War I veterans who marched down the Avenue de l'Opéra and demonstrated in front of the Ministry of Finance. Their pensions had hardly permitted them to buy a package of cigarettes a month, but they felt humiliated to be told, in effect, that their service was now worth nothing.

Colonial Wars and the Death of the Fourth Republic

The Loss of Vietnam. The tremendous blow French national pride had suffered with the defeat in 1940 increased France's determination to maintain the integrity of its empire. The French believed the colonies were necessary to maintain their nation's world standing. After the surrender of the Japanese, the French repossessed Vietnam a piece at a time. In October 1945, they reinstalled themselves in Saigon; the following March, they did the same in Hanoi. Their reentry into the northern capital had been prepared by an agreement reached with the local Communist and nationalist leader Ho Chi Minh on 6 March 1946. This accord recognized the northern part of the country as a separate republic, possessing its own parliament and army and having control over local finances. France thereby appeared to be the first European state to come to terms with a native nationalist movement. For Ho Chi Minh's political organization, the Viet-Minh,[54] the pact was a first step toward a totally independent and unified Vietnam.

The local army commander, General Philippe Leclerc, was glad things had gone so well, and to emphasize his good intentions, he ordered his military vehicles to be painted with both French and Viet-Minh insignias. He deplored the Communist presence, but felt that problems had to be solved politically, rather than militarily. "France," he wrote, "will no longer be able to collar a coalescent mass of 24 million people possessed with a xenophobic and, possibly nationalist, ideology."[55] However, the French high commissioner, Admiral Thierry d'Argenlieu, thought differently. Profiting by indecision in Paris, he organized a separate state in South Vietnam, which also had its own government and army. In August 1946, while the French government was negotiating at Fontainebleau with Ho Chi Minh on the future status of Vietnam, he called together his own conference at Dalat to establish an Indochinese Federation comprised of Cochin China, Laos, and Cambodia. D'Argenlieu's action torpedoed the Fontainebleau talks. Foreign Minister Georges Bidault blamed the breakdown on Ho Chi Minh, thereby suggesting implausibly that the Communists were prepared to start an insurrection for what they hoped to get through negotiations. Such accusations were peripheral to the main issue, which was whether France had any real national interest in holding on to this bit of territory in Southeast Asia. The Paris government could not make up its mind, but there were others who could.

On 23 November 1946, following a series of confrontations between French and Viet-Minh troops in Haiphong, the French cruiser *Suffren* opened fire on the port, killing about six thousand persons. Four weeks later, the Vietnamese Communists retaliated by attacking Hanoi and declaring the start of a war of liberation. The opening years of the Vietnam conflict were inconclusive and unexciting, and initially most of the French people paid it scant attention. The Cold War in Europe and inflation were more immediate concerns. Since no conscripts were sent to Indochina, the fracas was dismissed as the concern of the professional soldiers and the Foreign Legion mercenaries who seemed more than able to handle a rabble enemy army. Moreover, d'Argenlieu had convinced many people that Ho Chi Minh had no real following in the country.

The fighting took on a new dimension when Mao Zedong's Communists came to power in China in 1949. Now the Viet-Minh were able to secure sufficient arms and supplies to push for control of the Tonkin delta. The French army, backed with aid from the United States, was able to stem their advance and maintain a stalemate. However, after five years with no end in sight, the French back home started to become restive. It seemed absurd to squander lives and resources on a country that would eventually be governed by Vietnamese, no matter which side won. Besides, Ho Chi Minh might be a revolutionary, but he came by it honestly. Had he not admitted, "It was not in Moscow that I learned what revolution was, but in Paris, in the capital of Liberty, Equality and Fraternity"?

Then, there was the problem of Bao Dai, the man whom the French government was trying to put forth as the emperor of a united Vietnam. Bao Dai had a well-earned reputation as a playboy more concerned with living it up on the Riviera than with the well-being of his subjects back home. On 28 August 1953, at a conference at Rambouillet, Vice-Premier Paul Reynaud demanded that the would-be ruler set a good example by stopping his gambling. To which Bao Dai replied meretriciously, "If you were to go into the Salles de Jeux [gambling rooms], you would meet more French colonels than Vietnamese."[56] The French Vietnamese policy clearly was in confusion. Even Vincent Auriol, the president of the Republic, had difficulty finding out who was in charge. Premier Joseph Laniel could not control his subordinates. His ministry was described as "manufactured, like his speeches, with scissors and paste." Although the government had recognized the right of Bao Dai to rule a completely independent Vietnam, it was impossible to achieve that goal without a military victory.

General Henri Navarre, the local French army commander in Vietnam, thought he could provide it. He would coax the head of the Viet-Minh army, General Vo Nguyen Giap, into a futile assault against Dien Bien Phu, the French base lying athwart the main enemy supply route to China, some two hundred air miles from Hanoi. Navarre was so confident of his superiority in men and matériel that he committed only nine out of the hundred battalions at his disposal to the operation. He intended to supply the 20,000-man garrison by air.

Giap accepted the challenge and slowly marshalled his forces. In four months, he had assembled an army of twenty-eight infantry battalions and had implanted over two hundred guns in the hills commanding the Dien Bien Phu valley. On 13 March 1954, the all-out attack began. The Communist artillery quickly made the tiny French airfield unserviceable, while Giap's shock troops cleared the French from their peripheral strong points and threw them back onto their main base in the village. Although the French fought heroically, they were soon cut off. After six weeks of constant siege, their position became hopeless.[57] Dien Bien Phu fell on 7 May. The French did not surrender; they were literally overwhelmed. Of the 13,000 prisoners, only 3,000 survived to return home. The defeat was not irreparable militarily, but it was catastrophic politically.

On 17 June 1954, Pierre Mendès-France of the Radical party became premier and swore to bring a satisfactory end to the war by 20 July or resign. He doubted he would succeed. A nine-power conference convened in Geneva and, three hours before the expiration of Mendès-France's deadline, reached an agreement. The premier's ploy proved to be one of his best trumps because it warned the Viet-Minh that if they allowed this opportunity to pass, Mendès-France's successor might be less willing to come to terms. Despite the loss of Dien Bien Phu, the French still had a formidable military presence in the country.

In the settlement, all the territory north of the 17th parallel was surrendered to the absolute control of the Viet-Minh. South Vietnam would remain with France, but was promised eventual independence. The division of the country was provisional, pending a general referendum to be held within two years. The French received the news that they had lost part of their colonial possessions without rejoicing, but nevertheless the agreement was popular. The National Assembly ratified it with an overwhelming vote of 471 to 14. The war had defied the efforts of eleven governments to bring it to a close. It had cost $8.5 billion (of which $6.8 billion came directly from the French budget); it had consumed the lives of 92,000 men of the expeditionary army (19,000 French, 43,000 Indochinese, and the rest Foreign Legionnaires) and wounded 114,000 more. It had never been popular with the French people, yet it had dragged on for eight and a half years and could conceivably have lasted longer.

Mendès-France was the most successful premier of the Fourth Republic. He sold the French on the need to join the security pact of the North Atlantic Treaty Organization. He set the plan in motion for Tunisian and Moroccan independence, and he convinced the French to support the Geneva accords on Vietnam by threatening to draft Frenchmen to fight there.

The loss of Vietnam was followed by the end of French control in its other overseas possessions: Morocco, Tunisia, and Equatorial Africa. But the colonial troubles of the Fourth Republic were far from over. Within six months after the end of the fighting in Vietnam, France was at war in Algeria.

The Algerian War. The series of terrorist attacks that broke the tranquillity of Algeria's major coastal cities at the end of October 1954 seemed at first to be no more than temporary disturbances. The assaults caused some loss of life, but did minimal damage to property and seemingly had little effect on the attitudes of the Muslim population. The attacks, however, had been well planned. As early as 1947, a group of young Muslim extremists had begun stockpiling arms and recruiting militants for an eventual uprising. Over the next seven years, the leaders of the intended rebellion held hundreds of secret meetings in Algiers, Cairo, Bern, and Geneva to crystallize their plans. In March 1954, they formed a special Revolutionary Committee to prepare for direct action. They divided Algeria into revolutionary districts, placing each under local commanders to handle military op-

An armored personnel carrier, mounting a thirty-caliber machine gun, patrols the frontier between Algeria and Tunis near the city of Tébessa. The French built an electric fence between the two countries to stop Muslim rebels from smuggling in supplies.

erations, and laid the groundwork for a political organization known as the Muslim National Liberation Front (*Front de Libération National* or *FLN*).

Even had the French been able to appreciate the dynamics of this truly determined liberation movement, they would not have considered Algerian independence negotiable. Few then regarded Algeria as a mere colony. Since 1871, when its representatives were allowed to sit in the National Assembly, Algeria had been constitutionally a direct part of metropolitan France. The country had been divided into départements administered by Paris-appointed prefects. Both in relative and in absolute terms, Algeria had the largest population of European settlers[58] of any French overseas possession; they comprised about 10 percent of the total population of nine million. The French presence was massive. The *colons*, or settlers, monopolized the local government; owned the best agricultural land (which they claimed, truthfully, to have been responsible for developing); controlled over nine-tenths of the country's industry; dominated the educational system; and had even turned the great mosque in Algiers into a Roman Catholic cathedral. French civil status was theoretically open to all Muslims who were willing to be Gallicized, but integration was a screen behind which the *colons* maintained their ascendancy. For example, they were able to frustrate the implementation of the 1947 Algerian Statute that had given the Muslims half the seats on a local legislature that was to assist the governor-general in implementing policy.

The *colons* now formed their own terrorist organizations to fight both the FLN and any French government that dared try to make concessions to the rebels. Some even formed a special committee of public safety to plot the overthrow of the Republic. Such subversive activity could flourish only because of the complicity of the local administration and, more importantly, the sympathy and support of the French army, which, after three years of fighting, seemed to have prevailed militarily. The weak and confused Paris government abdicated more of its powers to the military. In January 1957, following a series of FLN terrorist attacks in

Algiers, the government invested General Jacques Massu, the commander of the 10th Paratroop Division, with full police powers. Massu applied them with such violence that many people back home were alarmed and began to wonder if French civilization was only a sham.[59] The *colons* were threatening the Paris government with continued violence, and possibly civil war, if it made any concessions to the Algerian nationalists. The settlers regarded each cabinet crisis as an opportunity for their supporters to form a government.

Many French did not think that the retention of Algeria was worth the destruction of their own country. The old days when France ruled over an apathetic Muslim population were gone and would never return. Now keeping Algeria in the fold would require a permanent occupation force. The economic and political costs of such a policy were more than most cared to pay. In May 1958, a new ministry, headed by Pierre Pflimlin, advocated direct armistice negotiations with the FLN.

The *Algérie française* extremists believed the time had come to save the state by bringing the French army to power. On 13 May, the day the new government presented itself to the National Assembly for formal investiture, a crowd of eight thousand people, composed mostly of young men and students, and encouraged and supported by the paratroopers, attacked and occupied the building of the Government-General in Algiers. The riot's leaders urged General Massu to become the head of a newly formed Committee of Public Safety. One of its members, Léon Delbecque, declared that he would recognize no government's orders unless that government were headed by General de Gaulle. On 15 May, General Raoul Salan, the man to whom the Paris government had assigned the task of maintaining order, concluded a speech before a crowd assembled in the Algiers forum with the cry "Vive de Gaulle!" The French army had often played a political role in modern French history, but not since the Boulanger affair of the 1880s had army leaders taken such direct steps to overturn a regime. Many career officers were ready to support such a move. To them, the loss of Indochina had been an act of betrayal. They felt that any national liberation movement was bound to be Communist and had to be crushed. They also believed that the government of the Fourth Republic could not be relied upon to protect the security of France. "We centurions," reflected the paratroop hero in a best-selling novel, "are the last defenders of man's innocence against all those who want to enslave it in the name of original sin, against the Communists who refuse to have their children christened, never accept the conversion of an adult and are always ready to question it, but also against certain Christians who only talk of faults and forget about redemption."[60] Until this time, the prospect of de Gaulle's return to power had aroused little support, but now it seemed the perfect way to keep Algeria French.

The Return of de Gaulle. De Gaulle was hardly taken by surprise. Within six hours after Salan's pronunciamento, he replied that he was ready to assume the powers of the Republic. On 19 May, he held a press conference at the Hôtel Palais d'Orsay in Paris in which he expressed sympathy for the Algerian settlers' frustration with the Paris government. "How could such a population fail to revolt in the long run?" he asked. "It is absolutely normal and natural; and, then, it cries Vive de Gaulle as all Frenchmen do, in anguish and in hope." He praised the army for helping "to prevent this emotion from turning into disorder" and carefully tried to appease the principal groups that might oppose his resumption of power. Thus, his kindest words were for Guy Mollet, the leader of the Socialists, whose support he deemed absolutely crucial.

De Gaulle had made it plain that he would only come to power constitutionally, but he said that it was "obvious that this could not be done according to the rites and procedure that are so habitual that everyone is tired of them," and he proposed that the National Assembly directly invest him with full powers. Then, after making yet another declaration of his devotion to parliamentary democracy, he said he would return to his village of Colombey-les-deux-églises and "remain there at the disposal of the country."[61] The government began immediate discussions with de Gaulle, but while it was trying to establish a proper course of action, the rebels struck again.

On Saturday, 24 May, parachute units, acting under the orders of the Committee of Public Safety, seized the island of Corsica. The government had few resources on which it could rely: the army was Gaullist; the national gendarmerie and the Paris police were unreliable; and the labor unions were reluctant to call a general strike.[62] Moreover, the French people seemed indifferent. Parisians left the capital for their usual weekend in the country in greater numbers than before. Meanwhile, de Gaulle forestalled a Committee of Public Safety plan to seize power on the mainland by announcing that he had begun to form a government. Later, it was claimed that he had saved his country from civil war, but by then not very many French citizens were willing to die to save the Fourth Republic.

President René Coty, after persuading the current government to resign to avoid civil war, formally designated de Gaulle the new premier. On 1 June, de Gaulle presented himself to the National Assembly for confirmation of his powers. He read a short speech, asking for full powers to rule France for six months, during which he would reestablish order and restore unity. He made it clear, however, that he wanted to give France a new constitution, in which "the executive and the legislative branches must be separate and apart."[63] He was confirmed 327 to 224, with 37 abstentions.

During the twelve-year life of the Fourth Republic, governments were changed, on an average, about twice a year. The longest ministry, that of Guy Mollet (1956–1957), lasted sixteen months; the shortest, those of Robert Schuman (1948) and Henri Queuille (1950), were overthrown the same day they presented themselves to the National Assembly. An enormous amount of time—something over 300 days—was lost in negotiations to find a new government. The more the ministries changed, the more they remained the same. The ministers were interchangeable and constantly reappeared after a slight reshuffling of portfolios. This rapid turnover was almost identical to the experience of the Third Republic, especially the period between the wars. Article 51 of the 1946 constitution allowed for dissolution of the National Assembly and new elections if two cabinet crises—i.e., a formal vote of no confidence by an absolute majority of the deputies—occurred within a period of eighteen months. But the Council of Ministers, which exercised the power, was reluctant to take any steps that might increase the already existent divisions among the parties of the ruling coalition. Consequently, most governments left office before the specified constitutional provisions could be fulfilled: the governments either fell apart from internal feuding or resigned after losing a majority vote. Article 51 was used only once—in 1955, when the Radical Edgar Faure dissolved the National Assembly. Faure was subsequently thrown out of his own party for such audacity. The instability of the Fourth Republic was heightened because the country's two most powerful political forces—Communism and Gaullism—refused to accept the governmental system and were actively committed to its destruction.

The Fourth Republic ended, as had its three predecessors, with a savior assuming power. The French had a tradition of authoritarian, charismatic leaders. De Gaulle said he had no desire to save France by abolishing its basic liberties. Universal suffrage would continue as the source of all power, and the government would remain responsible to an elected assembly. "Why should I, at 67, begin a career as a dictator?" he asked.[64] His constitution, drafted by a specially appointed committee, perpetuated much of the parliamentary structure of the previous system. On paper, at least, the prime minister (the premier or president of the Council of Ministers under the Third and Fourth Republics) would continue to formulate and conduct state policy. However, the Fifth Republic differed significantly from its two immediate predecessors. The presidency was hardly the position of a figurehead. It was the focal point for the entire system, shifting the initiative of governance away from the legislature to the executive branch, which now had a commanding and independent advantage.

The French people endorsed the Fifth Republic constitution, on 28 September 1958, by a majority of nearly 80 percent. Remarkably, a substantial part of the working class and a large number of Communists voted for it. The parliamentary elections the following November were, by and large, a repeat performance. Most candidates, no matter what party, tried to get elected by professing loyalty to and faith in de Gaulle. The "Gaullist" party, the Union for the New Republic (*Union de la nouvelle république* or *UNR*), a hastily assembled collection of supporters and identifiers, emerged after the second round with 189 of the 467 seats in the assembly (over 40 percent). Leftist parties were the big losers. The Communists saw their strength dwindle from 145 in the previous legislature to a mere 10. The Socialists were down from 88 to 40. Even the middle-of-the-road Radicals, once the most prestigious of French parties, dropped from 55 to 13. With guaranteed support from other rightist parties, de Gaulle could rule as he chose. He appointed his own man, Michel Debré, to be prime minister and began to intervene actively in the business of government, all the while pretending he was above parties. "I am a man," he claimed, "who belongs to no one and who belongs to everyone."[65] He still freely identified himself with the French general will, but his skill as a politician stemmed from his ability to make his pretensions appear true or, as Georges Bidault put it, to make people believe that they owned "a piece of the True Cross of Lorraine."[66]

POSTWAR ITALY

Inauguration of a Republic

Constitutional Guarantees. Because of his close association with Fascism, King Victor Emmanuel III was not very popular. His strongest friends, the traditional ruling classes, who were similarly compromised, were currently in disarray and unable to give him their traditional support. The king hoped to protect his dynasty with a ruse. He would retire, not abdicate, and give his more popular son Umberto authority to act in his stead by naming him lieutenant-general of the realm.

The liberation brought a return of party government. The survival of any leader depended on the support he received from Italy's two major forces—the Marxists and the Catholics—and on the approval of the powerful Committee of National Liberation (CLN). In the year after the deliverance of Rome, on 4 June 1944, the moderate Labor Democrat Ivanoe Bonomi presided over the government. In June 1945, he was succeeded by Ferruccio Parri, a respected non-Communist leader of the northern armed resistance. Parri, a member of the small laic and republican Action party (*Partito d'azione*), became premier when the CLN deadlocked between the candidacies of Pietro Nenni (Socialist) and Alcide De Gasperi (Christian Democrat). Parri's government marked the furthest swing to the Left in postwar Italian politics. His vigorous attempt to purge the government and the bureaucracy of its Fascist elements was his undoing. In late autumn, the Conservatives succeeded in effecting his ouster, arguing that the purge should be halted so that the state could return to law and order. The government was also criticized for doing little to resolve the economic crisis or quiet Sicilian separatism. In December 1945, De Gasperi became premier, a post he held repeatedly until 1953. Christian Democrats, in fact, maintained a monopoly on the premiership until the early 1980s, but even then they continued to retain most of the cabinet posts.

Among the important items of business for these early governments was to prepare a referendum to decide the fate of the monarchy. Victor Emmanuel, fearful of the results, finally did abdicate, but the gesture came too late. The vote, held on 2 June 1946, showed that 54 percent of the electorate (12,717,923 to 10,719,284) favored scrapping the monarchy for a republic. The country had split along geographical lines: the south, including Rome, voted to retain the monarchy by 64 percent; in the more populous, industrially advanced north, the reverse was true. The vote was the first free election held in Italy since 1922. Some monarchists refused to accept its results and proposed rallying the south against the north. The new king, Umberto II, realized such a fight was useless and quietly went into exile. He had been his country's monarch for only thirty-four days.

At the same time the Italians sealed the fate of the monarchy, they also voted for a constituent assembly to draft a new Italian constitution. The results gave the newly formed Christian Democratic party (*Democrazia cristiana*) 35.2 percent of the vote and 207 seats in the assembly, the Socialists got 20.7 percent and 115 seats, and the Communists received 19 percent and 104 seats. The once powerful Liberals won only 6.8 percent and 41 seats.

The new constitution, which came into force in January 1948, was a curious blend of old and new. It guaranteed the inviolability of personal liberty, but perpetuated, in Article 13, preventive detention. The punitive legislation of the Fascist period was not automatically invalidated. People still could be charged with publishing falsehoods likely to disturb the public peace. They could be prohibited (until 1961) from moving from one locality to another unless they had a specific job offer. They could be ordered into exile without trial because they were believed to be a security risk. They could also be imprisoned on the ambiguous charge of *vilipendio*. Under the penal code, persons and institutions had honor that could be damaged by public criticism even when the attack was true. Thus, anyone could be jailed for speaking ill of the state, the armed forces, the police, the Catholic church, or a public official.[67]

The constitution recognized the rights of workers to join trade unions and engage in collective bargaining. However, the Fascist laws controlling labor migration still remained in force. A new law passed in 1949 reaffirmed the state's monopoly on regulating access to jobs. Thus, it was not unconstitutional to restrict a worker's employment to the area of his or her official residence. A worker who wanted to get a job elsewhere had to register in that area, but to register in another area, one had to have held a job elsewhere. The choice was to stay put or migrate illegally. In fact, the law was often violated, but workers who did so were usually paid much less than the going rate by their employers (who were also breaking the law). The legislation, rationalized as a means of controlling unemployment, was supported by powerful special interests. Industrialists favored it because they could hire labor at lower wages; the big agrarian groups liked it because it thwarted the emigration of cheap farm labor to the cities; the Communists welcomed it because they feared an influx of unintegrated workers; and municipal politicians approved it because the migration of unskilled labor to the cities would strain their social and educational systems. The prohibitions lasted until 1961.

Many articles of the 1937 Fascist Code of Public Security were still in force. During a state of emergency, provincial prefects had the authority to maintain order by whatever means they deemed necessary—even to the suspension of civil liberties. The recognition of the Lateran pacts as the law of the land likewise abridged freedom. Divorce was still illegal. The Roman Catholic clergy continued to enjoy special privileges. And criminal sanctions were applied to those who "either by word or deed" publicly offended or insulted the Sovereign Pontiff. Article 21 of the constitution officially recognized censorship. The article stated that everyone could freely "manifest his own thought by word, [and] by writing" as long as this was not "contrary to good morals." Thus, the publication, broadcasting, or performing of anything that violated this ambiguous standard was prohibited. An office to enforce this provision was established in the Ministry of Tourism and Spectacles. All scripts for movies, plays (until 1962), and radio and television shows had to be approved prior to public presentation.

Although the constitution guaranteed freedom of religion, Italy continued to be a virtual confessional state. Only Roman Catholics had the right to proselytize freely. Those who publicly questioned the validity of the 1929 Concordat could be prosecuted for offending the state religion. A 1931 Fascist law on public security was continually used to harass such Protestant evangelical denominations as the Church of Christ. Roman Catholic priests who were under ecclesiastical censure were still treated as second-class citizens and prevented from becoming state civil servants, schoolteachers, or municipal councillors. The Vatican, one of the principal defenders of state censorship, used Article 21 to frustrate any hostile social and political criticism.

Yet the constitution contained some attractive new features. A Constitutional Court was established that incorporated the American principle of judicial review. Under the old 1848 *Statuto*, the constitution could be amended by ordinary legislation, making it possible to use the democratic system to destroy the system. This was, in fact, what happened during the Fascist era. Now, such laws could be ruled unconstitutional, making a return to dictatorship more difficult. Another innovation recognized the country's diversity by creating nineteen federalized regions (later raised to 20) with limited powers of home rule. In addition, there were special grants of autonomy for the three frontier areas of Val d'Aosta, Trentino–Alto Adige, and Friuli–Venezia Giulia and for the two islands of Sicily and Sardinia. The move was intended to discourage local separatism. In Sicily, for example, there was a movement to become the forty-ninth state of the United States. Regionalization conferred on these units certain powers of finance and control over public services: the maintenance of schools, roads, health, and abandoned children. These powers were exercised through regional councils and assemblies that were established over the following two decades by statute.

The constitution established a parliamentary system with a bicameral legislature: the Chamber of Deputies and the Senate, to which the cabinet—the Council of Ministers—was legally responsible. The president, Italy's chief of state, appointed the prime minister, who then formed a government, provided it received the confidence of the legislature. In this multiparty system, ministries changed frequently: between 1945 and 1960, on an average of every nine months. Initially, however, there was no great instability because of the predominant position of the Christian Democratic party. Its leader, Alcide De Gasperi, served uninterrupted as prime minister from December 1945 to August 1953. His party continued to be the backbone of every government.

The Formation of Parties. Modern party government was an unknown commodity. Even before the Fascist period, political groups were not genuinely representative nor were they well organized. The groups in parliament had been formed mostly around individuals whose position was based on local influence rather than on any political program. Only the Socialists and the Popular party (*Partito popolare*) had really possessed permanent organization that provided a basis on which a postwar party structure could be built.

The Christian Democrats were the Popular party's reincarnation. De Gasperi, their leader, was one of the few members who had genuine professional experience. He had not only served under Don Sturzo before the Popolari were outlawed in 1924, but had also been a member of the Austro-Hungarian parliament before World War I. The Fascists arrested him in 1927, releasing him two years later after the Vatican intervened on his behalf. During most of the Fascist dictatorship, De Gasperi worked as a librarian in the Vatican. He felt that "governing a state creates an intimate tie with God our Father and . . . a responsibility which is immediate toward the people, but toward a people seen as a mediator of the divine will that governs us."[68] It was therefore natural for his party to look to the papacy for support. In many Italian towns and villages, the party headquarters was located next-door to the church.

During the 1920s, the papacy had sacrificed the Popolari to form an association with Mussolini. Now, however, with the Fascists in disgrace and the monarchists in disarray, there were no strong rightist parties around to challenge the parties of the Left. Present necessity dictated that the Christian Democrats receive papal endorsement. Nevertheless, Pius XII disagreed with many of the party's modernist positions, specifically, the establishment of public health services, free public education, and religious freedom. Pius usually made little distinction between Communists and Socialists and was disturbed to learn that the first postwar government of the Christian Democrats included representatives from both of these parties.

De Gasperi had formed his first cabinets with the anticlerical Socialists and Communists because government without them would have been difficult; together they controlled more seats in the Chamber than his own Christian Democrats. Besides, it was a time of national reconciliation, and the Marxists were likewise committed to social legislation and industrial reform. Still there was something ominous in their joint declaration of October 1946, "to achieve the concentration of all popular forces in the struggle against the conservative reactionary forces and [to work] for the conquest of power on the part of the working classes."[69]

The strength of the Christian Democratic party, as well as its weakness, derived from its diversity and its ability to maintain a certain amount of cohesion among its factions and their various social, regional, personal, and political interests. The right wing was a staunch champion of the rights and prerogatives of the papacy and the privileges of the rich and well-born, while the party's reformist wing was more socially conscious and committed to Christian charity and public service. De Gasperi spent most of his political life trying to steer a middle course between the extremists on the Left and the reactionaries on the Right inside as well as outside his own party. Many members of the traditional Italian Right had joined the Christian Democratic party in hopes of bringing about a conservative restoration. Committed, usually elderly, monarchists joined the Italian Democratic Party of Monarchical Unity (*Partito democratico italiano di unità monarchica*), while die-hard former Fascists joined the essentially Rome-based Italian Social Movement (*Movimento sociale italiano*).

The Communist party (*Partito comunista italiano*), led by Palmiro Togliatti, was the second most important party in Italy. The Communists showed a willingness to play by constitutional rules, but only insofar as doing so served their long-range purpose. Like other Marxist-Leninist parties, they subscribed to the rules of democratic centralism. No one could be sure whether they would maintain a pluralistic system should they actually come to power. The party won considerable popularity because many of its members had been willing to risk their lives in the armed struggle against Mussolini and the Germans. They also appeared to be one of the few parties that was sincerely committed to social change and to the improvement of the lot of the lower classes. Togliatti set his initial postwar strategy at a meeting at Salerno in March 1944.[70] He said that it was his intention to create a "new party" that would work with the Christian Democrats, the Socialists, and other parties to build a new society within the present system.

Operating under this new Popular Front strategy, the Communists helped draft the liberal democratic constitution and were even willing to support the inclusion of the 1929 Concordat. Their members served in all of De Gasperi's cabinets until they became too threatening and were thrown out in May 1947. Even during the Moscow-inspired protest riots against the Marshall Plan and against the inclusion of Italy in the western security alliance, the North Atlantic Treaty, Togliatti preferred to try to come to power through the ballot box. Had the Communists managed to pull it off, Togliatti would not have been the firm supporter of democracy as he pretended, although he would not have slavishly followed the lead of the Soviet Union. Stalin purportedly so distrusted Togliatti that he tried to entice him away from active leadership of the Italian Communist party by offering him the post of secretary-general of the Cominform in 1951. Togliatti's resignation would have cleared the way for the succession of Pietro Secchia, a man more willing to follow directives from Moscow. Whether the reports of Stalin's mistrust are true or not, Togliatti undoubtedly had his own ideas about a separate road to authoritarian socialism.

The Communists, unable to reenter a government coalition, much less gain power on their own, concentrated their energies on regional development and reform. The center of their local power base lay in the industrial centers of the north, the so-called Red Belt regions of Tuscany, Emilia-Romagna, and Umbria. For example, after 1946 they controlled the government of Bologna, making it a showpiece of urban reform. They rescued the historic district, adapting the old buildings to modern needs by installing nurseries, community centers, and public libraries in old palaces, monasteries, and churches. They built retirement homes and expanded health care, improved sanitation, and promoted traffic reform. As the Italians became more prosperous and political dogmatism lessened, the Communist party abandoned its commitment to the dictatorship of the proletariat and under a new liberal leader, Enrico Berlinguer (secretary of the party from 1972 until his death in 1984), seemingly endorsed democracy, even accepting that Italy should "in principle" remain a member of the North Atlantic Treaty Organization. These changes helped to calm many fears about Communist intentions, but did not bring the party any closer to national power.

The Communists managed to bring about this transformation of philosophy without destroying the unity of their party. The Socialists did not have it so easy.

From the time of the liberation, the Socialists could not agree on whether to be revolutionary or evolutionary, whether to work within the system or to overthrow it. The divisions, which were old ones dating back to the nineteenth century, resulted in constant confusion, bewilderment, and bemusement—all adding up to a loss of influence. The unity achieved in the Italian Socialist Party of Proletarian Unity (*Partito socialista di unità proletaria*) after the liberation did not last long. In 1947, the party's right—that is, nonviolent—wing formed its own faction, the Italian Workers' Socialist party (*Partito socialista dei lavoratori italiani*), in protest over the continued alliance with the Communists. Its leader, Giuseppe Saragat, believed that the mutual hatred of the proletariat and the middle class had contributed to the triumph of Fascism and was determined to prevent this from happening again. "We have seen," he said, "that always when the proletariat has linked to itself the workers of the middle classes by means of a truly democratic policy, there has been progress; and it is precisely when the proletariat has rebuffed them that there have been catastrophes."[71]

Further defections from the main party followed, resulting in the establishment of still more Socialist parties. The pro-Communist radicals who remained in the original party followed the leadership of Pietro Nenni, whose fellow traveler positions made it impossible for the Socialists to build an effective loyal opposition to the conservative Christian Democrats. A net result of the Socialists' ineffectiveness was the continued success of the Christian Democrats. Indeed, Saragat's moderates believed that the best way to achieve social justice and prevent a return of monopolistic capitalism was through continued cooperation with the Christian Democrats, even though this party contained many of the elements that had once supported Mussolini's dictatorship.

The failure of the Socialists to achieve unity was one of the most important negative factors of Italian politics in the postwar era, but support from the moderate wing was necessary for De Gasperi to remove the Communists from his cabinet in 1947, a move the Vatican and the United States welcomed. Indeed, some suggested that the Americans had threatened to withhold credits if this were not accomplished. In time, however, the virtual stranglehold the party had on the reins of power made its leaders increasingly more concerned with promoting special interests and less responsive to change and reform. Anti-Communism alone was not sufficient to create a dynamic ruling tradition or to develop an effective social conscience.

The Fragility of Centrist Government. The elections of April 1948—in which over one hundred parties ran candidates—produced a landslide victory for the Christian Democrats, who received 48.5 percent of the vote, giving them control of 305 of the 574 seats in the lower chamber. Despite Vatican threats that anyone who voted Communist was committing a mortal sin, the Communists came in second with a substantial 31 percent of the vote and 183 seats. The Vatican now tried to induce De Gasperi to form a one-party Roman Catholic government, but the prime minister refused and added representatives from the Liberal, Republican, and moderate Socialist parties to his cabinet. De Gasperi wisely attempted to avoid the acrimonious division between clericals and anticlericals that had so clouded the political atmosphere of the nineteenth century.

Under the Christian Democrats, the country was dominated by some of the groups that had earlier supported Mussolini: big business, landowners, and the Roman Catholic church. For the most part, organized labor was not under the thumb of the Christian Democrats, but because the working-class movements were so rent by schisms and factionalism, the conservatives were able to resist their demands for greater participation in political and economic decision making. The situation had parallels in the working of the Italian parliamentary system in the generation before World War I. For a decade and a half following the liberation, the Christian Democratic party became "the natural focus of opportunists and self-serving interests,"[72] behaving as if its anti-Communism excused an all-too-frequent association with financial and moral corruption. In betraying the public trust, it helped to bring parliamentary democracy into disrepute. De Gasperi spent much of his time trying to keep the Communists at bay in the legislature and the reactionaries at bay in his own party. Although he tried to maintain a reasonable independence from the church, his political strength depended critically on the influence the Vatican exercised over one-third of the Italian electorate.

Consequently, Roman Catholic influence grew steadily and was frequently decisive in determining who would advance in public service. The church was active in the censorship of the arts. It obtained state subsidies for parochial schools and carried religious instruction into the state schools. The semiofficial Catholic Action society constantly pushed for the formation of a rightist coalition of Christian Democrats, monarchists, and neo-Fascists. Its head, Luigi Gedda, threatened to form a new authoritarian church party despite De Gasperi's opposition.

The Christian Democrats' campaign rhetoric proclaimed the humanization of capitalism through social welfare. The role of government was to protect small businesses, small farmers, shopkeepers, and artisans and the poorer regions of the country. The party's left wing did take these things seriously, but many more party members were not particularly sensitive to the economic problems of underdogs. By 1953, the popularity of the Christian Democrats had slipped perceptibly. In preparation for the elections, the government passed a law reminiscent of the Acerbo Law of the Fascist period, which enabled a party with only a bare plurality of the votes to take two-thirds of the seats in parliament. The Christian Democrats failed to do so and thereby lost power in the Chamber of Deputies.[73] The 1953 election was a clear victory for the extremes. The monarchists and Fascists gained one-eighth of the seats in the Chamber; the Communists increased their strength, particularly in rural areas where dissatisfaction over the government's failure to enact an effective program of land reform ran high. When De Gasperi found he could not organize a strong government, he resigned and retired from politics. He died one year later.

The decline of centrist government initiated a period of increased political instability. For the next five years, a series of minority left-of-center ministries ruled Italy. They simply tried to hold their own against the political extremes.

The legislative immobility, together with a succession of political scandals, blighted the faith of Italians in centrist government. About 40 percent of them voted for extremist parties. "If only *he* were back, there would be order," people would say. They were referring to Mussolini. The Duce's widow, Donna Rachele, capitalizing on renewed sympathy for Fascism, opened a restaurant near Forlì in northern Italy. Featured on her menu were such delights as "spaghetti Blackshirt," "beefsteak Benito," and "Fascist Empire sponge cake." The government's fear of the extremists and unwillingness to push for further reform meant that Fascist civil and criminal law and Fascist civil and criminal trial procedure continued in force.

All in all, it is remarkable that representative institutions were as strong as they were, considering that most of the adult population had never known democratic government; that (as late as 1957) about 90 percent of the people had only five years or less of formal education; that most of the country south of Rome had hardly evolved from feudalism; and that practically all the political parties of post-war Italy officially embraced philosophies that, if carried to their logical extreme, would fundamentally deny the right of other organizations to function. Part of the answer lies in the caliber of the country's leaders; many of them were sensible men who sincerely wanted to build a new society on the discredited ruins of Fascism, even though the odds against them were great.

Although the legislators were ultimately accountable to the voters, the judges seemed accountable to no one. As a consequence, for the average Italian, justice was at best an abstract commodity. The courts sometimes took as long as three to six years to settle a routine case involving an automobile accident. More serious affairs could go through as many as four trials, with each court reaching a different verdict because each tried the case over from the beginning. Furthermore, the judiciary was so completely immersed in politics that rightist judges tended to impose their own conservative morals on the law while leftist judges viewed the courts as another element in the class struggle.[74] Frequently, basic civil liberties got lost in the shuffle. A certain police state mentality left over from the Fascist era still permeated the system. Arrests for sedition and disturbance of the peace were often made on the slightest suspicion. Because Italy had no bail, suspects in felony cases (whether they were accused of stealing a toy airplane or a Boeing 707) could be held in jail as long as four years before their case might come to trial. Yearly, thousands of individuals, including hundreds of motorists involved in automobile accidents, were routinely detained for questioning; sometimes they spent many months behind bars before being released without ever having been brought to trial. Only in 1972 were judges given discretionary authority to grant provisional liberty. Gaetano Salvemini, a distinguished historian and anti-Fascist, once remarked that if the police were to accuse him of raping the statue of the little Madonna on top of the Milan cathedral, he "would think first of escaping and only later of defending [himself] against the charge."[75]

The Economic Miracle

Foreign Aid and Reconstruction. The Fascist system had recklessly squandered national resources in a futile pursuit of glory: in 1935, the Italians attacked Ethiopia; from 1936 to 1939, they fought in Spain; then they conquered Albania; in 1940, they attacked France and Britain and then Greece. In 1941, they went marching into Yugoslavia. By 1943, the destruction that Mussolini had so freely brought to others had finally come home. For two years, it swept the entire length of the peninsula, leaving the Italians destitute and homeless. In addition, almost 450,000 people—30 percent of them civilians—had lost their lives. Over one-third of the nation's highways were destroyed or heavily damaged; 8,000 bridges were blown apart; 40 percent of the railroad stations were unusable; and 75 percent of the rolling stock was irreparable. The gross national product had tumbled to half of its level in 1938.

The war had been financed by lavish deficit spending, which expanded the amount of money in circulation by eighteen times and bloated the entire credit structure. At the time of the liberation, the Italian price index was twenty-five times its 1938 level. Yet prices continued to rise because money hoarded during the war reappeared, and the Allied military government put a new currency in circulation. Credit, unregulated by the government, expanded at a precipitous rate. Between July 1946 and September 1947, the Bank of Italy and other private banks loaned out some 590 billion lira (about $1.7 billion), more than the market could comfortably absorb. National production, though increasing, still remained below its prewar level. Only those fortunate workers whose wage scales were pegged to a cost of living index kept pace with inflation. Most Italians suffered terribly. The inflation also seriously affected Italy's foreign exchange. Between 1945 and May 1947, the lira depreciated from 100 to 906 to the dollar, while bad harvests drastically cut the supply and raised the cost of food. The ensuing discontent was a passport for the success of Communism.

The Allies could not afford the political risks of Italian pauperism, but as long as British and American troops directly held power in the north (which they did until December 1945), there was little danger of a Communist takeover. The military government controlled the allocation of raw materials and opposed any policy for the redistribution of wealth. The Americans defined "socialistic solutions" rather broadly and usually supported the Italian conservatives who opposed the imposition of controls and drastic reforms. The factories and plants, which had been commandeered and operated by special factory councils of the local resistance, were restored to their former owners. The National Liberation Committees were prevented from controlling local government.

De Gasperi wanted to revitalize the Italian economy, not revolutionize it. He favored market liberalization and eliminated most of the controls imposed by Mussolini on agriculture and industry. Nevertheless, the Christian Democrats wanted recovery to occur within the existing framework of the established business and industrial interests. This laissez-faire style of economics intensified the already serious inflation inherited from the Fascist era, endangering the Christian Democratic program of social progress. Matters could no longer be left to sort themselves out.

On 30 May 1947, De Gasperi transformed his committee on credit and saving into a sort of economic general staff. He appointed Professor Luigi Einaudi to be his deputy premier and ordered him to stabilize Italian finances. Einaudi was a staunch anti-Fascist and a liberal classical economist who preferred to curb inflation by the traditional methods of restricting credit and raising the discount rate. He ordered an increase in commercial bank reserves and forbade the Treasury to draw money from the state bank without specific legislation. The strategy exceeded expectations. Prices fell, foreign exchange stabilized, speculation declined, and savings increased. Italy began to invest in the raw materials and equipment necessary for industrial growth.

Unemployment, however, remained high, rising to almost two million in 1947. Einaudi held fast to his tight money policy, believing that a stable monetary system would automatically produce investment and growth. Indeed, Italy's recession proved temporary. In 1948, production began to rise and unemployment started to fall. The following year, Italians were producing more than they had before the war. The progress continued. Over the next two decades, the economy grew at more than five percent a year.[76] Einaudi was rewarded for his service by being elected the first president of Italy under the new constitution that went into effect in 1948. He served for seven years (1948–1955).

State Proprietorship. As long as inflation was kept in check, the Christian Democratic leaders saw no need to draft a general plan for the country's economic growth. Besides the state already exercised a commanding position in the economy. Most of the major Italian enterprises were already monopolies or semimonopolies in which the state had a direct financial interest. This situation dated from the Great Depression, when the Fascist government acquired vast amounts of stock in

Italian companies to save them from bankruptcy. In 1933, these holdings were organized into the Institute of Industrial Reconstruction (IIR), a conglomerate that ultimately administered a complex of 125 joint stock companies. After World War II, the institute included about one-quarter of Italy's industrial capital, divided into several main subsidiaries.

One subsidiary, *Finmare*, controlled most of Italy's shipping; *Fincantieri* accounted for four-fifths of its shipbuilding; *Finsider* controlled two-thirds of the country's iron and steel industry; *Fin-Meccanica* directed an assortment of engineering and mechanical companies, including automobile production (Alfa Romeo), electrical appliances, electronics, and optical instruments; *Stet* ran a complex of urban and interurban telephone services; and *Finelettrica* directed (until electricity was nationalized in 1962) one-fourth of the electrical power industry. The state also held the paramount interest in three of Italy's largest commercial banks (the Banca Commerciale, the Banco di Credito, and the Banca di Roma). In addition, it controlled radio and television broadcasting, the Italian Air Lines, and a potpourri of glass, paper, and plastics companies. By continuing the holding company pattern, the state demonstrated a desire to provide direction for economic development and expansion, albeit along rather different lines than French national planning.

Thus, in 1953, the state established another holding company, the National Association of Hydrocarbons (NAH), to administer its oil and natural gas interests. The holding company participated in every aspect of the industry from exploration and drilling to transportation, refining, and marketing. Subsidiaries of this company produced drilling equipment, developed atomic power, and operated a chain of motels. The government acquired control over the entire natural gas production of the Po valley and, under the direction of Enrico Mattei, built this monopoly into one of the most important elements of Italy's postwar industrial expansion. Mattei often acted on his own initiative; he negotiated an agreement with the Soviet Union to have Soviet oil transported by pipeline through Eastern Europe to Italy. Before his death in 1962, he had developed the NAH into one of the world's largest state hydrocarbon industries.

The IIR was a crucial element in promoting Italy's "economic miracle." Its enterprises operated within the framework of the market economy, but they possessed certain advantages not shared by private companies: the government would never allow any of its companies to default or go bankrupt, no matter how much money it lost (shipbuilding and the mechanical industries often had deficits), and state enterprises never had much difficulty obtaining investment capital. Government ownership of industry was a blend of corporatism and capitalism. The state rarely possessed all of the stock in the companies it controlled. The rest was held by private investors, who shared seats on the boards of directors with the government. Through such arrangements, the state could keep the politicians at arm's length while providing the necessary capital investment to create a modern economy. This government-fueled boom in investment encouraged others to put their money to work, including the Catholic church.

The modern wealth of the Vatican came from the assets it had received from the 1929 Concordat with Mussolini. Using this windfall wisely, the church amassed one of the greatest financial empires in Italy and gained control of hundreds of Italian industries. It directed one of the five main units of the State Institute for Industrial Reconstruction, *Finsider*, which rolled about two-thirds of Italian steel and also produced metal tubing, cement, and pig iron.[77] The church's principal investments were in real estate, however. Its *Società generale immobiliare (SGI)* was one of the largest hotel, office, and apartment building promoters in the world.[78] SGI's gross assets were worth around $50 million in 1955; twelve years later, their value had climbed to $170 million.[79]

Italian economic vitality was also evident in great private industrial firms like Fiat for automobiles, Pirelli for tires, Olivetti for office equipment, Beretta for armaments, Montecatini Edison for chemicals, and Snia Viscosa for textiles, to name just a few. In addition, Italy's tourist industry was Europe's largest, providing important seasonal employment for hundreds of thousands of people from Venetian gondoliers to Neapolitan waiters. Through these invisible exports, the Italians lived off their country's natural beauty and the art treasures in its museums. Yet, Italy's economic growth was due as much and perhaps even more to the country's exuberant "home industries." Many of these small-scale enterprises were owned by families who worked for themselves, usually with no more than seven employees.[80] These businesses, which turned out such products as knitted wear, jewelry, household goods, straw hats, machine tools, and precision equipment, worked long hours and kept costs low, enhancing their competitiveness. Moreover, their limited inventories and small outlays for equipment made them better able to take advantage of changes in the market than were larger, more established concerns. Only a small number of these small enterprises operated openly. Italy had one of the largest underground economies in Europe. The output from these under-the-table businesses, which avoided government control and taxation, probably added from 15 to 30 percent to the gross national product.

The popular view of the Italians as a people who spend long hours lounging around in idle chitchat belies the hard work that they performed to make their country one of Europe's industrial powerhouses. However, prosperity was not achieved by hard work alone. The Marshall Plan provided investment capital, but equally important was the boost offered by favorable terms of trade, especially low-cost raw materials, credit, and improved technology. While the standard of living of many Italians was now comparable to that of other Western European countries, Italy had one of the lowest per capita incomes.[81] Wealth was not distributed evenly. The greatest gains in industrial growth came in the area of the country that was already the most prosperous—north of the line traced by the Po River across the Lombardian plain from Piedmont to Venetia with particular concentration on the region around Milan. Italy's poorhouse continued to be the south, the old kingdom of Naples, the *mezzogiorno*, with the islands of Sicily and Sardinia.

The Problem of the South. The area south of Rome contained over one-third of the country's people and land area, but in 1950, it produced only one-fifth of the country's gross national product. The area had few natural resources. The sun had burned its soil; its roads were poor; and its people bore the weight of poverty, superstition, and violence. Its social structure had existed almost unchanged since the Middle Ages. The south was usually the last area to receive government aid, and private investors preferred to place their funds in already established markets where returns were surer and higher. Unification (the *Risorgimento*) had brought few benefits. Efforts to solve the problems of the south never seemed to get much farther than the discussion stage. The people who lived there were distinctly Mediterranean and had a dramatically different social culture and work ethic from that of the northerners. Centuries of foreign domination and exploitation had taught southerners to feel little obligation to serve the public interest or society as a whole; it was said that they put more emphasis on being clever than on being industrious.[82] They had a reputation of being warmhearted and compassionate, but

The more things change, the more they stay the same. Despite the economic miracle, life for many Italians went on much as it had before. Naples contained some of Europe's worst slums.

extremely reluctant to cooperate or compromise. Northerners generally regarded them as unfit for modern society and, indeed, somewhat barbaric. Nevertheless, after World War II, the politicians recognized that, unless something were done to bridge the gap between the two Italies, the prosperity of the entire country would suffer.

In 1950, the Christian Democratic government established the *Cassa per il mezzogiorno*, a credit institution with special authority to promote the social and economic growth of the south. Priority was given to the long-term improvement of agriculture with additional subsidies going to the development of water supplies, transportation, communications, industry, and tourism. The state hoped to entice private industry into the area by creating a modern infrastructure and by agreeing to advance up to 70 percent of the cost of land and equipment for the construction of new factories. The state-controlled Institute for Industrial Reconstruction was required to make three-fifths of its new investments in the south, and from 1950 to 1960, the Italian government spent about $6 billion on development in the area. The results were disappointing. The south was treated as a colony of the imperial industrial north. Frequently, the Christian Democrats used the Cassa per il mezzogiorno as a source of political patronage and dispensed its funds to likely supporters. On the positive side, though, the Cassa helped to reduce the traditional power of the landlords, but it encouraged thousands of young men to move elsewhere.

In 1960, the south had a per capita income of $297 a year, compared to $702 for the rest of the country. With the exception of certain regional complexes, such as the steel plants of Taranto and the petrochemical refineries at Gela, the south was hardly conducive to industrial development. Southern workers were largely unskilled and were ill equipped to work in the new, more highly automated factories, which required less, but more highly skilled, labor than the older plants. In addition, the region lacked the necessary infrastructure to support profitable industry; roads and other transportation facilities were still so poor, for example, that transportation costs were prohibitive. Energy was also a problem. The south lacked the hydroelectric power of the north, and with the discovery of new reserves of methane gas in the north, the energy gap between north and south widened. Agriculture was as backward as industry. It proved easier to break up large estates and decree the elimination of small, marginal farms than to develop the expertise to make the farms productive. Even when agriculture improved, greedy middlemen siphoned off the profits, leaving the producers as impoverished as before. Private industry, reluctant to follow the lead of the government, continued to invest in the more profitable north. Consequently, no matter how much the south improved, the rest of the country continued to grow at a faster rate.

One of the chief forces retarding the economic development of the south was local politics. For example, in western Sicily one of the strongest bulwarks against modernization was the *Mafia*, the criminal organization that sold protection against itself. This society, which developed in feudal times, owed its position and influence to its hold over the island's scarce resources. Its leaders would thus oppose the construction of aqueducts or dams because these projects might endanger the power they had over the peasants who depended on Mafia-controlled artesian wells. The *mafiosi* also ran a wide variety of rackets: they engaged in the recovery of stolen property; allocated monopolies to shopkeepers and artisans; managed the sale of plots in cemeteries; acted as middlemen for fishermen and farmers; and manufactured and sold devotional candles and religious relics. Among the items a Mafia enterprise exported to the United States in 1962 were "twenty suits of armour of Joan of Arc, twenty monastic gowns worn by St. Francis of Assisi, fifty rosaries alleged to have belonged to Bernadette, and . . . the wand carried by Moses when he led the children of Israel into the Promised Land."[83]

After the war, the Mafia took advantage of the power vacuum resulting from the political collapse of Fascism, and assumed direct control of the government in half the villages of Sicily. At first, many mafiosi were promoters of Sicilian separatism. When the central government granted Sicily local autonomy in May 1946, however, many mafiosi became supporters and allies of the Christian Democrats. Younger dons saw association with Italy's main political party as an avenue to new wealth and power. Extorting money from a factory owner or a construction company could be more profitable than terrorizing goat farmers. Owning real estate in Palermo brought more power than controlling olive trees in Corleone. The revenues from drug trafficking were astronomical compared to the sale of bogus religious relics. To these opportunists, the plan to develop the south was simply a means of increasing their wealth and influence, and their affiliation with the Christian Democrats made them virtually immune from prosecution.

But such corruption and terrorism were self-defeating. Sicilians abandoned their homeland in droves—in the decade between 1951 and 1961, some 400,000 left, more than 10 percent of the population. Most of these were young men who went north to find work, leaving behind their women and children and elderly parents. Capital from the mainland also disappeared as investors found the payment of protection a needless business expense. Thus, these sections of Sicily participated even less than other parts of the *mezzogiorno* in Italy's great economic miracle.[84]

POSTSCRIPT   Governments could no longer exist on promises alone. People expected them to provide more services and perform more duties than they had done in the past, chief among these being social security. During World War I, governments had become involved in all aspects of the nation's economy, but after the conflict was over, most states returned to the status quo ante. The result was unmitigated inflation and depression. After 1945, however, recovery would not be left to unpredictable market forces. Growth would be planned. Technocrats, nonelected officials, and experts with power exceeding those of elected officials would resolve economic problems once left to legislatures.

People took the rise of the public sector in stride. They had become used to wartime controls and welcomed the expanded welfare programs. In Britain, Aneurin Bevan hailed the success of the national health program: "Society becomes more wholesome, more serene, and spiritually healthier, if it knows that its citizens have at the back of their consciousness the knowledge that not only themselves, but all their fellows, have access when ill, to the best that medical skill can provide."[85] Yet the best in practice was often a far cry from what was first envisioned. The social services in all countries were overloaded. Furthermore, the benefits of economic growth all too often failed to be distributed equally throughout society. But despite such problems, great reforms all contributed to weakening the old society, making the economies more progressive, and making Europeans less class-conscious.

An immense change had, indeed, occurred. The average standard of living had risen dramatically. The boom created more opportunities for career advancement and, to that extent, broke down barriers to upward social mobility. Furthermore, benefits that were once considered radical were now taken for granted: free education and medical care, unemployment compensation, old-age pensions, family subsidies, and retirement income. During the 1950s, Western European peoples were better off than they ever had been; their rate of economic growth was historically unprecedented. Unemployment virtually disappeared, and income and the benefits of national productivity were more equitably distributed. Vast demographic changes had occurred as people flocked out of small towns and rural areas into the larger cities. By the decade of the 1960s, most Western Europeans had become more "middle class" in their outlook. Although all the major countries continued to have their share of have-nots, the postwar social revolution was based on the assumptions that all people should be guaranteed a minimum level of subsistence and that great differences in wealth were an insult to civilized society.

ENDNOTES

1.   Clement R. Attlee, *As It Happened* (New York: Viking Press, 1954), 229.
2.   Winston S. Churchill, *The Hinge of Fate* (Boston: Houghton, Mifflin, 1950), 959.

3. During the 1930s, the average output of French workers was consistently inferior to that of workers in most of the other major industrial nations. In 1938, the British worker outproduced the French worker by 22 percent, but American workers outproduced their French counterparts by more than four times.

4. "Constitution of the Italian Republic," Articles 3 and 36 in Norman Kogan, *The Government of Italy* (New York: Thomas Y. Crowell, 1964), 188–89, 193.

5. Winston S. Churchill, *Victory, War Speeches* (London: Cassell, 1946), 189.

6. In the popular vote, no party actually received a majority. Out of 25 million votes cast, Labour won 12 million, the Conservatives and their allies about 10 million, and the Liberals, as usual grossly underrepresented, 2.5 million.

7. The loan was advanced at a scant 2 percent interest. John Maynard Keynes, who negotiated the loan from Washington, managed to get an additional $1.25 billion from Canada. More from the United States would come later. From 1945 to 1950, Britain received slightly over $7 billion in Marshall Plan aid.

8. *Annual Register, 1946*, 101.

9. The practice was discontinued in 1955 when the Exchequer handled all such financing directly.

10. Roy Harrod, *The British Economy* (New York: McGraw-Hill, 1963), 106.

11. *Annual Register, 1946* (London: Longmans, 1946), 28.

12. Kenneth O. Morgan, *Labour in Power, 1951–1954* (Oxford: Clarendon Press, 1984), 151–63.

13. Attlee, *As It Happened*, 233.

14. *Hansard*, 418, col. 1900.

15. *Annual Register, 1947*, 78.

16. The production indexes, using 1937 as 100, were as follows: 94 in 1938; 90 in 1946; 98 in 1947; 109 in 1948; 116 in 1949; and 124 in 1950. *United Nations Statistical Yearbook, 1949–50* (New York: United Nations, 1950), 139.

17. Attlee, *As It Happened*, 290.

18. The Tories and their allies won 321 seats; Labour, 295; and the Liberals, 6.

19. *The Diaries of Sir Alexander Cadogan* (London: Cassell, 1971), 786.

20. *A King's Story, The Memoirs of the Duke of Windsor* (New York: G. P. Putnam's Sons, 1947), 180.

21. Winston Churchill served again from October 1951 to April 1955, Anthony Eden from April 1955 to January 1957, Harold Macmillan from January 1957 to October 1963, and Alex Douglas-Home from October 1963 to October 1964.

22. The Economic Survey for 1951 predicted defense spending would double within the next fiscal year, causing an adverse reduction in the exports of coal and metal products.

23. Harold Macmillan, *Riding the Storm* (New York: Harper and Row, 1971), 181.

24. The figures are based on the number and the capital value of estates over 100,000 pounds on which duty was paid.

25. See Trevor D. Burridge, *Clement Attlee: A Political Biography* (London: Jonathan Cape, 1985); and Kenneth Harris, *Attlee* (New York: Norton, 1982).

26. Attlee, *As It Happened*, 31.

27. See Brian Crozier, *De Gaulle* (London: Eyre Methuen, 1974).

28. Especially, Basil Liddell Hart, Jean-Baptiste Estienne, and Colonel J. F. C. Fuller.

29. General Eisenhower explained this predicament: "If de Gaulle was a loyal Frenchman, [the professional soldiers] had to regard themselves as cowards. Naturally, the officers did not choose to think of themselves in this light; rather they considered themselves as loyal Frenchmen carrying out the orders of constituted civilian authority, and it followed that they officially and personally regarded de Gaulle as a deserter." Dwight D. Eisenhower, *Crusade in Europe* (New York: Doubleday, 1948), 84.

30. Churchill, *The Hinge of Fate*, 958.

31. In 1944, production was about one-third of what it had been in 1937. The output of wheat had been 9,800 metric tons in 1938, but was only 4,210 metric tons in 1945. The output of potatoes was 17,310 metric tons in 1938; 6,060 in 1945. The

output of sugar beets was 7,980 metric tons in 1938; 4,470 in 1945. The output of wine was 60,300 hectoliters in 1938; 28,600 seven years later.

32. From an index of 311 in 1944 to 461 in 1945; 706 in 1946; 1,049 in 1947 and its all-time high 1,664 in 1948. Brian R. Mitchell, *European Historical Statistics, 1750–1970* (New York: Columbia University Press, 1975), 253, 269, 280, 282, 745.

33. Charles de Gaulle, *War Memoirs, Salvation* (New York: Simon and Schuster, 1960), 8.

34. Ibid., 20.

35. Quoted by Jules Roy, *The Trial of Marshal Pétain* (New York, 1968), 18.

36. Ibid., 67–68.

37. In their first two years of operation, the special courts handled about 125,000 cases of collaboration; thereafter the number of trials diminished rapidly. Around 40,000 accused were found guilty of *indignité nationale* and deprived of their civil and political rights (sometimes the right to live in France) for varying periods. An equal number received prison sentences. Another 2,000 were condemned to death, but less than 800 sentences were carried out. Within five years after the end of the war, most of those still in jail received amnesties. The High Court sat for the last time in July 1949, and soon all trials ceased. They had become too unpopular; few people wanted to be reminded of the inglorious war years.

38. Roosevelt assumed that the British and Americans would administer France until a suitable government was found. In the meantime, he would allow de Gaulle's Committee for National Liberation to assume responsibility for maintaining public order in the areas of liberated France outside the battle zones, but French politics would have to serve Allied strategy. De Gaulle was not content with these arrangements. He had already prepared a list of candidates for every important post in the French government, including prefects in the départements; as the country was liberated, he had these men immediately installed in their assigned positions. In Paris, substitute ministers acted as stand-ins, pending the arrival of proper designates. Thus, de Gaulle hoped to frustrate any plans for an Allied military government. The strategy paid off. After the liberation of Paris, the Allies recognized the fait accompli and accorded de Gaulle the recognition they had previously denied him.

39. The Radical party, which had ruled the parliamentary destiny of France during the last years of the Third Republic, won only 29 seats.

40. De Gaulle, *War Memoirs, Salvation*, 271–72.

41. Ibid., 325.

42. The Communists controlled 182 delegates—the largest single representation.

43. Raymond Aron, "The Political 'System' of the Fourth Republic" in James Friguglietti and Emmet Kennedy, *The Shaping of Modern France* (New York: Macmillan, 1969), 528–29.

44. Its resources were later sold to its employees, and it reemerged as *Le Monde*.

45. These were the *Crédit Lyonnais*, the *Société Générale*, the *Banque Nationale pour le Commerce et l'Industrie*, and the *Comptoire Nationale d'Escompte de Paris*.

46. Alexander Werth, *France, 1940–1955* (New York: Henry Holt, 1956), 223.

47. The government controlled 77 percent of the capital in 1947, 65 percent in 1950, and 56 percent in 1958.

48. But the government continued to exercise restrictions on the allocation of resources in the building industry.

49. Total U.S. aid to France between 1945 and 1962 was $4.7 billion.

50. In 1949, military expenditures amounted to 19 percent of total state spending. By 1952, because of rearmament and the costs of fighting the Indochinese War, the military budget had climbed to 35 percent, or 1,290 billion francs ($3.7 billion).

51. No official statistical surveys of industry and agriculture had been made since the Great Depression. Businesses guarded production figures like peasants hoarding gold Napoleons.

52. By 1953, annual coal production had risen to 56.5 million tons, a 35 percent in-

crease since 1945 and 1.5 million tons above the previous all-time high set in 1929. The steel industry exceeded its 1929 production by 10 percent, and the output of electricity increased over two and a half times, while consumption more than tripled.

53. On the vote over the admission of Germany to the North Atlantic Treaty Organization, the Socialists split 86 for to 18 against, the MRP 16 to 54, the Radicals 61 to 28, the Conservatives 75 to 25, and the Gaullists 38 to 20. Only the Communists, in voting against, displayed complete unanimity.

54. The Viet-Minh had been founded in 1941 to resist the Japanese. Ten years later, it was transformed into the Fatherland Front, an organization that included the Workers' party and the North Vietnamese army.

55. Vincent Auriol, *Journal du Septennat*, vol. 1 (Paris: Armand Colin, 1970), 663.

56. Ibid., 7:406.

57. The only thing that might have saved the French was a massive air strike by the Americans. Secretary of State John Foster Dulles and the Joint Chiefs of Staff favored intervention, but President Eisenhower had no intention of letting himself be dragged into this war.

58. These were largely of French extraction blended with a sizable minority of Spanish, Italians, and other Mediterranean peoples who adopted or, like the Jewish natives, were accorded French citizenship. Very few of the settlers were descendants of the early landed colons who had arrived shortly after the conquest. Most were poor whites who lived in the large European cities. They were members of the lower-middle or laboring classes and strongly resisted any change in the system that allowed them to lord it over the indigenous Muslims.

59. The inquisitorial techniques of the French army were already being compared to those of the Gestapo. One of the victims, Henri Alleg, chillingly recalled one of his tormentors, a blond "youth with a sympathetic face, who could talk of the sessions of torture I had undergone as if they were a football match that he remembered and could congratulate me without spite as he would a champion athlete. A few days later I saw him, shriveled up and disfigured by hatred, hitting a Moslem who did not go fast enough down the staircase." Henri Alleg, *The Question* (New York: George Braziller, 1958), 104–5.

60. Jean Lartéguy, *The Centurions* (New York: Dutton, 1962), 370.

61. The text of the conference on 19 May is in *Major Addresses, Statements and Press Conferences of General Charles de Gaulle* (New York: French Embassy, n.d.), 1–6.

62. On 29 May, René Pleven told a meeting of the Council of Ministers: "Let's not waste words. We no longer have power. The Minister of Algeria can no longer cross the Mediterranean. The Minister of National Defense no longer has an army. The Minister of the Interior has no police." J. R. Tournoux, *Secrets d'état* (Paris: Plon, 1960), 361.

63. *Major Addresses, Statements and Press Conferences of General Charles de Gaulle*, 8.

64. Ibid., 6.

65. Ibid., 2.

66. Tournoux, *Secrets d'état*, 426.

67. "Only the weakest institutions," Wayland Kennet observed, "lay claim to respect by criminal sanctions." Wayland Kennet, *The Montesi Scandal* (New York: Doubleday, 1958), 247.

68. Shepard B. Clough and Salvatore Saladino, *A History of Modern Italy* (New York: Columbia University Press, 1968), 547.

69. Ibid., 544.

70. C. Grant Amyot, *The Italian Communist Party: The Crisis of the Popular Front Strategy* (New York: St. Martin's Press, 1981), 41–51.

71. Clough and Saladino, *A History of Modern Italy*, 547.

72. Kogan, *The Government of Italy*, 52–53.

73. Not the least disappointed at the results was the Eisenhower administration, which

had poured vast amounts of money into Italy to try to help De Gasperi's faction win.

74. Frederic Spotts and Theodor Wieser, *Italy: A Difficult Democracy* (Cambridge: Cambridge University Press, 1986), 158–66.

75. John Clarke Adams and Paolo Barile, *The Government of Republican Italy* (Boston: Houghton Mifflin, 1972), 219.

76. Using 1938 as the base year of 100, the index of industrial production had fallen to 29 in 1945. But in 1949, it was again 100; in 1950, it was 127; in 1954, 189. By the early 1960s, it had climbed to over 300; a decade later, it was over 500. Thus, in the quarter century after the war, it had risen a fantastic eighteen times. Mitchell, *European Historical Statistics*, 357–58.

77. It also held paramount interest in such diverse enterprises as the Bank of Rome, the General Insurance Company, the Industrial and Commercial Finance Company, the Italian Gas Company, the Vittorio Olcess Textile Company, and the Pantanella Flour and Spaghetti Company. Corrado Pallenberg, *Vatican Finances* (London: Owen, 1971), 105–16.

78. The SGI was responsible for the construction of Rome's famed Hotel Cavalieri Hilton; it financed the huge Paris headquarters of Pan American Air Lines at 90 Avenue des Champs Elysées; it constructed and owned the six-hundred-foot skyscraper that housed the stock exchange in Montreal, Canada; and it developed the five blocks of apartments and offices of the luxurious Watergate Hotel complex in Washington, D.C. Ibid., 102–5.

79. Nino Lo Bello, *The Vatican Empire* (New York: Trident, 1968), 907.

80. Two cities where the small business ethic has been practiced for generations are the Tuscan towns of Prato and Carrara. In Prato the main industry is textiles, produced in 15,000 different workshops, many comprising only family members. Carrara, the marble capital of the world, is loaded with artisans who render the models sent to them by artists throughout the world into large-scale sculptures. See Denis Mack Smith, *Italy* (Amsterdam: Time-Life Books, 1986), 59–65, 135–139.

81. In 1955: Italy: $464; the Netherlands: $892; France: $969; Germany: $975; and Britain: $1,152. Shepard Clough, *The Economic History of Modern Italy* (New York: Columbia, 1964), 289.

82. Adams and Barile, *The Government of Republican Italy*, 14–22.

83. Norman Lewis, *The Honoured Society* (London: Collins, 1964), 39–40.

84. Lewis, *The Honoured Society*, 205–6.

85. Aneurin Bevan, *In Place of Fear* (London: Heinemann, 1952), 100.

CHAPTER 4

THE COUNTRIES OF THE COMMUNIST BLOC

PREFACE   The war had disrupted Stalin's drive to create his personal brand of socialism and had exposed the Soviet people to alien influences. The German occupation had temporarily cut off most of European Russia from control by Moscow. The Nazi conquerors, although more adept in terrorizing the local populations than in exploiting discontent with Stalinist rule, did allow the formation of a Committee for the Liberation of the Peoples of Russia to work for the abolition of Communist controls and the emancipation of the Russian minorities. Established in September 1944 under the leadership of Colonel-General Andrei Vlasov, it had no influence on the course of German operations.[1] Nevertheless, it caused great alarm among Stalinist leaders.

Despite the government's efforts to keep contacts with the Allies at a minimum, the war gave many Soviet people an opportunity to see life outside their country and to discover that other European nations had a life-style superior to their own. Stalin warned his people to beware of the tinsel of Western society, but this did not assuage his fear that anyone tainted by outside influences was potentially disloyal. He had already banished certain national minorities whom he could not trust[2] and had ordered returning prisoners of war to be arrested and sent to work camps in the east to isolate them from the rest of the population.

Ideological purity had been one of the casualties of the war. To help maintain morale, the Communist leaders had returned tsarist heroes to the national pantheon; allowed the Russian Orthodox church to reestablish its patriarchate and resume the training of priests; encouraged Soviet writers to extol patriotism instead of Marxist-Leninism; and relaxed membership standards for the Communist party.[3] But as soon as the German armies were pushed from the soil of Russia, the campaign to return to rigid orthodoxy began. Only when the Soviets were firmly entrenched in Eastern Europe did the full winter of repression begin, as the Cold War became a necessary ingredient in Stalin's reassertion of control.

No flight of genius was needed to figure out that the defeat of Nazi Germany would leave the Soviet Union the dominant power in Eastern and Central Europe. When Winston Churchill visited Moscow in October 1944, he tried to uphold the interests of the West. The Soviet armies were then in Romania and Bulgaria. The British prime minister proposed that the Soviet Union "have ninety percent predominance in Romania, for [Britain] to have ninety percent of the say in Greece, and go fifty-fifty about Yugoslavia?" Churchill wrote the figures on a sheet of paper, adding Bulgaria, which he gave 75 percent to the Soviets and 25 percent to all the other countries, and Hungary, which would be split fifty-fifty. The prime minister passed the paper to Stalin who, after a moment's reflection, put a large blue check on the document and shoved it back across the table to Churchill.[4]

But the Western powers were not fighting the kind of war that would ensure them political influence in Eastern Europe, nor had their foreign policy ever guaranteed the security of this area. Churchill vainly hoped that by juggling percentages he could induce Stalin to treat the interests of those nations with some measure of generosity. But Stalin was not inclined to tolerate independence. His aims went beyond mere military control. He wanted not only to establish Soviet suzerainty over the area but also to ensure that the political systems of Eastern Europe conformed to Moscow's standard. To this end, he intended to fill their governments with reliable native leaders even though such dedicated Stalinists were currently in short supply. Until more leaders could be developed, Stalin planned to work through controlled coalitions, a process that might take several years.

Communism had not been an important force in Eastern Europe before World War II. Béla Kun's government in Hungary had fallen in 1920 after less than a year in power; a Marxist insurrection in Bulgaria in 1923 had also failed miserably; and in Yugoslavia a conspiracy of junior army officers was easily suppressed in 1932. Communist cells had existed in various Eastern European universities, but nowhere, save in Czechoslovakia,[5] the area's most highly industrialized state, did anything like a mass party following exist. In a sense, however, the absence of strong, native Communist parties and leaders was a blessing in disguise for Stalin. He had no reason to fear competition and could more easily create subservient regimes once the non-Communist parties had been eliminated and proper machinery for control was in place. This process followed a distinct pattern.

THE SOVIET STATE IN THE AFTERMATH OF VICTORY

Rebuilding Communism

Bitter Spoils. The Soviet victory parade on 24 June 1945 had been carefully rehearsed and was performed with precision and élan despite the gray overcast sky and persistent drizzle. "Little streams of rain [trickled] from the peaks of the men's caps, but the unanimous spiritual uplift was so great that none bothered to notice it," wrote Marshal Georgi Zhukov, who took the salute from horseback in front of the Kremlin walls. The jubilation reached its peak when two hundred captured German battle standards were flung on the concrete pavement before Lenin's tomb. But, as Zhukov sadly recalled, so many had died in battle and were not alive "to see this happy day, the day of our triumph."[6]

The Soviet Union's losses were truly horrendous; they were even more appalling than those suffered a generation earlier on the killing grounds of the Marne and Champagne, which had previously set the standard for systematic slaughter. More Soviet soldiers died in the defense of Stalingrad than the Americans lost altogether. The siege of Leningrad took upwards of a million lives. The entire war resulted in the death of some 25 million, at least half of whom were civilians.[7] Seven million soldiers were killed in battle, the rest died as German prisoners. The fighting laid waste to 800,000 square miles of the country's most productive land, leaving 25 million people homeless. Overall, 30 percent of the national wealth was destroyed, but the percentage of steel and coal production lost was close to 60 percent. In the German-occupied areas, 1,209,000 of 2,567,000 residential buildings were destroyed, along with 32,850 large and medium-size industrial enterprises, 82,000 schools, and tens of thousands of hospitals, museums, and stores.[8] Stalin, fearing that other nations might try to exploit Soviet weakness, refused to release damage figures. In the Soviet view, such losses were more than enough justification for the acquisition (since 1939) of 262,000 square miles of new territories with their 22,162,000 inhabitants.

After four years of the bloodiest war in their history, the Soviet people deserved a rest, but Stalin asked them for new sacrifices. There could be no relaxation. Not only must the structures destroyed by the war be rebuilt, but, more importantly, the ideological laxity of the war years must be ended. Stalin took full credit for the salvation of his country and shunted most of the famous army commanders into obscurity, denigrating their achievements to enhance his own reputation. Nikita Khrushchev, Stalin's eventual successor, wrote that "he tried to inculcate in the people the version that all victories gained by the Soviet nation during the Great Patriotic War were due to the courage, daring, and genius of Stalin and to no one else."[9] The official Stalinist history of the war also largely ignored the contribution the Soviet Union's allies made to the defeat of Hitler.

At the war's end, Stalin was sixty-six years old and firmly set in his ways. He still delighted in humiliating his subordinates. Milovan Djilas of Yugoslavia remembered a Kremlin dinner where Stalin proposed that all the guests guess the outside temperature and drink the number of vodkas corresponding to the degrees they guessed wrong. Djilas was appalled and recalled those suppers held by Peter the Great, "at which they gorged and drank themselves into a stupor while ordaining the fate of Russia and the Russian people."[10] Two and a half years later, Djilas met the Communist dictator again and found him worse, ravaged now by "conspicuous signs of his senility." Despite his physical decline, Stalin fought hard to force the Soviet Union back into the orthodox path it had trod during the 1930s. Ever fearful of a threat to his authority, he governed in an atmosphere of suspicion, distrust, and tyrannical subjectivity. Anyone, no matter how high his position, could be apprehended on any charge and had absolutely no legal protection.Marshal Nikolai Bulganin once remarked, after coming home from an evening at the Kremlin, "You come to Stalin's table as a friend, but you never know if you'll go home by yourself or if you'll be given a ride to prison."[11]

A New Wave of Repression. Since the Great Terror, the composition of the Politburo had remained fairly stable; Stalin kept its members in line by playing them off against one another, giving none the chance to establish a power base from which to challenge his leadership. By the end of the war, however, two of its members—Andrei Zhdanov and Georgi Malenkov—had risen to special prominence. Malenkov held important positions in the government, notably on the State Committee of Defense, and Zhdanov had become the first secretary of the Leningrad party organization following Sergei Kirov's assassination. Zhdanov had been transferred to Moscow in 1945 and made a secretary of the Central Committee, thereby becoming the most important man in the party behind Stalin. Zhdanov, an ideological fanatic who had fashioned the cultural doctrine of socialist realism, was now assigned the task of purifying Soviet cultural life from the corrupt influences of cosmopolitanism.

The *Zhdanovschina*, a pejorative term for the new purge,[12] opened with an attack on creative artists, specifically novelists, dramatists, filmmakers, and composers. It then moved to the government bureaucracy, the party cadres, and the military hierarchies. But Zhdanov did not live to carry it through to its conclusion. On 31 August 1948, shortly after he had restored Stalinist orthodoxy to the Soviet Composers' Union, he died of a heart attack. Zhdanov was publicly mourned, the Ukrainian city of Mariupol was renamed in his honor, and the anniversary of his death was officially commemorated. But Stalin shed few tears at his passing. Months before, Stalin had replaced him as his top deputy with Malenkov. Stalin blamed Zhdanov for his failure to turn the Cominform into a major weapon of the Cold War and his failure to prevent the defection of Yugoslavia.[13] In domestic politics, he blamed him for not extending the Zhdanovschina into the biological sciences. Stalin now undertook to rectify this sin of omission.

Stalin considered himself the supreme authority in the field of genetics. In 1938, he had Trofim Lysenko, a Ukrainian agronomist and biologist, appointed president of the Academy of Agricultural Sciences. Lysenko was a strong opponent of those who accepted the chromosome theory of heredity. He explained genetic evolution as the inheritance of acquired characteristics and maintained that heritable change could be accomplished through alteration of the environment. Thus, he claimed that scientists could produce a better crop of winter wheat by subjecting grain to freezing temperatures. Such a contention complemented the ideological belief that human character could be changed and that a new and better Soviet citizen could be produced in a proper social environment.

In 1948, the quack geneticist received full backing from the party Central Committee and instituted a reign of terror among his colleagues in the academy. He ousted everyone who did not endorse his attack on cytogenetics in favor of natural selection. He conceived a grand plan to change the climate of Russia and increase agricultural productivity by planting oak seedlings in dense clusters as protection against the hot dry winds of Central Asia. This "Great Stalin Plan for the Transformation of Nature" was a great fiasco, but until Stalin's death in 1953, Lysenko remained an absolute dictator in the field of biology. The purge was not an isolated event. Not only did it retard and pervert the study of genetics, but it also had a profound effect on the fields of psychology and sociology. It also discouraged experimentation and development in the fields of computers and cybernetics, an omission that would cost the Soviets dearly a generation later.

Official endorsement of Lysenko's pseudoscientific beliefs came at a time when Stalin was aiming his purge more directly at the politicians. During the war, the Communist party had risen to a position of power and prestige that it had not enjoyed since the early 1930s before the great show trials. The party had been instrumental in organizing the successful resistance to Nazi aggression. Its agents were responsible for mobilizing civilian resistance and organizing partisan activity in the occupied areas. Party members joined the army in great numbers—70 percent of the Leningrad organization served at the front and 90 percent of the members from Odessa and Sevastopol. Three and a half million party members, or 60 percent of its total membership, had been in the armed forces.[14] The party's prestige was too high for Stalin's comfort. From 1947 to 1952, he called no sessions of the Central Committee, despite the statutory limit of four months. He ignored the party hierarchy and directed the affairs of state through the Secretariat of the Politburo. The secret police continued to be responsible to him alone.

The purge of the party, directed by Malenkov, began with an attack on the "Leningrad Center." By 1949, he had replaced the entire five-man Secretariat of the Leningrad City Committee and had appointed one of his protégés, Vasili Andrianov, to the position of chairman. Former Zhdanov supporters, such as Nikolai Voznesensky, were weeded out. Stalin opposed Voznesensky's wholesale price reforms and expelled him from the Politburo and stripped him of his post as chairman of State Planning. In Stalin's view, Voznesensky's concept of economic planning did not depend sufficiently on direction from the central administrative authority.[15] Nevertheless, he kept Voznesensky around, occasionally even inviting him to dinner at the Kremlin.[16] Eventually, Stalin tired of the game and ordered Voznesensky arrested and shot. Just as he had done during the Great Terror of the 1930s, Stalin took a personal interest in the investigation and preparation of treason cases. Evidence against the Leningrad organization was fabricated by Lavrenti Beria's deputy, Viktor Abakumov, the one-time head of the NKVD hit squad SMERSH. The verdicts had already been decided.

The purge spread from the party into the government bureaucracy and the armed forces. Stalin demoted and replaced Admiral Ivan Yumashev, the commander-in-chief of the navy; Marshal Nikolai Voronov, the commander of the artillery; Marshal Semyon Bogdanov, the commander of the armored corps; and General Iosif Shikin, the head of the Army Political Directorate. Air Marshal Aleksandr Novikov, denounced by Stalin's pilot son Vasili, was charged with accepting defective airplanes and thrown in prison. Marshal Zhukov was disgraced.[17] In 1949, Stalin separated the party from the government by forcing the members of the Politburo to resign their ministerial positions. Later the same year, he brought Nikita Khrushchev, party boss of the Ukraine, to Moscow to offset the growing influence of Malenkov and Beria. Khrushchev was named First Secretary of the Moscow Party Committee with a seat on the ruling Secretariat. But

Khrushchev realized that nobody, no matter what his position or how much he appeared to be in official favor, was safe. "Everything depended on what Stalin happened to be thinking when he glanced in your direction," he wrote.[18]

Stalin was convinced that Zionism threatened the Soviet Union. His anti-Semitism had recently been inflamed by the demonstrations that greeted Golda Meir when she visited Moscow as the new Israeli foreign secretary in October 1949. Stalin was shocked at the deference the Soviet Jews paid to this representative of a foreign power.[19] On his own initiative, he launched a campaign of "anticosmopolitanism." He ordered Jews purged from the party and the bureaucracy and had Jewish cultural institutions dissolved. He also instituted a quota system to limit Jewish personnel in universities, scientific institutes, and factories. Lazar Kaganovich, who was Jewish by ancestry, directed the campaign; its purpose, not unlike that of the Nazi Nuremberg Laws, was to destroy all Jewish influence in the state, especially in the arts, and to turn Jews into second-class citizens. Important Jewish figures were arrested and sent to detention camps.[20] Many never returned. Stalin directed his greatest fury against those Jews who had not become culturally Russian. He ordered the murder of the Yiddish actor Solomon Mikhoels. Stalin wanted Mikhoels dead because he was a leader of the Jewish Anti-Fascist Committee, which was suspect for having solicited donations from the United States. According to one version, Mikhoels was shot in Minsk during a performance of *King Lear*.[21] The actor's death was then explained as a traffic accident. There were other executions and arrests. Vyacheslav Molotov's Jewish wife was suspected of being connected with the Anti-Fascist League and arrested. Molotov was unhappy, but continued to serve Stalin.

Return to the Five-Year Plans. During the war, overall production had fallen by 23 percent with certain sectors more seriously affected: pig iron had dropped by 41 percent, oil by 38 percent, timber by 48 percent, cement by 66 percent, and sugar by 79 percent. Consumer goods were off 41 percent. Yet the economy began a slow recovery. In the Fourth Five-Year Plan, introduced on 18 March 1946, Stalin gave top priority to repairing the ravaged areas of the country and to rebuilding the country's heavy industry. He believed that only by tripling industrial production over prewar output could the Soviet Union protect itself against capitalist agression. Special emphasis was put on the production of strategic minerals, armaments, nuclear energy, heavy machinery, and transportation equipment. People were required to work a forty-eight hour week. In return, they could expect barely adequate housing and few consumer goods.[22]

The Fourth Plan envisaged a 28 percent increase over the 1940 level in industry, but set only a 7 percent goal in agriculture. Even this modest amount was too ambitious. The war had hit the agricultural sector the hardest. As in the 1930s, agricultural workers were asked to make superhuman sacrifices, but now labor was in even shorter supply. The peasantry had suffered high casualties during the war. Once the conflict was over, higher pay in industry discouraged many survivors from returning to the farms. Much of the Ukraine, the most productive agricultural region, had been a battlefield. Livestock had been slaughtered by the millions. The Germans had destroyed 2,890 tractor stations. As a result of this devastation, collectivization in the Ukraine had broken down, with the peasants appropriating many acres of kolkhoz land for their personal use. To make matters worse, 1946 was a year of drought and disastrous harvests. State planners had little sympathy for the privations suffered by the peasantry. They expected the peasants to fulfill their quotas no matter how unrealistic. Lacking consumer goods with which to encourage the peasants to produce, the regime resorted to force. The planners tried to bring more and more land under cultivation and increase the yield per acre. But to meet these goals, the obligatory deliveries had to be raised, killing incentive. When Khrushchev complained about the famine conditions in the countryside, Stalin accused him of "writing memoranda to prove that the Ukraine was unable to take care of itself."[23] Beneath Stalin's accusation lurked the basic animosity he, and many other Communist leaders, felt toward the peasantry. To Stalin, low productivity contained the seeds of counterrevolution. He preferred to believe his own propaganda about the well-fed peasants happy in their rustic utopia.

As a result of these policies, Soviet agriculture recovered slowly. By 1953, the year Stalin died, gross agricultural output was no higher than it had been in 1940 despite the extension of the Soviet frontiers. Livestock and wheat showed some improvement, but most cereals still lagged behind their earlier levels.[24] All aspects of agricultural production had become politicized. Disputes over whether to plant spring or winter wheat, or whether to plow deeply or not, were part of the struggle for power and were resolved on political, not agricultural, grounds. This politicization only worsened the already sorry state of Soviet agriculture.

City dwellers also suffered deprivations. Since 1940, the average amount of urban living space had declined from 54 square feet per capita to 48 square feet. The standard of living had dropped as well. By 1950, a Soviet laborer had to work almost 1 hour for a quart of milk, 4 hours for a dozen eggs, 22 hours for a pound of tea, 72 hours for a pair of women's shoes, and 376 hours for a man's wool suit. The currency devaluation of 1947 cut drastically into savings and income—currency was exchanged at the rate of 10 to 1, ordinary state bonds at two-thirds, and bank deposits at a third to a half. As a result, people had to work harder to maintain marginal comforts. Still, people no longer lived in canvas tents and the ruins of bombed-out buildings as millions had done at the end of the war.

A Fifth Five-Year Plan began to be drafted in January 1951, but its directives were not revealed publicly until August 1952. Capital and military goods, including a nuclear buildup, remained a top priority with consumer goods coming in last. The start of the Korean War in 1950 had made the production of tanks more important than tractors. The regime blithely pretended that it no longer had a grain problem.[25] In *Economic Problems of Socialism in the U.S.S.R.*, published in 1952, Stalin revealed that political enthusiasm could not transcend the laws of cause and effect, but gave little hope for any fundamental change. He emphasized that the Soviet system would remain committed to rigid socialist planning. Characteristically, Stalin wanted to have it both ways—rigid planning and increased production. He also liked to keep his subordinates guessing; that way, no matter what course of action he eventually chose, he could take the credit if it worked and blame others if it did not.

At the Nineteenth Party Congress in October 1952, the first in over thirteen years, Stalin announced his intention to replace the Politburo and Orgburo with a larger, more flexible "Presidium to the Central Committee of the Communist Party of the Soviet Union." This new group would have twenty-five members and eleven alternates and would include a larger percentage of government administrators as opposed to mere party functionaries. A secret inner bureau, its composition determined by Stalin, would dominate this new enlarged group. Stalin now had a framework in which he could play off the older elite by threatening to replace them with younger, less experienced but more trustworthy *apparatchiki*. The change seemed a prelude to a purge of the old guard. Vyacheslav Molotov and Anastas Mikoyan were already out of favor, and Klementi Voroshilov had to telephone Stalin before each meeting of the Politburo to see if he would be allowed to attend. Beria had to endure the humiliation of not having his associates re-elected to the Central Committee. Two new lieutenants, Malenkov and Khrushchev, played prominent parts in the congress's proceedings. Malenkov gave the main report of the Central Committee, usually the duty of an heir presumptive, while Khrushchev gave the report on the new party rules. Of the 125 members elected to the Central Committee, 79 were new faces. The congress endorsed the Fifth Five-Year Plan, published the previous month, and asserted the need for strict hierarchy in party ranks with added supervisory authority for the top echelons. The secret police were given greater authority over party members.

Stalin now proceeded with the next step, the so-called Doctors' Plot. In November 1952, a group of Kremlin doctors—six of whom were Jewish—were arrested on the charge that they had poisoned prominent Soviet officials, including Zhdanov. Five of the doctors were accused of working for the American intelligence through an international Jewish organization, the other three were supposedly British agents. Beria was berated for not having uncovered the plot sooner. *Pravda*, which publicized the arrests in January 1953, called for tighter discipline and greater vigilance. Building on his campaign of anti-Semitism and counter-espionage, Stalin was clearly setting the stage for a resumption of the Great Terror of the 1930s. How far this would have gone and how many lives it would have claimed will never be known. Stalin died from a cerebral hemorrhage on 5 March 1953 before the second bloodletting could get under way.

Stalin's Heirs

An Interregnum. Stalin's chief henchmen gathered at his dacha at Kuntsevo as soon as they were informed he had suffered a stroke. They arranged shifts for an around-the-clock vigil. Over the next three days, they witnessed the dictator's death agonies.[26] Voroshilov, Kaganovich, Malenkov, Bulganin, and Khrushchev appeared genuinely grieved, but none let his sorrow dispel his fears of the others. Since the Soviet system had no provisions for a formal succession of power, Malenkov and Beria formed an alliance of convenience—they had shared the day shift during the death watch. In the first government following Stalin's departure, they seized the most important posts. Malenkov took the chairmanship of the Council of Ministers and secretaryship of the Communist party, while Beria took the Ministry of State Security and the Ministry of Internal Affairs, now merged into a single organization. The members of Stalin's Presidium were reduced in numbers from twenty-five to ten, most of whom had been in the old Politburo.

The Malenkov-Beria affiliation could not maintain its cohesion—each man was too afraid of the other. The other members of the Presidium also distrusted anyone who held a top position in the party or the government. Malenkov tried to conduct business as usual, but he was hardly capable of filling Stalin's shoes. He lost his post as party senior secretary after only ten days. A five-man directorate replaced him. The most powerful member of this group was Khrushchev, who now became the prime mover in a plot against Beria. The conspirators, looking for a way to arrest the regime's chief policeman, finally decided to do it at a special session of the Presidium in June. They assembled a gendarmerie of eleven Soviet marshals and generals who, at a prearranged signal, entered the council chamber with guns drawn and arrested Beria. The indictment charged Beria with trying "to set the Ministry of Internal Affairs above the Party and Government in order to seize power and liquidate the Soviet worker-peasant system for the purpose of restoring capitalism and the domination of the bourgeoisie."[27] He was sentenced to death and shot. His associates were also liquidated. Subsequently, Beria's full-page picture was cut from the *Great Soviet Encyclopedia* and replaced by an article about whaling in the Bering Straits.

In February 1955, Bulganin replaced Malenkov, Beria's one-time ally, as premier. The campaign against Malenkov had begun two months earlier when his policy of producing more consumer goods at the expense of heavy industry was denounced as a threat to the national security. Khrushchev, with the support of the military leaders, had planned the attack.

The Rise of Khrushchev. The shakeup in the Kremlin gave Khrushchev the opportunity to become first among equals in the collective leadership. However, as important as he became, he was never able to establish a true one-man rule and could never really ignore the views of his colleagues. Khrushchev cloaked his ambition through a policy of de-Stalinization that had already begun shortly after the dictator's death with the termination of the "Doctors' Plot." Those who had not died under torture were released and exonerated. After the execution of Beria, the party reasserted its control over the secret police, taking away its status as a separate government ministry with power over a wide spectrum of economic activities. New laws forbade administrative arrest and disbanded slave labor camps. Coercion continued, but it became more indirect. Now nonconformists were more likely to be deprived of benefits, subjected to education or mass media persuasion, or exiled to mental health facilities than to find the secret police knocking on the door in the middle of the night. Khrushchev also advocated economic reforms, concentrating first on easing restrictions in agriculture. He tried to increase incentives by raising the prices the state paid the peasants for their quotas of food, reducing the taxes on produce from the collective farms' private plots, and allowing the kolkhozy to set their own work schedules. He also started to break up the great centralized administrative empires that had directed agricultural affairs from the remoteness of their Moscow headquarters. He embarked on dramatic projects, most notably one to reclaim 90 million acres of uncultivated land in Kazakhstan and southwestern Siberia, an area as large as all the farmland in Britain, France, and Spain. Khrushchev emphasized that this "virgin lands" scheme could achieve enormous gains at relatively low cost.

Khrushchev's driving force was even more in evidence in February 1956 at the Twentieth Congress of the Communist party when he delivered a scathing denunciation of Stalin and the "cult of the individual." The speech was remarkable for the vehemence of its attack against a man whom many had regarded as a god. Khrushchev tried to depict Stalin's reign of terror as an aberration of Leninism rather than its logical extension. Where Lenin tried to "induce people to follow him without using compulsion," Stalin violated "all existing norms of morality and of Soviet laws."[28] Further, Stalin had left the country unprepared to face the Germans in 1941, contributing to a series of defeats, though he later broadcast the lie that all victories came from his own "courage, daring and genius." Khrushchev also attacked Stalin for more recent sins: his fabrication of the Leningrad Affair, his responsibility for the break with Yugoslavia, his role in the trumped-up Doctors' Plot, and his disastrous agricultural policy. Khrushchev held up to ridicule the myth that all progress in the Soviet Union since Stalin took charge was due to his leadership.

De-Stalinization was not attractive to some members of the current leadership who feared it might pose a threat to their own existence.[29] While Khrushchev had the support of a few trusted associates, the initiative for the policy was undoubtedly his. His decision to destroy Stalin's reputation was a deliberate effort to strengthen the Soviet Union by getting rid of the shackles of the past. Among other things, he intended to replace the hard line in foreign policy with a policy of "peaceful coexistence" with the West. Improving relations with the United States and the countries of Western Europe would allow more resources to be diverted from military needs to improving the basic economy. It would also lead to more cooperative, less adversarial relations with the people of the Eastern bloc. Stalinism had petrified Soviet society making progress and improvement impossible. As long as the Soviet regime continued to make war against its own people, the country would remain backward and would fall progressively farther behind the nations of the European Community. Stalin had showed that the only way to preserve the Communist system was through naked force. Khrushchev thought that political relaxation would promote new levels of prosperity. But the sins of the past could not be purged by only a little reform. Once started, de-Stalinization proved difficult to stop. In time its own irreversible dynamic would ultimately consign Marxist-Leninism to the dustbin of history.

Khrushchev turned anti-Stalinism to his advantage by denouncing his rivals for violating the principles of collective leadership. Thus, the campaign became a means to weaken the power of the Stalinist old guard—Molotov, Kaganovich, and Malenkov. Khrushchev appealed for support to those in the party and the government who had fearsome and bitter memories of the sufferings caused by the Great Purge. His speech was intended to be secret and therefore only for domestic consumption among a privileged few. But, leaked to the world through the Italian Communist party, it had a significant effect on the political life of the Eastern European satellites and provoked crises in Poland and Hungary. The Stalinists in the Presidium and the Central Committee saw these crises as their chance to strike back, and in December 1956, they forced Khrushchev to abandon his efforts to decentralize the economy. But their victory was only temporary.

Khrushchev had been steadily building up personal alliances among the cadres, and he currently had the support of more than one-third of the membership of the Central Committee. The five members elected to the Presidium immediately after the Twentieth Party Congress were his supporters, as was the chairman of the new Committee for State Security, General Ivan Serov, and the general Soviet prosecutor, Roman Rudenko, formerly the Soviet prosecutor at the Nuremberg trials. Most of these men had served Khrushchev when he had been party boss of the Ukraine or first secretary of the Moscow party organization. With them behind him, Khrushchev was ready to counterattack.

On 17 February 1957, he took a step toward the decentralization of industry by pushing through the Central Committee a resolution to reorganize the State Economic Commission. The following May, at a meeting of the Supreme Soviet, he succeeded in abolishing ten National Republic and fifteen Union Republic ministries. This move gained him the support of Marshal Zhukov, who favored decentralizing the economy as a protection against aerial attack.[30] At the meeting of the Presidium in June 1957, Khrushchev's opponents voted seven to four to replace him with Molotov. Khrushchev boldly appealed the result directly to the Central Committee, which reversed the decision of the Presidium by a solid majority. The Central Committee, although nominally superior to the Presidium or the earlier Politburo had never before exercised its power. By supporting Khrushchev, it allowed him to purge the Presidium.

Khrushchev shunted Molotov off to Outer Mongolia as ambassador; he put Malenkov in charge of a hydroelectric station in Kazakhstan; he gave Bulganin the sinecure of chairman of the board of the state bank; and he entrusted Kaganovich with the production of cement in the Urals. Next, he reasserted the position of the Communist party in affairs of state. Emerging as spokesman for the party's liberal wing, Khrushchev advocated producing more consumer goods and presented his policy of peaceful coexistence as an alternative to the Leninist theory of the inevitability of war with the capitalist nations.

Dictatorship in Different Clothes. In February 1958, Khrushchev became both the chairman of the Council of Ministers and the first secretary of the Communist party. But the arrangement did not signal a return to the cult of personality. Although Khrushchev was able to dominate the party, he never succeeded in placing himself above it. Not only did circumstances oppose such a move, but the age of terror had died with Stalin. Khrushchev had a style of leadership that was dramatically different from that of his predecessors—some called him the first Western politician in Russian history.[31] Once he had fought hard for Stalin's General Line, now he was leaving it in ruins. He did not lose his taste for dictatorship, however. He was a pragmatist rather than a theoretician, an opportunist as well as a dreamer. He related well to people and enjoyed giving them practical advice on how things should be done. He had a vulgarity that both repelled and attracted. He once remarked that Stalin had known that the Soviet Union did not win World War II by itself, but had "admitted it only to himself in the toilet."[32] This common touch gave Khrushchev the ability to swap friendly stories with workers, but his bonhomie could be deceptive. For example, he could assure the peasants he was looking after their interests while preparing legislation to convert their collective farms into state farms and to deprive them of their family vegetable plots. Yet, despite his bullying, he was not bloodthirsty. His great short-coming was his belief that he could bring great changes to the Soviet system without changing the basic nature of the totalitarian state. He, therefore, continued to rely on a command society and to enhance his place in it. He removed the old elements of the Communist party and even replaced most of the old district secretaries with his own men; he reorganized the entire Army High Command until almost every important military office was occupied by soldiers who had served with or under him at Stalingrad during October-December 1942.[33] He did not tolerate politically ambitious generals, including Marshal Zhukov whom he denounced for "Bonapartism" and removed from the Presidium in October 1957.[34] Khrushchev also had his erstwhile ally Bulganin dropped from the Presidium in September 1958. Bulganin had voted against Khrushchev on an important vote the previous year.

During this housecleaning, Khrushchev continued his efforts to alter the Stalinist economic system. The powers of the local economic administration were enhanced. Regional planning councils, or *sovnarkhozy*, were created and made directly responsible for industrial development within their area. Khrushchev scrapped the Sixth Five-Year Plan, adopted in 1956, which was intended to prepare the Soviet Union to surpass the industrial productivity of the United States, and put forth his own Seven-Year Plan at a special, early meeting of the Twenty-First Communist Party Congress in January 1959. In this plan, Khrushchev outlined an ambitious program to increase the supply of consumer goods in order, as he explained, to eradicate class distinctions and ensure the flowering of the spirit of true Communism. Khrushchev, now appearing as the party's leading theoretician, said that with "the victory of Socialism, the USSR [had] entered a new historical period of gradual passage from socialism to communism," and that the new plan would reflect this change by creating "the material and technological basis of Communism."[35] A significant reordering of economic priorities was essential. No longer would heavy industry, iron and steel, and capital goods automatically take precedence. Thus, Khrushchev pitted himself against one of the country's most powerful interest groups—the military-industrial complex or, as the Soviets called them, the "metal-eaters." Khrushchev believed that, with proper reorganization, productivity could be increased in the agricultural and light industrial sectors without seriously curtailing defense and capital goods expenditures. He hoped to accomplish this by increasing the enthusiasm of the Soviet people for work, among other things.

The masses, however, failed to respond, especially those in the rural areas. In the first five years after Stalin's death, the Soviet economy had shown gradual, if unspectacular, improvement. In 1958, wheat production reached a postwar high of 76.6 million metric tons. However, the next five years saw an overall slide of 42 percent. In 1963, the Soviets produced only 49.7 million metric tons,[36] and began to purchase grain from abroad. Khrushchev's boast that he would make the Soviet Union as productive as the United States now seemed a joke. His great virgin lands scheme had been a debacle. Initially, it had appeared to be a success, but after a few years the original nutrients in the soil were exhausted; since they were not replenished with adequate fertilizer, the yields began to tumble. Khrushchev had ignored previous cautions that the Asian steppes were too arid and saline to produce wheat. Now the warnings came back to haunt him. The virgin lands were becoming a dust bowl. The venture was also plagued by the usual Soviet mismanagement, administrative chaos, and decisions based on ideology rather than economics. The Asian steppes lacked the basic infrastructure to accommodate a new agricultural work force, which was mostly "volunteer" labor drawn from the Komsolmol youth organization and army recruits. Furthermore, Khrushchev's plan to make "Agriculture keep step with industry" did not find favor with Gosplan bureaucrats who were reluctant to restrict steel production and armaments so more funds could be allocated to agriculture. Tension with the West over the status of Berlin brought even greater demands for military expenditures.[37] Khrushchev had recognized the necessity of taking bold measures to cure the agricultural backwardness of the Soviet Union, but his policies succeeded only in increasing the polarization between the peasants and the workers who lived in the great industrial centers of the five-year plans. To add to his problems, Khrushchev also ran into trouble in his campaign of de-Stalinization.

The Thaw Was Too Good to Last. At the Twenty-Second Party Congress in 1961, Khrushchev continued his attack on Stalin's heritage. He revealed that Stalin was directly responsible for the assassination of Kirov in 1934 and that false documents supplied by the Nazis had led to Marshal Mikhail Tukhachevsky's execution. Khrushchev also renounced Stalin's thesis that the closer a society came to Communism, the more intense its class struggle became—a 1937 thesis that served to justify the Great Terror. Khrushchev openly attacked certain Soviet leaders, namely, Malenkov, Molotov, Voroshilov, and Kaganovich, for their participation in the crimes of the Stalinist era. The Congress voted to remove Stalin's embalmed body from Lenin's tomb on Red Square. During the debate D. A. Lazurkina, one of the delegates, claimed she had a visitation from Lenin. "Yesterday I consulted Ilyich as if he were alive in front of me, and he told me, 'It is unpleasant for me to lie next to Stalin, who brought so much misfortune to the Party.' "[38] (Stalin was reburied in a plot in front of the Kremlin wall.) The Congress also decided to replace one quarter of the membership of the Presidium and the Central Committee at all regular elections. This move was intended to winnow out the old leaders and prevent the return of a personality cult. Khrushchev also promised that the Soviet state would begin to wither away and be replaced by communal autonomy. As part of this withering away, the coercive state organs would disappear. Nevertheless, the Communist party would still direct the economy.[39] But Khrushchev's goals were contradictory. The Marxist-Leninist system and the authority of the party could not be preserved without centralization, coercion, and punition.

The decline of Stalinism promised an end to socialist realism and a lessening of state interference in the cultural life of the nation. The novelist Ilya Ehrenburg described the period as "the Thaw." And the poet Yevgeni Yevtushenko wrote that it was "a rough spring, a difficult spring with late frosts and cold winds, a spring which takes a step to the left, then a step to the right, then a step back, but which is certain, nevertheless, to go on and take two or three steps forward."[40] By 1961, Yevtushenko was widely regarded, both inside and outside his country, as the chief spokesman of the post-Stalinist generation of young writers. In that year he published *Babii Yar*, a poetic memorial to the thousands of Jews who were murdered by the Nazis in a ravine outside Kiev. The Soviet Union had never recognized that the Jews suffered more at the hands of the Germans than any other national group. In pointing out that the massacre site was marked by no special memorial—it was, in fact, currently being used as a garbage dump—Yevtushenko was actually criticizing the anti-Semitism that was still rampant in the Soviet Union.[41] Yevtushenko claimed Khrushchev had personally authorized the poem's publication.

One of the highlights of the thaw was the publication of *One Day in the Life of Ivan Denisovich*, the sensational novel by Aleksandr Solzhenitsyn, that first appeared in the November 1962 issue of the literary journal *Novy Mir*. The book's action takes place, with true classical unity, on a single day and in a single place in a Siberian concentration camp in January 1951. The hero-narrator, Ivan Denisovich Shukhov, is in the eighth year of a ten-year sentence for espionage. In 1942, Shukhov had been captured by the Germans, escaped, and rejoined the Soviet army. The authorities believed the Germans intentionally released him to betray his country. Shukhov confessed because he felt he had no other choice: "If he did not sign, he was as good as buried. But if he did, he'd still go on living a while, so he signed."[42] Shukhov's companions in prison have also been sentenced for crimes they did not commit. Thus, the prison becomes a microcosm for the entire Stalinist state. The book is filled with references to the forced collectivization of the peasants, the mass liquidation of the kulaks, the systematic persecution of the ethnic minorities and religious groups, the Great Purges of the 1930s, and the return to repression after World War II. Thus, Solzhenitsyn exposed the basic injustices of Soviet society in a way never before allowed in print. As with *Babii Yar*, the novel's publication was supposedly authorized by Khrushchev.

Khrushchev, however, was under tremendous pressure from colleagues who were ill at ease with such revisionism and feared its consequences. Khrushchev himself was having second thoughts. He saw that liberalization could ultimately undermine the power of the Communist party and his control over it. The official counterattack began on 1 December 1962, when Khrushchev and some of his cronies visited an art show sponsored by the Moscow section of the Artists Union. Most of the canvases were painted in the officially approved socialist realist style, but an adjoining room contained a special display of abstract art. When Khrushchev saw these paintings, he became furious and launched into an obviously premeditated tirade. He wanted to know how painters dared perpetrate such an outrage.

In the next several months, musicians and writers, as well as artists, came under attack. But the new hard line could not save Khrushchev from his own transgressions and contradictions, specifically, from his failed agricultural policy and setbacks in foreign affairs.

His virgin lands scheme had wasted precious resources to little effect. He had failed to resolve the conflicts over economic priorities—the "metal eaters" and militarists versus the decentralizers and consumer goods advocates. He had allowed relations with China to deteriorate and had embarked on an unpopular rapprochement with West Germany. The base of Soviet authority in Eastern Europe had considerably deteriorated. Many of the Soviet Union's problems transcended Khrushchev's personal responsibility, but his contradictory policies hardly helped. He had abandoned Stalin's collision course with the West in favor of peaceful coexistence, yet his last great adventure brought the country to the brink of war with the United States over the installation of missiles in Cuba. Khrushchev's restless energy could not compensate for his lack of coherence and efficiency. The world press liked to see him in action, banging his fists on tables and taking off his shoe at the United Nations, but his colleagues found these antics an embarrassment. Khrushchev knew that he would either have to carry out another purge of the Presidium or risk losing his position. He therefore planned a new plenary session of the Central Committee to launch a vast administrative and power reorganization. However, in October 1964, before the session could take place, his opponents toppled him from power. Leonid Brezhnev replaced Khrushchev as party first secretary, and Aleksei Kosygin became chairman of the Council of Ministries. These men, who came from the party apparatus, had benefited by the elimination of the Stalinist old guard; Khrushchev had brought them to prominence, appointing Brezhnev president of the Soviet Union and Kosygin head of the Gosplan.

On 17 October 1964, *Pravda* denounced Khrushchev for his "hare-brained schemes, half-baked conclusions and hasty decisions and actions, divorced from reality; bragging and bluster; attraction to rule by fiat; unwillingness to take into account what science and practical experience have already discovered." He, henceforth, became a nonperson and lived out the rest of his life in virtual isolation. He was not buried in Red Square, but nevertheless was interred in a prestigious Moscow cemetery that also holds the remains of Chekhov and Gogol.

COMMUNIST HEGEMONY IN EASTERN EUROPE

The Stalinization of Eastern Europe. The process had a textbook quality. In most countries it was carried out in three phases. The first began with the organization of a coalition of anti-Fascist parties. These groups ran the political gamut from Communist to socialist, from peasant to middle class. Most of the non-Communist groups respected political freedoms. The Communists also pretended to favor a representative democracy, while insinuating their members and supporters into positions of responsibility, particularly in the Ministry of Interior and armed forces. This initial phase could last anywhere from six months, as in Romania and Bulgaria, to more than three years, as in Czechoslovakia. Some countries, like Poland and East Germany omitted this phase. The second stage usually occurred when the Communists felt they were sufficiently well entrenched to go on the offensive, first against all political groups outside the coalition and then against the non-Communist parties within. In this phase, non-Communist parties ostensibly shared power with the Communists, but in fact their independence was in the process of extinction. Their leaders were in prison or had been transformed into obedient stooges. In the third or last phase, the Communists ruled alone, having completely destroyed opposition of every kind throughout the country.[43]

The Soviets assured subservience and uniformity through a series of institutions backed up by the presence of the Red Army, which had liberated most of Eastern Europe from the German yoke. The Communist Information Bureau, established in 1947 as a counter to the Marshall Plan, replaced the dissolved Comintern as an agency for controlling foreign Communist parties. Its new mission, foreshadowed in April 1945 by the French Communist leader, Jacques Duclos, in an article in *Cahiers du Communisme (Communist Notebooks)*, was to reorganize international Communism to prepare for a resumption of revolutionary militancy under a tightly centralized bureaucracy. The Soviet embassies provided most of the on-the-spot supervision; the ambassador usually acted in the capacity of a proconsul with the authority to use military force should that prove necessary. Educational, social, political, and economic systems became monotonously standardized. The constitutions followed the Soviet model.

The Soviets looked on Eastern Europe both as a security zone and as a storehouse of goods and services to be exploited for the benefit of the crippled Soviet economy. The Soviets insisted on uniformity. They established five-year plans, demanded the nationalization of basic industries, and insisted on the collectivization of agriculture. In 1949, they established the Council for Mutual Economic Assistance, or Comecon, to make sure that all the economies of the bloc were geared first to the needs of the Soviet Union and then to the demands of the area as a whole. Through a series of bilateral treaties, the Soviets bound the foreign trade of each satellite directly to the Soviet Union. The satellites were obliged to consult directly with their Soviet masters on all important questions. The Soviets insisted on frequent purges in the local Communist parties to ensure constant loyalty and prevent deviation from the party line. Opposition, real or imaginary, resulted in imprisonment or death.

Bulgaria

A Smooth Takeover. The process of Stalinization was most readily accomplished in Bulgaria where the people were traditionally friendly toward Russia and had never declared war on the Soviet Union. On 9 September 1944, the day after the Red Army entered the country, the Fatherland Front (a collection of left-wing elements including the Agrarian Union, Social Democrats, Communists, and some progressive republicans known as the Zveno) overthrew the pro-German Sofia government and began a thorough purge of the former ruling classes. Kimon Georgiev, a leader of the Zveno and a former premier (1934), headed the new government, but the Communists took the posts of vice-premier and minister of the interior (the department in charge of national police) and used them as a base from which they proceeded to capture power. Interior Minister Anton Uygov staffed the national gendarmerie with Communists and put party members into provincial and village administrations. These appointees then began harassing the non-Communist parties in the Fatherland Front. Opposition newspapers were closed, their leaders were arrested, and the lives of their party members were threatened.

Comintern-trained Georgi Dimitrov, one-time defendant at the Reichstag fire trial, directed the campaign from Moscow. As the Communists completed their control of the Fatherland Front, they intensified the attack on all opposition parties, breaking up their meetings and terrorizing their supporters. The Communists bluntly warned that all those who did not vote for Communist candidates in the elections of 18 November 1945 would experience another Saint Bartholomew's night, a reference to a bloody massacre of French Protestants in the sixteenth century. Dimitrov returned home to preside over the last stages of the takeover. He had not set foot in his country for twenty-two years.

When the national elections were held in 1945, the Fatherland Front claimed it captured 88 percent of the vote, making it appear that a vast majority of the voters clearly favored a Communist-dominated, Soviet-supported government. The British and Americans protested this rigged election as a gross violation of the Declaration of Liberated Europe and refused to recognize the validity of the results. Stalin, therefore, promised that he would "advise" the Bulgarian government to include two representatives of opposition parties. But nothing really changed. The West accused the Soviets of a lack of good faith, but withheld recognition only until a Bulgarian peace treaty was signed in February 1947.

The Creation of a One-Party Dictatorship. In December 1945, the Communists declared that the Fatherland Front was the real leader of the people since it ensured "the possibility of being masters of their own destiny." They insisted ominously that "vigilance of the people against its open and hidden enemies must increase."[44] All free political expression now disappeared. In September 1946, a referendum scrapped the monarchy in favor of a republic, and Georgiev was removed as premier. Most of the key leaders of the Socialist party and the Agrarian Union were placed under arrest.

The following month, on 27 October, elections were held for a National Constituent Assembly. The Fatherland Front won by a landslide, and Dimitrov at last emerged from behind the scenes to take charge himself. Political repression intensified. In June 1947, Nikola Petkov, head of the Agrarian Union, the most popular and best-known opposition leader in the country, was arrested and charged with conspiring with Bulgarian army officers to overthrow the government. His trial was conducted in a style reminiscent of the old Moscow purge trials, complete with Communist-controlled groups all over the country demanding his death. The Sofia Miners' Union said that capital punishment would inspire the miners to "harder work and greater achievement in the production field." The court obliged, and the sentence was carried out on 23 September.

By the end of 1947, all non-Communist parties had ceased to exist. Moscow-trained functionaries ran the government ministries. The new Bulgarian constitution mirrored the 1936 Soviet constitution. On 28 December 1947, a far-reaching program to control the entire economy began with the nationalization of all mines and industries and the collectivization of agriculture. By the end of the following year, the last year of the Bulgarian Two-Year Plan, very little private trade remained. The Bulgarian Communists proved so thoroughly Soviet in style that when Dimitrov died in July 1949, he was embalmed, like Lenin, and his corpse was put on public display in the old Sofia cathedral.[45]

Romania

A Tradition of Russophobia. The Communist takeover in Romania proved troublesome and took longer to accomplish than in Bulgaria. Part of the problem was the endemic suspicion and mistrust that the Romanian people had for anything Russian: ill feelings toward the Russians had existed since the formation of the

Romanian state in the nineteenth century.[46] The Romanians had already abandoned their ties with the Axis by the time the Red Army entered Bucharest in August 1944. A group of generals, headed by General Constantin Sănătescu, ran the government. Sănătescu had come to power as a result of a coup against the dictatorship of Marshal Ion Antonescu. King Michael announced the end of the war against the Allies and, on 25 August, declared war on Hitler. The Romanian army, which had already suffered about 500,000 casualties fighting the Soviet Union, now joined the Red Army in the assault against the Germans in Hungary and Slovakia. Thus, Romania helped the Soviets extend their control over Central Europe. In appreciation, Stalin gave King Michael the Soviet Union's highest decoration: the Order of Victory.

At the time of King Michael's coup, the Romanian Communist party, which had been officially outlawed since 1924, had perhaps 1,000 members; the number of hard-core Stalinists or "Muscovites" was considerably smaller and included a sizable number of non-Romanians. Nevertheless, the Soviets began imposing their authority on the country. Many areas were currently ruled by the Red Army either directly or through local appointees, and only in Wallachia and southern Transylvania was the old administration still functioning. In December, the Soviets denounced both the premier and the minister of interior for being soft on Fascism and forced their resignations. Both posts were then given to the elderly, more reliable General Nicolas Radescu.

Shortly after the Yalta Conference in February 1945, Stalin sent his chief hatchet man, Andrei Vyshinsky, Soviet deputy foreign minister, to Romania to pressure King Michael into replacing the present government with one totally controlled by the Communists. By this time, the Communists had infiltrated the other political parties, especially the Ploughman's Front. This agrarian party already had a number of crypto-Communists who talked "democracy" and "social and political reform" while pressing forward with their agenda of Stalinization.

A Stalinist Agenda. On 24 February 1945, a clash in Bucharest between Communist and non-Communist workers gave the Communists a pretext for occupying the headquarters of the Romanian army and disarming the local garrison. Vyshinsky forced King Michael to create the National Democratic Front, amalgamating the Communists and the left-wing Social Democrats with the Ploughman's Front and some liberals. Petru Groza of the Ploughman's Front, headed the new cabinet, which emerged on 6 March. The Communists took charge of the three crucial ministries of Interior, Justice, and Foreign Affairs. Only two of the cabinet posts were held by members of "bourgeois" parties. This coalition government lasted for the next two years.

During this time, the government enacted a major land reform and nationalized the National Bank of Romania, but the Soviets devoted most of their attention to gaining control of Romania's natural resources, particularly its petroleum, timber, and chemicals. They accomplished this through special agencies, or *Sovroms*, that had been created by economic and commercial treaties between Romania and the Soviet Union. At the same time, the "home" Communists, led by Party Secretary Gheorghe Gheorghiu-Dej, worked to gain uncontested control of the Romanian Communist party. Once the peace treaty was signed in February 1947, and the British and Americans had recognized the Romanian government, the Stalinists abandoned all restraints. They muzzled, then dissolved, the opposition parties, arresting their leaders and trying them for conspiracy. They fused the non-Communist parties of the National Democratic Front with the Communist party.

In November 1947, they forced the king to abdicate, and Romania became a People's Republic with a Soviet-style constitution. Stalin continued to push for the complete subordination of the Romanian economy to the demands of the Soviet Empire. He was clearly more interested in exploiting this former enemy state than in creating socialism.[47] But such organized looting would eventually backfire. The Romanian Communist leaders were in no position to object, but they were still nationalists and became increasingly uncomfortable in their role of servitude.

Poland

Free Soviet-Style Elections. Russia had been meddling in Polish affairs since the Poles came into existence. But Stalinization was, of course, a more recent form of intervention. It began with the Soviet invasion of eastern Poland on 17 September 1939 and continued with the subsequent partition of the country in accordance with the secret treaty with Hitler. This period lasted until June 1941, when the Germans launched Operation Barbarossa. During that year and a half, the Poles were given a taste of the meaning of Soviet tutelage: the Communists deported about 10 percent of the area's inhabitants and liquidated many of the old Polish elites, including the murder of thousands of army officers and other leaders in Katyn Forest.

In 1944, before the end of the war with Germany, the Soviets established their own Polish government in exile, the National Council of the Homeland, which was completely dominated by the Polish Communist Workers' party. On 22 July 1944, after the liberation of some Polish territory by the Red Army, the Polish Committee of National Liberation was set up and declared itself the unique representative of the will of the Polish people. At the end of the year, it became the provisional government and was immediately recognized by the Soviet Union. But because Roosevelt and Churchill at Yalta insisted upon broader representation, the council was expanded to include more non-Communists. Even so, the Polish Communists remained very much in charge, controlling the police and the armed forces. In March 1945, the Soviets arrested sixteen leaders of the Polish underground who had been loyal to the London government in exile. The men were taken into custody while attending a Soviet-sponsored conference to determine the composition of a government of national unity; they had been invited to the conference under a pledge of safe conduct. All sixteen were charged with subversion against the Red Army and sent to Moscow for trial. The British and Americans protested that such conduct violated the Declaration of Liberated Europe, but Stalin told the Western leaders to mind their own business, adding that he resented being dictated to.[48] He would later explain that the arrests were necessary because the Red Army was "forced to protect its units and its rear-lines against saboteurs and those who create disorder."[49]

The Process of Communization. The Soviets also began bringing the areas taken from Germany under Communist control. They had established a separate Ministry of Regained Territories, entrusted directly to the general secretary of the Polish Communist party, Wladyslaw Gomulka, who had spent the war years in the Polish underground. Thus, even before the complete Soviet takeover of Poland, there already existed a Communist state within the state. Moscow insisted that the usual pattern of Stalinization be followed. Non-Communist parties were harassed, especially those formerly associated with the London government in exile. Opponents were tried and imprisoned or executed. The socialist parties were fused with the Communists into a United Workers party.

Elections took place in January 1947, as a pro forma honoring of the promises in the Potsdam accords, but the results were shockingly fraudulent. Many of the campaign workers of the important Peasant party had already been put in jail before election day. The party was awarded only 28 seats, compared to the 394 accorded the Communist-Socialist coalition. Peasant party leader Stanislaw Mikolajczyk was denounced as an agent of Western imperialism. In October, fearing he would be arrested, he fled the country. The British and Americans protested, but without effect. The elections led to the adoption of a Soviet-style constitution.

Gomulka, although a willing actor in the creation of a one-party state, believed that the Polish Communists should be allowed to chart an independent road to socialism. He therefore opposed compulsory collectivization of agriculture and did not approve the Cominform's supervision of Polish domestic affairs. This stand brought him into direct opposition to the Stalinist group headed by Boleslaw Bierut and Edward Ochab. The Stalinists accused Gomulka of being a bourgeois reactionary and stripped him of his party and government posts and in 1951 put him under house arrest. By then the Polish Communist party had become a faithful replica of the Soviet party. Gomulka's fate was not unique; the purge of deviationist elements eventually encompassed many other comrades who also wanted independence from Soviet tutelage. The housecleaning was carried out by the Polish security police under the direction of the NKVD, but proved less bloody than similar purges in other Eastern European countries.

The government now headed by Bierut pushed for the complete integration of the Polish and Soviet economies. All nonparty organizations were either dissolved or were coopted by the new regime. Only the Catholic church retained any measure of independence. Consequently, the Stalinists launched a campaign of increasing intensity against the church and its institutions. The Stalinists nationalized the church's publishing houses, dissolved its youth groups, secularized its schools, seized the assets of its charitable organization, *Caritas*, and confiscated all its estates over fifty hectares without compensation.

In April 1950, the Polish Catholic church had signed an agreement with the Communist government; in this pact, the first of its kind, the church promised to respect the authority of the state in temporal matters in exchange for the preservation of its jurisdiction in spiritual matters, including recognition of the authority of the pope. The state soon began to violate this concordat, however. It restricted religious instruction, harassed priests, claimed the right to make church appointments, and demanded that all church dignitaries take an oath of loyalty to the Communist state. Those who refused were arrested including Stefan Cardinal Wyszynski who was confined to a monastery in 1953. Despite the persecution, the church remained, as in the past, a symbol of Polish independence. Support for Catholicism became a form of political protest against the regime.[50]

Hungary

A Losing Battle. In Hungary, the Soviets initially displayed a sense of moderation. Hungary became a republic again in 1946 and was directed by a non-Communist coalition until 1947, while the Communists marshalled their forces. Stalin's spearbearers, Ernö Gerö, Imre Nagy, and Matyas Rákosi, returned from Moscow to join forces with local Communist underground leaders, such as Laszlo Rajk and János Kádár. The Communists also augmented their political strength through an aggressive policy of recruitment—from a few thousand adherents, party membership soon reached 200,000—and through associations with other parties. Thus, they formed an alliance with the Social Democrats and tried to do the same with the agrarian Smallholders party.

The Smallholders had gained immense popularity because of their commitment to land reform, which had broken up the estates of the Magyar gentry and created hundreds of thousands of new peasant proprietors. Even in areas with working-class majorities, the gains of the Smallholders were impressive. In the Budapest municipal elections of 2 October 1945, they won 51 percent of the vote, demonstrating the proletariat's lack of confidence in the Communist–Social Democrat ticket. The chairman of the Allied Control Commission, Marshal Klimenti Voroshilov, became alarmed and summoned the leaders of the Smallholders party to a meeting in an attempt to limit the number of parliamentary seats the Smallholders would be allowed to win in the forthcoming national elections on 4 November 1945. Voroshilov first proposed 40 percent, but when the Smallholders protested, he raised it to 45 percent. Again the Smallholders refused. Voroshilov said his last offer was 47.5 percent. The Smallholders still found it unacceptable and refused any preelection deal, but promised vaguely to work with the other parties of the "Independence Front" to create a common policy.

The Smallholders won 57 percent of the total seats in parliament. The Communists and Social Democrats each got only 17 percent. But despite their majority, the Smallholders were pressured into forming a coalition ministry in which the Communists obtained the key Ministry of Interior with control of the police. The result was predictable.

The Extinction of the Opposition. The Communists gradually assumed control of the other main instrumentalities of power: the armed forces and the trade unions. They denounced the Smallholders party as a haven of Fascists and bourgeois reactionaries and vilified its general secretary, Béla Kovács. In February 1947, he was arrested and never seen alive again. Presumably, he was executed, but not before he had been forced to denounce his friend Premier Ferenc Nagy for espionage against the Soviet Union. The allegation was made public in May, when Nagy was on holiday in Switzerland. The Communists demanded Nagy's resignation and threatened to arrest his son unless he complied. Nagy agreed, but said he would do so only after the boy had joined him in Switzerland. Soviet Foreign Minister Molotov claimed he did not understand the concern of the British and Americans, since events in Hungary did not threaten any Allied interests.[51]

The Communists extended their attack against the Smallholders to include all other political groupings. At the start of 1948, the only non-Communist party still in existence was the Social Democratic party. Its independence ended in June, when it was forced to merge with the Communists into the newly named Hungarian Workers party. The attack on the political opposition was accompanied by an offensive against the Reformed Calvinist, Evangelical Lutheran, and Roman Catholic churches. The regime mobilized and pressured the faithful, confiscated church property, and closed down church schools. The police maintained a record of those who attended religious services. To show that nobody was safe, the regime arrested Joseph Cardinal Mindszenty, the primate of the Hungarian Catholic church. The regime charged him with conspiring to restore the landlord-capitalist order and the Habsburg regime. In February 1949, a people's court sentenced the cardinal to life imprisonment for treason and espionage. He had also been charged with currency violations.

The creation of a one-party state and Soviet domination of Hungary were now virtually complete. In April 1949, new parliamentary elections were held. No opposition candidates appeared on the ballot. The Communists now began an attack against all those within their ranks whom they felt were not sufficiently Stalinist. One of the first to be arrested was the foreign minister Laszlo Rajk.

Rajk's Communist credentials were impeccable, but he had two failings: he was a personal rival of Rákosi, and he had not been an émigré in Moscow during the war. The Stalinists accused Rajk and his associates of acting as agents of Tito of Yugoslavia and the Western imperialists. His trial in September 1949 was worthy of the great Stalinist show trials of the 1930s. The witnesses had been interrogated constantly to make sure they would follow the prosecution's script. Rajk and his codefendants all confessed. Rajk, à la Lev Kamenev, even declared in advance that he considered the sentence of the court to be a just one.[52] He was sentenced to death and hanged. Thus, Rajk fell victim to the very police state he had helped to create. On his orders, many of the leaders of the Smallholders and Social Democrats had been tortured and sent to the scaffold. In appearance, however, he was far from odious. Rajk was tall and handsome, almost courtly; he had a solid reputation based on his service in the Spanish Civil War and in the anti-Nazi underground. Rákosi, in contrast, was short and dumpy, with a bullet head that sat on his shoulders as if he had no neck; generally, he was coarse and rude, although he could be charming when he tried. He had spent the war in Moscow and owed his position to Stalin's favor. The two men were a study in contrasts, but contrasts in evil.

Czechoslovakia

A Tradition of Accommodation. The Czechs tried to ward off Soviet interference by voluntarily including Communists in the postwar government. Communism had a stronger popular following here than in any neighboring state. The National Front was composed entirely of parties in existence before 1938, namely, the Social Democrats, Communists, and the People's Catholic party. The Communists controlled the crucial Ministry of Interior, but the voluntary withdrawal of the Red Army in December 1945 left the local party without the military backup that had been critical for a takeover elsewhere.[53] But of all the Eastern countries, Czechoslovakia seemed to present the best chance for the Communist party to come to power legally. In the first postwar parliamentary elections, held by free and secret ballot in May 1946, the Communists managed to win an impressive 38 percent of the popular vote, receiving support from both working-class and agricultural districts. President Edvard Beneš therefore invited party leader Klement Gottwald to be premier. The Moscow-trained Gottwald formed a ministry with nine Communists and seventeen non-Communists.

Beneš, one of the principal architects of Czech democracy, apparently had been under no specific Communist pressure to appoint Gottwald, but did so in the hope of maintaining his country's independence within the Soviet orbit. He realized that Czechoslovakia's ultimate fate was directly related to the postwar relationship between the Soviet Union and the Western powers. If these two power blocs could cooperate, then Czech democracy could survive. He also hoped that the Communists "having already come so far on the way to real power [would] understand that they must impose some restraint on themselves, that while they need not retreat anywhere they must have the patience to choose the correct moment for continuing in a reasonable way along the evolutionary road."[54]

In 1943, Beneš had forestalled the creation of a Moscow-sponsored Czech exile government by going to Moscow to conclude a Soviet-Czechoslovak Friendship Treaty in which both states agreed "to maintain close and friendly co-operation after the re-establishment of peace and to regulate their actions according to the principles of mutual respect of their independence and sovereignty and non-interference in the internal affairs of the other signatory."[55] Throughout the ne-gotiations, Beneš had been repeatedly assured that the Soviets were not interested in interfering in Czech affairs. He was therefore confident that his country would be allowed to exist as a bridge between the two superpowers. Soon, however, Stalin let the Czechs know their optimism was misplaced.

When the Czechoslovak government unanimously accepted the invitation of the United States to participate in the Marshall Plan for European Economic Recovery on 7 July 1947, Stalin informed Gottwald, who was in Moscow at the time with other Czech officials, that the real aim of the Marshall Plan was to "create a Western bloc and isolate the Soviet Union with loans." Stalin warned that he would regard Czechoslovak participation as a "proof to the people of the U.S.S.R. of the fact that [the Czechs] have allowed [themselves] to be used as an instrument against the U.S.S.R., something which neither the Soviet public nor the Soviet Government could tolerate."[56] The Soviet leader insisted that the in-vitation be rejected. The Czechs obediently complied.

The Coup in Prague. Henceforth, Stalin resolved to take no chances. As it no longer seemed likely that the Czech Communists would capture a majority of the votes in a free election, he approved the usual tactics of subversion, beginning with an attempt by the Communist Interior Minister, Vaclav Nosek, to purge the National Police Force. On 12 February 1948, the non-Communists in the cabinet demanded that this subversion cease, but Nosek, backed by Premier Gottwald, refused. On 21 February, twelve ministers from the Catholic, National Socialist, and Slovak Democratic parties resigned in protest; they anticipated that President Beneš would refuse to accept their resignations, thereby forcing the Communists to back down. But Beneš feared that if he intervened, the Communists would start an insurrection, providing the Soviets with an excuse to enter Czechoslovakia to restore order.

Meanwhile, on 19 February, Soviet Ambassador Valerian Zorin had arrived in Prague to arrange a *coup d'état*. Communist "Action Committees" and trade union militias were hastily organized, armed with new rifles, and let loose in the streets. They seized the Czech radio network and threatened a general strike unless Beneš formed a new government, giving the Communists an absolute majority of the posts. Beneš caved in. On 25 February, he appointed a Communist-controlled government with Gottwald retaining his post as premier. The only important post occupied by a non-Communist was the Foreign Ministry, which was given to Jan Masaryk, the son of the founder of the republic. Masaryk had decided to stay on in "the faint hope that he would be able to soften the impact of Communist ruthlessness for a short time, and perhaps aid others in leaving the country."[57] But within two weeks he was dead.

Shortly before sunrise on 10 March, his crumpled, pajama-clad body was found in the courtyard of Czernin Palace, thirty feet below a small bathroom window in the minister's third-floor apartment. Gottwald announced that Masaryk had taken his own life in a fit of despondency. In reality, one of Zorin's terrorist squads had murdered him. The assassins had suffocated him with bed pillows and thrown him feet first out the window.[58] The Communists feared that Masaryk would flee to the West, from which he could make radio appeals to his fellow Czechs. These events completely crushed Beneš, and he resigned the presidency, thereby allowing the Communist boss Gottwald to take his place.

To the West, the Communist coup in Czechoslovakia was especially shocking; it destroyed any lingering illusions that cooperation with the Soviet Union was possible. The Czechs had been a symbol of hope. They alone of all Eastern European peoples had managed to create a functioning democracy. Now, for the second time in less than a decade, their aspirations had been crushed under the heel of totalitarianism. But some people felt that the Czechs themselves were hardly blameless, that they had not fought hard enough to preserve the values they cherished. One of the harshest judgments came from the American ambassador in Prague, Laurence Steinhardt, who wrote bluntly that the Czechs "have never seemed able to exercise firmness, courage and noble traits in time of crisis but rather have chosen to bow to political storms which have ravaged about the country."[59] This unfair assessment revealed the degree of frustration that the West felt at being unable to prevent the consolidation of Communist power in Eastern Europe. No other state in Eastern Europe, except Yugoslavia where the circumstances were different, had been able to prevent a Soviet takeover.

Although the Prague coup seemed to establish Stalin's unquestioned control over Eastern Europe, at the very time it occurred, the independent-minded Yugoslavs were creating serious difficulties for the Soviet dictator. In fact, the Soviets had not ended the Eastern European peoples' longings to control their own destinies. Forcing a state to become Communist did not make it less nationalist. Independence could be smothered by fear, but forcing a people into submission did not make them loyal or reliable.

Yugoslavia

Apparent Compliance. At the end of the war, the Yugoslav Communist party, backed by its powerful army of Partisans, had established clear control of the National Liberation Front. It had replaced the monarchy with a republic and prevented the older ruling parties from participating in the national elections of 11 November 1945, thus gaining 96 percent of the vote and control of the country. But the Yugoslav Communists did not need such chicanery to win. As the driving force in the resistance against Nazi Germany, they were the closest the country had to a party of national unity, although no amount of popularity could overcome the state's basic ethnic differences. Although the Communist party leader Josip Tito admired the Communist system, he did not believe the Soviet Union had created its most perfect example. Furthermore, he had no particular respect for Soviet leaders, in whose company he often felt ill at ease. Once, coming home from a state dinner at the Kremlin, he remarked, "I don't know what the devil is wrong with these Russians that they drink so much—plain decadence."[60] Of course, it was not just the Soviet capacity to down large quantities of alcoholic beverages that made an eventual declaration of independence from "Big Brother" inevitable.

Still, the new Yugoslav constitution of January 1946 followed the Soviet model in creating a federal system of separate republics and autonomous regions, with a Council of Nationalities designed to give the major ethnic groups specific representation. The Communists established immediate control over the economy by nationalizing those enterprises that the Germans had confiscated during the war and by expropriating the businesses and industries of Nazi collaborators. Their sole ambition seemed to be to turn the country into a faithful replica of the Soviet Union. In 1947, Tito officially abolished the monarchy.

If the Soviets had any objection, it was that "the Yugoslavs were taking the Marxist socioeconomic model somewhat too seriously." Moscow, possibly fearing that the Yugoslavs would create the Communist utopia first, advised them to "relax a bit . . . be less virginal, less doctrinaire."[61] In a speech made three months after the end of the war, Tito proclaimed that the "most significant foreign policy event in the history of the new Yugoslavia" was "the signing of the Treaty of Mutual Assistance, Friendship and Economic and Cultural Cooperation" (11 April 1945) that established "indestructible links with the Soviet Union [for] the guarantee of our security and of great value for the development of our country."[62] But Tito left no doubt that the liberation of his country was essentially the work of the Partisans. In fact, serious friction between Yugoslavia and the Soviet leaders had arisen soon after Belgrade had been liberated in the autumn of 1944, when the Yugoslavs protested the raping and looting of civilians by Red Army soldiers in northeastern Yugoslavia, the only part of the country the Russians had occupied. The Russian commander Marshal Ivan Konev was not sympathetic. He angrily rejected the charge as an attempt to smear the honor of the glorious Red Army. Like most Soviet military leaders, he belittled others' contribution to the defeat of Nazi Germany. The Soviets also made much of their gifts of wheat to the Belgrade government even though the grain "was in fact wheat that the Germans had collected from Yugoslav peasants and had stored on Yugoslav territory"; the Soviets "looked upon that wheat, and much else besides, simply as their spoils of war."[63] The Yugoslavs were confused and annoyed by this insistence on eternal gratitude.

Profile: Josip Broz Tito (1892–1980)

Unlike other Eastern European Communist leaders, who had come back to their countries in the baggage trains of the Red Army, Tito had stayed in his country to fight. He was a genuine national hero, a modern-day version of those legendary Slavic warriors who had risked everything for the freedom of their people. He therefore possessed the stature to forge the strong national authority from which he could challenge Stalin by taking an audacious, independent line. He had been born Josip Broz, the seventh of fifteen children of a blacksmith in the rural village of Kumroveć in Croatia.[64] (His revolutionary name of Tito became firmly affixed only during World War II.) Josip remembered a childhood of constant scarcity. He had very few years of formal education—the Croatian peasants believed formal schooling was unnecessary. At the age of twelve, he began to work as a cowherd. At fifteen, he left his village to learn the trade of a locksmith. He became acquainted with machines and farm production, but only in metalworking was this knowledge more than·superficial. Tito had an ear for languages, however. He spoke Serbo-Croatian, Slovenian, Russian, French, German, and English, but could not express himself fluently except in his own native dialect. This difficulty gave rise to rumors that he was not really Yugoslav, but Russian or even German.

Service in the Austro-Hungarian army led to his lifelong association with Communism. Captured by the Russians in the Brusilov offensive in 1916, he was freed two years later during the Revolution, when he joined the Bolsheviks. He returned home to work as a trade union agitator. Imprisoned in 1928 for revolutionary activities, he left for Moscow to work for the Comintern upon his release in 1934. Although he was introduced to the major works of Marx, Lenin, and Stalin, his knowledge of Communism was slight. In the party schools in Moscow, loyalty was more highly prized than social and economic theory. In 1937, in the midst of the Great Terror, Stalin named him head of the Yugoslav Communist party.

Party work gave Tito a mission. He had a strong romantic view of history and found personal meaning in the messianic struggle of the working class. He also believed that his success in helping the proletariat of his country fulfill its historical destiny entitled him to assume greater responsibilities. His real talents as a political organizer were revealed during World War II, although even his efforts could not eliminate the divisions that had plagued Yugoslavia before the war. Tito and his Partisan army not only had to fight the German invaders, but also had to contend with the Chetniks, a force used by King Alexander to support his royal dictatorship. The Chetnicks, led by General Draza Mihailović, had links to the Serbian government in exile. In 1943, however, after the Teheran Conference, Churchill halted further supply drops and missions to the Chetniks because he believed that the Partisans were more effective in fighting the Germans, and he also believed they would be easier to work with after the liberation.[65] By the autumn of 1944, before the Soviet army arrived, Tito's forces had taken advantage of the general German disengagement to liberate most of the country, even managing to help capture Belgrade. Thus, they were accustomed to making critical military and political decisions without considering what might be acceptable to Moscow. In September 1944, Tito went to Moscow where he obtained Stalin's promise to withdraw the Red Army from Yugoslavia as soon as the war with Germany was over. Tito treated the Soviet dictator with respect, but he had not come to Moscow to lick his boots. As the commander of a successful national army, Tito was accustomed to giving orders, not taking them.

Tito had led his forces with a mixture of courage and common sense; he combined a singleness of purpose with the flexibility necessary to achieve his goals.[66] He could be jovial, but also utterly ruthless. Later as chief of state, he developed a taste for a luxurious life-style, including splendid uniforms that he believed befit his position. Formerly, however, he had shared all the hazards and hardships of war with his Partisans who had responded to his leadership with a willingness to make great sacrifices. Probably for the first time since the founding of the Yugoslav state, many had been inspired to fight together for a common cause. Yugoslavia was a country in which a true sense of natural cohesion was always a scarce commodity. The state had come apart during World War II, and Tito put it back together. The unity lasted, at least as long as he remained alive. Having a common enemy in the Soviet Union helped.

An Aborted Satellite. The first *public* sign of Soviet-Yugoslav difficulties after the war came in the dispute over the Adriatic seaport of Trieste. The city had been given to Italy in 1920, but now its status had yet to be determined. Both Italy and Yugoslavia wanted it. The city proper was populated by Italians, but most of the inhabitants of the surrounding areas were Slavs. At first, Stalin supported Yugoslavia's claims, but he grew alarmed at Tito's determination to create a power base in the Balkans and changed his mind.[67] Stalin was also concerned with promoting the Italian Communist party. In February 1947, the Paris Peace Treaty created a free territory in which Trieste was put under the joint military government of the United States and Great Britain. Yugoslavia was allowed to govern the Istrian Peninsula. In the meantime, Tito had advanced plans to create a Balkan confederation with Yugoslavia, Albania, and Bulgaria. In December 1947, Stalin, fearing that this would upset the balance of power in Yugoslavia's favor, summoned Tito and Bulgarian leader Dimitrov to Moscow for discussions. But Tito pleaded ill health and sent Milovan Djilas instead. Stalin viewed Tito's insubordination as "not only heresy but the denial of the Soviet Union's 'sacred rights.' "[68] In the months that followed, tension with Moscow increased with an angry exchange of letters.[69] In that time, Stalin completed the takeover of Czechoslovakia, possibly as a warning to the Yugoslav Communists of what could happen should they become too independent.

In June 1948, Yugoslavia was expelled from the Cominform. The news was announced appropriately by the Czechoslovak Communist party newspaper, *Rude Pravo*. The article denounced the Yugoslavs for Bukharinist opportunism, petty bourgeois nationalism, Menshevism, Trotskyism, adventurism, Turkish terrorism, and, worst of all, the pursuit of "an unfriendly policy toward the Soviet Union." The formal resolution of banishment, which had been signed by representatives from all the Iron Curtain parties, plus the Communist parties of France and Italy, accused the Yugoslav Communists of serious violations of Marxist-Leninist doctrine, including the denial of the (Stalinist) dogma that the class struggle intensifies during the period of transition from capitalism to socialism. The Yugoslavs were lambasted for disregarding class differentiation among the peasantry, belittling "the role of the party in the political life of the country," having no "inner party democracy," and violating the doctrine "of the equality of the Communist Parties." Cutting through all this verbiage, the real issue was that "the Yugoslav leaders think that they can maintain Yugoslavia's independence and build socialism without the support of the Communist parties of other countries, without the support of the Peoples' Democracies, without the support of the Soviet Union."

Stalin once boasted to Khrushchev, "I will shake my little finger and there will be no more Tito."[70] The boast simply showed how little he understood the limitations of his country's power and the character of the man he believed he could crush so easily. As Djilas pointed out, the Soviets were caught in their own trap: they had committed themselves to the cult of the leader and were in no position to resist the cult of Tito, which "would serve to strengthen Yugoslavia's capacity for independent resistance."[71] The break with Moscow seemingly left the Yugoslavs isolated and exposed to Soviet intervention. However, the subversion that usually accompanied such a move was doomed to fail because of the personal stature of Tito and the tight-knit political organization over which he ruled. Many of Tito's supporters had been with him during the war and were ready to follow him in another struggle to maintain Yugoslav independence—if need be, against the Soviets.

Independence did not make the Yugoslavs any less Communist, however. Tito did not favor the development of representative government. Indeed, in the first two or three years after the liberation, his ideology was as doctrinaire as Stalin's. After the schism, however, Tito became more flexible and, by Stalin's definition, more heretical. Tito did not emphasize collectivization of agriculture and, in 1953, actually allowed peasants to withdraw from land cooperatives they had previously joined. The private farm sector increased significantly as a result. Yugoslav workers also had considerably more say in the running of factories than did workers in other Communist countries. Tito simultaneously increased his contacts with the countries of the West. Britain and the United States proved more than willing to give him aid—even military assistance—without question. Being able to play off the East and West obviously had its advantages.

Trying to Keep the Faith

Reform in Poland. Tito had dramatized Soviet relations with the Eastern bloc by denouncing the Stalinist leaders of the Eastern European satellites: "These men have their hands soaked in blood, have staged trials, given false information, sentenced innocent men to death." He was, in effect, saying that as long as such men remained in power, there could be no real rapprochement with the Soviet Union. The death of Stalin aroused hope that direct Soviet interference in the affairs of Eastern Europe would decline. Indeed, Moscow's New Course, which called for a certain amount of economic decentralization and an easing of the tension of the Cold War, seemed to promise better times. The program did not come soon enough to prevent the riots in East Berlin in June 1953 and the less serious demonstrations in Pilsen in Czechoslovakia, however. Elsewhere people wanted change but seemed content to wait for it. Khrushchev wanted to put relations among the Soviet-bloc states on a more rational and, he hoped, firmer basis. However, the promise of a new era raised expectations of greater independence. His speech at the Twentieth Party Congress in February 1956 seemed to indicate that the Soviets no longer regarded their system as the only model for Communism.

All the Eastern European satellites had demands, but only in Poland and Hungary did the situation become really dangerous. In Warsaw, almost as if on cue, the leading Polish Stalinist Boleslaw Bierut died in March 1956, opening the way for a reshuffling of forces within the government. Prime Minister Josef Cyrankiewicz said that the new policy would include improving living standards, restoring intraparty democracy, and developing the political initiative of individuals and of the masses. He recognized that economic grievances were widespread and that reforms were needed.

But the Poles were unwilling to wait. On 28 June 1956, in the city of Poznan, a peaceful demonstration by workers from the Stalin Engineering Works quickly turned into a political protest against the government. The government called out the troops and restored order within a day and a half, but the seeds of unrest continued to germinate. The government at first blamed the riots on agents of the imperialist powers—an explanation in perfect harmony with the views of the Soviet Union. Then, the party line began to take a more realistic turn. The regime now conceded that the Poznan workers had legitimate grievances and demands that had to be recognized. This about-face displeased the Soviets.

Marshals Bulganin and Zhukov arrived during the July meeting of the Polish Central Committee to put the matter straight. Bulganin dismissed the explanation that the disturbances were due to economic unrest and clung to the version that they were caused by agents provocateurs. The Polish leaders disagreed. They refused to launch a Soviet-style repression, proposing instead that further democratization was needed. In their view, the Poznan rising was a profound reflection of the country's political and social problems; it should be analyzed and evaluated and answered with far-reaching concessions and reforms. But before they could institute reforms, the Polish leaders had to ensure that the Soviets would not intervene (six Red Army divisions were currently stationed in the country). To do so, the Poles had to prove that they were in control of the situation. Although the reformers wanted to replace the Stalinist party chief Edward Ochab whose authority had been critically weakened, they feared this move might trigger a pro-Soviet coup.

The reformers tried to consolidate their position by calling for the return to power of a number of leaders who had been removed from government in the purges of the late 1940s and early 1950s. They especially wanted to bring back former First Secretary Wladyslaw Gomulka, who, they felt, could command the support of the party rank and file while at the same time not alarming the Soviets. For their part, the Soviets were watching for any signs that the Poles intended to defect from the Warsaw Pact. "In short," said Khrushchev, "it looked to us as though developments in Poland were rushing forward on the crest of a giant anti-Soviet wave. Meetings were being held all over the country, and we were afraid Poland might break away from us at any moment."[72] Khrushchev formally requested an invitation to attend the meeting of the Polish Central Committee, on 19 October, at which a new Politburo would be elected. The Poles recommended that he come later. He came anyway and brought with him Marshal Ivan Konev, the commander-in-chief of the Soviet ground forces and deputy minister of defense. As a precaution, Khrushchev ordered the Soviet troops stationed in Silesia to be moved closer to Warsaw. The Soviet leader had already reconciled himself to the appointment of Gomulka as first secretary, but he wanted to make sure that this would not involve a significant loss of Soviet authority. On 21 October 1956, the Polish Communist leaders elected Gomulka as party secretary, but allowed Ochab to retain a seat on the Politburo.

Gomulka began his rule by insisting on the dismissal of various pro-Soviet ministers, including Minister of Defense Marshal Konstantin Rokossovsky, a Soviet citizen of Polish birth. He also demanded that the Soviet units heading toward Warsaw be returned to their bases, but at the same time he assured the Soviet leaders that Poland would continue to be a firm partner in the Soviet alliance. Khrushchev, apparently convinced, ordered the Soviet units to halt. "We believed him when he said he realized we faced a common enemy, Western imperialism," he wrote.[73] Despite their desire for independence, the Poles still relied on the Soviet Union to guarantee the territorial integrity of their country, which included land taken from Germany. To dramatize the fact, Gomulka made Khrushchev an honorary citizen of Szczecin, the former German city of Stettin on the Oder. Khrushchev, who realized the implications of the honor, was only too willing to accept. Gomulka knew that he would have to act with extreme caution; any hint that Polish economic and political reforms could endanger Soviet security might result in Soviet intervention. Ironically, however, Gomulka had become popular precisely because of Soviet meddling.

In time, the Polish Communist system gradually became less dogmatic and more pragmatic. Contact with the West increased. The collectivization of agriculture was halted, and within less than a decade, private farmers held 85 percent of all arable lands and accounted for almost 90 percent of total production. Most industry remained nationalized, but private enterprise continued to exist and was actually encouraged. Despite official censorship, some freedom of expression was allowed. Yet, for all its liberalization, Poland remained a one-party dictatorship. Gomulka was a dedicated Communist, not, as some had hoped, a democrat in disguise. Khrushchev said he was glad the Polish crisis had not produced a showdown: "an armed clash between Soviet soldiers and Polish workers [would have] been a fierce one—and the most welcome one of all for the enemies of the Soviet Union, of Communism, and of Poland."[74] As the Soviets proved by their handling of the more volatile situation in Hungary, they would hardly have been squeamish about forcing a satellite back into obedience if they had thought it necessary.

Counterrevolution in Hungary. In June 1953, three months after Stalin's death, the new Kremlin rulers informed Hungarian party leader Matyas Rákosi and some of his lieutenants, including Ernö Gerö, that the days of a Stalinist-style leadership were over. Budapest already had a workers' strike, and the Kremlin leaders feared that without reform the country might soon be at the brink of chaos. They allowed Rákosi to remain as general-secretary, but they wanted the authority of the party to be separated from the state. Rákosi was forced to relinquish his post as prime minister in favor of his political rival, Imre Nagy. Nagy wanted to return the country to a rule of law, ending the police state and one-man rule.

Nagy also wanted to relax economic controls, which would allow the return of small-scale private enterprise and the disbanding of collective farms. In April 1955, however, the old hard-liners, led by Rákosi, forced Nagy to resign and moved to strip him of his party membership. Turning back the clock proved difficult, however. In July 1956, following Khrushchev's secret speech, Anastas Mikoyan engineered the election of Gerö as the new Hungarian party chief at a meeting of the Hungarian Central Committee. However, Gerö, once a Rákosi protégé, was not entirely acceptable to the party's "moderates," who favored more liberalization and the return of Imre Nagy. Consequently, Gerö had difficulty consolidating his position.

Meanwhile, dissatisfied Hungarian intellectuals were pressuring for democratization. Delegates to the Hungarian Writers' Union, which met in September, stressed the importance of artistic freedom and the necessity of concluding "a stubborn, protective alliance among ourselves to tell the truth."[75] Election of the union's new executive board resulted in the wholesale ouster of the old Stalinists. Journals and papers henceforth spoke openly of the necessity of breaking with the past. In its 6 October 1956 edition, the Communist party paper, *Szabad Nep (Free People)*, covered the reinterment of four victims of the purge trials of 1949 and wrote that the ceremony was also a remembrance of "the dark practices of tyranny, lawlessness, slander and defrauding of the people."[76] The editorial reflected a national mood. Over the next two weeks, the Writers' Union called for a democratically elected national leadership, the Journalists' Union insisted on new laws permitting a free press, and the students at the Technical College of Budapest demanded an end to compulsory Russian language courses and a reduction in the hours devoted to the study of Marxist-Leninism. Such agitation would not have been so successful had not the ruling party itself been so badly split. Few of its members actually considered abandoning Communism, but they did debate what form Communism should take. To many, the choice seemed to be between the hard line of Ernö Gerö and the liberalization of Imre Nagy.

Nagy had recently been reinstated in the party and restored to regular membership in the Hungarian Academy of Sciences. Tension was particularly high, and an editorial in *Szabad Nep* on 23 October warned college students to be "on guard under all circumstances lest their democratic and socialist unity be disrupted by some sort of provocation."[77] Already the Hungarian protest movement was taking a newer, more dangerous turn.

The news of Gomulka's success in Poland prompted a group of writers and university students to organize a sympathy demonstration in front of the Polish embassy in Budapest. On the afternoon of 23 October, some 50,000 people thronged the streets carrying Polish and Hungarian flags from which the Communist emblems had been removed and singing the "Internationale," the "Anthem of Kossuth," and the "Marseillaise." Toward evening, the bulk of the crowd had coalesced in the square before the House of Parliament, while others gathered in front of the broadcasting headquarters where Gerö was scheduled to address the nation at eight o'clock. His speech would be carried to those in the streets via

A Red Army major is one of the casualties of the bloody Budapest revolt in October 1956. However, the Soviets soon restored order with their T-34 tanks.

loudspeakers. Gerö had recently returned from the Crimea, where he had met with Khrushchev and Tito, and most of those in the crowd assumed he would announce significant concessions. But Gerö's address, actually a remote transcription from party headquarters, was just the opposite: We "condemn those who strive to spread the poison among our youth and who have taken advantage of the democratic freedom insured by our state to working people to carry out a demonstration of a nationalist character."[78] The speech, which lasted just over ten minutes, ended with an appeal to party unity. Gerö's intransigence inflamed an already nasty situation, and when units of the dreaded Hungarian Security Police (*Allamvédelmi Hatósag* or AVH) who were protecting the radio building opened fire on the crowd, Budapest erupted into civil war. People raided ammunition depots and police stations for weapons. They destroyed Soviet bookstores. They toppled the huge bronze statue of Stalin on Dozso Gyorgy Street. They seized and wrecked the newspaper offices of the Communist paper *Szabad Nep*. All over the city, members of the crowd clashed with the forces of order. Gerö proclaimed martial law and called upon the Soviets to support his tottering regime. On 24 October, between one and two o'clock in the morning, Soviet motorized units entered the city. At the same time, the Hungarian party Central Committee met and agreed to make Imre Nagy prime minister in an apparent effort to restore popular confidence in the national leadership. Later that day, Anastas Mikoyan and Mikhail Suslov arrived from Moscow, just in time for one of the most decisive events of the Hungarian revolt.

On 25 October, demonstrators in front of the House of Parliament were gunned down by troops of the hated AVH; many were killed or wounded (as were several members of a Soviet tank crew stationed in the center of the square). The crowd returned the fire. The skirmish convinced Mikoyan and Suslov that Gerö had no hope of bringing the situation under control; they replaced him with János Kádár, a former Stalinist loyalist whom Rákosi had imprisoned for being "an imperialist agent." From all appearances, the Soviets seemed inclined to be conciliatory. But the situation in Hungary was significantly different from Poland where the Gomulka government could count on solid support from the working class and the army. Hungary was becoming federalized; local provincial councils were taking charge of their own affairs and making demands on the Budapest government. The Hungarian Communist party had lost considerable authority and was on the verge of disintegration.

A new government that included non-Communists was organized on 27 October 1956. The next day, Nagy made a radio address to the Hungarian people. He said that his government supported "those new organs of democratic self-government which have sprung up at the people's initiative and [would] strive to find a place for them in the administrative machinery."[79] Appealing to the crowds to lay down their arms, he declared an amnesty for those who had participated in the fighting. He promised to begin negotiations with the Soviets for the withdrawal of their forces from Hungary. Over the next several days, the Nagy government began returning the country to the status that had existed before the Stalinist takeover. It ordered the reorganization of the armed forces, decreed the construction of a new unified democratic police force, and on 30 October proclaimed the restoration of the multiparty system to put "the country's Government on the basis of democratic cooperation between the coalition parties, reborn in 1945."[80] Also on 30 October, Cardinal Mindszenty was released in response to rebel demands that all persecuted religious leaders be rehabilitated. Mindszenty returned to Budapest prepared to take up where he had left off; he even formed a new Christian Democratic party. The narrow-minded cardinal had little appreciation of the current situation, however. Nor for that matter did Nagy himself. Nagy had hardly envisaged the rebirth of a true representative system when he and his fellow group of "Muscovites" returned home after World War II to carry out the Communist revolution. He might have been willing to change with the time, but the Soviets were not.

They viewed the collapse of Communist authority with the greatest alarm and were particularly concerned when Nagy announced on 1 November that he intended to withdraw Hungary from the Warsaw Treaty and proclaim it a neutral state. For Khrushchev, allowing Hungary to pull out of the Soviet bloc would have been political suicide. As a matter of fact, at the end of October, the Presidium had already unanimously resolved to crush the Nagy government, in order, as Khrushchev put it, to "help the working classes of Hungary in its struggle against the counter-revolution."[81] But before the Soviets ordered their troops into action, they took special pains to assure themselves of the support of other Communist countries.[82] Khrushchev personally obtained the concurrence of the leaders of Poland, Romania, Bulgaria, and Yugoslavia.[83]

The Red Army began its advance on Budapest before dawn on the morning of 4 November 1956. Up until the last moment, the Soviets had continued negotiations with the Nagy government, offering hope of a peaceful solution. A four-man Hungarian military delegation, including Minister of Defense General Pal Maléter, came to Soviet headquarters in Tokol for talks, lured there with a promise of safe conduct. The men were arrested shortly after they arrived. The Soviets had more difficulty with the Hungarian army and the armed freedom fighters of Budapest, but the issue was never in doubt. The Nagy government disappeared. Nagy sought asylum in the Yugoslav embassy. Later, guaranteed immunity from arrest, he left, but was kidnapped by the Soviets and taken to Romania. Cardinal Mindszenty sought refuge in the American embassy where he remained cooped up as a none-too-welcome guest for the next fifteen years.[84]

On the heels of the Red Army came members of the Soviet-sponsored Revolutionary Worker-Peasant Government led by party secretary János Kádár. Kádár promised to work for Hungarian national independence and sovereignty and to institute certain economic, administrative, and industrial reforms. Although the new regime was a front for Soviet rule, Hungary was, in fact, far more independent than before the revolt began. The Soviet Union gradually abandoned its exploitative trade practices over the Hungarian economy. And, in time, Kádár became more liberal; in the 1960s, his slogan would be "Those who are not against us are with us." But this was no comfort in 1956.

The Soviet repression resulted in about 25,000 casualties. About 20,000 Hungarians were arrested for political crimes, of whom 2,000 were executed, including Imre Nagy and Pal Maléter. During the revolt, about 200,000 Hungarians fled to Austria; most of these were young people, including many of Hungary's most talented and ambitious citizens. The revolt's strongest supporters and leading participants were often the very people whom the Communist regime had groomed to become the country's ruling elite. These cadres were old enough to recognize the brutality and hypocrisy of totalitarianism and still young enough not to be cynical. Few ever returned permanently to Hungary.

Khrushchev claimed that Soviet intervention was necessary to protect the Hungarian working class. "We, the Soviet Union, support the revolutionary forces of the world," he wrote. "We do so out of our international obligations. We wholeheartedly join in the struggle being waged by the working classes under the red banner emblazoned with the slogan, 'Proletarians of the world unite.' We are against the export of counterrevolution. That is why it would be unthinkable and unforgivable for us to refuse help to the working class of any country in its struggle against the forces of capitalism."[85] Although in practice the "Khrushchev Doctrine" was less bloodthirsty than the old Stalinism, it was extremely open-ended, and few Hungarians were willing to give it the benefit of the doubt.

Communist party leaders in the West almost universally sided with Khrushchev—at least at first. Their fear of the effects of de-Stalinization made them conveniently willing to ignore the crushing of a true working-class movement in Hungary. Nevertheless, the Hungarian October uprising had caused a split in the ranks of European leftists. It brought to an end many of the existing alliances between the Communists and socialists. It had forced Communists to reappraise their loyalty to the Soviet Union. Intellectuals, disgusted by the ossified Communist ideology, quit the party in droves. Communist sympathizers, or fellow travelers as they were called, almost ceased to exist.[86] The hard-liners in the party did not have an easy time retaining their influence. Reformists demanded changes that eventually led to the development of Eurocommunism in which Communist politicians seemingly accepted democracy and expressed their willingness to play the parliamentary game. After Hungary, Communists found it hazardous to be attached to the Soviet Union. Even as the Eurocommunist movement developed, the credibility of the Soviet Union continued to decline as its system became more economically backward and its hold over its satellites more tenuous.

POSTSCRIPT   As events in Yugoslavia had shown, Stalin had overestimated his power in Eastern Europe. His experience with Tito made him determined to take no further chances. He ordered a thorough purge of nationalist tendencies in Bulgaria, Poland, Hungary, Romania, and Czechoslovakia, placing their governments and Communist parties more firmly in the hands of trusted Muscovites. Traditional Soviet-style show trials followed, with most of the suspected "Titoists" being liquidated after summary hearings. The Soviet Union tried to strengthen its hold over the satellites by concluding bilateral treaties to enforce economic subservience. As a result, many local industries were put under direct Soviet management, and within five years Stalinization appeared complete. The Stalinization campaign impressed the British and American governments as primary evidence that Stalin was motivated by the desire to extend Soviet power westward rather than by a desire for security. After the coup in Prague, nothing that the Stalinist government could have done would have convinced the West that the Soviet dictator was not aiming at European, or even world, domination. Considering how the Soviets had institutionalized the expansion of their power, the assumption was not wholly unreasonable.

In "Stalin's Heirs," Yevtushenko wrote of the difficulty of de-Stalinization in a society shaped according to Stalin's will:

No, Stalin has not given up.
He thinks he can cheat death
We carried him from the mausoleum.
But how to remove Stalin's heirs from Stalin! . . .

They, the former henchmen,
hate this era of emptied prison camps
and auditoriums full of people listening to poets.[87]

Khrushchev was a different sort of dictator from his murderous predecessor. Khrushchev claimed he sincerely wanted to raise the standard of living of Soviet citizens because he believed that only this would ensure the survival of the Communist system. "It's time for us to realize that the teachings of Marx, Engels and Lenin cannot be hammered into people's heads only in the classroom and newspapers and at political rallies; agitation and propaganda on behalf of Soviet power must also be carried on in our restaurants and cafeterias. Our people must be able to use their wages to buy high-quality products manufactured under socialism if they are ultimately to accept our system and reject capitalism."[88] Although he talked about dismantling the coercive apparatus of the state, he seemed more sincere about using it to his own advantage.

The collective leadership that followed Khrushchev abandoned de-Stalinization, permitted the secret police to resume some of their earlier judicial prerogatives, scrapped Khrushchev's efforts at economic reorganization, and reaffirmed the need for central control. The satellite states were discouraged from taking an independent path to socialist development, and Soviet influence was pushed into areas of the world—Africa, India, Cuba, and Southeast Asia—that had formerly been considered outside the immediate Soviet sphere of interest. Khrushchev could not create a human face for Soviet Communism, although he did present a human side to his own extraordinary personality. But his successors failed to do even that. Brezhnev developed the doctrine that the Soviet Union had the right and duty to interfere in the internal policies of the satellite states to protect the socialist system. Perhaps he believed the relative ease with which Moscow's will had originally been imposed augered well for continued domination.

As future events showed, however, the Soviet Union would have neither the strength nor the will to maintain indefinite control over its rebellious satellites. Although for the time being Tito was the only Eastern European Communist leader who could chart an independent course for his country's affairs, his example gave the other Eastern European countries hope that, in the right circumstances, their own deliverance might be possible and even ordained.

ENDNOTES

1. Vlasov was a Soviet war hero who had become disgusted with the brutality and corruption of Stalinism. He wanted to organize fighting divisions from Russian prisoners of war, but the Germans were wary of arming men they might not be able to control. Vlasov ultimately surrendered to the Americans; they turned him over to the Russians, who hanged him.

2. The Volga Germans, the Crimean Tatars, some Caucasus Muslims (principally the Karachai, Balkars, Ingushi, and Chechens), and the Kalmyks were sent to Central Asia and Siberia. The deportees were rounded up by the NKVD with only several hours to get ready and loaded into cattle trucks bound for the uninhabited regions in the east. Nikita Khrushchev claimed the Ukrainians avoided a similar fate "only because there were too many of them and there was no place to which to deport them." Nikita Khrushchev, *Khrushchev Remembers: The Last Testament* (Boston: Little, Brown, 1974), 596.

3. From 1941 to 1945, the party increased its membership from 3.5 to almost 6 million, suffering a loss of discipline in the process.

4. "It was all settled in no more time than it takes to set down," Churchill observed. Winston S. Churchill, *Triumph and Tragedy* (Boston: Houghton Mifflin, 1953), 227.

5. In the years following the Great Depression, something like 10 percent of the Czech electorate voted Communist.

6. Georgi Zhukov, *The Memoirs of Marshal Zhukov* (New York: Delacorte Press, 1971), 654.

7. Ironically, some who survived owed their lives to the Great Terror. "If I hadn't been in a camp in 1941," recalled a former political prisoner, "I would have been called up, and a Russian soldier's chance of surviving till 1945 was practically nil .... I don't suppose you often hear people say, as I do, 'Thank God for Stalin and Yezhov,' though in fact, hundreds of thousands of people who were in camps right through the war were saved that way." Alexander Werth, *Russia: Hopes and Fears* (New York: Simon and Schuster, 1969), 85.

8. A. M. Prokhorov, ed., *Great Soviet Encyclopedia*, vols. 7 and 21 (New York: Macmillan, 1975, 1978), 29, 141.

9. Khrushchev, *Khrushchev Remembers*, 594.

10. Milovan Djilas, *Conversations with Stalin*, (New York: Harcourt, Brace and World, 1962), 151.

11. Khrushchev, *Khrushchev Remembers*, 258.

12. Literally, the bad rule or the bad regime of Zhdanov.

13. Werner G. Hahn, *Postwar Soviet Politics: The Fall of Zhdanov and the Defeat of Moderation, 1946–53* (Ithaca: Cornell University Press, 1982), 102.

14. *Information U.S.S.R.* (New York: Macmillan, 1962), 215.

15. Robert Conquest, *Power and Policy in the U.S.S.R.* (London: Macmillan, 1962), 109.

16. Khrushchev, *Khrushchev Remembers*, 251.

17. All resumed their careers after Stalin's death. Yumashev became the head of the Voroshilov Naval Academy, Voronov the president of the Artillery Academy, Bogdanov the head of the Soviet Tank Academy, Novikov the commander of Strategic Aviation, and Shikin an official of the Central Committee of the Communist party. Zhukov became deputy minister of defense.

18. Khrushchev, *Khrushchev Remembers*, 257–58.

19. Ronald Hingley, *Joseph Stalin: Man and Legend* (New York: McGraw-Hill, 1974), 406–7.

20. Stuart Kahan, *The Wolf of the Kremlin* (New York: William Morrow, 1987), 250–51.

21. Ibid., 251.

22. Warren Bartlett Walsh, *Russia and the Soviet Union* (Ann Arbor: University of Michigan Press, 1968), 538–39.

23. Khrushchev, *Khrushchev Remembers*, 234.

24. In 1953, there were 56.6 million cows, up from 47.8 million in 1940, 28.5 million pigs versus 22.5 million, and 94.3 million sheep versus 66.6 million. The number of horses was less in 1953, 15.3 million down from 17.7 million. When one adjusts for the addition of Latvia, Lithuania, and Estonia, these gains (or losses) seem less (or more) significant. Brian R. Mitchell, *European Historical Statistics* (New York: Columbia University Press, 1975), 316–17. In 1950, 31.8 million hectoliters of wheat were grown. In 1953 it was 41.3 million hectoliters, but these gains came at the expense of rye, barley, oats, and maize, all of which dropped on an average of more than 50 percent without compensating for the addition of the Baltic states. Ibid., 262, 273.

25. Timothy Dunmore, *Soviet Politics, 1945–53* (New York: St. Martin's Press, 1984), 86.

26. His daughter shared the grisly details as if the dictator's final agony somehow helped atone for the misery he had caused others. "The hemorrhaging had gradually spread to the rest of the brain. . . . His breathing became shorter and shorter. For the last twelve hours the lack of oxygen was acute. His face altered and became dark. His lips turned black and features grew unrecognizable. The last hours were nothing but a slow strangulation." Svetlana Alliluyeva, *Twenty Letters to a Friend* (New York: Harper and Row, 1967), 10.

27. Conquest, *Power and Policy*, 440.

28. Nathaniel Weyl, ed., *The Anatomy of Terror: Khrushchev's Revelations about Stalin's Regime* (Westport: Greenwood Press, 1956), 26.

29. On the other hand, some suggested that the Stalinists actually encouraged the policy because they hoped that a denunciation of the personality cult would thwart Khrushchev's own rise to the top.

30. The reorganization also increased the general's power. Of the eight central ministries that remained, all but two were now included in the Defense Department.

31. Edward Crankshaw, *Khrushchev: A Career* (New York: Viking, 1966), 214.

32. Khrushchev, *Khrushchev Remembers*, 225.

33. Alan Clark, *Barbarossa* (New York: William Morrow, 1965), 506.

34. Zhukov's disgrace was a singular act of ingratitude. During the leadership contro-

versy the previous June, Zhukov had performed a valuable service for Khrushchev by flying Khrushchev's Central Committee supporters in the provinces to Moscow by military aircraft.

35. Conquest, *Power and Policy*, 361.

36. Mitchell, *European Historical Statistics*, 273.

37. In the murky world of Soviet politics, two main explanations of the interaction of domestic affairs with foreign affairs have been advanced. According to one, Khrushchev provoked the Berlin crisis to divert attention to foreign affairs and thereby quiet his critics. If so, the tactic backfired, for the heavy industry lobby used the crisis to its own advantage. The other explanation contradicts the first, to wit: Khrushchev, realizing he had overreached himself, agreed to greater military expenditures and prompted the crisis as a pretext.

38. Comrade Lazurkina had been a survivor of a Stalinist prison and at the Twenty-Second Congress related that in spite of her arrest she had never lost faith in his leadership. Roy Medvedev, *Let History Judge* (New York: Columbia University Press, 1989), 524–25.

39. Roger Pethybridge, *A History of Postwar Russia* (New York: New American Library, 1966), 242–49.

40. Yevgeny Yevtushenko, *A Precocious Autobiography* (New York: Dutton, 1963), 100.

41. It was not exactly a trade-off, nor was it intended to be, but eventually the Soviet authorities did erect a commemorative statue at Babii Yar. The memorial made no reference to the fact that the victims had been Jews; in a later edition of his poem, Yevtushenko was forced to add that the Nazis killed Russians as well as Jews.

42. Alexander Solzhenitsyn, *One Day in the Life of Ivan Denisovich* (New York: Praeger, 1963), 19.

43. Hugh Seton-Watson, *The Pattern of the Communist Revolution* (London: Methuen, 1953), 248–56.

44. *Foreign Relations of the United States*, 1945, IV, 416.

45. In 1990, following the end of the Communist system, Dimitrov's remains were removed and cremated.

46. During the nineteenth century, Romania had an ongoing dispute with Russia over the ownership of Bessarabia, which Russia had acquired from the Turks in 1812. However, in 1859, the southern part was incorporated in the newly created Romania. Russia managed to get it back in 1878, but at the end of World War I, all Bessarabia became Romanian. The seesaw was not finished. The Red Army occupied Bessarabia in 1940. The Romanians again ruled it from 1941 to 1944. The Soviets "liberated" it at the end of World War II. Throughout all this, neither the Romanians nor the Russians bothered to consult the wishes of the local Moldavian peoples.

47. In part, this was a natural consequence of the war. It was difficult for the Soviets to forgive a nation that, among other things, had fought alongside the Germans in their offensive at Stalingrad.

48. *Stalin's Correspondence with Churchill and Attlee, 1941–1945* (New York: Capricorn Books, 1965), 331.

49. Ibid., 348.

50. Václav Benes and Norman Pounds, *Poland* (New York: Praeger, 1970), 282–90.

51. *Foreign Relations of the United States*, 1947, IV, 191.

52. David Irving, *Uprising* (London: Hodder and Stoughton, 1981), 70.

53. Stalin demanded and received Ruthenia, the eastern tail of Czechoslovakia—a bit of territory that had never been part of the historic Russian state. Its acquisition more than compensated for the withdrawal of the Red Army because it extended Soviet territory across the Carpathian Mountains and gave them a common frontier with Hungary.

54. Edvard Beneš, *Memoirs* (Boston: Houghton Mifflin, 1954), 285.

55. Ibid., 256.

56. *Foreign Relations of the United States*, 1947, III, 319.

57. Ibid., 1948, IV, 742.

58. Claire Sterling, *The Masaryk Case* (New York: Harper and Row, 1969).

59. The judgment became even more extreme: "From the American viewpoint, it seems despicable that, with the exception of a few students, not a single person from the President of the Republic down to the humblest citizen even uttered a public word in defense of their political liberties." *Foreign Relations of the United States*, 1948, IV, 752.

60. Milovan Djilas, *Conversations with Stalin* (New York: Harcourt, Brace and World, 1962), 115.

61. George Zaninovich, *The Development of Socialist Yugoslavia* (Baltimore: John Hopkins Press, 1968), 57.

62. Henry Christman, ed., *The Essential Tito* (New York: St. Martin's Press, 1970).

63. Djilas, *Conversations with Stalin*, 92.

64. For a sympathetic biography, see Phyllis Auty, *Tito: A Biography* (New York: McGraw-Hill, 1970).

65. Walter R. Roberts, *Tito, Mihailovic and the Allies, 1941–1945* (New Brunswick: Rutgers University Press, 1973) 187–253.

66. Fitzroy Maclean, *The Heretic: The Life and Times of Josip Broz-Tito* (New York: Harper, 1957), 194–98.

67. Tito was also intending to annex Albania.

68. *Documents on International Affairs, 1947–1948*, 348–87.

69. Ibid., 175.

70. Weyl, *The Anatomy of Terror*, 55.

71. Milovan Djilas, *Tito: The Story from the Inside* (New York: Harcourt Brace Jovanovich, 1980), 30.

72. Khrushchev, *Khrushchev Remembers*, 199–200.

73. Ibid., 205.

74. Ibid., 204.

75. Paul E. Zinner, ed., *National Communism and Popular Revolt in Eastern Europe* (New York: Columbia University, 1956), 383.

76. Ibid., 385.

77. Ibid., 396.

78. Ibid., 404.

79. Ibid., 430–31.

80. Ibid., 431.

81. Khrushchev, *Khrushchev Remembers*, 417.

82. The Red Chinese leader, Mao Zedong, had earlier advised the Soviets against military intervention in Poland and his representative Liu Shaoqi now told Khrushchev that it was not necessary to use armed force in Hungary. He said the Soviets should withdraw "and let the working class build itself up and deal with counterrevolution on its own." Ibid., 418. Khrushchev replied that the opposite might well be true, that the Hungarian working class, if left to its own devices, might take a fancy to counterrevolution. Later, he claimed that his argument changed Mao's mind.

83. Why Tito agreed is not clear since Hungarian independence would clearly have been in his interest. Possibly, he was opposed to any popular uprising against a Communist system, or perhaps he felt that since he could not change Soviet intentions, he should go along in the hope of obtaining some future Soviet concession. As it turned out, Khrushchev's visit to Tito was pro forma, because the Soviets had already finalized their military plans.

84. Irving, *Uprising*, 507–8, 539–41, 547.

85. Khrushchev, *Khrushchev Remembers*, 428.

86. Fernec Fehér and Agnes Heller, *Hungary 1956 Revisited* (London: Allen and Unwin, 1983), 42–49.

87. *The Poetry of Yevgeny Yevtushenko*, trans. George Reavy (London: Calder and Boyars, 1965), 165.

88. Khrushchev, *Khrushchev Remembers*, 147.

CHAPTER 5

THE BATTLES OF THE COLD WAR, 1949–1962

PREFACE   Soviet puppet regimes had been installed in Bulgaria and Romania, the Communists were trying to foment rebellion in Iran, and it seemed likely that they intended to invade Turkey and seize the Black Sea straits. Harry Truman was nettled. On 5 January 1946, the American president warned his secretary of state, James Byrnes, that "unless Russia is faced with an iron fist and strong language, another war is in the making." The Russians, he insisted, only understood one language, "how many divisions have you?" Truman thought the time for compromise was over. "I'm tired of babying the Soviets,"[1] he said.

The power vacuum in Central Europe, caused by the defeat of Nazi Germany, invited a confrontation between the Americans and the Soviets. The Americans quickly replaced their wartime portrait of Stalin as kindly Uncle Joe with that of a power-hungry barbarian. The Soviet Union, once the noble ally in the fight against tyranny, had become a huge octopus with evil, thrashing tentacles reaching out to seize the world. The Americans saw their duty to keep this monster at bay. They were superbly equipped for such a task.

The United States emerged from World War II far more powerful than it had been when the war began. The war had been waged overseas, not on American soil, and American losses had not been crippling. Indeed, many Americans not directly affected by the war had a notion of battle, derived from Hollywood movies, as a relatively clean affair in which the good guys always finished first and most survived intact. The hellish nature of combat, especially as it had been waged on the Eastern Front, was beyond their comprehension. Roosevelt and his military chiefs made sure that the Americans fought a different kind of war. They saved lives by insisting on the maximum use of machines and firepower rather than masses of infantry divisions.

The Soviets, who had squandered human lives more freely, did not believe that the Americans appreciated their sacrifice, nor did they think the United States was willing to recognize their legitimate security interests. The Soviets thought American insistence on free elections in Eastern Europe was just a ploy to install anti-Soviet, anti-Communist governments in the region. The Soviets were determined to control what they had conquered and establish a huge strategic territorial barrier from the Baltic to the Black Sea to protect them against future attack.

Truman found the Soviet goals offensive. He thought it outrageous that at Potsdam the Americans "were faced with an accomplished fact and we were by circumstances almost forced to agree to Russian occupation of Eastern Poland and the occupation of that part of Germany east of the Oder River by Poland."[2] The failure of the postwar negotiations to change this situation only further frustrated the president. Clearly, the only way the Soviets could be budged from Eastern Europe was by military force. The Americans still believed in the self-determination of peoples, and they still wanted to make the world safe for democracy. Now they had to think in terms of new alliances and rearmament programs instead.

The ability of the United States and the Soviet Union to determine Europe's fate was in sharp contrast to the situation after World War I when neither state had played a major role in the continent's affairs. Moreover, their confrontation was not confined to Europe but encompassed the Far East, the Middle East, and the Western Hemisphere. Nevertheless, the focus of the Cold War was always in Europe. Here it began and here it would have to be resolved.

THE POLICY OF CONTAINMENT

A Military Equation

The North Atlantic Treaty Organization. The Stalinization of Eastern Europe prompted the governments of Britain, France, Belgium, the Netherlands, and Luxembourg to conclude a treaty for collective self-defense. The agreement, signed at Brussels in March 1948, specified that an attack on any one of the signatories would oblige the others to respond with "all the military and other aid and assistance in their power." Such a commitment was intended "to fortify and preserve the principles of democracy, personal freedom and political liberty, the constitutional traditions and the rule of law, which are [the] common heritage."[3] However, when the Brussels treaty was signed, the Western European countries had scant means of protecting themselves. Only the United States could guarantee their security, but there was, as yet, no indication of how this would be done.

The Soviet coup in Prague did induce the U.S. Senate to adopt a resolution, on 11 June 1948, to support regional defense pacts with military assistance "if such aid were shown to be in the interest of the United States." But this intent did not take more tangible form until after the start of the Berlin crisis, when the

THE NORTH ATLANTIC
TREATY ORGANIZATION
AND
THE WARSAW PACT

NATO Members, 1949–1955
Warsaw Pact Members, 1954

Map 3

North Atlantic Treaty was signed on 4 April 1949. The heart of this agreement
was contained in Article 5: "The Parties agree that an armed attack against one
or more of them in Europe or North America shall be considered an attack against
them all" and will commit them "individually and in concert with the other
Parties" to take such action deemed necessary, "including the use of armed force,

to restore and maintain the security of the North Atlantic area."[4] The signatories—the five Brussels Pact countries, plus the United States, Canada, Denmark, Italy, Norway, Iceland, and Portugal[5]—also agreed to establish a permanent council to help "maintain and develop their individual and collective capacity to resist armed attack."

No more would the United States send troops to Europe only *after* the outbreak of war. Once the Senate ratified the treaty, the United States had a long-range commitment to preserve the status quo in time of peace and was bound to an extensive military aid program. The Truman administration, though, gave the impression that the American role would be restricted to strategic bombing and keeping sea lanes open, and that the bulk of any ground troops would come from the Europeans themselves. Like the British in an earlier time, the Americans appeared willing to fight to the last soldier of their allies. In fact, the European governments had grave doubts about the sincerity of the United States toward its new commitments. With the forces currently at their disposal, the North Atlantic Treaty Organization (NATO) partners could fight no more than a delaying action that would—they hoped—give the United States time to deploy its nuclear weaponry. But the atomic bomb suddenly seemed less a deterrent than before, when on 23 September 1949, the world learned that the Soviets had set off their first atomic explosion. The news acted as a tonic; Truman's $1.5 billion military aid program sailed through Congress.

Europeans were more apprehensive. Many believed that improved economic and social conditions alone would be sufficient to prevent the spread of Communism. Some feared that building strong defense forces would provoke the very war they were trying to prevent. Emanuel Shinwell, Labour's secretary of state for war, remarked that it was no use getting free dentures if you were going to get your head blown off. The Italian Communist leader Palmiro Togliatti, in his speech against ratification of the North Atlantic Treaty, warned, "The pact that you are about to sign will ensure that Italy will be a military objective and a theater of war if it breaks out, or as I should say, wherever it breaks out. Italy is one of those countries which will be 'a carpet of atom bombs,' as the American strategists so elegantly express it."[6] Fears that Stalin was planning to attack Western Europe did not seem so farfetched, and many Europeans were thinking that it was better to be Red than Dead.

The North Atlantic Alliance, according to Lord Ismay, the organization's first secretary-general, was created to keep the Russians out, the Americans in, and the Germans down. The NATO alliance developed gradually, concentrating first on standardization of weapons and equipment. The planners also worked to develop a strategic concept of integrated defense and to provide a program for the production and supply of armaments. Despite such activity, the NATO alliance would hardly have deterred a determined aggressor. It existed primarily as an alarm system to warn of the drastic consequences that could arise should its resolve be tested. Stalin, no doubt, concluded that challenging the status quo in Europe was too hazardous. In any event, he was soon forced to focus his attention on events in another part of the world, where the risks proved difficult to calculate.

The Korean War. At the end of the war in the Far East, the Allies agreed that all Japanese troops north of the 38th parallel in Korea would surrender to the Soviet Union and all those south of the 38th parallel would surrender to the United States. The line was established for military convenience and was not intended to be a final political frontier. However, like the zonal boundaries in Germany, the Korean demarcation line became permanent. The discussions over unification broke down in September 1947, and the United States turned the problem over to the United Nations (UN), which resolved that the Koreans themselves should decide the issue in a nationwide referendum. The Soviets refused to cooperate, so only the south voted. The results led to the creation of the Republic of Korea (ROK) in August 1948. One month later, the Soviets established a separate state in the north and began supplying it with tanks, aircraft, and heavy artillery—more apparently than would be required for defense. The Americans, in the meantime, withdrew most of their forces from the ROK as a signal that the peninsula was outside their sphere of interest. In January 1950, Secretary of State Dean Acheson said the U.S. Pacific Ocean defense perimeter ran along the Aleutians to Japan and south to the Ryukyu Islands. His statement proved to be an invitation for aggression.

On 25 June 1950, the North Koreans launched their armies across the 38th parallel. Stalin had not approved the move and apparently was as surprised as the Americans that it had occurred. President Truman was in the library of his home in Independence, Missouri, when Secretary of State Acheson called to inform him of the attack. Truman returned to Washington the next day. As he contemplated what action to take, he made several assumptions: He assumed that the Communist bloc was monolithic and that Stalin had ordered the North Koreans to act. He thought of earlier examples of aggression against Manchuria, Ethiopia, and Austria, and he remembered "how each time that the democracies failed to act it had encouraged the aggressors to keep going ahead." He believed that if "the Communists were permitted to force their way into the Republic of Korea without opposition from the free world, no small nation would have the courage to resist threats and aggression by stronger Communist neighbors. If this was allowed to go unchallenged it would mean a third World War, just as similar incidents had brought on the Second World War."[7] Truman feared the Communists might strike next in Yugoslavia or Germany. He ordered the U.S. Eighth Army hastily flown to South Korea to keep the peninsula from falling into Communist hands. Then he requested a special session of the United Nations Security Council to endorse an American-sponsored resolution declaring North Korea guilty of a breach of peace and recommending that the UN members give South Korea all aid necessary to repel the attackers and reestablish peace and security. Fortunately, the Soviet Union did not attend,[8] and the motion passed unanimously (9 to 0 with Yugoslavia abstaining). The Americans established a unified UN command under the direction of General Douglas MacArthur. Forty-eight states responded with some form of assistance. Truman viewed this as a test of American world leadership; he had not bothered to consult Congress for proper authorization for his action. The Cold War had begun to distort the American Constitution.

The Korean War lasted over three years. The North Koreans almost won the day. Within two months, they had captured all of Korea except the southeast corner around Pusan. Their failure to break the American perimeter allowed MacArthur to launch a daring counterstroke. In September, his amphibious landing at the western port of Inchon, two hundred miles behind the North Korean front lines, brought about the complete disintegration of the North Korean army and put American troops at the 38th parallel. It was one of the most spectacular military operations of modern times and encouraged Truman to turn it into a major Cold War victory by liberating the whole of Korea. MacArthur assured him that the Americans had nothing to fear from the Red Chinese who might view American forces on the Manchurian frontier as a threat to their security. On 27 September, a Joint Chiefs of Staff instruction gave him authorization to go on.[9] American forces reached the Yalu River at the end of October.

On 26 November, however, the Chinese Communists counterattacked with an army of 300,000 men. They found the American forces badly divided, vulnerable, and incapable of supporting each other. MacArthur had divided his forces in the face of an obvious Chinese threat, a mistake in military preparedness for which he rightly deserved criticism. By January 1951, the Chinese had pushed the American forces some sixty miles south of the 38th parallel. The Americans held and eventually recovered some lost ground, but they never managed to push the battle lines much beyond the 38th parallel. Americans, who had grown up believing that they had never lost a war, were outraged, but the frustration must have been just as intense in the Kremlin. Stalin could hardly rejoice at Mao Zedong's entry into the war, which would give the Chinese a sphere of influence in the Korean Peninsula. Nor could he welcome the increased strain put on the Communist system by the need to supply the military and economic needs of the North Koreans. The Soviets in turn required more goods and services from their Eastern European satellites. The reactions of the Eastern Europeans to the pressure for increased production ranged from apathy to various forms of resistance including absenteeism and occasional strikes. The mounting resentment would soon have more dramatic expression in Poland and Hungary. Equally alarming to the Soviets was the effect the war had on the NATO alliance.

The war pushed the United States into a massive program of rearmament. From 1950 to 1953, American defense spending almost quadrupled, rising from $11.9 billion to $43.6 billion. Similar dramatic increases occurred in all the other NATO countries. The NATO members also considerably enhanced and unified their command and organization. This consolidation of the alliance made it easier to reintegrate the Federal Republic of Germany into Western European security affairs, virtually ending the occupation. In December 1950, General Dwight D. Eisenhower became supreme commander of all the alliance forces in Europe, from Norway to the Mediterranean and from Turkey to the Atlantic Ocean. The American presence in Europe was now overwhelming. American foreign policy, in effect, determined the defense policies of all the NATO members, with the ultimate weapon, the atomic bomb, subject only to American control. In fact, the separate nuclear capacities of the superpowers bound them together in a special power relationship outside any alliance system and crystallized the lines of demarcation between East and West in what became known as a balance of terror. However, the determination of the United States and its allies, acting together under the banners of the UN to halt the aggression of the North Koreans, undoubtedly had a chilling effect on other regional adventurers who might contemplate trying the same thing.

Nuclear Politics

The Posture of Liberation. The Soviets exploded their first atomic bomb on 29 August 1949. That was sooner than the Washington experts had expected. President Truman could not believe that "those asiatics" had been capable of building something so complicated. He was alarmed, but, so he claimed, not panicked. He at once ordered the secretaries of state and defense and the chairman of the Atomic Energy Commission (AEC) to prepare a technical, military, and political analysis "as to whether and in what manner the United States should undertake the development and possible production of 'super' atomic weapons."[10] Such weapons would have a thousand times the power of the device dropped on Hiroshima.

Research on the thermonuclear process had been under way since 1942, but had not received a high priority. Some scientists doubted that a weapon of this magnitude could be built. The AEC gave the task of examining the possibility to the General Advisory Committee (GAC), headed by Robert Oppenheimer. Its discussions were held in strict secrecy; the American people were never informed, much less consulted. The GAC recommended that research and development of fissionable weapons be accelerated, but it did not favor making the development of a superbomb a high priority. Its objections were technical, political, ecological, and moral. The committee pointed out that a single such bomb could devastate a vast area, threaten the environment with radioactive fallout, and become a weapon of genocide. The committee saw a "unique opportunity of providing by example some limitations on the totality of war and thus limiting the fear and arousing the hopes of mankind."[11] The GAC conclusions, minus some technical data, were released to the public and sent to President Truman for the final decision. Truman rejected the advice. In doing so, he relied strongly on the arguments of Edward Teller and Teller's associates who maintained that developing the superbomb could assure the United States of its paramount position in the struggle against world Communism. Teller argued that the Soviets would, in time, build their own superbomb anyway, leaving the United States at a great disadvantage.[12]

As a companion piece to the study of nuclear feasibility, Truman had also requested a broad foreign policy statement from his diplomatic and military chiefs. Shepherded by Dean Acheson, this State-Defense study team produced a special brief for the necessity of active American participation in world affairs. The study argued that the United States had to develop a military posture in excess of that required to protect the western hemisphere and essential lines of communication with its allies. More specifically, the United States should develop and stockpile all types of improved weapons, conventional as well as atomic, and augment the military and economic assistance it provided to its allies and to other countries in which it had special interests. The experts insisted on maintaining the policy of containment, but not the balance of power as it currently existed. Thus, the United States, while increasing its will and means to resist Communist aggression and subversion, "should take dynamic steps to reduce the power and influence of the Kremlin inside the Soviet Union and other areas under its control. The objective would be the establishment of friendly regimes not under Kremlin domination. Such action is essential to engage the Kremlin's attention, keep it off balance and force an increased expenditure of Soviet resources in counteraction."[13]

Truman never specifically endorsed these recommendations (rearmament actually occurred in response to the demands of the Korean War), but much of the study became an accepted part of American foreign policy, if only, at times, rhetorically. For example, Acheson's successor, John Foster Dulles, talked a great deal about replacing the policy of containment with a policy of liberation, but his words were largely for domestic consumption. The United States remained basically a proponent of the status quo. Americans hoped that the Soviet system would eventually collapse under its own contradictions and weaknesses, which the State-Defense study identified as "universal suspicion, fear, and denunciation"; Soviet survival and power depended "on intricately devised mechanisms of coercion." In a brilliant analysis, which at the time seemed to be wishful thinking, the report characterized the Soviet monolith as a system with no natural cohesion "held together by the iron curtain around it and the iron bars within it." Therefore, relationships within the Soviet bloc were bound to be fragile. Nationalism remained the most potent emotional-political force and was all the more dangerous to the survival of the Soviet system because the Communist leaders demanded that their satellites "accept not only the imperial authority of Moscow but that they believe in and proclaim the ideological primacy and infallibility of the Kremlin." The report concluded: "In short, Soviet ideas and practices run counter to the best and potentially the strongest instincts of men, and deny their most fundamental aspirations."[14] And the Soviet regime, if faced with the determination of the free world to defend itself, would "become convinced of the falsity of its assumptions" and allow workable agreements to be formulated. At the very least, the Soviets could be induced "to coexistence on tolerable terms with the non-Soviet world."[15]

The New Arms Race. Superbomb weaponry added a new dimension to the strategy of power politics. It was no longer possible, as in the past, to redress a balance of power through war without the risk of mutual annihilation. The Americans exploded their first hydrogen bomb on 8 May 1951; the Soviets had their first successful firing on 12 August 1953. Throughout the 1950s and into the 1960s, both countries built up their arsenals far beyond any rational equation of self-defense, stockpiling thousands of warheads with the collective capacity to destroy the enemy many times over. In neither country did the public have any influence in stopping the kilotonnage race.

During this period of nuclear expansion, the Soviet Union made various attempts to break out of its encirclement. Some sort of revisionism seemed justified by the vast increase in its military strength. This certainly would have been a valid assumption half a century earlier, but now anticipated gains could not overcome the risks. The territorial status quo, established in Europe after the 1948 Berlin crisis, therefore remained fixed as the two superpowers engaged in a will-o'-the-wisp arms race of horrendous proportions. The buildup emphasized technology and invention: the development of better delivery systems and smaller, more powerful warheads. Each side feared that the other might produce a weapon of destruction so powerful and diabolical that nothing could deter its use.

Hitler had prompted people to think of foreign policy in terms of blueprints and time tables: a remilitarized Rhineland, then an annexed Austria, next a destroyed Czechoslovakia, an invaded Poland, and a conquered France. The superpowers, therefore, tended to regard each move made by their adversary as part of a plan to master the universe. In this atmosphere, correct judgments were hard to come by, and both parties frequently ignored or downplayed their adversary's weakness. For example, the U.S. Secretary of State John Foster Dulles (1953–1959) consistently exaggerated the menace of the Communists whom he felt were malevolently hostile to the values of the free world. Since he believed that any sort of accommodation with them was impossible, he had little incentive to take many positive steps toward easing the tensions of the Cold War.

Dulles's intransigence worried many Europeans who feared they were being forced to accept annihilation without representation. Antinuclear movements developed in all the countries of Western Europe. Some were hardly even-handed. They denounced the threat of the United States, but not that of the Soviet Union. However, many people were genuinely afraid that the nuclear umbrella could become a shroud. The situation became more complex with nuclear proliferation. Britain joined the "nuclear club" in 1952; France followed in 1960. China exploded its first bomb four years later. It seemed that almost every country that wanted a bomb might eventually have one. These weapons might even fall into the hands of terrorist groups who could use them to hold nations hostage. A horrible picture emerged of bombs being smuggled in suitcases into great metropolitan areas and detonated by remote control. What did deterrence mean when the threat of the nuclear winter was worldwide and so pervasive? Nobody could be safe again, especially the Europeans who were in the trenches of the Cold War.

Some small efforts were made to defuse the situation. Partly to deflect criticism that the United States only thought of nuclear energy in terms of destruction, in the early 1950s, President Dwight D. Eisenhower launched his "atoms for peace program," which emphasized beneficial civilian uses of atomic energy. In 1952, the United Nations established its first disarmament commission to coordinate plans for the reduction of conventional and nuclear weaponry. However, unless the superpowers themselves were able to reach agreement, the problem proved insoluble.

TOWARD PEACEFUL COEXISTENCE

De-Stalinization

A Collective Leadership. Protecting vested interests seemed to be as important as ensuring national security as the military and industrial leaders formed an alliance to push for greater defense expenditures. They routinely overestimated the strength of their adversaries. Washington operated under the assumption that Soviet power was monolithic despite its economic problems and the growing restiveness in Eastern Europe and among the Soviet Union's non-Russian peoples. During the transitional period that followed Stalin's death, Soviet foreign policy appeared less forceful and less abrasive and even somewhat conciliatory. In a speech before the Supreme Soviet on 8 August 1953, Prime Minister Georgi Malenkov claimed that there were no outstanding disputes that could not be solved by mutual agreement: "We stand, as we have always stood, for the peaceful coexistence of the two [Communist and capitalist] systems. We hold that there are no objective reasons for clashes between the United States of America and the Soviet Union. The security of the two states and the world, and the development of trade between the United States of America and the Soviet Union, can be ensured on the basis of normal relations between the two countries."[16] The Kremlin's collective leadership still ruled in an atmosphere of insecurity and suspicion and remained apprehensive of the strength of the West; nevertheless, they believed that a more reasonable, less threatening foreign policy might forestall the rearmament of Germany and enable them to divert resources from military to consumer goods, thereby strengthening their system at home and improving their ties with the satellites. Washington dismissed the Soviet overtures as a ploy to make the West lower its guard.

Nevertheless, at the Conference of Foreign Ministers held in Berlin from 25 January to 18 February 1954, the Soviet Union and the Western powers made an attempt—the first in five years—to reach an agreement on European security. Neither side as yet seemed willing to alter the existing status quo. Vyacheslav Molotov proposed that all foreign troops be withdrawn from Germany so that it could become a neutral state. Reunification would follow, accompanied by a general European security treaty open to all European states that promised to settle their disputes by peaceful means. He said that in the event of aggression, an attack against one state would be considered an attack against all, and "each one of the parties, in the exercise of the right of individual or collective self-defense, shall assist the state or states which had been so attacked by all the means at its disposal."[17] Molotov's use of the language of the North Atlantic Treaty was a neat touch in a scheme that seemed designed to destroy NATO. Furthermore, the West did not think much of the Soviet Union's proposal to withdraw its troops from Europe, provided the United States did the same. The Soviet armies would only cross the Bug River, the border between the Soviet Union and Europe, while the American armies would withdraw across the Atlantic Ocean. The West refused to discuss the matter. Again the Soviets appeared to have deliberately courted Western intransigence to give them an excuse to reassert their power.

At Moscow in November 1954, the Soviets opened their own conference on European security at which they revealed a plan to create their own military alliance to counter NATO. The agreement, eventually called the Warsaw Pact, would give the Soviets a perfect excuse to maintain their armies in Eastern Europe where they could intervene in their satellites' domestic affairs when necessary. Nevertheless, by 1954, Soviet foreign policy was outwardly less Stalinist. Though Molotov continued as foreign minister, Nikita Khrushchev, the first secretary of the Central Committee of the Communist party and the new *primus inter pares* of the ruling circle, actually conducted foreign policy. In style at least, Khrushchev was a refreshing departure from previous Soviet leaders. Despite a certain ruthlessness, he enjoyed socializing—he was seen so frequently at official receptions with a bottomless glass in his hand that it was rumored he had a "drinking problem"—and he professed a seemingly genuine desire to reduce international tensions. Where Stalin had insisted that the solution of the Austrian problem had to wait for an agreement over Germany, Khrushchev was willing to pull Soviet troops out of Austria in exchange for Austrian neutrality. There was a good bit of method to his decision. A neutral Austria flanking an already neutral Switzerland created a huge neck of neutral territory that blocked north-south NATO communications. In a most remarkable move, Khrushchev also sought to improve relations with Yugoslavia.

Efforts at Conciliation. Stalin was hardly entombed, when, on 29 April 1953, the Kremlin sounded out Belgrade on the prospect of normalizing relations. The Soviets encouraged their satellites to follow suit. On 10 October 1954, the Soviets signed a barter agreement with Yugoslavia under which the Soviets would trade their manufactured articles for an equal value of Yugoslav raw materials. At a meeting of the ruling Presidium in March 1955, the unimaginative Molotov openly criticized the new policy, objecting to any attempt to reestablish relations with a country whose policies were so anti-Soviet and so far removed from Communism. Khrushchev pressed ahead anyway, and at the end of May, accompanied by Defense Minister Nikolai Bulganin, he paid Tito a personal visit. Molotov was excluded from the official Soviet delegation. Khrushchev did not want any hint of Stalinism to mar this major ideological turnaround. In essence, Khrushchev was giving up on the Stalinist claims to impose ideological purity on the peoples of Eastern Europe. By tacitly admitting that there was a separate path to socialism, he was ending the pretense of a Soviet monolith. Thus, Khrushchev's visit was a kind of apology for previous Soviet excesses.

Tito, however, did not seem impressed. He met his guests at the Belgrade airport, but refused to smile. Khrushchev appealed to the "ties of an age-old fraternal friendship and joint struggle against the . . . fascist invaders, in the years of the Second World War." He said that he sincerely regretted the Soviet-Yugoslav parting of the ways, which he blamed on "enemies of the people, the contemptible agents of imperialism who fraudulently wormed their way into the ranks of our Party." He promised to "take all the necessary steps in order to remove all the obstacles to make the relations between our states completely normal."[18] Throughout the visit, Tito remained exceedingly formal. He suspected that Khrushchev was primarily interested in weakening the associations that Yugoslavia had made with the countries of the West.

On 28 February 1953, Tito had concluded a Treaty of Friendship and Assistance with Greece and Turkey to safeguard the peace and security of the Balkans. The agreement had called for the formulation of plans for the common defense and increased technical, economic, and cultural cooperation. It also invited the other states of the region to join under the same conditions and rights. Moscow viewed this treaty, which linked Yugoslavia with two members of the North Atlantic Alliance, with special alarm. Tito denied any intention of formally seeking admission to NATO, but four months later he declared that he was willing to cooperate with the Western allies in creating a system of collective security. Since Yugoslavia was already receiving American military aid, the Soviets surmised that Tito was deliberately trying to undermine the Soviet position in Europe. In August 1954, the Balkan treaty became a formal defensive alliance, obliging each of the signatories to come to each other's aid should any one be attacked. The Stalin-Tito feud had cost the Soviets dearly and obviously would not be laid to rest with one trip to Belgrade.

Khrushchev also inaugurated a new foreign policy toward the nonaligned countries of Asia. At the end of 1954, he, again in the company of Marshal Bulganin, visited India, Burma, and Afghanistan. Everywhere they went, the two leaders professed devotion to the doctrine of peaceful coexistence and respect for the sovereignty of nations. They offered to provide each country with economic assistance and to engage in scientific, technical, and cultural exchange programs. Such assistance and cooperation were to be the cornerstone of their policy to gain influence among the underdeveloped nations. With the failures of the Stalinist period and the uncertain power relationships among the succeeding Soviet leaders, the Soviet Union was in need of new directions. Although Khrushchev constantly preached peaceful coexistence, ironically his foreign policy became more adventuresome as his position became more secure. Indeed, he resurrected the practices of the past, complete with the old Soviet world view, and seemed to have no great desire to end the Cold War. Whether this shift reflected Khrushchev's own views or his fears that he might be replaced should he show too much flexibility is not certain. Khrushchev, more than any previous Soviet leader, was a proponent of peaceful coexistence, but as long as the Americans were determined to maintain and strengthen their nuclear superiority, the Soviet Union could not afford to relax lest this be taken as a sign of weakness. For this reason, the Soviets refused to consider German reunification before all foreign troops were withdrawn from Europe. They knew this condition was unacceptable to the United States. But even had the Americans agreed to disband NATO and disengage from European affairs, the Soviets would certainly not have agreed to dismantle their East German satellite regime. Agreeing on disarmament was just as difficult. Both the Soviet Union and the United States favored an end to the arms race and the conversion of atomic energy to peaceful uses, but they were stymied by their inability to devise a workable system of inspection and control.

At the summit conference in Geneva attended by the Soviet Union, France, Britain, and the United States (18–23 July 1955), President Eisenhower proposed an "Open Skies" plan, whereby the United States and the Soviet Union would have the right to photograph each other's territory and would exchange blueprints of military installations. This scheme, Eisenhower explained, would "convince the world that we are providing as between ourselves against the possibility of great surprise attack, thus lessening danger and relaxing tension."[19] Earlier over dessert at their first official dinner, Eisenhower had told Khrushchev that they should control the threat of thermonuclear weapons. Their countries had enough bombs to wipe out the entire northern hemisphere from fallout alone. Khrushchev agreed: "We get your dust, you get our dust, the winds blow and nobody's safe."[20]

However, the Soviets found the Open Skies plan of dubious reciprocal benefit. They already had access to general information on American military installations by subscribing to various U.S. newspapers and publications, whereas if they allowed the Americans unrestricted access to Soviet installations, the Americans would have the opportunity to gather information they could not get from any other source. Besides, the Soviets viewed the American bases in Europe and the Middle East—not those in the United States—as the real threat to their security. They therefore rejected all proposals to inspect or monitor their military establishments, claiming this would be a grave violation of national sovereignty—a point that was hard to refute. Nor did the Americans seem particularly anxious to lessen East-West tensions. Eisenhower continued to call for free elections in Germany and Eastern Europe, a matter the Soviets did not consider open for discussion. Secretary of State Dulles went even further—he advocated the liberation of Eastern Europe.

However, the atmosphere at the Geneva Summit Conference was noticeably free of name calling and bullying. Both Khrushchev and Eisenhower were plainly eager to make good impressions and privately had complimentary things to say about each other. (Khrushchev, though, thought Secretary of State Dulles "a cur.") British Prime Minister Harold Macmillan, however, considered Khrushchev fat and ugly with pig eyes, while to French Foreign Minister Antoine Pinay he was coarse with "fat paws."[21] The British and French, though, had to watch the "Big Two" from positions of inferiority. The sessions were detailed and extensive, but produced no solutions to the problems of disarmament and European security. Yet, even without detente, the superpowers had at least tacitly agreed to avoid the threat of a nuclear showdown.

The Suez Crisis

Egyptian Resentment of the West. The British were committed to decolonization; and the French, after their defeats in Indo-China and the decline in their control over North Africa, had no other choice. But the transfer of authority from Europeans to local native leaders brought great confusion and instability. Most of the new Third World leaders had been inadequately prepared for self-government by the colonial powers; now they tried to establish their identities by stridently denouncing Western neocolonialism and making a great virtue of not taking sides in the Cold War. Many tried to play off one side against the other, a game that was not devoid of risks.

Egypt, with its Suez Canal, had long been an area of special British interest. Under a 1936 treaty, Britain was allowed to keep a force of 10,000 men near the canal, but in 1954, under pressure from the Egyptian government of Gamal Abdel Nasser, the British agreed to remove them. Nasser had come to power as a result of a military coup on 23 July 1952, which had overthrown King Farouq, a ruler long associated with corruption, indifference, and subservience to the interests of the West. The new Egyptian regime's abrogation of the canal-forces treaty was a bitter draught for the British government, which had constantly maintained that British military presence at Suez was essential for the security of the canal. Prime

Minister Anthony Eden, trying to put the agreement in the best possible light, said that "Britain would be more likely to be able to influence Egyptian policy when [this] main cause of Egyptian antipathy to Britain was removed."[22] The British, still a paramount power in the Middle East, wanted to remain on good terms with Egypt as part of their policy to keep the peace between the Israelis and the Arabs.

On 14 May 1948, the United Nations had proclaimed the existence of the state of Israel, bringing to an end the old British League of Nations mandate in Palestine. The General Assembly recommended the creation of a Jewish state and an Arab state, but the Arabs refused to recognize the existence of the Jewish state. The day after Israel came into existence, Egypt, Iraq, Jordan, Lebanon, and Syria invaded its territory. During the ensuing Israeli "War of Independence," Israel took some of the land that had been previously allotted to the Arabs, but lost some it had received—some territory across the Jordan River and the Gaza Strip. The fighting ceased in January 1949. In May 1950, France, Britain, and the United States issued the Tripartite Declaration in which they pledged to take immediate action, both inside and outside the United Nations, should Israel or any of the Arab states try to violate the current frontiers or change the armistice lines.

The Egyptians proved most troublesome. In violation of the 1949 accords and international law, they refused to allow Israeli ships to use the Suez Canal and mounted coastal artillery at the southern tip of the Sinai Peninsula to prevent Israeli ships from passing through the Straits of Tiran. Thus, the Egyptians had effectively blocked Israeli maritime contacts with Africa and the Far East. Constant border clashes occurred and seemed part of an organized plan. In 1955, following a series of raids and counterraids across the demarcation line in the Gaza Strip, Israel attacked an Egyptian military outpost in the Sinai desert.

Nasser was determined to avenge the affront. The attack also gave him an opportunity to attempt the all-out destruction of the state of Israel, a feat that would earn him the highest esteem from his own people and the Arab world in general. First, he concentrated on building up his army, making the British, French, and Americans extremely nervous in the process. The United States refused to sell additional weapons to Egypt, but the Soviets took this opportunity to extend their influence into an area from which they had been heretofore excluded. They allowed Egypt to buy large amounts of military hardware through Czechoslovakia, including tanks, armored troop carriers, artillery pieces, combat aircraft, destroyers, torpedo boats, and submarines. Nasser paid for this hardware by mortgaging future Egyptian cotton crops and cutting down on investment in his country's economic development. Alarmed at the rise of Soviet influence in Egypt, the Americans offered Nasser financial assistance to build a high dam at Aswan on the Upper Nile. Washington hoped that with proper handling Nasser could become a force for Middle Eastern stability. However, while accepting aid from the West, Nasser continued to cultivate the Communist powers. On 16 May 1956, he ostentatiously recognized Red China, for example. The Americans began to have second thoughts and, in July 1956, withdrew their offer to help Nasser finance the dam. They were confident that the Soviet Union, troubled by the unrest in Poland and Hungary, would be unable to take advantage of the situation.

Nasser responded, not with an appeal to Moscow, but by announcing, on 26 July, that he would nationalize the Suez Canal and use its tolls to finance the building of the dam. The shock wave hit Paris and London especially hard. The security and prosperity of Western Europe depended upon Middle Eastern petroleum that came through the Suez Canal. Nobody believed the Egyptians were capable of running the canal by themselves, but that was not the point. Prime Minister Eden wanted Nasser gone. He believed him no better than Hitler and was determined not to allow him "to have his thumb on [Britain's] windpipe." He insisted he would protect Britain's essential interests even if this meant going to war and even if the British had to act alone.[23] Eden already knew that he could count on French support to bring Nasser into line. The French feared that if Nasser were not curbed, the Algerian rebels would seek his backing in their struggle for independence from France. The French were also suffering from the same Munich complex as the British. This notion that Nasser was another Hitler who must be stopped before it was too late provided French leaders with a certain moral justification and a faith that their decisions would receive public support.[24] Eden also believed that the Americans "did not exclude the use of force if all other methods failed."[25] The British and the French military began drawing up contingency plans for an invasion of Egypt at the end of July 1956, determining what units would be involved. At the same time, the British and French fleets were mobilized for service in the Mediterranean, measures described as "precautionary."[26]

In August, representatives of the countries who were major users of the Suez waterway met in London. They endorsed an American plan to establish a special international organization to operate, maintain, and develop the canal. Nasser, however, immediately denounced the scheme as a derogation of national sovereignty "provocative to the people of Egypt." Such a summary rejection convinced Britain and France that the time had come for sterner measures. The British were convinced that a failure to preserve the balance of power in the Middle East would end their status as a world power. But the United States, upon whom both counted for support, was reluctant to engage in force. Washington felt that keeping the canal open was more important than punishing Nasser. Eisenhower, in his press conference of 11 September, flatly opposed intervention: "We established the United Nations to abolish aggression, and I am not going to be a party to aggression."

Eden tried to cover all bases, all the while continuing his military buildup and clandestine maneuvers to depose Nasser. At the same time, the French strengthened their ties with Israel. They had no difficulty obtaining the Israelis' agreement to cooperate in an Anglo-French war against Egypt. Israeli Prime Minister David Ben Gurion was looking for an opportunity to launch a preemptive strike to curb Egypt's growing military power. He also wanted certain strategic bases in the Sinai Peninsula, including Sharm el-Sheik, which would unblock the entrance to the Gulf of Aqaba and open the Israeli port of Eilat. Nevertheless, Moshe Dayan, chief of staff of the Israeli army, was doubtful whether Israel without the support of the British and French "would have launched her campaign; and if she had, its character, both military and political, would have been different."[27]

In London, on 21 September, the users of the canal brought forth another plan: they would create an association to manage the canal, hire pilots, and organize navigation. This idea had no more chance of being approved by Nasser than the others. The French suspected that it was a deliberate American ploy to forestall any Anglo-French move against Egypt. Time was on Nasser's side. He was now a hero to his own people and the most significant leader in the Arab world. The Egyptians had demonstrated that they could run the canal and maintain free passage without outside help. The United Nations Security Council discussed the Suez crisis in October. The British and French introduced a resolution that called upon the Egyptian government to recognize the rights of the canal users to operate the canal, but opposed any solution that left control of the waterway in Egyptian hands. On 13 October 1956, the Soviet Union obligingly vetoed the Anglo-French resolution.

Resort to Arms. On 22 October, representatives of Britain, France, and Israel met at a secluded villa in the Paris suburb of Sèvres. The delegations were headed by British Foreign Secretary Selwin Lloyd, French Premier Guy Mollet, and Israeli Prime Minister Ben Gurion. The basic plan to attack Egypt had already been drafted two months before: code-named Operation Musketeer, it called for an Anglo-French airborne operation against Alexandria, followed by an infantry advance on Cairo. The attack had initially been scheduled to begin on 13 September, but Eden's elaborate efforts to tranquilize the Americans by waiting for the Security Council meeting had led to one delay after another. The plan became "Musketeer Revised," essentially the same plan as before with the initial objective changed from Alexandria to Port Said. At the Sèvres meeting, the British insisted on having a proper pretext before beginning the attack.

The British wanted the Israelis to attack first so that they could claim Anglo-French intervention was necessary to prevent the conflict from spreading. The French agreed. According to General André Beaufre, the operation's deputy commander, the French and British would become a United Nations "advanced guard and might lead with equal certainty to the political results at which we aim."[28] This last reference was to the overthrow of Nasser, now the operation's principal aim. The political objective of getting rid of the Egyptian leader confused the operation, however. What was the main military objective now—securing the canal or occupying Cairo?

The meeting broke up without agreement, but later the Israelis agreed to strike first, provided they were required to hold out alone for no more than thirty-six hours. France had been actively supplying the Israeli armed forces with new military hardware since August. The Israeli high command felt confident they could mobilize the army in three days and advance rapidly into the Sinai to defeat the Egyptian army; this offensive would be followed by double thrusts, one north to the Gaza Strip, one south to the Gulf of Aqaba. The Israelis calculated that the Soviet Union was too involved with affairs in Hungary to give Egypt much support and that the Americans would be distracted by the presidential election campaign.

The attack began on the evening of 29 October. Before dawn of the following day, the Israelis had swept halfway to Ismailia. Soviet Premier Bulganin warned, "there are countries now which need not have sent a navy or air force to the coasts of Britain, but could have used other means, such as rocket technique. We are filled with determination to use force to crush the aggressors and to restore peace in the [Middle] East."[29] But nobody really believed the Soviets would begin a world war over Egypt, a country not vital to their national security. The Americans warned the Israelis and the Egyptians to stop all military action and withdraw their forces to a distance of ten miles from the canal.

Eden tried unsuccessfully to convince Eisenhower that the Americans should join the British and French in taking immediate, decisive action to stop hostilities. The prime minister did not think that the American refusal to participate meant opposition to the British and French taking action by themselves. The British, without previously informing the Americans, demanded "temporary" Anglo-French occupation of Port Said, Ismailia, and Suez, which would have placed the canal in British and French hands. However, the real aim all along had been, in Eden's words, to "knock Nasser off his perch."[30] Therefore the British never intended for the Egyptians to take the twelve-hour ultimatum seriously. In any case, its terms would only have applied to Egypt since Israeli forces were not yet within ten miles of the canal. Nasser rejected the British demand, and on the evening of 31 October, the Anglo-French bombardment of the Egyptian Air Force began.

World reaction was instantaneous and almost universally hostile. Britain and France vetoed Security Council consideration of the attack, but the General Assembly, by a vote of 64 to 5, the largest majority in UN history, passed a resolution for a cease-fire. The French and British responded that they would stop their "police action" only if the UN organized a special task force (acceptable to both Israel and Egypt) to keep the peace. The operation against Port Said was launched on 5 November as scheduled. But, by now, the goal of ousting Nasser had been scaled down to simply holding the canal until the arrival of the United Nations Special Force. But the intended advance along the canal to Ismailia and Suez never took place. Israel and Egypt accepted a cease-fire, and the British had to follow suit. Eden realized that he had run out of excuses.[31] The United States had applied tremendous pressure to force the British to suspend operations. Heavy trading against the pound had weakened the British economy. Eden was in poor health, still weak after a recent gallbladder operation. Pleading ill health, he resigned as prime minister.

General Beaufre, a key participant in the Suez affair, believed it was a major turning point: "Before Suez, European prestige was still intact in the eyes of the Third World and the victor nations of 1945 had maintained their solidarity. After Suez, prestige and solidarity had vanished. This was the end of the empire, the end of an epoch."[32] Eden again tried to justify his actions with historical comparisons: "I thought and think that failure to act would have brought the worst of consequences, just as I think the world would have suffered less if Hitler had been resisted in the Rhine, in Austria or in Czechoslovakia rather than in Poland."[33] Eden had not come to grips with the serious damage British and French prestige had suffered nor with the loss of their position in the Mediterranean. Far from humiliating Nasser, much less removing him from power, the Suez crisis had made him a hero. His nationalization of the Suez Canal epitomized the longings of the Arab world for emancipation from Western tutelage. The Egyptian army had made a very poor showing on the battlefield, but Nasser had no difficulty transforming military defeat into political victory. He captured the imagination of the Middle Eastern world with his call for Arab nationalism, thereby confirming his own legitimacy and leadership.[34] Nasserism became a powerful expression of pan-Arab sentiment that lasted long after his sudden death from a heart attack in 1970. Since then other leaders have tried to take his place by echoing his appeal to Arab nationalism.

Israel did succeed in opening the Gulf of Aqaba, but the crisis did not add perceptibly to Israeli security. The British and French attack on Egypt and its consequences accelerated the decline of these two nations as world powers, thereby continuing a process that had begun with World War I. The crisis was a stunning example of their inability to take any significant action, whether good or bad, without the approval of the United States. The Americans now became the paramount power in the Middle East. They felt they had no other choice if they were to keep the Soviets at bay. As for the Soviets, the Hungarian uprising had prevented them from turning the situation to their advantage, an indication of the dangers of being overextended in a part of the world that was not crucial to their national security. The Soviets wanted to protect Eastern Europe against possible defection as much as the United States wanted to protect the Middle East from Soviet intervention. Consequently, the Soviet reaction to the Suez crisis, like that of the United States toward events in Hungary, was more remarkable for words than deeds.[35] Both superpowers had learned how to pull their punches. Consequently, the 1956 crisis brought no alteration in the East-West balance. By now the politics of the Cold War seemed almost predictable.

Until 1957, the Americans had the capacity to attack the Soviet Union directly without the Soviets being able to strike at the United States. That immunity came to an end with the launching of the first Soviet space satellite—*Sputnik*. This new development heightened European fears that the two superpowers might be deterred from striking at each other's homelands and confine their attacks to the other's positions in Europe instead. Indeed, NATO strategy emphasized the use of short-range, or tactical, nuclear weapons to compensate for the numerical superiority of the Soviet armed forces. At the same time, some Europeans doubted whether the Americans would really defend Europe at all. In frustration, the European people took to the streets. Protesters in Western European countries marched on American military bases where atomic weapons were stockpiled and on facilities where nuclear research was carried out. In Eastern Europe, the Soviets encouraged antinuclear demonstrations against the policies of the Western powers, especially against the buildup of an American nuclear arsenal in West Germany. Despite the protest, the likelihood of a slowdown in the arms race remained remote as long as so many security issues between East and West remained unresolved.

The Emergence of a Third Force

Western European Integration and the German Problem. Superpower control of European affairs had been the dominant factor in European politics since the end of World War II. Thus, the Geneva summit of 1955, like previous such meetings on European security, was mainly a Soviet-American duet. The British and French were on stage; they even had a few lines from time to time (both sponsored their own disarmament plans), but clearly they filled the roles of choristers. On occasion, the Soviets were outright condescending, secretly rejoicing that French and British political influence was waning in those areas in which the Soviet Union was trying to advance. The Americans, although less overtly obnoxious, also kept their own counsel. Neither superpower treated the European states as sovereign entities entitled to make their own decisions without outside interference. The United States allowed much more freedom of action than did the Soviets, but the Suez crisis clearly showed that there were limits to how much the Americans would tolerate. Both the Soviets and the Americans formed their spheres of interest into alliances and bound them together militarily, politically, and economically. But whereas Soviet rule in Eastern Europe led to economic backwardness, rebellion, and smoldering ethnic hatred, American tutelage of Western Europe resulted in the creation of a secure and sophisticated community on the way to becoming a third superpower.

Although the "European Movement" had many intellectual ancestors, its true parentage was the most fundamental of imperatives—necessity. The dramatic events of the Cold War boosted unification in the form of the Marshall Plan, which required Western European nations to promote integration across national boundaries. The Berlin crisis and the Soviet rape of Czechoslovakia in 1948 hastened the formation of a Western European military alliance in NATO. There were attempts to bring about a similar political association. A Council of Europe convened in Strasbourg in 1949 to establish "a closer unity" among the states of Western Europe.[36] However, no one was willing to give this body supranational powers despite the belief that such an organization could help prevent Germany from once again threatening the peace of Europe.

The necessity of containing the ambitions of the Germans was as urgent as containing the ambitions of the Soviets. Germany was obviously not going to become a pastoral state, and with the remarkable prospects for European recovery offered by the Marshall Plan, it showed every indication of once again becoming an economic powerhouse. Such a state would be impossible to keep in a position of international inferiority, especially considering its strategic geographic position, which it could use to exploit the divisions of the Cold War to its advantage. The process toward German independence had already begun.

On 22 November 1949, Chancellor Konrad Adenauer achieved the first tangible recognition of sovereignty for the Federal Republic with the Petersberg agreement, which allowed West Germany to "reestablish consular and commercial relations with those countries where such relations appear advantageous."[37] The Allies also agreed to stop dismantling the equipment in a number of chemical factories and steel plants and recognized Germany's right to rebuild its commercial fleet. The price for these concessions was Germany's agreement to allow a special international authority to regulate the industrial production of the Ruhr valley. Adenauer accepted willingly. He hoped that the internationalization of the resources of the Ruhr would enable him to further his policy of reconciliation with France; the latter, in turn, was a means through which Germany could once again return to a position of prominence in European affairs.

The French, however, saw German cooperation as a means of enhancing their security. They realized that it was preferable to integrate an independent Germany within the Western alliance than to perpetuate the kind of control that had so poisoned relations between the two countries after World War I. On 9 May 1950, French Foreign Minister Robert Schuman formally proposed the creation of the European Coal and Steel Community in which France and Germany would place those industries under a common authority, thereby integrating the iron ore deposits of Lorraine with the adjacent coal reserves of the Saar and Ruhr. The economic advantages were secondary to the political benefits—Germany would be deprived of control over vital national resources as a guarantee against future aggression. The treaty included the Netherlands, Belgium, Luxembourg, and Italy as well as Germany and France and cleared the way for similar integration in military affairs.

The United States guaranteed the security of Western Europe, but it had never intended to do the job by itself. The Americans believed that the Europeans, including the West Germans, had to demonstrate a commitment to their own security. The Americans regarded the Federal Republic as the first line of defense against Soviet aggression. Therefore, it seemed logical, especially after the Berlin Blockade, that Germany should be included in NATO, which had been created in April 1949 to protect all the signatories against a Soviet attack.[38] The Americans hoped to ease the anxieties of the French by allowing German militarization to occur only within an international framework.[39]

Questions still remained about how far the Bonn government could be trusted. Even in Germany itself, some people had doubts about remilitarization. The Social Democrats were vehemently against it. University students and other young people clearly expressed their attitude with the slogan *"ohne mich"* (freely translated, "count me out"). Leaders of the Evangelical church, like Pastor Martin Niemöller, denounced it and launched a popular campaign against it. Adenauer himself had once opposed an armed Germany, which he had associated with Prussianism, but now his ideas had changed. He believed that German armament was a necessary ingredient in the restoration of German sovereignty, and he proposed that a German contingent be integrated into a general Western European defense force. The creation of a German army within the framework of a general Western alliance would lead to the end of Allied occupation.

Meanwhile the French were working to limit the possible damage and proposed the Pleven Plan of the European Defense Community. This scheme was a sort of military equivalent to the Schuman Plan. The nations of West Europe would pool their armies and operate under a common military budget and joint command. Thus, German contingents would be outnumbered by the more numerous units from the other countries. Germany would have no need to develop a separate ministry of defense or a general staff. Many of the features of the Pleven Plan found their way into the text of the final treaty, signed on 26 May 1952.

The Fate of the European Defense Community. The Federal Republic agreed to integrate its armed forces into the European Defense Community in exchange for the full recognition of sovereignty including the abolition of the Allied High Commission. Under this agreement, the British, French, and Americans would continue to station armed forces in the Federal Republic and would retain their prerogatives in Berlin. They also reserved the right to intervene in German affairs to preserve the democratic system and would retain their interest in German reunification. The agreement cleared the Bundestag without difficulty. On 30 August 1954, however, the French National Assembly rejected it by a vote of 319 to 264, with 43 abstentions. The parliamentary divisions say much about the political chaos in the last days of the Fourth Republic. The Gaullists and the Communists were united in opposition, the Catholic Popular Republicans were in favor, and the Socialists and the Radicals were badly split. Many French still believed that German aggression was more plausible than Soviet aggression. They criticized the British for not committing more of their troops to the European army. Some opponents feared that France, with a large part of its military strength absorbed in the European Defense Community, would be unable to defend its interests in the rest of the world.

German rearmament therefore had to be achieved in other ways. The United States paved the way for the creation of a German ministry of defense by allowing the Federal Republic to assume responsibility for all questions concerning the Allied occupying forces in a Commission for the Federal Government. Meanwhile British Prime Minister Eden cleared the path for a European army by giving the Western European Union (WEU), created in 1948, power to regulate the size of the national armed forces. In 1955, the Federal Republic established a formal Ministry of Defense and conferred commissions on the first officers of the new German army. Germany (and Italy) then became official members of the WEU. Ironically, the union allowed Germany more independence in the development of its military establishment than would have been permitted under the defunct European Defense Community. The Federal Republic also joined NATO in 1955. The creation of a supranational authority to curb Germany's control over its warmaking potential was followed by the general economic integration of Western Europe.[40]

The Treaty of Rome. On 1 January 1958, France, Italy, the German Federal Republic, Belgium, Luxembourg, and the Netherlands, joined hands in the European Economic Community (EEC or Common Market).[41] The action followed the ratification of the Treaty of Rome the previous year. According to this arrangement, goods produced in the member countries could travel freely within all the member countries without tariffs or other taxes and duties. A common level of protection against nonmember countries would be set by averaging the preexisting tariffs of the member states. The agreement also provided for the free movement of workers and gave business firms the right to provide unrestricted services anywhere in the Community. Restrictions on the movement of capital would also end.[42] In Article 119, the Treaty of Rome laid down the principle of "equal remuneration for equal work as between men and women workers." The provision sprang from the desire to avoid giving a competitive advantage to member states that practiced wage discrimination, but it had social implications. Members were to be in full compliance with the provisions of the treaty after a transition period of twelve years.[43]

The organization had a full set of institutions, including a permanent bureaucracy. Its executive and chief decision-making body was the Council, which consisted of the six foreign ministers of the member countries and represented their individual political interests.[44] The Council was assisted by the Commission, which was divided into several branches according to function; each major branch was headed by a commissioner who prepared policy recommendations for presentation to the Council.[45] The Commission was composed of career functionaries who formulated objective policy for the whole Community. The Community's legislature was the Assembly, later to be known as the European Parliament; its members, appointed by the member states in approximate ratio to the strength of the country's political parties, rendered advice on proposals submitted to it by the Council. The judicial arm of the Common Market was the European Court of Justice, which ensured compliance with the treaties, acted on complaints of member states, and settled disputes between institutions. The Common Market organizations were scattered among several cities to distribute the political and economic benefits. The Council was in Brussels, the Assembly in Strasbourg, and the Court of Justice in Kirchberg, just north of Luxembourg City.[46] Together the states of the Community had a population of 170 million. Many of the architects of the Community hoped it would be the first step in the creation of a European political union, a United States of Europe.

The United States favored the organization of the Common Market for several reasons. For one thing, the Americans believed it would continue the work of the sixteen-nation Organization for European Economic Cooperation developed out of the Marshall Plan. The Americans thought that pooling the collective energies of the European countries, establishing common institutions, and harmonizing their social policies would be an effective way to confront Soviet power. Furthermore, the economic strength of the Common Market, added to the unified military force created by NATO, would eventually enable the Europeans to assume a larger role in guaranteeing their own security. In this sense, it was a proper substitute for the stillborn European Defense Community and could provide a way for an independent, economically strong Germany, without a taste for nationalist adventurism, to regain its place in the council of nations. For this reason, the Common Market also had the support of the French, who were looking for ways to harness German power. The Germans themselves were delighted by this opportunity to return to respectability. They did not feel that they had sacrificed their dream of unification, since unification was hardly practical at the moment.[47]

The timing was propitious for European cooperation. Moderate parties were in office, and all states endorsed liberal market economies. Furthermore, the Suez crisis of 1956 with its threat of cutting off Europe's access to Middle Eastern oil had prompted the feeling that the individual European states were no longer capable of protecting their prosperity by unilateral action. They also realized that if they were ever to move away from the tutelage of the superpowers, they would have to act as a unit.

European federalism had scant appeal in Great Britain, however. Winston Churchill had once talked about creating a United States of Europe, but he was careful to exclude his own country. The British were reluctant to consider themselves Europeans, whom they traditionally had distrusted, and preferred instead to base their security on the United States and their own nuclear capability. Nor did the British want to undertake any commitments that might imply a loss of their own sovereignty. They felt that they could cooperate with the members of the Community without sacrificing any freedom of action. According to the British, their associations with the Commonwealth prevented their participation in the Community. As a result of their aloofness, they played no part in the development of the Common Market and thus had no opportunity to influence it.

The Common Market, like any such organization, had the effect of both expanding and restricting trade. That the forces of growth were more important than those of constriction was due in large part to the economic development that had already occurred before the organization came into existence. Businesses rushed to take advantage of the new prosperity. In the first decade of the Common Market, trade among its members quadrupled, while trade between the Common Market and the rest of the world only doubled. France, which in 1958 had returned to economic stability and peace under the leadership of Charles de Gaulle, was able to reduce the deficits in its foreign exchange. Germany became one of the world's major trading nations; its exports almost equaled the total exports of the other five countries combined.[48] Eastern Europe, once a major customer of the Common Market countries, now received an insignificant two percent of their exports.[49] Eastern Europe's exports to France and Germany, formerly its best customers, also temporarily declined. In time, however, the Common Market countries would expand their exports to Eastern Europe because what the West had to sell could no longer be furnished by the Soviet Union. This gave Western Europe added political leverage.

Showdown of the Superpowers

Berlin Revisited. In June 1957, Khrushchev pried the Stalinist hard-liners from the Presidium, but his power was still not secure. He felt under constant pressure to maintain the initiative at all costs, particularly in foreign affairs. Now the inclusion of the Federal Republic in NATO raised the specter of German militarism. Furthermore, Khrushchev had few domestic triumphs to which he could point. Although industrial productivity had shown some improvement, agriculture, the sector in which he claimed particular expertise, was in a sorry state. On the other hand, the Soviets had made progress in armaments. By 1958, they had developed long-range bombers capable of striking the United States. They had fired an experimental intercontinental ballistic missile (ICBM) a distance of 4,500 miles and, on 4 October 1957, had launched an artificial satellite (*Sputnik*) into orbit around the earth. Soon they might be able to hit targets throughout the world at will. The Americans had started worrying about a "missile gap."

Under a traditional balance-of-power system, the increased military strength of the Soviet Union—its new nuclear capacity combined with its existing advantage in ground forces—would have entitled it to demand certain concessions. Khrushchev thought this should still be the case. On 10 November 1958 in Moscow, Khrushchev told a group of visiting Polish party officials that the time had come "for the signatories of the Potsdam Agreement to discard the remnants of the occupation regime in Berlin and thereby make it possible to create a normal situation in the capital of the German Democratic Republic."[50] Two and a half weeks later, he followed these words with an ultimatum: if the West had not reached a suitable agreement with Moscow on the status of Berlin within six months (i.e., by 27 May 1959), the Soviets would hand over control over access to the city to the East German government. If the Western powers challenged this arrangement by force, they would face Soviet guns.

Khrushchev probably never expected these extreme demands to be met—however much he may have desired to force the Western powers out of Berlin, it is doubtful that he actually believed he could do it. In fact, his immediate goals were quite different: he hoped that, in the aftermath of the Hungarian revolt, a bold flourish in foreign affairs would confirm the basic dynamics of the Soviet system; more specifically, he wanted to foment a Berlin crisis, which he could then use as a lever to prevent the United States from supplying the new West German army with tactical nuclear weapons. On 10 November 1958, he gave the impression he believed this had already occurred: "The German militarists—with the blessing of the Western Powers, and primarily the United States are receiving nuclear weapons. The Federal Republic already has American rockets which can be fitted with nuclear warheads."[51] The Soviets apparently feared a preemptive strike from the Germans more than they feared an attack from the Americans.

The Soviets had strongly endorsed the Rapacki Plan, which the Polish Foreign Minister Adam Rapacki had revealed in a speech to the United Nations General Assembly in October 1957. This scheme called for an atom-free zone in Central Europe, chiefly in the two Germanies and in Poland. The United States had rejected the scheme because it provided "no method for balanced and equitable limitations of military capabilities and would perpetuate the basic cause of tension in Europe by accepting the continuation of the division of Germany."[52] Now Khrushchev was going to try to convince the Americans to change their mind.

The Americans regarded the current status of Berlin as a matter that was not subject to compromise. They therefore decided to call the Soviet's bluff, ignoring the fact that the Soviets had more troops in the area. But relative troop strength was no longer very important. Khrushchev himself had said that nations could no longer calculate "the alignment of forces on the basis of who has the most men." That might have been possible in the age of fists or bayonets, but "when the machine gun appeared, the side with more troops no longer necessarily had the advantage. And now with the atomic bomb, the number of troops on each side makes practically no difference to the alignment of real power and the outcome of a war. The more troops on a side, the more bomb fodder."[53] The Soviets proposed a conference of heads of state to discuss the Berlin issue, while at the same time making threats about the dire consequences of nuclear war if the Berlin crisis were not resolved. But such propaganda did little to weaken the NATO alliance.

Khrushchev, realizing that his belligerent attitude had not accomplished much, became conciliatory. In March 1959, he said that the deadline he set for the solution of the Berlin situation was no longer fixed, and he publicly acknowledged the rights of the Western allies to maintain troops in the city. The crisis had passed—until the next time. Meanwhile, behind the bluster, the Soviets had been working to put their relations with the United States on a more rational basis.

Deputy Premier Anastas Mikoyan had first tested the waters in an "informal" trip to the United States the previous January. His efforts resulted in a cultural exchange: the Soviets agreed to send an exhibit to the trade show to be held at New York's Colosseum; the Americans agreed to mount an exhibit at the Sokolniky Park fair scheduled for Moscow the following July.[54]

The spring of 1959 also brought an exchange of American industrialists and Soviet engineers who looked into various aspects of each other's economies, particularly shipbuilding. In June 1959, Eisenhower invited Khrushchev to visit the United States. Khrushchev arrived in Washington on 15 September. He stayed in the United States almost two weeks and covered a lot of territory: he had lunch with some movie stars at the Twentieth Century Fox studios in Hollywood; talked with American labor leaders in the Mark Hopkins Hotel in San Francisco; inspected a stand of hybrid corn on an Iowa farm; and had a *tête-à-tête* with Eisenhower at the president's retreat at Camp David. The Camp David meeting came just before Khrushchev returned home, and the intimate atmosphere seemed to inspire the two leaders to a new cordiality.[55] Journalists were soon talking about the "Spirit of Camp David." The sharp about-face was typical of the Khrushchev years: he conducted a spasmodic foreign policy that alternated between periods of crisis and detente. Such ambivalence flowed naturally from the state of siege in which Khrushchev constantly felt himself. Relations with China were worsening, and Khrushchev feared the ambitions of Mao Zedong: Mao is "a nationalist . . . bursting with an impatient desire to rule the world."[56] For his part, Mao was openly critical of Khrushchev's foreign policy; peaceful coexistence, he said, was a bourgeois pacifist notion. Khrushchev could hope to quiet these Chinese slanders only by achieving some dramatic success.

The Camp David meeting set the stage for a summit meeting in Paris that finally began on 16 May 1960 after prolonged disagreements over the agenda. But no sooner had the leaders of the United States, the Soviet Union, Britain, and France seated themselves at the conference table than Khrushchev launched a broadside. He demanded that the United States condemn its spy plane flights that had violated Soviet airspace and that those guilty of such actions be punished. Khrushchev was referring to the capture two weeks before of Gary Powers, the pilot of a U-2 plane that had crashed some 1,200 miles within the Soviet Union. The Soviets had removed the plane's aerial photography equipment intact. Eisenhower had first lied about the flight because he believed the equipment and the pilot could have not survived the crash.[57] Khrushchev gave him a chance to put the blame on his subordinates, but Eisenhower candidly admitted he knew about the flights and assumed full personal responsibility. He gave Khrushchev no satisfaction except to say that there would be no more U-2 flights. He now accused Khrushchev of coming "all the way from Moscow to Paris with the sole intention of sabotaging this meeting on which so much of the hopes of the world have rested."[58]

Khrushchev, in a press conference two days later, declared that the Soviet Union would "not tolerate insults, we have our pride and our dignity. We represent a mighty socialist state." He promised that in the future not only would such planes be shot down, *but* the bases from which they flew would be attacked. Khrushchev was under tremendous pressure from the hard-liners at home. Had he not complained so much publicly, they might have accused him of not taking Soviet security seriously. Some believe he was not serious about negotiating at Paris and that he used the U-2 incident to break up the summit. More likely, he had hoped to make some progress toward a limited test ban treaty and toward a resolution of

The Berlin Wall winds around the Brandenburg gate, now cut off from the West. The Soviets began sealing off their zone from those of West Berlin on 13 August 1961, gradually replacing the early temporary cinder block and barbed wire barrier with a more substantial structure of concrete sections. The entire area east of the boundary, including "Checkpoint Charlie," was off-limits. Anyone caught there without permission could be shot.

the German problem that would keep nuclear weapons out of the hands of the "revanchist" West German military. This scenario would explain why he gave Eisenhower an opportunity to deny that he had sent the U-2 into Soviet airspace. The U-2 incident had forced Khrushchev to show how tough he was and to come home with a diplomatic success. But, when it became clear that Eisenhower was not prepared to make significant concessions, Khrushchev chose to save face by torpedoing the summit.[59] Khrushchev made a blustery speech in which he again promised "to conclude a peace treaty with the German Democratic Republic, to draw a line under the Second World War and thereby to deprive the Western powers of the right to have occupation troops in West Berlin."[60] Then he left Paris and flew to East Berlin, where he repeated his threats. Perhaps the history of European affairs would have taken a different turn if Eisenhower, in that tense encounter in Paris, had given Khrushchev more help in repairing his already damaged reputation.

The U-2 incident and the failed summit were the latest in a long string of Soviet defeats. In his years at the helm, Khrushchev had achieved no notable success in foreign affairs. His German policy had failed. So had his efforts to significantly increase Soviet influence in the Third World. He had had no success in making the United Nations more responsible to the Soviet will.[61] He had also failed to head off a rupture with Communist China. When he traveled abroad, he often reacted with incredible cloddishness when he was subjected to criticism of the sort he was unaccustomed to hearing at home. In New York at the Fifteenth Session of the United Nations General Assembly, he responded to an unfavorable speech by delegates from the Philippines by taking off his shoe and pounding it on the desk. He was probably sincere in wanting to find some common security agreement with the West, but as long as the U.S. policy of encirclement continued, he felt his country would always negotiate at a disadvantage. As recent trouble in the satellites had indicated, the Communist bloc seemed threatened more by erosion from within than from the West.

Khrushchev certainly knew he could not force the Western powers out of Berlin short of an atomic war, but he was not averse to provoking another crisis there to strengthen the Soviet position. At a meeting in Vienna, on 3–4 June 1961, with the newly elected American president, John F. Kennedy, Khrushchev warned that if the Americans were not willing to resolve the German question by negotiation, the Soviets would conclude a unilateral agreement with the Democratic Republic. When Khrushchev returned home, he issued an ultimatum, informing the signatories of the Potsdam agreement that they had until the end of the year to reach a settlement. In the meantime, on 13 August 1961, the Soviets, after secret preparations, sent their troops into position along the city's border, sealing off West Berlin from East Berlin. The Allies protested but accepted the change without armed resistance. The situation, however, remained tense for the next several months. General Lucius Clay, the hero of the 1948 blockade, was sent to the city, and the American garrison was reinforced with 15,000 troops, sent to Berlin via the autobahn. On 21 August, the Soviet Union announced its intention to resume nuclear testing, which had been discontinued since November 1958; over the next two months, there were some fifty explosions, culminating on 30 October with a blast of 57 megatons (Soviet propaganda claimed it was 100 megatons!).

The third 1961 Berlin crisis could be counted a Soviet success. As on previous occasions, the Soviets took the initiative and decided how far they wanted to push. This time they discovered that although the West reiterated its intention to remain in Berlin, it would not actively oppose alteration of the city's four-power status. Henceforth, any negotiations on Germany would have to proceed from the assumption that the division of the country was permanent. On 13 August 1961, to drive this point home, the East Germans began to seal off their border with the West by stringing serpentine barbed wire around their section of Berlin. Two days later, they began installing the first slabs of concrete. Khrushchev had feared Western reprisals and had made his approval of the construction of the more permanent structure conditional on the West doing nothing.[62]

The Berlin crisis strengthened Khrushchev's hand in dealing with his foreign and domestic enemies. At the Twenty-Second Communist Party Congress in October and November 1961, he lambasted the leaders of the Albanian Communist party for perpetuating the Stalinist cult of the individual and deliberately slandering the Soviet Union. The real issue was not Soviet-Albanian relations. Khrushchev was actually attacking the Albanians' main supporters, the Red Chinese. In his closing remarks, he said sarcastically that if "the Chinese comrades wish to make efforts towards normalizing the relations between the Albanian Party of Labor and the fraternal parties, there is hardly anyone who can communicate to the solution of this problem more than the Communist Party of China."[63] The Sino-Soviet schism had now become public, but how this split would affect the overall conduct of Soviet foreign policy was not yet clear. The Soviet leaders seemed to have given up hope that they could prevent the Chinese from developing an independent nuclear capacity, or that they could control West German rearmament, but they still had a strong desire to achieve a position in the world commensurate with their military strength.

The Cuban Missile Crisis. Although Khrushchev boasted that the Soviet Union possessed "indisputable superiority in rocketry and nuclear arms,"[64] he realized that the Soviet atomic arsenal was quantitatively inferior to that of the United States. His efforts to overcome this deficiency led Khrushchev into one of the most desperate gambles of the Cold War: his attempt to install medium-range and intermediate-range ballistic missiles on the island of Cuba.

American Central Intelligence chief John A. McCone had already warned President Kennedy that the Soviets might try to install such weapons in Cuba. McCone reasoned that the attempt would be made so the Soviets could "greatly improve their bargaining position vis-à-vis the United States, for whatever use they cared to make of it."[65] But Kennedy and his advisers simply did not believe that the Kremlin would deliberately commit such a reckless act. The Americans assumed that the Soviets would behave rationally and, that before they embarked on a specific course of action, they would have examined their options and considered the consequences that might follow. However, the fact that the Soviets were capable of doing such cost-benefit analysis did not mean that they would necessarily arrive at the same supposedly logical conclusions as the experts in Washington. There were simply too many unknowns—the exact relationship between Khrushchev and his Politburo colleagues being one of the most important. As for Khrushchev himself, he seemed determined to teach the Americans a lesson no matter what the cost:

> The Americans had surrounded our country with military bases and threatened us with nuclear weapons, and now they would learn just what it feels like to have enemy missiles pointing at you; we'd be doing nothing more than giving them a little of their own medicine. And it was high time America learned what it feels like to have her own land and her own people threatened. We Soviets have suffered three wars over the last century; World War I, the Civil War, and World War II. America has never had to fight a war on her own soil, at least not in the past fifty years. She has sent troops abroad to fight in the two world wars and made a fortune as a result. America has shed a few drops of her own blood while making billions by bleeding the rest of the world dry.[66]

The Cuban missile crisis lasted thirteen days—from Monday, 15 October 1961, when aerial photographs taken by U-2 spy planes revealed the presence of the missile sites, to Sunday, 28 October, when Khrushchev agreed to dismantle the weapons and return them to the Soviet Union. Kennedy had recently read *The Guns of August* by Barbara Tuchman and was impressed that the major European powers in 1914 seemed to have tumbled into war "through stupidity, individual idiosyncrasies, misunderstandings, and personal complexes of inferiority and grandeur."[67] He therefore took special pains to be in constant contact with Khrushchev and to leave him in no doubt that the United States was totally committed to eliminating Soviet missiles from Cuba. He underlined American determination by proclaiming a naval blockade of Cuba, and when this failed to effect a withdrawal, he warned Khrushchev that either the Soviets would have to remove the missiles or the United States would do it for them. Faced with American determination to regard the presence of Soviet missiles in Cuba as a *casus belli,* Khrushchev backed down. As a trade-off of sorts, Kennedy promised to respect the sovereignty of Cuba and to close a couple of (marginal) air bases in Turkey.

Throughout the crisis, the American president made a conscious effort not to behave arrogantly; he made it clear that the U.S. objective was only the removal of the missiles, not the humiliation of Khrushchev. Kennedy did not believe that the Soviet Union would regard the Cuban adventure as vital to its own security: "Thus, if hostilities were to come, it would be either because our national interests collided which, because of their united interests and our purposely limited objec-

The Soviets display their military strength at the forty-fifth anniversary of the Bolshevik revolution on 7 November 1962. A "Scud" moves past party leaders assembled on the reviewing stand of Lenin's tomb in Red Square. This intermediate-range missile could travel 175 miles and carry a nuclear, chemical, or conventional warhead. It was designed to strike at cities and major enemy control centers.

tives, seemed unlikely—or because of our failure or their failure to understand the other's objectives."[68]

Khrushchev later explained the whole missile business as a Soviet effort to prevent the Americans from sponsoring another attempt to invade Cuba as they had in April 1961 at the Bay of Pigs: "We had no other way of helping them meet the American threat, except to install our missiles on the island, so as to confront the aggressive forces of the United States with a dilemma: if you invade Cuba, you'll have to face a nuclear attack against your own cities. Our intention was to install the missiles not to wage war against the U.S. but to prevent the U.S. from invading Cuba and thus starting a war."[69] But if the Soviets had merely wanted to protect the regime of Fidel Castro, they could have done so with less risk by sending a contingent of troops to Cuba to act as a deterrent in the same way American troops guaranteed Berlin from outside attack. The installation of offensive weapons ninety miles from Florida, with a range capable of destroying "New York, Chicago, and the other huge industrial cities, not to mention a little village like Washington,"[70] would openly invite the very attack the Soviets said they were trying to avoid. In fact, some analysts assumed that the missiles were sent to Cuba for that very reason. According to this scenario, the American bombing of Cuba would cause such confusion at home and arouse such animosity abroad that it would wreck the NATO alliance and allow the Soviets to move with impunity against Berlin or some other area of the world. However, if this hypothesis were true, why did Khrushchev withdraw the missiles before an American attack? It has also been suggested that the Soviets installed the missiles to use as bargaining chips to get the United States to dismantle its atomic bases in Turkey, Italy, and England. If so, the quid pro quo would not have resulted in any significant increase in Soviet security; the bulk of the Americans' missile strike force was not located in these overseas bases, although the Americans did remove their Jupiter missiles from Turkey a few months after the crisis. Perhaps Khrushchev was once again only testing American intentions; President Kennedy thought so. But why choose Cuba, a place thousands of miles from the Soviet Union? If the United States showed itself ready to stand firm in Berlin, how much more willing would it be to do so when the threat was only ninety miles off its shores?

POSTSCRIPT   The Cold War was more about geography than ideology. Stalin had drawn the Eastern European frontiers to maximize the influence of the Soviet Union. Much of this effort was aimed at recovering the territories lost in World War I; hence, the Soviets reintegrated the Baltic states, regained chunks of the Ukraine and Belorussia from Poland, and obtained Bessarabia from Romania. But the Soviets also took additional pieces of territory to increase their strategic advantage. They carved out an enclave around Königsberg, renamed Kaliningrad, in order to obtain another port on the Baltic and to interpose themselves between Lithuania and Poland. (This new acquisition, which was not contiguous with a Soviet-Russian ethnic base, was sure to be the source of future troubles.) They chopped off the Ruthenian tail of Czechoslovakia to put themselves on the other side of the Carpathian Mountains and give them a common frontier with Hungary. They extended their Moldavian territory to the mouth of the Danube, a truly international waterway that flows through or along a dozen states. All in all, these additions increased Soviet influence.

By the 1950s, however, the Soviets were finding it increasingly difficult to maintain the kind of political control these changes facilitated. A series of adventures outside Europe added to their sense of vulnerability. The two superpowers came closest to blows in the Cuban missile crisis, which ironically led to a period of relaxation in their relations. The following year, the United States and the Soviet Union concluded a treaty banning the testing of nuclear weapons in the atmosphere and in the oceans. They also installed a special telegraph circuit—a hot line—between their capitals to allow their leaders instant communication in the event of a future crisis. These fail-safe procedures, which were passed along to the Soviets, had been developed by the United States. The Cold War was not over, but there was a new realization that no crisis was worth escalating into actual warfare.

The skirmishes of the Cold War resulted in no great victories, only occasional tactical advantages. By the late 1960s, both sides, although not yet willing to change their basic goals and beliefs, had recognized that the old ways were too costly and too dangerous. The new Kremlin leaders had grown up in Stalin's era, but they proved more flexible and significantly less bloodthirsty than he. Still, contradictions remained. The Soviets no longer wantonly plundered the resources of their satellites, but they refused to relinquish their control, even though it was becoming ever more costly. The Soviets also had to cope with the effects of such crises as Berlin, Korea, and Cuba, which had strengthened the resolve of the Western alliance and endangered the very security the Soviets were trying to protect.

Clearly, a relaxation of tension with the West was in the Soviets' best interests, considering the backwardness of their economy, their bureaucratic bungling, inadequate mechanization, and woeful lack of incentives. Soviet farmers, for example, were about one-tenth as productive as their

American counterparts; as a result, the country was plagued with chronic shortages. Increasingly, the Soviet Union had to rely on food purchases from abroad, paid for by increased sales of gold. The Soviets also needed technical assistance and investment capital to modernize their ailing industry. Shifting scarce resources from arms and munitions to more productive ventures would help them close the widening gap with the more highly productive countries of the West.

At the beginning of the Cold War, an extension of Soviet power into Western Europe seemed not only possible but imminent. By the mid-1960s, it was the least likely scenario. Nevertheless, American calculations were still based on such an eventuality, while the Soviets still feared an American preemptive strike against them. Almost by habit, as well as by vested interest, the two cold warriors followed their old paths of rivalry; each country was reluctant to give way lest the other take advantage of the show of weakness. Yet ironically, as mentioned earlier, this balance of the superpowers created one of the longest periods of peace in European history. Not since 1945 had any European state fought another. These decades of peace permitted the less-than-superpower European states, at least those in the West, to develop their economic and political strength to the stage where they could determine their own destinies free from outside domination.

ENDNOTES

1. Harry S Truman, *Memoirs*, vol. 1 (Garden City, N.Y.: Doubleday, 1955), 552.
2. Ibid., 551–52.
3. *Command Papers*, Cmd. 7599 (London: H.M.S.O., 1948).
4. *Documents on International Affairs, 1949–1950*, 258.
5. Turkey and Greece joined in 1952, and West Germany in May 1955.
6. *Documents on International Affairs, 1949–1950*, 256.
7. Truman, *Memoirs*, 2:333.
8. Stalin had temporarily withdrawn his representatives in a protest against the refusal to give the Red Chinese a seat on the Security Council following Mao Zedong's victory the previous year over the Nationalists of Jiang Jieshi (Chiang Kai-shek).
9. Acheson, *Present at the Creation* (New York: Norton, 1969), 453.
10. Truman, *Memoirs*, 2:309.
11. "The GAC Report of October 30, 1949," in Herbert F. York, *The Advisors, Oppenheimer, Teller, and the Superbomb* (San Francisco: W. H. Freeman, 1976), 152–59.
12. Ibid., 65–74.
13. NSC-68, "A Report by the Secretaries of State and Defense on 'United States Objectives and Programs for National Security April 7, 1950,'" reprinted in *Naval War College Review* (May–June 1975):51–108.
14. Ibid., 62–63.
15. Ibid., 57–58.
16. *Documents on International Affairs, 1953*, 30.
17. *Documents on International Affairs, 1954*, 32.
18. *Documents on International Affairs, 1955*, 265–66.

19. Ibid., 40.
20. Michael R. Beschloss, *Mayday: Eisenhower, Khrushchev and the U-2 Affair* (New York: Harper and Row, 1986), 102.
21. Ibid., 103–4.
22. *Annual Register 1954*, 35.
23. Anthony Eden, *Full Circle* (Boston: Houghton Mifflin, 1960), 475. Eden wrote: "Some say Nasser is no Hitler or Mussolini. Allowing for a difference in scale, I am not so sure. He has followed Hitler's pattern, even to concentration camps and the propagation of *Mein Kampf* among his officers. He had understood and used the Goebbels pattern of propaganda in all its lying ruthlessness." Ibid., 481.
24. William Roger Louis and Roger Owen, eds., *Suez 1956: The Crisis and its Consequences* (Oxford: Clarendon Press, 1989), 134–38.
25. Eden, *Full Circle*, 488.
26. Donald Neff, *Warriors at Suez* (New York: Simon and Schuster, 1981), 289.
27. Moshe Dayan, *Diary of the Sinai Campaign, 1956* (London: Sphere Books, 1967), 11.
28. André Beaufre, *The Suez Expedition, 1956* (New York: Frederick Praeger, 1969), 74.
29. Eden, *Full Circle*, 620.
30. Selwyn I. Troen and Moshe Shemesh, eds., *The Suez-Sinai Crisis 1956: Retrospective and Reappraisal* (New York: Columbia University Press, 1990), 17–18.
31. Eden, *Full Circle*, 624.
32. Beaufre, *Suez Expedition*, 14.
33. Eden, *Full Circle*, 626.
34. Troen and Shemesh, *Suez-Sinai Crisis*, 150–60.
35. Louis and Owen, *Suez 1956*, 233–53.
36. Richard Vaughn, *Post-War Integration in Europe: Documents of Modern History* (New York: St. Martin's Press, 1976), 43. The states were Belgium, Denmark, France, Ireland, Italy, Luxembourg, Netherlands, Norway, Sweden, and Great Britain.
37. *Documents on Germany under Occupation, 1945–1954* (London: Oxford University Press, 1955), 440.
38. See the discussion of NATO earlier in this chapter.
39. In the Petersberg protocol (1950). *Documents on Germany under Occupation*, 445.
40. See Arnold J. Zurcher, *The Struggle to Unite Europe, 1940–1958* (New York: New York University Press, 1958).
41. The European Atomic Energy Community (Euratom) was created at the same time to engage in a common program of scientific research for the peaceful use of atomic energy. However, this organization remained fairly weak because several nations, especially France, refused to provide it with adequate funding. Later Euratom and the Common Market were consolidated into the European Community.
42. Carl H. Fulda, "The Legal Structure of the European Community," in *France and the European Community*, ed. by Sidney N. Fisher (Columbus: Ohio State University Press, 1964), 21–34.
43. See Finn B. Jensen, *The Common Market: Economic Integration of Europe* (Philadelphia: Lippincott, 1965); Katharine Savage, *The Story of the Common Market* (New York: Walck, 1970); John Paxton, *The Developing Common Market: The Structure of the EEC in Theory and Practice* (London: Macmillan, 1976); and Steven J. Warnecke, *The European Community* (New York: Council for European Studies, 1978).
44. Sometimes when less important decisions were taken, the foreign ministers might be replaced by the ministers of agriculture, finance, or other branches of government if their expertise was deemed necessary.
45. Over time these senior posts became the fiefs of certain countries. Thus, the commissioner of agriculture was traditionally from the Netherlands, the director-general was French, and so forth.
46. See Anthony J. C. Kerr, *The Common Market and How it Works* (New York: Perga-

mon Press, 1986), Chapter 3.

47. William Diebold, Jr., "The Process of European Integration," in Lawrence B. Krause, ed., *The Common Market: Progress and Controversy* (Englewood Cliffs, N.J.: Prentice-Hall, 1964), 34–39.

48. Brian R. Mitchell, *European Historical Statistics* (New York: Columbia University Press, 1975), 498.

49. John P. de Gara, *Trade Relations between the Common Market and the Eastern Bloc* (Bruges: De Tempel, 1964), 36.

50. Nikita Khrushchev, *For Victory in Peaceful Competition with Capitalism* (New York: Dutton, 1960), 738.

51. Ibid., 736.

52. *Survey of International Affairs*, 1956–58, 564.

53. In remarks to Chinese Communist leader Mao Zedong. Nikita Khrushchev, *Khrushchev Remembers: The Last Testament* (Boston: Little, Brown, 1974), 470.

54. Khrushchev came to see the capitalists' display but, as he stated later, was not terribly impressed: "The Americans wanted to impress Russians with a lot of fancy gadgets." Ibid., 366.

55. However, the nastier, more disgusting (but characteristic) aspects of the Cold War seemed hardly to have changed. From Khrushchev's stay at Camp David, the American Central Intelligence Agency (CIA) obtained a specimen of the Soviet leader's feces from which they hoped to ascertain the state of his general health.

56. Khrushchev, *Khrushchev Remembers*, 474.

57. The Soviets interrogated Gary Powers for two months, then put him on trial in August 1960. The televised trial was the greatest show trial of the Cold War. The court sentenced Powers to ten years deprivation of liberty. In February 1962, he was exchanged for Soviet master spy Rudolf Abel.

58. *Documents of International Affairs 1960*, 31.

59. Beschloss, *Mayday*, 374–82.

60. Ibid., 36.

61. Khrushchev had wanted to change the office of secretary-general into an executive troika that would include one representative from the West, one from the Soviet Union, and one from the uncommitted nations.

62. Peter Wyden, *Wall: The Inside Story of Divided Berlin* (New York: Simon and Schuster, 1989), 85–90.

63. Nikita Khrushchev, *Khrushchev Speaks* (Ann Arbor: University of Michigan Press, 1963), 433.

64. Ibid., 426.

65. Elie Abel, *The Missile Crisis* (New York: Bantam, 1966), 13.

66. Khrushchev, *Khrushchev Remembers*, 494.

67. Robert Kennedy, *Thirteen Days* (New York: W. W. Norton, 1971), 40.

68. Ibid., 103–4.

69. Khrushchev, *Khrushchev Remembers*, 511.

70. Khrushchev, Ibid., 496.

PART TWO

SOCIETY AND CULTURE, 1945–1990

CHAPTER 6

THE URBAN ASCENDENCY

PREFACE Despite the massive destruction of people and property, World War I had spared most of Europe's cities, at least those not in the direct path of battle. Cannons had pounded Paris and Antwerp; zeppelins had bombed London and towns along the southeastern English coast; gunboats had opened up on Belgrade; and bombers had struck western Germany. Nevertheless, the technology of the Great War was not sufficiently developed to enable warring nations to hit targets very remote from the battlefield. Besides, the belligerents felt a certain reluctance to pursue strictly civilian targets. None of these restrictions applied to World War II, which left very few cities of strategic value intact.

The Germans were certainly not squeamish about leveling enemy cities. Paris was spared because Wehrmacht commander, Dietrich von Choltitz, refused to carry out the Führer's order to destroy it,[1] and Rome was saved by becoming an open city. But others, including Warsaw, London, Rotterdam, Valenciennes, Coventry, Milan, Leningrad, Kiev, and Stalingrad—the list goes on—were not so fortunate. Neither were cities in Germany itself. The Allies repeatedly struck Berlin, Cologne, and Hamburg. In the last year of the war, the British and Americans bombed Germany with practically every plane that could get off the ground. One-third of Germany's buildings were completely destroyed, another 44 percent partially so. In Cologne, 66 percent of the city was demolished and 93 percent of Düsseldorf was seriously damaged.[2] Dresden was gutted in one great terror raid. Fire storms and bombings alone killed 500,000 Germans.[3] The center of Berlin was in complete ruins. Bombs and shells had wrecked or flattened one-fifth of the city's 250,000 buildings and damaged another 150,000. Vital public services, including power plants, transportation, and police and fire protection had ceased functioning. Untreated sewage sluiced through the city's waterways. Almost all of Berlin's bridges that had not already been bombed had been blown up in the last days of the fighting. Streets and roads were choked with rubble. Dead bodies floated in the lakes and canals and were hidden under the debris. The restoration of gas utilities throughout Berlin had a macabre by-product: the suicide rate suddenly increased in those districts.[4]

By 1945, all Europeans from Belfast to the Urals showed at least some signs of neurosis. When the guns fell silent, they were left to clean away the fragments of buildings, bury the bodies, restore public services, and provide temporary shelter for the homeless. The cities became places of refuge for thousands of displaced persons. Refugees reasoned that no matter how miserable life was in the cities, it was still safer than in the country-side. The great migration continued even after order had been restored. Urban life meant prosperity and escape from boredom. By the 1980s, more than 80 percent of the people of Western Europe and 60 percent of those in Eastern Europe lived in urban areas.[5] Cities had long played an impor-tant role in European life, but never before had they been so prominent; never before had their values and problems so shaped the life of European nations.

CITY DYNAMICS

Town Planning and Reconstruction

The Experience of Western Europe. Repairing the damage of war was a task beyond the resources of private enterprise. People everywhere expected govern-ment would assume a major role in recovery and development. Nevertheless, urban planning took different forms in the various Western European countries. In Bel-gium, France, and Italy, which already had strong traditions of urban physical design, engineers and architects played a dominant role. But in Great Britain, the Netherlands, and Denmark, where planning had often been less specialized and more liberal, land-use policies continued to depend more upon private interests. Yet even in these countries, central control increased as land became scarcer.

The Netherlands had a long history of town planning. By the end of the nine-teenth century the Dutch had managed to devise a national spatial policy that provided for the needs of a steadily growing population by encouraging develop-ment through economic incentives. In 1958, with Amsterdam's population ap-proaching a million, the government forbade further expansion inside the city's municipal boundaries and concentrated on developing separate residential districts north and south of the city. At the same time, it took steps to preserve a green belt between its major cities by limiting new construction in other areas of the country.

In Italy, planning was less rational, and urban growth was more chaotic. Squat-ters frequently took over vacant lands that had been designated for parks or in-dustrial areas and threw up makeshift dwellings that lacked the normal amenities of sanitation, electricity, and heat. Approximately 800,000 such people lived on the outskirts of Rome in "houses" built without the necessary permits on land that the inhabitants did not own; frequently, the squatter settlements were near already established public housing.[6] The authorities occasionally tried to tear down these shanty towns, but as soon as the bulldozers left, the squatters rebuilt their villages.

Le Corbusier's Swiss Pavilion at the Cité Universitaire (1930–1932) shows off the architect's severe functional style; it incorporates his characteristic slab structure on stilts. Le Corbusier believed that the massive simplicity of an American grain elevator was functional architecture at its best.

Some of these houses had a certain air of permanence despite having been put together one room and one floor at a time. The residents even demanded, and sometimes received, proper city services including a bus stop.

The French tried to avoid unregulated growth by creating new towns, or satellite cities, filled with apartments and located outside many of the large urban areas. In France, three-fourths of urban dwellers would ultimately live in apartment houses.[7] To create this new housing, the government established planning offices in eight designated metropolitan areas and asked Le Corbusier (Edouard Jeanneret), one of the country's most famous architects, to help develop a standard housing formula. No town planner had thought more about the relation of people to their environment. "Le Corbu" saw the city as an architectural landscape, a vital element of human geography, a dimensional truth that reflected human activity at its moment of use.[8] He wanted his creations to provide more than clean, healthy housing: set within a rational infrastructure, they would organize work and provide the necessary amenities for free time. He proposed the linear city (*la ville radieuse*) as a proper balance between the workplace and the home, with human activity organized around a geometric grid.

In 1946, he began the construction of the *unité d'habitation* at Marseilles. This was a reinforced concrete block of 337 units, built on a slab supported above the ground on pilings or *pilotis*. Le Corbusier created a proper social mix by including apartments of various sizes, from one-room studios to large duplexes for families. Every other floor contained large interior streets, and the sixth and seventh levels enclosed a vast shopping mall. The major center of public activity, however, was the roof, which featured an artificial mountain range, a gymnasium, two solariums, a 1,000-foot cinder track, a swimming pool, a day nursery, a kindergarten, and an open air theater. It was one of the great roofs of the world. Le Corbusier elevated social activities far above street level to remove recreation from the "fungus" that had eaten up the pavements of Paris. He found it illogical that "one entire superficie of a town should be unused and reserved for a flirtation between the tiles and the stars."[9]

In the Marseilles project, Le Corbusier tried to apply the same concept to apartment living that he had attempted in a workers' housing development he had designed after World War I for the town of Pessac, near Bordeaux. In this earlier project, he had also wanted to replace "the brutality, squalor, and stupidity [of the typical town] with machines for living in." Trouble was, not many French seemed to appreciate living in Le Corbusier's cubist, architectural masterpieces. At Pessac, they had modified the houses to make them more cozy. They had replaced the horizontal windows with cottage windows, tacked on additional rooms, and hung the family wash on the roof terraces. They had also decorated the stark exteriors with plaster swans, flower boxes, and fake stone veneers.[10] In Marseilles, the residents preferred to shop and take their recreation closer to the ground so the space provided for such activities went largely unused. People called the Marseilles project the *"maison du fada"* (the nut house). Le Corbusier was offended and never designed another such building in France. His later apartments at Nantes, Briey-en-Forêt, and Firminy followed conventional designs. The French government also grew tired of such visionary planning. The costs of trying to control the whole range of urban activity were too high. After 1955, the government embarked on a policy of liberalization with greater opportunities for the private sector.

The Germans favored new urban construction, but they also wanted to save and restore as much of their ruined real estate as possible. Their passion to preserve the fronts of bombed-out buildings gave their cities a curious appearance—starkly modern facades frequently stood alongside German empire baroque. Much of the first building after the war was of inferior quality, however, due to the necessity to provide immediate housing for the millions of refugees who poured into the urban regions around Hamburg and in the Ruhr, the Rhineland, and the south. Later, spatial planning and design became more important, but this new emphasis led to a constant tug of war between private developers and public authorities who wanted to use planning as an element in the creation of a modern progressive society.[11]

Communist Development. The Communists associated cities with capitalist exploitation and therefore believed they had a duty to make radical changes in the urban environment in order to create a new society. Soviet leaders were also committed to changing their essentially agrarian country into an industrial powerhouse. In 1931, they officially decreed that urban society was the basis of modern Communism and announced that town planning should be dedicated to the dynamics of the work ethic. In the Soviet view, people lived in cities for the purpose of building socialism. In general, the Soviets preferred to transform their older cities by expanding into new districts away from the historical centers. Certain cities, however, had to be completely rebuilt. At Stalingrad, for example, new apartment complexes resembling rectangular boxes were built to house the workers near fortresslike factories laid out along a geometric grid. Cities like Stalingrad, which had suffered extensive damage during the war, were fairly easy to repair because there was no imperative to preserve important architectural monuments. However, the older towns with their historical and cultural treasures were another matter.

The war had brought a new reverence for the artifacts of the past despite their tsarist associations. Restoring the classical architecture of Leningrad, the city of the Revolution and the thousand-day siege, became high priority. As part of this commitment, the Communists allowed many of the city's old prerevolutionary street names to be revived, including that of the main thoroughfare, which again became the Nevskii Prospekt. At the same time, however, Leningrad had to accommodate a new influx of people. During the war, the city had lost about 2 million of its inhabitants, leaving it with a population of 639,000. By September 1945, the population had skyrocketed to double its size in 1940. Most of the recent migrants came from the rural areas of the Ukraine, Byelorussia, and the Tatar Republic and had few work skills suited to an urban environment.

The Leningrad experience was not unique. All the major Soviet cities experienced similar population growth. By the 1980s, the Soviet Union had 297 cities with more than 100,000 inhabitants, and about 75 percent of all Soviets lived in cities with more than 2,000 inhabitants.[12] Soviet planners estimated that by the middle of the twenty-first century that number would rise to 95 percent. Most of the increased population was housed in great superblocks that sprawled endlessly into the suburbs. Since very few Soviets possessed private motor cars, the residents of these apartment blocks became prisoners of public transportation. The complexes were occupied mostly by younger families, while older couples, pensioners, government officials, and students lived in the older residential districts. Only they could enjoy the old walking character of urban life.

Profile: Moscow and Paris

Paris

Both the Soviets and the French regarded their respective capital cities as the center of the world, the focus of their centralized state, and the heart of their civilization and art. Decisions affecting the world had been made in both Paris and Moscow. Each city had begun modestly and had grown outward in ever-widening circles, relentlessly pushing beyond a series of defensive walls. When these were torn down, they were replaced by boulevards, then by belts of housing, and finally by more boulevards and more housing.

Moscow, the center of the world's last great empire, was little damaged by the war. Therefore, the Soviets could simply continue the great plan for the city's transformation that had been developed in 1935. Already the center of the city had been transformed by the construction of new buildings—the most conspicuous being the Stalinist wedding-cake skyscrapers with their tall spires—and broad highways. The width of Gorki Street, Moscow's main thoroughfare, was more than tripled from its original forty feet. Moscow was to be the Soviet Union's model city, and its development was carefully controlled. Postwar planners limited its population to 5 million persons, a maximum they intended to enforce through the use of internal passports that allowed settlement only by special permission.[13] But these plans proved unrealistic. By 1965, the city's population exceeded 7 million people. The surrounding regions with their semi-isolated suburban subcommunities added another 28 million. The 1971 plan predicted that the population of the metropolitan area would grow to over 50 million by the year 2000. At the end of the 1980s, Moscow's population already approached 9 million people.[14]

In its headlong rush to create a new world metropolis, the Soviet government launched a massive housing program, extending the city's official limits and pushing the subway farther into the suburbs. Although the large expenditures on public utilities and apartments drained investment capital from other parts of the economy, the quality of the new construction was frequently shoddy. The social costs were also very high. The minimum size of each habitation cluster was 50,000 people. The huge apartment buildings, which were often built without connecting streets or integrated neighborhood services, remained isolated units, giving their residents no sense of neighborhood.

On average, people spent between two and four hours a day commuting to and from work. Shopping for food might add another two hours. Understandably, people placed an enormous premium on weekend leisure activities: theater, movies, sports, or watching television. Realizing this, the regime tried to encourage people to participate in social activities around their workplace. Women, especially, took advantage of these services as a relief from the demands placed upon them at home.[15] In their collectives, they could nurture friendships and enjoy some relaxation.[16] Moscow had a conspicuous absence of public restaurants, cafés, or marketplaces where friends could meet to chat and retreat from an overbearing political system. Shops were drab and lacked merchandise. The displays in the windows were frequently just an indication of what the store would sell if it had any goods to sell. Soviet planners did not consider shopping to be a valuable social or recreational activity.

The drabness of Moscow life resulted in high rates of public intoxication. To handle the drunkenness, the regime created a special police squad to round up the drunks and take them to one of the city's twelve sobering-up stations where they would be detained forty-eight hours. There was never a shortage of people to arrest. The special squads handled over 140,000 cases a year. They plucked tipsy Muscovites off the streets and responded to calls from shops, subway stations, factories and offices, and private homes. A person who was arrested three times in one year could be sentenced to a labor camp. Yet, alcohol was very expensive. A bottle of vodka in a state liquor store cost two-days wages, but black marketeers got twice that amount. Muscovites also drank home brew, hair tonic, eau de cologne, aftershave lotion, and medicinal alcohol.

Paris was more charitable to its drunks. The police seldom bothered them as long as they did not block traffic. Many drunks had the good sense to stay out of the way and sleep it off on side streets. Paris was also more tolerant toward its clochards. The Nazis had had no patience with such derelicts and cleared them off the streets. After the occupation, the bums came back, much to the delight of the Parisians who considered them part of the landscape. Paris contained all the activities, vices, and services appropriate to a great international metropolis: boutiques, world-class restaurants, fashion houses, five-star hotels, street vendors, and Gypsy children who picked your pocket. The city took in half of all the money tourists spent in France.

But Paris was also a working town, the center of activity for government and industry; it provided a livelihood for at least a quarter of the nation's population. Ever since World War I, the Paris region had been the country's largest industrial area—a preeminence that had caused many of its districts to become blighted with inadequate sanitation and pollution. Indeed, Paris was the center of just about every French economic activity except mining and truffle gathering. After Tokyo, New York, and London, it was the largest metropolitan area in the world. In 1964, the number of departements in the Paris region increased from three to eight; the city constituted an entire departement by itself. The nearer and outer suburbs beyond the city proper included 279 towns, over half with populations exceeding 10,000 people. At the end of the 1980s, Paris itself had 8.5 million inhabitants,[17] but most of the recent growth was in the areas of low-cost housing in the suburbs. Surrounding the city was a drab industrial belt of chemical plants, steel mills, textile plants, and automobile factories, the so-called Red suburbs, where the workers lived in public housing and traditionally voted Communist.

In Paris itself, the working class lived in the older sections around the Hôtel de Ville and to the east of the Latin Quarter, while the rich monopolized the districts in the western part of town near the Bois du Boulogne. Central Paris, the historic and artistic Paris of legend and lovers, covered only two percent or roughly eight square miles of the entire metropolitan area. This Paris retained much of its old character; in many areas it was still the Paris of Baron Haussmann, the great city planner of Napoleon III in the mid-nineteenth century. Here the old facades were preserved although many of the quarters were giving way to offices, luxury apartments, and condos.

More songs have probably been written about Paris than about any other city. Paris was, by legend, the city where everyone fell in love. Indeed, the city had a charm all its own. It was an easy city to navigate. Its public transportation was convenient and highly efficient, but it was still a place where people walked. It offered a cultural and social richness—day or night, at any season of the year—that few other metropolises could emulate. The weekly activity publication, *Pariscop*, contained almost 150 pages of activities: places to eat, sporting events, theaters and movie houses, music halls, clubs, and cabarets appealing to every sort of taste and perversion, from poetry readings and troubadours to the most explicit forms of pornography. Paris gave its inhabitants every reason to spend their discretionary income. Parisians were clearly not bored. Yet Paris had a divorce rate double that of the rest of the country.

The Material Ethic

For Love of a Car. A sense of alienation and a feeling of entrapment were not exclusive to Communist societies. In the so-called capitalist West, however, the pangs of desperation were alleviated by material opportunity. In the twenty years following World War II, Western Europe experienced its greatest period of sustained material growth. People expected their governments to ensure the continuation of this prosperity and to provide the consumer goods and comfortable lifestyle to which they had grown accustomed. They wanted protection against unemployment, poverty, and disease. Keynesian economics seemed to provide the perfect mechanism for balancing central direction with market forces.

In virtually all Western European countries, people with steady jobs were told that they had a right to a private automobile. The automobile industry, led by the British, Germans, and French, had consolidated itself into a few leading companies that were able to produce cars for a mass market. After World War II, these companies concentrated on small-car production. The idea of attracting lower-income buyers was not new; it dated back to the Austin Seven in Great Britain, the Fiat Topolino (Little Mouse) in Italy, and the Volkswagen in Germany in the 1930s. In 1947, the French state-owned Renault Company launched its popular 4 CV (750 cc), a four-seater with a rear engine and rear-wheel drive. At first, all these cars were colored desert-sand yellow from supplies of paint confiscated from Rommel's Afrika Korps. By 1950, the factories were turning out approximately 400 cars a day, with 20 percent of the sales going overseas. The Renault factory then employed 50,000 workers. The success of the 4 CV was followed, in 1956, with that of the more stylish Dauphine, which sold for $1,600, about $400 less than its nearest competitor. Soon most of the other major European car manufacturers were trying to duplicate Renault's success.

The reconstruction of the German motor car industry was aided by massive assistance from the United States. The Volkswagen Company, under Heinz Nordhoff, captured the popular car market while Opel, under the direction of General Motors, went after middle-income buyers. Nordhoff reputedly had a Nazi past that

The Mercedes-Benz was the status symbol par excellence throughout Germany and the rest of Europe. On this assembly line at the Daimler Benz factory at Stuttgart, several lines of 250 series cars pass a final inspection.

the British authorities were willing to overlook. Fiat, the largest company in Italy, had been badly damaged by the war but, within five years, had again risen to prominence with the moderately priced four-cylinder 1400, which featured unitary body construction and synchromeshed gears. Great Britain's entry in the mass auto market was the Morris Minor, unveiled in 1950. Over one million units were produced in its first decade of production. It continued to be produced for another ten years with virtually no modifications.[18] The European motor car industry, initially protected by import controls, enjoyed twenty years of continuous expansion. West German production rose from 219,000 private cars a year to 3,380,000; French production went from 257,000 to 2,168,000 units; the British from 523,000 to 1,729,000 units; and the Italian from 100,000 to 1,477,000.[19] Production increased in Eastern Europe as well, but on a much smaller scale than in the West.[20]

In Western Europe, new housing developments were always linked by roadway as well as rail to the great urban centers; in contrast, Eastern European countries rarely built more than train and subway connections. Almost all Western European countries constructed superhighways, the most famous being the German autobahns. These roadways, which had been started by the Nazis to make it easier to move their armies, were greatly expanded by the Federal Republic. The autobahns had no speed limits. The average cruising speed was around 125 kilometers or 78 miles per hour, but the fastest "flyers" usually drove their high-powered Mercedes-Benzes, Porsches, or BMWs at speeds in excess of 220 kilometers or 138 miles. The Germans claimed that the fastest drivers were the best drivers, but Germany, along with France, had the highest automobile death rate in Europe.

Greater mobility brought greater headaches in the form of monumental traffic jams, especially in older cities that had been built for the horse and buggy and for pedestrians. The supply of parking places could not keep up with the demand, and drivers left their cars anywhere there was room: on the grass in public parks, on sidewalks, and at the corners of intersections. Constabularies and police departments struck back with the "Denver boot," a bright orange clamp that attached to a wheel and immobilized the vehicle. To get the boot removed, the scofflaw had to pay a hefty fine on the spot. Many European cities also adopted bans against horn blowing. In Paris, where honking had been considered a constitutional right, the policy of prohibition proved a surprising success.

All urban planners tried to accommodate the design of their historical city centers to the invasion of vehicular traffic. Traffic was rerouted, certain streets became one way, boulevards were widened, and sidewalks were narrowed. Overpasses and underpasses were built. In Paris, an east-west freeway reduced the width of the Seine River. Cities tried to encourage people to use public transportation by making constant improvements and keeping the cost of commuting low. Meanwhile private developers built shopping malls away from the center of town. These vast multi-unit commercial centers came complete with their own free or low-cost parking facilities. Europeans liked these concentrated supermarkets, whether in or outside the towns. Here, they could buy everything from light bulbs to salami, from wines and spirits to Valencia oranges, from peanut butter to *paté de foie gras*. Having to go to five separate stores to get meat, milk, bread, beer, and vegetables no longer seemed quaint to those caught in the daily grind. Reducing the time spent on basic chores increased time for leisure and relaxation. It no longer seemed so important to know the butcher personally.

The Entertainment Center. As expectations for more material possessions increased, so did the demands for greater convenience. Within a generation after the end of the war, many Western Europeans had a more comfortable life-style than that enjoyed by ancien-régime monarchs whose drafty palaces lacked central heat, indoor plumbing, and electric lights. Most modern households did not have servants to do the dirty work, but they did have an abundance of helpful appliances. The most important of these was undoubtedly the television set. It did not clean the house, but it helped take one's mind off a dirty one.

In 1950, only Britain and the Soviet Union had national television, but by the end of the decade all the other European countries had established their own broadcasting systems. By 1970, Western Europe had 75 million sets, the Soviet Union another 30 million.[21] These quantities would double over the next twenty years until more Europeans owned television sets than had previously owned radios. The increased concentration of people in urban areas, where they could easily be reached by the relatively short-range television signals, made this explosion in viewership feasible. (Even the practicality of cable television, which appeared later, required a concentration of viewers.) Furthermore, since Europeans now spent relatively fewer hours at their jobs, they had more free time to lounge around.

The power of the electronic eye alarmed many intellectuals who lamented that cultural standards were declining. Dubious that television would ever live up to its high aesthetic promise, they blamed it for promoting indifference and apathy and predicted it would create a generation of illiterates. Nevertheless, the masses loved it and watched it three to four hours a day.

Television broadcasting in the Soviet Union was a state monopoly that presented the state's point of view. Lenin had said that it was the duty of the press to propagandize, agitate, and organize. Television continued this tradition and became a participant in the development of socialism, an assistant that would help the party accomplish its task. Soviet leaders admitted this propagandistic purpose quite openly and somewhat self-righteously. Consequently, Soviet television presented a consistently positive image of society and made no attempt to separate information from ideology. Domestic achievements were always presented in the most favorable light with heavy emphasis on the fulfillment of production quotas and lavish praise for exemplary workers whose pictures were on display in their factories. In a sense, television became the nation's "honor board." No matter what the program, viewers were reminded that they were working to build Communism and were encouraged to be more productive.[22] Soviet television was also expected to point up the contradictions inherent in the capitalistic system and therefore concentrated on strikes, labor violence, class conflict, social decadence, and crime. The principal source of this news was TASS (Telegraph Agency of the Soviet Union), founded in 1925, which got its information largely from Western television broadcasts. The State Committee for Radio and Television in Moscow approved all programming for 123 regional centers; its director was a government minister.

Sporting events were televised to instill pride in the Soviet system, which took the credit for the achievements of the athletes. Similarly, broadcasts of opera, ballet, and symphony orchestra performances were intended to promote cultural pride. Educational programs taught people, especially children, about the sacrifices of earlier generations. Soviet television favored documentaries and dramas that depicted the heroic struggles of World War II. Television not only attempted to make higher education available to those who did not go to the university, but also offered programs on literature, science, and the arts aimed at university students. Broadcasting to regional audiences was frequently a daunting task, considering that the Soviet Union included 129 ethnic groups, and 89 languages. This difficulty was somewhat offset by the general knowledge of the Russian language, a compulsory subject in all the nation's schools. Soviet television also broadcast Russian language classes as well as instruction in other languages, particularly French, Spanish, English, and German.

The regime wanted to give all Soviet citizens access to five channels through satellite and cable hookups, but most could receive only one channel. Moscow, the center of state broadcasting, had four channels, which carried national events, regional news, educational programs, films, and concerts. Most Soviet citizens could afford a black and white set although its cost—between 200 and 300 rubles—was equivalent to two months' salary. Color television, which had been available in the Soviet Union since 1967, cost twice that amount. Only one in twenty television owners had color.

In France, television broadcasting was also a state monopoly that operated on three channels through the ORTF (Office for French Radio and Television Transmission). The politicians of the Fourth Republic generally practiced a hands-off policy, allowing commentators a certain latitude and independence in presenting material unfavorable to the government. This policy changed with the advent of Charles de Gaulle. The general, who faced a hostile press, wanted to avoid as much additional grief as possible. Criticism dried up; those who persisted were fired or reassigned. Not until de Gaulle left office was the ORTF allowed to reestablish its own identity. News programs and political commentary formed only a small part of French television's offerings, however. Viewing fare ran the gamut from the sublime to the ridiculous, from grand opera to the silliest of game shows. Through it all, the French broadcasters retained a strong compulsion to educate.

One of the most prominent shows in the 1970s was "Screen Dossier," which featured a movie about some historical person or event followed by a high-level discussion of its meaning and relevance. The experts tried to outshine each other with brilliant analyses. For example, a film about Admiral Horatio Nelson, starring Laurence Olivier, drew commentary from historians, naval experts, and the great-grand-nephew of the commander of Napoleon's fleet, Admiral Pierre de Villeneuve, who refused to acknowledge that his famous ancestor had committed suicide. The ORTF also presented dramatizations of French novels. By initiating this type of programming, it managed to keep foreign imports down to less than 20 percent of the total. French television also included a hefty diet of boxing, soccer, bicycling, horse racing, and road racing. In addition, it had a *"Soirée policière"* that showed cops and robbers movies.

At first, there was no commercial advertising. Then ads were presented in one chunk at the beginning of the viewing evening, just after the children's programs. Often this parade of thirty-second time bites was the most entertaining fifteen minutes of the evening. Pressure mounted to make French television more commercial. In the early 1970s, ORTF officials, facing persistent difficulties in balancing their budgets, allowed brand names to be introduced into programs. Sporting events were named after products, and private charities were allowed to solicit donations.[23] Some thought that the time had come to privatize the networks completely. This did not happen, but the state did loosen its control, permitting the number of channels to double, including the addition of an all-movie channel.

The Italian television industry, which was part of the state-owned RAI (Italian Radio-Television) company, also concentrated its commercials in a lively segment before the evening's main entertainment, but there the similarity ended. The Italian television corporation took elaborate precautions to avoid political domination by any one faction. Each news program had as many as six anchors, each representing one of the major political parties. Another way the company's directors protected themselves against the slings and arrows of controversy was to take refuge in the past. Italian television was strong on historical drama and culture. Its programming was generally of high quality, with many of its feature films being produced by the country's leading film directors—Vittorio da Sica, Federico Fellini, and Roberto Rossellini. Multipart dramatizations of novels were especially favored. Even then, the RAI had to take care lest a political or religious leader infer an insult from the dramatization of a novel or a past event. Nevertheless, Italian television managed to present rather hard-hitting historical drama. It successfully showed the seamy side of the pontificate of Alexander VI including his incestuous relationship with his daughter Lucrezia. However, one of Italy's most popular programs was also one of its most tasteless. In April 1987, the television impresario Umberto Smolia launched "Colpo grosso" ("Big Hit"). The format was an update of the traditional striptease in which, for extra points, a contestant could join the act. Viewership of the program surpassed 5 million a night.

The Dutch tried to avoid political arguments over programming by conceding regular television time to any group that had an established membership of more than 100,000 members. These groups included advocates of homosexual rights, abortion and sterilization, group marriage, and nuclear disarmament. The Dutch bragged that their television was the freest and most open in the world. Hilversum, a city twenty miles east of Amsterdam, not only was home to the Dutch broadcasting company, but became the headquarters for the largest associations. The conservatives, the Roman Catholic church, the Protestant church, and the socialists divided the lion's share of programming time. If others felt that their views were not adequately represented, they could try to form their own group. Despite their diversity, the major interest groups could not afford to be too heavy-handed if they wanted to attract an audience. Accordingly, they kept their opinion programs down to a minimum and tried to steer clear of controversy elsewhere. One way of doing so was to buy foreign programs—for example, "Bonanza," "Dallas," and "Falcon Crest" from the United States—all of which were presented in their original versions with Dutch subtitles.

In Germany, the regional governments, the Länder, were responsible for licensing television stations. As a result, various regional stations were established with the most powerful located in major urban areas, like Hamburg, Cologne, and Munich, where the viewing audiences were the largest. These giants determined the bulk of the programming. Sports, news programs, and detective shows were popular fare, but other offerings also attracted viewers. "Tutti-Frutti," a spin-off of "Colpo grosso," added wacky filmstrips and, like its parent version, was immensely popular.[24] Such bawdiness was a far cry from German television's origins in 1935, when it was required to imprint the image of the Führer in the hearts of the German people. The quality of much German programming was rather low. People debated whether "Sesame Street" was a desirable program for German children, but stations had no hesitancy about buying other American programs for their viewers. "Dallas" was hugely popular here as well.

The British had begun regular transmissions of high-definition television back in 1936, but had yet to develop an audience. Consequently, only 10,000 people watched the coronation of George VI in May 1937. Sales for the limited number of television sets were slow, and the government was reluctant to finance a program of expansion. Despite the lack of additional subsidies, the BBC directors were determined not to raise monies through commercial sponsorship. At the same time, they realized that if this new medium were ever to attract a wide audience, it would have to make concessions to the tastes of the British people. Hence, the last program to be televised before the BBC went out of business on 1 September 1939 for the duration of World War II was a Mickey Mouse cartoon.[25]

The BBC resumed broadcasting in June 1946 and remained the only source of television programming in the British Isles until 1955 when commercial television broke the government monopoly. Lord Reith, the BBC's founding father, likened this intrusion to an assault by "smallpox, bubonic plague, and the Black Death."[26] Nevertheless, the competition proved to be a blessing. Under a new director, Hugh Greene, BBC television became less stodgy and academic. The number of channels expanded, as did the variety of programming. Vulgarity, which was certainly not alien to British audiences, came into its own. Comedians like Benny Hill made a career of chasing scantily clad females. In the famous "Steptoe and Son," a junk dealer constantly bickered with his family, especially his son; in "Till Death Do Us Part," the inspiration for American television's "All in the Family," the balding middle-aged cockney Alf Garnett ranted and raved against every ethnic, social, or religious group he hated—and he hated them all. Whenever the queen's name was mentioned, he became a superpatriot. The British loved it and made Alf Garnett a national hero.

When the BBC was at the top of its form, it set an enviable standard of excellence. Its dramatic adaptations of novels, historical series, and cultural programs established its reputation at home and abroad. The U.S. Public Broadcasting System benefited from the availability of such programs as "Upstairs, Downstairs," "Elizabeth R," "Civilization," "The Ascent of Man," "The Fall of Eagles," and "The Flame Trees of Thicka." Even the Roman Empire soap opera "I Claudius" traveled extremely well. Amplifying its original mission to educate, the BBC produced some riveting documentaries. "The War Game," which dealt with the aftermath of an atomic attack on Britain, chillingly understated its grisly effects. Another documentary, chronicling the effects of smoking, lampooned the romanticized ads of the tobacco companies by showing Marlboro country to be inhabited by a lot of wheezing cowboys on their last legs from cancer and emphysema.[27]

The medium of television was a natural for a highly literate people such as the British. They kept their programming remarkably free of political and commercial pressure. The BBC was thus able to criticize British politicians mercilessly often with a great deal of insight and black humor. A popular program of political satire once had a feature showing a puppet version of Prime Minister Margaret Thatcher at the hairdressers. "Make it a style that's universally popular," she tells the barber, whereupon he promptly cuts off her head. On 5 October 1969, the BBC received the gratitude of millions when it first presented "Monty Python's Flying Circus," showcasing the most zany bunch of comic geniuses to come along since the Marx Brothers.

If television could make stars out of people playing fictitious characters, it could also make heroes out of performers who played themselves. Nowhere was this truer than in the realm of professional sports.

Modern Sports

Urban Nationalism. Modern European sports enthusiasts marked their year with playing seasons just as medieval peasants marked theirs with religious festivals. The sporting year began in the fall with soccer. It then proceeded through the winter with hockey and into the spring and summer with bicycling and tennis. Between times, there were skiing events, motorcar grand prix, horse racing, boxing, and basketball—one of the very few sports the Europeans adopted from the United States. Modern commercial sports were vastly different from the old upper-class competitions played for fun in English public schools.

Soccer, already established as a solid team sport before the war, was far and away the most popular. This game, like rugby and field hockey, began its modern development in Britain during the last half of the nineteenth century.[28] Reportedly, it was spread abroad by railroad construction crews who played it in their time off. In any case, working-class players took over from the aristocrats, formed their own clubs, and held regular matches in front of paying audiences. Increased professionalization, bigger purses, better communications, and improved organization spread the competition nationally and internationally. The World Cup competition drew greater radio, television, and live audiences than any other sporting event.

The attraction of soccer lay in its simplicity. It did not require a great deal of money to play, equipment was minimal, and a flat playing surface was all that was necessary to get started. In time, vast stadiums were built, such as Berlin's 35,000-seat Grunewald Arena, which was finished before World War I. Soccer action was fast paced, continuous, constantly changing, and ever-fluid. All players, with the exception of the goalkeeper, were expected to attack or defend whichever was necessary, whenever necessary. Fortunes changed frequently and instantaneously, and a player was constantly required to balance his own egocentrism with the necessity of playing as a member of a team. Thus, the player had to be both aggressive and cooperative, individualistic but helpful. Timing and setting up scoring opportunities were paramount.

The age of television turned the game into great theater and the soccer players into superheroes. The teams had their own battle colors, legends, superstitions, groupies, and sacred victories.[29] They retained strong local and regional ties. In Britain, many of the most dedicated fans came from the industrial Midlands and the lower-class districts of London and Glasgow. When match day arrived, they

Belgian police confront angry soccer fans at Heysel stadium in Brussels, 29 May 1985. Moments later, the rioting spread to the stands. In the melee scores of people were trampled to death.

eagerly anticipated "the peaks of high tension and emotional drama that the game will bring, breaking their steady routine with surging moments of almost unbearable excitement."[30] The teams enhanced the reputation of the urban areas they represented. Bringing home a silver cup was tangible proof of the superiority of both the team and its region. Pep rallies were held to confirm this loyalty. Since soccer was so territorial, it was only natural that teams might perform less well on the turf of their opponents. Visitors coming to watch a match on home turf were often regarded as invaders. This hostility could lead to verbal insults and even violence.

The amount of hooliganism attached to soccer appeared to increase after the 1960s, especially in Great Britain. Fans attacked each other, the referees, players, and police officers. Following a match, the visitors' dressing room might be besieged. Postmatch demonstrations resulted in dented cars, broken shop windows, vandalized buses and trains, and even burned buildings. In 1985, incidents of violence were particularly numerous. Following a rampage at Luton in March, Prime Minister Thatcher called a special cabinet meeting to discuss emergency measures. An apprehensive sports minister, Neil McFarlane, canceled the annual Scotland versus England match at Wembley because he feared things might get out of hand. On 11 May, the Leeds fans ran wild on Birmingham City's field, injuring ninety-six police officers. One boy died after a wall collapsed on him. But the worst was yet to come.

On 29 May at the European Cup Finals in the Heysel stadium in Brussels, supporters of Turin's Juventus, a club owned by Fiat's boss Gianni Agnelli, began throwing pieces of crumbling masonry at the Belgian police. Then, a group of drunken Liverpool "Reds" fans charged Juventus's fans who retreated in panic. In the melee, a barrier collapsed. Thirty-eight people were killed. The riot was witnessed by hundreds of millions of people watching on television. (The game continued—Juventus beat Liverpool on a penalty kick.) The British Football Association conducted an investigation and banned all British teams from participation in matches on the Continent for one year. The Thatcher government enacted legislation prohibiting alcohol sales at English playing fields and outlawing special football trains and buses.[31]

Everybody had an opinion about what had gone wrong. Some believed that soccer violence was society in microcosm, a protest against inadequate living conditions and too few job opportunities. Others found explanations in the changing nature of the soccer crowds, especially those who stood in "the terraces." The spectators here were mostly white, young, working-class high school dropouts who were used to asserting tribal territoriality. With the disappearance of the old class solidarity and the erosion of traditional values, devotion to football provided the young with "a kind of surrogate community," giving them a way to demonstrate hardness and machismo and an opportunity for "mixing it up."[32] In a sense, this fierce pride and aggressive behavior were part of a larger context in which people viewed sports as an expression of national pride. In their first half century, the Olympiads had been more reflective of national rivalries and hostility than of international peace and harmony. The years after World War II were hardly an exception.

Olympic Nationalism. The Olympiads were halted for World War II as they had been for the world conflict a quarter of a century before. When the games resumed in 1948, the Cold War had begun and would continue to influence competition for the next generation and a half. The 1956 Melbourne games were held shortly after the Soviet Union had crushed the rebellion in Hungary. Anticipating trouble, Avery Brundage, the president of the International Olympic Committee, reminded people that the games were "contests between individuals and not between nations."[33] It did no good. A semifinal water polo match between the Soviet and Hungarian teams set off a riot in the stands as well as in the pool. But the worst violence ever to besmirch the games occurred in 1972 in Munich when eight Palestinian terrorists of the Black September group invaded the Olympic village and took nine Israeli athletes hostage. The gunmen demanded the release of two hundred Arabs being held in Israeli jails. The Israeli government refused and told the German government to do the best it could. In a final shootout at Furstenfeld- bruck airport, German sharpshooters managed to kill five of the terrorists but not before the terrorists had killed all their hostages. With this drama in progress, the Olympic games continued as before. When the full extent of the massacre became known, the games were called off—for one day. Any illusion that the Olympic games could insulate themselves from the imperfections of the world at large had been shattered forever. In certain quarters, using the games for specific political purposes even became respectable.

In early 1980, the United States decided to boycott the games in Moscow in protest against the Soviet invasion of Afghanistan the previous December. The action was part of a series of measures the Carter administration took against the Soviets, including an embargo on grain and on all sporting goods and Olympic- related products. President Jimmy Carter solicited international support for the policy, and ultimately sixty-one other countries also decided not to send teams. The games took place anyway, with eighty-five countries present.[34] The boycott proved mainly symbolic, hardly an adequate basis upon which to conduct foreign policy. It certainly did not persuade the Soviets to change their policy toward Afghanistan. The main damage was suffered by the 6,000 athletes who were de- prived of the chance to display their all-too-transitory skills. Four years later, the Soviets had an opportunity to return the favor by refusing to participate in the Los Angeles games. Most of the Eastern bloc countries followed suit. The absence of the Soviets weakened the quality of the competition, but gave the United States the opportunity to dominate the games in a way it had not been able to do in years. Never was American nationalism more on display or so blatant as in the television coverage of the events by the jingoistic commentators of the American Broadcasting Company.[35] The American athletes, especially the good-looking, fair-haired members of the gymnastics team, were hailed as heroes, shining examples of all that was good and noble about the United States. In a way, such adulation was in the Olympic tradition, but American pride was so narrowly focused that no other country could relate to it.

CHANGING ATTITUDES AND VALUES

A New Feminism

Guarantees—Written and Practical. Modern wars cannot be waged without the participation of women even though most of the fighting is done by men. Recognition that women's efforts were indispensable for success in World War I made it difficult to deny the "weaker sex" the same legal rights as men. Only France, Italy, Belgium, Switzerland, and Hungary refused.[36] This omission was finally rectified after World War II when women in these countries were finally granted equal social and economic rights.

The Italian constitution promised women equal pay for equal work and equal eligibility for public office. It protected them against working at night, hard or dangerous jobs, and termination of employment because of marriage or pregnancy. By law, women had the right to retain their maiden names, have an equal say in where the family lived, and determine how the children were to be educated. A woman could have her own bank account and could travel abroad without her husband's permission. If a woman worked for a firm employing more than thirty-five people, she could insist that the firm provide free nursery care for her minor children. Italy eliminated all the restrictions of the Fascist and pre-Fascist eras and replaced them with one of the most progressive packages of legal protection enjoyed by women in Europe.

Similarly, the 1946 French constitution guaranteed women legal, economic, and social equality as did the Basic Law (1949) of West Germany. And in the Soviet Union, much of the antifeminist legislation of the Stalin years was revoked after the dictator's death in 1953, as the Communist regime returned to the official liberalization of earlier times. The Soviet Union pretended that because socialism promoted the emancipation of everyone regardless of class, race, or sex, no separate women's issue had existed. This theme was echoed in the Soviet satellites, all of which drafted constitutions that insisted the sexes enjoyed the same rights and privileges.

The International Labor Office (ILO) of the United Nations boosted the cause of women's rights by drafting two pieces of model legislation that were designed to end discrimination against women in the workplace: the Equal Remuneration Convention (1951) and the Employment and Occupation Convention (1958). All the countries of Europe, except the United Kingdom, officially ratified these provisions. The British passed a more comprehensive Equal Pay Act and Sex Discrimination Act (1975), protecting women against discrimination in pay and working conditions and guaranteeing them equal educational opportunities and equal retirement compensation. The law also forbade discrimination in the provision of goods and services including housing. Other countries also showed their determination to go beyond the ILO provisions. In 1981, the French created a special Ministry for Women's Rights to help train women for technically advanced jobs and to promote women's cultural activities, including the sponsorship of literary competitions. The ministry also helped prepare new legislation on women's issues. In 1986, it became part of the Ministry for Social Security and Employment. Other countries had comparable commissions and councils that were entrusted with the task of promoting and monitoring women's rights. The Austrians had a Government Committee for Women's Affairs (1969); the Finns had a Council for Equality (1972); the Danes had an Equal Status Council (1975); the Dutch a Woman's Emancipation Council (1981) and a Woman's Arbitration Body; the Swedes an Equal Opportunities Research Commission (1983) and an Equal Opportunities Ombudsman; and the West Germans a Central Office for the Equality of Women (1979) and a Department of Women's Affairs (1986), which was part of the Federal Ministry of Youth, Family Affairs, Women and Health.[37]

Although women had more options and received more protection than before, the kind of egalitarian society promised by the postwar constitutions was a long way off. Many of the constitutional guarantees lacked proper legislative codification; and even where laws had been passed, many of them were not enforced. Women's groups therefore devoted less of their time to calling for new rights than to trying to obtain those already accorded. The struggle was not without hope. Women were better trained and educated than ever before; they were entering the labor force in greater numbers; and they were no longer willing to remain passive.

Women under Communism. Despite the laws on equality, Soviet men still considered women biologically inferior; women were loved, but not respected. Yet women comprised a greater percentage of the labor force than did men (50.9 percent in 1986) and also edged men in enrollment in higher education and in many of the professions. Sixty percent of the doctors were women and 72 percent of the schoolteachers. Nevertheless, equality eluded them. Ironically and importantly, the high female participation in medicine, education, and elsewhere did little to raise the status of women. It simply lowered the status of those professions. Women were conspicuous by their absence in leadership or managerial positions. The majority of Soviet women, old and young alike, continued to be employed in low-paying, manual labor jobs. They were especially numerous as street sweepers, window washers, painters, and hod-carriers. They accounted for more than one-third of the road construction crews. Educated women usually filled jobs beneath their skill levels and earned only 70 percent as much as their male counterparts. In industry, only two percent of the women earned the same as the men who performed the same job.

The full weight of child raising also fell on their shoulders. Stalin had preached the cult of motherhood, but had done little to relieve women's burdens by providing adequate child care facilities or a sufficient supply of relevant consumer goods. In addition to completing a full work schedule, women were expected to wait in long lines for the family's food. About the only thing that men waited in line for was vodka. The Soviet Union had serious shortages of baby care products and feminine hygiene and beauty products. If a woman wanted to make herself more attractive, she had to do so without basic cosmetics. When Estée Lauder opened a shop in Moscow at the end of the 1980s, it had to impose a four-item limit to control the demand despite the high prices of its products. At Lauder's a basic cosmetic budget could easily equal one-third of a woman's average monthly wage. Christian Dior's Moscow outlet also priced its products beyond the range of most Soviet consumers. In October 1990, the first Russian language edition of the *Ladies Home Journal* appeared in Moscow. Its 10,000 copies were quickly snapped up despite the fact that the seven-ruble cost was more than a day's pay for an average Russian woman. The magazine described a world beyond the reach of most of its readers. Upon reading the articles, including those on how to make the perfect dessert, how to look like fashion models, and why husbands should do more around the house, some Russian women were divided as to whether they should laugh or cry.[38] Small wonder that the Soviet Union, especially the Russian Republic, became a nation of one-child families. The social impact of this trend is still unclear.

Half of Soviet marriages ended in divorce. Women complained that men were rude and incapable of sustaining warm relationships. The grounds most frequently cited for divorce were adultery, poor fathering, and alcoholism. Many couples had married in order to obtain an apartment, and the apartment became the chief item in the property settlement. Frequently, the couple continued to live in the same apartment after the divorce because the former husband had no place else to go. The result was anger and often violence.

In the other nations of the Communist bloc, women also formed a high percentage of the active labor force. In the 1980s, they were 45 percent of the work force in Hungary, 46 percent in Czechoslovakia, 45 percent in Romania and Poland, and more than 47 percent in Bulgaria. As in the Soviet Union, women remained concentrated in the lower-paying jobs in the service sector. In Romania, the only woman in the ruling politburo was Elena Ceausescu, wife of the president. On the whole, Czech women were better educated than men, but they filled three-fourths of the lower-status jobs, mainly positions in retailing, the service sector, and health services. In Poland, the development of feminist sentiment had been complicated by the prominent position of the Catholic church, which regarded women primarily as wives and mothers. The Polish birth rate was high, and abortions, although legal, were performed less frequently than in any other country in Eastern Europe. In Hungary, feminism exercised an influence not found in other Eastern European countries, but it remained an urban phenomenon, concentrated mostly among the artistic and intellectual elite whose members found it difficult to organize into a national movement. Women in Communist countries were expected to follow the direction of the government. Their primary goal was to encourage the other members of their sex to fulfill the state's economic goals. In East Germany, Hungary, and Romania where the birth rate was low, women's societies were also required to encourage the production of more babies.

Female Rights in the Western Democracies. Nobody had given women their rights until they demanded them. However, women in the Western democracies had greater opportunities to organize and assert their strength than the women in Eastern Europe. In the early days of the feminist movement, solidarity among women often meant hostility to men. Following the lead of Simone de Beauvoir, women argued that they had to change the culture in which they lived. In her monumental work *The Second Sex*, de Beauvoir argued that women would never shed their second-class status until they became economically independent. "It is through gainful employment that women have traversed most of the distance that separated her from the male; and nothing else can guarantee her liberty in practice."[39] But economic equality was only part of the solution.

Western European women already had entered the labor force in increasing numbers, but as in Eastern Europe, many were concentrated in low-paying, low-status jobs; women accounted for a smaller number of the high-paying jobs in individual occupational groups than did men.[40] In France, 45 percent of the women were in "female professions" such as nursing and secretarial work. French women were also likely to work fewer hours per week than men and were usually the first to be let go during a recession. In Britain, women made up over 80 percent of the part-time work force and over three-fourths of those employed in food services, cleaning, and hairdressing. In Ireland, 93 percent of all typists were women, as were 61 percent of all textile workers. In Sweden, 78 percent of primary schoolteachers and 53 percent of the secondary schoolteachers were women. In Spain, employers could still dismiss pregnant women. Western European women, on average, earned between 65 percent (Germany) and 86 percent (Denmark) of the pay received by men.

In the 1960s and 1970s, the number of women's organizations grew dramatically. Many of these had their own newsletters and meeting places, coffee houses, and shelters. Some of these organizations had originated in the late nineteenth century. For example, Britain's National Council of Women dated from 1895; Italy's *Unione Femminile Nazionale* (National Female Union) had been founded in Milan in 1899; and the *Nederlandse Vereniging voor Vrouwenbelangen* (Netherlands Association for Women's Interests) had been established in 1894. These "traditional" groups wanted to remove the barriers to full female participation in the life of the nation while giving protection to working women and their children. However, most of the Western European women's organizations that came into existence after World War II were more narrowly focused. The *Parti Feministe Unifié* (United Feminist party) of Belgium wanted to ban the production of all nuclear and chemical weapons. The French *Ligue de Droit des Femmes* (Women's Rights League) campaigned for the elimination of physical and mental abuse of women, giving particular support to women who were trying to regain their children who had been kidnapped by Algerian fathers. The *Associazione Nazionale Donne Elettrici* (National League of Women Voters) campaigned for electoral reform and encouraged Italian women to exercise their right of suffrage. The Movement for the Ordination of Women pushed for the admission of women to the Anglican priesthood. Other European women's groups created facilities and support groups for lesbian women, divorced women, housewives, and working women. Sweden's *Alla Kvinnors Hus* provided sanctuary for women and children who were victims of physical or sexual abuse.

Such groups discovered that government authorities were extremely reluctant to become involved in domestic relations between a husband and his family no matter how violent. Women also found it difficult to persuade a traditionally male-dominated society to accept women in nontraditional roles. Many men still believed that the only true woman's job was that of housewife and mother, and they resented the competition that women presented when they succeeded in entering business and the professions. Women who did get their feet in the door found it difficult to advance into the upper echelons. In Italy, women still suffered from a rigid caste system within the family that rising affluence, ironically, did much to reinforce. When it was no longer necessary to have two incomes to make ends meet, many women quit work and returned to the home where their prestige was much greater. However, this phenomenon did not occur in France where motherhood did not have the same hallowed cachet. French working women got more support from the trade unions, which were generally willing to support women's causes. Moreover, Frenchwomen had impressive historical forebears: warriors like Joan of Arc (canonized in 1920) and Jeanne Hachette; painters like Berthe Morrisot, Elizabeth Vigée-Lebrun, and Rosa Bonheur; writers like Georges Sand, Marie-Madeleine de La Fayette, and Colette; and scientists like Marie Curie, Irène Joliet-Curie, and Emilie du Chatelet.[41] With such role models, Frenchwomen could confidently avoid feeling guilty for not devoting their talents to the so-called domestic pleasures, but many Frenchmen no doubt shared the sentiments of Voltaire, the lover of Madame du Chatelet, whom he praised by saying that "she was a great man whose only fault was in being a woman."[42] Moreover, other European women probably did not consider their French sisters as liberated as they seemed to be. In May 1991, France obtained the first woman premier in its history when President François Mitterrand appointed Edith Cresson to the post. Cresson's combative style did not seem very ladylike and earned her a certain amount of gratuitous criticism.

Until Cresson's appointment, the only major European nation with a female head of government had been Great Britain.[43] Many had served in lesser posts, however, as cabinet ministers, regional administrators, or legislators in national and provincial assemblies. Among the minor powers, Portugal had a female prime minister in Maria des Pintassilgo, who formed a two-week caretaker government in July 1979. Of longer duration was the election of Mary Robinson as president of Ireland in November 1990. Robinson, a Socialist and leading constitutional lawyer, campaigned on a platform of pluralism and women's rights. Government and business, however, continued to be dominated by an "old-boy" network, a group of chums whose bonding had been accomplished in their formative years when females were regarded as members of another race.

British women who might have challenged this exclusive male-club mentality tended to avoid political and social causes and devoted many hours to genteel charity instead. Consequently, women continued to be discriminated against in university enrollments and were less likely than their sisters on the Continent to enter a profession. Some women left the country to make careers elsewhere. But British women did not want to make a fuss; they put their class before their sex.

In Germany, however, the reduced numbers of men because of the war heightened women's prestige. Men still held a majority of the important positions in business and politics, but women were elected to national and state offices in increasing numbers. They were more prominent in the service sector than in the professions and suffered because of their popular image as *Hausfrau*, but they also held important positions in labor, industry, and education. German women were often obliged to do double duty. Working outside the home did not give them an excuse to neglect their wifely and motherly duties. Demanding husbands had little sympathy if dinner was not ready on time or if their shirts were not properly ironed. Some attributed the demands put on women to lingering authoritarian patterns in German society, possibly reinforced by traditional religious practices.[44] In any case, the superwoman work ethic continued to flourish.[45]

An Americanized Exterior

A Manner of Speaking. American English is a hungry language. It gobbles up foreign words and expressions with great voracity, creating an enormous linguistic resource in the process. The Americans are also generous in their linguistic exports, and therein lies the problem. Throughout Europe, defenders of linguistic purity mobilized in a grim stand against the back-across-the-ocean invasion. The French were especially alarmed and tried to rally their troops to defend the barricades. Already before the war, some words had crept in such as *pullover, knockout, cocktail, self-service, lunch, poker,* and *slapstick.* Now the struggle seemed to grow more desperate. The new arrivals included *hamburger, bulldozer, briefing, pipeline, timing, ketchup, motel, blockbuster, landing,* and *poster.* Those who tried to head off the onslaught proposed French equivalents. They wanted to call blue jeans *les salopettes;* the happy hunting ground would become *le pays de la chasse perpetuelle,* and a pie fight would be *une débâcle à patisserie*. But the contest was lost from the beginning. Borrowed words were here to stay. Not surprisingly, the most successful intruders were the words with the greatest cultural influence such as sports terms or words related to food, fashions, business, politics, and entertainment. The words entered the French language unchanged except in pronunciation, appearing in the masculine gender. Some Americanisms were modified slightly, but hardly enough to make a difference. A *bartender* became *un barman*; an *escalator*, once an *escalier roulant*, became an *escalateur*; a supermarket was a *supermarché*, and picnic survived as *piquenique*. There were *les holdups par les gangsters* and *le eye-liner avec eye-shadow*. Some nouns emerged in an abbreviated form: *un pull* for *a pullover*, *un trench* for *a trench coat*, and *le foot* for *football* (soccer). Curiously, however, *jogging* became *le footing*; and wrestling was *le catch* from the old-fashioned English phrase catch-as-catch-can.

Even linguistic purists had to recognize that some of their translations were conceptually inadequate. The *weekend*, an Anglicanism, was different from *la fin de semaine*, the latter referring more to location than to the leisurely interlude between work weeks; and a *fauteuil* was less comfortable as a seat than a *lounge chair*. Furthermore, the defenders of the French language could not overcome the growing tendency of the French to equate Americanisms with sophistication, just as the English upper classes often used French expressions to be snooty.

Articles and letters to the editor appeared in the European press, complaining that American speech was bastardizing the language. The perceived damage was usually worse than the reality, if indeed any damage had been done at all. More-over, European peoples who butchered their native tongues hardly needed help from the Americans. Slang was practiced generously in all countries, and elegance had nothing to do with it. But mounting watch on the linguistic beaches facing westward across the Atlantic seemed more worthwhile than building linguistic barricades against the forces of Babel at home. European youths listened to American popular music and mouthed the words of songs in American English. American speech patterns began to permeate foreign consciences. The British often used American expressions because they were class neutral and frequently more direct. At one time Europeans had tried to speak English with an Oxonian accent, but that was now being challenged by the accent of the American Midwest.

In England, some people maintained that language *was* the clearest form of class delineation.[46] One word was thus deemed better than another. For example, to *have one's bath* was considered Upper Class or U, while to *take a bath* was non–Upper Class (non-U). *Stays* were U, *corsets* were non-U; *jam* was U, *preserves* were non-U; *rich* was U, *wealthy* was non-U. Non-U speakers ate *dinner* at noon and took their *evening meal* at night, while U speakers had *lunch* in the middle of the day and *dinner* at night. Many non-U usages were Americanisms. A U father of an eleven year old remarked, "I tell my son he can go anywhere but to the toilet. To the lavatory, the loo, what-have-you. But the toilet—it grates on my ears."[47] Professor Alan Ross of the University of Birmingham maintained that the modern phenomenon of verbal distinctness came about with the creation of the new-rich class in the 1960s; old-line aristocrats lapsed into determined anachronism to set themselves off from the upstarts.

Fast Foods and Fashion. A restaurant in Wiesbaden advertised its pizza as "real American" and insisted that it tasted better. Most of this "junk food" might have been a caloric and cholesterol horror, but it was a boon to the timesavers and pinchpennies and frequently was quite palatable. American food culture was not just displayed on a few streets in a few locations, it was everywhere: McDonald's, Burger King, Colonel Sanders, Wendy's, Pizza Hut. The menus were reassuringly familiar, and the terminology was practically identical. Fries and Coke were fries and Coke in any land. So was a cheeseburger—hamburger *mit käse*, or *avec fromage*, or *con formaggio* did not make the grade.[48] Although the American impact on Europe was frequently overestimated, this was not the case in the imperialism of such proletarian bill of fare. Even Iron Curtain countries were not immune.

After fourteen years of negotiations, McDonalds opened its first *Big Mak* in Moscow, finally raising the golden arches on Pushkin Square in February 1990. The emporium had a seating capacity of 700, making it one of the largest hamburger joints in the world. Its 605 employees could serve 15,000 customers a day. Twenty-seven thousand people had filled out applications to work there. The $50 million deal had been closed by McDonald's Canadian subsidiary, which agreed to purchase all the restaurant's raw materials from Soviet producers in exchange for control of its own distribution plant, located just outside Moscow. Here, McDonald's had its own bakery, dairy, meat processing plant, and microbiology laboratory. It practiced quality control on its waiters, training them to look each customer in the eye and smile. The Muscovites loved the friendly service—so rare in their own native businesses—and stood in line as long as forty-five minutes to get served. By Soviet standards, the wait was short. A Big Mak, french fries, and milkshake initially cost 5.5 rubles, roughly half an average day's pay. The customers took their plastic forks and Styrofoam plates home as souvenirs.[49] That was a good thing too, for everywhere else in Europe the American fast-food craze had left litter in its wake—cast-off hamburger wrappers and red and white decorated boxes with the picture of an elderly, goateed gentleman in a string tie, the perpetrator of an American culinary delight known as "finger lickin' good." Everybody knew, of course, that Styrofoam coffee cups did not cause litter, people did.

Fast-food restaurants were merely one aspect of a food merchandising onslaught that included a wide range of products that found their way down European gullets.[50] The product that best expressed the American style and philosophy of eating was breakfast cereal. Although corn flakes and other cereals had already been established in Europe after World War I, these were now joined by an array of breakfast foods with designer names like "Captain Crunch" and "Frosted Mini-wheats." In the meantime, Europeans had developed their own, less spectacular versions. The British had created *Wheatabix*, which received the endorsement "By-appointment-to-Her-Majesty-the-Queen." The cereal was a kind of wheat cake that turned soggy as soon as the milk hit it, creating an instant mush. The British pretended that they designed it that way.

Such products adapted themselves well to the urban rushing-off-to-the-job environment. In families where eating in a hurry, often alone, was not a necessity, breakfast could be more in keeping with local culture: kippers and fried bread for the British, "bouncers" egg and ham on bread for the Dutch, a boiled egg and *wurst* on pumpernickel for the Germans. The French still had croissants and the Italians polenta (cornmeal mush). However, even these so-called traditional breakfasts were not eaten every morning—they were expensive and took too long to prepare.

American-style convenience foods, based on improved food technology and mass production, affected other aspects of the European diet. Tomato ketchup and baked beans did not exert the same kind of social influence on the European food culture as fast-food restaurants and packaged breakfasts, but they were immensely popular items nevertheless. The war of the colas—Pepsi versus Coke—was fought out on European battlefields with the persistence of the dynastic wars of bygone years. That the popularity of such sugary fizz-water might have contributed to a diminished consumption of alcohol was possible but not proven, especially not in France where alcoholism still killed more people than in all the other Western European nations combined.

The faster-paced urban societies of Europe also found sustenance in other American exports. High fashion was still associated with the great *couturiers* of Paris and Rome, but leisure and sports attire was becoming increasingly Americanized, especially among the young. It was frequently impossible, even in Moscow, to tell nationality from attire. Jeans, T-shirts, and sweat suits all became internationalized. The keen observer might be able to pick out national characteristics from the shoes, but not from the ankles up. European youths adored pullovers with American university logos. American informality of dress was not only comfortable, but it conveyed a sort of proletarian chic.

The Sexual Revolution

Contraception and Abortion. After World War II, Europeans entered the greatest period of sexual transformation in their history.[51] This change was variously ascribed to the trauma of two world wars, the weakening of religious ties, the drive for equality by women, the availability of contraception and abortion, and the ease with which people could terminate their marriages. Many countries had recognized adultery, cruelty, and desertion as legitimate grounds for divorce before World War II. Now, they recognized divorce by mutual consent.[52]

By the 1960s, people had the time, money, and desire to practice as well as accept new forms of sexual behavior. They were also more willing to talk about it publicly. Orgasms, masturbation, and homosexuality were discussed freely in the press and on television. Women no longer regarded sex as a painful duty, but as a natural right. Not having "good sex" was dysfunctional. Women demanded an end to all restraints that controlled their sexuality and fertility. Through protests and political lobbying, they won a great deal of control over their own bodies. Contraception was legalized and often subsidized through public health services.[53] In any case, it was readily available in all Western European countries save Ireland. In Eastern Europe, contraception, though legal, was constrained by the inadequate supplies and low quality of contraceptive devices. Condoms, when available, were generally of such poor quality that they broke during use. In the Soviet Union, more than half of the women had no reliable form of birth control. Some even believed that contraception was dangerous for one's health. Consequently, for every 100 live births, there were 106 abortions—the highest rate in the world. Abortion was clearly the Soviet Union's standard form of birth control—an estimated 50 million were performed in the 1970s and 1980s. An average woman underwent between five and six abortions; some had as many as twenty-five.

In 1920, the Soviet Union had become the first European country to legalize abortion, only to see it prohibited again under Stalin in 1936. The prohibition lasted until the dictator's death in 1953. The 1938 Swedish law legalizing abortion was the first of its kind in Western Europe. This measure was liberalized in 1975 to grant a free abortion on request up to the eighteenth week of pregnancy. After that, obtaining an abortion was less routine, but in general any Swedish woman could get an abortion unless the abortion presented a danger to *her* life. By the 1980s, most of the countries of Western Europe had laws permitting abortion.

The British abortion law dated from 1967. Denmark adopted one in 1973, West Germany and France in 1974, Italy in 1975, Finland and Austria in 1978, Norway in 1979, and Spain in 1985. Many countries imposed restrictions, however. In Britain, abortion was available with the approval of two doctors, provided that the pregnancy presented a threat to the woman's physical or mental health. In the Netherlands, the abortion had to be performed in a special licensed hospital. In France, a woman had first to receive special counseling and then wait a week. In Germany, the waiting period was three days. Luxembourg permitted abortion in cases of rape or if the fetus was malformed or presented a danger to the woman's health. Doctors in Britain, Austria, and Italy could refuse to perform an abortion on grounds of personal conscience. Under a 1985 Spanish law, abortion was permitted in the first trimester if the pregnancy resulted from a rape, and in the first twenty-two weeks if the fetus was malformed.[54] Abortion was still listed as a crime in the Swiss penal code, but the practice was permitted if the woman's life were in danger. Enforcement of the code was left to the cantons' discretion. Geneva once enjoyed a reputation as one of the abortion centers of Europe. French women unable to obtain abortions in their own country flocked there in great numbers for "routine" D and Cs (dilation and curettage). Abortion was prohibited only in Belgium and Ireland. In September 1983, in a national referendum, Irish voters approved adding the ban to the constitution. Consequently, many women went to other countries to terminate their pregnancies.

The number of legal abortions in France in 1986 was 166,797; 88,540 were performed in the German Federal Republic in 1987; 174,652 in the United Kingdom in 1987; and 84,540 in Hungary in 1987. In 1984 in Italy, 228,377 abortions were performed, most of them in the industrial north. Hospitals could not keep up with the demand. Many more unauthorized abortions, through shame or ignorance, were reputedly undertaken in rural areas.[55] In Romania, the Ceausescu regime allowed abortions only for women over forty years old and for those with four or more children. Women who wanted to travel outside the country were checked before they left and after they returned to ensure they did not have an abortion while abroad.

Pornography. By reputation, France was the country of the dirty postcard par excellence. There Americans and British could buy all those books that had been banned in their own countries—from the unexpurgated edition of D. H. Lawrence's *Lady Chatterley's Lover* to Henry Miller's *Tropic of Cancer* and collections of dirty limericks. However, the French market was not as open as most people believed. Charles de Gaulle began a crackdown on hard-core pornography. The distinction of being the first European country to remove *all* restrictions on explicit materials therefore went to Denmark.

In 1969, the Danes permitted the publication of all pornographic material and allowed it to be distributed to anyone over the age of sixteen. Copenhagen's porno merchants celebrated the law with a "Sex 69" fair. Porn shops, "film centers," and a wide variety of magazines grew like mushrooms. "Private clubs" catered to various pornographic tastes. Tourists came to Denmark by the thousands, some on charter flights. But the Danish pornography boom did not last long. The craze ran its course, the tourists had their fill and left, and at the end of the summer season, over 80 percent of the smut shops closed. Knud Thestrup, the Danish minister of justice who had introduced the bill abolishing the indecency statutes, had predicted the novelty would soon wear off.[56] The Danes felt vindicated. Their society was freer and studies showed it had suffered no ill effects. Incidents of rape and exhibitionism remained about the same, but child molestation had decreased.

Other countries followed the Danish example. The end of restrictive legislation in Germany produced a new class of porno-entrepreneurs like Beate Uhse who opened a sex shop, the first in an empire of such boutiques that spread throughout Germany. Uhse became one of her country's most successful businesswomen and a national celebrity. She was featured in articles and appeared on television talk shows. Her face became as familiar as that of a movie star.[57] The marketing of pornography was so prevalent in European cities that few natives paid much attention to it. London had Soho, where peep shows nestled side-by-side with the ethnic restaurants for which the area was once best known. In Paris, those who found the show at the vaunted Folies-Bergère or the Lido too tame could visit the famous Crazy Horse Saloon, a topless bar. Other night clubs featured acts that were even more revealing. Public advertising also began to feature nudity. Nude beaches appeared in many countries. Every age and every society of modern Europe has in some way commercialized sex. Nevertheless, few periods since the decline of the Roman Empire have been more openly "permissive" than the postwar era.

The accelerated breakdown of conventional morality and the increased mobility of populations led to a wide spread of sexually transmitted diseases. Syphilis became epidemic in 1944 and 1945, but the use of penicillin, which had been discovered in 1939, gave the authorities the means to bring the disease under control. Postwar treatment was initially so effective that optimists predicted that syphilis would soon entirely disappear. This was not the case as its revival in the 1960s showed, but the concern over the increased incidence of this once-dread disease were soon directed at a "new" ailment that was both noncurable and deadly.

The AIDS Pandemic. Acquired immune deficiency syndrome, or AIDS, first began to spread in an observable way in 1981. The virus had probably been existent before then, although its current, deadly form may have been a recent mutation. The disease was carried in blood and semen and spread chiefly in urban areas.[58] Hemophiliacs, recipients of blood transfusions, and heroin addicts were all high risk, but most of the early cases of AIDS were contracted by homosexuals and by those with multiple sex partners. As such, the disease became a matter of instant shame. Some moralists even considered it evidence of God's judgment. People with common sense, though, realized that such a disease has no regard for sexual preference, and they looked to science to find the cause and develop a cure.

In Europe, AIDS was first detected in Copenhagen, one of Europe's most sexually tolerant cities. All of the Danish victims had direct or indirect links to infected persons in New York, Los Angeles, and San Francisco.[59] Soon, instances of AIDS were discovered in France, England, West Germany, Spain, Portugal, Belgium, Switzerland, and Portugal. All of the victims had connections with infected people in either the United States or Africa. The Africans, suffering from a different strain, spread the disease mostly through heterosexual contact. Modern aerial transportation and the increased movement of peoples rapidly escalated the disease into a pandemic. The world was not only smaller, it had become more socially and sexually permissive. It also used more hypodermic needles and gave more blood transfusions.[60]

In June 1983, Dr. Luc Montagnier, director of the Pasteur Institute in Paris, confirmed that his research team had isolated the AIDS virus. The initial discovery had been made the previous January by Françoise Barre. (The technology enabling her to do so had only become available as recently as 1978.) The Pasteur Institute's breakthrough did not take the scientific world by storm. Indeed, the National Cancer Institute (NCI) at Bethesda, Maryland, where similar work was in progress, was positively hostile. The NCI's leading retrovirologist, Dr. Robert Gallo, even insinuated that the French results had been contaminated. The NCI's reluctance to credit the work of French "amateurs" was a disturbing example of scientific nationalism that cost precious time in fighting the epidemic.[61] French researchers even had difficulty getting their articles published in American journals.

Finally, in April 1984, the NCI announced its own discovery of the virus. The French protested this slap in the face without success. Their work continued to be slighted. In 1985, the Pasteur Institute filed a lawsuit against the NCI demanding a share in the royalties that the NCI had received from its patent of an AIDS blood test. Montagnier had strong evidence that Gallo had used French research samples to make his discovery, but the French were suing for more than the money, which would be theirs from a patent on the blood test. They wanted full credit for their accomplishment.[62] The matter was settled out of court in March 1987, when President Ronald Reagan and Premier Jacques Chirac signed an agreement recognizing Montagnier and Gallo as co-discoverers. The incident was probably the first time heads of government helped to resolve a question of who should take credit for discovering a virus. The virus was named human immunodeficiency virus, or HIV.

During the first half of the 1980s, European health officials viewed AIDS as an American problem because the United States continued to be the most heavily infected part of the world, with two-thirds of its cases occurring in New York City. In time, however, the steady increase of AIDS cases in Europe changed their attitude. From 1984 to 1988, the number of reported instances in Europe jumped from 880 to 20,000. France had about one-third of the total; over half of the cases were concentrated in the Paris region. French medical demographers believed these figures were too conservative and estimated that as many as a quarter of a million people were HIV positive. The French also led Europe in treatment of the disease. While their antiviral drug HPA-23 was not a cure, AIDS sufferers from around the world flocked to Paris, feeling they had nothing to lose. This migration included American movie star Rock Hudson, whose affliction helped to increase public awareness of AIDS. American patients were gratified that the French viewed AIDS as just another disease like leukemia, not a moral judgment.[63] Cases of AIDS also rose dramatically in Italy where most of the infections—about 70 percent—involved drug users, the opposite of northern Europe where AIDS continued to be a disease primarily affecting homosexuals.[64]

Communist bloc countries considered AIDS a capitalist disease, something to be expected from a decadent society. The Soviets even asserted that the virus had been developed in the biological warfare laboratories of the CIA. They maintained that the Soviet Union had no AIDS cases because it was virtually free of drug abuse and had only 70,000 homosexuals, all of whom were registered with the Ministry of Health. By the end of the 1980s, however, the Soviets had come to their senses. They either refused to reveal or did not know the precise number of confirmed cases of AIDS, but they were plainly worried. *Pravda* estimated that 15 million Soviet people would be infected with AIDS by the year 2000.[65] Soviet authorities now concentrated on finding solutions, but the backward nature of Soviet health services made this extremely difficult. The system had problems handling even rudimentary infectious diseases. Encouraging safe sex was difficult when the economy could not even produce enough condoms. Moreover, there was a chronic shortage of diagnostic kits. In 1986, the Ministry of Health set a goal of establishing 1,000 diagnostic testing centers throughout the Soviet Union to perform 1.5 million tests a month.[66] However, announcing goals was one thing, achieving them another. In the meantime, the Soviets concentrated on screening Africans and other foreigners, deporting anyone who tested positive.

One of the primary ways AIDS was transmitted was through intravenous injections. In the West, most such transmittals occurred through the use of "dirty" needles by drug users; in the Soviet Union, the contamination happened in hospitals. In 1988, a group of mothers and children contracted the disease in a Ukrainian hospital where unsterilized syringes were reused. There was insufficient alcohol to clean the needles because people would drink it. Romania experienced an even worse scandal, which came to light only after the death of President Nicolae Ceausescu in December 1989. Tests carried out on children in pediatric hospitals showed that one-third of them had AIDS. They most likely had contracted the disease through the reuse of dirty needles and through the traditional Romanian practice of injecting minute quantities of adult blood into children to make them stronger. The Ceausescu regime had ordered the testing stopped, pretending that AIDS existed only in capitalist countries.[67]

AIDS was also present elsewhere in Eastern Europe.[68] East Germany admitted to having 4,000 victims, the highest number in Eastern Europe and, in January 1990, signed an agreement with West Germany for AIDS assistance. Yugoslavia was reported to have more AIDS cases than Romania. The fall of the repressive dictatorships brought a more honest attitude toward the disease, but the desperate state of health care and the greater freedoms encouraged its spread. Condoms remained in short supply, as did lifesaving syringes, diagnostic testing, and treatment facilities. Poland simply denied AIDS patients entrance to hospitals. Sexual promiscuity, a heightened use of illicit drugs, and increasing contacts with foreigners put these societies at high risk. In 1990, the World Health Organization detected a shifting pattern of HIV transmission away from Europe and North America to Africa, parts of the Caribbean, and Latin America. It was a small consolation.

POSTSCRIPT   After World War II, Europe's cities defined the strength, values, and identity of their respective nations as never before. They called the tune in art, music, and sports and provided the arena for the further emancipation of women, which proved to be a necessity for continued national prosperity. No modern society could exist without the active participation of its female population. French Premier Edith Cresson said that it was easier to do without men. "I say, in general, that you can replace men everywhere except in private life," she quipped.[69]

Women became more prominent in the European work force because they were increasingly holding down jobs that had been male monopolies. In addition, the nature of work itself was changing. Women gained ground in the sectors that used new technology: banking, insurance, biotechnology, and information management. Even if women did not achieve executive positions in proportion to their numbers, they did account for a significant minority of supervisory positions. Women now enjoyed the same property and inheritance rights as men. They had similar educational opportunities and could file for divorce. Along with these practical gains, women began to demand an end to the gender prejudices inherent in their languages and argued that their cultures should be studied from a woman's perspective.[70] They also wanted to serve in the armed forces in combat roles.

Men, though, continued to dominate, especially in professional team sports. Thanks to the increased coverage provided by modern electronics, the playing field became sacred turf. Jet transportation enabled teams to maintain a widely dispersed schedule, and satellite transmissions and instant play-by-play transformed the weekly game into something resembling a historical force. For television viewers, professional sports satisfied the search for identity and enabled the most determined layabout to participate vicariously in the great cult of youth. Sports promoters presented the matches as theater, creating a sort of urban nationalism that transcended class.

The most significant change in the way people entertained themselves, however, was in their new attitudes toward morality. Saint Augustine believed that marriage was the only place for sex and that its only purpose was procreation. But now the more respected prophets were those like Havelock Ellis and Sigmund Freud who wrote that sex was natural and desirable, pleasurable for men and women alike. The old strict moral codes crumbled before this new attitude. The great sexual revolution after 1945 led to the widespread liberalization of the laws on divorce and abortion and to a freer attitude toward sexual mores. However, the sudden intrusion of the deadly AIDS virus again made people cautious. In 1990, the World Health Organization predicted that between 8 and 10 million people worldwide would contract the fatal disease during the following decade. The greatest relative increase would occur in women and children.[71]

The last chapter on the bitter AIDS discovery controversy has yet to be written. In the 1987 agreement, the Pasteur Institute agreed to split the revenues coming from the invention of the blood test with American researchers. However, in December 1991, following the disclosure that the U.S. Department of Health and Human Services had withheld crucial data supporting the French claim to prior discovery, the Pasteur Institute, backed by the French government, demanded that the earlier agreement be renegotiated.[72] There were few scientists who were by then reluctant to accord the French the credit they deserved. However, many people were more inclined to reserve their highest accolades for those who would eventually produce a cure for the disease.

ENDNOTES

1. See Larry Collins and Dominique Lapierre, *Is Paris Burning?* (New York: Simon and Schuster, 1965).
2. *Survey of International Affairs: Four-Power Control in Germany and Austria* (1956), 7–11.
3. By comparison, German air raids killed 58,000 British civilians.
4. John McGinnis, *Military Government Journal* (Amherst, Mass.: University of Massachusetts Press, 1974), 304.
5. In 1986, the percentage of the population living in cities of more than 2,000 people was 91.4 in Spain; 88.5 in the Netherlands, 87.8 in the United Kingdom, 80 in the German Federal Republic; 76.8 in the German Democratic Republic; 74.7 in

Czechoslovakia; 73.4 in France; 65.8 in the Soviet Union; 65.2 in Bulgaria; 60.7 in Poland; and 50.5 in Romania. United Nations, *1968 Demographic Yearbook* (New York: United Nations, 1968), 199–302.

6. Leonardo Benevolo, *The History of the City* (Cambridge, Mass: MIT Press, 1980), 967–1008.

7. In contrast, the British preferred row houses to huge apartment complexes, and about three-fourths of their new buildings took this form.

8. See Carlo Cresti, *Le Corbusier* (London: Hamlyn, 1969) and Maurice Besset, *Who Was Le Corbusier?* (Geneva: Skira, 1968).

9. Le Corbusier, *Towards a New Architecture* (London: John Rodker, 1931), 60–61.

10. In 1980, the Bâtiments de France assumed the authority to approve all future construction projects at Pessac in the hope of eventually restoring the district to its original condition, but many of the houses' owners put up a stiff resistance. Fiona Gleizes, "For Living, It's Hard to Beat a House," *Newsweek*, 8 March 1990, 28.

11. See David H. McKay, *Planning and Politics in Western Europe* (New York: St. Martin's Press, 1982).

12. United Nations, *1988 Demographic Yearbook*, 302, 330–33.

13. B. Michael Frolic, "Moscow: The Socialist Alternative," in H. Wentworth Eldredge, *World Capitals: Toward Guided Urbanization* (New York: Doubleday, 1975), 309–15.

14. The population of Leningrad, the Soviet Union's second largest city, was about 4.5 million. United Nations, *1988 Demographic Yearbook*, 330–33.

15. Francine du Plessix Gray, *Soviet Women: Walking the Tightrope* (New York: Doubleday, 1989), 183.

16. Ibid., 185–86.

17. United Nations, *1988 Demographic Yearbook*, 322.

18. Marco Ruiz, ed., *One Hundred Years of the Automobile, 1886–1986* (New York: Gallery Books, 1985), 78–86.

19. Brian R. Mitchell, *European Historical Statistics, 1750–1970* (New York: University of Columbia Press, 1975), 469.

20. Private car production in the Soviet Union rose from less than 500 to 294,000 with most of these cars intended for official use; Czech production went from 24,500 to 132,400; East German from 7,200 to 12,100; and Polish from less than 100 to 47,000. Ibid., 469.

21. The Soviets were second only to the United States in overall number.

22. Jean Philippe Rapp and Roger Burkhardt, "Heroes, Workers and the Party Line" (Geneva: Swiss Television, 1979). Distributed by the Corporation for Public Broadcasting, David Fanning, Executive Producer.

23. Ruth Thomas, *Broadcasting and Democracy in France* (Philadelphia: Temple University Press, 1976), 117.

24. It gave rise to yet another version that debuted on Spanish television in 1991.

25. The BBC ceased broadcasting because the television antenna was a perfect direction finder for German aircraft. Asa Briggs, *The BBC: The First Fifty Years* (London: Oxford University Press, 1985), 155–71.

26. Timothy Green, *The Universal Eye: The World of Television* (New York: Stein and Day, 1972), 83.

27. The British also had an independent television network that tried to be less intellectual, more informal, and more regional than the BBC. It too had its share of great successes, chief among these being the action serials "The Avengers," "The Saint," and "The Prisoner."

28. The basic rules established in 1862 have never changed, namely, that the ball must be moved with the feet and may not be aimed at another player. Joan M. Chandler, *Television and National Sport: The United States and Britain* (Chicago: University of Illinois Press, 1988), 132–52.

29. Desmond Morris, *The Soccer Tribe* (London: Jonathan Cape, 1981), 114.

30. Ibid., 234.

31. H. V. Hodson, *The Annual Register, 1985* (London: Longman, 1985), 456–57.

32. Richard Holt, *Sport and the British: A Modern History* (New York: Oxford University Press, 1990), 337–39.

33. Richard Espy, *The Politics of the Olympic Games* (Berkeley: University of California Press, 1981), 40.

34. Ibid., 188–97.

35. Randy Roberts and James S. Olson, *Winning Is the Only Thing: Sports in America since 1945* (Baltimore: Johns Hopkins University Press, 1989), 207.

36. Some countries had already accorded women the right to vote before the war. Finland had done so in 1906, Norway in 1907, and Denmark in 1915.

37. See the appropriate national entries in *Women's Movements of the World*, edited by Sally Shreir (Burnt Mill, Harlow, Essex: Longman, 1988).

38. Thom Shanker, "Sorry, Natasha, U.S. magazine is dreamland," *Chicago Tribune*, October 7, 1990, 1, 18.

39. Simone de Beauvoir, *The Second Sex* (New York: Alfred Knopf, 1976), 679.

40. By the 1980s, women comprised over 49 percent of the active work force in Sweden, 45 percent in Norway, 43 percent in Great Britain, 40 percent in Belgium, 38 percent in West Germany, 37 percent in France, 36 percent in Italy, and 33 percent in Luxembourg and the Netherlands.

41. Madame du Chatelet, the author of the physics text *Institutions de physique* (1740), possessed a confidence in her abilities that spoke directly to women of all ages: "It may be that there are metaphysicians and philosophers whose learning is greater than mine, although I have not met them. Yet, they are but frail humans, too, and have their faults; so, when I add the sum total of my graces, I confess that I am inferior to no one." Margaret Alic, *Hypathia's Heritage: A History of Women in Science from Antiquity through the Nineteenth Century* (Boston: Beacon Press, 1986), 147.

42. Alic, *Hypathia's Heritage*, 139.

43. In Norway, though, Gro Harlem Bruntland had served twice as prime minister.

44. Uta Ranke-Heinemann in her book *Eunuchs for the Kingdom of Heaven: Women, Sexuality, and the Catholic Church* (New York: Doubleday, 1991) attacked the Roman Catholic church for its sexism in vilifying women as the cause of men's passions and lust. Ranke-Heinemann felt that in emphasizing theological gymnastics, the church had failed to teach men and women to be more humane and kinder to each other. The German Catholic church took the book in stride. *Chicago Tribune*, 3 March 1991, Books, 7.

45. See Shari Steiner, *The Female Factor: A Study of Women in Five Western European Societies* (New York: Putnam, 1977).

46. Alan Ross, "U and Non-U," in Nancy Mitford, ed., *Noblesse Oblige* (New York: Harpers, 1956), 56–58.

47. *International Herald Tribune*, 20 November 1969.

48. In all fairness, the all-meat patty, as well as the sausage known in the United States as the hot dog, originally came from Germany. But the Americans knew a good thing and turned these items into true foods for the international market. The cheeseburger seems to be an American refinement.

49. Thomas Moore, "For the Leninists It's Mac in the U.S.S.R.," *U.S. News and World Report*, 12 February 1990, 11; Ann Blackman, "Moscow's Big Mak Attack," *Time*, 5 February 1990, 51.

50. Magnus Pyke, "The Influence of American Foods and Food Technology in Europe," in C. W. E. Bigsby, *Superculture: American Popular Culture and Europe* (Bowling Green, Ohio: Bowling Green University Press, 1975), 83–95.

51. Alfred Kinsey's works, published after World War II, were highly influential in Europe. *Sexual Behavior in the Human Male* (New York: W. B. Saunders, 1948) and *Sexual Behavior in the Human Female* (New York: W. B. Saunders, 1953).

52. Germany and Switzerland recognized the irretrievable breakdown of a marriage. In Ireland, a popular referendum in June 1986 on a proposal to legalize divorce was defeated with 63.5 percent against the measure.

53. Certain fundamentalist Protestant churches and the Roman Catholic church staunchly opposed all "artificial" contraception. The Catholic church regarded the "rhythm method" as the only acceptable form of birth control.

54. The law was bitterly opposed by the Spanish bishops who threatened to excommunicate anyone who received or assisted an abortion.

55. United Nations, 1988 Demographic Yearbook, 393–94.

56. Jan Sjöby, "Denmark and Pitfalls of Pornography," International Herald Tribune, 30 August 1979.

57. Steiner, The Female Factor, 210–11.

58. The term AIDS unfortunately is not very adaptable phonetically outside the English language. The French, though, had their own analogous acronym in SIDA (Syndrome d'Immuno-Déficience Acquise).

59. Mirko D. Grmek, History of AIDS: Emergence and Origin of a Modern Pandemic (Princeton, N.J.: Princeton University Press, 1990), 21–22.

60. Ibid., 109.

61. Randy Shilts, And the Band Played On: Politics, People, and the AIDS Epidemic (New York: Penguin Books, 1988), 372.

62. Ibid., 592.

63. Ibid., 562.

64. Grmek, History of AIDS, 194.

65. Jerome E. Groopman, "Red Scare, AIDS in the U.S.S.R.," The New Republic, 17 April 1989, 25.

66. Ibid., 27.

67. See Eloise Salholz, "Watching the Babies Die," Newsweek, 19 February 1990, 63; and Andrew Purvis, "Rumania's Other Tragedy," Time, 19 February 1990, 74.

68. "A sneak attack of Eastern Europe," U.S. News and World Report, 19 February 1990, 11.

69. Sharon Waxman, "For Cresson, honeymoon is over," Chicago Tribune, 20 July 1991.

70. Bonnie S. Anderson and Judith P. Zinsser, A History of Their Own: Women in Europe, vol. 2 (New York: Harper and Row, 1988), 426–29.

71. Anne-Christine d'Adesky, "WHO predicts dramatic rise in global AIDS toll: Women and children newly affected," UN Chronicle (December 1990), 66–68.

72. Chicago Tribune, 31 December 1991, Section 1, 1 and 12.

CHAPTER 7

HIGH BROW, LOW BROW

PREFACE Popular culture and elite culture had been rivals since, at least, the beginning of the twentieth century. After World War II, however, the contest seemed to gather intensity, although it was hardly a fight to the death. The two could coexist, albeit with a certain amount of snobbishness from one and spite from the other. Cultural elites who prided themselves on their refined taste and looked down their noses at those who preferred more basic forms of entertainment could always point to history to justify their attitudes. Indeed, great works of art, practically by definition, proved more durable than those of lesser quality, which were produced for a mass market and maximum revenues. Elites could also count on governmental support. Those aspects of culture deemed to be of the highest quality and worthy of preservation had always enjoyed a certain amount of official favoritism.

In music, government subsidies favored the works of the great masters, allowing them to be performed in appropriate surroundings. This was especially true of grand opera. More than most other forms of musical creativity, opera became a matter of national pride. Opera houses were cultural basilicas, places of reverence and worship as well as centers for entertainment.[1] World War II, unfortunately, had not been kind to these great edifices. Practically all of Germany's more than fifty opera houses were either partially or totally destroyed. The casualty list included the prestigious Berlin Staatsoper and the Munich Bayerische Staatsoper. Italy's opera houses, the most numerous in Europe after Germany, had also experienced extensive material damage, including the severe bombing of La Scala in Milan, the nation's best-loved opera house. In Austria, another world-famous building, the Staatsoper, had suffered even worse damage from an attack in 1945 that left only the vestibule and the loggia standing.

When the fighting stopped, nations and cities frequently gave the highest priority to the reconstruction of their opera houses and concert halls, often in a form as close to the original as possible. In Vienna, private homes had to wait while the opera-loving Viennese rebuilt the Staatsoper.[2]

Despite all the special attention lavished on opera and other high-brow forms of musical entertainment, these never won a truly mass audience. Popular entertainment was to be found elsewhere. Young audiences, in particular, liked the music from the United States, with its Afro-American cultural roots. They turned its musicians into folk heroes, made many of them multimillionaires, and accorded them the status of poets, prophets, and social revolutionaries. The most significant musical export was rock and roll, which, thanks to the speed of communications and the physical presence of the American military, arrived in Europe as fast as it did at home. The Europeans assimilated rock and roll so well that they were soon contributing to its development. In Britain popular musicians gave the genre a new life of titanic proportions.

The presence of the United States was also felt in the world of the visual arts. European painters and sculptors had crossed the Atlantic after World War I, and the fusion of their energy and talent with that of the Americans had produced a true international art style. Much of this new modern art was confusing and controversial and left spectators and traditionalists perplexed and bewildered. Giorgio de Chirico, the principal founder of metaphysical painting, remarked with great disillusionment, "No one enjoys modern art, neither those who do it, nor those who buy it. They are all afraid to tell the truth."[3] But such a statement could hardly be taken seriously considering that modern art encompassed many more diverse styles than the art of almost any previous age.

THE VISUAL IMAGE

Post-Modernism

The Nonobjective Renaissance. Abstract expressionism, the artistic style that held sway after 1945, seemed ideally suited to the confusion and anxiety of the age of mutually assured destruction. Actually, however, the style first developed in Europe prior to World War I and gradually spread throughout the world.[4] Eventually, New York City became the center for abstract expressionism, but many of its most famous practitioners were European expatriates. Although these painters came from diverse backgrounds and were fiercely individualistic, they shared common nonobjective roots. They were determined to create a new art that was resistant to and independent of the restraints of a materialistic society.[5] Many were in their forties when World War II ended.

Arshile Gorky, a Turkish-Armenian who came to the United States in 1920 when he was sixteen, created a series of biomorphic paintings, splashed with bold contrasting colors, in which all the abstract objects seem to be in the process of transforming themselves into something more alarming. His close friend Willem de Kooning, born in Rotterdam in 1904, was equally nonobjective, but painted with more dynamic brush strokes that he slashed across the canvas in jagged, architectural lines, aggressively conveying the power of the haphazard—a form of dramatic creativity that had first appeared in the surrealist automatic painting of the 1920s. This form of artistic spontaneity with its revolt against academic conformity influenced Wyoming-born Jackson Pollock, who created the drip technique.[6] Pollock stood on a stepladder or a chair and poured paint from a bucket onto a canvas or board. He used commercial pigments applied directly from a can. Pollock would also fling or splash his colors without predetermined patterns. The physical process itself was thus part of the artistic result and became known as action painting.

This form of creativity, largely divorced from geometric traditions, showed that abstract expressionism was not so much a style as an artistic concept. If its practitioners had anything in common, it was their strong individuality. Still, despite its amorphous internationalism, some practitioners of abstract expressionism were influenced by more traditional antecedents.

In France, for example, many abstract artists preferred a more Cartesian and less free-spirited approach. Pierre Soulages imposed formalistic black strips on a colorful background to produce depth and perspective in the restrained manner of oriental calligraphy. Roger Bissière, who created the geometric abstract school, blended strong lyrical color with the cubist tradition of Cézanne. Meanwhile Jean Bazaine drew on a wide range of periods and cultures, claiming not only Cézanne and Rembrandt but also Paolo Uccello, Van Eyck, and Vermeer as his artistic forebears. In addition, he said he was influenced by African art, Hindu, Chinese, and primitive Greek sculpture, and the religious aspect of medieval art.[7] Bazaine was looking for something beyond painting and trying to express a universal truth. In his abstract landscapes, he attempted to give greater dimension to the external world.[8] For him, unlike Pollock, abstract painting was a matter of precision, an eternal quest for the essential. Sometimes he repainted his canvases as much as fifty times "to get an effect which seemed to [him] to express a truth, or a more accurate and more profound aspect of reality."[9] His fellow countryman, Alfred Manessier, agreed. Manessier saw abstract painting as the means by which he would achieve "a higher sense of reality and take account of what was essential in himself."[10] In his paintings, a flowing geometry of irregular shapes moved through a sea of color.

In general, though, the abstract expressionist revolution seemed to float freely in time. Although its European roots were obvious, encompassing the whole expressive tradition of modern art from Cézanne onwards, it leapfrogged so rapidly across national boundaries that any predominant tendencies soon got jet lag. Creative techniques also varied. Some artists painted conventionally to gain better control of gesture and texture; the so-called color-field painters pushed a wide variety of materials to their limits to form powerful images with the force of randomness. Consequently, abstractionism cannot be appreciated by relying on comfortable generalizations, but only by concentrating on the specific output of individual painters.

Art and Popular Culture. Not all artists wanted to divorce creativity from the recognizable—far from it. For every artist who wanted to retreat into a purer, abstract world, at least as many wanted their art to represent the figurative world around them. Their goal was to produce a graphic depiction of the real world of machines, science, and consumerism. They wanted an art that embraced the garish and the smelly city environment of popular taste—an art that was the essence of modern society. In their view, art should reflect modern urban culture, not a pastoral wilderness. Necessarily, their art built upon the banal and the vulgar.

Nonobjective art was inaccessible; it was foreign and distant from most viewers. In art museums, spectators passed quickly through the rooms where it hung. They found it dull. Popular art, on the other hand, spoke directly to many people. It was the art of the billboard, the poster, the comic strip, and sometimes the obscene graffiti on the walls of buildings. It appeared in cigarette, clothing, and perfume advertisements, enlivened newspapers, and flashed across television screens.

In 1956, the Whitechapel Art Gallery in London hosted an exhibition called "This is Tomorrow." The show featured the works of the Independent Group, young artists who were fascinated by the new popular urban culture epitomized by postwar America. The exhibit proposed to introduce viewers into a series of modern environments; its tone was set by the entrance display, a collage by Richard Hamilton entitled *Just What is it that Makes Today's Homes so Different, so Appealing?* The collage consisted of a series of images that included all the artifacts of modern society: a television set, a tape recorder, a vacuum cleaner, a canned ham, a suite of boxy furniture with a black lacquer cocktail table, a Ford logo on a dark lampshade. A stripper, clad only in pasties and a bow around her waist, reclined on the sofa with a lampshade on her head. In the left foreground was a body builder in posing strap carrying a huge lollipop labeled "tootsie pop." A picture of the cover of a "young romance" comic book hung on the wall; a movie theater could be seen through the window. There was a picture of the moon on the ceiling.

The collage's creator was demonstrating the intellectual parameters of pop art, whose qualities he described as transcendent, witty, sexy, youthful, and glamorous.[11] Hamilton was touting and satirizing the extravagant pleasures of American consumerism in a postausterity Britain. Other practitioners of the style hardly needed Hamilton to tell them how to tout the new economy of abundance.

The Swede Claus Oldenburg, who spent many of his early years in the United States with his diplomat father, carried the artistic lampoon of postwar commercialism to absurd heights with great canvas-filled, sculptural creations of everyday food items: an eleven-foot-long ice cream cone (*Floor Cone*), a huge piece of cake (*Floor Cake*), and a giant hamburger (*Floor Burger*). "I am for U.S. Government Inspected Art, Grade A art, Regular Price art, Yellow Ripe art, Extra Fancy art, Ready-to-eat art, Fully cleaned art, Spend less art, Eat better art, Ham art, pork art, chicken art, tomato art, banana art, apple art, turkey art, cake art, cookie art," he wrote.[12] Oldenburg carried his architectural-scale concepts into the construction of a monumental *Clothespin*, a *Giant Ice Bag* (with a mechanism inside to make it move), a *Lipstick (Ascending) on Caterpillar Tracks*, a *Baseball Bat*, and a *Giant 3-Way Plug*.[13] Equally arresting were certain projects that never were realized—the *Good Humor Bar* proposed for Park Avenue in New York City, *Scissors in Motion* intended to replace the Washington Monument, and the two toilet balls designed to float on the Thames River near the Houses of Parliament. He also proposed a new facade for the Chicago Museum of Contemporary Art in the shape of a geometric mouse. Oldenburg's surrealistic concept of the menace of everyday objects both glorified and mocked the mechanistic society that had given them birth.

Pop art had a dual nationality—Britain and the United States—and a dual ancestry—the urban consumer society and the world of Dada.[14] In the postwar era, everyday objects were made in such quantity that they no longer possessed any distinction independent of their utility. If in a disposable society everything seemed to collapse in a welter of cultural egalitarianism, then perhaps the disposable had to be taken more seriously.

Roy Lichtenstein found the inspiration for his art in the comic strip. He cribbed from the pages of actual war and romance comics, enlarging them to monumental proportions. His famous triptych, entitled *As I Opened Fire*, was taken from "Wingmate of Doom" in the Detective Comics book *All-American Men of War* series. A fighter plane is shooting off its 50-caliber guns, with each succeeding section being a close-up of the preceding panel. The title proceeds: (1) "As I opened fire, I knew why Tex hadn't buzzed me . . . if he had . . . (BRAT!); (2) The enemy would have been warned (BRATATATATA!); (3) That my ship was below them . . . (BRATATATA)." Each panel measured 5 feet 8 inches by 4 feet 8 inches.

One critic wrote that Lichtenstein was searching for a modern paradisiacal mythology, "an imaginary folk culture, a coherent world of stereotyped action that seemed at once to echo and second the apparently sophisticated world of avant-garde gestures."[15] If true, his pretension was disturbing. Few pop artists deserved to be taken that seriously. Merely blowing up images found in a comic book failed to make a case that Lichtenstein's achievement was very significant. Nor could the works of other artists. Jasper Johns, for example, put sculp-metal over an ordinary flashlight and mounted it on a piece of wood. Jeff Koons copied a vinyl, inflatable rabbit in stainless steel. And Andy Warhol created thirty-two red and white polymer paintings of *Campbell's Soup Cans*; the paintings differed only in the flavors that gave them their titles: *Onion, Scotch Broth, Pepper Pot, Chicken Gumbo*, and so on. The pictures, which individually measured 20 by 16 inches, were arranged in four rows of eight paintings. Warhol, arguably one of the most pretentious and least talented artists of the modern age, explained that he painted because he wanted to be a machine. "I think it would be terrific if everybody was alike," he said.[16] Warhol achieved the ultimate in pop art when he began simply signing the labels of the soup cans themselves, thereby creating a work of art from his name alone.

The Spectator as Participant

The New Tendency. In much post–World War II art, the viewer was given a central place in the aesthetic process. The artists of this genre thought it their duty to involve the spectators by provoking their optical and tactile reactions. The separate status of the object was thereby weakened for the object had no independent value without the active role of the spectator.

Spectator involvement had already been solicited by Alexander Calder, whose form of kinetic art, called the "mobile," was intended to encourage viewer participation. However, the beginning of a coherent movement came with the artists of the *Nouvelle tendance*. According to Karl Gerstner, the New Tendency aimed to establish reciprocity between the viewer and the artist. "What we are trying to achieve," he explained, "is for your joy before the work of art to be no longer that of an admirer but of a partner." Gerstner said that art was a means of "procuring visual sensations" bringing out the active participation of the viewer.[17] If artistic standards needed any further shove into the chasm of chaos, this was it. Artists who worked this vein wanted to move art out of the museums and the galleries into a larger optical environment. They wanted to create a pictorial experience on an urban scale, sometimes static, sometimes kinetic, but mostly ephemeral.

Nicolas Uriburu used water for his canvas. In 1968, he dumped thirty kilograms of fluorescent sodium into the Grand Canal of Venice, turning the water green

Bulgarian-born Christo Javacheff has wrapped the Pont Neuf with 430,000 square feet of silky sandstone-colored cloth, held in place with seven miles of cable. The project, completed on 7 October 1985 after two weeks' work, cost $2.1 million and involved a team of divers, mountain climbers, tree cutters, and other technicians. Christo got the idea for projects like this in Sofia, where the Communist regime used him and other art students to embellish the landscape to impress Western visitors passing through the country on the Orient Express.

over a three-kilometer length. Uriburu said he was probing the relationship between the durable and the fleeting. He was so pleased with the green canal that he later repeated the exercise first in New York's East River and then in the Seine River at Paris, giving the conception a certain rakish internationalism.

The Bulgarian Christo Javacheff pursued another form of artistic expression by inventing the technique of *empaquetage*. Christo wanted to wrap anything that was technically capable of being wrapped. Some of his packaging projects included the Art Museum at Bern and the trees along the Champs Élysées in Paris. He also hung a curtain across a valley in Rifle, Colorado, and covered a million square feet of a craggy inlet near Sydney, Australia, with a blanket of polypropylene plastic. The eighty-foot cliffs of Little Bay took almost a month to "wrap." A team of sixty volunteers sewed the fabric together and tacked it to the rock with staples fired from ramset guns. The artist explained that containing an object exposed "its commonness in a beautiful and relaxed manner."[18] Spectators had to pay twenty cents to see the result. Christo said he was trying to return objects and institutions to a state of nothingness. From 1985 to 1991, he worked on a $26 million project to open 1,340 twenty-foot blue umbrellas along a twelve-mile stretch of land in Japan and 1,760 similar yellow umbrellas along eighteen miles of California hills. When all the umbrellas were unfurled, Christo announced enigmatically, "The project mirrors the people around it."[19]

Other examples of unmarketable eccentric action or conceptual art involved such projects as tracing various lines and designs on a piece of land, ploughing a pattern in a field with a tractor, piling up masses of earth in temporary sculptural forms, and creating a pattern in the sand by running back and forth at low tide. Roland Balandi wanted to enclose the Arc de Triomphe in Paris with a plastic dome where artificial snow would continually swirl about.

Yves Klein, a former judo instructor and merchant seaman, hit upon another sort of happening in his *Anthropometries*. These were monochromatic paintings using nude women as brushes. The first such creation was produced before a roomful of spectators at the Galérie Internationale d'Art Contemporaine in Paris on 9 March 1960. While an orchestra played Klein's "Monotone Symphony," consisting naturally of one note, two blue-splotched women flopped around on a canvas stretched out on the floor. Klein had patented the intense cobalt blue color as "Klein International Blue"; he was so fond of it that he created a whole series of paintings using it alone.

Anything Goes and Usually Does. Avant-garde art was collapsing under the presumption that anything new should be taken seriously. Museums and galleries seemed game for virtually any concept. Hence, Walter de Maria, claiming that a concept could be "just as strong in ideas as real sensations,"[20] filled three rooms in a Munich gallery with a layer of dirt two feet deep. Joseph Beuys, an artist from Düsseldorf, filled an open space with an assortment of large objects. Included were an operating table, a battery with wires and canisters, a stretcher, and a Red Cross blanket, which was hung on the wall. The clutter was supposed to suggest a concentration camp. Lygia Clark expressed her concept of the pleasures and traumas of life in the uterus by creating a series of tentlike pouches, or stages, through which visitors were invited to crawl. Clark was nonchalant about her objects, most of which were disposable. What mattered was the concept behind them: "What remained of importance was only the act."[21] The work appeared at the Venice Biennial. Keith Arnatt painted pictures on which were written words like "OOF" or "KEITH ARNATT IS AN ARTIST," while Robert Barry hung a sign on an outside door that read: "For the exhibition, the gallery will be closed."[22] The latter was a great stroke of Dada, showing that conceptual art not only did not need gallery space for its venue, but need not be art at all.

Inanity reached its apogee with the mercifully short-lived "movement" known as body art. Here the artist's own body became the exposition space, both the subject and object of the art work. The artist might spit water from his mouth like a fountain or wrap himself in thongs and rope like a trussed chicken. The occasions would be preserved with photographs. Body art in its most gruesome incarnation involved self-mutilation, like the slashing of shoulders and arms with razor blades to re-create pagan rituals. In 1969, at the age of twenty-nine, Austrian artist Rudolf Schwarzkogler literally killed himself for his art. To critic Robert Hughes, the gesture had an emblematic value: "Having nothing to say, and nowhere to go but further out, he lopped himself and called it art."[23]

Most artists who challenged the conventional standards of art desired more destruction and absurdity for its own sake. Even the Dadists did not believe that anti-art devices formed an adequate basis on which a sound art could be built. Marcel Duchamp was astonished when latter-day pop artists talked about the significance of his ready-mades: "I threw the bottlerack and the urinal into their faces as a challenge and now they admire them for their aesthetic beauty," he wrote in surprise.[24] Shortly before his death in 1968 at the age of eighty-one, Duchamp complained that the artists of this postwar generation were too integrated into society. "In my day," he reflected, "artists wanted to be outcasts, pariahs."[25] Duchamp's indictment was a bitter condemnation of an age when each new artistic monstrosity could be peddled to some collector as an investment.

MUSIC: CLASSICAL AND POPULAR

Musical Theater

The Production of Grand Opera. With the reconstruction of Europe's great opera houses came the reestablishment of their traditional repertoire. Europe's leading houses were museums where the great works of the great composers of the past, predominantly those of the nineteenth century, were on constant display. Both economics and audience preference limited the performance of works by contemporary composers. Rumor had it that a composer had to be dead or almost dead to have a work performed at the Paris Opera. On the other hand, the Hamburg Opera, one of the oldest in Europe, felt an express obligation to mount the works of living composers. And La Scala, while still emphasizing the "oldies," sometimes included as many as four contemporary works in its almost year-long season. But no opera house could afford to neglect the tried and true. Simply put, modern works did not sell tickets.

Opera houses were more willing to take chances in the staging of operas than in the choice of the operas themselves. One of the great revolutions in stagecraft came at Bayreuth, the home of the Wagnerian musical dramas. Production resumed in 1951 under the direction of Richard Wagner's grandsons Wieland and Wolfgang. Together they completely changed the nature of Bayreuth productions. They junked all the exaggerated neoromantic naturalism with its lavish, realistic sets, heavy props, and overblown stage effects complete with fire-belching dragons and Rhinemaidens swimming around while suspended on cables. In its place, they adopted streamlined, stylized sets based on a geometric use of space. In this, they were following in the footsteps of the great Swiss *metteur en scène*, Adolphe Appia, who stripped his sets to their bare essentials in an attempt to transcend external reality. Appia set the mood not with painted flats, but through the skillful use of light. He used economy and simplicity to emphasize the dramatic vision created by the music. Wieland Wagner claimed that he used the stylistic elements of modern art to render the operas as timeless "archetypal musical theater."[26]

This concept was carried beyond Bayreuth by Günther Schneider-Siemssen, the chief set designer at the Vienna Staatsoper. In addition to his home turf, Schneider-Siemssen productions appeared in Stuttgart, Cologne, Frankfurt, Düsseldorf, Munich, Geneva, Zurich, Sofia, London, Buenos Aires, Moscow, and New York. In his textbook, *The Stage as Cosmic Space*, he explained that to create a scene on stage was to point toward a cosmic, existential nexus, which was the essence of all great cultures.[27] Schneider-Siemssen's sets had an ethereal quality in which gravity apparently disappeared. He believed that the stage designer's task was to portray spiritual and religious striving, to create a theater of the future that would influence all the arts.[28]

Rudolf Bing, the Viennese impresario, who became general-manager of the Metropolitan Opera in New York, once described his function as preserving the great works of the past in excellent modern frames.[29] But the packaging did not have to follow the stylistic dictates of directors like Schneider-Siemssen. Franco Zeffirelli used a more traditional approach. Zeffirelli sought to give authenticity to his productions, at least those definable historically, by imitating the decor appropriate to the period in which the action occurred. Thus, he tried to make the inside of a church or a palace look as realistic as possible by piling detail upon detail.

Stage designers who followed no specific concept, let alone any ideology, tried to bring out the qualities of the work in accordance with their personal artistic image. They were thus able to draw upon whatever styles—realist, surrealist, impressionist, expressionist—they thought would highlight the specific work to be performed. For example, Jean-Pierre Ponelle constructed an entire town for Rossini's *Barber of Seville*. He made the town fit in perspective with the opera's main playing areas—the town square, the barber shop, and Doctor Bartolo's house—by putting the latter on a turntable stage. In this way, he integrated each element into a definite landscape with its own social conditions, climate, and mores.[30]

If the leading designers took their talents from one opera house to another, so did the singers. In fact, the ease of travel and the publicity obtained through radio and television helped the star system, already present in Europe's prestigious houses before the war, to become more firmly entrenched. Because many great singers tended to become associated with certain parts, the leading roles in the large opera houses came to be rotated among a pool of relatively few singers. Getting the talents of one of these singers could often make the difference between a routine performance and a great success. Singers with international reputations usually did not sign long-term contracts with one house, but kept themselves free to shuttle around. Thus, in the course of a year, Placido Domingo might sing at Covent Garden, La Scala, the Met, Chicago, San Francisco, Sydney, and places in between. In the large houses, casting became less nationalistic. It was not unusual to do an *Aida*, say, with an American tenor, a Polish soprano, an Italian baritone, a German mezzo-soprano, and a Bulgarian bass. This conglomeration of nationalities often forced the opera houses to present the operas in their original language rather than the language of the country where they were being performed, as had often been the custom in the nineteenth century.

American singers, as if to counterbalance the European operatic migration to the United States, routinely appeared in all the leading opera houses of Europe. Europe had more opera houses than the United States and gave singers a greater opportunity to gain experience. James McCracken, for example, started out singing small parts at the Metropolitan Opera, then migrated to Zurich where he improved his talent with larger roles. Ultimately, he came back home when the Met mounted a new production of *Otello* to showcase his talents. Nevertheless, he also continued to sing in Europe.

The Return of Naturalism. Styles in opera composition roughly paralleled the artistic or literary movements of the time. Following the great periods of classicism and romanticism, opera had developed in more abstract directions: impressionism, symbolism, and expressionism. Composers such as Claude Debussy (*Pelléas and Mélisande*, 1902), Richard Strauss (*Electra*, 1909), and Béla Bartók (*Duke Bluebeard's Castle*, 1918) depicted character and situation through allusion and relied on the music to reveal the inner emotions of the characters. Russian composers like Nikolai Rimsky-Korsakov (*The Golden Cockerel*, 1909), Igor Stravinsky (*The Nightingale*, 1914) and Sergei Prokofiev (*The Love of Three Oranges*, 1921) composed works of fantasy and escape in which exotic color, satire, and fantasy were interwoven. In all these operas, the characters stood apart from society. Of course, such themes never completely dominated opera composition. Many composers, including Gustave Charpentier (*Louise*, 1900), Giacomo Puccini (*Madame Butterfly*, 1904), and Italo Montemezzi (*The Love of Three Kings*, 1913), had always held fast to the realistic and melodramatic tradition. However, fantasy and exaggeration became less popular after World War I. Modern audiences wanted characters they could identify with, individuals whose dilemmas reflected their own. The return to dramatic naturalism dominated opera production for the next two generations and became the mainstay of opera production after World War II.

In Great Britain, naturalism was most strongly associated with the works of Benjamin Britten, who did more than any other composer since Henry Purcell (*Dido and Aeneas*, 1689) to stimulate the development of English national opera. In restoring his country's confidence in musical drama, Britten was able to establish a distinctive tradition in his own right. His *Peter Grimes*, performed at the re-opening of the Sadler's Wells Theater in June 1945, was a psychological drama about an English fisherman who is wrongly suspected of killing two of his apprentices. To escape his fears and rage, he drowns himself. In this work, Britten combined set arias with the composite character of the crowd, using lyrical orchestral passages to heighten the mood. The opera incorporates many different musical elements—sea chanteys, dance-hall tunes, church music. *Peter Grimes* was an instant success and propelled its creator into the first rank of contemporary opera composers. It was translated into eight languages and was soon performed throughout the world.

Peter Grimes marked the beginning of a period of great productivity for its composer. Over the next eighteen years, Britten wrote sixteen stage works, eight of which were full-length operas. The most famous of these was his adaptation of Herman Melville's novel, *Billy Budd*, which appeared in 1951. *Billy Budd*, recognized as one of Britten's greatest works, again had as its theme the psychological anguish of a hero victimized by an unjust accusation. Billy Budd, the main character, is menaced by the villainous Claggert until he unintentionally kills his tormentor, an act for which he is court-martialed and hanged. The opera, written only for male voices, consists mostly of recitatives; its dramatically powerful themes are often briefly expressed so the audience will not be distracted from the mood of impending violence and doom. The three main characters are all strongly developed: Billy Budd's goodness is contrasted with Claggert's villainy. Captain Vere has noble, but flawed, intentions that force him to perform a duty alien to his humanity. The work quickly found a solid place in the British repertory.

Italian opera fell on lean times for several decades after World War I—most of the great composers of the post-Verdian generation were approaching the end of their careers—and not until the appearance of Gian-Carlo Menotti did someone arrive to carry on the tradition. Though born in Italy and influenced by the Italian operatic tradition, Menotti emigrated to the United States in 1927, when he was sixteen. He is probably best-known for his television opera *Amahl and the Night Visitors* (1951), which had its premiere on the NBC Television Opera Theatre and was shown every Christmas for many years thereafter. His short opera *The Medium* (1946) was made into a film that won prizes at both the Venice and Cannes film festivals in 1951. His other works include *Amelia Goes to the Ball* (1937), *The Saint of Bleeker Street* (1954), *The Last Savage* (1963), and *Help! Help! the Globolinks* (1968). All of these were in the Italian operatic tradition of tonal melody, in which the human voice is given preeminence. Menotti's rhythms were natural and easily remembered and were supported by a light and open orchestration. He also invariably wrote about ideas: "I haven't written one single opera," he said, "that doesn't have some sort of philosophical idea or social statement behind it."[31]

This was especially true of his first full-length, and possibly greatest, opera, *The Consul* (1950). The opera includes fully developed arias, duets, trios, and ensembles, but the composer believed its real strength was its recitatives, which sustained the work's dramatic development. Written in the *verismo* tradition, the opera takes political oppression as its theme. Set in some authoritarian country, the plot concerns the efforts of Magda, the wife of a political suspect, to obtain a visa to leave the country and join her husband in exile. Her failure leads to her suicide. Menotti wrote the libretto for *The Consul* himself, as he did for all his works (typically, it was in English), because he was more comfortable matching the music with his own poetry. The results are extraordinarily powerful, as in Magda's aria:

> *To this we've come:*
> *that men withhold the world from men;*
> *no ship nor shore from him who drowns at sea,*
> *no home nor grave for him who dies on land.*[32]

By choosing a contemporary theme, Menotti hoped to make the work more accessible to the public. *The Consul* premiered on Broadway at the Ethel Barrymore Theater on 15 March 1950. It was greeted with tremendous acclaim and ran for a solid eight months. It then went on a tour that included performances in leading European cities. At La Scala in Milan, it became a victim of the Cold War. At the first performance, somebody shouted "Down with the Americans," and throughout the rest of the performance people blew whistles.[33] The Communists denounced it as blatant anti-Soviet propaganda. However, despite the controversy and criticism, *The Consul* remains one of the most significant operatic works of the post–World War II era.

The Soviet Imperative. In the Soviet Union, composers and directors had to adjust their creative styles to the demands of the state. For example, naturalistic set designs might reproduce the past, but had to reflect more than a desire for authenticity. Socialist realism dictated that realistic sets be socially realistic sets. That is, they had to release the works from their historical period so that they could speak with the voice of the present. The past could only be presented in a manner that reflected positively on the Communist society of the present. Contemporary operas were expected to depict the triumph of Communism. Their characters could be ordinary peasants or heroes fighting the forces of Fascism.

During World War II, the regime had encouraged Soviet composers to write music that would raise morale and reinforce traditional Russian patriotism. This new mandated usefulness made the composers respectable once again. (Sergei Prokofiev, for one, responded with his great epic *War and Peace*.) But the honeymoon ended in 1947.

The regime launched a vicious attack on Vano Muradeli's opera *The Great Friendship*, which the Bolshoi Theater had mounted to commemorate the thirtieth anniversary of the 1917 Bolshevik Revolution. *The Great Friendship* concerned the warm association between the Georgian and Russian peoples. The censors, however, judged the treatment of the subject false, artificial, and symptomatic of the general heresy currently existing among Soviet composers. They called the music weak, confused, and cacophonous and castigated the opera for having no memorable arias. They damned its ear-splitting sounds: "Occasional lines and scenes, making a pretense of melodiousness, are suddenly interrupted by discordant noises, alien to a normal human ear, which produces a depressing effect on the listener."[34] Dimitri Shostakovich, Prokofiev, and Aram Khachaturian were also singled out as composers who had become infatuated with "confused, neuro-pathological combinations" that transformed music "into a chaotic agglomeration of sounds." The organizational committee of the Union of Soviet Composers was denounced for being a "hotbed of formalistic distortions."[35]

From 17 to 26 February 1948, Stalin's deputy Andrei Zhdanov chaired the meetings of the Moscow Composers Union. He denounced its members for formalistic and antidemocratic tendencies and ordered them to come forward one by one to confess their sins. Muradeli praised Zhdanov for encouraging the Soviet composers to fight unswervingly "for the great ideals of building up Communist society in our country." Shostakovich said he was effusively grateful to the party for its criticism and solemnly swore to "try again and again to create symphonic works close to the spirit of the people from the standpoint of ideological subject matter, musical language and form." Prokofiev, who was in poor health and did not attend, made his genuflection in writing. He tried to explain that, in recent years, he had used atonal music only sporadically and without much sympathy, "mainly for the sake of contrast, in order to bring tonal passages to the fore." He said that his fear of creating immobility on the stage had led him to use recitative more than cantilena in his operas, but he promised that his forthcoming *Tale of a Real Man* would include "trios, duets, and contrapuntally developed choruses, for which I will make use of some interesting Northern Russian folk songs [as well as] lucid melody, and as far as possible, a simple harmonic language."[36] The musicians' meeting closed by giving thanks to Stalin for his personal suggestions on the creation of Soviet classical opera. The composers pledged to concentrate on producing realistic music that would reflect the struggles of the Soviet people.

Prokofiev immediately came forth with *A Tale of a Real Man,* a patriotic drama about a World War II pilot who loses both of his legs fighting the Germans. An old commissar in the hospital urges him to conquer his subsequent depression by becoming a real Soviet man. The pilot gets outfitted with wooden legs, climbs back into the cockpit, and returns to the fray. Presumed lost on his last mission, he nevertheless makes it back and is reunited with his fiancée, who loves him despite his handicap. The two embrace and look forward to their new life together. The music was perhaps the most traditional of the composer's works, featuring some popular-style melodies, even a waltz and a rumba; nevertheless, it was deemed not melodious enough. The authorities condemned it as modernistic and antimelodic trickery and denounced its treatment of the Soviet people as a gross distortion. Though already in rehearsal, the work was summarily withdrawn. It was not performed publicly until 1960.

Censorship also continued to dog the path of Shostakovich, who also tried to make his peace with the regime. He even acted as a cultural ambassador abroad and joined the government in its attacks on the musical avant-garde. Even after the death of Stalin, he remained cautious, composing within the general guidelines of socialist realism. In 1959, he wrote *Moscow, the Cherry Trees,* a musical comedy about the current housing shortage. He also revised his *Lady Macbeth of the Mtzensk District,* which had been damned in 1936 as "fidgety, screaming, neurotic . . . coarse, primitive, and vulgar."[37] It was difficult to tell how political or honest the revision was because doing musical penance was not as pressing in the Khrushchev era as it had been under Stalin. However, the new version, renamed

Katerina Izmaylova, did soften the earlier work's dissonant edge in an attempt to deliver it from its "eccentricities."

At the same time the Soviets were forcing conformity on their own composers, they continued to attack those of Western Europe and the United States with increasing ferocity. Tikhon Khrennikov, the newly appointed leader of the Composers Union, claimed he was unable to name a single Western composer who was not infected with "formalistic diseases, subjectivism and mysticism, and lack of ideological principles." The most odious of these reactionaries was Igor Stravinsky, with Paul Hindemith, Ernst Krenek, Alban Berg, Benjamin Britten, Max Brand, and Gian-Carlo Menotti not far behind. Khrennikov stigmatized their works as a "reversion to the primitive savage cultures of prehistoric society; eroticism is glorified along with psychopathology, sexual perversion, amorality and the shamelessness of the contemporary bourgeois heroes of the Twentieth Century."[38] Only after Stalin's death was this harsh judgment abandoned. In the 1960s, Stravinsky was finally allowed to visit his homeland where he was treated to performances of his works.

The Blockbuster Musical. In 1990, Peter Hoffmann, one of Germany's most famous Wagnerian tenors, decided to take a vacation from the opera stage. He signed a two-year contract to portray the title role in the Hamburg production of Andrew Lloyd Webber's *Phantom of the Opera*. Hoffmann, having sung a full range of music from classical to rock and roll, wanted to perform one of the most significant roles written for the contemporary stage. His defection highlighted what many people had known for some time—that Andrew Lloyd Webber was a remarkable musical talent. Lloyd Webber became a superstar in an age when that description was rarely applied to composers; he was a throwback to the sacred monsters of the nineteenth century. Lloyd Webber's musical antecedents were diverse; he drew as much from the great American musical dramas of Victor Herbert, Jerome Kern, and Irving Berlin as from the grand opera lyricism of Giacomo Puccini.

At a time when the New York and London musical stages were languishing in nonharmonic doldrums and grand opera was becoming more allegorical, thematically more moral and philosophical, Lloyd Webber brought modern musical theater back to life with a string of successes including *Jesus Christ Super Star* (1971), *Evita* (1976), *Cats* (1981), *Starlight Express* (1984), *The Phantom of the Opera* (1986), and *Aspects of Love* (1989). Although he was often accused of being superficial and facile, he wrote music people enjoyed hearing and wanted to hear again. If his orchestrations did not quite measure up to the sophistication of the masters, his tunes were eminently hummable and spoke to the desires of a latter-day romantic age as much the music of the great composers of the past did to theirs. His stories were basic, and he had no social or political ax to grind. His shows had an international appeal. *The Phantom of the Opera* with its great themes of profane and happily-ever-after love enchanted audiences simultaneously in London, New York, Los Angeles, Hamburg, Tokyo, Toronto, Stockholm, Vienna, and Chicago. Moreover, *Phantom*, like other Lloyd Webber hits, created an entire industry. Its spin-offs included cast albums, books, souvenir programs, T-shirts, coffee mugs, pins, posters, bathroom towels, and Phantom masks.

Lloyd Webber's success, though not surpassed, was at least duplicated by the French composer Claude-Michel Schönberg, who gave the world the two megahits of *Les Misérables* (1980) and *Miss Saigon* (1990). These musicals, also written in a traditional operatic style, shared a common organizational link with *Phantom* in that all three were produced by British impresario Cameron Mackintosh. (He had also been responsible for the "now and forever" mounting of *Cats*, which in 1991 entered its second decade of continuous performances at the New London Theater.) In the age of the celebrity, these shows were virtually star-proof because they depended more on their comfortably melodious scores and energetic staging than on the personalities singing them.

When American composer Leonard Bernstein saw *Miss Saigon* on Broadway, he realized after five minutes that he was not going to hear any musical talent in the score, so he "just sat back and watched the lighting cues and had a wonderful time."[39] What he saw, among other stage effects and overblown production numbers, was a helicopter drop from the fly space and hover over the set to reenact the flight of the Americans from the embassy at Saigon during the Vietnam War. Rarely had musicals created such joy in going to the theater. As Mackintosh acknowledged, "You can remind people of your existence, but you cannot persuade. Word of mouth does that. In a long run, that is what any show depends on."[40]

In the six years after its London premiere in September 1986, *Les Misérables* was performed 12,200 times in twenty-three worldwide productions; its performances were seen by 19.2 million people.[41] The story, following Victor Hugo's novel, is set in France in 1830—a period that might not seem to have much historical relevance for modern audiences. Yet when they left the theater after hearing the last rousing chorus of the musical's revolutionary theme, many were ready to return to Louis Philippe's Paris—at least on the stage—to hear the rousing chorus about revolution and the rights of the people to be free:

> *Do you hear the people sing?*
> *Say, do you hear the distant drums?*
> *It is the future that they bring*
> *When tomorrow comes.*[42]

The Rock Mania

The New World Influence. The Americanization of European musical tastes had begun in the years immediately prior to World War I when Tin Pan Alley songs were imported into British music halls. In 1912, the American Ragtime Octette did a turn around the continent. The new beat influenced such serious composers as Claude Debussy ("Golliwog's Cakewalk") and Darius Milhaud ("The Cow on the Roof") as well as Igor Stravinsky. Following World War I, American jazz carved out a permanent place in European culture. One branch developed into the commercial, sweet variety known as swing; the other, much prized by connoisseurs, remained raucous and more directly attached to its black African roots. The French called this version *le jazz hot*.

The American musical presence in Europe was boosted by the actual physical presence of American soldiers in both world wars. After 1945, the Americans not only stayed around as occupation troops, but their Armed Forces Radio Network beamed American popular music all over Europe, reducing the normal waiting period for cultural transmission to zero. Any European with a radio could now hear American popular music as soon as it appeared in the United States. American popular singers became as popular as movie stars. In the early 1950s, balladeers such as Frank Sinatra, Johnny Ray, and Frankie Laine seemed to epitomize the relaxed, comfortable American life-style that most of Europe's youth wanted to emulate.

Europeans, plagued by class traditions, were slow to develop the American rock and roll teenage subculture, but this changed as increasing economic independence gave young people the means to indulge their musical tastes without worrying what others thought. They listened to American rock and roll singers like Elvis Presley, Chuck Berry, and Little Richard—all three of whom burst on the musical scene around 1954–1955. In 1955, Bill Haley's "Shake, Rattle, and Roll" made the British record charts. The spirit of revolt and overt sexuality that came with such songs was irresistible. In England, Teddy Boys and Rockers—lower-class and lower-middle-class youth groups, who developed their own exaggerated masculine subculture of violence and vandalism[43]—were particularly addicted to loud pulsating music. Youths in other European cities followed suit. Hamburg, Germany, became a sort of proving ground where would-be emulators could play loud, fast, raw music.[44] The groups that came here were often more remarkable for their frenzy and noise than their talent. However, among the groups playing a gig in one of Hamburg's nightclubs was an unknown combo from Liverpool, England, which called itself the Beatles.

The Rise of the Groups. In 1961, Brian Epstein, a Liverpool record store owner, went to hear the Beatles playing in a Liverpool dive called the Cavern. The place was located in a cellar. Epstein found them "ill-presented, unkempt . . . with untidy hair."[45] Still, he liked their hard rock and rhythm and blues "Mersey Sound" and became their manager.[46] He was determined to make them bigger than Elvis.

Epstein first worked on elevating their social status. He got them to cut out their smart-alecky stage repartee, curb their drinking, and limit their smoking. He had them appear in public wearing conservative narrow-lapel mohair jackets with their hair in bangs—not too long, not too short—always properly washed and combed. Frequently, they wore ties and black nylon socks. All this upgrading carried the risk that the Beatles would lose some of their lower-class fans who identified with the scruffy, working-class look. Epstein, though, created something more universally appealing and decidedly more commercial.[47] Establishing the collective identity of a group constituted a break with the solo performer acts of the 1950s.

The Beatles' music was not only upbeat and melodic, it was written largely by themselves. Their song "I Want to Hold Your Hand" (1964), which quickly climbed to the top of the charts, was hailed as the most popular rock song since Elvis's "All Shook Up." The Beatles sang it to instant success in New York in February 1964 when they appeared on the "Ed Sullivan Show," the TV vaudeville hour that launched their American career. For foreign rock stars, success in the United States was essential in the climb to superstardom.

Almost singlehandedly, the Beatles launched a second pop explosion—the last the rock and roll craze produced. According to true believers, the advent of the Beatles brought about a significant shift in people's "sexual behavior and even helped change their political beliefs."[48] The Beatles' fans regarded them as demigods and copied their hair style, manner of speech, and dress. They lined the walls of their rooms with Beatles' pictures. Every detail of the Beatles' personal lives became a matter of international concern. Drummer Ringo Starr's tonsillectomy in December 1964 set off a worldwide vigil. In 1985, Queen Elizabeth II gave each member of the group an M.B.E. (Member of the British Empire).

In August 1966, with Beatlemania at its height, guitarist John Lennon told a reporter from the *London Evening Standard* that Christianity would eventually end. Lennon claimed that the Beatles were "more popular than Jesus," adding that, although Jesus was right, the religious leader's "disciples were thick and ordinary." Lennon confessed, "It's them twisting it that ruins it for me."[49] The British took the remarks in stride, after all Lennon had not said the Beatles were better than

Protected by New York police officers, **the Beatles make a hasty exit** from Carnegie Hall to avoid getting crushed by enthusiastic admirers. The Liverpool quartet just played to two sold-out houses in a pair of Lincoln's Day concerts on 12 February 1964.

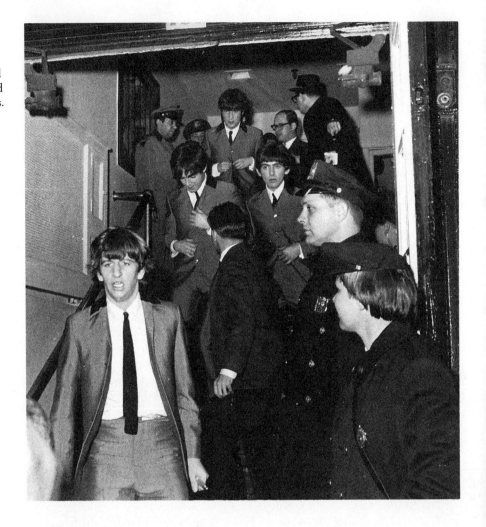

Jesus, only that they were more popular, which to some sounded plausible. In the United States, however, the words hit hard. Many Americans were indignant at such blasphemy. In the South, they threw Beatles' records on bonfires; many radio stations stopped playing their music. There were even threats of violence. The Beatles were scheduled to begin an American tour. Something had to be done to calm the furor.

Lennon was pressured into making an apology of sorts. He did so in Chicago. "I wasn't saying whatever they're saying I was saying. I'm sorry I said it really. I never meant it to be a lousy antireligious thing. I apologize if that will make you happy."[50] The tour could now proceed. It was a great success, but it was the last the Beatles ever made. Afterwards, they satisfied their screaming fans with performances in a recording studio. Their popularity did not diminish. The release of their album *Sgt. Pepper's Lonely Hearts Club Band* in 1967 prompted one reviewer to hail it as a major factor in bringing Western civilization closer to unification than it had been "since the Congress of Vienna in 1815."[51]

Many of the rock groups that followed the Beatles were more outrageous. They had more loose ends, were more raucous and disrespectful, and were certainly nastier and more petulant. They were also degenerate, sexy, and antisocial. The

Rolling Stones, who presumed to replace the Beatles as trendsetters, cast themselves in the role of outlaws, leaving their hair uncombed and dressing as if they had just sauntered in off the mean streets.[52] They were arrogant and lewd, but they fulfilled their fans' fantasies about glamour, success, and fame. One critic wrote: "More than the Beatles, whose personal appeal derived in large part from their talent as songmakers, the people would gladly pay to see the Rolling Stones just stand around and look like pop stars."[53] From their debut at the Crawdaddy Club in Richmond, England, in February 1963, they grew into an international cult. Their loud, persistent songs often with explicit lyrics were sometimes banned. Where the Beatles wanted to hold your hand, the Stones proposed "Let's Spend the Night Together" (1967). The Beatles projected a certain mellow boyish bonhomie, the Stones a high-decibel wickedness. Members of the group had brushes with the law: they smoked pot, were into various other controlled substances, and had wild parties with nude women. It was said they practiced Satanism. All this added to their mystique and popularity.

The Rolling Stones style was much copied, especially in the United States, but it reached its height in the British youth culture of the 1960s. The fans apparently cared more about the Stones' message of a liberated life-style and their doctrine of liberation from social and sexual frustration than they did about the quality of the group's musicianship. Still, despite all their antics, the Stones sometimes seemed sincere about creating good music.

That could not be said about many other practitioners of rock, especially these groups that played a new form known as punk rock, a genre that took musical self-indulgence to its raucous, uncompromising limits. Typical was a group known as the Sex Pistols who debuted in 1975. The ensemble was completely manufactured. Lead singer John Lydon (a.k.a. Jonny Rotten) had been recruited primarily for his ability to sneer and posture. He had little musical experience before he joined. As part of his performance, Rotten would throw empty beer bottles at the audience, blow his nose, and make obscene gestures. During the performance, other members of the quartet might spit in the air, vomit, or become even more vulgar. Sometimes they wore safety pins through their cheeks. The music of the Sex Pistols was repetitive, tribal, electronic, and ear-shattering, but their showmanship carried the day. Sex Pistol performances were hectic, outrageous, and vulgar.[54] They touted their drug and alcohol abuse and their sexual prowess. They intended to be ugly, and their songs reflected it.

Nevertheless, the group seemed to be capable of creating the true sense of community that many rock fans craved, while being its lowest common denominator. In Britain, punk rock spoke for those who felt they had no stake in the present society. Many of its fans were unemployed and cared nothing for their country's traditions.

One of the Sex Pistols' ditties, "God Save the Queen," called Elizabeth II a moron. The song was released during the Silver Jubilee of her reign. Another, "Anarchy in the U.K.," extolled nihilism: "I'm an antichrist, Don't know what I want, But I know how to get it, I want to destroy."[55] These songs appeared in *Never Mind the Bollocks, Here's the Sex Pistols*, an album that was briefly banned from display in Britain. The record company that released it subsequently canceled its contract with the group because some executives thought the Sex Pistols were preaching anarchy.[56] The group lasted less than five years, destroyed by its own excesses. Rotten feared he was being turned into something chic and quit. Lead bassist John Ritchie (a.k.a. Sid Vicious) died of an overdose of heroin after he had murdered his girl friend. The story of their relationship became the subject of the Alex Cox film *Sid and Nancy* (1986).

The Sex Pistols' squalid values represented the darkest side of rock culture, an exercise in outrageous media hype and little else. The group guitarist Steve Jones confessed that their antisocial posture was a sham. He said he only joined the group to meet girls and get drunk. "I was really a football hooligan. I went to matches and bashed people. Punk was the perfect way to do what I wanted to do—cause trouble—and get paid for it."[57]

Outside Britain, the boom and blast school of musicality also had aficionados. The amount of money rock music generated, the number of careers it supported, the hefty amount of taxes and revenues it produced appeared to make it worthy of respect. The rock movement produced a succession of talented musicians and frauds. Every time the style appeared exhausted and about to fade, another singer or group would come along to give it a new vitality and perhaps take the movement into yet another, although not necessarily a better, direction.

POSTSCRIPT   Art and music are dialectical: one movement contains the seeds of its own transformation or, at least, the means through which new schools can be developed and different techniques can be tested and formed. The period after World War II was one of significant cultural creativity, although whether it surpassed the great golden or silver ages of yesteryear was debatable.

In the visual arts, the modern synthesis, coming on the heels of the great artistic outpourings of the past, had yet to run its course and, considering its variety, was conceivably impossible to exhaust, much less objectively evaluate. The resultant frustration may have encouraged the very lack of standards that carried artistic expression to the point of absurdity. That many conscientious, talented artists were still at work encouraged people to ask questions about the fundamental nature of artistic creation and the basic definition of an artist. While some had a sneaking suspicion that much work being passed off as art was really a product of adolescent self-indulgence or even fraud, the fact remained that no matter how outlandish some new form of artistic expression might be, a museum or gallery would take it seriously and afford it space.

Art, though, like music evolves. It does not necessarily progress or improve. So the fight over what constitutes art continues. The traditionalists held that art was about values that were communicated by beauty and that there was no such thing as ugly art. Nor was art created for itself. Art, they maintained, was not a suicide pact that people had to follow even when it went over a cliff. Others said that art was the fulfillment of a human need, something that made people think and feel at the same time. It was something that took them someplace they had not been before even if it involved that great leap into space.

ENDNOTES

1. Milan's La Scala, for example, reinforced the religious identity by opening its season on 7 December, the feast day of Saint Ambrose, the city's patron saint.

2. Joseph Wechsberg, *The Opera* (London: Weidenfeld and Nicolson, 1972), 245.

3. Cima Star, "Modern Art: It's Awful," *International Tribune*, 16 June 1970.

4. H. W. Janson, *History of Art* (Englewood Cliffs, N.J.: Prentice-Hall, 1986), 695–715.

5. Norbert Lynton, *The Story of Modern Art* (Ithaca, N.Y.: Cornell University Press, 1980), 226–46; Charles Harrison, "Abstract Expressionism," in Tony Richardson and Nikos Stangos, ed., *Concepts of Modern Art* (New York: Harper and Row, 1974), 168–201.

6. Pollock said there was no such thing as "American painting" any more than there could be American physics or American mathematics. The basic problems of contemporary artistic creation were universal. Jean-Clarence Lambert, *La peinture abstraite* (Lausanne: Editions Rencontre, 1967), 71.

7. Jean Bazaine interview, L'Oeil, *The Selective Eye* (New York: Random House, 1955), 50.

8. Lambert, *La peinture abstraite*, 149–50.

9. *The Selective Eye*, 50.

10. Lambert, *La peinture abstraite*, 178–79.

11. Edward Lucie-Smith, *Late Modern: The Visual Arts since 1945* (New York: Praeger, 1969), 135.

12. Kirk Varnedoe and Adam Gopnik, *High and Low: Modern Culture and Popular Art* (New York: Museum of Modern Art, 1990), 351.

13. Ellen H. Johnson, *Modern Art and the Object: A Century of Changing Attitudes* (New York: Harper and Row, 1976), 156–65.

14. H. Harvard Arnason, *Modern Art* (New York: Harry Abrams, n.d.), 575–601.

15. Varnedoe and Gopnik, *High and Low*, 212.

16. Richardson and Stangos, *Concepts of Modern Art*, 231.

17. Gerstner gave his description in 1964. Frank Popper, *Art—Action and Participation* (New York: New York University Press, 1975), 15.

18. *Time*, 14 November 1969, 50.

19. *Time*, 21 October 1991, 99.

20. *Time*, 22 November 1968, 75.

21. Ibid., 77.

22. Ibid., 18 December 1972, 112.

23. Robert Hughes, "The Decline and Fall of the Avant-Garde," *Time*, 18 December 1972, 111–12.

24. Edward Lucie-Smith, "Pop Art" in Richardson and Stangos, *Concepts of Modern Art*, 226.

25. *Time*, 24 September 1973, 102.

26. Stanley Sadie, ed., *The New Grove Dictionary of Music and Musicians*, vol. 13 (London: Macmillan, 1980), 636.

27. Günther Schneider-Siemssen, *Die Bühne als kosmischer Raum* (Vienna: Bergland Verlag, 1976).

28. Rudolf Hartmann, ed., *Opera* (New York: William Morrow, 1977), 55.

29. Wechsberg, *The Opera*, 250.

30. Hartmann, *Opera*, 129.

31. Joel Honig, "The Menotti Theorem," *Opera News* (June 1991), 15.

32. Gian-Carlo Menotti, *The Consul* (New York: G. Shirmer, 1950), act II, scene 2.

33. John Gruen, *Menotti: A Biography* (New York: Macmillan, 1978), 99–102.

34. Nicolas Slonimsky, *Music since 1900* (New York: Coleman-Ross, 1949), 684.

35. Ibid., 684.

36. David Ewen, *Encyclopedia of the Opera* (New York: Hill and Wang, 1955), 494.

37. Sadie, *The New Grove Dictionary of Music*, 19:265.

38. Ibid., 695.

39. David Patrick Sterns, "Bernstein's Last Hurrah," *Connoisseur* (September 1991), 106.

40. William A. Henry, "They Just Keep Rolling Along," *Time*, 2 September 1991, 73.
41. Ibid., 73.
42. Alain Boubil and James Fenton, *Les Misérables* (London: Alain Boubil Music, Ltd.: 1985).
43. The Teds adopted exaggerated Edwardian dress; the Rockers donned black leather motorcycle costumes to fit their favorite mode of transportation.
44. Jim Miller, *The Rolling Stone Illustrated History of Rock and Roll* (New York: Random House, 1980), 170.
45. Ray Coleman, *The Man Who Made the Beatles: An Intimate Biography of Brian Epstein* (New York: McGraw-Hill, 1989), xi.
46. David Dalton and Lenny Kaye, *Rock 100* (New York: Grosset and Dunlap, 1977), 89–94.
47. Ibid., 100–102.
48. Miller, *Rolling Stone Illustrated History*, 181.
49. Dalton and Kaye, *Rock 100*, 281.
50. Ibid., 283.
51. Miller, *Rolling Stone Illustrated History*, 183.
52. See Tim Dowley, *The Rolling Stones* (New York: Hippocrene Books, 1983).
53. Lloyd Grossman, *A Social History of Rock Music from the Greasers to Glitter Rock* (New York: David McKay, 1976), 49.
54. Miller, *Rolling Stone Illustrated History*, 451–62.
55. "The Sex Pistols Are Here," *Time*, 16 January 1978, 62.
56. "The Sex Pistols," *Stereo* (February 1978), 132.
57. Irwin Stambler, ed., *Encyclopedia of Pop Rock and Song* (New York: St. Martin's Press, 1989), 609.

PART THREE

THE REUNIFICATION OF EUROPE, 1962–1991

CHAPTER 8

A TIME FOR DETENTE, 1962–1985

PREFACE   The Europeans were increasingly reluctant to follow the superpowers wherever they might lead. They were naturally uneasy that their foreign policy was being fashioned in Washington and Moscow. Eastern Europeans had learned they must accept a subservient place in the Warsaw Pact bloc or risk Soviet intervention. The countries in the West had come to expect more freedom of action, but within the North Atlantic Treaty Organization (NATO), they were still very much junior partners. They never felt that the Americans took their advice seriously. President John F. Kennedy seemed an exception, however. He appeared to be a different kind of cold warrior, more sympathetic and more willing to listen than his predecessors. Relatively young, friendly, and handsome, he made nice speeches and liked to show off his pretty wife. Many European politicians tried to develop their own Kennedy-like style while ordinary people kept a picture of him in their homes.

Kennedy's recklessness during the Cuban missile crisis of October 1962 helped jar the Europeans back to reality. Nikita Khrushchev touched off the confrontation by trying to put medium-range weapons close to American soil, but Kennedy's reaction was disturbingly reckless. Without consulting his allies or trying to persuade Khrushchev to retreat through quiet, diplomatic channels, he provocatively threatened the Soviets with nuclear war via television. Although the governments of the NATO countries supported his action, Europeans nevertheless believed that Kennedy was risking war to show his voters how tough he could be. They asked how all this posturing might affect their own security. Cynics among them suspected that Khrushchev and Kennedy were accomplices in a gigantic theatrical presentation.

The crisis begged many questions. Was the crisis worth the risk? Had a few missiles on the island of Cuba really changed the current balance of power? Was not the United States ringing the Soviet Union with even more menacing weapons? Could not the confrontation in the Caribbean have produced an explosion in Europe? Would the Soviets react by making another move against Berlin? Some Europeans feared the worst and made a run on food stores. Newspapers expressed greater concerns. The *Manchester Weekly Guardian* was shocked that the Americans would even consider dropping an atomic bomb.[1] André Fontaine of *Le Monde* observed darkly that "never since the last war ended has any confrontation between the Big Two so closely grazed the brink of catastrophe."[2] In the end, most Western Europeans still believed in the worth of the Atlantic alliance, but some were more than willing to call down a plague on both superpower houses.

The crisis led to a renewed arms race. The Soviets felt they had to erase the humiliation by building up their nuclear arsenal, especially in intercontinental ballistic missiles. The Americans pushed the development of Polaris missiles, which were fired from submarines, and other, land-based missiles. They began a new round of talks with their partners in NATO to facilitate the new strategy, especially the British on whose land the new weapons would primarily be based. They also beefed up their military presence throughout the rest of the alliance countries. Western European opposition leaders responded by calling for more independence in national defense policy. Antinuclear protests increased. Although the British agreed to equip their submarines with the new Polaris missiles, they refused to have these units integrated totally within NATO.[3] French president Charles de Gaulle went a step further. He removed his military forces entirely from the NATO command.

The Soviets, recovering from the desultory Khrushchev era, convinced themselves that their ideology was triumphant. With optimistic boldness, they pushed their influence into parts of the world heretofore considered off-limits—Ethiopia, Angola, and Latin America—and reinforced the centralization of their own government. However, their Achilles heel continued to be Eastern Europe where the threat of defection was constantly present. In 1968, it was the turn of Czechoslovakia. The Kremlin, however, did not want a repeat of its ruthless crushing of the Hungarians in 1956 and handled the Czechoslovaks with relative restraint. The Soviet leaders wanted to keep the lid on the satellites, but they tried to do so by stimulating a greater willingness to cooperate. They also hoped to gain access to Western technology, which was essential to invigorate their flagging economy. Finally, although the Soviet leaders were slow to realize it, the Soviet Union no longer had the resources to project its will as it had done in the past.

The United States also encountered limitations on its power, for which, in a sense, it had only itself to blame. Massive expenditures on weapons of war had diverted resources from problems at home. The Americans had enhanced their influence in Europe, but in doing so, they had also helped those they once nurtured to grow sturdy. The creation of the European Community was an American success story, but offspring do not remain children forever and often grow up to challenge their parents. The Cold War had outlived its usefulness as a means of boosting Western integration. If the Europeans wanted to increase their prosperity, if the Soviets and the Americans wanted to survive as great powers, they would have to end their rivalries in Europe. But old habits were hard to break.

THE INTEGRATION OF WESTERN EUROPE

The Politics of Grandeur

The End of the War in Algeria. Before France could again become the paramount power in Western Europe, the Algerian war had to end. But ending it was a dangerous task because those who had helped return Charles de Gaulle to power expected him to do everything possible to keep Algeria part of France. De Gaulle, though, came to realize that the Algerian affair could destroy French unity; and he therefore made secret contact with the Algerian rebel leaders to explore ways to bring the conflict to an end—hopefully with a maximum amount of respect for French rights. It was a difficult juggling act.

The National Liberation Front leaders were stubborn; they wanted France to withdraw from Algeria unconditionally. The *colons*, or Algerian settlers, were equally intransigent. They wanted to maintain their power and position, and when they got wind of the behind-the-scenes negotiations, they took to the streets in protest. In January 1960, a group of extremists seized control of downtown Algiers and had to be dispersed by military force. When de Gaulle pushed ahead, opening up formal talks with the rebel leadership at the resort city of Evian-les-Bains on Lake Geneva, the opposition went underground. They formed a Secret Army Organization (*Organization de l'armée secrète* or OAS) and began a campaign of terror, bringing the war home. In Paris, bombs exploded at the place Vendôme, the stock exchange, and even in the Palais-Bourbon, home of the French National Assembly. In April 1961, a cabal of generals, led by Maurice Challe and Raoul Salan, took control of Algiers and tried to rally the colonial garrisons and the Foreign Legion for an invasion of France itself. The government was clearly worried. De Gaulle went on television to forbid all French citizens to obey the rebels' orders. For the first time in history, a president of France ordered soldiers to disobey commands of their superior officers. The revolt collapsed after three days. Many professional soldiers were sympathetic to the mutineers, but had no intention of jeopardizing their careers for a venture that lacked a reasonable chance of success. Conscripts, who made up the bulk of troop strength in Algeria, were not eager to join a war against their own government. De Gaulle emerged shaken, but triumphant. More than ever, he was determined to bring the war to an end.

Most of the French people were sick of the bloodshed that threatened the lives of their sons and drained the country of its other vital resources. In March 1962, 90 percent of the voters endorsed the Evian accords in a referendum that recognized the sovereignty of Algeria. Although the treaty contained safeguards for the property and personal security of those colons who chose to remain in Algeria, the French settlers left the country in droves. Almost 800,000 came to France, a country they little knew, and whose inhabitants they feared would treat them with hostility. Their suspicions were exaggerated. Within a generation, the pieds-noirs were largely assimilated into French society.

De Gaulle's Grand Design. At the same time de Gaulle ended the war in Algeria, he took vigorous steps to end the inflation that had plagued the country since the end of World War II and that was fueled by a dramatic increase in demand. De Gaulle's financial experts carried out a policy of austerity. They devalued the franc by 17.5 percent in order to attract foreign investment and boost exports. Then, they increased taxes and reduced government expenditures. They also ended certain subsidies to nationalized industries, ordering them to balance receipts with expenses. These measures helped change the traditionally protectionist nature of the French economy; protectionist policies had been adopted in the first place because French goods and services (aside from certain luxury products) were poor competitors on the world market. The planners realized that the economy had to be globalized if the country were to hold its own with its partners in the Common Market and with the major industrial powers in the rest of the world.[4] As a vital element in this process, the French franc had to become convertible.

De Gaulle created the "new franc," a hard currency achieved by moving the decimal point two notches to the left, thereby converting 500 old francs to 5 new francs. But there was more substance to the new franc than that. The new unit was a symbol of de Gaulle's determination to achieve monetary stability and to avoid another round of inflation that would cause further devaluation. The government therefore began to balance its budget and improve efficiency. Creating a hard currency was part of de Gaulle's plan to make Paris the principal money market of the European Community. Managing the French economy was his way of restoring France to its place as a great power, able to counterbalance the increasing importance of Germany and determine the destiny of Europe.

The policy got off to a good start. French goods became less expensive; increased sales abroad boosted foreign reserves; and production continued to rise.[5] In 1963, France adopted a stabilization plan aimed at controlling prices and wages and at reducing the budget deficits. The government then tried to stimulate the economy by trying to funnel private savings into capital investment and to increase the international competitiveness of French companies by making them larger. De Gaulle realized that even though the world was getting smaller and nations were becoming more interdependent, French industry had to develop economies of scale.

De Gaulle also wanted to free himself from the day-to-day management of politics and establish an independent base from which he could dominate the political process. Under the 1958 constitution, a college of 80,000 electors chosen by the local units of government elected the president. De Gaulle wanted this procedure changed so he could be elected by direct popular vote, thereby giving him a true national constituency. In 1962, he presented this proposal to the French electorate, which adopted it by a 62 percent majority. Later that year, the Gaullist Union for the New Republic swept the parliamentary elections, giving him control of the legislature. He replaced the premier, Michel Debré, whom he did not consider a very effective manager of domestic affairs, with Georges Pompidou, whom he was grooming as his successor. Now de Gaulle could concentrate his efforts almost exclusively on trying to increase French influence abroad. "France cannot be France without grandeur," he had written in his memoirs.[6] He wanted to steer a middle course between the superpowers, with France holding the balance of power among the states of Western Europe and in the Third World.

It was essential that France not lose ground to Germany. France had an edge militarily because it possessed the atomic bomb, but this alone was not enough. De Gaulle wanted Germany's support in creating a European Political Union, a new organization that would have its own parliamentary assembly and would preside over the reform of NATO. De Gaulle could no longer tolerate NATO in its American-dominated form. He artfully concealed his intention to use the new arrangement as a springboard for world leadership by convincing Konrad Adenauer that the union was a means through which Germany could enhance its own international status. But convincing other European leaders proved much harder, and the scheme never got off the ground. This failure prompted de Gaulle to diminish British influence in European affairs in order to establish a bilateral arrangement with West Germany.

A Franco-German treaty was signed in Paris on 22 January 1963.[7] The agreement obliged the two nations to consult on all foreign policy questions concerning the other members of the European Community and the states of Eastern Europe. They also agreed to hold mutual discussions on anything involving NATO, carry on joint research in the development of armaments, and harmonize their military strategy and tactics. The treaty did not mention nuclear weapons—Adenauer was not interested in acquiring them. De Gaulle wanted German technical know-how, but did not want to share French results. He hoped that Europe would one day be able to defend itself rather than having to rely on the United States, a country he doubted had any long-range commitment to European security.

The treaty was the high-water mark in his attempt to bolster French influence through an association with Germany. It was also the last foreign policy association of de Gaulle and Adenauer. The German chancellor retired later that year and was replaced by Ludwig Erhard, a man who did not hold an association with France in such high regard. De Gaulle, however, continued to pursue the policy of independence by developing his own country's nuclear deterrence.[8] The French could not possibly match the nuclear capacity of the United States, so their *force de frappe* (strike force) was intended to be more diplomatic than military and was aimed primarily at reinforcing French influence in European and world affairs. Ironically, though, it would also ensure that the Americans would not abandon Europe, since the use of French nuclear weapons automatically would involve the United States.

In 1965, de Gaulle, now seventy-five years old, ran for reelection as president of France. Expecting an easy victory against his two challengers, he was dismayed when he received only 44 percent of the vote and was forced into a runoff election with François Mitterrand. Mitterrand had the support of most of the parties of the Left, including the Communists. In the second round, de Gaulle won by 55 percent, hardly a landslide considering who he was. Nevertheless, he did not feel that he should significantly alter his policy of national greatness. In 1966, in a further display of independence, he withdrew his country from the military structure of the NATO alliance. France remained part of the NATO political structure, however. (As a result, NATO headquarters was moved from Paris to Brussels.) De Gaulle, who did not view Soviet westward expansion as a realistic eventuality, felt the American troop presence in his country provided less protection than his *force de frappe*. Besides, France could still enjoy American nuclear protection. Thus, in all but an extreme emergency, the Europeans themselves would maintain the European balance of power. However, the decision to go it alone so strained French resources that it threatened social stability at home. In playing to the world, de Gaulle had neglected the mounting discontent of his own people.

The Events of May 1968. The end of the Gaullist era began with a student protest at the University of Nanterre in the Paris suburbs. The leaders, radicalized by the war in Vietnam and abuses in the educational system, put forth a vague leftist program that called for the support of "democratic" forces in the United States and in the Federal Republic of Germany. Some radicals, hoping to bring down the bourgeois system, raised abstract, philosophical questions about the validity of hierarchical institutions as a valid basis for modern French society. The students arrogated to themselves the right to use force against those who did not agree with their lofty pretensions of social reform. The protest spread to Paris proper where the demonstrators were joined by young workers. Many of these workers were not yet members of unions and felt threatened by the high rate of unemployment in their age group, which made their jobs insecure; they found radical politics appealing. Demonstrations on the Left Bank on 3 May 1968 led the police to occupy the Sorbonne, the seat of the science and letters faculty of the University of Paris. The police beat the demonstrators with billy clubs and made arrests willy-nilly. Soon the Latin Quarter looked like a war zone. Police cars were stoned, autos were overturned, pavements were torn up, and trees were cut down. Fourteen barricades were thrown up on the avenue Gay-Lussac. The smell of tear gas hung over the area like a pall. On 13 May, a crowd estimated at 650,000 people, which included the leaders of the opposition, like Socialists Mitterrand and Guy Mollet, converged on the place Denfert-Rochereau and demanded de Gaulle's resignation. At the same time, students occupied important university buildings, and de Gaulle's opponents in the National Assembly tried to introduce a motion of censure. Despite the unrest, de Gaulle left for Bucharest to visit Romanian president Nicolae Ceausescu to pursue his East/West policy of mediation. The revolt continued.

A wave of strikes swept the city. At one time, between 9 and 10 million workers, out of a total labor force of 17 million, stopped work. Unlike the students, the striking workers had bread-and-butter grievances. They were protesting the Gaullist policy of austerity and stabilization that had reduced their standard of living. They wanted an increase in the minimum wage and an improvement in benefits. The gap between skilled and unskilled labor had become larger, and many young workers sensed that they were bearing the brunt of an austerity policy that was benefiting chiefly the bankers and the technocrats. The protest extended to other classes of workers as well. Wildcat strikes brought services to a standstill. Trains did not run, and airplanes did not fly. Customs officers abandoned their posts.[9] Gasoline scarcities developed. The post offices were closed. The workers seized control of the Renault factory while the students "liberated" the Sorbonne and declared it under permanent occupation.[10]

De Gaulle hastily returned from Romania. On 24 May, he tried to restore calm by making a television address to the nation as he had done during the Algerian war. The appeal did not work, and the disorder continued. But time was on his side. The demonstrators had difficulty agreeing on a common program of reform. Paris was a mess. Trash and broken glass littered the streets, making it hard for people to go about their daily tasks. There were wanton acts of vandalism. A crowd of students attacked the stock exchange and, crying "down with the temple of capitalism," set it on fire. Automobiles were smashed as symbols of the consumer society. A great deal of the destruction occurred in the more modest sections of the city and had the greatest effect on people of lesser means. Cafés remained shuttered, bakeries and food stores stayed closed. Sympathy rapidly turned to disgust.

Many young workers now discovered they had little in common with the students, many of whom came from the comfortable middle classes and were, in fact, the offspring of the government ministers, company presidents, diplomats, and industrialists of the French elite. The unfocused kind of revolution that the silver-spoon students advocated offered uncertain rewards for unanswered questions. The skilled workers, who were already enjoying the benefits of modern materialism— cars, electric appliances, and electronic gadgets—never really joined the protest. Farmers, whose standard of living had increased since the end of the war, also remained aloof. The Communist party, under great pressure to throw in its lot with the militants, had actually found much in Gaullism with which it could agree, especially the policy to weaken the American-led alliance. They did not want a revolution under such tenuous circumstances. The younger workers booed the party union officers when they tried to restore order in the factories, but the leadership finally succeeded in regaining control over its followers.

On 30 May, de Gaulle made another address on the radio. This time he was better received. De Gaulle dissolved the National Assembly and ordered new elections. He transformed the prefects into commissioners of the Republic, ordering them to take extraordinary steps to maintain order.[11] This was the de Gaulle of old, successfully beating back the forces of anarchy. The police threw the students out of the Sorbonne, cleaners swept the trash from the streets, glaziers repaired the broken windows, and sidewalk cafés brought out the chairs and reopened for business.

France paid dearly for the affair of May. The franc had been put under so much pressure that the government contemplated another devaluation. It was the end of French pretensions to become the premier capital market of Europe. The myth of Gallic superiority and de Gaulle's grand design lay in ruins. The general, faced with a precipitous decline in his domestic popularity, no longer had a popular base on which to build his claim to international leadership. De Gaulle's moral prestige had always been based on an unshakable claim to represent the French general will, and he was not content to serve out the remaining four years of his presidential term in limbo. Looking for a way to recover his popular support, he proposed another change in the constitution. The referendum had two parts: one would increase regional autonomy; the other would make the Senate more representative of the country's social and economic needs. Although neither proposition seemed to have much popular support, de Gaulle made the vote a matter of confidence. The referendum failed—by 47 to 53 percent—and de Gaulle gave up the presidency, leaving office without a formal letter of resignation.

He retired to his home at Colombey-les-Deux-Églises, where he died in November 1970. He was buried in the local village cemetery, and his grave soon became a pilgrimage site. Whatever his arrogance, his special sense of purpose, his resemblance to a latter-day monarch, he had restored the unity of France on at least two occasions. But the country he loved so much lacked the desire to measure up to his costly ideal of greatness. The European Community was becoming too strong to allow one nation to entertain such ambitions.

The Strength of the Common Market

Britain Tries to Join. The growing strength of the Common Market produced a policy change in Great Britain. The British first proposed establishing a free-trade zone in which the Western European states would abolish tariffs among themselves. When the French vetoed the plan, the British proceeded to create the European Free Trade Association (EFTA) of non-Common Market countries—the so-called Outer Seven—in conjunction with Austria, Sweden, Portugal, Switzerland, Norway, and Denmark. The EFTA, supposedly an alternative to the Common Market, was really an attempt to match the Common Market's economic power. In the first decade of the EFTA, trade between its members jumped by two and a half times, but the British did not share in this increase. The British boom, begun in the early 1950s, was slowing down, and the country's balance of payments was in deficit. The British were, therefore, forced to recognize that their decision not to join the Common Market had been a mistake. At the same time, the Kennedy administration, believing that European economic unity was a vital ingredient of the Western alliance, put pressure on the British to join.

In 1961, the Conservative government of Harold Macmillan (1957–1963) began formal negotiations for membership. This move was prompted more by a lack of faith in Britain's power to halt its own decline than by any great enthusiasm to join forces with the rest of Europe. Furthermore, for Britain to abandon its special relationships with the countries of the Commonwealth seemed a betrayal of its history. The paucity of domestic support for the move reflected this ambivalence. Politicians in both major parties feared a loss of their nation's sovereignty. Certain economic interest groups, like the farmers, feared the new competition would mean a loss of revenue and lead to higher costs. Some private citizens feared they would be inundated with nasty influences from abroad.[12] The Labour party put forth a series of conditions. The government worked to gain special protection for British agriculture and to demonstrate to the voters that it was not going to make too many concessions. However, the question of whether Britain would be allowed to join the Common Market was not a matter for British voters to decide.

On 14 January 1963, President de Gaulle announced that his country could no longer support British membership. De Gaulle feared that Britain's traditional ties with the United States would prevent the British from establishing a closer relationship with Europe, but more importantly, he suspected that British membership might weaken his leadership of Europe. The European Community had definitely enhanced the French political presence. By depicting Britain as a Trojan horse for the interests of the Americans, de Gaulle found allies in other Common Market countries. He wanted a consortium approach to European integration, a Europe of separate parts in which each nation's sovereignty would be reaffirmed, not diminished. British membership would detract from his consortium arrangement with Germany, so he publicly torpedoed British membership the week before the signing of the Franco-German treaty.

The French leader's insistence on more national integrity clashed with the notion of integration that the economic planners in other Common Market countries desired. Most of them favored a federated Europe—a concept advanced by Germany's Walter Hallstein, chairman of the European Community Commission. These planners wanted a European parliament with the authority to approve the Community's budget, while de Gaulle opposed reaching decisions by majority vote. To make his point, de Gaulle ordered the French representatives on the Common Market Council home from Brussels.[13] He insisted on the right of veto, and only when this was accorded—in the Luxembourg Agreement of 1967—did he end the French boycott. As long as de Gaulle's policy prevailed, the institutions of the European Community could not neutralize the power of its member states.

De Gaulle won another point in 1967, when he again dashed British hopes of joining the Common Market.[14] The general wanted to promote the modernization of the French economy, so it could keep pace with the other members of the Common Market, and to protect it against undesirable political and cultural consequences of American investment. His singular determination to fashion Europe in his own image fanned European fears of French domination. Other Community members did not regard the entry of Britain or the American presence in Europe as a liability. Jean Monnet, the founding father of the Common Market, believed that the absence of the British would fetter Europe's civilizing mission: "The British have a better understanding than the continentals of institutions and how to use them. Continentals tend to believe that problems are solved by men . . . but without institutions they reach no great and enduring decisions. This the British have long understood."[15] Such support encouraged the British to try a third time—but only after de Gaulle had left office.

The Conservative government of Edward Heath (1970–1974) began negotiations for the final attempt in July 1970. Under the Treaty of Accession, signed in Brussels on 22 January 1972, Britain abandoned its special economic ties with the Commonwealth and with the United States and accepted a diminished role for sterling. It had to meet all requirements for membership within three years.[16] The French gave the arrangement their blessing. President Georges Pompidou (1969–1974) supported British entry as a balance against a strong Germany. The British Labour party, however, in another of its reversals, took a firm stand against membership and fought it to the end without success.

Denmark and Ireland entered the Common Market at the same time as the British in 1973, thereby creating the Community of Nine. (In a referendum, Norway decided to stay out.) The European Community now had a combined population of 257 million people; it was responsible for 26 percent of the world's exports and over 27 percent of its imports. Further increases would occur in 1981 when Greece became a member—some say merely to prevent the Turks from also joining—and in 1986 when Spain and Portugal joined. By that time, Austria and Norway had displayed interest in becoming members, as had Switzerland and Sweden, to say nothing of Yugoslavia and Turkey.

The Community in Operation. Agriculture was the glue that held the Common Market together, but finding a common policy proved to be the organization's most controversial and structurally most difficult task.[17] The Community contained some of the best farmland in the world. With a vast diversity of soils and climates, stretching from the Arctic to the Mediterranean seas, from the Atlantic Ocean to the Aegean, the region produced an enormous variety of crops and livestock, most of which enjoyed a certain amount of protection against foreign competition. The reasons for this were both political and emotional. National legislatures had deferred to farming interests, endorsing, sincerely or otherwise, an agrarian romanticism in which farmers were depicted as the soul of the nation. This protectionism was supposed to end with the Common Market, but the practice continued, becoming even more complicated.

For example, the Germans wanted to continue their industrial expansion without alarming the French. So, they agreed to guarantee French wheat at a price adequate to meet its costs of production.[18] They also protected their own farmers who might be hurt by this policy; and, for good measure, they protected the small family farms because they believed them to be historically and socially important. Such props inflated costs and stimulated overproduction, resulting in huge surpluses. As a result, the wealthier farmers got wealthier, while the marginal farmers, whom the policy was designed to benefit, fell farther behind. Most of the German farms remained small and inefficient, the so-called dwarf-farms. Moreover, the consumers did not receive any economic benefits. In fact, they were hurt twice: they paid higher taxes and had to pay high fixed prices for farm products.

Common Market import duties were based on a variable price structure. When the world market price was low, tariffs would be adjusted accordingly. Often, when it was to its advantage, the Common Market found ways to exclude foreign imports altogether. For example, the Common Market prohibited imports of American beef by claiming that it contained too many hormones that were harmful to peoples' health. On the other hand, the Common Market saw nothing wrong with dumping its surpluses on the world market at prices 20 to 50 percent below market price to beat down the competition. Thus, the Common Market countries protected all sorts of products for all sorts of political, economic, moral, and social reasons. The results were sometimes impressive, like the great "wine lakes" and "butter mountains" that appeared in the 1970s. But, by committing such large resources to the agricultural sector, member states deprived the more dynamic industrial and urban sectors of the investment needed for further growth.

In trying to even out advantages and disadvantages between countries, member states collected "compensatory amounts" on goods crossing national frontiers. They thereby collected customs in disguise, making a mockery of economic unity. Agricultural policy, for example, protected from the mechanics of the free market, tried to reconcile the irreconcilable. The pricing needs and demands of the food-importing countries, like Great Britain and West Germany, constantly conflicted with the pricing needs and supplies of the food-exporting countries, like France. Food-importing countries were not enthusiastic about favoring the agricultural sector, whose expenses drained as much as 75 percent of the European Community budget, but bringing about significant change was difficult. Unable to rearrange this fundamental priority, the British compensated by successfully obtaining, in the 1982 Fontainebleau agreement, a rebate on their budget contributions.

Planners responded to the overstimulation of agriculture by pushing for greater modernization of the farming sector and for more functionalism, or product specialization. For example, they wanted Britain and Ireland to concentrate on the production of beef, France to produce wheat, and Italy to grow fruit and vegetables. But, not surprisingly, such plans lacked the support of the producers they were designed to eliminate—producers who frequently possessed the political power to protect their special position. Dramatic rural protests became a feature of agricultural politics in the Common Market. Since the decisions taken in Brussels influenced the income of all Common Market farmers, the farmers used whatever leverage they had to get special treatment. One tactic was to dump their produce in a village square, block the roads with their tractors, mobilize their lobbyists, and call in the media. Consequently, eliminating, or even controlling, price guarantees to producers was extremely difficult.[19] In 1987, the Commission sought to cut the farm subsidies, but at the same time moved to raise tariffs. This helped to reduce the dumping of surplus goods on the world market, but those who did not benefit from the scheme fought to have it changed. As a result, the Common Market was unable to take a clear position on protectionism or free trade with nations outside the Community.

However, pressure to remove all internal barriers to trade continued. In July 1987, the Common Market adopted the Single Act of European Union. This law, which was based on a study entitled "Completing the Internal Market," advocated eliminating all exchange controls and restrictions on the movement of labor and capital to achieve a completely integrated market by 1992. All countries would then have a standard "value-added tax."[20] Monetary compensation would no longer be paid on agricultural goods. State aid to industry would be controlled to prevent certain industries from gaining a competitive edge. The Single European Act also reversed de Gaulle's policy of unanimity by providing for majority voting by the European Community Council and envisaged an expanded role for the European parliament. This push for integration came at a time when European business had become more integrated and more multinational through mergers and takeovers. It was also determined to compete with the United States and Japan for a greater share of the world market.

A Community-funded study, the Cecchini report, indicated that a single European market would raise gross national productivity by at least six percent and lead to greater expenditure on research and development. Consumers would benefit from lower prices and a greater variety of goods. Governments would save money from the elimination of border formalities and lower expenditures on regulation. While few people believed that the task would be finished by the time targeted for its completion, the progress achieved was surprising. Long-term movements of capital were freed, and short-term movements were liberalized. Telecommunications were targeted for deregulation. An additional boost to integration occurred in October 1990, when Great Britain, traditionally reluctant to yield more of its economic sovereignty to the Community, announced that it would tie the pound to the other European currencies. In joining the system, Britain pledged to adjust its economic policies and interest rates to ensure that its currency stayed within a certain range of the nine currencies already in the system. (Only Portugal and Greece now remained outside.) Under current arrangements, central banks had to intervene if currencies drifted outside the prescribed limits. The announcement was greeted with a surge of stock prices on the London exchange. The Confederation of British Industry was pleased because the stabilization of the pound against the other European currencies would result in more predictable export prices for British businesses. However, the British government still refused to consider a single currency, a long-time goal of European Community planners.

Other steps toward complete integration proved equally thorny. Still to be resolved were problems concerning the standardization of labor relations, the harmonization of corporate taxation, the reduction of variations in indirect taxes among members, the elimination of visas, the creation of an internal energy market, the formulation of an environmental protection policy, the creation of a single market for banking and securities, and—most importantly—the establishment of a single central bank and a single currency. Further integration along these lines came close to the marrow of statehood, especially since the pretensions of the Common Market went beyond mere economics.

Article 119 of the Treaty of Rome, concerning equal pay for equal work, was economic in origin, but it took the Community into the controversial world of sex discrimination. The European Court of Justice ruled that Article 119 committed the members of the European Community "to ensure social progress and seek the constant improvement of the living and working conditions of their peoples."[21] Enforcement, though, depended on the national courts and legislatures, a difficult proposition considering the enormous differences in attitudes and customs in the various Common Market countries.[22] For example, Great Britain's tradition-based, common-law political system posed an inherent obstacle to the application of this fundamental right. British law respected the right of the individual to do all that was not prohibited, but "fundamental rights" could not be used to strike down the acts of Parliament.[23] Therefore, European Community law could not have a direct effect, even though it was treaty law. The negative consequences of this were largely moral. Unless a state specifically decided to enact the European Court's rulings, there could be no real compliance, especially on social, as opposed to economic, matters. The court was still feeling its way in this new domain of international jurisprudence.[24] In many countries, the rights of women did not receive the highest priority. The Community, therefore, refrained from legislating social progress and from trying to force the least progressive members to bring about change. Furthermore, as memories of World War II grew dimmer and with them the likelihood that Germany might again disrupt the peace, the Common Market nations became more reluctant to surrender further national sovereignty to a group of experts meeting in Brussels or legislating in Strasbourg. Thus, de Gaulle's fear that supranationalism would deprive France of its sovereignty proved exaggerated, but on that issue he fashioned his own policy of greatness.

The Reign in Spain

The Twilight of the Franco Regime. The government of General Francisco Franco was based on the fundamental political principle that might makes right. But this did not mean that he could do entirely as he chose. The support he received from the aristocracy, the landowners, and the Catholic church was conditional on his respecting their traditional rights, something he had little difficulty doing. However, it was his military victory in the Spanish Civil War in 1939 that had established his legitimacy and confirmed his position as Caudillo "by the grace of God." Franco remained the supreme commander of the armed forces, the chief of the government of the Spanish state, and the chief of the Movement—that is, of the state's only legal political organization. Theoretically, he could pass any law or issue any decree he chose and had no constitutional limitations on his power save God and history. He ruled both as president and prime minister until 1973, two years before his death, when ill health forced him to hand over the active affairs of state to others. Even before that, however, Franco had already allowed his ministers a good deal of initiative. As long as he thought they were carrying out the overall goals of his regime, he interfered little in the running of their departments. Franco believed that his destiny was to re-create the greatness of Spain's monarchical past and, in the process, destroy the evils of democracy and separatism. The other states of Western Europe regarded Franco's Spain as a pariah.

In 1947, as the first step to restoring the Spanish monarchy, he promulgated the Law of Succession, which set out the job description for the future monarch: male, Spanish, Catholic, at least thirty years old, and willing to uphold the fundamental laws of the regime and the Movement.[25] Franco, in tandem with the enactment of the Law of Succession, established a Council of the Realm as a special prop for the consolidation of authoritarianism. The council had power to declare war and rule on all laws passed by the Cortes, the national legislature, which had only advisory powers. Not until 1969 did Franco announce a specific candidate for king in the person of the thirty-one-year-old Juan Carlos, the grandson of Alfonso XIII, Spain's last reigning monarch who had gone into exile in 1931. In doing this, Franco skipped over Juan Carlos's father Don Juan, the legitimate heir, because Don Juan favored a limited monarchy instead of one-man rule. Despite his antipathy toward the regime, however, Don Juan favored a restoration and allowed his son to be educated in Spain to further that prospect.

As the Cold War heated up, the Atlantic community states began to soften their harsh attitude toward Franco's dictatorship. In 1948, France opened its Spanish frontier. Spain was considered for Marshall Plan aid. This came to nothing, but in 1949 the regime managed to negotiate a $25 million loan from the Chase National Bank; the following year, the U.S. Congress approved a $62.5 million loan. Spain was not invited to join NATO, but in 1953, it signed the Pact of Madrid, granting the United States the right to construct three air bases and one naval base and lease them for ten years in exchange for military and economic aid.[26] The Americans reserved the right to use these facilities to launch a nuclear attack on the Soviet Union. Not all Spaniards were as enthusiastic as Franco about the Madrid agreement because they feared the incorporation of Spain into the American and European security zone might involve the country in a war between the superpowers. In 1955, Spain received some consolation when it became a member of the United Nations.

Increased interaction with the West began to modify the restrictive nature of the regime, although this was not immediately apparent. Freedom of the press and association were still severely restricted. The police had wide discretionary powers to arrest and detain suspected enemies. Officials had the authority to restrict privileges and might take away driver's licenses or passports or have dissidents discharged from their employment. If politics seemed business as usual, such was not the case in economics. Within a generation after World War II, Spain had moved from a primarily agricultural economy toward an advanced industrialized society. Improvement was slow at first. The Franco regime wanted to make the economy self-sufficient in the autarkic manner of Fascist Italy. This entailed high tariffs, trade quotas, price regulation, and special protection and subsidies to a whole host of industries. In the 1950s, however, a new class of technocrats, many associated with the Catholic movement *Opus Dei* (Work of God), began pressuring for the modernization of the Spanish economy as a necessary prelude for integration into the Western Europe markets. Opus Dei, an order recognized by the Vatican in 1943 as a secular institute, had originally concentrated on spreading Catholicism throughout state institutions, especially the universities. In 1952, it opened the University of Navarre at Pamplona, the only Spanish secular institution of higher learning devoted mainly to Catholic principles. The organization's members were also prominent in business and finance. Some of them strongly supported the antiliberal economics of the Franco regime, but another, ultimately more important, group wanted to bring about reform through rapid capitalistic growth. They hoped to neutralize politics through prosperity.[27] Although essentially favoring the interests of the upper-middle class, the reformers believed that employers had to recognize the rights of the working class if they wanted to increase productivity. Many of Franco's ministers were members of Opus Dei.

In 1957, the technocrats of Opus Dei succeeded in centralizing all the ministries dealing with economic policy into the single Office of Economic Coordination and Planning. The timing was fortuitous as that was the year the Treaty of Rome was signed. Spain then began to dismantle the apparatus of autarky. The country's balance of payments was stabilized. Controls were dropped, foreign investment was encouraged. Slowly, Spain was converted to a market economy. The results were palpable. During the 1940s and 1950s, Spain's industrial productivity grew at a respectable 7 percent per year; in the 1960s, the growth rate rose to 11 percent. This gain of 50 percent over the previous decade was especially impressive because it came when the overall levels of industrial productivity were greatly superior to those at the beginning of the period. By 1969, Spanish industrial production was 5.69 times higher than in 1949.[28] By comparison, agriculture remained backward. Its gains were very modest compared to those in industry.[29]

The rehabilitation of the Franco regime and the foreign loans that came as a result provided real benefits for the Spanish economy. Spain needed the loans because it could not earn enough foreign capital from its exports to pay for foreign capital goods. In addition, Spain received foreign exchange from the money its nationals working abroad sent home. In 1973, a quarter of a million Spaniards were working in Germany, and twice that number were in France, many of them in unskilled or manual labor jobs. Spain further relied on tourism, which during the 1970s brought in $3 billion a year.[30] The devaluation of the peseta in 1959 made Spain one of the cheapest vacation spots in Europe.

The Spanish technocrats borrowed their concept of planning from the French. In their desire to expand private investment, however, they were more willing to ignore the social costs and worried less about the development of the public sector. Taxes fell heavier on those with lower incomes than on the very wealthy who traditionally were unaccustomed to paying their fair share. As a result, Spain still had a large underclass for whom poverty continued to be a way of life. The amount of begging and the malnutrition, especially in backward areas, were startling. Emigration from rural to urban areas created the surplus population necessary for the expansion of the industrial and service sectors. Nevertheless, unsolved social problems led to growing resentment of the Franco regime. Workers' strikes and student protests broke out in many areas, but the Basque national resistance was the most serious form of radicalism. In December 1973, Basque extremists managed to kill the president of the government, Luis Carrero Blanco, a strong advocate of authoritarianism. The assassins blew Carrero Blanco's car with him in it four stories high to the roof of a Jesuit monastery. The army went on alert, but no attempt at a coup followed the assassination. Until his death, the Caudillo enjoyed such popularity, or encouraged such apathy, that at no point was he in any real danger of being toppled.

Reconstructing Spanish Democracy. General Franco hoped that his designated successor would preserve the character of his regime after the general had been laid to rest in his tomb in the Valley of the Fallen. As long as Franco lived, Juan Carlos was in a difficult position. The regime's hard-liners did not trust him; the leftists thought him a stooge. For many moderates, however, Juan Carlos represented the best hope for a transition to a peaceful and more liberal Spain. The prince guarded his counsel so carefully it was difficult to predict what he might do when he came into his inheritance. He said as little as possible, studiously avoiding involvement in the affairs of state while the Caudillo lived. Remarkably, Franco made no direct attempt to indoctrinate him, no doubt hoping that Juan Carlos would do the right thing when the time came.

The time came on 20 November 1975. Even before Franco breathed his last, however, his regime was no longer the one he had originally created. The country was more prosperous than it had ever been in its history. Much of this progress had taken place despite Franco's efforts or desires. It simply happened without much opposition. Franco's authoritarianism, no matter how objectionable, did provide a stable environment for steady economic growth. The Spanish people seemed content to wait patiently until the Caudillo died before making comparable changes in their political system. The Civil War had been so traumatic that few wanted to resolve their differences again in a bloody manner. Franco's long reign gave them the opportunity to outlive their extremism. That Franco had fought so hard to extinguish democracy made the successful transformation to Western-style parliamentary institutions the more remarkable. Much of the credit for this transition was due to the thirty-seven-year-old king.

Juan Carlos knew that the survival of the monarchy and the future well-being of his country depended on the successful dismantling of the Franco state. In doing this, Juan Carlos proved a skilled politician. At first, he treaded very carefully, trying not to antagonize those who feared he would go too far, but reassuring those who feared he would not go far enough. He was lucky in that he did not face any strong competition. The elimination of Carrero Blanco had removed one possible source of opposition; Franco's failure to nominate a new president of the Council of the Realm had removed another.

The king tried to run his first government with men who had Francoist credentials, but were personally loyal to him. He appointed Torcuato Fernández Miranda to head the Council of the Realm and the Cortes. Fernández Miranda was flexible and could be relied upon to help neutralize the rightist opposition. He also retained Carlos Arias Navarro, Carrero Blanco's successor, as prime minister. Although Juan Carlos made it clear to the ministers of his first government that his aim was the complete democratization of the Spanish political system, the government could not agree on a program of political reform. There was much squabbling and not much progress.[31] Meanwhile unrest and public protest increased in Madrid, Barcelona, the Basque country, and elsewhere. The Communist and Socialist opposition formed an alliance in the *Coordinacion Democrática* (Democratic Coordination) to which the Christian Democrats, the Carlists, and the trade unions added their strength. The Francoist forces were calling for a crackdown. In July 1976, the king dismissed Arias and replaced him with Adolfo Suárez González.

Suárez continued the process of democratization with great success. He turned the Franco apparatus against itself and, within a year, had dismantled it beyond recognition. In July 1976, using the very legal instruments Franco had created, he suppressed the police state Tribunal of Public Order. In November, he and Fernández Miranda persuaded the Francoist Cortes, which had been only a rubber stamp, to vote itself out of existence by passing the Law of Political Reform, which called for the election of a new bicameral Cortes by universal suffrage. In February 1977, the Law of Political Associations legalized all political parties except the Communist party. (Two months later, the Communists achieved legal status, after promising to accept the monarchy and respect the state's political institutions.) In March, labor unions were legalized, thereby destroying the old Francoist labor syndicates. As fears spread that the army was plotting to seize power, Juan Carlos worked to keep it loyal. He had a great institutional advantage. The officers could not act against him as a politician without challenging his authority as the chief of the Spanish state and commander-in-chief of the armed forces. Such treason would have destroyed everything they had sworn to uphold.

In June, Spain held free elections for the first time since 1936. The campaign lasted a month; 18 million people, almost 80 percent of the entire electorate, came to the polls. The voters overwhelmingly rejected the parties of the extremes. Of the 350 seats in the *Congreso* (Congress), the lower house in the new Cortes, the right-wing neo-Francoist party *Alianza Popular* (Popular Alliance) won only 16 (five percent of the popular vote); the Communist party (*Partido Comunista Español*), despite its professed willingness to play by democratic rules, got only 20 seats (nine percent of the popular vote). The big winners were the moderate coalition *Union de Centro Democrático* (Union for the Democratic Center), led by Suárez, with 165 seats (34.3 percent of the popular vote) and the *Partido Socialista Obrero Española* (Socialist Workers' party), led by Felipe González Márquez, which captured 118 seats (28.5 percent of the popular vote). These two parties also dominated the upper chamber, the *Senado*. The Christian Democratic party of José Mariá Gil Robles, a prominent politician of the Second Republic, had been practically wiped out. The Spanish people, having rejected the parties of the center to their misfortune in 1936, had now embraced them with a vengeance.

Since 1975, Spain had been so concerned with political reorganization that economic problems were often ignored. The country's heavy industries needed further rationalization; unemployment was on the rise, and an increase in the world price of oil cut into foreign exchange. In 1977, the inflation rate reached more than 24 percent. A proposed policy of austerity was unpopular and shook people's faith in the Suárez government. Nevertheless, the workers and left-wing parties agreed to make sacrifices in exchange for a promise of social reform, including a more equitable tax structure.

Meanwhile, a committee of the Congreso worked to draft a new constitution. The process, wending its way through many amendments, compromises, and alterations in committees, took fifteen months to complete. The final document, which passed both houses of the Cortes in October 1978, created a parliamentary monarchy based on liberty, justice, equality, and political pluralism. The drafters were determined not to repeat some of the mistakes of the 1931 constitution. Therefore, although the constitution did not establish a state religion, it did promise to maintain relations with the Catholic church and other religions. Similarly, although education was to be free and public, the constitution promised that the state would aid private schools, i.e., mostly Catholic schools. While the constitution affirmed the unity of the Spanish state, it recognized the right to autonomy of the various nationalities, including the right of these ethnic minorities to teach their local language and fly their own flag. The provision did not go far enough for the Basques but went too far for the neo-Francoist Popular Alliance. Nevertheless, almost 88 percent of the Spanish people gave the constitution their approval.[32]

The first elections held under this constitution on 1 March 1979 changed the distribution of power very little; both the Democratic Union and the Socialist Workers' party picked up three seats at the expense of the smaller parties, including the Communists who had aggressively campaigned as a party of Western democracy. The Spanish Right suffered a further loss and was not even represented in most of the country. Yet Franco's legacy persisted. Some senior officers of the Spanish army harbored strong desires for the old days. Largely out of touch with the rest of the country and lacking any real support among the general population, they nevertheless continued to conspire against the democratic regime. The Suárez government's failure to improve the economy and deal with a mounting wave of Basque terrorism—Basque gunmen liked to kill Castilian police officers—led to an attempted coup in Madrid. The rebels wanted to dissolve the Cortes and create a new military government of national unity. They made their move on 23 February 1981, when the Congreso had assembled to vote on the investiture of a new prime minister. (Suárez, buffeted by dissension in his own party and in the Cortes, had just resigned.) The conspirators believed that the king secretly welcomed such a move and would accede to their fait accompli.

Two hundred members of the Guardia Civil, led by Lieutenant-Colonel Antonio Tejero Molina, burst into the Congreso with guns at the ready. It was 6:20 P.M. One of the police officers fired some shots into the ceiling prompting the deputies to dive for cover. Tejero announced he would obey no one save Lieutenant-General Jaime Milans del Bosch, captain-general of Valencia and the conspiracy's leader. Milans telephoned the country's other military leaders, telling them he was acting "in the name of the king." Juan Carlos, however, began calling the same generals, telling them that his name was being used in vain and ordering them to support the legitimate government. He was not always successful. General Alfonso Armanda Comyn tried to exploit the coup by intriguing to get himself named head of the government in the style of General de Gaulle. In the end, though, most of the generals obeyed their commander-in-chief. That same night the king addressed the nation on television. He declared that he would not tolerate any subversion of the constitution.

The coup collapsed, but it had been a close call. Had the king not acted decisively, the conspirators might have succeeded in undoing the democratic achievements of the past four years. It was one of Juan Carlos's finest hours. His strong stand for democracy kept the army in line and convinced many hidebound republicans that the monarchy had some value after all. Juan Carlos was determined to avoid the blunder of his grandfather, Alfonso XIII, who in 1923 violated the constitution by turning the government over to a dictator. The king feared, however, that the democratic system that he had helped create might not survive if it constantly had to depend on such extraordinary efforts. The day after the coup, he advised the leaders of the Cortes to promote concord and unity and recommended against taking revenge on the armed forces.[33] Only a small proportion of those involved in the coup were actually brought to justice. Thirty-three were tried, most of whom received relatively light sentences. The chief conspirators Milans, Tejero, and Armanda received the maximum—thirty years. The fledgling Spanish democracy, although badly shaken, had successfully survived its first major threat.

Leopoldo Calvo Sotelo, who succeeded Suárez, took steps to restore confidence by intensifying the war against terrorism. He also negotiated the entrance of Spain into the NATO alliance. In doing this, the government hoped to find a new role for the military besides meddling in domestic politics. Still, some feared that the 1981 coup would not be the last time the army would try to seize power. The Socialists, who had increased their strength throughout the country, were especially apprehensive that the military might try to prevent them from ever assuming power.

The Socialist secretary-general Felipe González had worked hard to make his party respectable. He had eliminated Marxist ideology as a central component of the party's philosophy and had excluded the party's left-wingers from all positions of importance. He had also abandoned the nationalization of industry as a political objective. Now González put pragmatism ahead of ideology and concentrated on fighting unemployment, protecting democracy, and achieving administrative reform. His popularity was phenomenal; he was the only Spanish leader who was affectionately referred to by his first name. He believed that refashioning socialism was the best insurance against Communism and a revival of Francoism.

The Socialist Workers' party swept the elections of October 1982 with 48 percent of the popular vote, capturing 210 of the 350 seats in the Congreso. This was an increase of 120 over the January 1979 balloting. The Communists practically disappeared, dropping from 20 to 5 seats. The Union for the Democratic Center fell catastrophically from 168 seats to a scant 13. Many of the Democratic Union's former supporters had voted Socialist. The rightist Popular Alliance led by Manuel Fraga Iribarne became the second largest party. Fraga had been the minister of information and tourism in the Franco government. The elections gave Spain a virtual two-party system. The Spanish army pledged to respect the election results.

González downplayed his lopsided victory. At the age of forty, he was the youngest government leader in Europe. He had epitomized the aspirations of the Spanish for the consolidation of the democratic system and their desire to integrate their country with the rest of Western Europe. Yet, Spain had a 16 percent unemployment rate and a 12 percent inflation rate and also faced a significant threat in the form of Basque terrorism. Furthermore, a significant part of the electorate had voted for an opposition party whose roots lay in the former authoritarian system. Nevertheless, the Socialist victory showed that the Spanish people's hope for a new beginning outweighed their longing for the past. The Socialists dominated Spanish politics for the rest of the decade. They became a centrist party, a party of moderation, the kind of political organization that Spaniards had previously ignored at their peril.

Privatization of the British Welfare State

The Faltering Consensus. In the nineteenth century, the British created a liberal democracy by extending the right to vote, but after World War I, political liberalization was no longer enough. People now had greater demands. They expected government help in raising their standard of living. All major political parties adopted the rhetoric of compassion, beginning with the promise to veterans that Britain would be made a fit place for heroes to live in. Even people who felt no moral obligation to share their privileges with others nevertheless recognized that some welfare legislation was necessary to maintain constitutional and institutional stability. The Conservative governments of the 1920s and 1930s could point to some successes in expanding the public sector, but generally they dragged their feet on making any real economic and social changes.

During World War II, the promises were taken more seriously. Both major parties agreed that the inequities of the present system could not be corrected without more state intervention. They agreed that the British people should have proper medical assistance, subsidized housing, and improved education. They agreed to provide care for disadvantaged children, the mentally and physically disabled, and the elderly. They also accepted the principles of Keynesian economics, in particular, that the state has a major role to play in guaranteeing a stable economy with full employment and a steady rate of growth. Accordingly, they believed the government should keep a tight rein over the country's monetary system and expected it to manipulate prices, income levels, and foreign exchange. They also favored, or at least accepted, the direct ownership of certain industries, including coal, steel, transportation, and public utilities.

Although the Conservative and Labour parties disagreed on the reasons for nationalization—the former finding its worth primarily in economic development, the latter believing it was necessary to promote economic equality—both advocated developing national priorities and solving problems through the tripartite cooperation of government, labor, and industry. The "beer and sandwiches" approach extended from the national level down to local units and assumed that all decisions must be reached through compromise.[34] Although the communality of Conservative-Labour belief was more often fiction than fact, the areas of consensus seemed more important than those of disagreement. The Conservatives did not attack the welfare state directly, although they disagreed vehemently with the Labour party over how it was to be financed, how the growing power of the trade unions should be treated, and how wealth should be distributed.[35] Much of the Conservatives' later criticism of Labour, whether justified or not, stemmed from the relatively poor performance of the British economy compared to other European countries.

West Germany and France grew at a rate of between 3 and 5 percent per year, while Britain squeezed out a bare 2 percent. Some people warned that the country would fall behind Italy or even Portugal and blamed the welfare state for a multitude of sins: failure to shake British industry out of its hidebound ways, failure to make labor more productive, and failure to promote class harmony. None of this was new. Before World War II, people had complained about worsening labor relations, the rise of class hatred, and the declining productivity of industry. Only now the stakes were higher. The existence of the welfare state depended on a healthy, growing economy. In many ways, growth was more important to Labour than to the Conservatives because Labour's constituents were traditionally those less well off.

By the 1970s, social security benefits were taken for granted. People were used to the improved health care resulting from the National Health Service, and they expected the state to subsidize their housing and guarantee their well-being. The cost of such benefits, however, was rising. One answer was to reduce benefits—a politically risky proposition. Failing that, the answer was to increase revenues. Monies could be obtained in various ways. The government could levy taxes on property, goods, or income; it could borrow, or it could promote a policy of inflation, which would enable it to pay its bills with depreciated currency. But each option entailed social and economic costs even assuming the government made an effort to be fair. In any case, the cost of living would rise, which would inevitably precipitate a demand for higher wages. From the 1960s through the 1980s, the Conservative and Labour governments struggled fitfully to raise revenues to maintain services, increase the standard of living, ensure full employment, and improve productivity.

Harold Macmillan did not live up to his 1959 election promises to increase British productivity. His government sponsored a host of studies and reiterated a heightened commitment to planning, and in 1962 it urged employers to hold the line on pay increases at two percent to aid the economy. Under pressure, however, it allowed as much as three times that amount for civil servants and workers in nationalized industries. People complained that the moratorium was unfair. Meanwhile domestic production remained about the same. Disenchantment with the Conservatives' performance resulted in Labour and Liberal party victories in the 1962 by-elections. The improvement in the British standard of living in the previous decade had contributed to high expectations about continuing prosperity that the Conservatives seemed incapable of sustaining. In 1961, the index of industrial production had risen about 1 percent over the previous year; in 1962, it was up just over 3 percent; and in 1963, it remained about the same as in the previous year.[36] From 1963 to 1964, the index of industrial production shot up by more than 13 percent, but the increase came too late to restore Macmillan's popularity. Thanks to de Gaulle, he had also failed to bring his country into the Common Market. And, in March 1963, his administration was faced with a major sex scandal. Secretary of state for war, John Profumo, had an affair with a call girl who also shared her attractions with a naval attaché from the Soviet embassy. Profumo at first lied about his involvement, then had to admit he had "misled" his colleagues. Macmillan was an innocent party, but his position as leader was shaken nevertheless. In October, following a prostate operation, he announced his resignation and turned over the leadership of his party to Sir Alec Douglas-Home, a lackluster crossover from the House of Lords.[37] Douglas-Home had little time to put his own stamp on British politics before he was faced with a general election.

The Conservatives promised more public housing. Labour promised a reduction in medical costs, an improvement in education, and an increase in insurance benefits. The programs would be paid for out of revenues from higher productivity— a familiar promise. Labour won—its first government (1964–1970) since Attlee's victory in 1945—controlling the Commons with a slim majority of four seats.[38] Harold Wilson, the new prime minister, sought to turn Britain around. His goals were to reverse the deficit in the balance of payments, increase industrial productivity, and stabilize prices. The government produced a "National Plan" to control and stimulate growth primarily through technological modernization. The results were disappointing. Only in 1968 did the index of industrial productivity reach 6 percent; for the rest of Labour's term in office, the index hovered around 2 to 3 percent growth per year. From 1966 to 1967, there was no growth at all.[39]

In 1970, the Conservatives again took charge under their new leader Edward Heath. Heath, like his predecessors, promised more than he delivered. He wanted to reduce expenditures, cut taxes, stimulate investment, and expand productivity. But as before, inflationary wage demands and the loss of working days through stoppages and strikes squandered human and material resources and further weakened the country's industrial base. Furthermore, a war in the Middle East in 1973 led to a significant rise in the price of oil, which greatly affected all European economies. Everything suddenly became more expensive; at least, everything that was dependent on petroleum, plastics, transportation, and fertilizers. The consumer price index skyrocketed, pushing the inflation rate into double digits. Between 1974 and 1978, prices doubled, especially in the public sector. The value of the pound began to tumble, pushing up the cost of imports. Heath could not control inflation in time for the 1974 elections. Although the Conservatives outpolled Labour, they fell three seats short of a plurality. Labour, still led by Harold Wilson, formed the first minority government since 1929. By calling another election eight months later, however, Wilson was able to gain a majority of three seats, small but adequate. He resigned in 1976 and was replaced by James Callaghan (1976– 1979), the former foreign secretary and the first prime minister since the war who had never been to a university. Callaghan always thought himself less bright than he actually was.

Britain was still plagued by inflation, but Callaghan was reluctant to shrink the money supply and begin a program of austerity for fear of jeopardizing the jobs of his working-class constituents. But if inflation were to be brought under control, a higher rate of unemployment seemed inevitable. Labour bit the bullet and, in July 1976, adopted a tighter monetary policy, slashing public spending by one million pounds. It also applied for a loan from the International Monetary Fund. Still the cost of living continued to rise. In October, the government trimmed another 2.5 million pounds. Unemployment rose to 1.5 million people. The situation was reminiscent of the early 1930s when Ramsay MacDonald had tightened the nation's belt in order to get credits from New York bankers. Prime Minister Callaghan placed the blame on Keynesian manipulation of the economy. He said that the inflation had been caused by boosting public spending to increase employment. Indeed, previous administrations, including those of the Tories, had tried to maintain a high standard of living through increased spending.

In a 1976 speech, Callaghan told the Labour Party Conference that the nation could no longer afford a policy of cutting taxes and engaging in deficit spending.[40] His task seemed impossible. He tried to hold the line on wages, knowing the country could not afford such inflationary increases. One way of doing this was through high levels of unemployment, a practice he found intolerable.[41] The government tried to limit public employees to a five percent increase. It intended to enforce these guidelines against private corporations by refusing to order goods from companies that violated them. The Trade Union Congress opposed the policy.

The floodgates opened in the winter of 1978 when the Ford Motor Company, which had had a very profitable year, decided to give its workers a pay increase of 17 percent. This prompted the road transport workers to demand 25 percent and, when they did not get it, to go on strike. Shop stewards in other industries came out in favor of secondary picketing, which encouraged workers in businesses totally unconnected to the original dispute to show their solidarity by also downing their tools. Consequently, workers from garbage collectors and gravediggers to nursery school attendants also stopped work. The disruption of services, the nondelivery of goods, and the loss of purchasing power damaged the economy further. Industrial output fell by one-third. This "winter of discontent" helped return the Conservatives to power in the general elections of March 1979. Ironically, the Labour party did not lose support; its national vote was actually higher than it had been five years earlier. Rather the Conservatives, who had abstained in 1974, returned to vote in great numbers. They feared more labor unrest and welcomed the lower taxes that their party promised. Callaghan, on leaving office, felt that it was a miracle that he had stayed as long as he had.[42]

Britain had lagged behind the other industrial powers of Europe since the beginning of the century, but the British could not agree on whether the reasons for the "decline" were technical or psychological or both. British industry suffered from a lack of investment, especially in new manufacturing techniques. Moreover the products the British tried to sell failed to claim their share of either the world market or the domestic market. The reasons were sometimes easy to see. For centuries, the British had been claiming "British is best" when in fact it was not. British products were often poorly designed, badly marketed, late in delivery, and inadequately serviced. Some products, such as the British motorcycle, clung to old-fashioned technology. The Japanese had created a bike that could be started by pushing a button on the handlebars, but the British models still used the old kick starter that took several hard pumps to produce an ignition. As a result, the British motorcycle industry went into recession. Even British souvenirs—T-shirts, horse brasses, china ashtrays—frequently came from abroad. Britain was no longer the workshop of the world and had not been for decades. The British themselves frequently preferred foreign goods to those produced at home.

Also blamed for the British malaise was the class-ridden educational system that failed to train a properly skilled work force. Universities and secondary schools often put a premium on the liberal arts to the neglect of science, engineering, and technology. Futhermore, business executives had lower social prestige than in more aggressive societies. Many of the technicians and entrepreneurs that Britain did produce left the country to find work in the Commonwealth countries or the United States. American and Canadian universities are full of examples of this "brain drain." Some critics preferred to blame the welfare state itself for Britain's faults, blaming it for inflation, the lack of resources, the fall in the standard of service, and the decline in self-reliance. They accused the welfare state of diminishing Britain's creative vitality by subsidizing unproductive industries and by overregulating and overtaxing. In their view, the welfare state stripped resources from the more vital private sector, did not respond to individual needs, and failed to involve people in decisions that affected their lives.[43] Many of the arguments were ideological and emotional, and many tended to overlook the achievements of the welfare state.[44] But whatever its faults, most commentators agreed that the British people would have to work harder and produce more if their benefits were to increase.

Thatcherism. Margaret Thatcher, the new prime minister (1979–1990), thought she had the answer. Thatcher, the first woman to become the head of government in British history (unless one counts the Tudor and Stuart queens), had strong opinions about what was wrong with the country. Labour leader James Callaghan had already rejected the Keynesian concept of managing demand, but this was only the beginning of a solution. Thatcher wanted to blast the state out of its command position over economic affairs and restore the free market. She was prepared to take on the establishment, specifically, the civil servants and government planners whom she derided for telling the British people what they should eat, how they should be housed, and under what conditions they should work. Thatcher wanted a decisive break with what she saw as an all powerful paternalistic government that turned its citizens into dependent beneficiaries.[45] Her strong, aggressive personality, which would have been accepted as normal in a man, seemed unfeminine in a woman. Tory backbencher Julian Critchley quipped that Thatcher had an urge to hit British institutions with her handbag. Despite such sexism, her impact was enormous. And she soon established a base of popular support that transcended her base in her own party.

Thatcher believed that all those who worked for their money should be allowed to accumulate wealth by keeping a larger share of it. She therefore began by cutting income taxes. The 1979 budget clipped the highest rate from 98 percent to 60 percent, and the basic rate from 33 to 30 percent.[46] It exempted the first 5,000 pounds of investment income from tax altogether. More cuts followed. In the 1988 budget, the upper rate dropped to 40 percent, the basic rate to 25 percent. The new taxation policy increased the gap between high- and low-wage earners, but also made it possible for more Britons to buy their own homes, accelerating a trend that had begun in the early 1970s. The Thatcher government chose a "salami-

Prime Minister Thatcher celebrates the victory of her party in the elections of 1983. The Conservatives won 397 of the 650 seats in the Commons. This solid majority convinced many of them that they no longer need pay lip service to the welfare state.

slicer" style of reform. It began by selling public housing units to tenants, eventually privatizing whole rows of public housing. It then reduced subsidies to public
housing. Next it tried to stimulate private housing development by relaxing rent
controls on new buildings and on new tenancies.[47] Owner occupation increased
from 50 to over 64 percent.

Privatization was the cornerstone of the government's policy to reverse collectivization and revitalize the national economy. Thatcher proceeded to assault state-
owned industries, which, she thought, were inefficient in meeting public demand
and in encouraging working-class productivity. The problem, as she saw it, lay in
the *fact* of public ownership itself. Costs would never be reduced and efficiency
would never be achieved as long as industries lacked the discipline of the marketplace, and the government paid for their losses. Allowing the market to work
would reduce inflation, make labor more productive, and stimulate the kind of
investment that would make the country's industry more competitive. In practice,
privatization led to the sale of such public services as British Telecommunications,
British Gas, British Airways, British Airports Authority, British Petroleum, and
ten water companies. In addition, the government got rid of Rolls Royce, Jaguar,
Sealink, Vickers Shipbuilding, National Bus Company, British Rail Hotels, and
Royal Ordinance, to name a few of the more prominent.[48] Most of these divesti-
tures were accomplished either by offering shares on the open market or through
private sales. In a few cases, such as British Steel, joint ventures were worked out
between the government and the private sector. Critics of privatization countered
that most of the privatized industries were already operating at a profit and thus
were already performing well while less efficient industries remained state property.
In response, the government pointed to the benefits the taxpayers received from
reduced government spending and from the billions of additional pounds pumped
into the public treasury. It took pride in the growing number of households that
owned shares of stocks.

In 1979, only seven percent of British citizens held shares; in 1988, that number
had almost trebled. Of the 600,000 workers transferred from the public to the
private sector between 1979 and 1986, over half became shareholders, many in
the enterprises where they worked. For example, in 1983, the employees of British
Airways agreed to accept minimal wage increases for two years in exchange for a
profit-sharing plan that would give them shares in the company's stock. The government gave tax breaks to those who participated in such programs.[49] The government hoped this grass-roots capitalism would weaken the trade unions. Whatever the reasoning, many of the initial employee-shareholders did benefit when
the value of their investments increased as the economy improved. Instead of
focusing on preventing unemployment, the government emphasized removing obstacles to growth. To this end, the Tories curbed the power of the trade unions
and facilitated the free exchange of goods and services and the movement of
capital. The main weapon of control over the economy that was still in the state
arsenal was the power to regulate interest rates.

From 1973 to 1979, the British economy continued to plod along, growing at
an annual rate of 1.5 percent; but from 1983 to 1989, the rate of growth jumped
to 3.5 percent per year. The Conservatives believed that this improvement vindicated their policy, even though overall output was only slightly more than it
had been twenty years earlier.[50] Although inflation declined, it did not go away,
and it still exceeded that of Italy and France. Moreover, unemployment had
emerged on a scale unseen since the Great Depression. By January 1986, 14 percent
of the labor force, or 3.4 million people, were out of work—an enormous rate for

a society that had been taught that employment was a fundamental right.[51] The impact was felt all over Britain. At the same time, the number of British households living below the poverty line increased,[52] and the gap between the rich and the poor widened.

Prime Minister Thatcher was so confident that she was steering the right course that she planned to denationalize large public utilities, in particular water and electricity. The government also wanted to trim government expenditures for the social security program. While full benefits for the most needy would be retained, benefits for others would be drastically reduced. Thatcher believed that handouts discouraged self-reliance and independence and lowered people's incentive to find work. She instituted a means test for receiving social security benefits and achieved additional savings by changing the way benefits were calculated. The unemployed had to show evidence they were actively looking for employment in order to continue receiving benefits. Eventually, under Thatcher's plan, the national government would transfer the responsibility of paying room and board allowances to local authorities. She also talked about cutting child allowances and streamlining the popular National Health Service as well as raising the fees for its services. Thatcher thought the private health care sector should be enlarged. Altogether, she planned so many alterations in welfare services that many suspected that the Conservative government intended more than mere reformation. Ironically, a majority of the British people did not agree with much of what Thatcher was doing. They favored more welfare, not less, and preferred an expansion of public spending to a cut in taxes. Yet such opinions were not sufficiently focused to threaten the Conservatives' parliamentary majority.

Part of the reason for the Tories' success was the inability of the Labour opposition to heal its divisions and mount an effective challenge. The presence of radical groups within the Labour party, such as the faction called the Militant Tendency, made it difficult for the party to agree on a course of action. Moreover, the party's left wing wanted further nationalizations and advocated unilateral nuclear disarmament. Tony Benn, the leader of this radical faction, was an avowed Marxist who believed that the capitalists were trying to overthrow the democratic system. He attempted to become the deputy leader of the party in 1981, failing by a whisker. Throughout the rest of the decade, Labour continued to suffer from ideological confusion.

Thatcher's popularity received a great boost in April 1982, when Argentina seized the Falkland Islands. By grabbing these islands, which had been British for the last 150 years, the generals who ran Argentina hoped to gain a quick foreign policy success that would redeem their declining popularity. Thatcher rallied the country to defend the Falklanders' right of self-determination. During the month or more required to assemble and transport a military force 8,000 miles to the South Atlantic, Thatcher tried negotiations. When these failed to remove the Argentines, she ordered a counterinvasion. The attack began on 21 May, with the establishment of a bridgehead at San Carlos Bay on East Falkland Island. Three and a half weeks later, on 14 June, the British forced the surrender of the main Argentine army. There were only 255 British casualties. The British greeted the victory with great ebullience. When Thatcher heard the news of the Argentine defeat, she appeared at the door of the prime minister's residence at 10 Downing Street and shouted, "Rejoice! Rejoice!" She had reason to be happy. Her handling of the crisis made her one of the most popular leaders of the postwar era. The crisis also helped her divert attention from the social stress caused by her domestic policies.

A trace of magnanimity toward the losers surfaced in a proposal that the Lord's Prayer be recited in Spanish as well as English at the commemorative service in St. Paul's Cathedral. The suggestion was rejected.[53] The British were smug and self-righteous about their victory, but this did not mean that the Argentine generals, who had cynically provoked the war, were any less disreputable, although they were hardly on a par with Hitler. Throughout the affair, Thatcher had mirrored the Churchillian spirit to remain resolute in pursuit of justice. She saw the war, not as a rivalry between two states, but as a test of the resolve of Western democratic nations to stand up to the aggression of dictators. The Falklands' conflict was her fight for a new international order. It was her way of saying that Britain was on the road to recovery from its period of socialist decline.[54] The ability of Britain to mount such a venture, however, was due more to the added revenues it was getting from the sale of North Sea oil, which came pouring forth almost at the moment she entered office, than to Thatcher's messianic determination to refashion British politics. The North Sea windfall also enabled Britain to reduce its budget deficit and mobilize capital for long-term investment.

Thatcher's popularity began to slide after the 1987 elections. Those elections gave her party a one-hundred–seat edge over Labour in the House of Commons, but the economy turned sour, inflation rose into the double digits, investment slowed, and productivity began to decline. Thatcher reacted by pushing up interest rates, to as much as 15 percent, and by reforming the local tax structure. She instituted a "poll tax," substituting the current property tax with a flat rate on every adult. This new means of getting revenue hit the poorer classes especially hard and produced weeks of public demonstrations, culminating in a particularly bloody riot in Trafalgar Square in March 1990. The Tories began losing by-elections to Labour. Thatcher's loss of popularity also extended to within her own party. Many of her colleagues tired of her tirades; they resented her confrontational style and her zest to solve nonexistent problems. Since the last election, almost her entire cabinet had either resigned or been fired. In November 1990, with the Labour party leading ten points or more in the polls, former Defense Minister Richard Heseltine challenged her for party leadership, forcing her into a second round of balloting. However, before this took place, Thatcher resigned. She clearly had become the problem that threatened to split the party. Her replacement was the modest, low-key John Major. Shortly after taking office, he began to talk about a "social market" economy and a more "caring" government. Clearly, the British people wanted their government to provide more, not fewer, public services.

Toward German Reunification

A Search for National Identity. The defeat of Germany in 1945 dealt a serious blow to the country's sense of national identity. The Nazi regime was so linked with the spirit of the people that discrediting one affected the other. Love of country in all its political or nonpolitical manifestations was now suspect. Political leadership passed into the hands of the Allies, who determined the shape and character of the disunited country. The eventual solidification of Germany into two sections, each with its own government, seemed to spell the end of German unity. Although the Western powers were locked in a cold war with the Soviet Union, both sides accepted partition as the best way to guarantee the stability of Europe. Whatever reconstruction the German Federal Republic and the German Democratic Republic (GDR) would achieve would have to be accomplished at the bidding and the expense of Germany's former enemies.

Of the two Germanies, the eastern regime had the most difficulty establishing its own legitimacy and integrity. The Soviets hailed the GDR as the true Germany, a classless state of peasants and workers separated from the imperialistic and capitalistic Federal Republic. Yet the Soviets were not above sacrificing their satellite if it served their interests. At Geneva in 1955, the Soviet Union tried to prevent the Federal Republic from joining any Western military alliance by proposing the reunification of Germany as a neutral state through free elections. Britain, France, and the United States did not take the bait. But the Soviet overtures showed the GDR leaders the fragility of their tenure. Until the 1970s, the only countries that had exchanged ambassadors with East Germany were those of the Communist bloc and some newly emergent nations. This was largely due to the Hallstein Doctrine, the West German threat to break diplomatic relations with nations that recognized the GDR. East Germany tried to become a more viable state by creating a cult of economic progress, but promised improvements failed to materialize. Its consumer goods and industrial productivity lagged a generation behind those of the West. The Communist leaders' boast that they had ended exploitation fell on deaf ears. While the regime continued to preach that only under socialism did science and technology serve human needs, East German workers continued to devise ways to flee to the West. The GDR clung to its close association with the Soviet Union. It hailed the policy of detente pursued by Leonid Brezhnev as the correct course of action. But the relaxation of tensions between East and West presented real problems. East Germany had constructed its ideology around continued tension with the other Germany. This proved to be a very weak reed.

The West Germans also had problems of identity, but the Allies permitted them a longer leash. Spared the subservience that was mandatory in the East, the Federal Republic was able to develop a viable parliamentary system. The Cold War also enabled the Federal Republic to assert its independence rather rapidly, even though that independence was firmly tied to the Western alliance. The most tangible proof of West German sovereignty was its inclusion in the NATO alliance in 1955 and the rebuilding of its army. These came as a direct result of the Western need to develop an additional bulwark against Soviet expansionism. Thus, at a time when the East Germans were coming increasingly under the control of the Soviets, the West Germans were able to win more freedom. The reemergence of West Germany as a major power was also due to its *Wirtschaftswunder* (economic miracle), which gave real substance to the West German sense of identity and self-confidence. One of the proudest symbols of that ascendancy was the Mercedes-Benz, an artifact that combined elegant design with authoritative style. The West Germans reveled in their materialism; such pride had not been seen since the boom years of the German Reich prior to World War I. The preamble of the West German constitution claimed West Germany would carry the torch of German freedom and unity through free self-determination,[55] and the country's great industrial expansion suggested this might be more than an optimistic dream. A new generation, unsullied by Hitlerism, had developed the confidence to exercise power without guilt to make their nation once again the arbiter of Europe.

Eastern Politics. Konrad Adenauer had apparently failed to appreciate the threat that de Gaulle's European union presented to the NATO alliance. But unlike de Gaulle, Adenauer was not unduly alarmed at American dominance, which he regarded as necessary to protect Germany against aggression and guarantee the integrity of West Berlin. Furthermore, the 1954 agreements, which underscored the responsibility of the Big Three in German reunification, limited Germany's options. The bilateral cooperation between Germany and France, upon which de Gaulle counted to make his independent Europe a reality, did not survive Adenauer's retirement. The Germans saw no reason to undertake an uncertain association with France, especially since de Gaulle was not inclined to commit his country's nuclear capacity to the common defense of Europe. Even had de Gaulle been willing, the *force de frappe* was hardly in the same league with the striking power of the United States. German military cooperation with the United States therefore expanded.

The government of Ludwig Erhard (1963–1966) was under considerable pressure from "German Gaullists" to become more independent of the United States. The chancellor's determination to remain on good terms with both France *and* the United States prompted de Gaulle, on the eve of his withdrawal from NATO, to link French support for German reunification to support for his defense policy. The scheme to separate Bonn from Washington backfired. The Erhard government remained a staunch member of NATO, believing that the eventual reunification of Germany could only be achieved through the Atlantic alliance, with an undiluted American presence. The Germans concluded that de Gaulle's nuclear defense policy would result in their subservience to France. They figured that the American nuclear umbrella came with fewer strings. Besides, German leadership in the Common Market provided a secure base from which Germany could assert an increasingly active role in foreign policy. They also believed German industrial strength would prove especially valuable in dealing with the economically backward states of the Soviet bloc. Accordingly, the Germans began changing their strategy on reunification.

One flaw in these calculations was the chancellor himself. Erhard lacked the stature of his predecessor. He had been an able economics minister, but in becoming chancellor, he had risen to his level of incompetence. He was always more at home with numbers than with people, and his enforcement of a secondary policy like the Hallstein Doctrine was pathetic. Even before his fall, Erhard had damaged the cohesion of his own party.

The new government was a Grand Coalition of Christian Democrats and Socialists (1966–1969), led by Kurt Georg Kiesinger of the CDU as chancellor and Social Democrat Willy Brandt as foreign minister. These leaders recognized that German reunification need not be a prerequisite for the normalization of relations with the East. In its new *Ostpolitik* (Eastern policy), the West German government acknowledged that the Federal Republic did not have an exclusive right to represent all Germans and abandoned the Hallstein Doctrine. The concession paved the way for the inclusion of both Germanies in the United Nations. (East Germany established diplomatic relations with other Western European states, the United States, and most other major powers.) Two important events in 1968 allowed the West Germans greater freedom of action. De Gaulle, faced with the riots in Paris, began concentrating more on domestic affairs. The Soviets sent troops to Prague, Czechoslovakia, in a desperate effort to hold their crumbling satellite empire together. The West Germans, freed of French competition, decided they would not try to exploit Soviet insecurities.

In 1969, Willy Brandt formed his own government supported by votes from the small Free Democratic party. In the five years (1969–1974) he remained chancellor, he helped change the face of West German relations with the Soviet bloc countries. In Moscow on 12 August 1970, he signed an agreement with the Soviet Union in which both countries promised to respect "without restriction" the territorial integrity of *all* European states, including the present frontier between West and East Germany and the Oder-Neisse line between East Germany and Poland.

Four months later, the Brandt government drove the point home by signing a similar accord in Warsaw. Again the Federal Republic recognized the Oder-Neisse boundary between Poland and the GDR. During the visit, Brandt made an important symbolic gesture. He placed a wreath on the Polish war memorial and dropped to his knees in prayer. The Catholic Poles were genuinely touched.

The Ostpolitik bore further fruit. In September 1971, the Soviets officially recognized the independent status of West Berlin in a Four-Power treaty. In December 1972, the Federal Republic and the GDR extended de facto recognition to each other, with an exchange of permanent representatives (not ambassadors).[56] In June 1973, West Germany and Czechoslovakia signed an agreement in which the 1938 Munich Agreement, which had been concluded under the threat of force, was declared null and void. The treaty also included a mutual renunciation of force, respect for the inviolability of frontiers, and a pledge to settle all disputes peacefully. Taken together, the agreements signed between 1970 and 1973 amounted to a collective Locarno in which the Germans showed they had no desire to change the territorial status quo established at the end of World War II. By undoing the past insofar as it was possible, they hoped to clear the way for the eventual reunification of their country.

The foreign policy of Willy Brandt and Konrad Adenauer stood in dramatic contrast. Under Adenauer, the Federal Republic considered itself the only legitimate German state and the only one capable of representing Germany's interests. Adenauer dramatized the foreign menace to help spur his country's recovery and revitalize its sense of purpose. He felt that Germany's final borders could be established only by an eventual peace treaty. He believed that reunification had to come before detente. Brandt, however, recognized that confrontation was no longer necessary for a Germany that was economically one of the world's strongest states as well as one of the most secure. Thus Germany could afford to be more conciliatory. Brandt's doctrine of "two states of one nation" indicated that henceforth the Federal Republic's relations with the GDR would be characterized by mutual exchange and cooperation. Accordingly, Brandt agreed to respect the inviolability of East Germany's frontiers. He believed that detente would pave the way for reunification, but he and his colleagues were also aware that if the Soviet Union opposed reunification, then reunification would not take place. They also knew that other Europeans did not want the two Germanies to become one Germany. Although a generation had passed since the war, memories of German aggression and atrocities were still vivid, and many Europeans still believed the Germans were not to be trusted. A popular joke went: "What do you get if the Germans unite? Out of the way." Therefore it only seemed reasonable that the Germans should make the best of partition.

Helmut Schmidt, the Social Democratic leader who followed Brandt as chancellor (1974–1982), believed that West Germany had to gain Soviet acceptance of the Federal Republic's right to help improve the living standards of Germans living under Communism.[57] Schmidt recognized Germany's strategic position in the defense of the democratic West, but at the same time, he was determined to continue and strengthen the Ostpolitik. His negotiations with the Soviets focused on two principal areas: economic exchange and the status of Berlin. Clearly, the Germans wanted to be free of the tutelage of the superpowers; but, as Schmidt recognized, this was not likely as long as the Europeans could not achieve proper integration or agree on common objectives. Schmidt was less obvious and possibly more sincere than de Gaulle in advocating European independence (he certainly was less exclusionary when it came to Great Britain), but the idea of fortress Europe was a strong component in his thoughts. The Europeans, he believed, had "a right to protect and defend [themselves] against any attempt to force foreign rule or dictatorial social and governmental forms." The chance that the Europeans could defend themselves successfully would increase if, through its own unification process, Western Europe were to develop into a great power.[58] Naturally, a re-unified Germany would be expected to play a significant role in that amalgam.

Building Socialism in the GDR. The Stalinist regime of Walter Ulbricht had become rancid. The long-time political boss of the East German Communist party had weathered many changes and threats. He had survived demands for his resignation during the Berlin riots of 1953; maintained rigidity in the face of de-Stalinization and the denunciation of the cult of personality; and secured the GDR's borders by fostering the erection of the Berlin Wall in 1961. But Ulbricht's insistence on full freedom of action for his country in its foreign relations clashed with the broader interests of the Soviet Union for detente and led to his ouster as party chief in May 1971.[59] (Ulbricht remained as head of state, however, until his death in 1976.) His place was taken by Erich Honecker, a man created in Ulbricht's image but without his force or determination. Honecker emphasized economic improvement over ideological purity. He concentrated on raising national income and on such projects as expanding public housing and producing more consumer goods. Honecker's accession to power coincided with the new Ostpolitik of the Federal Republic, which had produced the first "basic treaty" between the two countries. The agreement prompted Honecker to suggest a new formula for separate socialist nationhood: "There are not two states of a single nation," he explained, "but instead two nations in states of different social orders."[60] Because East Germany was the heir to everything progressive, it was a legitimate historical German entity.

On 7 October 1979, at the official commemoration of the thirtieth anniversary of the founding of the GDR, Honecker hailed the triumph of socialism in East Germany as a turning point in the history of the German people and of Europe:

> The course and results of the socialist revolution on German soil once again confirm the correctness and triumphant nature of the ideas of Marxism-Leninism. It has become perfectly clear that our workers' and farmers' state is the guardian of the revolutionary traditions of the German working class and the humanistic heritage of the German people.[61]

However, the state's increased contacts with the West were producing greater indebtedness. A marked deterioration in the terms of trade, especially the increase in the world price of oil, made its balance of payments worse. The Soviet Union, the main supplier of raw materials to East Germany, raised its prices, thereby adding to the trade deficit. Naturally, East German consumers bore the cost of such adversity. Growth in retail trade slowed, and the supply of consumer goods fell. Demands for political liberalization began to be heard, spurred on by the protest movements in the other Eastern European countries, especially Poland. Honecker tried to avoid a crisis that might endanger his position, but the regime over which he presided was in deep trouble and would soon lose its ability to survive.[62]

DISCORD IN THE EASTERN BLOC

The Degeneration of Soviet Power

The Brezhnev Succession. Nikita Khrushchev had a buccaneer's spirit. While talking peaceful coexistence, he threatened war. Part of his daring undoubtedly came from his frustration at having his country encircled with enemy military bases. To this was added the humiliation he suffered from the U-2 spy plane flights. Only in 1960, after ten years of trying, were the Soviets finally able to shoot one of these intruders down. Perhaps a more prudent man would have tempered his frustration with caution, but that was not Khrushchev's style. He provoked two crises at Berlin and followed these with an attempt to place missiles on the island of Cuba. The risks were too great for his Kremlin colleagues. In October 1964, they forced him to resign.

Leonid Brezhnev, his successor (1964–1982) and former protégé, was more cautious. He wanted to stabilize his country's foreign relations, while carrying out a massive arms buildup that would make the Soviet Union invulnerable to attack. The experiences of World War II influenced Brezhnev, as they had Khrushchev, and he was determined that the Soviet Union would not be caught off guard again. He wanted to be able to conduct foreign policy from a position of nuclear parity with the United States. At the same time, however, he realized that the next war would have no winners. His goal, set out at the Twenty-third Congress of the Communist party in 1966, was to safeguard the earth from another world war by practicing peaceful coexistence with states that had different social systems.[63] Yet while Brezhnev wanted to participate in building a new world order, the Soviets also wanted to retain what they had, especially their sphere of influence in Eastern Europe, and, if possible, to transform themselves from a continental to a global power.

The policy of de-Stalinization, which discontinued Soviet economic exploitation of the satellites and loosened its political control over them, did not mean that the Communist leaders were ready to allow the satellites to chart their own course in politics and economics. The events of the 1950s had showed that Eastern Europe could no longer be considered an unqualified asset, but it was still vital as the outer defense perimeter of the Soviet Union. Even so, the Soviets had to ask themselves if the advantages outweighed the liabilities. The Eastern European peoples were undergoing a nationalistic renaissance and could hardly be considered reliable allies. Furthermore, their economies were a mess and needed constant assistance from the Soviet Union. Accordingly, Brezhnev tried to establish more business-like relations with the satellites. He was prepared to tolerate some latitude and diversity, but he insisted that the states remain members of the Warsaw Pact and that their policies not threaten Soviet strategic interests. However, it was difficult to determine how much local autonomy was compatible with Soviet hegemony.

The Soviets still feared a rearmed Germany. For this reason, Stalin's offer to accept reunification (with the proviso that the country be neutralized) may not have been insincere. Brezhnev tried to strengthen Soviet ties with the GDR. At the same time, he pursued improved relations with the Federal Republic. The Soviets had also tried to exploit de Gaulle's dissatisfaction with NATO and his growing differences with West Germany by expressing concern about German militarization. But trying to maintain close relations with both Germany and France has always been historically difficult. Being on friendly terms with one has usually resulted in alienating the other. Brezhnev's timing was particularly bad. The Federal Republic, like the other nations of Western Europe, had yet to get over its outrage at the Soviet invasion of Czechoslovakia in August 1968.

The Prague Spring. While other Eastern European satellites had sought to extricate themselves from the crushing pressure of Soviet tutelage, the Czechoslovaks seemed content to remain an obedient satellite. During the 1960s, however, many people inside and outside the Czechoslovak Communist party concluded that an independent road to socialism was necessary if the country were to develop economically. When Klement Gottwald died in March 1953, his body was embalmed and put on display in a Prague mausoleum in the manner of Lenin and Stalin, but the hope of burying his system with him seemed forlorn. Antonín Novotný, an unfaltering Stalinist, became his successor.

The new secretary-general proceeded to consolidate his hold on power with a wave of arrests and persecutions. In the aftermath of Stalin's death, the Soviets were urging the Hungarian and Polish party leaders to relax their police states to calm popular discontent, but left the Czechoslovaks practically alone. Khrushchev apparently had more confidence in Novotný than in Hungary's Matyas Rákosi or Poland's Boleslaw Bierut. Indeed, considering Czechoslovak quiescence during the events of 1956, the trust did not seem misplaced. While the Polish and Hungarian Communists were purging themselves of Stalinists, the Czechoslovak party continued with basically the same faces. In 1957, Novotný also assumed the Czechoslovak presidency. Although some opposed his growing personal power, the dissidents, many of them intellectuals, presented no threat to the regime. Indeed, Novotný felt so secure that he set about eliminating the last vestiges of capitalism by abolishing private farms and single-proprietor businesses. Members of the old middle class were dismissed from their jobs and forced to take unskilled or manual labor jobs. In 1960, the party boasted that Czechoslovakia had achieved the highest level of socialism outside the Soviet Union. The new constitution contained an article pledging cooperation with the Soviet Union and the other countries of the Eastern bloc.[64]

De-Stalinization in the Soviet Union troubled the Czechoslovak hard-liners, however, and they resorted to a series of cosmetic changes. They sent the corpse of Gottwald to the crematorium, dismantled Stalin's monument in Prague, and rehabilitated some prominent Communist victims of earlier purges. Novotný found scapegoats for previous excesses and mistakes in Gottwald and his henchmen. Emulating Khrushchev, Novotný removed the Stalinists from the party hierarchy and the government and replaced them with younger men. But this new leadership was not as dependable as Novotný thought. Many had lost their early reverence for the Soviet system as the proper model for socialist development. They wanted to reform the Communist system, but believed this was impossible under Novotný. Furthermore, the Slovaks wanted an end to Czech centralization. The Czechoslovak Communist party appeared to be breaking down into its national units as an anti-Novotný coalition formed in the party Central Committee.

The party secretary of Slovakia, Alexander Dubček, led the rebellion against Novotný at the Central Committee meeting in November 1967. Novotný called upon the Soviets for support. Brezhnev came to Prague in December, but remained noncommittal. During his visit, the Soviet leader consulted with Dubček. Brezhnev's apparent lack of support for Novotný emboldened the reformers, and they pushed for Novotný's ouster. On 5 January 1968, Dubček became first secretary of the Communist party, although Novotný retained his post as Czechoslovak president. The forty-six-year-old Dubček was a compromise candidate, a Slovak with good Communist credentials. He seemed to be a typical *apparatchik*.[65] Between the wars, he had lived in the Soviet Union where he attended primary and secondary schools; he had stayed there again from 1955 to 1958 and studied at a higher political school in Moscow. Novotný had found him reliable and had selected him to be the first secretary of the Slovak party in 1963.

Shortly after becoming first secretary, Dubček went to Moscow for consultations, the tenor of which can be gathered from one of his speeches published soon after his return. Dubček insisted that he did not intend to change the general nature of Czechoslovak internal and foreign policy, but he did promise reform: the adoption of new methods and a rapid advance in science and technology. He also pledged to develop socialist democracy.[66] The "new direction" sounded like the old Communist double-talk, but Dubček did not intend to conduct business as usual, and he had more than enough support to carry out his plans. Demands for real change came from many quarters and from all parts of the country in countless meetings and rallies. On 22 March, Novotný was forced to relinquish the post of president. A mass resignation of his supporters from their leadership positions followed.[67] General Ludvik Svoboda, who had helped deliver the country to Communism in 1948, became the new president, the perfect man to forestall possible Soviet interference.

The reform continued on many levels. While Dubček and his associates tried to create Communism "with a human face" by bringing about change within the party, others tried to force the pace of reform while ignoring the party. Already by March the mass media were publishing information and news with little restriction, but without official approval. Radio and television followed suit. As millions of people expressed support for the reform process, demands arose for an investigation into the death of Tomás G. Masaryk, the foreign minister who had been murdered after the 1948 Communist takeover. On 5 April 1968, the Czechoslovak Communist party adopted an Action Program that reiterated the party's right to maintain its leadership role as a guarantor of progress, but acknowledged that freedom of expression, "a broad scope for social initiative, a frank exchange of views, and the democratization of the whole social and political system have literally become a necessity if socialist society is to remain dynamic."[68] The program promised to guarantee freedom of speech and curb the authority of the secret police. It also advocated a greater role for free enterprise in the economy. In May, the Dubček government officially abolished censorship. But could the party continue in power if Czechoslovakia adopted real democracy? The Czechoslovak Communist party momentarily enjoyed great popularity, but it could no longer control the pace of democratization. The Soviets knew that it would only be a question of time before Czechoslovakia would dismantle its Communist system.

Shortly after Novotný's ouster as president, Brezhnev, supported by Wladyslaw Gomulka of Poland and Ulbricht of East Germany, warned of unpleasant consequences if the Czechoslovaks were to continue on their current path of reform. Relations with Czechoslovakia grew noticeably worse. In May, Dubček again went to Moscow to try to reassure the Kremlin leaders that his reforms presented no threat to Soviet security and were compatible with socialism. Even while he spoke, however, other Warsaw Pact countries were carrying out military maneuvers in southern Poland just across the Czech border, and the Soviets were increasing their military force in Czechoslovakia to about 30,000 troops. The Kremlin feared it might lose control of all Eastern Europe. On the night of 20–21 August, units of the Red Army crossed into Czechoslovakia. The Soviet troops were supported by forces from Poland, the GDR, Hungary, and Bulgaria. The 500,000-man army made it the largest military action since the end of World War II. Of the Eastern bloc countries, only Romania condemned the action and refused to participate. The Romanians had no sympathy for Dubček's policies of liberalization, but they understandably opposed foreign intervention in another nation's domestic affairs.

The Soviets tried to make their aggression more palatable by claiming that the Czechoslovak Communist party had invited them in to give fraternal assistance to the Czechoslovak people. Unfortunately for this ploy, the Soviets could not find any Communist leader who would admit he made such a request. They therefore asserted that they had a right to intervene to preserve socialism in Eastern Europe whenever they thought it was necessary. The "Brezhnev Doctrine" was the high-water mark of Soviet pretensions of control over the satellites. It stated that every Communist party was "responsible not only to its own people but also to all socialist countries and to the entire Communist movement."[69] The policy stipulated that each socialist country maintained its independence only because it was part of the socialist commonwealth backed by the power of the Soviet Union. In essence, the doctrine was a throwback to the Stalinist practice of maintaining "friendly" governments in Eastern Europe for the strategic needs of the Soviet Union.

The Czechoslovaks met the invasion with passive resistance. They even tried to talk to the Soviet soldiers and convince them to respect their rights, but to no avail. The Soviets arrested Dubček and his associates, but found it impossible to put together a coherent government to run the country.[70] President Svoboda went to Moscow to negotiate, but insisted that Dubček and the other imprisoned leaders be allowed to participate in the talks. The Soviets reluctantly agreed. They managed to convince Svoboda to accept their fifteen-point protocol, however. This program effectively destroyed the reform movement and removed its leaders from positions of power. The process of "normalization" led to the ouster of Dubček. Gustáv Husák replaced him on 17 April 1969. Husák was also a Slovak, but he was more willing to give the Kremlin what it wanted and presided over the wholesale dismissal of reformers from the government, the party, the trade unions, the universities, and the mass media.[71] The Husák regime jailed many reformers for being counterrevolutionaries,[72] but it did not carry out a bloodletting as had occurred in Hungary in 1956. Dubček was treated relatively leniently, for example. He was first appointed ambassador to Turkey and then received a minor post in the State Forestry Service in Bratislava. The Hungarian uprising and the Prague Spring also differed in another respect. In 1956, the Hungarian leaders had clearly forsaken Communism; in 1968, the Czechoslovak government was trying to put a human face on it. The Soviets, however, considered both movements dangerous because both aimed at independence from Moscow.

Restricting the Use of Force. By the end of the 1960s, the Soviets had been able to overcome their ten-year inferiority in intercontinental ballistic missiles and had actually surpassed the United States in overall number of missiles. Not only had the Soviets increased their strategic rocket forces, thereby adopting the American policy of deterring aggression through the threat of massive retaliation, but they had also achieved an across-the-board increase in their conventional military strength. They thus had the capability of conducting their rivalry with the United States on a global scale. This new position of strength, which was roughly comparable to American military power, assured that the Soviets could enter any serious Strategic Arms Limitations Talks (SALT) without being disadvantaged. After numerous delays, such negotiations finally got underway at Helsinki on 17 November 1969. Despite the international tensions that existed as a result of the war in Vietnam and the conflict in the Middle East, the superpowers finally produced an agreement on 26 May 1972.

One of the things that helped convince the Soviets that it was in their interest to sign an agreement at this time was the triangular policy of National Security Affairs Adviser Henry Kissinger who hoped to gain leverage against the Soviets by using the Red Chinese. Kissinger had secretly gone to China in July 1971 to talk directly with Zhou Enlai. This diplomacy cleared the way for the admission of the People's Republic of China to the United Nations—Taiwan unceremoniously lost its Security Council seat—and its diplomatic recognition by the United States. President Richard M. Nixon cemented the deal in a historic visit to Beijing in February 1972. The Communist Chinese were obviously more afraid of the ambitions of the Soviets than they were of the Americans. Periodic military skirmishes had erupted on their northern border, and the Soviets had built an air base in Mongolia.

The first SALT agreement prohibited deployment of antiballistic systems, set limits on strategic delivery systems, and defined technical issues related to such things as radar and testing; it also included provisions for monitoring the treaty through electronic and other surveillance. The United States recognized what it heretofore was reluctant to do: that the Soviet Union had a right to full nuclear parity. The SALT treaty was followed with a general agreement that tried to reduce tensions further. In Moscow on 22 June 1973, President Nixon and Chairman Brezhnev pledged to "refrain from the threat or use of force against the other Party, against the allies of the other Party, and against other countries, in circumstances which may endanger international peace and security."[73] They also promised to cooperate in a wide range of activities, including trade, health, and science.[74] The Soviet-American summit did not so much remove basic problems, as underscore the obsolescence of the policy of confrontation. Nevertheless, some viewed the Soviet move as only a ploy to lull Europe into a more sympathetic attitude toward the Soviet Union in order to erode American influence. Critics also believed that the Soviets were using detente to convince the American public, already undergoing a new mood of isolationism because of the loss of the Vietnam War, that they should reduce their military commitment to Europe. At the very least, it seemed clear that the Soviets wanted international acceptance of the territorial changes that had been made in Europe after World War II.

In July 1975, thirty-five nations met in Helsinki, Finland, for the grand conference on European Security and Cooperation. Over two years of negotiations had been needed to produce the Final Document that was signed on 1 August. The ceremony took seventeen minutes. The Helsinki accord was one of intent rather than actual commitment, but it resolved many issues stemming from World War II—at least on paper. The Soviets specifically recognized the inviolability of all current European frontiers, while the Western democracies insisted on a clause in which the signatories promised to respect "fundamental freedoms, including freedom of thought, conscience, religion, or belief." The signatories also pledged to accord each other most-favored-nation treatment in trade and to facilitate "the freer and wider dissemination of information of all kinds." They pledged to cooperate in the fields of science, technology, and the environment, to facilitate wider travel, and to ease restrictions on movements of citizens, especially families, from one state to another. Finally, they expressed a desire "to search for peaceful solutions to all outstanding differences."[75] The agreement had a little in it for everyone and was comfortably void of sanctions. Although the agreement was a symbol that the two superpowers were becoming less confrontational in Europe, their interests continued to clash in other parts of the world: the Middle East, Africa, and Southeast Asia.

American president Jimmy Carter (1977–1981) took the moral high ground in a campaign of human rights throughout the world—a latter-day example of Wilson's desire to make the world safe for democracy. Nevertheless, Carter signed a second SALT treaty with the Soviets at a summit meeting in Vienna on 18 June

1979. SALT II set a limit of 2,250 on strategic delivery systems and cruise missiles whose range exceeded 600 kilometers. It also allowed the Soviets a 308 to 0 advantage in silo-based intercontinental ballistic missiles. The American Senate was reluctant to ratify the arrangement. A majority of the senators feared that the president had conceded too many advantages to the Soviets, thereby increasing the likelihood of a Soviet first strike. Detente received a further blow when the Soviets invaded Afghanistan in December 1979 to secure Communist rule against local Afghani freedom fighters or *Mujahideen*; the invasion marked the beginning of a bloody eight-year war. In January 1980, Carter effectively withdrew the SALT treaty from consideration. The administration took further action by suspending American participation in the Olympic games set for Moscow in the summer of 1980 and canceling American grain sales to the Soviet Union. Increased expenditure on armaments accompanied the breakdown of detente. Throughout the years of Carter's administration, more and more money was allocated for high-tech weaponry, including smart bombs, cruise missiles, and stealth technology.

A Brief Return of the Cold War. Ronald Reagan, who succeeded Carter in 1981, was also an ideologue but in a different way. Reagan believed that the United States was a chosen nation, the only country in the world whose entire system was based on the words "we the people." Reagan made hatred of the Communist Soviet Union a main feature of his campaign for the presidency in 1980; upon his accession to office in January 1981, it became clear that this was not just campaign rhetoric. The new president had an abiding hostility toward the Soviet Union, which he called the "evil empire." To show he meant business, he continued the arms buildup of his predecessor. Reagan liked big weapons systems, the most impressive of which was the Strategic Defense Initiative. Dubbed "Star Wars," it was envisioned as a vast, movable, stratospheric Maginot Line composed of laser beams that would shoot down all enemy missiles targeted on the United States, giving the country absolute immunity from attack. The possibility of developing advanced technology with such precision seemed remote. Progress in armaments' development had made it feasible for missiles to intercept and shoot down other incoming missiles, although not with the infallible precision necessary to make the United States invulnerable to attack. The Reagan administration believed otherwise.[76] The president was so confident that this new technology would end a superpower showdown that he offered to share it with other nations.

The Soviets, already lagging behind the United States in the sophistication of their weaponry, feared that Star Wars or even a system approaching Star Wars could prompt the United States into carrying out a first strike. They did not believe that the Americans were simply interested in bargaining from strength, and it seemed preposterous that the United States would actually give away the Star Wars secret. The Soviets feared that Reagan was actually preparing the United States to fight a nuclear war it would win. In May 1981, Yuri Andropov, the chairman of the Soviet secret police, made a secret speech to the Politburo in which he revealed that the KGB was cooperating with Soviet military intelligence to ascertain the exact timing of such an operation. For example, KGB operators in London were monitoring the number of lighted windows and automobile traffic at all government buildings and military installations outside the usual working hours to report any deviation from the norm. In 1982, when Andropov at the age of sixty-eight succeeded Brezhnev as head of the Communist party (1982–1984), fear of nuclear attack reached its height. Andropov claimed that the Reagan administration had imperial ambitions, and he doubted "whether Washington has

A visibly ailing **Leonid Brezhnev inaugurates a memorial building complex in Kiev** on 9 May 1981. He is accompanied by Soviet Defense Minister Dimitri Ustinov and the First Secretary of the Ukrainian Party, Vladimir Shcherbitsky. The gerontocrats' hold over the destiny of the Soviet Union was approaching its end.

any brakes at all preventing it from crossing the mark before which any sober-minded person must stop."[77] In November 1981, the KGB center in Moscow believed that American armed forces had been put on alert as a prelude to the countdown of an attack. The Soviet fears, of course, proved to have been exaggerated. Though unknown in the West, the crisis was one of the last great nuclear alarms of the postwar period.

When Andropov died in February 1984, he was succeeded by the colorless, stolid, and if anything more conservative Konstantin Chernenko, who was seventy-three. Brezhnev (who was seventy-six when he died), Andropov, and Chernenko all came from a class of leaders whose careers had profited from the purges of the 1930s.[78] This gerontocracy no longer represented many of the post-Stalinist leaders who were uncomfortable with straitjacket ideological formulas. The younger generation believed the security of the country depended on its ability to modernize its economy, even if this meant introducing the incentives of the marketplace. Such a policy had not been seen since the New Economic Policy of the 1920s. This pressure for reform would grow in strength and eventually lead the country away from Communist-dominated government.

The Restive Satellites

The Frailty of Allegiance. The Soviets maintained control of their satellites through their domination of government and party leaders. The Soviet ambassadors acted as the regime's proconsuls and could call on the Red Army to back up their authority if necessary. However, tight Soviet control had led to economic backwardness and popular hostility born of dark memories of lives broken and families destroyed. The Communist path had all too often led to a graveyard. All the satellites suffered from the same deficiencies and scarcities that plagued the Soviet economy: shoddy and insufficient consumer goods, declining worker productivity, low rates of growth, wasted resources, and environmental pollution. While the market economies of Western Europe flourished, the economies of Eastern Europe were plagued by gross mismanagement, antiquated equipment, and bloated bureaucracies. Pricing structures bore little relationship to actual costs or customer demand. Restrictive and hostile to change and innovation, Eastern European industry used technology reminiscent of an earlier age. Khrushchev had talked about allowing the satellite states to develop their own socialist systems, but whenever the Soviet Union was faced with divergence, it endeavored to bring the irregulars back into line. The Brezhnev Doctrine was merely the latest example.

Western European Communism seemed to present an alternative, however. "Eurocommunists" contended that political power was dependent on the free will of the electorate in a multiparty system with a mixed economy. Detente and the policy of Ostpolitik had made strict orthodoxy passé.

Communist rule was especially fragile in Poland where five attempts to shake loose from Soviet domination were made between 1956 and 1981. Each crisis had been preceded by predictable complaints and predictable demands: the expansion of political freedom, the end of central economic planning, and independence from the Soviet Union. The 1956 crisis, which had brought Gomulka to power, had, at first, expanded freedom of speech and halted the persecution of the Roman Catholic church, but under Soviet pressure and with Gomulka's own preference for authoritarianism, repression had returned. Gomulka hardly enhanced his popularity by announcing price increases (as much as 20 percent) on a range of basic commodities. At the same time, he tried to boost production by offering new incentives. Many Poles viewed this program as a trick to induce them to work harder for fewer benefits. Gomulka launched his austerity program just before Christmas on 12 December 1970. Two days later, shipyard workers in Gdansk (formerly Danzig), Gdynia, and Sopot went on strike to protest the price increases. The strike led to clashes with the police and an attempt to burn down the regional Communist party headquarters. The violence spread to other cities throughout Poland. In an attempt to restore order, the Communist party, at a special Central Committee meeting on 20 December 1970, deposed Gomulka and replaced him with Edward Gierek. Gierek immediately promised the Poles a higher standard of living and a greater degree of worker participation in running the factories. The new party chief did not rescind the decrees of the previous week, but did promise a two-year freeze on prices.[79] The turmoil, however, continued through the rest of the decade, an indication that the Communist party leadership was incapable of changing its basic authoritarian style or providing the Polish people with a decent standard of living.

The new leadership's answer was to take advantage of the current mood of detente to borrow as much money as it could from the West to invest in the development of Polish industry. Much of the money, however, was used to buy off the workers with higher wages rather than to improve capital equipment. Although it guaranteed worker satisfaction in the short run, such a policy of bribery was bound to backfire. If Poland were to be considered a good capital risk, it would eventually have to repay the loans. But without fundamental economic changes that would enable it to produce goods the West wanted in exchange, repaying the loans would prove difficult. The Poles tried to meet their foreign obligations by exporting agricultural products, but this put a heavy strain on their own domestic market.

Although Poland had some of the best farmland in northern Europe, and the regime had backed away from the policy of collectivization begun after World War II, food production did not keep pace with demand. Farming techniques had changed little from those employed half a century earlier. Mechanized equipment was scarce, and the government was not eager to remedy the situation because doing so might enhance the position of the private farmers. Therefore, the more efficient private sector was frequently deprived of fertilizers and other supplies necessary for increased output. Agricultural exports, especially in meat, caused domestic shortages. In June 1976, the government raised the price of food to reflect the limited supply. Immediately, workers in Warsaw and Radom went out on strike. The authorities backed down and rescinded the increases. Aware of their growing power, workers and intellectuals began to organize. Their petitions demanded respect for the rule of law and civil rights. In October 1978, the election of Karol Wojtyla as pope (John Paul II), the first Pole to be so honored, gave a tremendous boost to the aspirations of the Polish Catholic church to bring an end to Communism. But the most persistent irritant proved to be the high cost of food; it constantly stoked the fires of discontent. In July 1980, the regime raised the price of meat by as much as 60 percent. Gierek went on nationwide television to try to explain the necessity for such hikes.

The lesson in economics fell on deaf ears. This time the workers did not have to take to the streets. Instead, they used their recently organized committees to negotiate wage increases to match the price increases. Such collective bargaining was heretofore unheard of in a Communist state. The regime opportunistically tried to limit the damage by satisfying those workers with the most muscle at the expense of the weaker groups. This divide-and-conquer policy did not work. The Lenin shipyards at the Baltic port of Gdansk, the locus of previous strife, went out on strike. In addition to their grievances over pay and benefits, the workers demanded the democratization of Polish society, the lifting of restrictions on the Catholic church, and an end to the Communist monopoly of the trade unions. The Gdansk shipbuilders, led by Lech Walesa, demanded the legal recognition of Solidarity, an independent federation of trade unions that would act as the workers' main collective bargaining unit. The protest was too strong for the government and the seriously divided Communist party.

In the Gdansk Agreement of 31 August 1980, the government recognized the legitimacy of Solidarity, thereby becoming the first Communist state to recognize an independent trade union. The workers had the support of dissident intellectuals and the Catholic church, which had traditionally played a strong political role in protecting Polish nationalism. Standing behind the claim of the Catholic church to be the moral guardian of the Polish people was Pope John Paul II who intended to use his influence to defend the Polish Catholic church's prerogatives by encouraging more political activism. The Soviets feared the Gdansk Agreement could lead to Polish defection from the Warsaw Pact and the end of their control in

Thirty-seven-year-old electronics technician **Lech Walesa inspires fellow workers** at the Lenin shipyards in Gdansk in May 1980. The discontent of the shipbuilders led to the establishment of the first independent trade union movement in the Communist bloc.

Eastern Europe. They considered military intervention, but were not eager to take such action. They knew that intervention would end detente and any hope of future arms control agreements, both of which were essential to allow the Soviet Union to shift its resources from armaments production to economic development. Furthermore, at a Warsaw Pact meeting in December 1980, all of the other satellite countries opted for a political solution, preferring to let the Polish leadership re-establish order by itself. The satellites decided that the best way to bring Solidarity to heel was for the Polish army itself to mount a coup.

Moscow found a candidate in General Wojciech Jaruzelski, a Politburo member and currently a minister of the government without portfolio. In the fall of 1981, the Soviet leaders pressured the Polish Communist party to make Jaruzelski its leader. On 13 December, Jaruzelski proclaimed martial law, and the following year, he ordered 6,000 members of Solidarity, including Walesa, placed under arrest. Despite the crackdown, Jaruzelski ruled with a certain amount of moderation, at least by Communist standards. He tried to co-opt Solidarity's campaign for more worker participation in the management of factories by creating new, non-Solidarity trade unions to handle complaints. These new groups remained under party control. He allowed non-Communist candidates in parliamentary elections, and once he had lifted martial law and released the Solidarity leaders, he tolerated a certain amount of freedom of speech. The policy of "normalization" offended Polish Communist hard-liners, who unsuccessfully tried to have him removed. But no amount of official moderation could restore credibility to the Polish Communist regime.

Jaruzelski's motives were the subject of controversy. Some regarded him as a dedicated Communist ideologue who willingly served the interests of his foreign masters; others saw him as a hero who acted in the best interests of his country in helping to prevent a Soviet takeover. The sharp division reflected the nature of survival in a Soviet satellite. In a broader sense, it posed the dilemma of how to judge collaboration. Jaruzelski's supporters said that the general had prevented a war that would have drowned the Poles in a sea of blood; others claimed that he had declared war on his own people. Michael Jagiello, the first ranking Communist official to resign in protest over the imposition of martial law, said that Jaruzelski was an example of a patriotic Pole who found himself tragically trapped in the Communist system. In Jagiello's view, Jaruzelski's greatest political error was that he kept his illusions too long: "He failed to recognize the collapse of socialism until his last years." His actions were well-intentioned, but misguided.[80]

The Spread of Reform. The Soviet Union had further cause for alarm. Crushing the Prague Spring in 1968 in Czechoslovakia did not stop the steady erosion of faith in the Communist system. The regime of Gustáv Husák, who succeeded Alexander Dubček, had restored stability, but tension lay just under the surface. In January 1977, three hundred Czech intellectuals circulated a petition, "Charter 77," which condemned the current wave of political repression. The protest was quickly and brutally suppressed, but its drafters were not exterminated.[81] Even after Husák's purge of the party, no one wanted to go back to the Stalinist tactics of the past. Many Czech citizens, deprived of an open forum in which to vent their opposition, turned to religious activity as a means of keeping the protest alive. Thus the Czechoslovak Catholic church served the same purpose as its Polish counterpart in providing an avenue through which people could express their opposition to Communism.

In Hungary, the government of János Kádár rebuilt the Communist party after Soviet tanks invaded the country in 1956 following Hungary's withdrawal from the Warsaw Pact. Kádár was a politician who wanted to survive, and to do so he tried to build up a constituency in his own country independent of close Soviet direction. He launched a middle-of-the-road economic program, called "the New Economic Mechanism," which featured a departure from rigid central control. Henceforth, factory managers would be allowed to set their own wages, contract for their own supplies—even from abroad—and set their own standards of efficiency with the intent of turning a profit. Individual enterprises were therefore able to reduce waste and adjust their output to the demands of the market.

In agriculture, the New Economic Mechanism heralded the end of the policy of collectivization. Individual farmers could now set their own quotas and manage their own time and labor. As a consequence, agricultural production increased so much that the Hungarians were able not only to feed their own people but also to produce a surplus for export. The quality and variety of produce also expanded. At the same time, the New Economic Mechanism created problems for a system that, by its nature, seemed impervious to change. Resources flowed into the new sectors, leaving the old industries to wallow in inefficiency. The older leaders who feared that any movement away from centralized control would weaken their influence began to fret. Moreover, the increased imports of Western goods added to Hungary's foreign debt. Unable to pay its bills, the government launched a policy of austerity, which increased the cost of living and stunted economic growth.

In Romania and Bulgaria, popular resentment of the current regimes was less marked. Bulgaria was perhaps the most servile and docile of all the Soviet satellites. The Bulgarians, whose pattern of trustworthiness was set by Georgi Dimitrov, the first postwar leader of the Bulgarian Communist party, identified strongly with the Bolshevik revolutionary tradition and political example. For this support, Moscow rewarded them with extensive political backing and economic assistance. Dimitrov's successors (Vulko Chervenkov in 1949 and Todor Zhivkov in 1954) continued his loyal policies, even to the extent of accepting the Soviet view that bilateral relations with Moscow were the best way to deal with regional Balkan problems. (Bulgaria had once entertained the idea of conducting an independent regional diplomacy with its neighbors, Yugoslavia, Greece, Romania, and Turkey, with which it had much in common economically.) Under Soviet tutelage, Bulgaria had completely collectivized its agriculture, but allowed some decentralization of its industry. Although it extended invitations to foreign capitalists to invest in Bulgarian enterprises, there was no comparable relaxation of political control.[82]

Zhivkov increasingly consolidated his position, and at his direction, the new 1971 constitution recognized the Communist party as the leading force in the society and the state. A state council became the chief organ of power with both executive and legislative authority. Zhivkov became its chairman and was thus well placed when the 1975 Helsinki accords and Eurocommunism began to offer a promise of liberalization. As compensation for such tight political control, Bulgaria undertook a program of economic expansion in the early 1980s, known as the New Economic Model (NEM). The intent was to institute technological changes to make Bulgaria more competitive with the nations of the West while, at the same time, increasing the supply of consumer goods. The latter was deemed essential to prevent the Bulgarian people from catching the Polish virus. By decentralizing industry, the NEM aimed to make the economy more self-sufficient and competitive. But the great improvement did not occur. The quality of Bulgarian goods did not improve, and Bulgaria's trade balance worsened as the country became more dependent on imported energy. In addition, after years of strict central control, Bulgarian economic planners and factory managers simply did not have the expertise to achieve new levels of productivity. Living standards remained depressed, the bureaucracy continued to be indolent and corrupt, and the leadership grew increasingly remote and isolated from the population. In the mid-1980s, a noticeable cooling of relations between the leaders of the Bulgarian Communist party and the Kremlin put their continued tenure increasingly in doubt.

In Romania, the dictatorship of Nicolae Ceausescu seemed unshakable. Both Ceausescu and his predecessor Gheorghe Gheorghiu-Dej, who died in 1965, held fast to the Communist system, tolerating no criticism from their people and no show of disrespect for the Soviet Union. Such protestations of loyalty convinced the Soviets to withdraw their troops from the country in 1958. They also had tolerated a removal of the "Muscovites" from the government, thereby allowing the Romanians to nationalize their party in much the same way as Tito had done in Yugoslavia. Without the immediate threat of Soviet intervention, the Romanians were able to embark on their own program of industrial development and even direct their own foreign policy to a certain extent.

In the late 1950s, the Romanians began an independent program of industrialization, thereby flouting the Soviet mutual economic assistance program under which Romania was to concentrate on expanding its agricultural sector and export primary products to the satellite countries to the north. During the time of the Sino-Soviet split, the Romanians continued to maintain relations with Beijing, insisting that Moscow respect the independence of other Communist parties and not interfere in their internal affairs. They thus opposed the Soviet intervention in Czechoslovakia and the Warsaw Pact intervention in Poland. The Romanians proceeded to expand relations with the West, paying special attention to the United States from which they hoped to secure huge development loans. The Soviets did not believe these deviations from the satellite norm posed a threat to the continuation of Soviet power in Eastern Europe and therefore tolerated them. Indeed, a stern political dictatorship free of the contagion of reformist tendencies was a positive asset, counterbalancing the unpleasant examples of Poland, Hungary, and Czechoslovakia. Furthermore, the country was not as strategically important as the satellites that protected the Soviet Union from a direct assault by NATO forces.

Ceausescu tightened his hold on the countryside, completing the process of collectivization by obliterating farming villages and relocating their inhabitants to high-rise apartment complexes. He deemed it necessary to destroy all attachment to the land in order to carry out his crash program of industrial development. He also enhanced his central control with a policy of cadre rotation that prevented upper-echelon bureaucrats from establishing a power base in the administration by moving them to a new position after two or three years. He also passed out important state positions to members of his family, including his wife Elena. In 1974, after he became president and commander-in-chief of the Romanian armed forces, he appointed her the first deputy prime minister and president of the Romanian Academy. In all, Ceausescu found important jobs for an estimated forty members of his tightly run clan.[83] The dictator's reliance on members of his own family was prompted by his fear of his own people, a paranoia that rivaled Stalin's.

Repression was also a hallmark of the regime. Owning an unregistered typewriter was illegal. Contact with foreigners was strictly limited—it was permitted only in the presence of at least two officials—and citizens were required to report any such contact they had or suspected others of having. Critics of the regime often disappeared without a trace. Protests and strikes, of which there were few, were suppressed with summary executions. The secret police were everywhere, moving about quite openly; their agents, dressed in black leather jackets, watched suspects with little subtlety. They infiltrated every department of government. Many of these men were orphans who were specially recruited because their primary allegiance would be to the regime, not to their families. In exchange for their loyalty, they were rewarded with a high standard of living. Few others in the state could match the secret police in data processing and high-tech communications.

The Ceausescu regime retained and expanded its power by rekindling old ethnic hatreds. Ceausescu targeted the two million Hungarians who lived mostly in Transylvania and the more widely dispersed, but less numerous, Jews. Anti-Semitism needed little encouragement. During the war, the Romanians had actively participated in the killing process. As a result, the Jewish population had dropped from 800,000 to a little over 400,000. The decline continued after 1945, and by the early 1980s, only 35,000 Jews remained in Romania. The Ceausescu regime depicted the Romanian Jews as seditious and traitorous, but also established ties with Israel, the only satellite state to do so.

At a time when other Eastern European satellites were going through a period of liberalization, repression continued full tilt in Romania. Political control absorbed a tremendous portion of the state's time and resources. Improving the general standard of living was of secondary concern. As a result, the Romanians were among Europe's poorest peoples. Shortages of consumer goods were the norm; food was frequently scarce. Despite sizable oil reserves, there were shortages of energy. Ceausescu's compulsion to liquidate a foreign debt of $10 billion led him to sell petroleum and food abroad. Working conditions were among the most miserable in the Eastern bloc, being little better than in the nineteenth century; industrial pollution was menacingly bad, and wages were low. Romania's iron-fisted regime of dynastic socialism was without incentives; it was a system in which the most routine aspects of life were subject to regulation and control—from the temperature of private apartments (a chilly 59°F) to the number of children a woman was required to produce before she was forty-five years old (four). From all external indications, the Ceausescu system was a great success, but hatred and resentment smoldered just below the surface, waiting for an opportunity to claim a terrible vengeance.

POSTSCRIPT   The Cold War divided Europe into two broad zones of confrontation, but it also led to the resolution of age-old conflicts. The nations in Western Europe, which had been at each others' throats for centuries, abandoned their mercantilistic barriers and sought unity in formal cooperation. The states of the European Community used their combined economic power to emerge as a third international force. The nations in the Warsaw Pact, still fettered by rigid economic centralism and Communist exploitation, grew relatively weaker and in many respects more divided. In Western Europe, where greater political independence was possible, the movement for integration was strong, while the supposedly monolithic Soviet bloc was alive with ethnic and political tensions.

The momentary collapse of authoritarianism in Czechoslovakia in 1968, a feat heretofore believed impossible in a Communist country, was a foretaste of what would happen in Spain in the next decade after Franco's death. The Spanish, however, did not have to worry about foreign intervention. They could transform their system with the support and encouragement of outside powers. Their rapid progress toward democracy after so many years as a dictatorship was until then unique in Western European history.

The Soviets' efforts to bring reluctant satellites back into the fold showed how crucial they considered the control of Eastern Europe to be to their own security. Czechoslovakia was important strategically because it guarded the border with West Germany. Poland guaranteed the Soviet Union's lines of communication to East Germany. But the Soviets also feared the influence that Eastern European movements would have within their own country. Letting go might provoke demands for reform in the Ukraine, in the Baltic states, and among other nationalities that resented Muscovite control over their affairs. The ethnic diversity and nationalistic yearnings of the Soviet minorities had always been a major historical concern. To tolerate self-determination in one part of the empire might open dangerous floodgates elsewhere. Maintaining control of such restive peoples was an increasingly difficult task, however, and would become more costly and dangerous as time went on. Eventually, the Soviet Union might have to choose which it would keep and which it would let go. In the meantime, the best way to minimize the damage was through a relaxation of tensions with the West.

Detente would reduce the need for a powerful and costly military establishment, allowing resources to be put to better use elsewhere. But as long as the nations of the Atlantic community feared Soviet expansionism, there could be no hope for real accommodation. The strategy of NATO, largely set by the United States, was geared to the unlikely assumption that the Soviets, given the opportunity, would send their armies all the way to the English Channel. In historical terms, such expansionism was not farfetched.

Russian power had grown steadily since the eighteenth century, creating the empire that the Soviets inherited and managed to extend. That much of this power was in the process of dissolution hardly seemed possible. The Soviet Union was the last great empire of Europe, and its power and unity seemed capable of enduring for centuries. The Soviets paradoxically assumed the right to guarantee their satellites a socialist form of government, but nevertheless took a pledge of noninterference in their affairs. The promise of noninterference eventually turned out to be genuine as the Soviets, like so many imperial masters before them, came to realize the impossibility of dictating the passions of the peoples over whom they ruled.

ENDNOTES

1. *Atlas,* November 1962, 405.
2. Ibid., 406.

3. The British insisted that they would control these weapons during a non-NATO crisis.

4. See François Caron, *An Economic History of Modern France* (New York: Columbia University Press, 1979), 205–19.

5. In 1958, the index of industrial production was 191; in 1959, 193; in 1960, 208; in 1962, 220; and in 1963, 233. It rose steadily throughout the rest of the decade until 1969 when it was 341. Brian R. Mitchell, *European Historical Statistics* (New York: Columbia University, 1975), 358.

6. Charles de Gaulle, *Mémoires de guerre* (Paris: Plon, 1954), vol. 1, 5.

7. The signing was accomplished in the immediate aftermath of de Gaulle's vetoing of Britain's entry into the Common Market, an action he had taken without prior consultation with Adenauer.

8. See especially Wilfrid L. Kohl, *French Nuclear Diplomacy* (Princeton: Princeton University Press, 1971), 123–77.

9. It was rumored that wealthy people, prohibited by the currency restrictions from transferring large amounts of capital abroad, took advantage of the open frontiers by loading up the trunks of their cars with banknotes and driving unchallenged into Switzerland.

10. Eyewitness accounts appeared in Claude Durand, dir., *Le livre noir des journées de mai* (Paris: Éditions du Seuil, 1986).

11. France-Soir, *Les journées de mai* (Paris: Librarie Hachette, 1969).

12. The push to join the Common Market came during the same period that Britain was enacting the Immigration Act of 1962 to limit the amount of colored immigration from the multiracial nations of the Commonwealth.

13. The Rome Treaty, which gave the Common Market Council certain powers to make decisions binding on the member states, provided for no power of enforcement.

14. The effort this time was made by the Labour government of Harold Wilson. Earlier the Labour party had been opposed to joining the Common Market.

15. Jean Monnet, *Memoirs* (Garden City, N.Y.: Doubleday and Company, 1978), 451.

16. On 17 February, the British Parliament passed the necessary enabling legislation to bring British law into accord with that of the European Community. The British officially joined on 1 January 1973.

17. G. N. Minshull, *The New Europe: An Economic Geography of the EEC* (New York: Holmes and Meier, 1985), 103–28.

18. Peter Coffey, *Main Economic Policy Areas of the EEC—Towards 1992* (Boston: Kluwer Academic Publishers, 1988), Part 2.

19. Guy de Bassompierre, *Changing the Guard in Brussels: An Insider's View of the EC Presidency* (New York: Praeger, 1988), 43–44.

20. The value-added tax is a tax that governments add to a product at each step of the productive chain. It must be paid whenever any improvements are added to the value of a product. It has been a great revenue enhancer, and its cost is naturally passed on to the consumer. Without standardization, producers in some countries could gain a competitive edge over those elsewhere.

21. The ruling involved the case of a female flight attendant of Sabena Airlines who was forced to retire because she had reached the age of forty, a restriction not applied to men. *Columbia Journal of Transnational Law*, 21 (1983): 640.

22. See Christopher McCridden, ed., *Women, Employment and European Equality Law* (London: Eclipse, 1987).

23. Peter Oliver, "Enforcing Community Rights in the English Courts," *Modern Law Review* 50 (1987): 881–907.

24. Stephen Wiseman, "Sex Discrimination: Some Recent Decisions of the European Court of Justice," *Columbia Journal of Transnational Law* 21 (1983): 621–40.

25. Stanley G. Payne, *The Franco Regime, 1936–1975* (Madison: University of Wisconsin Press, 1987), 372.

26. These were Moron Air Base near Seville, Torrejon Air Base near Madrid, Zaragoza

Air Base near Zaragoza, and Rota Naval Station near Rota. *Military Travel Guide* (Washington, D.C.: Raisor, 1985), 130.

27. Raymond Carr and Juan Pablo Fusi Aizpurua, *Spain: Dictatorship to Democracy* (London: Allen and Unwin, 1981), 29–31.

28. Mitchell, *European Historical Statistics*, 357–58.

29. Between 1939 and 1969, the annual production of wheat increased by 61 percent, that of barley 1.8 percent, potatoes by 37 percent, olives by 52 percent, and citrus fruits by 1.93 percent. The output of a crop like sugar beets, though, increased 5.91 percent. Ibid., 264, 274, 286, 287.

30. Carr and Aizpurua, *Spain*, 57–58.

31. David Gilmour, *The Transformation of Spain: From Franco to the Constitutional Monarchy* (London: Quartet Books, 1985), 139–44.

32. Ibid., 195–201.

33. Paul Preston, *The Triumph of Democracy in Spain* (London: Methuen, 1986), 203–4.

34. Stephen P. Savage and Lynton Robins, eds., *Public Policy under Thatcher* (New York: St. Martin's Press, 1990), 2–4.

35. Peter Jenkins, *Mrs. Thatcher's Revolution* (Cambridge, Mass.: Harvard University Press, 1988), 3–6.

36. Mitchell, *European Historical Statistics*, 358.

37. Douglas-Home had renounced his family title as the fourteenth earl of Home. No member of the House of Lords had been allowed to head a British government since the marquess of Salisbury in 1886–1902. In 1963, when Douglas-Home stood for election to the Commons as prime minister, he technically was a member of neither house.

38. Alfred F. Havighurst, *Britain in Transition in the Twentieth Century* (Chicago: University of Chicago Press, 1979), 506–7.

39. Mitchell, *European Historical Statistics*, 358.

40. Kenneth Harris, *Thatcher* (Boston: Little, Brown, 1988), 66.

41. James Callaghan, *Time and Chance* (London: Collins, 1987), 417–18.

42. Ibid., 563–64.

43. Paul Wilding, "The debate about the welfare state," in Bill Jones, ed., *Political Issues in Britain* (Manchester: Manchester University Press, 1989), 185–92.

44. Although their views were more curious than cogent, the Marxists thought the welfare state was a gigantic ploy to keep the workers subservient by pandering to their basic needs. Radical feminists believed the welfare state contributed to the subordination of women.

45. Denis Kavanagh, *Thatcherism and British Politics* (Oxford: Oxford University Press, 1987), 252.

46. The 98 percent rate amounted to 83 percent on earned income and another 15 percent on investment income.

47. "Margaret Thatcher's Ten Years, A Singular Prime Minister," *The Economist*, 29 April 1989, 20–21.

48. Savage and Robins, *Public Policy under Thatcher*, 34–41.

49. Jones, *Political Issues in Britain*, 141–43.

50. Savage and Robins, *Public Policy under Thatcher*, 43–44.

51. Jones, *Political Issues in Britain*, 160–66.

52. Jenkins, *Mrs. Thatcher's Revolution*, 373.

53. *The Annual Register* (1982), 7–18.

54. Harris, *Thatcher*, 134–39.

55. John J. Wuest and Manfred C. Vernon, *New Source Book in Major European Governments* (Cleveland: World Publishing Company, 1966), 291.

56. Helga Haftendorn, *Security and Detente: Conflicting Priorities in German Foreign Policy* (New York: Praeger, 1985), 225–30.

57. Helmut Schmidt, *Men and Powers: A Political Retrospective* (New York: Random House, 1989), 19.

58. Ibid., 386.
59. Ulbricht, for example, wanted full recognition of East German sovereignty with exclusive control of the access routes leading into West Berlin, something the Soviets, let alone the other responsible powers, were not prepared to yield.
60. Harold James, *A German Identity, 1770–1990* (New York: Routledge, 1989), 173.
61. Heinz Heitzer, *D.D.R.: An Historical Outline* (Dresden: Berlag Zeit im Bild, 1981), 244.
62. Mike Dennis, *German Democratic Republic: Politics, Economics and Society* (London: Pinter, 1988), 41.
63. Jonathan Steel, *Soviet Power: The Kremlin's Foreign Policy—Brezhnev to Andropov* (New York: Simon and Schuster, 1983), 23.
64. Hans Renner, *A History of Czechoslovakia since 1945* (London: Routledge, 1989), 25–33.
65. H. Gordon Skilling, *Czechoslovakia's Interrupted Revolution* (Princeton: Princeton University Press, 1976), 185.
66. The speech appeared in *Rudé právo* on 2 February 1968. Robin A. Remington, ed., *Winter in Prague: Documents of Czechoslovak Communism in Crisis* (Cambridge, Mass.: M.I.T. Press, 1969), 40.
67. Novotný's final fall from power was triggered by the defection to the West of Major General Jan Sejna. Sejna, a personal friend of Novotný, had been chief of the secretariat of the Ministry of Defense and therefore knew the highest secrets of the Czech military and the Warsaw Pact. His flight to the waiting arms of the U.S. Central Intelligence Agency hopelessly compromised Novotný and his clique.
68. Remington, *Winter in Prague*, 16.
69. The Brezhnev Doctrine was printed in *Pravda* on 26 September 1968. Alvin Z. Rubenstein, *Soviet Foreign Policy since World War II: Imperial and Global* (Boston: Little, Brown, 1985), 95.
70. Philip Windsor, *Czechoslovakia, 1968: Reform, Repression, and Resistance* (New York: Columbia University Press, 1969), 102–30.
71. Jirí Pelican, *Socialist Opposition in Eastern Europe: The Czechoslovak Example* (New York: St. Martin's Press, 1976), 35–44.
72. Vladimir Kusin, *From Dubček to Charter 77: A Study of Normalization in Czechoslovakia, 1968–1978* (New York: St. Martin's Press, 1978), 109–18.
73. *Annual Register of World Events* (1973), 524.
74. By way of implementation, it was subsequently agreed to pool information on cancer research and to make joint preparations for a rendezvous in orbit of American and Soviet space ships in 1975.
75. *New York Times*, 30 July 1965, 8.
76. The president's first introduction to the concept apparently came from a Hollywood thriller of the 1940s in which enemy planes were knocked out of the sky with an electrical beam.
77. Oleg Gordievsky, "Inside the KGB: A Double Agent's Tale," *Time*, 22 October 1990, 82.
78. Brezhnev's increasing senility toward the end of his rule occasioned many jokes and anecdotes. The leader's speech, for example, was so slurred and his diction was so poor that he had difficulty pronouncing the name of the country: Union of Soviet Socialist Republics. "Socialist" in Russian is *Sotsailisticheskikh*. Brezhnev would reduce the seven syllables to three so it sounded like *sososkikh*—the Russian word for sausage.
79. Leslie Holmes, *Politics in the Communist World* (Oxford: Clarendon Press, 1986), 303–5.
80. *Chicago Tribune*, 23 September 1990, 26.
81. Janusz Bugajski, *Czechoslovakia: Charter 77's Decade of Dissent* (New York: Praeger, 1987), 8–51.

82. R. J. Crampton, *A Short History of Modern Bulgaria* (Cambridge: Cambridge University Press, 1987), 173–209.

83. One of his brothers, Ilie, became an army general and deputy defense minister; another brother, Nicolae Andruta, became a police general and deputy minister of the interior; a third brother, Ion, was head of state economic planning; and a fourth, Florea, was an editor of the Communist newspaper, *Scinteia*. Ceausescu also took care of his in-laws, making one brother-in-law a party secretary in charge of agriculture and putting another in charge of trade unions. Ceausescu's youngest son, reputedly the regime's crown prince, became party secretary in Sibiu province in southern Transylvania, headquarters of a powerful military and security garrison.

CHAPTER 9

THE COLLAPSE OF THE SOVIET EMPIRE

PREFACE   German and Soviet expansionism threatened the independence of the other European states through much of the twentieth century. The collapse of the Nazi empire in the defeat of World War II left a power vacuum into which the Soviet Union expanded. However, the Soviet Union did not seem content to establish its authority only in Eastern Europe. The Western European states, buttressed by the might and insistence of the United States, formed the Atlantic Alliance to keep such power contained.

The European equilibrium changed from a multilateral system into a bipolar system, an arrangement long believed to be inherently unstable. Indeed, the point was proved in the Cuban missile crisis, the most serious of a series of confrontations between the superpowers. However, weapons of mass destruction had shown their limited nature as much as they had shown their gargantuan possibilities. Assertions to the contrary, both the U.S.A. and the U.S.S.R. knew that nuclear wars were not winnable. The showdown over Cuba was a sobering experience. Afterwards, relations between the two states became more restrained, each side having learned that there was a point beyond which it dared not push.

Yet behind its powerful facade, the Communist world was coming apart. The Soviet state, which had been expected to last for many more generations, collapsed in only three years. Such a peacetime transformation was unprecedented in European history. The forces of nationalism and ethnic hatred, long kept in check by the Soviet Holy Alliance, burst forth with sudden vigor. In Eastern Europe a dangerous multipolar world emerged with more opportunities, more crises, and more bloodshed. The new countries that took shape had little prior experience in running their own affairs. Ending the Cold War had been such an article of faith in the chancelleries of Western Europe that few politicians had considered the dangers that might arise once that goal was achieved. A new era began just as Europe had become successful in ironing out the uncertainties of the old.

THE DAY OF THE DEMOCRATIC REVOLUTION

A Radical in Office

The secretary-general of the Communist party of the Soviet Union, Konstantin Chernenko, died on 10 March 1985. His successor, Mikhail Sergeievich Gorbachev, was the youngest man on the Politburo. After being ruled by a gerontocracy for the past decade, the party and the Soviet Union now had a comparatively youthful, energetic leader. Gorbachev was fifty-four years old, nineteen years younger than his predecessor. The difference was more than just one of age. Gorbachev, and the men he subsequently brought to power with him, came from a new generation in Soviet politics. This group had risen to prominence after the purges of the Stalin era and had been too young to fight in World War II. Consequently, they were the country's first intact generation since World War I. Unlike their elders, they were ready to confront the country's shortcomings and were confident they could overcome its problems. Gorbachev himself was a convinced Communist who believed his "second revolution" could be achieved within the broad parameters of the present system. He still thought the Soviet system was basically superior to that of capitalism.

Until he became secretary-general, Gorbachev gave every indication that he was a faithful, dependable disciple of the regime. Hardworking, with a strong desire to please his superiors, he advanced steadily through the local party hierarchy in his home district of Stavropol, some 750 miles south of Moscow. He became first secretary in April 1970 when he was thirty-nine. His success in increasing agricultural output brought him to the attention of certain members of the Politburo.

Mikhail Gorbachev addresses the top officers of the Kremlin on 2 November 1987. After he had been first secretary of the Communist Party for two years, he began a revolution from above by telling the officials that Communism must be radically reformed in order for it to survive.

Thanks to them, he was brought to Moscow and elevated to the post of secretary of the party Central Committee in 1978. This appointment came toward the end of the Brezhnev period. Now known as the "years of crisis," this time of intense economic and political decline was probably the most corrupt of the postwar era. Gorbachev was put in charge of Soviet agriculture, a sector of the economy that was almost impervious to improvement. It was a hazardous assignment; Soviet agriculture had long been the graveyard of political careers. However, the fortuitous death of Leonid Brezhnev in 1982 opened new opportunities including membership in the ruling Politburo. Two years and two secretaries-general later, Gorbachev became its chief.

That Gorbachev's rule was not going to be business as usual became obvious at the early meetings he held with the managers of the country's factories and farms. At these sessions, he revealed things about the nation's lamentable state that had rarely been discussed in public before. Gorbachev described an economy where tens of thousands of factories produced goods nobody wanted, many enterprises stood idle, and thousands of collective farms were on the brink of collapse.[1] He wanted to introduce changes immediately without waiting until the older leaders had retired or died off.

Perestroika and Glasnost

Gorbachev was determined to make his policy of *glasnost* (openness) and *perestroika* (restructuring) irreversible. At the Communist party conference, which took place in Moscow from 28 June to 1 July 1988—the first such held since 1941—Gorbachev proposed a radical reform of the whole political system beginning with the demolition of the centralized, bureaucratic monolith that had led to the ossification of government and the alienation of the workers. He proposed infusing the system with democracy by creating a new representative body, the Congress of People's Deputies, that would elect the country's legislature, the Supreme Soviet. The Soviet would, in turn, elect the chairman (the chief of state), who would nominate the prime minister. Secret elections by competitive ballot would be held with the candidates chosen through a "lively and free expression of the will of the electorate."[2] Gorbachev also favored decentralizing power to give more responsibility to the local managers. Individual enterprise would be encouraged, and the economy would give more scope to private ownership.

The floor debate when Gorbachev's proposals were presented publicly for the first time was remarkable for its frankness and openness. Never during the past sixty years had Soviet citizens had such an opportunity to express their opinions openly. The conference voted to accept Gorbachev's proposals, but the vote was not unanimous. They became law at the end of the year with Gorbachev himself being elected as the new chairman of the Supreme Soviet.

Gorbachev next proposed a constitutional amendment (December 1988) to break the Communist party's exclusive hold over the electoral system. Henceforth, various other organizations could nominate candidates, who could have their own campaign organizations and present their own platforms. Moreover, candidates were required to actually live in the areas they represented. The first parliamentary elections under this new law (March 1989) saw a frenzied array of 3,000 candidates fighting for 1,500 offices. In some districts, as many as a dozen candidates vied for each seat, although in others only a single candidate emerged. The Communist party ran candidates in all the districts, but experienced a great electoral defeat. Thirty-eight regional or district Communist party secretaries throughout the country lost their positions. The party was voted out of office in Leningrad and Kiev. In Moscow, Boris Yeltsin, the onetime local Communist party chief, ran on an antiparty program and received 89.4 percent of the votes. Also victorious was Andrei Sakharov, the human rights activist and hydrogen bomb developer, who had been freed from internal exile in Gorki in 1986 at Gorbachev's orders and allowed to return to Moscow. The elections also showed the strength of nationalist candidates, especially those in the Baltic states.

Ironically, Gorbachev, who had created this electoral democracy, was now confronted with a collection of deputies who advocated everything from the breakup of the Soviet Union to curbs on the powers of the presidency.[3] In fact, the Soviet people, in the first real elections the country had held since the balloting for the Constituent Assembly in 1918, had again delivered a significant snub to the Communist party. Gorbachev tried to put the best possible face on the results. He said that the Communist party members who failed to be elected were conservatives who did not favor his campaign of liberalization. He denied that he was presiding over the dismantling of Communism, but claimed instead that his policies were putting its ideals into practice. To be a Communist, he maintained, meant "first of all to be consistently democratic and to put universal human values above everything else."[4] But he took no chances and strengthened his hand in his own party.

By January 1990, he had gotten rid of all twenty-five members of the Politburo and the Secretariat who had held office since the time of Brezhnev except himself and Eduard Shevardnadze, the foreign secretary. Bringing the party under his control was an essential element of perestroika, since Gorbachev wanted to transform the Communist party into the most progressive political force in the state. It was a daunting, and ultimately impossible, task, however. The party was more conservative than revolutionary and had long ago ceased to be a force for change. It was the party of the permanent ruling class, and its leaders were primarily concerned with holding on to their power and their perquisites. Still reeling from the trauma of Stalinism, they had learned to protect themselves against the danger of making decisions and, in doing so, had gradually lost control of the bureaucratic Soviet state.[5] Gorbachev wanted to streamline the party apparatus to make it more efficient in order to save it. However, the party was not part of the solution, but was itself the problem. Thus, the success of perestroika depended not on the rejuvenation of the Communist party, but on its removal from any significant role in the affairs of state. Gorbachev played a game of contradictions. He established his independence from the Communist party, but at the same time tried to hold it together under his control. By trying to turn it into a democratic organization, Gorbachev hastened its decline.

In February 1990, he convinced the Central Committee to change Article 6 of the Constitution, which Brezhnev had inserted in 1977. The article stated: "The leading and guiding force of Soviet society and the nucleus of its political system, of all state organizations and public organizations is the Communist Party of the Soviet Union." In removing Article 6, Gorbachev was ending all pretensions of one-party rule. He argued that the party should at last recognize that its political leadership could come only through free elections. The Soviet Constitution was amended accordingly.[6] In March 1990, Gorbachev also transformed the Soviet political system into a presidential form of government—a development that had no precedent in the previous political institutions of the country. The new powers gave the president the right to nominate the premier and other members of the cabinet, all of whom were accountable to him. The president could also suspend legislation, dissolve the legislature, and, in time of declared emergency, rule by decree. For example, he had the right to institute emergency decrees "to stabilize the country's socio-political life" for a period of eighteen months. He presided over a new council of federation composed of the presidents of the fifteen union republics. In effect, this council became the supreme decision-making body of the state. Gorbachev argued that such powers were needed to ensure that swift executive action could be taken. Although the president was to be elected by universal, popular suffrage, an exception was made for Gorbachev himself. He took office after securing a majority of the votes in the Congress of People's Deputies. Many feared that he was preparing for a return to dictatorship.

Meanwhile support for Communism was rapidly declining. Between January and September 1990, 1.5 million members quit the party. Those who stayed became engaged in bitter disputes over the organization's future. One faction, the Democratic Platform, wanted to abandon Leninism completely and become a general parliamentary party with no pretensions of being the vanguard of the proletariat. Another faction, the Marxist Platform, wanted to retain the party's revolutionary elitism and base its strength on the industrial working class. The Communist party also began to fragment into its ethnic components, which broke down further into independent and pro-Moscow factions. The Twenty-eighth Party Congress, which met in Moscow from 2 to 13 July 1990 and reelected Gorbachev as party leader, reiterated the principle of democratic centralism. That is, members could express their opinions on issues until the Central Committee had made a decision, then all would support it and conform to it. The party would act like any other parliamentary party in its external relationships, but would continue to be a vanguard party in its organizations in the workplace, the armed forces, and the homes. By now much of this resolve was romantic fantasy. Even if the Communist party could remain an important political organization, the authority of the central government had become so tenuous and the prevailing economic, social crisis, and ethnic problems so enormous that the country's very existence was in doubt.

The Nationality Question

In a wide arc, from the Baltic states in the northwest, through Belorussia to Moldavia in the south, and east to Georgia and across to Tadzhikistan, the Soviet Union was coming apart, collapsing into more than a dozen independent states. Lenin had believed that nationalism would disappear under Communism, but in reality, only the tight grip of Moscow and the Communist party had created a Pax Sovietica that kept nationalist and ethnic forces under control. When the force from the center disappeared, old passions and hatreds flared anew, culminating in demands for independence. The inability of perestroika to produce any improvement in the economy also convinced local leaders that they would have a better chance of recovery without the presence of Moscow.

In 1988, in the Caucasus, the national passions of the Armenians and the Azeris turned against each other. At issue was control of the district of Nagorno-Karabakh whose population of Christian Armenians had been included within the Muslim republic of Azerbaijan in 1921. Now the Armenians wanted to annex the district. The result was cross-border raids, "pacification" of villages, and riots that claimed the lives of hundreds of people and left thousands homeless. Moscow opposed any change in the borders and sent helicopters, artillery, and armored vehicles to the area to restore order. Using military force against civilians to quell internal unrest eroded army morale. Some officers openly protested the government's policy.[7] The ethnic violence accelerated both Armenian and Azeri demands for independence. No longer interested in preserving the Soviet Union, the Armenian government adopted a goal of independence within five years; it announced it would begin by recruiting its own "popular militia" and conducting its own foreign policy. In September 1989, the Azeris became the first Soviet people to declare their independence amid rumors that their country would merge with Iran. In January 1990, the Azerbaijan capital of Baku erupted in violence with a pogrom against the Armenians. The Soviets rushed in troops to keep the peace. But after two years, with no solution to the war in sight, Moscow ordered all the forces withdrawn to let the Azeris and the Armenians fight it out amongst themselves.

Christian Armenians were also harassed in other Muslim republics, where the new religious toleration that accompanied glasnost had led to a new assertiveness. In some Muslim republics, protesters called for Islam to be made the only official religion. Religious particularism went hand in hand with a new insistence on the primacy of the local culture, including the revival of the Arabic script instead of the Cyrillic alphabet forced upon them by Stalin in 1939.

The desire to retain their cultural integrity was also a primary factor in the drive of the Baltic republics for freedom from Moscow. Latvia, Lithuania, and Estonia had never really accepted their forceful incorporation into the Soviet Union in 1940. At the Communist party conference in June 1988, the non-Russian delegates from the Baltic states demanded greater political, economic, and cultural autonomy. Their demands were followed by the formation of People's Fronts in the three republics to continue to agitate for freedom. In November 1988, the Supreme Soviet of Estonia adopted a "Declaration of Sovereignty," which included the right to veto laws passed by the central government. Moscow promptly ruled the declaration null and void, but that hardly ended the matter. During 1990, all three Baltic states declared their independence. The Lithuanians began the process on 11 March; the Estonians followed suit with a more insistent declaration on 30 March, and the Latvians added their voice on 4 May.

Gorbachev answered the Lithuanian fait accompli by reinforcing the 30,000-man Soviet garrison and imposing an economic blockade on the country. He commanded the 1,500 Lithuanian soldiers who had deserted from the Soviet army to return to their units and ordered the Lithuanian people to turn in all firearms. Lithuanian president Vytautas Landsbergis, leader of the Sajudis nationalist movement, urged the deserters to seek sanctuary in churches and declared the Soviet decrees an unlawful interference in Lithuania's internal affairs. The Lithuanians were gambling that Gorbachev would not risk the end of perestroika by ordering a full-scale invasion to crush the revolt.

At one time, President Landsbergis, a former professor of music at Vilnius State Conservatory, had been more at home in front of a piano than on the barricades. Now he was his country's symbol of resistance. Landsbergis saw the crisis as a clear-cut question of whether the country belonged to the Lithuanians or the Russians. First, however, he had to determine how successfully Lithuania could withstand Soviet pressure. The country had fewer than 4 million people, 20 percent of whom were non-Lithuanians. Although Lithuania could produce enough food to feed itself, it was almost totally dependent on the Soviet Union for energy and raw materials. In short, the Soviets had the power to close down the Lithuanian economy and throw most of its people out of work. The Lithuanians decided to moderate their demands. On 29 June, they "suspended" their vote of independence. The Soviets then ended the blockade, and the two sides sat down to resolve their differences through discussions.

The declarations of sovereignty in the Baltic countries encouraged other independence movements. On 29 May 1990, Boris Yeltsin was elected the chairman of the Russian Supreme Soviet, thereby becoming the de facto president of the Russian republic. Shortly after coming to power, he asserted that his republic had the right to control its own natural resources, establish its own separate citizenship, proclaim the primacy of its legislation over that of the Soviet Union, and conduct its own foreign policy. The Russian republic operated from a greater position of strength than the Baltic states. It included slightly over half of the Soviet population and produced almost two-thirds of the Soviet Union's electricity, three-fourths of its natural gas, 90 percent of its oil, 55 percent of its coal, and 58 percent of its steel. The Russian district of Siberia supplied three and a half times more raw materials than the rest of the country combined. No matter what became of the Soviet Union, the Russian republic would remain a great power with the ability to dominate its neighbors. The separatist stance of the Russian federation put Yeltsin on a collision course with Gorbachev for leadership of the second revolution.

The Ukraine, the next most important republic, took similar moves toward sovereignty, aiming for control of its own economy and foreign affairs. The Ukraine, with a population of 52 million, roughly equivalent to that of France, inaugurated a system of coupons for the purchase of certain commodities, a first step in the creation of a Ukrainian currency. In addition, it declared itself a nuclear-free zone. Elsewhere Belorussia enacted measures to control exports to other republics. The Moldavian parliament declared its independence from the Soviet Union, renamed itself Moldovia, adopted its own flag, and declared Moldavian the official language. Many suspected that Moldavia wanted to reunite with Romania from which it was separated in 1940. This fear prompted the ethnic Russians who lived in a region of the Dniester River valley near the Moldavian capital of Kishinev to declare their independence from Moldavia, while the Gagauz minority of 150,000 people also demanded self-rule. The Moldavians who insisted on their own right of self-determination refused to recognize it for others.

Independence movements were also in progress in all of the other republics including Georgia, Kazakhstan, Turkmenistan, Uzbekistan, and Tadzhikistan. In the predominantly Muslim Central Asian republics, where ethnic and religious tensions took precedence over nationalist sentiments, Islamic fundamentalists insisted their religion should be the only state religion and that women again take the veil. The autonomy movement even spread to districts within republics and to cities. The Russian republic was also beset with demands for separatism, mostly from distinct ethnic groups such as the Chuvash, Buryat, Tatar, Karelian, and Bashkir peoples. In addition, the predominantly Muslim Chechen-Irgusk region proclaimed its "equality and independence," while the city of Nizhni-Novgorod petitioned for its own special status.

Gorbachev hoped that declarations of sovereignty did not necessarily mean a desire to sever all ties with the Soviet Union. Assuming that the independence-minded republics would recognize the economic advantages of maintaining some type of union, he tried to design a federation that would satisfy most local sensibilities. In June 1991, the Kremlin and nine constituent republics negotiated a new treaty of union that would turn the Soviet Union into a confederation. The treaty ended control by the central government, transferring to the republics the power to tax, control natural resources, and run the police. The initial phase would begin with the adherence of the Russian and Kazakhstan republics on 20 August 1991. But two days before the ceremony, a group of anti-perestroika Communists, calling themselves the Committee for the State of Emergency, arrested Gorbachev and seized control of the central government.

The Coup That Failed

The attempt to bring back the country's authoritarian past began on 18 August. It lasted three days. Gennadi Yanayev, the coup's acting president, tried to convince the Soviet people that the takeover was essential to restore order. The situation was out of control, he said, the country was disintegrating, the economic situation had gone from bad to disastrous, and nobody was in charge. Yanayev declared that the eight-member Committee for the State of Emergency stood for genuine democratic reforms. In the meantime, it prohibited all political opposition and claimed the power to rule by decree.

Gorbachev had been warned that a coup might be afoot, but he had dismissed the warnings. President George Bush and other American officials had given him information that a revolt was brewing, but Gorbachev did not lend it credence because he was "deeply convinced that only a paranoiac, a madman, [could] attempt a coup."[8] He was in his Crimean retreat at Foros working on the speech he would make at the treaty signing, when a special detachment of the KGB surrounded the house and held him incommunicado. The next morning, the world learned what had happened, when TASS announced the formation of the Committee for the State of Emergency.

The committee ordered army units to enter Moscow to seize vital areas, but it did not undertake a mass arrest of all potential opposition leaders. The coup leaders also failed to gain control of the communications network. Even if they had, their success would not have been assured. Even the ruthless Bolsheviks had accomplished their takeover only after several years of bitter fighting. Lenin knew that a revolution without a bloodbath was no revolution. The men of the Committee for the State of Emergency were not cast in the same mold—to their credit. But even had they been, the country had changed dramatically from the days of the Bolshevik coup. By now, the Soviet people had had their fill of murder carried out in the name of the working class. Perestroika had given them hope, making it difficult to turn back the clock. The plotters knew they lacked widespread support and were so eager to establish their legitimacy that they pretended that Gorbachev was merely undergoing treatment for physical exhaustion. In his first press conference, Yanayev said that he hoped that as soon as Gorbachev felt better he would resume his office and work with the committee. The plotters promised to continue his policies until then.

Many officials in the government decided to see which way the wind was blowing before committing themselves, but some with a clearer appreciation of what was at stake immediately denounced the coup as unconstitutional. On 19 August, Anatoli Sobchak, the mayor of Leningrad, called on the people of his city to come to the defense of the legitimate government. As a result, thousands flocked to the square in front of the Winter Palace to prevent army units from entering the center of the city. In Moscow, just after noon on the same day, Boris Yeltsin climbed on an armored truck parked outside the Russian republic headquarters and called for a general strike against this illegal seizure of power. His dramatic gesture prompted tens of thousands of people to converge on the square in front of the Russian parliament building to protect it from hostile army units. Many of the soldiers sent into Moscow by the coup leaders began to defect. People started to throw up barricades. Pizza Hut delivered 260 pizzas, 20 cases of Pepsi, and gallons of hot coffee to Yeltsin and his associates inside the Russian parliament building. By now, it was plain that the coup leaders could only persist in the takeover at

Clutching the text of his speech, **Boris Yeltsin denounces the August coup leaders** from atop a tank in front of the Russian parliament building. Yeltsin was the first freely elected president of the Russian Republic. He now takes charge of the democratic revolution, thereby eclipsing Gorbachev's power.

the expense of considerable bloodshed, and the military leaders were clearly reluctant to storm the Russian parliament building. With no means of enforcing their decrees, the coup started to come apart. The leaders began running for cover; some went into hiding; others committed suicide. Many officials, who had earlier been hesitant to choose sides, suddenly decided that they had supported the legitimate government all along.[9]

On 21 August, four of the conspirators went to see Gorbachev in the Crimea to seek his forgiveness but were promptly arrested. Gorbachev returned to Moscow early in the morning of 22 August. But although he was restored to his position, the authority he had once had was gone. The man of the hour was Yeltsin. His assertiveness and determination, his strong voice for reform, had determined the fate of the country. His influence soared. He did not forget the help that Pizza Hut had provided, however, and called the Moscow restaurant to thank it for its support.

Gorbachev, who had tried to reform the Communist party and make it the spearhead for reform, now watched it vanish as a political entity. Without fanfare he resigned his post of secretary-general. Throughout the Soviet Union, local republican leaders used the coup as an excuse to wipe away the last remnants of the Communist party. It was banned, its headquarters and offices sealed, its property confiscated, and its special commissaries and stores closed. Many of its apparatchiks found themselves without work. (On the other hand, some of the old party bosses managed to hold on by only slightly changing their stripes.) As a symbol of the new order, local governments began to topple the statues of Communist heroes. In Moscow, 10,000 people crammed the square in front of the KGB headquarters to watch construction cranes pull down the fourteen-ton statue of Feliks Dzerzhinsky, the founder of the Cheka. Afterwards, people scrawled the word "fascist" on the empty pedestal and smeared a swastika on the KGB building itself.[10] Throughout the country, statues of Lenin were removed from public squares and parks. Leningrad returned to its tsarist name of St. Petersburg.[11] There were discussions of whether Lenin's body should be removed from its tomb on Red Square.

The Continuing Crisis

The end of the Soviet Union as a centralized political force brought with it the end of the command economy upon which that unity was conditioned. In supporting perestroika, people were in effect betting on the chance of improvement, not on present strength. The inefficiency of management and labor and the prevalence of antiquated techniques—the very problems that had led to perestroika in the first place—resulted in a steady decline in productivity and increased shortages of goods. Under Stalin, economic development had been secondary to political control. The Gosplan had destroyed local economic integrity in order to disperse the industrial processes, thereby making it impossible for any factory to survive on its own. As a result, only a minority of the republics were self-sufficient in energy or in food production. All of them had to rely on the others for the goods and services necessary to complete the manufacturing process. For example, practically all of the country's locomotives were assembled in the Ukraine, but 800 different factories throughout the rest of the Soviet Union made their component parts. Distribution of resources and products depended on priorities established in Moscow.

The ongoing crisis of leadership and the battle of the republics over the control of their vital resources removed this coherence without putting anything better in its place. Despite his intent to carry out radical reforms, Gorbachev was reluctant to abandon central planning in favor of a true free market. His hesitation was not unique. After decades of expecting Big Brother to mind the store, the average Soviet had difficulty adapting to the idea of individual initiative. Private property was considered anti-people. Furthermore, the transition to privatization risked throwing millions of people out of work, an unthinkable social consequence. Even with minimal side effects, a free economy, with its mortgages, securities, fixed rates, and market surveys, was alien turf.

A 500-Day Plan, that had been presented to the Supreme Soviet in September 1990, proposed privatizing 80 percent of the economy. State enterprises would be turned into joint-stock companies; farmers would be allowed to withdraw from the collective farms, and prices would be set by the marketplace. Gorbachev, however, beset by doubts about how to carry out the transformation, dragged his feet. His compromise solution called for the transformation of the economy in four stages. Such gradualism condemned the economy to a series of half-measures that did little to halt the steady decline in output.[12]

The Soviet economy was in its worst condition since 1945. Along with the shortages of food and basic commodities, the quality of health care was declining, and housing was scarce. Beggars in large numbers began appearing on city streets. The crisis stemmed in large part from mismanagement, incompetence, and outright hoarding rather than an absence of resources. For example, the farms had the capacity to produce enough food to supply the entire country, but primitive storage facilities and inadequate methods of harvesting and distributing the crops led to a threat of scarcity. Potatoes were frequently stored in closed containers, the sprouted with the unsprouted, and sometimes were enclosed with onions—a system that guaranteed almost instant spoilage. In 1990, soldiers, factory workers, and students were sent into the fields to help harvest potatoes. Yet despite the added labor, much of the crop rotted in the fields. A bumper crop of wheat was harvested that year, but the surpluses did not reach the city markets because the regions, especially in the south and east, withheld their produce to barter for other goods. Many shipments did not reach Moscow because of deliberate sabotage. Communist party officials ordered huge quantities to be sent to remote warehouses in order to discredit perestroika.[13]

Some areas auctioned off their agricultural produce to the highest bidder. Furthermore, the republics were not above using food as an instrument of blackmail. The Ukraine, for example, threatened to stop sending grain to Russia unless Russia continued to sell it oil at a subsidized price.[14] A wide range of products, including meat, tobacco, and tea, disappeared from state stores. Of course, the Soviet economy had always been conspicuous for its shortages, especially in consumer goods. As a result, people had accumulated huge cash savings, estimated at hundreds of billions of rubles. The increased scarcities posed a huge inflationary threat as all the reserve currency now chased after fewer and fewer goods. Blackmarketing flourished. Gangsters emerged to provide "protection" for the owners of the cooperative enterprises and joint private ventures that were allowed to exist.

Clearly, the Soviet Union's new commitment to human rights and economic freedom could not be sustained without some improvement in the standard of living of its people. The threat of dictatorship had been temporarily removed, and Communism totally discredited with the collapse of the coup in August 1991. But the danger that this country without a democratic tradition would seek some sort of authoritarian solution and the threat of economic and financial upheaval were still present. Even if the republics managed to keep the wolf from the door, the conversion to a new economic order could not take place without rising unemployment and inflation. The old system, with all its faults, did manage to provide certain minimum goods and services at subsidized prices. For the new regime not to do at least that would be catastrophic.

Yet, under the new reforms, the basic relationship between the citizen and the state had been transformed. Instead of being viewed as a ward of the state with an obligation to serve a collective need, the citizen was now guaranteed rights as an individual. This transformation from a corporate structure in which rights were defined within the group to one in which they were to conform to individual needs and desires brought an emancipation heretofore unknown in the Soviet Union or in tsarist Russia. At the same time, however, it removed the state's obligation to provide people with birth-to-death protection.

Yeltsin's determination to create a market economy in Russia regardless of what the other republics might do made the role of President Gorbachev increasingly irrelevant. Yeltsin had fought for the triumph of the reform movement during the August coup, but with the economic situation worsening, the Russian leaders had to consider whether the democracy they had saved could be preserved. The debate in the halls of parliament was over whether to grant Boris Yeltsin the power to rule by decree to save the country from economic collapse.

REFORM IN EASTERN EUROPE

The Independence of the Satellites

Stalin had kept the satellites in line by the direct use of force; his decisions were backed by the power of the Red Army. His successors continued the policy, but allowed the states of Eastern Europe more leeway to make their own decisions as long as they did not threaten the integrity of the socialist system and the security of the Soviet Union. Brezhnev elevated Soviet hegemony into a doctrine in which

Moscow arrogated to itself the right to determine acceptable limits, to guarantee, as it were, the satellites a Communist form of government. However, when Gorbachev began his reforms, the people in the satellites tried to figure out how they could use the new policies to their own advantage. At first, it was not clear how far the reform process might go; nor was there even any assurance it would continue. Gorbachev himself seemed tentative. His desire to maintain a socialist order, albeit a reformed one, still held ominous implications for the peoples of the Soviet bloc countries who remembered the thaws of the past that had never endured. Of particular concern was the 1985 renewal of the Warsaw Treaty for another thirty years. By reinforcing the obligation of its members to cooperate closely in international affairs, the pact reaffirmed the leadership of Moscow and gave a certain amount of support to hard-line governments.

In Poland, the authorities enacted a new penal code that established summary court procedures denying the accused the right to legal counsel. The Czechoslovak Communist party confirmed the old ideological line, including the state's limited freedom within the Soviet orbit. In Hungary, conservatives in the ruling party seemed resistant to any changes that would endanger their long-held privileges. In Romania, Nicolae Ceausescu further consolidated his position; and in Bulgaria, Todor Zivikov enacted measures against the country's restive young people who were not engaged in "socially useful work."

In all the Eastern European countries, the economy was sluggish, the goals of central planning were in jeopardy, and trade deficits were rising. Leaders put on a brave front, but offered no new solutions. They enjoined the people to work harder and make greater sacrifices. As the Gorbachev reforms gained greater momentum in the Soviet Union, however, the clamor for change became more vocal. In 1987, Poland's Solidarity movement presented its alternative to a government recovery program by calling for a mixed economy, expansion of private enterprise, and self-government for the workers. In Hungary, populists, journalists, democrats within the Communist party, and intellectuals called for more pluralism in the government and in public life. Romania saw public demonstrations of protest. The Bulgarian Communists tried to ward off expressions of discontent by pursuing their own version of perestroika, but without much conviction or success.

In 1988, Gorbachev repudiated the Brezhnev doctrine. He declared that the Soviet Union would no longer use force to keep the present Eastern European governments in power. His pronouncement was a sentence of death to the Communist regimes of Eastern Europe. Within a year, they had all disappeared.

The ax dropped first in Poland in January 1989. After a year of strikes and pressure from Solidarity and other forces, the Polish United Workers' party was forced to end its monopoly on power and accept political and trade union pluralism. Now the opposition could run candidates in the parliamentary elections in June; however, the party managed to obtain a guarantee that it and its allies would automatically receive 299 seats of the 460 in the Sejm. The newly created 100-seat Senate would be freely elected, however. Without their guaranteed allotment, the Communists would have been virtually eliminated as a political force. Solidarity won 80 percent of the popular vote and 160 of the 161 allocated free seats in the Sejm and 92 of the seats in the Senate. When Lech Walesa, the head of Solidarity, persuaded the Communists' allies to desert and join his parliamentary group, he assured that the non-Communists would control the government. In September, for the first time since the end of World War II, a non-Communist prime minister became head of the government. Shortly afterwards, the Communists abandoned Marxist-Leninism and declared their intent to change into a new social democratic party. The end of Communism led to a profusion of new political parties. In a short time, over 250 had emerged.

The new Polish government proposed a rapid transition to a market economy, which led to a dramatic increase in unemployment. More than a third of the 4,500 state factories headed toward bankruptcy. Many of the small, marginal farms were also going out of business. The number of homeless increased dramatically.[15] To complicate matters, the Polish Catholic bishops began pushing for the abolition of the separation of church and state, leaving many Poles wondering if they had rid themselves of Communism only to fall into the arms of clericalism.[16]

In Hungary, the Communist Social Workers' party also lost its direction. Reformers gradually gained control and in October 1989 voted it out of existence. It reemerged as the Hungarian Socialist party. The rapid change caught the opposition by surprise, thereby depriving the Hungarian people of any sense they had participated directly in the transformation.

The end of Communism did not come as easily in Czechoslovakia where the party still felt strong enough to resist democratization. Nevertheless, with the retreat of Communism elsewhere in Eastern Europe, holding the line against the mounting opposition became increasingly difficult. The ruthless suppression of a student demonstration in Prague in November 1989 led to mass demonstrations in the capital and other major cities. The protests were followed by a general strike accompanied by demands for the abolition of the one-party state. In December, with the election of Václav Havel, the head of the democratic Civic Forum, as president, the rule of the Communist party came to an end. Czechoslovakia established a pluralistic political system with a market economy. President Havel was a great admirer of Thomas Jefferson and was determined that the Jeffersonian spirit would take root in his own country. But what that country would be was

Playwright Václav Havel flashes a victory sign from the balcony of the Prague Castle to the thousands of well-wishers who, on 29 December 1989, hail his election as president of Czechoslovakia. His occupancy of the castle signalled that Communist power was finally at an end, but Havel preferred to go on living at his top-floor apartment in one of the city's rundown districts.

still not certain because the Slovaks began to talk about establishing their own independent state.

In most of Eastern Europe, the end of Communism was achieved peacefully with virtually no loss of life. Romania proved the exception. At the beginning of 1989, the Ceausescu dictatorship still seemed firmly entrenched. Thus far, the most serious protest had been mounted by six retired Communist party officials who wrote an open letter criticizing the president for violating the constitution. The letter writers were put under house arrest. In November 1989, the Communist party confirmed its monopoly on power at its annual congress and rejected the reform movements taking place elsewhere as models to be followed at home. The regime continued to harass political opponents and subjected some of them to violence.

In December, the regime ordered Lázló Tökés, an activist Protestant clergyman and an ethnic Hungarian living in the city of Timisoara (Transylvania), to move to another part of the country. Tökés refused and continued to defend the religious and ethnic rights of his people. When the police attempted to arrest him, local Hungarians and Romanians intervened. On 16 December, the security forces fired on the demonstrators, killing hundreds, perhaps even thousands. Ceausescu was not concerned. He believed the situation had been brought under control and left the country on a state visit to Iran. The protest continued, however.

Ceausescu returned on 20 December and put the western part of the country under a state of emergency. On 21 December, he staged a progovernment rally in Bucharest. But the move backfired. The crowd turned against Ceausescu, and the army refused to intervene. Some military units even joined the demonstrators and attacked Communist party headquarters. Army officers, intellectuals, and anti-Ceausescu Communist officials hastily formed a National Salvation Front and declared the president deposed. Ceausescu and his wife fled the capital, but were soon captured. After a secret trial, they were found guilty of genocide and corruption, sentenced to death, and immediately shot. The National Salvation Front now took steps to dismantle Ceausescu's repressive regime, bringing the hated secret police, the Securitate, under the control of the army. Abortion was legalized, the village destruction program was halted, and the way was prepared for free, multiparty elections.

The year 1989 was one of the most significant in the history of Europe; it ended forty years in which Eastern Europe had been subjected to authoritarianism and isolated from the rest of Europe. It has been compared in importance to 1848, another year in which Europe was swept by revolution. After the overthrow.of the French monarchy in February 1848, the revolutionary fervor spread to Italy, Austria, Germany, and Poland. People demonstrated against their rulers, demanding an end to the reactionary regimes that had run European affairs since the collapse of the Napoleonic empire. As in 1989, the 1848 uprisings were led by men who had little previous governmental experience and who fanned the flames of nationalism.

However, the differences between 1848 and 1989 were just as apparent as their similarities. In the nineteenth century, democracy had few champions, and the forces of authority and reaction were still strong and willing to fight to survive. Consequently, the "Springtime of Nations" collapsed in a bloody repression. In contrast, in 1989, the protest movements of Eastern Europe were backed by strong popular support and had the tacit blessing of the only empire that had it within its power to destroy them. The restraint of Gorbachev plus the determination of the reformers ensured that change would occur and would remain largely peaceful.

The Suicide of Yugoslavia

Tito had created a federal system in order to diminish Yugoslavia's ethnic and religious hatreds and rivalries. His association of equals helped to minimize the power of Serbia and keep the lid on regional nationalism. He bolstered the socialist economy with massive loans from the West. His successors were not as capable at holding things together, nor were they necessarily eager to do so. They were more interested in reasserting their own regional identities than they were in furthering proletarian internationalism. With the monumental changes taking place in the other countries of Eastern Europe and the Soviet Union, Yugoslavians were ready to abandon Communism. Shortly after the fall of Ceausescu in Romania, Ante Markovic, the president of the Federal Executive Council, instituted a program that favored the privatization of state-owned enterprises and the reintroduction of political pluralism. The democratization movement continued. By March 1990, the Communist party, the League of Communists of Yugoslavia, had virtually ceased to function; many of its component ethnic parts simply reorganized themselves as social democratic parties. These, together with a hundred other parties, many with specific ethnic constituencies, began demanding significant changes in the overall organization of the state. By year's end, control of most of the component republics had passed to local nationalists. No longer compelled to stay together to protect itself against the Soviet threat, Yugoslavia had begun to break apart.

In December 1990, the Slovenes revised their constitution to create Slovenia as an independent, sovereign, and autonomous state. They warned that they would withdraw from the federation within six months if they could not reach an accommodation with the central government. When such efforts failed, the Slovenes declared their independence on 25 June 1991. The same day, Croatia followed suit. Yugoslavia, the state put together at the Paris Peace Conference in 1919–1920 as the Kingdom of the Serbs, Croats, and Slovenes, was ending for good. This was not the first time Yugoslavia had come apart. During World War II, a separate Fascist state had been established in Croatia, and the Nazis had partitioned the rest. However, Tito had managed to put the country back together and create a central government that lasted until his death in 1981. Since then, the political dynamic was centrifugal. In 1991, it again became bloody.

The Croatian declaration of independence was answered by action from the Serb-dominated Yugoslav national army. The military intervention was occasioned by a rebellion among the 600,000 Serbs who lived in enclaves and villages in the eastern part of Croatia. These Serbs were irate that the Roman Catholic Croatians had reduced their status from equal citizens to that of a national minority and had begun an intensive policy of cultural transformation that ranged from changing street names to mandating the use of the Latin alphabet and the Croatian language.[17] The Serbs remembered the massacres of their people under the Croatian Fascist regime during World War II. Serbian intervention was motivated by more than the desire to protect the Serbs in Croatia from harm, however. The breakup of Yugoslavia was destroying a Serbian dream of a Greater Serbia that went back at least a century.

The war was particularly nasty, as the Yugoslav forces were not always careful in their choice of targets. Civilians frequently came under fire. The Yugoslav army attacked the city of Vukovar with such frenzy that Serbian and Croatian property was destroyed without distinction. The army also ruthlessly shelled the old medieval port of Dubrovnik, the "Pearl of the Adriatic" and one of Europe's richest cultural treasures, in an apparent attempt to destroy Croatia's multimillion dollar tourist industry. The city had no military value.

The struggle between the Croats and the Serbs was the first full-scale European war since 1945, and the parties defied all efforts of the European Community to arrange a permanent cease-fire. No sooner were truces arranged than they were broken; by the end of 1991, there had been at least fifteen. The nations of the European Community condemned the killing and Serbia's obvious attempt to expand its boundaries at the expense of its breakaway neighbor; but outside of adopting economic sanctions, which proved ineffectual, they made no effort to intervene themselves. Times had changed since 1914 when the affairs of the Balkans could touch off a general war. Now none of the Great Powers had rivalries in Eastern Europe. The European Community tried to mediate the crisis without success— Yugoslavia had been a powder keg of superannuated xenophobia for centuries, an artifical concoction of disparate cultures. Spurred by Germany, the EC countries recognized the independence of Slovenia and Croatia on 15 January 1992. This action encouraged nearby Bosnia-Herzegovina to also declare independence and solicit similar recognition. Shortly afterwards, Macedonia followed suit. Yugoslavia now consisted of just two republics, Serbia and Montenegro, with less than 40 percent of its former territory and only 10.5 million of its nearly 24 million people.

Hope that self-determination would restore peace proved short-lived. Within days after the Bosnian declaration, Serbian troops invaded the country, purportedly to protect the Serbian minority. However, the Serbs in Bosnia, unlike those in Croatia, were not being threatened. Bosnia's Muslims (44 percent), Serbs (31 percent), and Croats (17 percent) had lived in relative harmony. The only justification for the Serbian action was a grab for more territory. Slobodan Milosevic, the fiery nationalist leader of the Serbs, also wanted to divert attention from his failure to reform the economy after the collapse of Communism. The country had an inflation rate of 500 percent a year and unemployment of 750,000.

In playing the nationalist card, Milosevic plunged his country deeper into debt, prolonged the solution of the country's real problems, and cut it off from the international community. The government in Belgrade proclaimed a new federal republic in an attempt to lay claim to the assets of former Yugoslavia: membership in the United Nations, the World Bank, and the International Monetary Fund, and ownership of the diplomatic establishment, including all of its embassies and consulates. In fact, though, as long as the aggression continued, the new state remained a pariah and could expect no help from abroad.

Even were hostilities to end, the future remained bleak. None of the new states was economically viable, and few of their products were able to compete on the world market. The prospect of restoring a measure of cooperation amongst them seemed unlikely. The nations of the EC did not like to see such chaos and ruin in the heart of Europe, but none of them wanted to intervene actively. They encouraged the United Nations to send its "blue berets," but such forces were not equipped to separate armies fighting in the field. The other nations believed that those who started the bloodshed had to end it. Unless the war spread to other states, the combatants would be allowed to continue to kill each other until they came to their senses or collapsed from exhaustion.

THE REUNIFICATION OF THE GERMAN STATE

The Revolt in East Germany

Erich Honecker's regime pretended that the reforms being carried out in the Soviet Union would have little effect on the way it conducted its own affairs, and it repressed dissent with its habitual heavy-handedness. On 17 January 1988, a pro-test organized by a small group of critics and dissidents at a ceremony commem-orating the slain Communist leaders Karl Liebknecht and Rosa Luxembourg re-sulted in the arrest of a hundred demonstrators. The government's action touched off a wave of public meetings and church services in favor of the detainees, prompt-ing the authorities not only to release them all, but even to allow some to emigrate to the West. The move was uncharacteristically generous.

Although many East Germans hoped Gorbachev's reforms would lead to change, the German Democratic Republic persisted in its hard-line policies. Later in 1988, it even forbade the distribution of the Soviet journal *Sputnik*, deeming it to be too liberal. The only deference paid to glasnost was the easing of travel restrictions to the West and some talk of formulating a new process for appealing administrative decisions. These sops did nothing to assuage popular dissatisfaction. In August 1989, the full extent of the discontent became clear when Hungary, Poland, and Czechoslovakia decided to open up their frontiers with East Germany.

Within three days after the announcements, 15,000 East Germans had fled their country to seek asylum in the West German embassies in Prague, Warsaw, and Budapest. In September, the Iron Curtain came down as the three countries al-lowed the escapees to continue their flight to West Germany. The exodus in-creased and soon involved 225,000 people—out of a population of 16 million. Most of those leaving were between the ages of twenty and forty, and many were skilled workers. They left behind a critical shortage of trained personnel. On 7 October, Gorbachev made a state visit to East Germany. His visit encouraged East Berliners to take advantage of the official celebrations to mount their own dem-onstrations. The crowds clashed with the police as the situation began to get out of control. On 18 October, Honecker was forced to resign his party and state posts.

Egon Krenz, his successor, promised more openness and tried to make up for lost time by embarking on a program of economic and political reform. But it was too late. During the second week of November, the country was shaken by a series of protests that brought close to one million demonstrators into the streets of the country's major cities. The most important occurred in Leipzig where open protests had been going on for weeks. One demonstration had drawn half a million people. These popular protest movements led to the mass resignation of the East German government and the Communist Politburo. On 9 November, the Central Com-mittee of the Communist party agreed to permit free travel to the West, thereby ending the era of the Wall. In Berlin, people from both sides came with hammers to tear down the Cold War's most hated symbol.

Krenz had prevented bloodshed by forbidding the use of firearms to crush the demonstrations. But he still thought that the East German state could be saved if all the political and social forces in the country could reach a consensus. Krenz claimed that the East German people had no interest in giving up their socialist society for capitalism.[18] He believed that no responsible leaders really wanted German unification at this time. He promised free, secret elections, but set no date.

In December, the Communist party held an emergency congress and changed its name to the Party of Democratic Socialism, apparently gambling that by com-mitting itself to change it could retain its influence. Many of the delegates at this conclave denounced the party's past corruption and wrongdoings. But the change of heart was insufficient to keep the party together. Within a few weeks, mem-bership dropped from 2.3 million to 1.6 million and continued to fall. A group of reformers, led by Hans Modrow, took charge, but their days as leaders were over. Now the protests were accompanied by demands for reunification. In January 1990,

The first legal anti-government demonstration in East Germany, in November 1989, brings one million Berliners into the streets to demand radical change. The protesters want an end to "cosmetic solutions," to state controls, and to repression.

Modrow went to Moscow to persuade Gorbachev to allow the creation of a united, but neutral Germany. Gorbachev was hesitant, but agreed. The West Germans did not. Meanwhile, the Soviet Union, Britain, the United States, and France opened a series of talks on how they could control the unification process, which was now accepted as inevitable. Out of the talks came the "two plus four" scheme in which the four victorious nations of World War II would join with East and West Germany to arrange the merger.

In March 1990, East Germans went to the polls in their first free, democratic elections to vote on how to proceed toward unification. Forty-eight percent voted for the Alliance for Germany, which advocated rapid unification. The Socialists who favored a more gradual transition came in second with 21 percent, while the former Communist party was third with only 16 percent. The new government, headed by Christian Democratic leader Lothar de Maizière, began immediate negotiations to join the two Germanies economically. On 1 July, East Germany officially agreed to surrender its economic and monetary sovereignty to Bonn.

The Triumph of Ostpolitik

The drive for German unification was a testament to the undiminished strength of nationalism, but its immediate impulse came from the people of East Germany who were disgusted with the abuses and inefficiency of four decades of Communist rule. They had not only been cut off from the rest of their country, in many cases

REUNITED GERMANY

0   50   100   150 km

SWEDEN

DENMARK

NORTH
SEA

BALTIC SEA

Kiel

Rostock

SCHLESWIG-
HOLSTEIN

MECKLENBURG-
WEST POMERANIA

Bremerhaven

Schwerin

Hamburg

HAMBURG

POLAND

BREMEN   Bremen

LOWER SAXONY

BRANDENBURG

Hannover

Brandenburg   BERLIN

Potsdam

NORTH RHINE-
WESTPHALIA

Magdeburg

SAXONY-ANHALT

Essen   Dortmund

Düsseldorf

Leipzig   SAXONY

Cologne

Dresden

Erfurt   Weimar

BONN

Chemnitz

HESSE   THURINGIA

BELGIUM

RHINELAND-   Wiesbaden
PALATINATE   Frankfurt

Mainz

LUX.

Mannheim

SAARLAND

CZECHOSLOVAKIA

Saarbrücken

Nuremberg

NETHERLANDS

Map 4

Stuttgart

BAVARIA

BADEN-
WÜRTTEMBERG

FRANCE

Freiburg

Munich

AUSTRIA

SWITZERLAND

from members of their families, but also from the great material prosperity that the West German people enjoyed. With the opening of the Berlin Wall on 9 November 1989, the flight of people rose to an unstanchable 2,000 per day, and the East German regime quickly lost any remaining viability. At the same time, the flood of refugees put a tremendous strain on the resources of the Federal Republic. These newcomers from the East were no longer welcomed with open arms.

The government of Chancellor Helmut Kohl was ideologically committed to unification as all the previous West German governments had been. The imperative could be found in the country's Basic Law. But West German politicians would have preferred for unification to be accomplished gradually. The present crisis, prompted by the popular revolution in East Germany, mandated that the process be accelerated. Otherwise, the Federal Republic would founder under the crush of millions of wound-be settlers. Unification could induce this feared horde to stay where it was. Furthermore, if the citizens of East Germany could not be persuaded to work in the regions where they lived, the East German economy would never become viable. Finally, a commitment to immediate unification paid Kohl great political dividends.

The chancellor suddenly saw his lackluster image transformed into that of a great German statesman. The timing was particularly fortuitous, coming when his Christian Democratic party was losing ground to the rival Social Democrats. When Kohl had gone to Berlin in November 1989 to help celebrate the opening of the Wall, he had been repeatedly booed. The experience profoundly disturbed him. To his credit, Kohl recognized the uniqueness of this moment in history. He cast off his previous doubts and threw himself into the struggle for unification with single-minded determination. Almost overnight he built up a Christian Democratic party as a force in East German politics, enabling it to score an upset victory in the March 1990 elections. Kohl even crisscrossed the border to campaign directly in East Germany. At a rally in Erfurt at the end of February, he declared, "We are one Germany! We are one people!"[19] Soon he was being touted as the chancellor of the German Fatherland. His opponents now criticized his blitzkrieg tactics for their recklessness and presumption.

Kohl's refusal to renounce all claims to the territories east of the Oder-Neisse frontier, lands once German but now part of Poland, earned him more critics. Although the Federal Republic had already recognized the loss of these lands in its 1970 treaty with Poland and in the 1975 Helsinki accords, which affirmed the inviolability of frontiers, Kohl maintained that only a united Germany could make the final decision. But such legalisms did not impress the international community. Poland, in particular, feared that without a specific guarantee a united Germany would seek to revise the eastern frontiers. Kohl backed down. He claimed he had been misunderstood and had the Bundestag and the East German parliament pass resolutions stating that a united Germany would unconditionally guarantee the inviolability of the border with Poland. The matter was finally laid to rest in five specific paragraphs of Article I of the Treaty on the Final Settlement with Respect to Germany, which included the obligation of Germany and Poland to confirm their existing border with a treaty that had the force of international law. Germany further pledged that it had "no territorial claims whatsoever against any other states and shall not assert any in the future." The four victorious powers of World War II added their own guarantees.[20]

Throughout the process, the Soviets showed a great willingness to compromise, which was all the more remarkable considering that they had lost 26 million people during World War II. At the beginning of 1990, Gorbachev had opposed reunification. When it appeared inevitable, he tried to weaken German sovereignty by postponing a decision on German military alliances. Eventually, the Soviets dropped even this qualifier. However, in the "two plus four" treaty, initialed in Moscow on 12 September 1990, Germany had to renounce the manufacture and possession of nuclear, biological, and chemical weapons and agree to reduce its armed forces to 370,000 troops. In exchange, Germany would be considered fully sovereign, have complete control over Berlin, and be free to join alliances as it saw fit, even NATO. The Soviets agreed to withdraw all of their troops by 1994.

The united German government promised to ease their repatriation through special subsidies, including building new barracks for them in the Soviet Union. The united German government also pledged to give the Soviet Union general economic aid.

After forty-five years, the division of Germany officially ended on 3 October 1990. It was celebrated with ceremonies and festivities throughout the country. In Berlin at the stroke of midnight, a German flag, seventy-two yards square and carried by fourteen schoolchildren from both the East and West, was hoisted on the 132-foot flagpole in front of the Reichstag building, while fireworks thundered overhead. Next came a performance of Beethoven's Ninth Symphony, culminating, appropriately, in the "Ode to Joy."

Taking Charge

Kohl ended 1990 as the chancellor of 78 million united Germans, his position cemented by a Christian Democratic electoral triumph that had reduced the Social Democrats to their weakest position since the days of Konrad Adenauer. Part of the reason for the Christian Democrats' success was the rosy picture Kohl painted of the cost of unification. He promised that East Germany could become "a flowering garden" in five years without raising taxes. Kohl believed the hard work the task ahead would entail would restore the moral strength of the German people, which during the years of affluence had been covered over with "a layer of butter and kiwi and shrimp."[21]

But East Germany was a basket case. It was West Germany's Albania, with much of the land having no value. Some areas were so polluted with deadly chemicals and nuclear by-products that many residents were sick with cancer or had already died from the disease. Six thousand miles of rivers had been contaminated with raw sewage and chemical wastes that had killed all life. Forty-four percent of the forests had been damaged by acid rain. Toxic dump sites were everywhere. If West German environmental standards were applied to the factories of the East,

Germans celebrate the reunification of their country at Berlin's Brandenburg gate, 3 October 1990.

half of them would have to close. Moreover, East Germany's five nuclear plants discharged so much radioactive steam into the air that they should have been shut down completely. The German Environment Ministry estimated that pollution in the East caused $18 billion worth of damage a year.[22] Moreover, as the Soviet forces began their repatriation, they left virtual junk heaps in the areas they had controlled. The hulks of broken-down motor vehicles and trashed weapons of war littered the landscape. The terrain they had used for artillery practice was permeated with unexploded shells. The soldiers stripped the buildings, taking the plumbing, woodwork, and anything else in scarce supply in their own country.

The first stage of German unification had taken place on 1 July 1990 when East Germany became a member of the Western economic community. The shock was instantaneous. Although East Germany had been an industrial powerhouse in the Communist bloc, its state-owned enterprises were highly inefficient compared to those in the West. Unable to compete, East German factories began to close in great numbers. Unemployment, which stood at 272,000 in July 1990, had almost quadrupled by the end of the year. An estimated 20 percent of the industrial workers and 50 percent of the agricultural workers were likely to lose their jobs.

The end of Communist domination also meant unemployment for thousands of party members and bureaucrats. The entire diplomatic corps, for example, was fired. These jobs, like those in other government departments, were filled with skilled non-Communists from the West. Even those East Germans who managed to retain their jobs often were not competitive by Western standards. Under Communism, they had not been required to work as hard or display the same initiative as workers in the West. Many West Germans looked down their noses at the "lazy Osties" and complained that all they wanted to do was live on handouts and sit around and drink coffee.

The East was clearly going to be a drain on the resources of the more prosperous West for some time to come. Kohl's promise not to raise taxes to pay for the transition proved to be election politics. Estimates of the cost of bringing the East up to the standard of living of the West ran as high as $2 trillion or more. The German government hoped that much of this money would come from private sources and set up a special department to try to sell former East German state property to potential investors.

Despite its immediate problems, Germany's economic power would be awesome once reunification was achieved. Many of Germany's neighbors feared that strength. Yet their fear seemed baseless since the development of German democracy and the firm integration of the country into the European Community had apparently solved the age-old problem of what to do with an aggressive, expansionist Germany. Chancellor Kohl believed that his country should flex its economic and political muscles only within the framework of a larger democratic union of states. Nevertheless, the union of the two medium-sized German states did create a new European superpower, which would no longer be content to defer to the leadership of the British and the French and, most likely, would again become the chief arbiter of European affairs.

WESTERN UNITY, EASTERN DIVISION

The Reinforcement of the European Community

The Americans believed they could continue to play a major role in the new Europe. But their influence was gradually declining. The high deficit spending of the Reagan years left the United States with a weakened economy and a soft dollar compared to the German mark, the Dutch guilder, or the Swiss franc. Following the collapse of Soviet power, the NATO alliance, through which American power had most directly affected the affairs of Europe, searched for a new mission. Thwarting an invasion from the east had been its sole raison d'être. Now that this threat had disappeared, the French thought it opportune to push for the creation of a new European military force outside the framework of the NATO alliance. The French had wanted such an independent military since the presidency of Charles de Gaulle and proposed to begin by raising the strength of an already existing Franco-German brigade to the size of a corps. The Germans seemed willing to cooperate in creating such a force, but the scheme alarmed the Americans.

At a meeting of the NATO powers in Rome, on 7 November 1991, President George Bush told the other members that if they wanted to go their own way on defense, they should come right out and say so. "Our premise is that the American role in the defense and affairs of Europe will not be made superfluous by European Union," he remarked in closed session. "If our premise is wrong, if, my friends, your ultimate aim is to provide independently for your own defense, the time to tell us is today."[23] Washington policymakers clearly could no longer chart the course of the Western alliance with full expectation of European compliance. Nevertheless, European leaders were not yet ready to sacrifice the stability and certainty of the NATO alliance system for something more indefinite. They agreed that the presence of the United States was vital to the security of Europe, but at the same time, they favored less reliance on nuclear weapons and more emphasis on multinational allied forces. They clearly wanted to assume more responsibility for their own security. Autonomy in matters of defense was a natural complement to the strength they had achieved from economic and political integration.

On 10 and 11 December 1991, the twelve countries of the European Community (EC) furthered the process of integration in a meeting at Maastricht in the southern Netherlands. On the first day of deliberations, the delegates adopted a broad financial arrangement directed toward monetary union. The scheme, first spelled out two years earlier by Jacques Delors, the president of the European Commission, envisaged a three-stage development for a common European currency. The Maastricht meeting created a timetable for these stages: in 1994, the EC would establish a European Monetary Institute as a prelude to establishing a central European bank; in 1997, it would inaugurate the European currency unit, or ecu, providing seven of the twelve EC members met certain stringent economic standards;[24] in 1999, it would adopt the ecu automatically even if fewer than a majority of states met the criteria. These measures seemed irreversible. The EC members expected that in time the ecu would be one of the world's strongest currencies.[25] Furthermore, a common currency, in Delors's view, would be a first step toward complete economic unity and would lead to coordinated policies on inflation, interest and exchange rates, and national budgets.

Despite the anticipated advantages of a common currency, the British reserved the right to opt out of any single-currency arrangement. They also received an "out" on social and political matters. Prime Minister John Major insisted that his country must be sovereign in defense and national security matters and must have the right to set its own policies on such things as vacations, maternity leave, and equality between men and women in the workplace. The British had even opposed describing the community as "federal"—known in Britain as the F-word.

The driving forces for European unity at the Maastricht meeting had been French president François Mitterand and German chancellor Kohl. Both agreed on the need for a common defense policy and greater harmonization of domestic policies. Their goal was to raise the EC to the status of a world power. Kohl was a convinced European who wanted to increase the power of the 518-member European Parliament as a way of bolstering Germany's democratic system and aiding its reunification. Despite his efforts, however, the Maastricht delegates hardly changed the powers of the European Parliament. They gave the assembly the right to monitor the EC budget, but not the right to initiate legislation. The conference did agree to expand joint action in the areas of industrial affairs, health, education, trade, environment, energy, culture, consumer protection, and tourism. The member nations also agreed to coordinate their judicial and immigration policies and to improve cooperation on police matters by forming a new international police force known as Europol. The richer members specifically promised to provide more aid to their poorer associates—Spain, Portugal, Greece, and Ireland. At the same time, the delegates reaffirmed national sovereignty by deciding that a common foreign and security policy could only be adopted by unanimous vote. Once adopted, however, the policy could be applied by a two-thirds majority.

The Americans approved of the Maastricht agreement. Beginning with the Marshall Plan, they had consistently supported the cause of European unity even though their own influence had suffered as a result. The adoption of a new European currency posed further risks to that influence. Foreign banks, for example, might decide to hold a greater proportion of ecus than dollars, thereby undermining the power of the dollar in international finance. Furthermore, the agricultural policy of the EC, which hurt the sale of American farm products, now seemed less likely to be changed.[26] Already, Washington had been trying to persuade the Europeans to modify their protectionist policies in talks held the past year under the auspices of the General Agreement on Tariffs and Trade (GATT). In addition to being anxious about economic repercussions, the Americans feared that Germany presented a challenge to their political leadership of the Western alliance.

Chancellor Kohl felt that Germany need no longer be constrained by the ugly record of its past. The nation's firm commitment to democracy and European unity gave it the right to play a leading role in European affairs. A week after the Maastricht meeting, Kohl announced that Germany would recognize the independence of the secessionist republics of Croatia and Slovenia. At the same time, the Bundesbank, which was independent from the government but usually followed government policy, raised the prime lending rate to eight percent. Kohl argued that in recognizing Croatia and Slovenia, Germany was simply acknowledging the obvious fact that Yugoslavia was already dead. Recognition might even help end the fighting. Meanwhile Helmut Schlesinger, the president of the German central bank, justified the increase in the lending rate as essential to holding the German rate of inflation at its current four percent. These explanations were not convincing outside Germany.

Germany's recognition of Croatia raised the specter of a revived Teutonic bloc in Eastern Europe where German investment was already significant. People recalled that Nazi Germany had once been allied to the Fascist Ustashi, which had ruled Croatia during World War II. Additionally, Germany's decision to promote an increase in the value of the mark put German needs first. The Germans had made their decisions unilaterally and expected their EC partners to adjust as best they could. In fact, despite their fears that recognition of Croatia and Slovenia might encourage the Serbs to more determined resistance, the other members of the EC did "ratify" the German action. They stipulated, though, that Croatia and Slovenia must commit themselves to respect human and minority rights, agree to settle all future border questions peacefully, and establish a democratic government.[27] Recognition took place as promised on 15 January 1992.[28] On the monetary issue, the other EC states also had to adjust to Germany's fait accompli by raising their own prime rates. Increasing the prime rate presented a real hardship for Britain and France as both these countries had planned to stimulate their own economic expansion with a cheap money policy. Germany's action also destroyed what remained of the Bretton Woods arrangement under which industrial nations were to coordinate the value of their currency with each other.

Kohl reacted to complaints that his country was becoming overbearing by remarking that Germany had no reason "to be ashamed" of its actions since it had "great concern [for] the fate of others." He pointed to the efforts the Germans had made to support the reforms in Eastern Europe and to the cooperative position Germany had taken during the process of reunification.[29] Many Europeans, however, could not rid themselves of the suspicion that the Germans were seeking European hegemony under a new guise; that is, that Germany intended to dominate the new European superstate, though now its weapons would be economic power and market strength rather than armies and the threat of war.

The Commonwealth of Independent States

The dissolution of the Soviet Union had moved the political weight of Europe westward and enhanced Germany's position. The age-old rivalry between Germany and Russia, which had contributed to the outbreak of both world wars, was being redefined in a new geopolitical arrangement. But while Western European nations had submerged their old rivalries in the common pursuit of greater material prosperity, Eastern European nations were entering a new period of deprivation and turmoil. Nowhere was this more evident than in the republics of the Soviet Union whose people, accustomed to being told what to do, headed toward an uncertain future along the newly charted path of democracy and free enterprise.

Following the collapse of the ill-fated August coup, the last hurrah of Soviet centralism, the Soviet Union rapidly unraveled. On 29 August, the Congress of People's Deputies suspended the activities of the Communist party and froze its bank accounts, giving the coup de grace to one of the country's greatest cohesive forces. The republics rapidly usurped the powers of the Kremlin. Gorbachev recognized the demise of the central authority, but he still hoped to preserve a semblance of unity by holding the remains of the once-centralized country together with a new economic union. At the beginning of September, Gorbachev convinced the leaders of ten republics to agree to transfer authority to an emergency State Council that would run the country until a new union government could be fashioned. This new council officially recognized the independence of Latvia, Lithuania, and Estonia, on 6 September, and began negotiations to withdraw the 200,000 or more Soviet troops stationed in the Baltics. The other republics agreed to maintain the Soviet Union's collective defense with a single central control over the nuclear arsenal. The council began working on a plan for economic union.

Meanwhile, the disintegration of central authority continued. Many of the Soviet republics wanted to maintain some sort of economic ties with the other republics, but they also wanted to control their own resources and run their own governments. They could not have it both ways. Secessionist fever accelerated. The Russian republic had assumed control of the Soviet money supply and had begun regulating trade in gold, diamonds, and foreign currency. Yeltsin had taken over the old Soviet Finance Ministry and consolidated the Russian and Soviet budgets. The Russian republic had even assumed responsibility for paying the sal-

Map 5

aries of the remaining Soviet officials, including that of Gorbachev. Yeltsin prepared to absorb the KGB's domestic and foreign intelligence operations into the bureaucracy of the Russian republic.

In November, the Ukraine refused to join any new confederation and scheduled a referendum on sovereignty for 1 December. The Ukrainian leaders expected 70 percent of the people to vote for independence. They made preparations to issue the republic's own currency and went ahead with plans to create their own armed forces. When Leonid Kravchuk, the Ukrainian leader, met with Russian officials, he spoke in Ukrainian and had his words translated into Russian even though he was fluent in Russian.[30] At one time, Kravchuk had been a loyal Kremlin-centered Communist who worked to eradicate Ukrainian nationalism, but he had quickly trimmed his sails in the aftermath of the August coup. "A man cannot keep the same views all his life," he glibly explained.[31] The Ukrainians voted for independence by an astounding majority of 90 percent. Kravchuk stated categorically that he would not take part in any new union treaty, and he even disavowed his previous commitment to economic union, suspending all further payments to the Soviet budget. Yeltsin stated that if Ukraine would not sign, neither would he.[32]

Gorbachev protested. He insisted on his right to overrule any attempt by a republic to nationalize the Soviet armed forces, but the threat sounded hollow. In any case, Yeltsin ignored the threat and arranged to meet with Kravchuk and Stanislav Shushkevich, the leader of the Belorussian parliament, to discuss the formation of a new Slavic union. The meeting took place at a country estate near the city of Brest on 7 and 8 December 1991. The talks produced the Commonwealth of Independent States, a loosely knit organization that would coordinate the economic, political, and military affairs of its sovereign members. It had no enforcement powers. The three leaders agreed to respect each other's territorial integrity and to guarantee equal rights and freedom to their citizens. They also pledged to sign cooperative agreements on a wide range of political and economic issues from education to foreign policy. The commonwealth would have its capital at Minsk in Belarus (Belorussia), not at Moscow. Its nuclear weapons would remain under joint control "without distribution or division."[33]

In the course of the meeting, the three leaders wrote the obituary of the Soviet Union: "The Union of Soviet Socialist Republics, as a subject of international law and a geopolitical reality, is ceasing its existence."[34] Yeltsin, to show the irrelevancy of the Gorbachev government, dialed the White House to inform President Bush about the meeting before Shushkevich phoned the Kremlin to tell Gorbachev. The leaders of the other republics were then also informed and told that they could join the commonwealth, if they wished.

Nursultan Nazarbayev, president of Kazakhstan, suspected that the Slavic presidents were trying to create a union along religious, ethnic, and cultural lines and was hesitant to join. He argued that Gorbachev's economic union plan should be given a chance to work.[35] However, 40 percent of the people in his Muslim country were ethnic Russians. The Kazakhs themselves were actually a minority among the state's 16 million citizens. Under the circumstances, joining the new commonwealth was probably the least divisive choice. Nazarbayev, therefore, changed his mind and even insisted that Kazakhstan be considered a founding member. The membership of Kazakhstan persuaded the other Central Asian republics—Uzbekistan, Turkmenistan, Tadzhikstan, and Kirghizia—to suppress their fear of Slavic hegemony and also join. In fact, any of these states would have had difficulty surviving economically without some sort of association with another power.

The new commonwealth members considered the disposition of the old Soviet Union's nuclear arsenal, consisting of an estimated 27,000 to 30,000 warheads, at a meeting in Alma-Ata, the capital of Kazakhstan, on 21 December 1991.[36] Moldova and Azerbaijan, both commonwealth members, also sent delegates. Other items on the agenda included economic cooperation, human rights, and the future of Gorbachev. Gorbachev had strongly opposed the commonwealth structure and had even suggested that the way Yeltsin had handled its creation raised questions about his moral standards.[37] Even at this late hour, Gorbachev still believed he had a role to play in forming a new union and insisted that he wanted to "stay the course." "I feel that the capital I've accumulated should be fully used for the freedom of my country and international relations," he added.[38] Although Gorbachev was now the head of a nonexistent state, Yeltsin wanted to obtain his formal resignation as soon as possible because he still could cause mischief. He might, for example, convoke a meeting of the Supreme Soviet even though it would not have a quorum without the representatives from Russia and Ukraine.

Gorbachev announced his decision to "discontinue" his activities as president of the Soviet Union on 25 December 1991. He was regretful and bitter at being forced from office, but in his speech he focused on his accomplishments during the six years and nine months he had held office. He took pride in having inaugurated a multitier economy, ended the Cold War and the arms race, and halted Soviet interference in other nations' internal affairs. He took credit for eliminating the totalitarian system and replacing it with freedom of the press, freedom of worship, representative legislatures, and a multiparty system. He hoped to be remembered for these reforms:

I consider it vitally important to preserve the democratic achievements which have been attained in the last few years. We have paid with all our history and tragic experience for these democratic achievements, and they are not to be abandoned, whatever the circumstances, and whatever the pretexts. Otherwise, all our hopes for the best will be buried. I am telling you all this honestly and straightforwardly because this is my moral duty.[39]

The Legacy

Yeltsin's government now braced for the protests that were expected to erupt after the elimination of most price supports and the consequent rise in the cost of food on 2 January 1992. Yeltsin believed that an abrupt move to a market economy, rather than the gradual approach Gorbachev had advocated, was necessary to change people's behavior. He hoped that market forces would eventually produce deep changes in the structure of the economy. Few people had any idea what economic competition meant or how to exchange goods and services without central direction. State planning had eliminated any rational connection between the costs of production and prices. Yeltsin and his advisers anticipated that a rise in prices would bring a rush of goods into the market. If producers had to pay real costs for their materials, capital, and labor, they would learn the lessons of supply and demand. Higher prices would encourage greater production.

As soon as the Russian government lifted the controls, prices skyrocketed. The average cost of basic commodities rose 300 to 500 percent. But the supply of staple goods did not always increase as anticipated. People waited in long lines to buy bread and gasoline. The crisis also caused the value of money to decline.[40] To meet expenses, the government tripled the amount of currency in circulation, issuing bills in new denominations of 200, 500, and 1,000 rubles. Consequently, producers of durable goods and agricultural products traded for other commodities rather than selling their goods for almost worthless paper. However primitive, reversion to a barter system may have been a necessary phase in the transition from a planned economy to a market economy. It enabled people to learn about the value of commodities and to master the rudiments of a price system. Under the old regime, money did not necessarily ensure the ability to purchase goods. Sometimes personal connections were needed. Small wonder that the old party and managerial elites were opposed to the new system and tried to sabotage it. This resistance from the old guard was the true reason Gorbachev's reforms could not have succeeded.

Yeltsin knew this and, convinced he was pursuing the right course, proceeded with plans to denationalize large parts of the Russian economy. He promised to sell to the private sector a whole range of enterprises, including thousands of stores, cafés, construction firms, food processing plants, and other light industry. Yeltsin wanted to commercialize small trade as a prelude to privatization. He hoped to attract extensive foreign investment and expertise to help run the large state enterprises, many of which would also, in time, be privatized. Agriculture would undergo major changes as well. Government subsidies to state and collective farms would end. Land would be sold to individuals and families, and the government's role would be restricted to technical assistance and credit.

Two weeks after the reforms went into effect, some 5,000 people demonstrated in Red Square, demanding a return to Communism. Photographs of the crowd indicate that the demonstrators and, hence, the dissatisfied populace were mostly middle-aged or older. Shortly afterwards, Yeltsin spoke to the Russian parliament and exhorted its members not to lose their nerve. The president said that the

Russian people had not lost hope and accused entrenched bureaucrats of standing in the way of change. He charged that those state organizations that still had a monopoly over the production and distribution of certain goods were purposely forcing up prices.[41] He also blamed "criminal elements." Yeltsin concluded by preaching patience, promising that the benefits of his program would become evident in the next six to eight months. "The legacy we received [from 74 years of Communism] is simply depressing—it's as though an enemy had occupied and managed our land."[42] Yeltsin knew, however, that Russia would have to have help from the West for his reforms to succeed. In making a plea for that assistance, he warned: "If the reform in Russia goes under, that means there will be a Cold War [which could] turn into a hot war. There is again going to be an arms race."[43]

The confusion afoot in Russia also appeared in the other republics. Many of their leaders thought Yeltsin was proceeding too fast. The leaders of some states, especially those bordering Russia, felt they had no choice but to go along with Yeltsin and allow their prices to increase. Otherwise they might be faced with hordes of Russians descending upon them to buy up goods at cheap subsidized rates that no longer existed in the Russian republic. The republics' leaders foundered in indecision and lack of planning. There were no blueprints for dismantling totalitarian systems. In charting a course toward the new, they constantly had to confront the old. They argued over fundamentals and tried to make up for years of isolation from the rest of the world. The worth of democracy was on trial. If it could not satisfy the basic needs of the people, democracy might fail. Such a breakdown had already occurred in the republics of Central Asia and in Georgia. Indeed, rival groups had pushed Georgia to the brink of civil war.

Zviad Gamsakhurdia, the president of Georgia, had been elected with 87 percent of the vote in the country's first free elections. He once had been an outspoken advocate of human rights and a strong nationalist who was imprisoned for his opposition to the Kremlin. In power, however, he had become increasingly dictatorial and arbitrary, closing down the opposition press and imprisoning his political opponents. Dissatisfaction with his rule increased and led to demands for his resignation. He refused and his opponents sought to topple him by force.

In December 1991, armed units of the so-called Military Council laid siege to his Government House headquarters in Tbilisi. After sixteen days of fighting, Gamsakhurdia fled the country for Armenia. But he remained in exile only ten days. Returning to western Georgia, he called for a crusade against the Tbilisi regime and began recruiting an army. The Russian government expressed hope that the Georgian people would be able to find a peaceful solution to their problems, but realized it could do little to mediate the crisis.[44] Georgia had declined to join in the new Commonwealth of Independent States, and Moscow was anxious to withdraw its remaining troops from the country as soon as possible. With their own transition problems, the Russians could not afford to sort out the turbulent affairs of the Transcaucasus. The leaders of the Georgian Military Council had set a dangerous precedent in overthrowing a legally elected government, especially since they were hardly the democrats they pretended to be.

Adjustment was also extremely difficult in the three Baltic states, which, although sovereign, still remained tied to Russia by a common currency and a common market. Their industries were dependent on the supply of raw materials that Russia made available to them at less than the world-market price. It would take many years before these ties of half a century could really be severed. In January 1992, Estonia declared a three-month state of emergency in the face of mounting fuel and food shortages. Its parliament voted 53–37 to establish a joint government-parliamentary commission to assume wide powers over production and

Throughout the Soviet Union, people toppled the statues of the great Communist heroes. Here, a statue of Lenin, which used to stand in the main square of Riga, lies on its back before being carted off to the scrap heap. For the Latvians, the monument's demise in August 1991 is more than the symbolic end of the Communist system; it is also a strong statement of their desire to become independent.

distribution. The elimination of price controls was postponed. Estonia still depended on Russia for 90 percent of its trade.[45]

While the commonwealth republics tried to create new political and economic institutions, they also engaged in the frequently bitter task of dividing up the tangible assets and liabilities of the old Soviet Union. They had to decide how to apportion the massive $80 billion foreign debt and how to divide their common cultural,[46] scientific, administrative, and military property. The states had already agreed to unified control of the Strategic Deterrent Force—that is, nuclear weapons and rockets. Yeltsin currently possessed the Soviet Union's nuclear codes.[47] The republics also recognized that each republic had control over its local property and natural resources. But conventional military hardware and diplomatic property had to be apportioned.[48] At first, both the Russians and the Ukrainians claimed the entire Black Sea fleet, but eventually, they agreed to divide it. Even then, deciding how the division should be carried out and settling a whole host of other claims proved to be a long and arduous task.

EPILOGUE   The statues that the Communist system erected to its heroes expressed its aspirations for a perfect society. In truth, however, many of the "heroes" represented were tyrants and murderers. Thus, it is not surprising that people celebrated the end of Communist rule by toppling the statues. Throughout the country, these monuments were desecrated and consigned literally to the scrap heap of history.[49]

Gorbachev, to his credit, had realized that a modern society could not be built upon a culture of cynicism and resentment. He interpreted perestroika as an effort to "break the back of the totalitarian monster" that repressed people intellectually and forced them "to conform with stereotypes."[50] Yet, in attempting to reform Communism, he hastened its end and left in its place mass confusion and a renewed, frequently aggressive nationalism. In his role as tsar-liberator, Gorbachev inaugurated the mightiest peacetime revolution of the twentieth century. The nations that emerged out of the debris of the Soviet Union began the laborious task of transforming the political, social, and economic institutions of their civilization. They had to reallocate power, define new property rights, and create different human values. None of them had any real experience with free institutions. They had always played by the rules of democratic centralism, which taught them that there was only one right way to do something and that all those who thought otherwise were enemies and saboteurs. Pluralism was an alien concept. There was a similar lack of comprehension when it came to a free market system. People looked to the state to set their priorities and provide them with protection. Profit was a political rather than an economic concept. Communism had also repressed religious and ethnic identity in favor of class identity. The collapse of central government released the pent-up forces of nationalism, frequently in their most intolerant and aggressive forms. Harmonizing the forces of disintegration and reintegration would take many years, understanding them would take many more. Progress could not be assured, but the age of mutually assured destruction seemed over. The United States and the remnants of the Soviet Union began to scale down their nuclear arsenals, removing land- and sea-based delivery systems. Their missiles were no longer targeted at each other's cities and bases.

The downfall of the Soviet empire was one of the great defining moments in history, ranking in importance with the two great political eras inaugurated by World War I and World War II. After both conflicts, Europe had sought to regain its stability in the face of political and economic collapse. Now, the great powers enjoyed a harmony that had not been present in such degree at any previous time in the twentieth century. When Boris Yeltsin spoke to the United Nations Security Council on 31 January 1992, thereby making his debut as the head of an independent Russia, he said: "Russia considers the United States and the West not as mere partners, but rather as allies. It is a basic prerequisite for, I would say, a revolution in peaceful cooperation among civilized nations."[51] It is fair to say that none of his listeners ever expected to hear a Russian leader utter such words during their lifetime. Yet the period in which they lived had taught them not to take too much for granted. They knew that revolutions, like Janus, wear two faces and that such upheavals have as often spawned betrayal as rejuvenation.

ENDNOTES

1. Vincent J. Schodolski and Charles M. Madigan, "The Gorbachev story," *Chicago Tribune*, 11 March 1990, section 1, 1.
2. Alan J. Day, ed., *The Annual Register, 1988* (London: Longman, 1988), 105.
3. Vincent J. Schodolski, "Soviet reforms sowed political whirlwind," *Chicago Tribune*, 24 March 1991, section 4, 4.
4. Gorbachev interview, *Time*, 4 June 1990, 31.
5. Gyula Józsa, "The Heart of Gorbachev's Reform Package: Rebuilding the Party Apparatus," *The Soviet Union, 1988–1989: Perestroika in Crisis?* (Boulder: Westview Press, 1990), 23–29.
6. *Annual Register, 1990*, 105–6.
7. *Chicago Tribune*, 19 May 1991, section 1, 18.
8. *Chicago Tribune*, 13 November 1991, section 1, 4. See also Mikhail Gorbachev, *The August Coup: The Truth and the Lessons* (New York: HarperCollins, 1991).
9. See *Time*, September 1991, 20–55 and *U.S. News and World Report*, 20 August 1991, 128–41.
10. *Chicago Tribune*, 23 August 1991, section 1, 5.
11. Approved by the Executive Council of the Russian republic, the change took effect on 1 October 1991.
12. However, the Supreme Soviet of the Russian Republic adopted the 500-Day Plan by 213 to 2. *Time*, 24 September 1990, 58–60.
13. *Chicago Tribune*, 24 November 1991, section 7, 2.
14. *Chicago Tribune*, 2 September 1991, section 1, 4.
15. Joseph A. Reaves, "Growing legions of homeless roam Poland," *Chicago Tribune*, 23 September 1991, section 1, 2.
16. James L. Graff, "Power to the Pulpit," *Time*, 20 May 1991, 40.
17. The Serbs were, of course, Eastern Orthodox in religion, spoke their own language, and used the Cyrillic alphabet.
18. Interview with Egon Krenz, *Time*, 11 December 1989, 47.
19. James O. Jackson, "Waiting for the Magic Words," *Time*, 5 March 1990, 29.
20. *Annual Register, 1990*, 566.
21. Interview with Helmut Kohl, *Time*, 25 June 1990, 38.
22. Ray Moseley, "E. Germans fear ecological crisis," *Chicago Tribune*, 4 February 1990, section 1, 23.
23. Ray Moseley, "French plan for army irks president," *Chicago Tribune*, 7 November 1991, section 1, 16.
24. For example, total government debt had to be below 60 percent, and budget deficits could not surpass 3 percent of gross national product. Only France and Luxembourg met those standards at the time of the Maastricht meeting.
25. *New York Times*, 10 December 1991, A1 and A6.
26. *New York Times*, 12 December 1991, A8.
27. *Time*, 30 December 1991, 29.
28. Recognition by the EC was buttressed by recognition by many of the other European states: Poland, Hungary, Bulgaria, Austria, Norway, Estonia, Latvia, Lithuania, Switzerland, and Sweden.
29. *Chicago Tribune*, 11 January 1992, section 1, 3.
30. *Wall Street Journal*, 25 November 1991, A14.
31. *Time*, 23 December 1991, 22.
32. Calling the independent republic "Ukraine," meaning "on the edge (of Russia)," instead of "the Ukraine" makes sense only to speakers of English because the Ukrainian language, like the Russian language, does not have articles. The Ukrainians distinguish between a province and a sovereign state in the prepositional phrase "in the Ukraine," but they still retained the form used in the days of nonindepend-

ence. Apparently, they were less concerned with establishing political correctness than Ukrainian groups outside the country that advocated the change.

33. There would be three nuclear buttons, each controlled by a member of the commonwealth. All would have to be pushed simultaneously to launch rockets. However, Yeltsin moved swiftly to bring all these weapons under his own command so that only he and the chief of staff of the Russian military had the power to effect a launch.

34. *Time*, 23 December 1991, 30.

35. Nazarbayev, like Kravchuk, had been the Communist party leader in his republic and only left the party after the August coup.

36. Yeltsin flew here directly from meetings in Brussels with NATO officials. One of the matters discussed in Brussels was the possibility of eventual Russian membership in NATO, a prospect that British Foreign Secretary Douglas Hurd said was "a long way off." *Chicago Tribune*, 21 December 1991, section 1, 3.

37. Interview with Mikhail Gorbachev, *Time*, 23 December 1991, 26.

38. Ibid., 26, 27.

39. The complete text of Gorbachev's address appeared in the *New York Times*, 26 December 1991, A6.

40. The average Russian worker earned 432 rubles a month in 1991. This was worth $758 at the official rate of exchange, but only $4 on the open market. *Los Angeles Times*, 4 January 1992, A3.

41. *Chicago Tribune*, 17 January 1992, section 1, 5.

42. *Los Angeles Times*, 30 December 1991, A8.

43. *Chicago Tribune*, 2 February 1992, section 1, 1.

44. *Chicago Tribune*, 17 January 1992, section 1, 4.

45. Ibid., section 1, 4.

46. The opening of the Winter Olympic Games in Albertville, France, on 8 February 1992 raised the immediate problem of how the commonwealth republics would enter their athletes. They decided to have the athletes represent their individual republics but participate as a united team. The athletes marched together at the opening ceremony, entering the stadium to the strains of Beethoven's "Ode to Joy." When a team member won a gold medal, the Olympic flag was hoisted and the Olympic anthem played.

47. Russia had been designated the recipient by Belarus (Belorussia), Kazakhstan, and Ukraine, the other republics possessing such weapons.

48. *Time*, 13 January 1992, 25–26.

49. Place-names also fell victim to the new mood of emancipation, changing too fast for mapmakers to keep pace. Leningrad again became St. Petersburg, Gorky was back to Nizhi-Novgorod, and Sverdlovsk returned to Yekaterinburg (named after Peter the Great's wife). Cities named for former party secretary generals were renamed: Brezhnev, Andropov, and Chernenko became Naberezhnye Chelny, Rybinsk, and Sharypovo, respectively. The names of lesser Communist officials and other heroes also disappeared. *Time*, 27 January 1992, 36.

50. Mikhail Gorbachev, "My Final Hours," *Time*, 11 May 1992, 42–43

51. *Chicago Tribune*, 1 February 1992, section 1, 1.

A NOTE ON BIBLIOGRAPHY

This book has been written using a combination of sources: document collections, newspaper accounts, memoirs, biographies, monographs and other special studies, general histories, and annuals. Full citation of these works has been given in the endnotes, which serve as a guide for further reading. The literature on the history of Europe in the twentieth century is so vast that any list of materials could only scratch the surface. Nonetheless, the following standard reference books, which contain extensive bibliographies, should provide a reasonably representative selection. These bibliographies contain sub-divisions of author, title, and subject.

Derek Howard Aldcroft and Richard Roger, *Bibliography of European economic and social history* (Manchester, England: Manchester University Press, 1984).

American Historical Association, *Guide to historical literature* (New York: Macmillan, 1961).

Gwyn M. Bayliss, *Bibliographic guide to the two World Wars: An annotated survey of English-language reference materials* (London: Bowker, 1977).

Dieter K. Buse and Juergen C. Doerr, *German Nationalism: A bibliographic approach* (New York: Garland, 1985).

Frances Chambers, *France* (Oxford, England: Clio Press, 1980).

Council of Foreign Relations, *Foreign affairs bibliography: A selected and annotated list of books on international relations 1919–* (New York: Harper, 1933–).

Alfred George Enser, *A subject bibliography of the First World War* (London: André Deutsch, 1979).

Alfred George Enser, *A subject bibliography of the Second World War* (Boulder, Colorado: Westview Press, 1977).

Stephen M. Horak, *Russia, the USSR, and Eastern Europe: A bibliographic guide to English language publications* (Littleton, Colorado: Libraries Unlimited, 1982).

Paul Louis Horecky, *East Central Europe: A guide to basic publications* (Chicago: University of Chicago Press, 1969).

Clara M. Lovett, *Contemporary Italy* (Washington, D.C.: Library of Congress, 1985).

Royal Historical Society, *Annual bibliography of British and Irish history* (Hassocks, England: Harvester Press, 1986–).

Albert John Walford, *Walford's Guide to reference material* (London: Library Association, 1982).

The Bibliographic Index, a cumulative bibliography of bibliographies (New York: The H. H. Wilson Company, 1937–1992) regularly examines about 2,800 periodicals and lists those works which contain the most extensive bibliographies. See also Theodore Besterman, *A world bibliography of bibliographies* (Lausanne: Societas Bibliographica, 1939–66) and its supplement, Alice F. Toomey, *A world bibliography of bibliographies, 1964–1974* (Totowa, N.J.: Rowman and Littlefield, 1977).

PHOTO CREDITS